D1597096

MYSTERIES IN HISTORY

MYSTERIES IN HISTORY

From Prehistory to the Present

PAUL D. ARON

A B C 🟢 C L I O

Santa Barbara, California   Denver, Colorado   Oxford, England

Library of Congress Cataloging-in-Publication Data

Aron, Paul, 1956 Sept. 15-
    Mysteries in history : from prehistory to the present / Paul D. Aron.
      p. cm.
    Includes bibliographical references.
    ISBN 1-85109-899-2 (hardcover : alk. paper) — ISBN 1-85109-900-X (eBook) 1. World history—
Miscellanea. I. Title.

    D24.A683 2006
    909—dc22

                                                                                2005024845

09   08   07   06   10   9   8   7   6   5   4   3   2   1

This book is also available on the World Wide Web as an eBook. Visit abc-clio.com for details.

ABC-CLIO, Inc.
130 Cremona Drive, P.O. Box 1911
Santa Barbara, California 93116-1911

*The Acquisitions Editor for this title was Simon Mason, the Project Editor was Carla Roberts,
the Media Editor was Sharon Daugherty, the Media Manager was Caroline Price, the Editorial Assistant
was Alisha Martinez, the Production Manager was Don Schmidt, and the Manufacturing Coordinator
was George Smyser.*

This book is printed on acid-free paper.
Manufactured in the United States of America

CONTENTS

5   THE FIRST GLOBAL AGE, 1450–1770   155

8   PROMISES AND PARADOXES, 1945–   375

PREFACE

In Josephine Tey's classic mystery story *The Daughter of Time,* Scotland Yard's Alan Grant is laid up in the hospital after falling through a trapdoor. Frustrated and bored, he takes it upon himself to solve a five-hundred-year-old case: the murder of "the princes in the tower."

The prime suspect in the case—indeed, the prime example of evil incarnate, to judge from Shakespeare's play and, before that, Thomas More's history—was King Richard III. This was a man accused of murdering two kings, of marrying (and then poisoning) the widow of one of his victims, and of drowning his own brother in a vat of wine. So the murder of his two young nephews, each of whom stood between Richard and the throne, seemed completely in character.

Grant, however, has his doubts. Stuck in bed, he keeps staring at a portrait of Richard, one in which the king appears far too kindly to have done anything so heinous. He assigns his visitors to investigate, and he discovers, to his shock and indignation, that More was a very unreliable source; for Sir Thomas, though quite literally a saint after his 1935 canonization, grew up in the household of Cardinal John Morton, a bitter enemy of Richard's. In other words, More had it in for Richard.

The true villains, Grant concludes, were More, who framed Richard, and the historians who followed, who were too lazy to notice.

What's the moral? That fictional detectives are better investigators than professional historians?

Hardly.

As Grant begrudgingly concedes, most of his "discoveries" about Richard had been discovered years, and in some cases centuries, earlier, by members of the same historical profession that he holds in such disdain. It was historians who analyzed More's sources and motives, who uncovered an account of the deaths written *before* More's, who pressured Westminster Abbey to open the tomb in which the remains of the princes were supposedly interred.

No Scotland Yard detective could have asked for a more tenacious investigation.

What Tey's story does illustrate is that the best mystery writing has lots in common with the best history writing. In both, things are not always as they at first seem; in both, the quest for a solution is jammed with surprises and challenges and thrills. As the historians in this book take on the greatest mysteries of all time, you can follow along, not just in the essays but also in the annotated references that follow each, which are in chronological rather than standard alphabetical order.

As for the princes, the tomb in the abbey was opened in 1933, and the skeletons were examined by Westminster's archivist and by the president of Great Britain's Anatomical Society. What the forensic evidence revealed was—

One rule about great mystery stories: Don't give away the ending.

ACKNOWLEDGMENTS

I am grateful for the assistance, at ABC-CLIO, of Ron Boehm, Sharon Daugherty, Carla Roberts, Simon Mason, and Peter Westwick.

PART 1

ORIGINS AND
EARLY CIVILIZATIONS

Were the Neandertals
Our Ancestors?

O N A N A UGUST DAY IN 1856, in the Neandertal Valley in northwestern Germany, a workman in a limestone quarry uncovered the bones of what he thought was a cave bear. He put them aside to show to Johann Fuhlrott, the local schoolteacher and an enthusiastic natural historian.

Fuhlrott immediately realized this was something much more significant than the bones of a bear. The head was about the size of a man's, but it was shaped differently, with a low forehead, bony ridges above the eyes, a large projecting nose, large front teeth, and a bulge protruding from the back. The body, to judge from the bones that were recovered, must also have resembled a man's, though he would have been shorter and stockier—and more powerful—than any normal man. Making the bones even more significant, Fuhlrott realized, was that they'd been found amid geological deposits of great antiquity.

The schoolteacher contacted Hermann Schaaflhausen, a professor of anatomy at the nearby University of Bonn. He, too, recognized that the bones were extraordinary: "a natural conformation hitherto not known to exist," as he later described them. Indeed, what the workman had uncovered, Schaaflhausen believed, was a new—or rather a very, very old—type of human being, one that would come to be called a Neandertal. Perhaps, Schaaflhausen may even have suspected, the Neandertals were ancient ancestors of modern man.

If the professor and the schoolteacher expected the scientific establishment to celebrate their discovery, they were sorely disappointed. Charles Darwin's theory of evolution, as spelled out in *The Origin of Species,* was still three years from its publication in 1859. To most scientists, the idea that humans evolved from any other species, let alone one represented by these bones, seemed entirely absurd. Rudolf Virchow, the leading pathologist of the day, examined the bones and declared that they belonged to a normal human being, albeit one suffering from some unusual disease. Other experts followed suit.

By the end of the nineteenth century, however, Darwinism prevailed in most scientific circles. Some scientists, such as Gabriel de Mortillet in France, took another look at the bones and argued that modern humans evolved from Neandertals. The discovery of more Neandertal remains—in France, Belgium, and Germany—buttressed their case. These fossils dated back to between 110,000 and 35,000 years ago, making it impossible to dismiss them as either diseased or modern.

But the majority of scientists, led by another Frenchman, Marcellin Boule, still adamantly rejected Neandertals as human ancestors. The skeletons may have been ancient, Boule conceded, but they were no kin of his. This bent-kneed, squat-necked, curve-spined Neandertal was more ape than human, Boule argued. If modern humans had anything at all to do with them, he suggested, it could only have been that our *real* human ancestors, whoever they were, might have wiped out this "degenerate species."

For most of the twentieth century, the scientific rift only widened. On the one side were Mortillet's followers, who viewed Neandertals as our direct, albeit primitive, ancestors. On the other side were those who, like Boule, saw the Neandertals as at best our distant cousins, an evolutionary dead end destined to be replaced by modern humans. Only in the past few years have scientists begun, very tentatively, to build a bridge across this bitter divide.

⌇

One reason why Boule's followers were able to dismiss the Neandertals, well into the twentieth century, was that they could put forward their own and much more reassuringly familiar candidate for human ancestor. This was the infamous Piltdown man, discovered in 1912. An amateur fossil hunter named Charles Dawson found the Piltdown bones at a common by that name in Sussex, England, and they were an immediate sensation. Unlike Neandertal's skull, Piltdown's was in most respects just like that of a modern human being. Only the apelike jaw seemed primitive, and even there the flat-topped teeth added a human touch. Here was an ancestor whom Boule would have been happy to call his own.

The problem was that Piltdown was a hoax. Someone, probably Dawson, had fused parts from a modern human skull with the jaw of an orangutan, then stained them to make them seem older. The teeth had been filed down to throw investigators off the track. It was not until 1953 that scientists thought to look at the teeth under a microscope, at which point the file marks were plainly visible.

Now the scientific momentum shifted in favor of Neandertals as human ancestors. Instead of emphasizing how different they were from us, scientists started focusing on the similarities. In 1957 two American anatomists, William Straus and A. J. E. Cave, took a new look at the very same fossil that had formed the basis of Boule's description of Neandertals as brutish and nonhuman. This was the La Chapelle-aux-Saints fossil, found in a cave in southern France in 1908.

The first thing Straus and Cave noticed was that the Chapelle-aux-Saints man suffered from arthritis. Boule noticed this, too, but he ignored the implications. To Straus and Cave, the arthritis explained the Neandertal's stooped posture, and the rest of the Neandertal man suddenly didn't seem so different from a modern human being. The two anatomists concluded that if Neandertal man "could be reincarnated and placed in a New York subway provided that he were bathed, shaved, and dressed in modern

Are there any Neandertals in the family? From left, Piltdown Man, Neandertal Man, and Cro-Magnon (modern) Man. *(Courtesy Department of Library Services, American Museum of Natural History)*

clothing—it is doubtful whether he would attract any more attention than some of its other denizens."

The post-Piltown period saw a reevaluation of Neandertal behavior as well as looks. In the 1960s the American anthropologist C. Loring Brace led the way with new studies of Neandertal tools, technology, and living arrangements. From the pattern of ashes they left behind, for example, Brace deduced that the Neandertals were baking their food in shallow pits not so different from those of later humans. Others noted that many Neandertal remains appeared to have been buried intentionally—a practice that was undeniably human. Carefully arranged bones of animals at various Neandertal sites seemed also to indicate some sort of ritual slaughter, and the Neandertal bones at the Yugoslavian site of Krapina were broken up in a way that hinted at cannibalism. These were rituals that, however macabre, were definitely human.

The glorification of Neandertals reached its high point in 1971, with the publication of Ralph Solecki's work at an Iraqi cave known as Shanidar. Soil samples taken from a Neandertal burial there found an extraordinarily high level of wildflower pollen, far more than could have been blown in on the wind or carried on animals' feet. Solecki inferred that the Shanidar Neandertals had placed offerings of flowers on their burial sites, and he called his book *The First Flower People*. As additional evidence of their humanity, Solecki noted that the remains of one of the older people buried there indicated he had a withered right arm and was blind. These conditions would certainly have led to his early death unless members of his family or tribe took care of him.

With Solecki's book, the Neandertals' transformation was complete. No longer the apelike brutes of Boule's imagination, they were now sort of proto hippies, a people in many ways more humane than modern humans. This was also the high point for what became known as the "regional continuity" theory, according to which modern humans evolved from Neandertals in Europe and the Middle East, and from other, similarly archaic people in other regions. But the Neandertal image (and with it, the regional continuity theory) was about to suffer another reversal. The attack this time came not from archaeologists or anthropologists, but from molecular biologists.

⌒⌒⌒

The biologists knew little about fossils, even less about archaeology or anthropology. But they knew a lot about a small segment of genetic material known as mitochondrial DNA, or mtDNA for short. A team of Berkeley biologists—Rebecca Cann, Mark Stoneking, and Allan Wilson—calculated the rate at which human mtDNA mutated, and in 1987 came up with a new estimate of human origins: about two hundred thousand years ago.

This hypothetical mother of the human race was dubbed Eve.

Here was a new human ancestor, and unlike Piltdown, this was no hoax. If the biologists were correct, and Eve lived about two hundred thousand years ago, then modern humans were on the scene more than a hundred thousand years earlier than scientists had previously thought likely. That meant the first modern humans were around well before the disappearance of Neandertals—some of whom still lived, judging from fossils found on the Iberian Peninsula, as recently as twenty-eight thousand years ago. Proponents of the idea that Neandertals were our ancestors were thrown into disarray; after all, if some Neandertals were more recent than modern humans, that made it much less likely that the former evolved into the latter. And if modern humans were around *before* Neandertals even appeared, as now seemed possible, then the evolution was an out-and-out impossibility. New methods of dating ancient remains supplied more evidence that modern humans dated back as far as, if not farther than, Neandertals. Scientists estimated that Neandertals were at various sites in the Middle East about sixty thousand years ago, well within the range they'd previously estimated. But the new dates for modern humans were a real shocker: it turned out that they were in the area about ninety thousand years ago—much earlier than previously thought.

Meanwhile, archaeologists were also redating sites in sub-Saharan Africa, where they found evidence of modern humans from as long as a hundred thousand years ago, and by some calculations up to two hundred thousand years ago. This dovetailed with the findings of the biologists that Eve's home—her Eden—had been in Africa. Cann, Stoneking, and Wilson had found that the mtDNA of modern Africans showed significantly more diversity than that of other races. They interpreted this to mean that Africans had had more time to evolve; hence the original human beings must have been African.

So, according to what became known as the "out of Africa" theory, the human race first emerged in Africa, then spread to the Middle East, and finally reached Europe. In the latter two continents, humans encountered the more primitive Neandertals, and—as was the case with so many other species who came into contact with humans—the Neandertals ended up extinct. By the early 1990s the "out of Africa" scenario had replaced regional continuity as the dominant theory.

The latest blow to regional continuity came in 1997, again from molecular biologists. Matthias Krings and his colleagues at the University of Munich managed to extract a snippet of mtDNA from the arm bone of an actual Neandertal—in fact, from Fuhlrott's original Neandertal man. They then compared the Neandertal mtDNA with that of living humans and discovered that they differed in 27 of the 379 spots they examined. (In contrast, the African mtDNA samples, which showed greater diversity than that of any other modern humans, differed from each other in only 8 spots.) The genetic distance between Neandertals and modern humans, Krings concluded, made it very unlikely that Neandertals were our ancestors.

✎

The regional continuity proponents didn't take any of this lying down. They questioned the validity of the genetic and dating evidence, and in 1999 they struck back with a dramatic discovery of their own. About ninety miles north of Lisbon, Portuguese archaeologists uncovered the skeleton of a 24,500-year-old boy who appeared to be part human, part Neandertal. The boy's face was that of an anatomically modern human, but his body and legs were Neandertal. The dating, which placed the boy after the pure Neandertals were extinct, seemed to indicate that the child was the descendant of generations of Neandertal and modern human hybrids.

If Neandertals and modern humans had interbred, the regional continuity proponents were quick to point out, they could hardly have been as unlike each other as the "out of Africa" advocates had argued.

The Portuguese discovery could have further polarized the field, leaving both sides defending seemingly irreconcilable evidence and theories. To some extent, that happened: longtime defenders of each lined up to hail the new find or to dismiss it. But their rhetoric seemed somewhat more muted than after past discoveries, perhaps because the focus of the debate was changing. Instead of arguing about whether Neandertals or other archaic humans evolved into modern humans, scientists were increasingly focusing on the issue of how Neandertals and moderns interacted.

Did they fight with each other? Did they learn from each other? Did they speak, or breed, or perhaps just ignore each other? Perhaps archaeologists or microbiologists—or practitioners of some entirely different discipline—will someday be able to answer these questions. For now, the answers are very speculative, albeit intriguing. The German anthropologist Gunter Brauer, for example, has proposed a more moderate version of the "out of Africa" scenario. According to Brauer, modern humans did indeed emerge from Africa, then went on from there to the rest of the world. But though they were in many ways different from the Neandertals they encountered in the Middle East and Europe, they were not so different that they couldn't interbreed with them. So, Brauer proposed, modern humans could have some Neandertal ancestors, even if the Neandertal genes are only a minuscule part of our makeup.

On the other side of the aisle, some proponents of regional continuity, such as the Tennessee anthropologist Fred Smith, readily conceded that a key genetic change in human makeup occurred in Africa. But Smith argued that the European and Middle Eastern Neandertals, far from being overrun by the newcomers, took them in and incorporated their genetic advantages. Neither Brauer's nor Smith's compromise was fully embraced, nor can it be said that there's anything near a consensus on the place of Neandertals in human prehistory. But a majority of scientists would now agree that, whatever the relationship between Neandertals and modern humans, the two overlapped in time and probably in place. So somewhere, most likely first in the Middle East and later in Europe, these two kinds of people—people far more different from each other than any of today's races, yet each possessing some recognizably human characteristics— first confronted each other.

No one knows for sure what happened next.

To Investigate Further

Leakey, Richard, and Roger Lewin. *Origins Reconsidered* (New York: Doubleday, 1992).

Leakey, who is best known for his discoveries of fossils much older than those relevant to the above discussion, is nonetheless insightful and provocative on the Neandertal question. He started off believing in regional continuity, partly because he found appealing the apparent inevitability of the emergence of modern humans from all sorts of archaic peoples around the globe. But he gradually came to lean toward "out of Africa," with its even more appealing implication that all the races of today's world are one people.

Trinkaus, Erik, and Pat Shipman. *The Neandertals* (New York: Alfred A. Knopf, 1993).

A comprehensive history of the Neandertal controversies. Trinkaus, an anthropologist, is one of the leading proponents of regional continuity, but his historiography is admirably unbiased. The book's only flaw is the authors' tendency to interject thumbnail sketches of the leading scientists, whose lives—at least as described here—were not, in general, as interesting as their discoveries or ideas.

Stringer, Christopher, and Clive Gamble. *In Search of the Neanderthals* (New York: Thames and Hudson, 1993).

Stringer is the leading proponent of the "out-of-Africa" theory, but like Trinkaus, he's fair to both sides. British authors such as Stringer, by the way, have stuck with the traditional "Neanderthal" spelling; most others now spell it "tal."

Shreeve, James. *The Neandertal Enigma* (New York: William Morrow, 1995).
A popular science writer's clear and often elegant account of the ongoing debate.

Mellars, Paul. *The Neanderthal Legacy* (Princeton, NJ: Princeton University Press, 1996).
A technical but useful overview of Neandertal behavior, especially how they may have organized their communities.

Krings, Matthias, Anne Stone, Ralf Schmitz, Heike Krainitzi, Mark Stoneking, and Svante Paabo. "Neandertal DNA Sequences and the Origin of Modern Humans." *Cell* 90 (July 11, 1997).
The mtDNA analysis of the 1856 Neandertal specimen.

Ward, Ryk ,and Christopher Stringer. "A Molecular Handle on the Neanderthals." *Nature* 388 (July 17, 1997).
A less technical summary of Krings's findings.

Duarte, Cidalia, Joan Mauricio, Paul Pettitt, Pedro Souto, Erik Trinkaus, Hans van der Plicht, and Joao Zilhao. "The Early Upper Paleolithic Human Skeleton from the Abrigo do Lagar Velho (Portugal) and Modern Human Emergence in Iberia." *Proceedings of the National Academy of Sciences* 96 (June 1999).
The discovery of a Neandertal-modern human hybrid.

Sykes, Bryan. *The Seven Daughters of Eve* (New York: Norton, 2001).
A DNA expert explains how different our DNA is from the Neandertals', and then argues that almost all Europeans descended from seven women. He even names them.

When Did the First People Arrive in America?

S OON AFTER COLUMBUS LANDED IN AMERICA, Europeans began speculating about the people of this New World. To Columbus himself there was no mystery: since he assumed he'd reached some island off the shore of India (as all of Asia was then sometimes known), he had few doubts about who these people were (or what to call them). But once it became clear that the Indians were not, in fact, Indians, theories about who they were and where they came from abounded.

One theory that was especially popular in Spain was that the Indians were survivors of the lost continent of Atlantis. Atlantis, according to stories dating back as far as Plato's dialogues, once stretched from Spain to America but had sunk in a great flood. The first to tie the people of Atlantis to those of America was Francisco López de Gómara; in 1552 he explained that the Indians had been stranded in America when Atlantis sunk. As evidence, Gómara pointed out that the Mexican Indians used the word "atl" for water.

Another persistent theory was that the Indians were descendants of the lost tribes of Israel, whose exile to Assyria had been chronicled in the Old Testament and who hadn't been heard from since. A Dutch theologian named Joannes Fredricus Luminus seems to have been the first to make the connection between Jews and American Indians, arguing in 1567 that both had big noses and strange burial customs.

The first to move beyond such myths toward a serious study of American Indians were Spanish friars, among them the Jesuit missionary José de Acosta. In 1589 Acosta hypothesized that the Indians had reached the New World via an overland route from Asia. Here was a man ahead of his time; by the twentieth century, most scholars agreed he was right on the mark.

This consensus began to emerge in the mid-nineteenth century after Charles Darwin theorized that human beings first evolved in Africa, then spread around the rest of the world. Fossil evidence seemed to bear Darwin out: Africa and Europe could boast of numerous archaeological sites indicating the presence of humans tens of thousands of years ago; America had none (or at least none that weren't strongly disputed). Advances in geology strengthened the case for an overland route by demonstrating that a land bridge once existed between Siberia and Alaska, where today the waters of the Bering Strait are found.

So it seemed the mystery had been solved. Native Americans were not truly native; they had come from Asia. But an equally intriguing mystery remained: *when* had they arrived?

Until the 1960s and 1970s this mystery also seemed nearly solved. The consensus was that people crossed into America about 12,000 years ago.

This was near the end of the last Ice Age, when so much of the earth's water was locked up in glaciers that the Bering land bridge, also known as Beringia, was left exposed. Beringia had, to be sure, an inhospitable climate—worse than that of Alaska and Siberia today. But the climate had warmed up enough for humans to survive in the area. Fossils found there indicate that woolly mammoths, steppe bison, wild horses, and caribou all lived in the region, and their human hunters might very well have followed them onto and across the land bridge. So the 12,000-year estimate made sense: any earlier, and it would have been too cold for people to survive so far north; any later, and the water from the melting glaciers would have submerged the land bridge and blocked the passage across.

This geological logic was buttressed by archaeological evidence. In 1908 a cowboy named George McJunkin was riding near the small town of Folsom, New Mexico, searching for a lost cow. Instead, he came across some bones with a stone spearpoint beside them. The bones were much too large to belong to a cow; intrigued, McJunkin took them back to the ranch house. There they stayed until 1925, when they landed on the desk of Jesse Figgins of the Colorado Museum of Natural History. Figgins easily identified the bones as those of a long-extinct form of bison that had roamed the plains at the end of the Ice Age. But it was the stone spearpoints McJunkin had found beside the bones that had the more far-reaching implications. If these spearpoints were manmade weapons used to kill the bison, that meant humans had been hunting (and living) in America during the Ice Age.

More indications of Ice Age hunters followed soon after. In 1932 two amateur collectors exploring near Clovis, New Mexico, found the bones of some animals with stone spearheads between the ribs. In this case, the animals turned out to be woolly mammoths, also extinct since the Ice Age. And with the spearpoints right between the ribs, there could be little doubt that people were in America during the Ice Age.

In the 1950s a University of Chicago scientist named Willard Libby developed "radiocarbon dating," which allowed scientists to determine the age of the Folsom and Clovis finds more precisely; they turned out to date back between 10,000 and 11,500 years ago—thus fitting in very neatly with the puzzle being pieced together.

So, too, did evidence that came right from the prehistoric Indians' mouths—or rather, teeth. After examining more than 200,000 prehistoric teeth from the remains of about 9,000 prehistoric Indians, anthropologist Christy Turner determined that all Native American teeth shared certain genetic traits with northeast Asian teeth. These traits were unique—no other people had them besides the North American Indians and the northeast Asians. From this, Turner concluded that the Indians' ancestors must have come from northeast Asia. What's more, by examining the differences between northeast Asian and American Indian teeth and by comparing them to general dental evolution patterns, Turner calculated that the two populations must have separated in the vicinity of—you guessed it—12,000 years ago.

If people first entered America about 12,000 years ago, that explained another mystery as well: the rapid extinction of mammoths, mastodons, saber-toothed cats, native camels, giant beavers, and other large animals that roamed North America until about 10,000 years ago. When the bones of these animals were found at sites dated 12,000 years or older, there were no human artifacts nearby. When human artifacts less than 10,000 years old were found at similar sites, none of these animals' bones were around. Only in finds dating back between 12,000 and 10,000 years ago, such as those at Clovis and Folsom, did human artifacts (for example, spearheads) and these bones appear together. From this, paleoecologist Paul Martin formulated his hypothesis of "Pleistocene overkill" in 1967. Martin was convinced that human hunters crossed the Bering land bridge about 12,000 years ago and then moved south through an ice-free corridor just east of the Canadian Rockies. Here they found mammals so completely unadapted to human predators that they quickly hunted them to extinction.

Not all scientists accepted Martin's arguments. Some countered that climatic changes, or at least some combination of human hunting and climate, could better account for the extinctions. But there was no denying that the extinctions were yet another indication that people had crossed the Bering land bridge about 12,000 years ago. The mystery of when the first Americans arrived was, it seemed, solved.

ᕼᵐᵐᕛ

In the 1970s and 1980s this consensus fell apart as not one, but many, archaeologists claimed to uncover evidence of a human presence in America earlier—in some cases, much earlier—than 12,000 years ago.

Between 1973 and 1977 James Adovasio excavated Meadowcroft Rock Shelter in southwest Pennsylvania. There he found remnants of baskets and small stone blades at levels that radiocarbon dating indicated were occupied almost 20,000 years ago.

In 1976 in a Chilean peat bog called Monte Verde, Tom Dillehay unearthed the wooden foundations of huts occupied 13,000 years ago. At even deeper levels he found three hearths and some tools made from pebbles that radiocarbon dating showed to be about 34,000 years old.

Also in 1976 the husband-and-wife archaeologist team of Alan Bryan and Ruth Gruhn found the skeleton of a mastodon with a stone point inside it, at a site called Taima-taima in Venezuela. Radiocarbon dating placed the kill 13,000 years ago.

In 1978 Niede Guidon dated some prehistoric art from a Brazilian rock shelter called Pedra Furada back to about 32,000 years ago, making it among the oldest art in the world. And in 2004, in a hillside near the South Carolina–Georgia border, Albert Goodyear dug up some tools that, he claimed, people made about 50,000 years ago.

How could these people have traversed a continent still covered with glaciers? And how did they get to America in the first place—before there was a land bridge across the Bering?

Proponents of a pre-12,000-year-old human presence in America have suggested a couple of possibilities. Some have suggested that people crossed into America during an earlier period when the land bridge was exposed but when conditions had warmed somewhat. And even during the heart of the Ice Age there may have been an ice-free corridor along which people might have headed south.

Another hypothesis, this one championed by the Canadian archaeologist Knut Fladmark, was that people traveled across the Bering Sea and down the west coast of the Americas by boat. The boats would have been very primitive, but perhaps the Pacific coast of North America might have sustained enough life for people to make it far enough south, after which they could have headed inland. After all, Fladmark pointed out, people reached Australia about 40,000 years ago—also from Asia—and there was never a land bridge between those continents.

Proponents of the traditional 12,000-year date have sharply attacked all of these findings and theories. One traditionalist, Brian Fagan, mockingly referred to the ice-free corridor as a "prehistoric superhighway" beckoning the Paleo-Indians south from Beringia into warmer climes. Even at the warmest points during the Ice Age, Fagan argued, this corridor could barely support animal or human life, and people had little incentive to venture into it.

As for Fladmark's boat theory, traditionalists responded that, though the distance between Asia and America across the Bering Strait was about the same as between Asia and Australia, the trip to Australia was across fairly placid, tropical seas. In contrast, the Bering Strait—even during the warmer times of the Ice Age—was full of dangerous ice floes, hardly an appealing trip for people who, from all other evidence, survived by hunting and not fishing.

How, then, have traditionalists explained the pre-12,000-year-old finds? Many have claimed that the findings were simply wrong. In some cases the artifacts supporting earlier dates may have been natural and not man-made: trees may have fallen in ways that could be mistaken for human dwellings, natural deposits may appear to be hearths, pebbles eroded by streams may seem to be tools. In other cases the dating process may have been corrupted; radiocarbon dating depends on finding organic material (which can be carbon-dated) at the same level as human artifacts (which can't be carbon-dated), and then assuming that the latter are the same age as the former—but all sorts of geological disturbances could result in older organic matter ending up in the same layer as more recent human artifacts.

Besides questioning the new finds, those who stand by the 12,000-year date also point to the relatively small number of them. In Europe and Asia, on the other hand, there are thousands of well-documented sites that have yielded numerous and indisputably human artifacts dating back more than 30,000 years. If people lived here more than 12,000 years ago, traditionalists insist, there ought to be more record of it. Or, as some have put it, the absence of evidence is evidence of absence.

But it's also possible that the relatively small number of sites indicate that the pre-Clovis people were few in number, or too mobile to leave much of a mark on the land. To a much greater extent than was the case just a few years ago, archaeologists are willing to entertain the possibility that at least some people were in America long before the Ice Age ended.

To Investigate Further

Fladmark, Knut. "Getting One's Berings." *Natural History,* November 1986.
This and the following articles from *Natural History* were part of a series on the first Americans written by specialists and reporting on their original research but in nontechnical terms. Fladmark's article considers the likelihood of Ice Age Americans migrating by boat.

Adovasio, J. M., and Ronald Carlisle. "Pennsylvania Pioneers." *Natural History,* December 1986.
A report on the Meadowcroft Rock Shelter excavations.

Turner, Christy. "Telltale Teeth." *Natural History,* January 1987.
Dental evidence of Indians' Asian ancestry.

Ruhlen, Merritt. "Voices from the Past." *Natural History,* March 1987.
What Indian languages reveal about the migrations to and in the Americas.

Dillehay, Tom. "By the Banks of the Chinchihuapi." *Natural History,* April 1987.
A report on the Monte Verde excavations.

Grayson, Donald. "Death by Natural Causes." *Natural History,* May 1987.
Considers whether human hunters or climate caused the extinction of North America's Ice Age animals.

Bryan, Alan. "Points of Order." *Natural History,* June 1987.
A report on excavations in Venezuela and Colombia by a leading proponent of Americans' greater antiquity.

Guidon, Niede. "Cliff Notes." *Natural History,* August 1987.
A report on the Pedra Furada excavations.

Martin, Paul. "Clovisia the Beautiful!" *Natural History,* October 1987.
A summary of the conservative case against New World peopling prior to 12,000 years ago.

Dillehay, Tom, and David Meltzer. *The First Americans: Search and Research.* Boca Raton, FL: CRC Press, 1991.
A collection of essays that go beyond discussions of particular sites to discuss general issues relating to the peopling of the Americas, and which compare the migrations to America with those of other places and other times. Technical but readable.

Dixon, E. James. *Quest for the Origins of the First Americans.* Albuquerque: University of New Mexico Press, 1993.
A highly speculative but fascinating analysis by a proponent of early settlement.

Fagan, Brian. *The Great Journey: The Peopling of Ancient America.* Gainesville: University Press of Florida, 2004.
A scholarly but nontechnical overview of the subject by an archaeologist who is conservative in his assessment of the site data but open to the possibility of pre-Clovis finds (even more so in this new edition than in the 1987 original). This essay is much indebted to Fagan's work.

Did Noah's Ark Exist?

IN 1853, WHILE DIGGING IN ANCIENT NINEVEH (in what is today Iraq), the archaeologist Hormuzd Rassam came upon the library of Ashurbanipal, an Assyrian king of the seventh century BC. Here Rassam found thousands of clay tablets inscribed with cuneiform symbols. Neither Rassam nor anyone else knew how to decipher the ancient script. The tablets were shipped off to the British Museum where they sat, unread, for nineteen years. In 1872, George Smith, a museum cataloguer who knew how to read cuneiform, was the first person——at least since two thousand years before——to read the tablets.

The tablets told the story of a flood strikingly similar to that in Genesis. Here, too, a god becomes fed up with humankind but decides to spare the life of one pious man. The god tells Utnapishtim, the Sumerian Noah, to build an ark and take aboard "the seed of all living things." Then comes the deluge, which lasts seven days instead of the biblical forty. Finally, Utnapishtim sends out a dove, a swallow, and a raven (in the Bible, it's a raven and a dove) to find land, and offers a sacrifice to the god who has spared him.

This flood story turned out to be a part of the Sumerian epic of *Gilgamesh*. Gilgamesh, the king of Uruk, wants to be immortal, so after many adventures he goes to visit Utnapishtim. Gilgamesh asks Utnapishtim his secret, and Utnapishtim responds by telling him the story of the flood. Utnapishtim also tells Gilgamesh that he might attain eternal life by staying awake for a week. Gilgamesh promptly falls asleep. As a consolation gift, Utnapishtim gives Gilgamesh a "plant of rejuvenation" that will let him live his life over again. Gilgamesh loses the plant to a snake.

Gilgamesh is a remarkably sophisticated work of literature, but it was the similarity to the flood story that excited not just Smith but the world. Were the authors of *Gilgamesh* and Genesis describing the same event? And if so, did that mean the flood really happened?

༺᠅༻

In 1929 archaeologist Leonard Woolley thought he found the answer. Woolley was excavating the Sumerian city of Ur, now in Iraq and traditionally thought to be the hometown of Abraham. Woolley found two layers of artifacts separated by a ten-foot layer of alluvium——sediment deposited by flowing water. He dated this layer to about 3500 BC.

Woolley cabled London: "We have found the Flood."

Other archaeologists soon found similar alluvial layers, though at varying levels. Max Mallowan, an archaeologist and the husband of mystery writer Agatha Christie, interpreted this to mean that various rivers had overflowed at various times, and that a couple of these floods, rather than a single great deluge, were behind the stories of *Gilgamesh* and Genesis.

Even so, the discovery that there may have been some historical event or events behind the flood excited biblical archaeologists. Other exciting discoveries followed, among them an engraved Egyptian stone celebrating the pharaoh's victories over his enemies and naming "Israel" as one of those enemies, and a stone in Palestine that mentioned the "House of David." By the middle of the twentieth century, the prominent biblical archaeologist William Albright could confidently proclaim: "Discovery after discovery has established the accuracy of innumerable details, and has brought increased recognition of the Bible as a source of history."

Since then, the consensus among archaeologists has gradually become more sober. It was not so much that they discovered anything that disproved the Bible as that they failed to turn up much new evidence related to it. The "Israel" of the Egyptian stone was pretty much all that indicated Israel may have been an enemy of Egypt, and translators argued about whether it was the same Israel. There was little to indicate an Egyptian influence in Palestine, and no sign whatsoever of a people wandering about the Sinai Peninsula. The "House of David" inscription was also challenged, and even those who accepted it had to concede there was little else to connect the David of the stone with the David of the Bible.

The flood receded even further from history, with fewer and fewer archaeologists willing to link the alluvial silt with the biblical story. Some scientists speculated that the deposits might have been left by wind, not water. Others dug elsewhere and found the silt at very different levels than Woolley did. Still others failed to find it at all, even when, like Woolley, they dug near Ur. Journalist Werner Keller, whose best-selling book *The Bible As History* generally found the Bible historically reliable, considered the flood "archaeologically not demonstrated."

The credibility of a historical flood was further eroded by various adventurers who claimed they'd found remnants of the ark itself. According to Genesis, the ark came to rest "upon the mountains of Ararat," which referred to a region, possibly in present-day Armenia. That sent explorers—or as they were sometimes called, arkeologists—up various mountains around the Middle East. As early as the first century BC, the Greek historian Nicolaus of Damascus claimed to have located the boat on Mount Baris. In 1887 John Joseph, whose titles included prince of Nouri, grand archdeacon of Babylon, and Episcopal head of the Nestorian Church of Malabar, reported finding the ark on Mount Agri Dagi, near the borders of Russia, Turkey, and Iran. John Joseph was later reported to be a mental patient from Napa, California. In 1917 a Russian aviator photographed the ark from the air; alas, the photos were lost during the Russian Revolution. Among the most publicized expeditions were those of French industrialist Fernand Navarra in 1952 and 1969. Navarra reported seeing the outlines of the ark beneath the ice on Mount Agri Dagi, and he returned with some sample wood. Carbon dating, however, placed the fragments between 300 and 800 AD. Such expeditions continued into the twenty-first century, but well before the twentieth was past, most scientists dismissed the flood as a matter of faith, not history.

For anthropologists, though, flood stories were more than just stories. They found similar stories in many ancient cultures besides that of the Hebrews and Sumerians. Indeed, the story in Genesis was, according to most biblical scholars, itself made up of two tales that were later combined. Native Americans, too, told a variety of flood tales. Clearly these were more than old weather reports. Regardless of whether there really was some huge flood, the stories provided insights into these cultures. Some of these insights may have been a bit far-fetched; the Freudian Otto Rank, for example, traced flood stories back to dreams resulting from bladder troubles. But the flood tales presented, as theologian J. David Pleins put it, "mythical variations on an enduring medley of psychic questions and social challenges faced by the peoples of that region over the centuries." The themes of the stories defined what was divine and what was human, what was just and what was unjust.

"Let us continue, then, to dig for the flood," wrote Pleins, "but let us also continue to let the flood story dig away at our deepest selves."

ᵒᵐᵐᵖ

In 1993 two geoscientists went looking for evidence of Noah's flood under water instead of land. With the Cold War over, geologists William Ryan and Walter Pitman joined a Russian team on a converted fishing trawler called the *Aquanaut*. The boat was tracking radioactive contamination from the Chernobyl nuclear plant disaster, but Ryan and Pitman used their own sophisticated sonar equipment to survey the northern part of the Black Sea. Nearly five hundred feet below the surface, they spotted beaches, river gorges, and sand dunes. They also brought up the remains of some freshwater shellfish, and some freshwater trapped in the sea's lower clays. The fossils dated back about 7,500 years. Ryan and Pitman concluded that about that long ago, the Black Sea must have been a freshwater lake.

Under the northern mouth of the Bosporus Strait, which connects the Black Sea and the Mediterranean, is a deep gorge apparently carved with tremendous speed and pressure. Ryan and Pitman believed saltwater from the rising Mediterranean Sea had cascaded through the strait, inundating the once freshwater of the Black Sea as well as about sixty thousand square miles of surrounding land. Unlike the river floods posited by Woolley and Mallowan, the Ryan-Pitman flood would have been a catastrophe of biblical proportions, one that could have displaced Hebrews and Sumerians alike. And the gradual rise of the Mediterranean, unlike a sudden river flood, would have given some Noahs and some Utnapishtims ample warning of the approaching cataclysm.

In 1999 the Ryan-Pitman team received a boost from Robert Ballard, locator of the sunken *Titanic* and the *Bismarck*. On the south side of the Black Sea, this time more than five hundred feet below the surface, Ballard also found a mix of fresh- and saltwater mollusks, also dating back 7,500 years or more.

"The extinction date of these freshwater species coincided with the arrival of the marine shellfish species that Ryan and Pitman had collected on the Black Sea's northern coast," Ballard wrote. "We had closed the circle. No one could dispute that a Great Flood had occurred approximately 7,500 years ago."

Actually, many did dispute it. Ballard made much of the remains of a wooden structure he found on the underwater coast, but this turned out to be just two hundred years old. And there were plenty of other questions about the Ryan-Pitman theory. Some geologists placed the Mediterranean's rise much earlier, too early to have imprinted itself on the memory of the people of the Bible or the *Gilgamesh*. Others thought the transition from fresh- to saltwater was gradual—too gradual to have created an earth-shattering event. Still others accepted that a great flood had occurred, but they doubted its connection to ancient myths. Even if water from the Mediterranean poured through the Bosporus, the Black Sea would still have risen gradually, leaving people years to flee. And a rising sea could hardly be mistaken for rain, even forty days of it.

Still, Ryan and Pitman had changed the terms of the debate. The flood of Noah and Utnapishtim was again a subject debated by those interested in history, as well as those interested in mythology.

To Investigate Further

Keller, Werner. *The Bible As History.* New York: William Morrow, 1981.
    Originally published in 1955, Keller's book has since sold more than ten million copies.

Kovacs, Maureen. *The Epic of Gilgamesh.* Stanford, CA: Stanford University Press, 1985.
    Kovacs provides an introduction as well as the translation.

Bailey, Lloyd. *Noah.* Columbia: University of South Carolina Press, 1989.
    How Noah has been interpreted through the ages.

Ryan, William, and Walter Pitman. *Noah's Flood.* New York: Simon and Schuster, 1998.
    Though archaeologists remained skeptical, many of Ryan and Pitman's fellow geologists found their theory plausible.

Ballard, Robert, with Malcolm McConnell. *Adventures in Ocean Exploration.* Washington, DC: National Geographic, 2001.
    A lavish celebration of explorers from Columbus and Cook to Cousteau and Ballard.

Friedman, Richard Elliott. *The Bible with Sources Revealed.* San Francisco: Harper SanFrancisco, 2003.
    Different colors and type styles identify the different sources of the Bible. In the "J" version of the story, an angry God becomes disgusted with humanity and floods the world; in the "P" version, the flood is part of a more orderly plan.

Pleins, J. David. *When the Great Abyss Opened.* Oxford, England: Oxford University Press, 2003.
    How religion and science have interpreted the flood.

What Happened to
the Harappans?

NOT OFTEN HAS IT BEEN GIVEN TO ARCHAEOLOGISTS, as it was given to Schliemann," wrote John Marshall in the *Illustrated London News* of September 20, 1924, "to light upon the remains of a long-forgotten civilization. It looks, however, at this moment, as if we were on the threshold of such a discovery in the plains of the Indus."

Marshall's dramatic announcement was actually something of an understatement. Thanks to Homer, the history—or at least the story—of Troy was well known long before Heinrich Schliemann dug for its remains. Before Marshall's discovery, no one even had an inkling that India might once have been the center of a civilization as old and as large and sophisticated as those of Sumer and Egypt. There was no *Iliad* or *Odyssey*, no Bible or *Gilgamesh*, to tell about the Harappan people. The only evidence of their civilization was buried under Marshall's mounds.

"Now, however," continued Marshall, "there has unexpectedly been unearthed, in the south of the Panjab and in Sind, an entirely new class of objects which have nothing in common with those previously known to us."

The Harappans were literate, though no literature has survived and no one has yet been able to decipher the short inscriptions found mostly on their seals. They were also technologically advanced, with bathrooms and toilets in many houses, and citywide drainage systems. They were sailors and traders, whose crafts have since been found throughout Mesopotamia. And they were urban: Marshall would uncover the cities of Harappa, which gave the civilization its name, and Mohenjo Daro, whose baked-brick buildings surrounded a high mound that was sort of an Indian acropolis. Later archaeologists would uncover other large cities.

The more Marshall dug, the more excited he became. "To the archaeologist the site of Mohenjo-daro is one of the most fascinating that can well be imagined," he wrote in February 1926. "The existence of roomy and well-built houses, and the relatively high degree of luxury denoted by their elaborate system of drainage, as well as by the character of many of the smaller antiquities found within, seem to betoken a social condition of the people far in advance of what was then prevailing in Mesopotamia and Egypt."

The Indus were also a remarkably—maybe unprecedentedly—peaceful people. Archaeologists found hardly any spears or arrows. Wrote historian Jane McIntosh: "It was an exceptionally well integrated state . . . where warfare was absent and everyone led

At Mohenjo Daro and Harappa (pictured here), archaeologists found evidence of a hitherto unknown Bronze Age civilization. *(Roger Wood/Corbis)*

a comfortable existence under the benevolent leadership of a dedicated priesthood." McIntosh saw the pacifism of the Indus people as a precursor to Gandhi's.

Yet unlike the Mesopotamian and Egyptian civilizations, which lasted for millennia, the Harappans' endured only about six hundred years. By 1900 BC, Mohenjo Daro and Harappa were abandoned. People continued to live in the surrounding areas, but there were no longer signs of luxury items or writing or urban life. The reasons for the civilization's demise, archaeologists hoped, might also be uncovered somewhere in the Indus Valley.

ᥨᥩ

Mortimer Wheeler, who excavated at both Mohenjo Daro and Harappa during the 1940s, believed the Harappan cities were destroyed by invaders from the north. At Mohenjo Daro, Wheeler found the skeletons of men, women, and children sprawled on the ground, some bearing the marks of axes or swords. These, Wheeler concluded, were the peace-loving victims of a more violent people.

"They had been left there by raiders who had no further use for the city which they had stormed," Wheeler wrote. "In that moment Mohenjo-daro was dead."

Who were these invaders? Though there was no Indus text to tell of them, later Indian literature provided clues. Religious works known as the Vedas described the battles of people who called themselves Aryans. In the greatest of these, the Rig Veda, the Aryan war god Indra destroys ninety forts and "rends forts as age consumes a garment." Among those conquered by the Aryans were the Dasas, a dark-skinned race that lived in fortified cities.

"It has in the past been supposed that [these forts] were mythical," Wheeler wrote. "The recent excavation of Harappa may be thought to have changed the picture. Here we have a highly evolved civilization of essentially non-Aryan type . . . now known to have employed massive fortifications, and known also to have dominated the river system of northwestern India at a time not distant from the likely period of the earlier Aryan invasions of that region. . . . Its ultimate extinction is . . . likely to have been completed by deliberate and large-scale destruction. It may be no mere chance that at a Late Period of Mohenjo-daro men, women, and children appear to have been massacred there."

"On circumstantial evidence," Wheeler concluded, "Indra stands accused."

The evidence was, however, very circumstantial. Other archaeologists, such as George Dales, noted that some of the apparent wounds on the Mohenjo Daro skeletons appeared to have been made weeks or months before the victims' deaths. Moreover, the skeletons were not found together in the citadel, where you'd expect a last stand, but scattered about the city, and the positions in which they were found could just as easily have indicated a hasty burial as a massacre. It wasn't even clear that they'd all died in the same time period.

"Nothing delights the archaeologist more than excavating the ruins of some ancient disaster—be it flood, earthquake, invasion, or massacre," wrote Dales in 1964. "The 'massacre' idea immediately ignited and has been used as a torch up to the present day by some historians, linguists, and archaeologists as visible, awful proof of the invasion of the subcontinent by Aryans. But what is the material evidence to substantiate the supposed invasion and massacre? Where are the burned fortresses, the arrowheads, weapons, pieces of armor, the smashed chariots and bodies of the invaders and defenders? Despite the extensive excavations at the largest Harappan sites, there is not a single bit of evidence that can be brought forth as unconditional proof of an armed conquest and destruction on the supposed scale of the Aryan invasion."

The Rig Veda evidence was also dubious. Nothing in the text could be tied to any particular location, and its descriptions of the forts don't resemble Harappa or Mohenjo

Daro. Many archaeologists believed that the purpose of the elevated areas of the cities was not defensive, as Wheeler assumed, but public or religious. At Mohenjo Daro, there was a Great Bath and a warehouse, neither of which had any military use. Nor were the walls of the city necessarily for defense; many believed they were used to buttress the elevated buildings. The forts described in the Rig Veda, if they existed at all, were as likely to have been in Iran or Central Asia as the Indus Valley.

Then there was the problem of dates. Most scholars think the Rig Veda was first written down sometime between 1500 BC and 1000 BC, hundreds of years after Harappa and Mohenjo Daro were abandoned. True, the Rig Veda first existed as an oral tradition, and it could have recalled events of a more distant past, but it was still a long stretch to tie its battles to the fall of the Indus cities. Indeed, many historians have come to see racist undertones in the effort to portray white Aryans as conquerors of darker-skinned Dasas. Well before Hitler defined non-Jews as Aryans, the term had come to imply a superior white race (though the Vedas mention skin color only a few times, and never judgmentally). Even as the Indus were portrayed as an advanced civilization, wrote anthropologist Kenneth Kennedy, "the myth of invasions destroying Harappan cities created a paradigm in which the Aryans could still be considered the fountainhead of Indian civilization." It also provided, Kennedy added, a precedent for the British colonizers who inherited the white man's burden.

༄

If Aryan invaders didn't destroy the Harappan cities, who—or what—was to blame?

Some archaeologists thought disruption of the Harappan trade with Mesopotamia was a factor. After about 2000 BC, the number of Mesopotamian artifacts found in the Indus Valley declined, indicating a decline in trade. But none of these artifacts seemed essential to the cities' survival, so the decline in trade was more likely to be an effect than a cause of the problem.

Another theory was that the Harappans wore out their environment, perhaps deforesting the region for the firewood that baked the bricks for their buildings. This, too, seemed unlikely: only a few hundred acres of forest would have been required to build Mohenjo Daro and Harappa.

McIntosh argued that changing crop patterns were to blame. At the same time that farmlands were declining in the Indus Valley, farmers replaced the traditional wheat and barley with rice and various millets. The new crops flourished to the south and east, and farmers gradually moved in those directions. The Harappans may also have been victims of their own extensive sanitation systems, McIntosh speculated, if wastewater contaminated the drinking water and spread disease.

Many scientists blamed environmental changes beyond the Harappans' control. H. J. Lambrick suggested that the Indus River shifted course, perhaps because of tectonic changes in the Himalayas, and Robert Raikes thought the river's waters became dammed upstream from Mohenjo Daro. Gurdip Singh cited the changing salinity of the region's lakes as evidence of declining rainfall. Others suggested the problem was too *much* water: deposits in and around Mohenjo Daro indicated the city experienced a number of substantial floods, though some archaeologists suspected the deposits might have been left by wind, not water.

Any of these factors would have caused stresses and strains, and some—such as a change in the course of the Indus River or a devastating flood—might very well have caused the Indus people to abandon even as important a city as Mohenjo Daro. But why didn't they rebuild elsewhere? Why did they stop making painted pottery and stamp seals, why did they stop constructing drainage systems, why did they stop writing? Why did they give up on a civilization that had reached such heights?

For some, the answer lay not in the civilization's environment but in its ideology.

Anthropologist Gregory Possehl noted that the Great Bath at Mohendo Daro was abandoned before the city itself. Since the bath—and water in general—clearly played an important role in the Indus religion and culture, the people must have somehow lost their faith. Wrote Possehl: "The fatal flaw was centrally, and most importantly, sociocultural in nature; not flood, avulsion, drought, trade, disease, locusts, invasion or any other of a myriad of 'natural' or 'outside' forces. A failed Indus ideology is . . . the sociocultural flaw."

Possehl could only guess at why the ideology failed, but he suspected it might have been the very harmony that McIntosh and others admired. "If the world stood still, the well-integrated, tightly organized sociocultural systems like the Indus Civilization would work pretty well," Possehl wrote. "But the world does not stand still and sociocultural systems of this highly integrated type, which does not require constant negotiation, are vulnerable to changing conditions, both external and internal. It might take six hundred years for the system to fail, but eventually the changing world catches up with them."

Historian Matthew Fitzsimons agreed. "The Harappans mastered some of the basic necessities for city-living that almost no one so far has managed," he wrote. "They had to have concentrated authority which in turn was sanctioned by religion. The upshot of this was a defective capacity to respond to change."

These historians found in the Indus civilization not only the origins of India's later peaceful ideologies but also less appealing traits. Its harmony stemmed in part from a highly stratified society in which everyone knew his or her place—as in a caste system. But just as the Aryans can't be cast as proto-Europeans, the Indus can't be definitively tied to later Indians. Both Aryan and Indus cultures influenced what was to come, probably in many ways, but we don't know enough of either to do more than speculate.

Similarly, we can't settle on a single explanation for the decline of the Indus civilization. Here, too, a combination of factors probably came into play. The process was gradual—Mohenjo Daro was in decline by 2200 BC, but other cities lasted until around 1800 BC—further lending itself to multiple explanations.

"The process of decline and collapse, as it appears in the archaeological record at key sites, unfolds in various ways," wrote archaeologist Nayanjot Lahiri. "It is not one event but different kinds of events which are in need of elucidation here, and this may explain why various types of hypotheses have been offered as well as why one may consider more than one explanation to be plausible."

To Investigate Further

Lahiri, Nayanjot, ed. *The Decline and Fall of the Indus Civilization.* Delhi: Permanent Black, 2000.
   A collection of diverse views, often illuminatingly juxtaposed, from archaeologists, scientists, and historians from the 1920s through the 1990s.

McIntosh, Jane. *A Peaceful Realm.* Cambridge, MA: Westview Press, 2002.
   An accessible, illustrated history.

Possehl, Gregory. *The Indus Civilization.* Walnut Creek, CA: AltaMira Press, 2002.
   A thorough overview of Indus technology, architecture, art, writing, and religion.

Did Atlantis Exist?

IN THE FOURTH CENTURY BC, PLATO reported that the Greek sage Solon, some two hundred years earlier, traveled to the Egyptian city of Sais. There a priest told him the story of a great island that lay in the Atlantic Ocean nine thousand years before.

It was, the priest told Solon, "an island opposite the strait which you call . . . the Pillars of Hercules, an island larger than Libya and Asia combined; from it travelers could in those days reach the other islands, and from them the whole opposite continent which surrounds what can truly be called the ocean."

"On this island of Atlantis," Plato continued in the *Timaeus,* "had arisen a powerful and remarkable dynasty of kings, who ruled the island, and many other islands as well and parts of the continent: in addition it controlled within the strait, Libya up to the borders of Egypt and Europe as far as Tyrrhenia [Italy]."

Plato wrote that according to Solon, the island's demise came about when it attempted to conquer Athens. The Athenians resisted and went on to free others who'd been enslaved. "At a later time," Solon went on, "there were earthquakes and floods of extraordinary violence, and in a single dreadful day and night, all your fighting men were swallowed up by the earth, and the island of Atlantis was similarly swallowed up by the sea and vanished."

Sometime after the *Timaeus,* Plato wrote a dialogue called the *Critias.* Here he offered many more details about the "marvelous beauty and inexhaustible profusion" of Atlantis. There were temples, gymnasiums, gardens, canals, and bridges; dockyards filled with warships; buildings of white, black, and yellow stone; walls of bronze; a palace "whose size and beauty were astonishing to see," and even a track for horse racing.

The *Critias* builds to the climactic moment when Zeus, angry at the arrogance of the Atlantians, summons all the gods. As Zeus is about to speak, Plato abruptly stopped writing, leaving philosophers to wonder, for the next two and a half millennia, what happened next. Others, too, including historians, archaeologists, oceanographers, and geologists, have wondered what happened to Atlantis, and whether it ever truly existed.

☙ ❧

There were plenty of theories, placing Atlantis anywhere from North America (this was first promulgated by Francis Bacon in 1626, not long after the English had settled there) to Morocco (this according to the French archaeologist Felix Berlioux, who claimed to have found Atlantis there in 1874). The most obvious place for Atlantis, of course, was where Plato said it was: in the Atlantic Ocean. That's where Ignatius

Donnelly put it in 1882. This was the same Donnelly who argued that Francis Bacon wrote Shakespeare's plays (and Marlowe's, for that matter), but on the subject of Atlantis, Donnelly seemed to have more logic on his side. To the Greeks of Plato's time, the Pillars of Hercules were the Straits of Gibraltar. Beyond that was the Atlantic.

To Donnelly, Atlantis was no mere island. It was a huge continent linking the prehistoric peoples of Europe and Asia with those of America. It was also "the true Antediluvian world; the Garden of Eden; the Gardens of the Hesperides; the Elysian Fields; the Gardens of Alcinous; the Mesomphals; the Olympos, the Asgard of the traditions of the ancient nations; representing a universal memory of a great land, where early mankind dwelt for ages in peace and happiness."

"The gods and goddesses of the ancient Greeks, the Phoenicians, the Hindoos, and the Scandinavians," Donnelly believed, "were simply the kings, queens, and heroes of Atlantis; and the acts attributed to them in mythology are a confused recollection of real historical events."

After Atlantis sank, its survivors made their way to both sides of the ocean. This explained, Donnelly argued, why both Egyptians and the pre-Columbian natives of America built pyramids, why similar plants and animals lived in Europe and America, and why people on both sides of the Atlantic told stories of a great flood. The islands of the Atlantic were once the mountains of Atlantis; the furrows on the ocean floor were once its riverbeds.

More sober scientists, even in the nineteenth century, recognized all sorts of problems with Donnelly's theory. Geologists attributed the canyons on the ocean floor to underwater currents, not drowned rivers. Increasingly, scientists subscribed to an evolutionist rather than diffusionist explanation for the comparable natural and cultural developments in Europe and America: comparable forces on both sides of the Atlantic, not a common ancestor, explained the similarities. To the extent that prehistoric people and animals did migrate to America, it was more likely from Asia than Europe. Finally, there was the problem of timing. Donnelly (and Plato) dated Atlantis nine thousand years before Solon, a period when—judging from all the archaeological evidence—humans were a lot more like cavemen than the gods of Olympus.

Atlantis, it seemed, was a fantasy, and it attracted its share of fantasists. Paul Schliemann, who identified himself as the grandson of Heinrich Schliemann, the archaeologist who discovered Troy, claimed his grandfather had left him a vase with the inscription "From King Kronos of Atlantis." When he broke open the vase, he found it contained Atlantean artifacts, though he never showed them to the public. It turned out Heinrich Schliemann had no grandson named Paul.

Then there were psychics like (in the nineteenth century) Madame Helena Blavatsky, who learned about Atlantis from a dead Tibetan named Koot Hoomi, and (in the twentieth) Edgar Cayce, who saw Atlantis in his trances. Cayce's Atlantis featured atomic energy and flying machines. Charles Berlitz, whose 1974 book delved into the Bermuda Triangle, followed that up with one in 1984 that described forces capable of not only pulling planes and ships into the Atlantic but also an island and its civilization.

All this was nonsense. Other than the *Timaeus* and the *Critias,* there is no evidence that Atlantis existed. None of the Greek historians mentioned Atlantis, except to quote Plato. Even Herodotus, who couldn't resist a good story, said nothing. Aristotle, who was Plato's pupil and knew him well, said bluntly that "he who had invented Atlantis let it sink again under the surface of the sea." By the mid-twentieth century, amid the hoaxes and fantasies, serious historians had concluded that Aristotle was right, and that Atlantis was pure fiction.

ᕼᕼᕼ

In 1967, archaeologist Spyridon Marinatos uncovered a city buried on the Aegean island of Thera. Here were exquisite frescoes and pottery from the Minoan civilization that flourished in the area after about 2000 BC. Here, too, were plenty of red, white, and black rocks, just like those Plato said were in Atlantis. Thera appeared to have been destroyed by volcanic eruptions, and seismologists such as Angelos Galanopoulos determined that between 1600 BC and 1400 BC a volcano opened a huge hole in the ocean, leaving much of Thera under the sea. The volcano also set off tsunamis that would have rolled over Crete, the center of Minoan civilization. The civilization may not have perished in Plato's "single dreadful day and night," but tsunamis may have so devastated Crete that it never recovered.

The archaeological and geological evidence was inconclusive, but this was a theory about Atlantis that had to be taken seriously.

"Atlantis did actually, physically exist, not in the Atlantic Ocean, on the grand scale of legend . . . but in a lesser, more familiar dimension, in a sea utterly familiar to Plato," wrote oceanographic engineer James Mavor. "Atlantis lay in the Aegean itself, and in a position and under circumstances that would have certainly insured that its destruction, which did in fact occur, could be remembered through time to the Greek era, and through Plato to us." How did Atlantis end up in the Aegean instead of the Atlantic?

Galanopoulos and others argued that, though in Plato's time the Pillars of Hercules meant the Straits of Gibraltar, they may have had a different meaning to Solon or to the Egyptian priests of Sais. Some speculated that Solon's description of Atlantis as larger than Libya and Asia may have been a mistranslation for *between* Libya and Asia; that is, in the Aegean. The Pillars of Hercules, then, would be the two southernmost headlands of the Peloponnese—not far from Thera or Crete.

There was still the problem of dates. Galanopoulos conceded that dating Atlantis to 9600 BC was "both incredible and impossible." So, he explained, Solon must have misinterpreted the Egyptian hieroglyphics. "When dimensions and dates are given in thousands, they are all ten times too great," Galanopoulos argued. "This seems to indicate that when Solon was transcribing the Egyptian writings, the word or symbol representing 100 was mistaken for that representing 1,000."

Instead of nine thousand years, there were a mere nine hundred years between Solon and Atlantis. That put Atlantis's fall in the same general time period as Crete's.

The Crete-as-Atlantis theory was by no means universally accepted. A majority of historians continued to argue that Thera was too small to fit Plato's description, that the Pillars were Gibraltar, that the volcanic eruption at Thera came too late to explain the fall of Crete (let alone Atlantis), that Plato never even mentioned a volcano, and that some of Thera and all of Crete were neither submerged nor lost.

Still, Atlantis could now be discussed in respectable circles. "The island of Crete was not swallowed up by the sea," historian Rodney Castleden wrote in 1998, "but perhaps the tradition was a misremembering of what happened to the Minoan trading empire. . . . It was as if the invisible network of trading routes and political controls had sunk to the bottom of the Aegean . . . metaphorically 'swallowed up by the sea.'"

Castleden, as well as many other historians, believed Crete was just one of the traditions on which Plato drew. Plato was familiar with earthquakes; one destroyed the coastal city of Helice around 373 BC, only twenty years before he wrote the *Timaeus* and the *Critias*. Plato may also have had in mind the Athenians' failed expedition to Syracuse, which took place in 413 BC. Some scholars speculated Atlantis was an allegory about Athens: instead of directly criticizing the Athenians for invading Syracuse, Plato may have chosen to write about how an earlier and even greater civilization was done in by its imperial ambitions. Within the dialogues there are also echoes of the Peloponnesian War, also within his lifetime. That war ended with Sparta's defeat of Athens in 404 BC. As with the Syracuse venture, the analogy was imperfect, but the message was clear: too much ambition was dangerous.

To make that point, Plato included in the *Timaeus* and the *Critias* elements of the history of Syracuse, Sparta, Athens, perhaps even Crete. By not directly criticizing contemporary Athens, he protected himself from the fate of his teacher, Socrates, who was executed in 399 BC. But Plato also knew these elements would resonate with his readers. The mix of actual and invented history makes it impossible to know whether Plato intended any of the Atlantis story to be taken literally, but that was not his concern. He was a philosopher, not a historian, and in works like the *Republic, Timaeus,* and *Critias* Plato expounded on good and bad states. Atlantis, though it never existed, provided a memorable example of both.

To Investigate Further

Donnelly, Ignatius. *Atlantis.* New York: Harper and Brothers, 1882.
    Atlantis as the explanation for, well, pretty much everything.

Galanopoulos, Angelos, and Edward Bacon. *Atlantis.* Indianapolis: Bobbs-Merrill, 1969.
    Galanopoulos also suggested the Aegean tsunamis reached Egypt and caused the ten plagues described in Exodus.

Kukal, Zdnek. *Atlantis in the Light of Modern Research.* Amsterdam: Elsevier, 1984.
A geologist's analysis.

Pellegrino, Charles. *Unearthing Atlantis.* New York: Random House, 1991.
A paleontologist's case for Thera-as-Atlantis.

Zangger, Eberhard. *The Flood from Heaven.* New York: William Morrow, 1992.
Zangger argued Troy was Plato's model for Atlantis.

Castleden, Rodney. *Atlantis Destroyed.* London: Routledge, 1998.
A credible defense of the links between Crete, Thera, and Atlantis.

Ellis, Richard. *Imagining Atlantis.* New York: Alfred A. Knopf, 1998.
An entertaining overview of the various theories, from the scientific to the loony.

Who Was Theseus?

THESEUS'S EXPLOITS WERE LEGION: he brought democracy to Athens, joined Jason and the Argonauts in their quest for the Golden Fleece, and fought (to a draw) the fierce women warriors known as the Amazons. But all of this paled before his greatest deed, the slaying of the minotaur. The story, which was told most fully by Plutarch in the first century A.D. but which was clearly known well before then, went this way:

The powerful King Minos, who ruled Greece from his palace in Crete, was married to Pasiphae, who fell in love with a beautiful bull. Pasiphae had the inventor Daedalus build her a wooden cow, so she could hide inside and mate with the bull. She then gave birth to the monstrous minotaur—half man, half bull, and unfortunately fond of human flesh.

Minos turned to Daedalus, who built a huge labyrinth to hold the minotaur. Into this labyrinth, every nine years, the king sent fourteen Athenian youths, at once feeding the minotaur and avenging the death of Minos's son, Androgeos, at the hands of the Athenians. None of the youths ever returned—at least until Theseus, the son of the Athenian king Aegus, volunteered to go. He promised his father he'd return, flying a white sail to celebrate his success.

Back in Crete, Minos's daughter, Ariadne, fell in love with the courageous youth and handed him a ball of thread. Theseus slew the minotaur, then followed the unwound thread out of the labyrinth. Thus ended the cruel sacrifice of the Athenian youths, and with it the dominance of Crete over Athens.

It was not so happy an ending for Ariadne, whom Theseus abandoned on his way back to Athens, or for Aegus, who threw himself off a cliff when he spotted his son's ship still rigged with a black sail. (Theseus had forgotten to make the switch.) But that at least had the benefit of hastening Theseus's ascension to the throne.

Plutarch's story, filled with supernatural elements, obviously belongs to the realm of mythology. But early historians wondered whether the myth might not have preserved some memory of a Cretan empire that, in a prehistoric age, ruled Greece. In 1900 Arthur Evans, the director of the Ashmolean Museum at Oxford, arrived in Crete. What he found convinced him, and many others, that Crete had not only been the center of a great empire, but also that the story of Theseus was not nearly as fantastic as it once seemed.

෴

Evans was ideally suited to excavate at Crete. A third-generation academic, he was an expert on ancient writing, in search of which he first went to Crete. He was also a supporter of Cretan independence, which stood him in good stead after the island was liberated from Turkish rule in 1899. Best of all, Evans had inherited a fortune from his father's paper business. This allowed him to bypass the usual tricky negotiations, and simply buy the land where he wanted to dig. Local tradition was clear about the site of Knossos, Minos's palace, being in the Kairatos Valley, and that's where Evans began digging.

Within weeks, it was clear that this was a remarkable site. Luckily, it had not been built over in Greek or Roman times, so workmen almost instantly reached the remains of a Bronze Age palace. And what a palace! It extended for many acres, and with its numerous dark rooms and passages, it immediately conjured up a labyrinth. Evans couldn't help but imagine ancient Athenian visitors returning home to tell tales of having been trapped in a seemingly endless maze. In the middle of the palace was a large courtyard. Could this have been the home, Evans wondered, of the creature mythologized as a minotaur?

Still in 1900, Evans made his most sensational discovery of all: a painting depicting a male youth in the act of somersaulting over the back of the bull, while two female youths stood by, apparently either spotting their companion or waiting their turn. More images of bulls and bull-leapers soon were found, some on engraved seals and some in the form of bronze or ivory statuettes.

An amazed Evans consulted with the obvious experts—Spanish bullfighters. He asked them whether the type of bull-leaping portrayed in the Cretan art was possible. The bull-fighters responded that it couldn't be done, at least if the bull-leapers hoped to survive. But the evidence was overwhelming that some form of bull-leaping had taken place here. Whatever artistic license might have been taken by the Cretan artists and by the Athenian storytellers, bulls were clearly an integral part of this culture. Perhaps the youths pictured were Greek captives trained for the arena like the gladiators of ancient Rome.

Evans named the culture "Minoan," after its legendary (or perhaps not so legendary) king. He was convinced that the Minoans had, as the Theseus story recalled, once ruled over Greece, dominating the mainland politically and artistically. It was the Minoans, Evans believed, who laid the foundations on which were built the later achievements of the classical Greeks. The poetry of Homer, the philosophy of Plato, the architecture of the Parthenon—all these were foreshadowed in the Minoan culture.

Evans's confidence in his ideas was bolstered by his discovery at Knossos of a number of clay tablets. It was to search for ancient writing, you'll recall, that Evans initially went to Crete. The tablets, written in alphabets that came to be known as Linear A and Linear B, clearly confirmed Evans's belief that the Minoans were not only artistic but also literate.

To preserve the glories of Minoan civilization, Evans in 1901 began to reconstruct the palace at Knossos. He rebuilt the long-gone upper walls and columns, as well as part of the palace roof. He hired a Swiss artist, Emile Gillieron, to restore the frescoes. The result was completely unlike any other archaeological site of his time or ours; instead of looking at mere foot-high remains, even tourists with no historical background could get a clear sense of the full scope and grandeur of Minoan art and architecture.

Evans's critics accused him of creating a postcard version of history. It was no longer possible, they argued, to tell how much of Minoan civilization he'd discovered and how

"Everywhere the bull!" wrote Arthur Evans of his discoveries at Knossos. The most famous and startling was this fresco, which portrayed a man vaulting over a charging bull, and led archaeologists to wonder whether there might not be some truth to the story of Theseus slaying the minotaur. *(Wolfgang Kaehler/Corbis)*

much he'd invented. By later archaeological standards, his critics were undoubtedly right; no archaeologist today would allow a reconstruction on the actual site of an excavation. In fairness to Evans, it ought to be added that he was far more careful about preserving a precise and photographic record of what he found than were many of his contemporaries. And, reluctant as critics might be to admit this, he also created a site so dramatic that visitors ever since could not help but share in his passion for the Minoans.

ꙮ

A more fundamental problem with Evans's view of Greek history emerged as other archaeologists, primarily Alan Wace in the 1920s and Carl Blegen in the 1930s, excavated sites on the Greek mainland. There they found evidence of a culture that was flourishing at the same time that the Minoans ruled Crete. This "Mycenaean" civilization was clearly independent of the Minoans, and at least as powerful if not as sophisticated as its neighbors to the south. Indeed, Wace and Blegen argued, the Mycenaeans may very well have conquered the Minoans and taken over Knossos, probably sometime after 1500 B.C.

In a way, this seemed further confirmation that the Theseus legend had some basis in history. The Athenians, like the Mycenaeans, were Greeks, so Theseus's triumph could stand for some actual battle or series of battles during which the Mycenaean Greeks defeated the bull-headed Cretans. Evans, however, would have none of this. So convinced was he of the Minoans' superiority that he insisted that only a natural catastrophe—perhaps an earthquake—could have ended their rule. And if some such disaster enabled the Mycenaeans to dislodge the Minoans from Knossos, there was still no question in Evans's mind that it was the Mycenaean military might, not their culture, that prevailed.

Evans's position became increasingly difficult after 1939, when Blegen, still excavating on the mainland, discovered more clay tablets written in Linear B, the same alphabet Evans had found at Knossos. True, the discovery might be interpreted to mean that the Minoans had brought their writing north and introduced it to the Greeks. But it also raised the possibility that Linear B—and writing in general—was a Mycenaean and not a Minoan invention.

Evans died in 1941, never having figured out what was written on his precious tablets. Eleven years later, Michael Ventris, an amateur cryptologist utilizing techniques developed during World War II, finally broke the code. The words written on the tablet were something of a disappointment; far from being great poetry or philosophy, they were mostly lists of goods that had been stored at Knossos and elsewhere. But Ventris's discovery was nonetheless extremely significant, for Linear B, it turned out, was a system of writing *Greek*—an archaic and difficult Greek, to be sure, but Greek nonetheless.

That meant that writing had come to Crete from Greece and not, as Evans had always maintained, the other way around. It remains possible that the Minoans had a writing of their own—Linear A, which has still not been decoded, may turn out to be Minoan—but after Ventris's breakthrough it was impossible to picture Mycenae as a mere outpost of Cretan civilization. On the contrary, the Mycenaean Greeks clearly had a powerful civilization of their own. And at some point, much earlier than Evans thought—and perhaps even led by a prince named Theseus—these Greeks had come to Crete, and conquered it.

⟋⟍⟍

Linear B did not, by any means, spell the end of the controversies surrounding the Minoans. By the 1960s, most archaeologists agreed that the Mycenaeans had conquered Crete, but there was no consensus on how they'd done so. Some archaeologists, notably Spyridon Marinatos, remained convinced that a natural catastrophe had so weakened the Minoans that it opened the door for the Mycenaeans.

That catastrophe, Marinatos believed, was the eruption of a volcano on the island of Thera, about seventy miles north of Crete. In 1967 Marinatos went to Thera, seeking proof. He soon uncovered more than he'd hoped for: preserved under a layer of volcanic ash was an entire Bronze Age town. There was no need for Evans-style restoration here; these houses were still remarkably intact, and many were filled with Minoan-style art and artifacts indicating that this had been a Cretan colony. The only thing missing were the people, who apparently had had enough time to flee before the volcano erupted.

This was an extraordinary discovery—a Cretan Pompeii but twice as old. But could a volcanic eruption on Thera have ended Cretan civilization? Marinatos believed so. He argued that the volcano may have been set off by earthquakes, which in turn caused tsunamis that devastated Crete. At the very least, he maintained, the earthquakes and tsunamis did enough damage to give the Mycenaeans their opening. Had he lived, Evans certainly would have felt vindicated by Marinatos's arguments.

Most archaeologists and other scientists, however, were not persuaded. For one thing, the dates didn't match. Most volcanologists placed the Thera eruption between 1600 and 1700 BC, more than a hundred years before the estimated date of the Minoan collapse. Moreover, in spite of the obvious volcanic damage at Thera, there were no significant deposits of ash on Crete. Nor was there evidence that water from tsunamis had reached Knossos, let alone damaged it. In fact, the archaeological evidence on Crete seemed to indicate that fire, not ash or water, had caused much of the destruction there.

So most scientists—though by no means all—have denied the Thera volcano a significant role in the downfall of Minoan civilization.

Does that mean that Theseus played the role instead? That Theseus (or the Greeks he came to represent) slew the minotaur (or rather the Minoans the monster came to represent)? These are questions that can't be fully answered, given the centuries that separate us from Plutarch's time, and Plutarch from Theseus's time. But that certainly doesn't mean that no progress has been made in answering them. On the contrary, the discoveries of the past hundred years have filled in some very believable details about what once seemed an entirely fictional story.

To Investigate Further

Evans, Arthur. *The Palace of Minos* (London: Macmillan, 1921–1936).
 Evans's own account of the discoveries at Knossos, in four volumes.

Ward, Anne, ed. *The Quest for Theseus* (New York: Praeger, 1970).
 Essays on how the Theseus legend originated and developed in art and literature, from the classical era to the present.

Wunderlich, Hans. *The Secret of Crete,* trans. from German by Richard Winston (New York: Macmillan, 1974).
 Wunderlich argues, provocatively but ultimately unconvincingly, that Knossos was never lived in, but was, like the Egyptian pyramids, a royal tomb.

Horwitz, Sylvia. *The Find of a Lifetime* (New York: Viking, 1981).
 A readable biography of Evans, with a balanced presentation of the controversies until its publication.

Hardy, D. A., et al. *Thera and the Aegean World III* (London: Thera Foundation, 1990).
 These proceedings of a major international conference, held in Thera in 1989, include more than a hundred papers by archaeologists and other scientists. The clear consensus was that the Theran eruption was *not* responsible for the end of Minoan civilization.

Fitton, J. Lesley. *The Discovery of the Greek Bronze Age* (Cambridge, MA: Harvard University Press, 1996).
 An authoritative account of the excavations at Troy, Mycenae, Knossos, Thera, and other Greek Bronze Age sites.

Who Built Stonehenge?

T HE PYRAMIDS OF EGYPT, the Parthenon of Greece, the Colosseum of Rome: all conjure up images of great civilizations, of pharaohs and philosophers, of emperors and epics.

Not so Stonehenge.

The massive stone remains on Salisbury Plain are surrounded, not by ancient cities, but by modern highways, heading eastward toward London. There are no hieroglyphics to decipher here, no Socratic dialogues to interpret. The Stone Age and Bronze Age people who built Stonehenge also built lesser stone monuments, and their remains are scattered around the countryside. But they left nothing else to explain how or why they managed as prodigious a feat of engineering as Stonehenge. The ancient inhabitants of Salisbury Plain appeared in other respects to have a culture that was barely above subsistence level, and until late in the twentieth century, historians had no qualms about calling these people "barbarians."

No wonder, then, that from medieval times on, those who studied this ancient circle of stones looked beyond Salisbury Plain to explain who built it. The twelfth-century welsh cleric Geoffrey of Monmouth attributed Stonehenge to Merlin, the wizard of King Arthur's court. According to Geoffrey's *History of the Kings of Britain,* the monument was commissioned by Arthur's uncle, one Aurelius Ambrosius. Ambrosius was looking for a suitably monumental way to commemorate a great victory over the Anglo-Saxon invaders. Merlin suggested taking a circle of stones from a place called Killarus in Ireland, and then arranged to float the premade monument to Britain.

In the seventeenth century, King James I was so intrigued by Stonehenge that he assigned his court architect, Inigo Jones, to investigate. After studying the monument, Jones could only agree with Geoffrey of Monmouth that the region's Stone Age or Bronze Age residents could not possibly have built it. "If destitute of the Knowledge, even to clothe themselves," Jones reasoned, "much less any Knowledge had they to erect stately structures, or such remarkable Works as Stone-Heng."

Jones concluded that a "Structure so exquisite" could only be the work of the Romans, and that it was a temple to an obscure Roman god.

The succeeding years saw continuing efforts to credit Stonehenge to builders from somewhere—almost anywhere—besides Britain. The Danes, the Belgae, and the Anglo-Saxons all had their backers, as did the ancient Celtic priests known as Druids.

The problem with all these theories was the same. Though radiocarbon dating would not be invented until the twentieth century, the cruder dating methods of earlier archaeologists indicated that Stonehenge was probably built before 1500 B.C. The Druids, most scholars also realized, arrived no earlier than 500 B.C., the Romans after that. That meant Stonehenge was built more than a millennium before either reached England.

So, well into the twentieth century, the question remained: Who built Stonehenge?

⟨∞⟩

An archaeologist's accidental discovery in 1953 pointed to a solution. On July 10, as part of his survey of the site, Richard Atkinson was preparing to photograph some seventeenth-century graffiti on a stone next to what's known as the Great Trilithon. He waited until late afternoon, hoping for a sharper contrast of light and shade. As he looked through the camera, Atkinson noticed that below the seventeenth-century inscription were other carvings.

One was of a dagger pointing to the ground. Nearby were four axes, of a type found in England at about the time of Stonehenge's erection.

It was the lone dagger, not the axes, that most excited Atkinson. Nothing like it had been found in England, or anywhere in northern Europe, for that matter. The most comparable artifact came from the royal graves of the citadel of Mycenae, in Greece.

Here, finally, was the link to a more sophisticated civilization, one that could reasonably have been expected to build something like Stonehenge. Even better, the daggers found in Mycenae dated to approximately 1500 B.C., about the same time Stonehenge was built, according to most experts of the 1950s. Unlike the Romans or the Druids, the Mycenaean connection made chronological sense.

Atkinson worked up an elaborate theory that Stonehenge was designed by an architect visiting from the more civilized Mediterranean. Perhaps, he speculated, there was even a Mycenaean prince buried on Salisbury Plain. The archaeological world, relieved to finally have a solution to the Stonehenge problem, embraced the theory.

But just as quickly as the Mycenaean consensus formed, it was soon torn apart. The 1960s brought the advent of a new form of radiocarbon dating, and suddenly archaeologists were confronted by strong evidence that Stonehenge was much older than previously thought—and much older than the Mycenaean civilization. The new radiocarbon dates confirmed that the citadel at Mycenae was built between 1600 and 1500 B.C., but they pushed the origins of Stonehenge way back, well before any Mediterranean influences could possibly be felt.

By this latest reckoning, the banks and outer ditch of the Stonehenge circle were begun in approximately 2950 B.C. Some wooden structures were added within the circle between about 2900 and 2400 B.C., then replaced by the familiar stone structure sometime soon after that.

The new dates undercut not just the Mycenaean theory but also the entire "diffusionist" mind-set that led to it. Stonehenge was simply too old to have been built by any of the great European civilizations, and non-European civilizations were too far away. For the first time, most scholars had to accept that the people who built Stonehenge were people who lived near Stonehenge, and that they did so without outside help. These apparently primitive people had somehow built one of the world's most enduring monuments.

𐎞

As if that wasn't impressive enough, the people who built Stonehenge had made their task stunningly more difficult by using stones that came from 150 miles away, in the Preseli Mountains of southwestern Wales.

The "bluestones" (which are actually more of a splotchy gray) were traced to their source by the geologist H. H. Thomas in 1932. The three rock types in the bluestones are unlike any rock found near Stonehenge, but Thomas found that the same three could be picked out of natural rock outcrops between the summits of Mounts Carnmenyn and Foel Trigarn in Wales.

How did the people of Salisbury Plain get these stones, some weighing five tons, from Wales to England?

Thomas's discovery led some to look anew at Geoffrey of Monmouth's tale about Merlin's magic. Perhaps, archaeologist Stuart Piggott suggested, there were some genuine oral traditions embedded in the folklore. After all, Geoffrey had written of Merlin getting the stones from the west (albeit from Ireland, not Wales). Geoffrey had also written of floating the stones to Stonehenge, perhaps a residual folk memory of ferrying them across the Irish Sea. And Geoffrey may have even provided a hint as to why the people who built Stonehenge would go to such lengths to bring the stones from afar, when there were plenty of other kinds of rocks right around Salisbury Plain: perhaps the builders of Stonehenge, like Geoffrey's Merlin, believed these rocks had magical properties.

Most historians thought Piggott's suggestions a bit far-fetched, especially in light of Geoffrey's generally garbled version of history. But that still left unanswered the question of how at least eighty-five and possibly more stones got from the Preseli Mountains to Salisbury Plain.

Some, most notably the geologist G. A. Kellaway, argued that the bluestones were carried by glaciers, not people. But most experts lined up against Kellaway, since they didn't believe that the most recent glaciation extended as far south as the Preselis or Salisbury Plain. Even if it did, it's highly unlikely that glaciers would have gathered up the bluestones from one small area in Wales and deposited them in another small area in England, as opposed to scattering them all about. The absence of any other bluestones south or east of the Bristol Channel (with the possible exception of one now in the Salisbury Museum but of disputed history) makes a strong case against the glacial theory.

So, unlikely as it may once have seemed, the most common explanation was that the people from the Salisbury Plain area had lashed some canoes together and carried the bluestones across the Irish Sea. The journey was further evidence that the people of Salisbury Plain possessed surprising and extraordinary technological expertise.

𐎞

With the diffusionists in disarray, the 1960s saw even more remarkable claims made on behalf of the people of Salisbury Plain. This time they came not from archaeologists or geologists, but from astronomers.

The sixties were not the first time astronomy had come into play. Back in the eighteenth century, William Stukely had noted that the principal line of Stonehenge was "where abouts the Sun rises, when the days are longest," and many others who studied the monument had found other ways in which it was oriented toward the sun, moon, or stars. Yet none of those studies created a stir anything like that made by the Boston University astronomer Gerald Hawkins. His brashly titled book *Stonehenge Decoded* was published in 1965 and became an international best-seller.

Hawkins found that the alignments among 165 key points in the monument strongly correlated with the rising and setting positions of the sun and the moon. Even more controversially, he argued that a circle of pits in Stonehenge known as the Aubrey Holes had been used to predict eclipses of the moon. Hawkins dubbed Stonehenge a "Neolithic computer."

Atkinson, still the premier authority on Stonehenge since his discovery of the "Mycenaean" carvings, struck back with the equally bluntly titled article "Moonshine on Stonehenge." Atkinson argued that there was a good chance the celestial alignments could have occurred by chance. As for the Aubrey Holes as an eclipse predictor, Atkinson pointed to evidence that the holes had been used as cremation pits and had been filled up very soon after they'd been dug.

To some extent, the debate that followed pitted astronomers against archaeologists, with the practitioners of each discipline frequently having a great deal of trouble understanding the other's technical arguments. Astronomers came up with a variety of other ways by which Stonehenge could have been used as an astronomical observatory, some of which were less easily dismissed than Hawkins's. But the astronomers had a tendency to emphasize how different points were aligned with the sun or the moon, while ignoring the fact that one of these supposedly aligned points might have been constructed hundreds or even a thousand years later than the other. Archaeologists were quick to poke holes in most of these theories.

By the end of the second millennium, though the debate continued, there were signs of a consensus. The wildest theories, like Hawkins's, were discredited, even among astronomers, but almost all archaeologists (including Atkinson) recognized that at least a few of the celestial alignments, particularly the solar ones, were more than a coincidence. Most likely, most agreed, the monument was never used as an observatory, at least in the modern sense, but the people of Stonehenge probably did observe the sun from there, perhaps as part of some prehistoric ritual.

Yet even this imprecise kind of astronomy indicated that the people of Salisbury Plain studied the sky, and had some sort of system for keeping track of their findings. Clearly the builders of Stonehenge, however primitive they were in some respects, were remarkably sophisticated in others. In that sense, the latest discoveries, while deepening our understanding of Stonehenge, also have deepened the mystery surrounding the people who built it.

To Investigate Further

Geoffrey of Monmouth, *The History of the Kings of Britain*, trans. Lewis Thorpe (London: The Folio Society, 1966).

Just as it was when Geoffrey finished it in 1138, the *History* is still entertaining, intriguing ... and ultimately unreliable.

Hawkins, Gerald. *Stonehenge Decoded* (Garden City, NY: Doubleday, 1965).

In spite of his flaws, Hawkins had a flair for drama, and the book still makes for exciting reading.

Atkinson, Richard. "Moonshine on Stonehenge." *Antiquity* 40, no. 159 (September 1966).

The leading archaeologist's response to Hawkins.

Hawkes, Jacquetta. "God in the Machine." *Antiquity* 41, no. 163 (September 1967).

Hawkes is rightly famous for saying that "every age gets the Stonehenge it desires, or deserves." Her words could just as appropriately be applied to just about every mystery of history in this book.

Chippindale, Christopher. *Stonehenge Complete* (Ithaca, NY: Cornell University Press, 1983).

Though "complete" can only be an overstatement when the subject is Stonehenge, the book is a very thorough historiography that includes just about "everything important, interesting, or odd that has been written or painted, discovered or felt, about the most extraordinary of all ancient buildings."

Castleden, Rodney. *The Making of Stonehenge* (London: Routledge, 1993).

A close look at each phase in the monument's rise and fall.

Cleal, R. M., K. Walker, and R. Montague. *Stonehenge in Its Landscape* (London: English Heritage, 1995).

A fat technical report that brings together all of the results of all of the twentieth century's crucial excavations.

North, John. *Stonehenge* (New York: The Free Press, 1996).

The latest and most thorough presentation of the astronomical thesis. North's thesis, which impressed many but convinced fewer, is that Stonehenge embodied many significant alignments, but that previous astronomers have failed to recognize them since they looked at the sun from the center of the monument, when they should have been doing so from outside the circle.

Souden, David. *Stonehenge* (London: Collins & Brown, 1997).

Commissioned by English Heritage, the quasi-independent agency that controls the monument, this is a clear exposition of the orthodox position, accepting some (but rejecting most) astronomical theories.

Cunliffe, Barry, and Colin Renfrew, eds. *Science and Stonehenge* (Oxford: Oxford University Press, 1997).

A collection of essays that grew out of a conference held after the appearance of Stonehenge in Its Landscape; includes the latest entries in the bluestone and astronomy debates.

Why Did the Pharaohs
Build the Pyramids?

IN ABOUT 450 B.C. Herodotus recounted a story about Khufu, a pharaoh so wicked that when he'd spent all his treasure, he sent his daughter to a brothel with orders to procure him a certain sum. Loyal daughter, she did so. But, hoping to be remembered for something besides the number of men she slept with, she also demanded from each man a present of a stone. With these she built one of the huge pyramids that still stand on the Gaza plateau, near the Nile River.

At the time Herodotus wrote, the pyramids were already a couple of millennia old. Yet the 2,000-plus years since haven't stemmed the flow of crackpot theories about the origins of the pyramids.

Some medieval writers believed they were the biblical granaries Joseph had used to store corn during Egypt's years of plenty. More recently, the pyramids have been described as sundials and calendars, astronomical observatories, surveying tools, and anchors for alien spacecraft.

Yet even Herodotus knew that the most widely accepted theory was that the pyramids were tombs for the pharaohs. Most reputable Egyptologists still believe that, and for good reason. The pyramids are ranged along the western bank of the Nile, which Egyptian myths tie to both the setting of the sun and the journey to an afterlife. Archaeologists have uncovered nearby ceremonial funeral boats in which the pharaohs were to sail to the afterworld. And the pyramids are surrounded by other tombs, presumably belonging to members of pharaohs' courts.

Most telling of all, many of the pyramids contained stone sarcophagi, or coffins. By the nineteenth century, some of the hierographic inscriptions on or near the sarcophagi were identified as spells to help the pharaohs pass from one world to the next.

The tomb theory lacked one critical piece of evidence, however: a body. During the nineteenth and early twentieth centuries, explorers and then archaeologists entered pyramid after pyramid. (There are more than eighty in various states along the Nile Valley, and perhaps others buried under the desert sand.) They would find what appeared to be the pharaoh's coffin, they would breathlessly open it, and—again and again—they would find it empty.

∽∿∾

The most widespread explanation for the empty tombs has always been that the pyramids were robbed. Of course, most robbers were more interested in finding the pharaohs' treasures than their bodies, but they certainly weren't likely to take any time to make sure the latter were properly preserved. Nor were they likely to leave behind any mummy covered in pure gold.

The first tomb robbers were probably ancient Egyptians themselves, judging from the elaborate efforts to foil them. At the pyramid of Amenemhet III at Hawara, for example, the entrance leads to a small empty chamber, which leads to a narrow passage going nowhere. In the roof of that passage was a huge stone weighing more than twenty-two tons. Slid sideways, it revealed an upper corridor, again seeming to lead nowhere. A hidden brick door in one wall led to a third passage, then there were two more sliding ceiling blocks before reaching an antechamber and finally the burial chamber.

Yet it was all in vain; the Egyptian tomb robbers could not be thwarted. Their determination frustrated not just archaeologists but also later treasure hunters, such as the ninth-century Arab ruler Abdullah Al Mamun. He left a detailed report on what he thought was the first expedition into Khufu's Great Pyramid.

After leading his party through a series of false passages and plugged entrances, he finally reached the burial chamber, where he found nothing but an empty sarcophagus.

The European explorers who arrived in Egypt after Napoleon's conquest were more interested in carved stone than jewels, but they were only marginally more respectful of the pharaoh's monuments than their Egyptian and Arab predecessors. In 1818 Giovanni Belzoni, an Italian circus strongman turned explorer, used battering rams to get through the walls of the pyramid of Khufu's son, Khafre. Belzoni was busy stocking up for his upcoming exhibit in London, but he stopped long enough to check for bodies in what appeared to be the burial chamber. The only bones to be found belonged to a bull, perhaps some sort of offering thrown into the sarcophagus by some earlier intruders who'd made off with the pharaoh's body.

The search—for treasure and bodies—paid off in 1923, when the British archaeologist Howard Carter unearthed the tomb of Tutankhamen. "King Tut" is now probably the best-known pharaoh, and rightly so, given the magnificent and intact treasure Carter found. This included a solid gold coffin and a golden mask on the pharaoh's body.

Alas, the discovery proved nothing about pyramids, for Tutankhamen wasn't buried in one. His tomb had been cut right into the rocks of Egypt's Valley of the Kings.

Even more disturbing for Carter's crew was the death of the earl of Carnarvon, a rich amateur archaeologist who funded the expedition. Soon after arriving at the Valley of the Kings, Carnarvon was found dead in Cairo. Two others who had entered the tomb died soon after—first the head of the Louvre's department of Egyptian antiquities, then the assistant keeper of Egyptian antiquities at New York's Metropolitan Museum of Art.

Inevitably this led to all sorts of absurd speculation about a curse. One report had it that Carter found a tablet in the tomb inscribed, "Death will slay with his wings whoever disturbs the peace of the pharaoh."

⟨⟩

Curse or no curse, the search continued.

If the pyramids were built as tombs for the pharaohs, they were certainly expensive ones. As Rudyard Kipling wrote: "Who shall doubt the secret hid/Under Cheops' pyramid/Is that some contractor did/Cheops out of millions?" Pictured here is the Great Pyramid of Cheops. *(Library of Congress)*

In 1925, just two years after the discovery of Tutankhamen's tomb, a team of American archaeologists under George Andrew Reisner was working near the foot of Khufu's Great Pyramid. A photographer trying to set up his tripod accidentally nicked out a piece of plaster from a hidden opening cut into the rock. That revealed part of a hundred-foot-deep shaft filled with masonry from top to bottom. It took two weeks to reach the bottom.

There Reisner found the coffin of Queen Hetepheres, Khufu's mother. Since the tomb had been so well hidden, Reisner hoped he might find an intact burial, but the sarcophagus was empty. Only after they'd gotten over their disappointment did archaeologists notice a plastered area on the wall of the chamber, behind which they found a small chest. Inside that were the embalmed viscera of the queen.

Reisner's guess—and he admitted it was only that—was that the queen must once have been buried elsewhere. Then, after robbers removed her body to get at jewels under its wrappings, her remains must have been reburied near her husband and son.

The hope of finding an intact burial in a pyramid was revived in 1951, when an Egyptian Egyptologist, Zacharia Goneim, uncovered the remains of a previously unknown pyramid at Saqqara, about six miles south of Giza. The pyramid had never been noticed before, since its builders never got beyond the foundation, which was then covered by the Sahara sands. At first, Goneim assumed an unfinished pyramid was unlikely to hold much of importance, let alone a pharaoh's remains. But his expectations rose as he followed a shallow trench into a tunnel. As he dug through three stone walls, he became even more excited; after all, no robber was likely to have taken the time to reseal a tomb on his way out. Jewels found in the pyramid seemed a further indication that here, at last, was a tomb the robbers never found.

Finally Goneim reached the burial chamber, which he identified as that of Sekhemkhet, a pharaoh about whom little was known, but a pharaoh nonetheless. When Goneim spotted a golden sarcophagus, he and his colleagues danced and wept and embraced each other. A few days later, in front of an audience of scholars and reporters, Goneim ordered the coffin opened. To his shock, it was empty.

⁓

The failure to find a pharaoh in his tomb has spawned numerous theories, many based on the mathematical regularities that Egyptologists saw in the pyramids. In the nineteenth century, for example, the Scottish astronomer Charles Piazzi Smyth "discovered" that the Great Pyramid had just enough "pyramid inches" to make it a scale model of the circumference of the earth. Unfortunately, Piazzi Smyth's careful calculations were based on measurements taken when massive mounds of debris still covered the base of the pyramid.

In 1974, physicist Kurt Mendelssohn contended that the pyramids were public works projects rather than tombs, and that their purpose was to create a national Egyptian identity for what had been scattered tribes. Mendelssohn's theory explained not just the lack of bodies but also another disturbing problem with the tomb theory, namely that many pharaohs appeared to build more than one of them. For example, Khufu's father, Snefru, had three pyramids, and it's hard to imagine he intended his remains to be divided among them. Khufu himself had only one pyramid, but it has three rooms that seem to have been designed as crypts.

Another theory that's gained many followers is that the pyramids were cenotaphs—monuments to the dead pharaohs but not their actual tombs, which were hidden elsewhere to keep them safe from robbers. That would explain why they were full of funereal trappings but no bodies.

Still, the majority of Egyptologists continue to believe that the pyramids were built primarily as tombs, even if they served some other purpose as well. They're surrounded by other tombs, albeit of lesser officials. Even if ancient and not-so-ancient robbers have stolen most every trace of them, the pharaohs' bodies once lay there.

The pyramids, in the consensus view, can best be understood as part of an architectural progression that began with rectangular, flat-topped tombs of mud brick, today called mastabas (in which bodies have been found). Then architects started placing one flat-topped structure on top of another, creating what became known as the "step pyramids," the most famous of which still stands south of Cairo at Saqqara. Finally, someone had the idea of filling in the steps, and the familiar slope of the pyramid was born, probably at Meidum, about forty miles south of Saqqara.

The architectural development coincided with theological changes. Texts found in mastabas indicate a belief that the pharaoh would climb to heaven on its steps. Later texts from the period of the true pyramids reflect a cult of the sun god, and describe the pharaohs rising on the rays of the sun. The sloping sides of the pyramid, resembling as they do the shape of the sun's rays shining down, were the new pathway to heaven.

Did the cult of the sun inspire Egyptian architects to design the pyramids? It seems at first glance unlikely that so many extra tons of stones had to be quarried, transported, and hauled into place just because a staircase was no longer considered an effective way to get to heaven. But, difficult as it is for us to understand it some four and a half thousand years later, the Egyptian people considered it well worth the effort. (And, in spite of the popular misconception that Hebrew slaves built the pyramids, it was Egyptians who did it.)

Almost everything that has lasted of Egyptian civilization has to do with death. It appears to have been the defining force in their religion, their literature, their art. For the pharaohs, the afterlife was a very real goal, whether via staircase or sunbeam. It's completely appropriate, therefore, that the monuments that define their civilization for posterity were also, almost certainly, designed to house their dead.

To Investigate Further

Herodotus. *The Histories*, trans. Aubrey de Selincourt (Middlesex, England: Penguin, 1954).
He's been called both the "father of history" and the "father of lies"; either way, his tales still rank among the most entertaining ever.

Proctor, Richard. *The Great Pyramid* (London: Chatto & Windus, 1883).
Khufu's pyramid as an astronomical observatory.

Carter, Howard. *The Tomb of Tutankhamen* (New York: E. P. Dutton, 1954).
How does it feel to find yourself face to face with a pharaoh from three thousand years ago? Carter captures the awe and excitement of his history-making discovery. Originally published in 1924.

Edwards, I. E. S. *The Pyramids of Egypt* (Middlesex, England: Viking, 1947).
Still the classic history of the pyramids and their cultural and religious significance.

Tompkins, Peter. *Secrets of the Great Pyramid* (New York: Harper & Row, 1971).
A fascinating but too uncritical compendium of alternative explanations for Khufu's tomb.

Mendelssohn, Kurt. *The Riddle of the Pyramids* (New York: Praeger, 1974).
The pyramids as a political statement.

Fagan, Brian. *The Rape of the Nile* (New York: Charles Scribner's Sons, 1975).
Tomb robbers, tourists, and archaeologists in Egypt through the ages, with a special focus on Belzoni: "the greatest plunderer of them all."

Johnson, Paul. *The Civilization of Ancient Egypt* (New York: Athenaeum, 1978).
    Its rise and fall, in one fact- and opinion-packed volume.

Bauval, Robert, and Adrian Gilbert. *The Orion Mystery* (New York: Crown, 1994).
    The latest case for an astronomical explanation; specifically, that the Giza pyramids were positioned to represent the three stars of Orion's belt.

Lehner, Mark. *The Complete Pyramids* (London: Thames & Hudson, 1997).
    Pyramid by pyramid, everything you wanted to know about each.

Was There Really a Trojan War?

J UST A FEW MILES FROM THE DARDANELLES, on the Asian side of the narrow strait that separates Greece from Turkey, stands a small hill known as Hisarlik.

This, according to Herodotus, Xenophon, Plutarch, and various other classical Greek and Roman writers, was the site of Troy, the Troy of Homer's *Iliad* and *Odyssey*. The classical Greeks were not sure whether Homer had ever actually seen Troy, but they had no doubt that the battles he described had taken place. Nor did they doubt that they'd taken place in and around Hisarlik.

In a world where humans were like gods (and gods were all too human), this was where the greatest of both clashed. It was to Troy that Paris, the son of Troy's King Priam, brought Helen, the most beautiful woman of the world, after he kidnapped her from her Greek home. It was to Troy that the Greek king Agamemnon led his troops to win her back. And it was at Troy that Achilles, the greatest of the Greek warriors, slayed Hector, Paris's brother. In the final scene of the *Iliad*, Priam met with Achilles to negotiate the return of his son's body, and a truce between the Greeks and the Trojans.

As readers of the *Odyssey* knew, the story didn't end there. With a fatal blow to Achilles's heel, Paris avenged his brother's death. And with the help of a giant wooden horse, the Greeks sneaked inside the Trojan walls and ultimately destroyed the city. So ended the golden age of Troy—and not so long after, the golden age of Greece as well.

The belief that all this actually happened—and happened at Hisarlik—drew later conquerors to the site. In 480 B.C., the Persian king Xerxes sacrificed a thousand bulls near Hisarlik, right before crossing the Dardanelles into Greece. A century and a half later, when Alexander the Great led his troops in the opposite direction, he honored Achilles with sacrifices near the same spot. Through the Middle Ages and the Renaissance, travelers continued to visit Hisarlik, convinced this was Troy.

Starting in the eighteenth century, scholars began to take a more skeptical approach. Many doubted there was a war at Troy, let alone the monumental clash of Homer's epics. Some even doubted there was a Homer, or at least a single man rather than a series of poets. After all, they noted, hundreds of years separated Herodotus from Homer, and hundreds more lay between the poet and the alleged golden age.

By the second half of the nineteenth century, only a minority of scholars believed that that the *Iliad* and the *Odyssey* recalled events that really happened. Even fewer believed that Troy, if it existed at all, was at Hisarlik. To most, the *Iliad* and the *Odyssey* were great literature, not history.

One man who remained convinced that Troy existed was Frank Calvert, the U.S. consul to the region and an amateur archaeologist. In the mid-1860s Calvert made a few preliminary excavations at Hisarlik, uncovering the remains of a temple from classical times and a wall from Alexander's time. This was encouraging, but it also convinced Calvert that there were many layers of history beneath Hisarlik and that the type of excavation necessary would require more money than he had.

Then, in 1868, Calvert invited to dinner Heinrich Schliemann, a visiting German millionaire with a passion for Homer. Schliemann, too, became convinced that Hisarlik was Troy. And, unlike Calvert, Schliemann had the money to do something about it.

⟅⟆

In 1870, he and his crew began digging. Schliemann believed that Homer's Troy was so ancient that it could only be found by burrowing deep into Hisarlik. So he opened up an enormous area of the hill, reaching straight down to solid bedrock. As he dug, he was disturbed to find various Stone Age objects, for these ought logically to be found beneath the Bronze or Iron Age city that Homer described. In May 1872 Schliemann admitted in his diary that he was "perplexed." Still, he kept digging.

Then, in May 1873, he struck gold—literally. As he later told the story, Schliemann feared how his workmen might react to the sight of gold. Telling them he'd just remembered it was his birthday, he said they should all take a break. Then he called his wife, Sophia, who secreted away the gold in her shawl. Only later did the couple examine their treasure, which surpassed Schliemann's dreams. There were exquisite works of gold and copper, including 2 gold crowns made of thousands of tiny pieces of threaded gold, 60 gold earrings, and 8,750 gold rings.

This must be, Schliemann concluded, the treasure of King Priam, including the jewelry of Helen. He later speculated that a member of the royal family had scooped up the treasure chest as the Greeks ransacked the city. The unfortunate Trojan was then buried under debris as the chest and the city went up in flames. A copper key found near the jewels must once have opened the chest, Schliemann surmised.

Still concerned for the treasure's safety, Schliemann sneaked it across the border into Greece. This did not sit well with the Turkish authorities, who took him to court. In 1875 Schliemann agreed to pay the Turkish government fifty thousand francs. In return, the Turks conceded that he was now the owner of a unique and undeniably valuable treasure.

But was it Priam's treasure, as Schliemann so quickly dubbed it? Privately, Schliemann admitted some doubts. Grand though the treasure was, it didn't explain the lack of other signs that Hisarlik was Homer's Troy. Schliemann had found remnants of a small prehistoric settlement, but none of the wide streets or towers or gates the poems had led him to expect.

He was determined to dig further, but the Turks, still furious about his smuggling the treasure out of their country, refused to grant him a permit. Schliemann, never one to sit around, decided to continue his search for the Trojan War elsewhere.

If he couldn't get to Priam's kingdom, he decided, he would go to Agamemnon's instead. Here, too, the classical writers offered directions, this time to Mycenae, located below Corinth on Greece's Argolic Peninsula. Mycenae was long thought to be the burial place of ancient Greek kings, and unlike Hisarlik, Mycenae boasted some visible and impressive ruins.

Schliemann's inspired idea was to dig outside the Mycenae walls, where no one had looked before. The results were even more spectacular than at Hisarlik. He found five graves with the remains of nineteen men and women and two infants, all covered in gold. The graves also contained bronze swords and daggers with gold- and silverwork, gold and silver cups and boxes, and hundreds of decorated gold pieces. The men's faces were covered with distinctive gold masks that seemed to be portraits. Schliemann, with his customary flair for the dramatic, announced that he had stared into the face of Agamemnon himself.

Now Schliemann was more convinced than ever that Homer had described real people and real battles. But the sumptuous cemetery at Mycenae made the small town at Hisarlik seem even less imposing, and the contrast nagged at Schliemann. Finally, in 1890, in return for a large cash payment, the Turks granted Schliemann a permit to continue his excavation of Hisarlik.

This time Schliemann dug near the western border of the hill, about twenty-five yards outside the city where he'd found Priam's treasure. There he uncovered the remains of a large building. This, finally, was a structure worthy of Homer's heroes; perhaps, Schliemann thought, this was Priam's palace. Better still, within the building's walls workers found remains of pottery with unmistakably Mycenaean shapes and decorations. This provided Schliemann with the link he'd sought between Mycenae and Troy. If they hadn't fought with each other, then they must at least have traded with each other.

Ironically, the 1890 finds also confirmed Schliemann's worst fears, for the new discoveries were found much nearer to the surface than the town Schliemann had excavated in the 1870s. This indicated that Homer's Troy had been built centuries later than the small settlement where Schliemann had found the treasure, so the treasure couldn't have belonged to Priam, or any other figure from the *Iliad*. Worse still, it meant that Schliemann, in his eagerness to quickly reach the bottom of the hill, had cut right through the remains of Homer's Troy. In doing so, he almost certainly destroyed some of the remains of the city he so desperately wanted to find.

☙

Schliemann died in 1890, so it was left to his onetime assistant, Wilhelm Dorpfeld, to continue the excavations. Dorpfeld assumed that the large house uncovered earlier that year was part of the Bronze Age city that Schliemann had sought, and he continued to dig to the west and the south of the original town. Over the course of 1893 and 1894 he found more large houses, a watchtower, and three hundred yards of the city wall. He also found lots more Mycenaean pottery.

Dorpfeld concluded that this was Homer's Troy. Indeed, the tower, the large houses, and the wide streets were much more in keeping with the poet's descriptions than any of the buildings Schliemann had uncovered. Dorpfeld's analysis of the layers at Hisarlik led him to conclude that Schliemann's small settlement was the second built at Hisarlik, and that it dated back to about 2500 B.C. Dorpfeld's Troy was the sixth city built on the same site, and was built between 1500 and 1000 B.C. The dating, though imprecise, put Dorpfeld's finds close enough to the traditional date for the Trojan War—about 1200 B.C.—to deepen his conviction that he had found Homer's Troy.

Dorpfeld's views prevailed for about forty years, when an American expedition under the direction of Carl Blegen arrived at Hisarlik. Blegen's digs, which lasted from 1932 to 1938, pointed to some serious problems with Dorpfeld's hypothesis. The destruction of the sixth Troy, Blegen determined, could not have been the result of a Greek invasion. At one part of the wall the foundation had shifted, while other parts seemed to have collapsed entirely. Blegen believed that type of damage couldn't be man-made—even by men with godlike qualities. He attributed it to an earthquake.

According to Blegen, it was the next settlement at Hisarlik—and the seventh overall—that was Homer's Troy. After the earthquake, the Trojans rebuilt their city, but in dramatically different ways. The large houses of the sixth Troy were now partitioned into small rooms, and the wide streets crammed with tiny houses, each with large storage jars sunk into their floors. All this indicated to Blegen a city under siege; with the Greeks outside the Trojan gates, every available space had to be filled by refugees and their goods. Blegen concluded that the seventh city fell soon after the sixth, so it still fit the traditional date for the Trojan War.

⚬⚭⚬

First Schliemann, then Dorpfeld, then Blegen: all three archaeologists believed they found Homer's Troy at Hisarlik, albeit at different levels.

All three would have been heartened by the work of subsequent scholars and archaeologists. Some of the most tantalizing evidence came from the remains of the Hittite civilization, which flourished in Turkey until sometime after 1200 B.C. During the 1970s and 1980s, scholars deciphered clay tablets found there, some of which listed the names of foreign kings and diplomats with whom the Hittites dealt. Some of these scholars have suggested that among the names were Hittite translations of Priam and Paris.

Back at Hisarlik, in the mid-1990s, the German archaeologist Manfred Korfmann used new remote sensing technology to trace the walls of the Dorpfeld-Blegen city well beyond the earlier limits. Korfmann's Troy was, even more than his predecessors', a citadel worthy of Homer's heroes. Korfmann's analysis also indicated that the Trojan walls would still have been visible in the eighth century B.C., when Homer might have visited the site.

Still, the majority of scholars today have been wary of jumping to any conclusions—or at least to conclusions as dramatic as those of Schliemann, Dorpfeld, or Blegen. The

Hittite tablets, they've stressed, are subject to a variety of interpretations and certainly don't constitute proof that there ever was a Paris or a Priam, let alone a Hector or a Helen, or an Achilles or an Agamemnon.

Most scholars admit that they can't say for sure whether the Trojan War ever took place. The *Iliad* and the *Odyssey* were products of a longing for a long-lost golden age, as well as a poet's very vivid imagination, and as such they certainly can't be considered a reliable historical account. But, just as Schliemann suspected, there can no longer be any doubt that the hill at Hisarlik was once a great city, as was the citadel of Mycenae. And though historians can't be certain about the names or the deeds of the people who lived at either, they consider it very likely that each knew a great deal about the other.

The people of Troy and the people of Mycenae talked with each other, traded with each other, and, quite conceivably, fought with each other. At least to that extent, Schliemann—and Homer—were right.

To Investigate Further

Schliemann, Heinrich. *Troy and Its Remains* (London: John Murray, 1875).
Schliemann's own account of his 1871–1873 excavation, including the discovery of Priam's treasure.

Blegen, Carl. *Troy and the Trojans* (New York: Praeger, 1963).
Blegen's version, based on his 1932–1938 excavations.

Cook, John M. *The Troad* (Oxford: Clarendon Press, 1973).
A study of the archaeology in and around Hisarlik, including a comprehensive survey of pre-Schliemann theories. Many of these theories located Troy near the Turkish village of Pinarbasi, and Schliemann himself dug there before turning to Hisarlik.

Wood, Michael. *In Search of the Trojan War* (New York: Facts on File, 1985).
A companion to a BBC program, this provides a good introduction to Troy historiography, along with an intriguing and provocative look at the Hittite evidence.

Calder, William, III, and David Traill. *Myth, Scandal, and History* (Detroit: Wayne State University Press, 1986).
A collection of essays portraying Schliemann as a pathological liar, a thesis more fully developed in Traill's 1995 biography.

Traill, David. *Schliemann of Troy* (New York: St. Martin's Press, 1995).
An extremely controversial, all-out attack on Schliemann, accusing him of—among other things—cheating his business partners; lying to gain American citizenship; failing to give credit to Frank Calvert; and, most devastating of all, making up the story of how and where he found Priam's treasure. According to Traill, Schliemann lied about hiding the treasure in his wife's shawl to conceal the fact that he'd actually gathered the objects in the treasure from a variety of places in and around Hisarlik, then bunched them together so he could pretend he'd made a dramatic discovery. Traill's damning evidence includes the indisputable fact that Schliemann's

wife was in Athens at the time of the discovery. Traill's critics argue that it would have been impossible for Schliemann to bring together so many objects, all of which were later shown to come from the same period. They also point out that the vast majority of his archaeological notes have turned out to be largely accurate. Traill's defenders (and other Schliemann detractors) counter that the evidence of Schliemann's lying in his other business and personal dealings is overwhelming. Schliemann, they contend, couldn't be a Dr. Jekyll at Hisarlik while being a Mr. Hyde elsewhere. The book is well worth reading, but don't lose sight of the fact that the questions raised are largely irrelevant to the larger question of what happened at Troy. After all, even Schliemann eventually conceded that the part of Troy he first excavated dated back to well before the Trojan War and that Priam's treasure could not, therefore, have belonged to Priam or any of his contemporaries.

Moorehead, Caroline. *Lost and Found* (New York: Viking, 1996).

As riveting as the history of Troy is the mysterious fate of Priam's treasure, entertainingly revealed in Moorehead's book. Schliemann left the treasure to the German government, which displayed it at Berlin's Museum for Prehistory. In 1945 the treasure disappeared, apparently lost forever. Then, in 1991, a Russian art historian and a curator at the Pushkin Museum in Moscow broke the story that the entire treasure was buried in the museum's vaults, having been seized by Soviet troops at the end of World War II.

Tolstikov, Vladimir, and Mikhail Treister. *The Gold of Troy,* trans. from the Russian by Christina Sever and Mila Bonnichsen (New York: Abrams, 1996).

In 1994 the Russians admitted they had the treasure and agreed to make it available to scholars and the public. This is the catalogue of the first public exhibition in almost fifty years. It includes essays defending Schliemann (and the treasure) against Traill's accusations.

Allen, Susan. *Finding the Walls of Troy* (Berkeley: University of California Press, 1999).

Schliemann, who didn't want to share the spotlight, later minimized Calvert's contribution; here Allen moves Calvert out of the more famous man's shadow.

PART 2

CLASSICAL TRADITIONS, MAJOR RELIGIONS, GIANT EMPIRES, 1000 BCE–500

Who Was Homer?

THE GREEKS WERE HAZY ABOUT HOMER. At first, they weren't even sure what they thought of his poems. The philosopher Xenophanes, writing in about 550 BC, denounced Homer for misrepresenting the gods, and Plato went so far as to urge his students not to read either the *Iliad* or the *Odyssey*. Even after Aristotle placed the poems atop the canon, there was little known about their author, other than some shifting folk traditions about a wandering blind bard. Herodotus, whose fifth-century reference to Homer is one of the earliest extant, could only guess that he lived "four hundred years before my time."

The Greeks, and then the Romans, were also unsure how Homer composed the poems. "They say that . . . Homer did not leave behind his poems in writing," wrote the Roman historian Josephus in the first century AD, "but that they were transmitted by memorization and put together out of the songs, and that therefore they contain many inconsistencies."

There were indeed inconsistencies. In the *Iliad*, for example, a warrior is described as groaning, even though he's already died. It was easy enough to see why Homer would have had trouble keeping track of everything in the poems: the *Iliad* has about 16,000 lines and the *Odyssey* 12,000. Moreover, and more amazingly, as Josephus noted, Homer apparently composed both without the aid of pen or paper. In 1795, the German scholar Friedrich Wolf added scholarship to Josephus's speculation. Wolf noted that, other than a passing and dubious reference in the *Iliad* to a tablet with "baneful signs," there was nothing in the poems that indicated Homer even knew what writing was. Wrote Wolf:

> The word *book* is nowhere, *writing* is nowhere, *reading* is nowhere, *letters* are nowhere; nothing in so many thousands of verses is arranged for reading, everything for hearing; there are no pacts or treaties except face to face; there is no source of report for old times except memory and rumor and monuments without writing; from that comes the diligent and, in the *Iliad*, strenuously repeated invocations of the Muses, the goddesses of memory; there is no inscription on the pillars and tombs that are sometimes mentioned; there is no other inscription of any kind; there is no coin or fabricated money; there is no use of writing in domestic matters or trade; there are no maps; finally there are no letter carriers and no letters.

Wolf concluded that Homer must have composed orally, and that the poems must have been passed on and revised for generations before some editor wrote them down. Wolf's work paralleled that of eighteenth-century scholars of the Old Testament who reached the conclusion that the first five books of the Bible were once a number of separate works that an editor had woven together. Just as Moses did not write the "Books of Moses," Homer did not write the *Iliad* or the *Odyssey,* except perhaps in some much shorter and irretrievable early version. The inconsistencies were not a lapse on the part of an author but of an editor.

Even if Homer existed, Wolf argued, the *Iliad* or the *Odyssey* could just as reasonably be credited to generations of anonymous bards. "I find it impossible to accept the belief to which we have become accustomed," Wolf wrote, "that these two works of a single genius burst forth suddenly from the darkness in all their brilliance, just as they are, with both the splendor of their parts and the many great virtues of the connected whole."

⸎

Nineteenth-century archaeologists, most notably Heinrich Schliemann, uncovered evidence that Troy existed and that the Trojan War of the *Iliad* was, at least in part, a real event. But the archaeological discoveries also revealed that the world of the Trojans and Mycenaeans was very different from Homer's descriptions. Nowhere in the poems was there anything resembling the huge Mycenaean tombs or palaces, or the tablets with Mycenaean writing called Linear B, or the centralized, hierarchical society those tablets revealed. Nowhere amid the archaeological finds was there evidence of independent chieftains like Achilles living in small houses and acting independently of the king.

Why the discrepancies? Homer might have intentionally fictionalized to create an image of men who were more like gods and gods who were more like men. To some extent, though, the poet seemed to have been describing his own age, a post-Mycenaean "Dark Age," maybe three hundred years after the events he described in the *Iliad* and the *Odyssey.* This placed Homer no later than the sixth century BC and, most historians thought, around the eighth century BC.

But locating Homer in time merely underscored the problem: the poems were composed during an age when writing no longer existed in Greece. It seemed inconceivable that without writing, any single poet could have remembered, let alone created, such long and complex masterpieces. Most scholars agreed with Wolf that while someone named Homer might once have existed and might have written some ur-epic, he was at most a link in an evolutionary chain that only much later culminated in the *Iliad* and the *Odyssey* as we know it.

That consensus lasted until the 1920s, when the American scholar Milman Parry developed a theory of how a single poet might indeed have composed the *Iliad* and the *Odyssey,* even without writing. Parry began by showing how the poems' famous epithets—repeatedly used phrases like "swift-footed Achilles" or "wine-dark sea"—served the rhythm of the poems' lines. Odysseus might be "noble Odysseus" or "city-sacking Odysseus," depending on which epithet fit the meter. Similarly, certain themes recurred throughout the poems. Such formulas made it much easier for a poet, even an oral poet, to compose and pass on long poems. Parry did not deny the *Iliad* and *Odyssey* were part

How could a single poet, living in an illiterate age, have written the *Iliad* and the *Odyssey*? *(Photo by Hulton Archive/Getty Images)*

of an oral tradition, but he showed how a single poet—Homer—could have played a central role in creating the poems.

Parry and his followers, most notably Albert Lord, did not just theorize about oral poems. In the 1930s they traveled around the Balkans, observing and recording the oral poems of the South Slavs. These poems, they found, used many of the same devices as the Homeric epics, including the formulaic repetition of phrases and themes. Lord even found a Slavic masterpiece, *The Wedding of Smailagic Meho,* which was about the same length as the *Odyssey.* Here was proof that a talented oral poet could write and recite an epic. Just as in the *Iliad* and the *Odyssey,* there were inconsistencies in the *Wedding*—a hero's name changed, as did a horse's color—but to Parry and Lord this was evidence that, like Homer, the Slavic poet was human.

౼౼౼

Not everyone embraced Parry's approach. For one thing, there was clearly more to the *Iliad* and the *Odyssey* than a series of easy-to-remember formulas.

"Is the contribution of individual genius to be submerged entirely in a collective poetic tradition?" asked classicist John Foley. "Is each occurrence of a particular formula or typical scene to be taken merely as a mechanical solution to the challenge of composing performance? Is Homer then to be understood as wholly insensitive to the narrative situations in which he deploys the traditional structures, so that suitability to immediate context is never a concern?"

Foley called the Parry approach "one-sided" in its focus on Homer's mechanics rather than his art. Classicist Joseph Russo agreed that formulas could not explain "the mysterious chemistry whereby gifted poets transmute mere words into verbal art." Other critics chipped away at Parry's work, conceding the existence of formulaic phrases and systems but reducing their numbers and significance.

Still others endorsed an updated version of Wolf's evolutionary thesis. Classicist Gregory Nagy, for example, went so far as to object to the way critics used Homer's name. "The usage of saying that 'Homer does this' or 'the poet intends that' may become risky for modern experts," Nagy wrote, "if they start thinking of 'Homer' in overly personalized terms, without regard for the traditional dynamics of composition and performance." Nagy suggested Homer wasn't a proper name, but a word he translated as "he who fits [the song] together."

Nagy's evolutionary approach dovetailed with the widespread critical deemphasis, in the late twentieth century, on authors as the sole force in shaping a text. In 1968 the critic Roland Barthes declared "the death of the author," and many critics proceeded to study the language of literature as something independent from an author's intentions. If authors no longer mattered, as Barthes maintained, maybe it was time to let go of one whose existence had always been as dubious as Homer's.

Still, even Nagy conceded there was something unsatisfying about crediting two of Western civilization's great literary achievements to a tradition instead of a person. "It is as if we have suddenly lost a cherished author," he wrote.

Nagy offered some consolation. "Surely, what we have really admired all along is not the author, about whom we never did really know anything historically, but the Homeric poems themselves," he wrote. "We may have lost a historical author whom we never knew anyway, but we have recovered in the process a mythical author who is more than just an author [and] who will come back to life with every new performance of his *Iliad* and *Odyssey.*"

To Investigate Further

Lattimore, Richard. *The Iliad.* Chicago: University of Chicago Press, 1961.
  Lattimore's translations are considered true to the originals, though Robert Fagles's versions are also widely admired.

Fitzgerald, Robert, trans. *The Odyssey.* New York: Farrar Straus, 1998.
  Originally published in 1961, Fitzgerald's translation remains the most accessible.

Morris, Ian, and Barry Powell. *A New Companion to Homer.* Leiden, Netherlands: Brill, 1997.
  Thirty leading scholars provide an overview of Homeric studies.

Graziosi, Barbara. *Inventing Homer.* New York: Cambridge University Press, 2002.
  How the ancient Greeks imagined Homer.

Nagy, Gregory. *Homeric Responses.* Austin: University of Texas Press, 2003.
  As in his 1996 *Homeric Questions,* Nagy argues that an oral tradition could and did produce the *Iliad* and the *Odyssey.*

Powell, Barry. *Homer.* Malden, MA: Blackwell Publishing, 2004.
  Neither Parry nor Lord said much about how oral poems were written down, and most scholars continued to assume generations of poets passed down the poems before someone eventually put them in writing. Powell's intriguing theory is that Homer himself dictated the poems to someone. Powell notes that the Greek alphabet came into being in the early eighth century BC, and he speculates that it might have been invented in part to record Homer's poems.

Who Wrote the Bible?

To orthodox Jews and fundamentalist Christians, the answer is clear: God, or in the case of the first five books of the Old Testament, Moses inspired by God. The problems with this answer were equally clear, even in ancient times. For starters, there was the fact that Moses would have to have described his own death. One Jewish tradition had it that Joshua wrote the account of Moses's death, but the Pentateuch also included plenty that took place long after Moses's or Joshua's time. The seventeenth-century philosophers Thomas Hobbes and Benedict de Spinoza were among the first to catalogue these events.

By the eighteenth century, scholars had concluded that though Moses may have written parts of the Bible, much was added later. This explained why there were often two versions of the same story. The Creation, for example. In *Genesis* 1, God creates heaven and earth, plants, animals, and finally, man and woman simultaneously and in his image. Then, in *Genesis* 2:4, the Creation begins again and in a very different order. This time God creates man before plants or other animals, and woman not in his own image but out of man. Similarly, there were two versions of the Covenant and the Flood.

Scholars also noticed that one version of each story referred to God as Elohim, the other as Yahweh. Elohim meant God, but Yahweh was a proper name. In 1780 the German scholar Johann Gottfried Eichorn decided that the Bible must originally have been two works that were later combined. Eichorn called the author of one version E (from Elohim), and the other J (from the German spelling Jahweh).

The two-author theory didn't last long. In the nineteenth century, scholars such as Hermann Hupfeld, Karl Heinrich Graf, and Abraham Kuenen found that the Elohim stories could be further split into two versions with distinct language and subject matter. Many of the Elohim stories focused on priests and laid out laws and rituals, as well as a system of tithing to support priests. These appeared to be written by a priest, so the author became known as P. Another German, W. M. L. De Wette, noted that *Deuteronomy* was written in an entirely different style from the first four books of Moses, and apparently authored by neither E nor J nor P. Its author was called D. Finally, there must have been an editor who wove together all four strands. This was R, for Redactor. In 1878 Julius Wellhausen consolidated these ideas in a work that firmly established the four-author, one-editor hypothesis. Since the theory held that the Bible was drawn from a number of different documents, it came to be known as the documentary theory.

In the century and a quarter since then, scholars have continued to untangle the biblical strands. Sometimes they've done so by identifying linguistic differences, which go well beyond different names for God. For example: J and P refer to Mount Sinai, whereas

E and D call it Horeb; only P uses the phrase "be fruitful and multiply"; only J uses the term "to know" to mean sex. Sometimes the distinctions are religious, such as P's emphasis on priestly prerogatives. J, E, and D describe a God who appears and speaks directly to man, whether as a burning bush or a voice from above; in P the only channel to God is the priesthood.

Biblical scholars continue to debate what passages belong to which writer, and which writer wrote when. But for almost all of them, the starting point remains the documentary theory.

⌘

Documentary theorists have not generally identified specific people to replace Moses as the authors of the Old Testament. Still, by following the different strands, they've gone a long way toward locating them in time and place.

J and E both wrote about a period when the Jews were split into two kingdoms: Judah in the south and Israel in the north. J's focus was on Judah: Abraham lives in Hebron, the capital of Judah, and God promises Abraham the land "from the river of Egypt to the great river, the river Euphrates." These were the borders of the kingdom of David, Judah's first king. J's portrait of Judah's royal family is generally favorable, E's less so. Conversely, E presents a far more favorable portrait of Israel. In E, for example, the Israelites buy the city of Shechem; in J, they massacre its inhabitants. All this makes it likely that J lived in Judah, E in Israel. Neither appears to know anything of the period after the Assyrians overran Israel. That means both lived after 950 BC, when the land was split, and before 722 BC, when Israel ceased to exist.

As for P, most scholars placed him later on the grounds that the hierarchical priestly religion seemed less primitive than that of J or E, or for that matter, D. That the others barely mention P's detailed laws further buttressed the theory that P came later. As early as 1865, Graf established the order of J-E-D-P. J wrote in ninth- or tenth-century BC Judah, E in eighth-century BC Israel, D in seventh-century BC Judah, and P in fifth- or sixth-century BC Babylon. These dates have by no means been universally accepted—some scholars have argued that J came later and P earlier, and others that P may never have been an independent work but rather a revision of J—but Graf's order remains the standard.

Among the most provocative recent theories is that of the biblical scholar Richard Elliott Friedman, who argued that J may have been a woman. Friedman noted that the women in J, among them Abigail, Rachel, Rebekah, and Delilah, achieved considerable power in a male-dominated world.

"The J stories are, on the whole, much more concerned with women and much more sensitive to women than are the E stories," Friedman wrote. "This does not make the author a woman. But it does mean that we cannot by any means be quick to think of this writer as a man."

The literary scholar Harold Bloom reached the same conclusion with more certitude. Bloom thought J lived in the court of Solomon, or at least nearby. She may even have been a princess. Wrote Bloom: "J was not a professional scribe but rather an immensely sophisticated, highly placed member of the Solomonic elite, enlightened and ironic."

Most scholars didn't buy Bloom's case, though many agreed with him that J was the most interesting writer of the four. J's stories include the best-known versions of the Creation, the Flood, the Covenant, and Sodom and Gomorrah. J's Yahweh has more than a different name than Elohim. He is an anthropomorphic God, haggling with Abraham and, as Bloom put it, "eccentrically irascible." He may have originated in an earlier stage of Judaism. J's attitude toward Yahweh, Bloom wrote, is "an imp who behaves sometimes as though he is rebelling against his Jewish mother."

"The work is different from the biblical works that are ascribed to authors who were priests (including E, P, and D) in many ways; notably, unlike the other source works of the Five Books of Moses, it does not contain a lengthy code of law," agreed Friedman. "It is rather the work of a literary artist, whose aim seems to have been partly that of the writer and partly that of the historian—to tell the story, and to tell it beautifully."

Bloom compared J to, among others, Shakespeare. "J is something other than a storyteller, a creator of personalities (human and divine), a national historian and prophet, or even an ancestor of the moral fictions of Wordsworth, George Eliot, and Tolstoy," he wrote. "There is always the other side of J: uncanny, tricky, sublime, ironic, a visionary of incommensurates, and so the direct ancestor of Kafka."

৵৽

The focus on the genius of J, or any of the Bible's authors, detracted from the achievement of R, the editor who sometime around the fourth century BC created what we now think of as the Old Testament. For some, like Bloom, R was the villain of the story since "but for him we would have a much fuller Book of J."

For many scholars, though, R was himself an artist worthy of admiration and study, and the present form of the Bible was as worthy a subject as any of its sources. Indeed, since the documentary theory is after all still a theory, some scholars have gone so far as to reject the possibility of any real literary analysis of the work of J or other sources. Some have pointed to the many disagreements about what passages belong to which author and have concluded there may not even have been a J. Others have pushed R's contribution earlier, perhaps to the seventh or sixth century BC. Still others have returned to the predocumentary theory that the Bible is not so much an interweaving of four distinct sources as a work that arose from oral traditions and underwent successive revisions.

For many of these scholars, it is R who was the true creative force behind the Bible. R. Norman Whybray praised R for a "high degree of imagination and . . . great freedom in the treatment of sources." Robert Alter wrote that source analysis "seems to me a good deal less interesting than the subtle workings of the literary whole represented by the redacted text." For these scholars, the contradictions and repetitions that documentary theorists used to determine who wrote what are part of what makes interpreting the Bible so complex and fascinating.

"It is small wonder," Alter wrote, "that the documentary hypothesis . . . has begun to look as though it has reached a point of diminishing returns, and many younger scholars, showing signs of restlessness with source criticism, have been exploring other approaches—literary, anthropological, sociological, and so forth."

"At the present time," agreed John Barton and John Muddiman, "the study of the Pentateuch is a matter of controversy such as it has scarcely been since the time of Wellhausen and Kuenen."

Does that mean we're back where we started, with a Bible whose author can't be known? In some sense, of course, that's the case; even Bloom can't identify a particular person with any certainty. But, as Barton and Muddiman continued, scholars' "continued discussion of the composition of the Pentateuch from earlier material shows that they do not consider that the situation is as desperate as Whybray proposes." Much progress has been made, and the process has immeasurably enriched our appreciation of the Bible, both as a literary work and as a historical document.

To Investigate Further

Friedman, Richard Elliott. *Who Wrote the Bible?* Englewood Cliffs, NJ: Prentice-Hall, 1987.
A clear and entertaining synthesis.

Bloom, Harold, and David Rosenberg. *The Book of J.* New York: Grove Weidenfeld, 1990.
Even critics who didn't buy Bloom's analysis admired Rosenberg's translation.

Alter, Robert. *Genesis.* New York: W. W. Norton, 1996.
Translation and commentary by the distinguished literary critic.

Friedman, Richard Elliott. *The Hidden Book in the Bible.* San Francisco: HarperSanFrancisco, 1998.
Friedman argues provocatively that J wrote much more of the Bible than is generally accepted, and that he (or she) covered the period from the Creation to the death of David.

Barton, John, and John Muddiman, eds. *The Oxford Bible Commentary.* Oxford, England: Oxford University Press, 2001.
Comprehensive and balanced.

Friedman, Richard Elliott. *The Bible with Sources Revealed.* San Francisco: HarperSanFrancisco, 2003.
Different colors and type styles identify J, E, D, P, R, and other possible sources.

Did Jesus Die on the Cross?

I T'S A CLASSIC "LOCKED DOOR" MYSTERY.
A man is executed: he is crucified, then a lance is plunged into his chest to make sure he's dead. His body is buried in a tomb, by some accounts guarded by experienced centurions. Two days later, the body is gone. More mysterious still, people who knew the man well report seeing him and talking to him. At first they suspect it's some sort of dream or hallucination, but they touch him and eat with him, Finally, they conclude the man has come back to life.

The man, of course, is Jesus of Nazareth. And his resurrection is not just the basis of Christianity but also a mystery that's intrigued historians for nearly two thousand years.

୧୩୬

Compared to most people of his period, Jesus had a pretty well-documented life.

The Roman historian Tacitus, writing early in the second century, mentioned that "Christus" had been sentenced to death by the Roman governor Pontius Pilate. Tacitus added that his death hadn't stopped the "pernicious superstition" of his followers.

Jewish sources were equally curt, with the exception of the first-century historian Josephus. Josephus recounted how, after Pilate condemned him to be crucified, Jesus "appeared . . . restored to life, for the prophets of God had prophesied these and countless other marvelous things about him." The phrasing was blatantly that of a believer, so most historians concluded that some later Christian copyist must have added it. Still, most also assumed that Josephus's original text must have made some mention of Jesus' death.

The Roman and Jewish sources offered mere mentions. To learn more about Jesus' "passion" or suffering, historians turned to the New Testament, in particular the gospels of Mark, Matthew, Luke, and John. The earliest extant versions of the gospels date from the fourth century, but most historians believe the originals were written between 70 and 110, or between 40 and 80 years after the resurrection. They tell the same basic story, including the last supper with his disciples; the betrayal by one of them, Judas Iscariot; the arrest, trial, crucifixion, and resurrection.

Beyond that, there are all sorts of inconsistencies. In Mark, which most historians think is the earliest of the gospels, three women find a young man in a white robe in the tomb; he turns out to be a messenger sent to tell them Jesus has been raised. A decade or so later, Matthew adds an earthquake, a dazzling light, and an actual appearance of Jesus before the women; then Jesus appears, on a mountain in Galilee, before his eleven disciples. (The twelfth, Judas, has hanged himself.) In Luke, written about the same time as Matthew, the number of women at the tomb is unspecified, two angels appear at the tomb, and the first appearance of the resurrected Jesus is not to the women but to two people on the road to Emmaus. And in John, one woman goes to the tomb, and Jesus makes a number of appearances.

Why can't the gospel writers get their stories straight? They disagree on the number of appearances, the people to whom Jesus appeared, the times and places of the appearance, as well as other details.

For many, the inconsistencies were reason enough to completely discredit the gospels as historical documents. More fundamentally, all of the resurrection stories—like those of Jesus' other miracles—defied rational belief. As early as the second century, the philosopher Celsus described the resurrection as a fantasy of disciples who were "so wrenched with grief at this failure that they hallucinated him risen from the dead."

By the eighteenth and nineteenth centuries, with rationalism replacing religious belief among most educated Westerners, variations of Celsus's view were standard, especially among the liberals who staffed the leading theology departments at German universities. In 1782, for example, Karl Friedrich Bahrdt came up with the "two nails" theory of the crucifixion: he concluded that Jesus' hands but not feet had been nailed to the cross, enabling him to walk after he was taken down. Bahrdt speculated that Jesus' followers supplied him with drugs to alleviate the pain and induce a deathlike faint; they then hid their leader and nursed him back to health. In 1835 David Friedrich Strauss dismissed as myth just about every gospel story. Strauss explained the resurrection as mass hysteria.

In America, too, rationalism reigned. In 1804, Thomas Jefferson decided to extract from the gospels what was genuine; what was left in the "Jefferson Bibles" were plenty of sayings and parables and a mere skeleton of the original narratives. No miracles, no proclamations of Jesus' divinity, and certainly no resurrection.

All this seemed reasonable in what was, after all, the "Age of Reason." By the twentieth century, even religious Christians were mostly satisfied to leave the history of Jesus to rationalist historians. What emerged was sort of a truce: Christians could concern themselves about faith, historians about history. For the former, there was Christ; for the latter, Jesus. And neither had to pay much attention to the other.

The truce held until the second half of the twentieth century.

涣

A number of factors revitalized the quest for the historical Jesus. Biblical scholars started moving from seminaries and church colleges to secular institutions, where they were free to take a new look at Jesus. Scholars from other disciplines, in particular cultural anthropology and the social sciences, became interested in the history of religion. Most significant of all was the discovery of a set of ancient documents. These would dramatically change how historians viewed the life and death of Jesus.

In December 1945, in an area of Upper Egypt known as Nag Hammadi, an Arab peasant named Muhammad Ali al-Samman was searching for some soft soil to fertilize his crops. He stumbled on a red earthenware jar. Breaking it open, he found thirteen papyrus books, bound in leather, along with some loose papyrus leaves. Some of these straw leaves he used to kindle a fire, but the rest eventually made their way to the Coptic Museum in Cairo.

Among the documents Muhammad Ali al-Samman found was one titled "the Gospel According to Thomas." Early church documents had mentioned Thomas's gospel (mostly disparagingly), but historians assumed it was lost forever. Yet here it was, in its entirety and almost perfectly preserved by the dry air of the Egyptian desert. Radiocarbon dating placed the papyrus leaves between 350 and 400, but some scholars, noting that Thomas consisted almost entirely of Jesus' own words, suspected that it was written closer to the time of Jesus himself, perhaps as early as the 50s. That would make Thomas earlier than Mark, Matthew, Luke, or John.

What did Thomas have to say about the resurrection? Absolutely nothing.

Now, a dead body coming back to life is hardly a minor biographical detail. It's hard to imagine Thomas would forget to mention it. Many historians concluded, therefore, that the resurrection was an invention, not of Jesus or his disciples, but of later Christians, probably Mark.

Thomas tuned modern scholars in to a debate that apparently raged throughout the first two centuries after Jesus' death. On the one side were the orthodox Christians who insisted (along with Mark, Matthew, Luke, and John) that Jesus had risen. Not only that, he rose bodily; the canonical gospels go to great length to stress that the risen Jesus didn't just appear before his followers. He talked to them; he ate with them; he invited them to touch them; he explicitly told them (in Luke) that he was "not a ghost."

Against this orthodox view stood the "Gnostics," of which Thomas represented just one variant. They, too, believed Jesus lived on—but not literally. For the Gnostics, Jesus appeared in ecstatic revelations, in visions, and in dreams. Much like Martin Luther more than a thousand years later or various Pentecostal congregations today, Gnostics believed that Jesus could inspire any individual at any time.

Why did orthodox Christians insist on a literal view of resurrection? Why did they so vehemently reject Gnosticism as heresy?

One leading Gnostic scholar, Elaine Pagels, has suggested that the answer had more to do with politics than religion. Resurrection, she argued, served to legitimize the power of the men who'd inherited the church leadership from the disciples who'd seen the risen Christ. If anyone could experience Christ on their own, that totally undercut their power. So, according to Pagels, it was crucial for the church leaders to stress (as Luke did) that the resurrected Lord stayed on earth for forty days, then ascended to heaven. Any sightings of Jesus after those forty days . . .well, they just didn't count.

⚬ᴗᴗᴗᴐ

By the 1980s and 1990s, a new and much more liberal consensus had replaced the previously dominant view of Jesus. With the resurrection reduced to a political ploy (albeit a brilliant one), theologians felt free to focus on Jesus' sayings rather than his death. Freed of his image as Messiah, Jesus emerged in a variety of guises: a peasant, a sage, a rabbi, a Buddha, a revolutionary, even a comic firing off one-liners.

Many of those who painted these portraits came together in 1985 in the "Jesus Seminar." Here members didn't just discuss or debate the historicity of the gospels; they voted on them. Playing on the tradition of printing Jesus' words in red ink, the scholars took turns dropping beads into a container. A red bead meant the particular piece of the gospel was "authentic." Pink meant "maybe." Gray: "probably not." And black was "definitely not."

The voting guaranteed publicity, as well as quite a bit of ridicule. Members welcomed the attention; for many, the historicity of Jesus was of more than academic interest. Founder Robert Funk saw the Jesus Seminar as a direct and intentional challenge to the Christian Right; an attempt to take control of the religious discourse away from the Pat Robertsons and the Jerry Falwells.

Yet Funk and his followers, unlike Robertson and Falwell, were serious scholars, and that presented them with an intellectual problem. There was plenty of evidence in the gospels for their view of Jesus as a sage wandering around the countryside, sort of a Jewish Socrates. Yet they couldn't just quote his sayings and parables and then ignore everything in the gospels, including Jesus' own words, about his death and resurrection.

So they took a variety of tacks. Some, like Burton Mack of the Institute for Antiquity and Christianity in California, argued that the passion was nothing but an invention of later orthodoxy: there was no incident in the temple, there was no last supper, Jesus probably didn't even die on a cross. John Dominic Crossan, a former priest who became a professor at DePaul University in Chicago, conceded there was a last supper but quipped that "everyone has a last supper—the trick is knowing about it in advance." Crossan concluded that the body of a crucified Jesus was unlikely to have escaped the fate of other crucified bodies—namely, to be eaten by wild dogs.

Not surprisingly, the Jesus Seminar generated a backlash, with conservative scholars accusing it of misleading readers into thinking that literary or historical analysis of the gospels could reveal the real Jesus. Many conservative scholars emphasized the extent to which gospels are imbued with foreshadowings of the crucifixion and resurrection, but for liberals these were just further examples of the inventiveness of the gospel writers.

By and large, variations of the liberal consensus hold sway in academic circles, where even feminist and gay Jesuses have poked up. Like Martin Luther, Robert Funk of the Jesus Seminar has taken his theses and nailed them—or perhaps taped them—to the church's door. Whether they'll stick remains to be seen.

To Investigate Further

The New Testament.
    A best-seller for almost two millennia.

Robinson, James, ed. *The Nag Hammadi Library in English* (San Francisco: Harper & Row, 1988).
    Translations from the Coptic, including the Gospel of Thomas.

Strauss, David Freidrich. *Life of Jesus Critically Examined* (Philadelphia: Fortress Press, 1972).
Originally published in German in 1835 and still a classic of rationalism.

Schweitzer, Albert. *The Quest of the Historical Jesus* (New York: Macmillan, 1955).
Originally published in German in 1906, Schweitzer's book offered a thorough historiography up to then. Schweitzer devoted his life to practicing medicine on the disease-beset coast of Africa, convincing many that he had much in common with the subject of his book.

Wilson, Edmund. *The Dead Sea Scrolls* (New York: Oxford University Press, 1969).
The 1947 discovery of these documents near the shore of the Dead Sea created even more furor than the Nag Hammadi find. Many, including Wilson, believed the texts would change our view of Christian origins by shedding light on a sect that had much in common with Jesus' early followers. Scandalously long delays in publishing the scrolls convinced many, again including Wilson, that church leaders were suppressing evidence because it challenged the uniqueness of Christianity. In the 1990s, after Wilson's death, the scrolls were finally opened to all scholars, and most concluded that they confirmed his basic claim that Christianity grew out of first-century Judaism. They've been a disappointment, however, to those who hoped to find a direct connection to Jesus. The first part of Wilson's book was originally published in 1955.

Schonfield, Hugh. *The Passover Plot* (Dorset, England: Element, 1965).
Paints Jesus as a political revolutionary who deliberately provoked the authorities, then arranged to be taken down from the cross alive so he could "rise" again.

Pagels, Elaine. *The Gnostic Gospels* (New York: Random House, 1979).
The politics of early Christianity as revealed through the Nag Hammadi documents.

Baigent, Michael, Richard Leigh, and Henry Lincoln. *Holy Bloody, Holy Grail* (New York: Dell, 1983).
The theory here, generally considered overly conspiratorial even among liberal theologians, is that Mary not only witnessed Jesus' resurrection, but also married him and fathered his child. The theory is also at the center of *The Da Vinci Code*, Dan Brown's 2003 best-selling novel in which the hero has to solve a murder committed by a Catholic organization bent on suppressing the truth about Jesus and Mary.

Crossan, John Dominic. *The Historical Jesus* (San Francisco: HarperCollins, 1991).
Jesus as Jewish peasant. Crossan writes clearly and passionately, making his later, more popular distillations of this work (of which the most notable is his 1995 book *Jesus: A Revolutionary Biography*) largely unnecessary.

Thiering, Barbara. *Jesus and the Riddle of the Dead Sea Scrolls* (San Francisco: HarperCollins, 1992).
A dissident scholar's view of the Dead Sea Scrolls as cryptograms about Jesus that reveal that he did not die on the cross but was later revived and traveled around the Mediterranean in the company of Peter and Paul.

Wilson, N. *Jesus: A Life* (New York: W. W. Norton, 1992).
Wilson's theory is that the man who appeared as the resurrected Jesus was one of his brothers, probably James, who took the opportunity to seize control over Jesus' movement.

Funk, Robert, Roy Hoover, and the Jesus Seminar. *The Five Gospels* (New York: Macmillan, 1993).

When the votes were in, only 18 percent of the words ascribed to Jesus in the gospels passed as authentic; postpublication votes moved on from his words to his deeds and, not surprisingly, the resurrection lost the election.

Sanders, E. P. *The Historical Figure of Jesus* (London: Allen Lane, 1993).

Jesus as a Jewish prophet who believed the world was about to end.

Spong, John Shelby. *Resurrection: Myth or Reality?* (San Francisco: HarperCollins, 1994).

An Episcopal bishop's intellectual journey from a literal to a more symbolic belief in Easter.

Mack, Burton. *Who Wrote the New Testament?* (San Francisco: HarperCollins, 1995).

Mack goes farther than most modern scholars, even secular ones, in exposing how the gospels were fictional mythologies only distantly related to the historical Jesus.

Funk, Robert. *Honest to Jesus* (San Francisco: HarperCollins, 1996).

As always, the founder of the Jesus Seminar is provocative and readable.

Johnson, Luke Timothy. *The Real Jesus* (San Francisco: HarperCollins, 1996).

A sharp attack on the Jesus Seminar and the "misguided" quest for the historical Jesus.

Shorto, Russell. *Gospel Truth* (New York: Riverhead Books, 1997).

A journalist's entertaining survey of the most recent searchers for the historical Jesus, in particular the members of the Jesus Seminar.

Allen, Charlotte. *The Human Christ* (New York: The Free Press, 1998).

A thorough account of the search for the historical Jesus, though sometimes colored by Allen's Catholicism.

Pagels, Elaine. *Beyond Belief* (New York: Random House, 2005).

Pagels's latest exploration of Thomas is more personal than in *The Gnostic Gospels*; she finds comfort and joy in a dissident Christianity.

What Were the Nazca Lines?

I N SEPTEMBER 1926, two archaeologists scrambled up the rocky slopes near the town of Nazca, in southwestern Peru. The Peruvian, Toribio Mejia, and the American, Alfred Kroeber, intended to check out a nearby cemetery. Then, as they stopped for a moment and looked down on the flat, stony desert, they noticed a series of long, straight lines stretching to the horizon. Both scholars assumed the lines were some sort of irrigation system, and neither gave them much thought beyond that.

It was not until the 1930s, when commercial airlines began flying over the desert, that pilots and passengers realized there were many more of these lines—and lots more to their origins. From the air, they could see hundreds of lines, many radiating outward from central points, some of them miles long and perfectly straight. There were also other forms, including triangles, rectangles, trapezoids, spirals, and several animal shapes. As anthropologist Anthony Aveni wrote, the view from the sky resembled an unerased blackboard at the end of a busy geometry class.

Back on the ground, archaeologists examined the lines and shapes and saw that they'd been made by simply brushing aside the pebbles that covered the desert. Underneath was a light sand that stood out all the more clearly because the darker pebbles now formed a border alongside the lines and shapes. Archaeologists also realized that, once created, these drawings could remain in their original condition indefinitely; the desert around Nazca was so dry (receiving about twenty minutes of rainfall a year) and so windless that the lines might very well be centuries or even millennia old. Indeed, the remains of pottery found alongside some of the lines seemed to indicate that some were more than two thousand years old.

What, scientists wondered, could have inspired the artists of the period to choose such a difficult canvas? And why would they have drawn patterns so large that, from ground level, they couldn't even be recognized? Perhaps, some speculated, the ancient Nazcans may have known how to fly, using some sort of primitive gliders or hot air balloons. Or perhaps, according to the most notorious explanation for the lines and shapes, they hadn't been drawn by the Nazcans but by visitors from outer space; according to this theory, the lines were landing strips and the shapes were landing bays for extraterrestrial aircraft.

The extraterrestrial theory, made famous by Erich von Daniken's worldwide bestseller *Chariots of the Gods?*, was pure fantasy. It was based on nothing more than a very superficial resemblance between a small segment of the desert drawings and a modern airport. But von Dainiken's book, like the theory that the ancient Nazcans could fly, at least offered some sort of explanation for the huge and mysterious etchings.

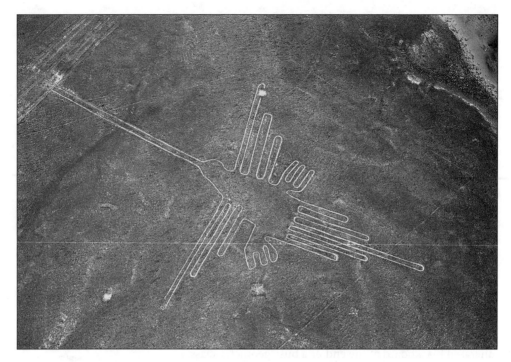

Since the Nazca lines—such as this massive hummingbird—could be seen only from the air, some scientists speculated that the ancient Peruvians may have known how to fly. *(Kevin Schafer/Corbis)*

How else could scientists account for these lines that were drawn in the sand—but could only be seen from the sky?

⟆

The first serious study of the Nazca lines came in 1941, when an American historian, Paul Kosok, visited the desert. Kosok, too, sought the mystery's solution by looking to the sky. His moment of inspiration came as he was watching the sun go down. Suddenly he noticed that it was setting almost exactly over the end of one of the long lines. A moment later, he realized that it was June 22, the shortest day in the year and the day when the sun sets farthest north of due west.

"With a great thrill we realized at once that we had apparently found the key to the riddle!" Kosok later recalled. "For undoubtedly the ancient Nazcans had constructed this line to mark the winter solstice. And if this were so, then the other markings might very likely be tied up in some way with astronomical and related activities."

Kosok had to leave the desert before he could conduct a more thorough study, so he enlisted the help of Maria Reiche, a German-born tutor of mathematics in Lima. By the end of the year Reiche had discovered that twelve other lines led to either the winter solstice or the summer solstice. The desert, Kosok and Reiche concluded, was "the largest astronomy book in the world." By marking crucial astronomical positions on the horizon, it also served as a giant calendar.

Critics of Kosok and Reiche argued that with so many lines running in so many different directions, it could easily be just a coincidence that some of them lined up with the sun. What was needed was a more systematic approach.

In 1968 Gerald Hawkins arrived in Peru, intent on providing just that. Hawkins seemed just the man for the job. He was an astronomer rather than an archaeologist, and his computer-assisted analysis of the alignments at Stonehenge had convinced him that those ruins had once been an astronomical observatory. Hawkins started by assigning a crew to fly over the desert and take a series of photographs that were used to plot an accurate map of the lines. Then he fed into the computer the positions of the sun, moon, and various stars along the horizon, adjusted to take into account the changes that gradually occurred over the past two thousand years. Finally, he selected 186 lines from one particular section of the desert.

Hawkins found that 39 of the 186 lines matched an astronomical position. That might sound impressive, but with so many astronomical positions to choose from, it was actually a huge disappointment. About 19 lines could have been expected to match some alignment by chance alone, and many of the other matches were actually "duplicates"—where a single line led to a winter solstice in one direction and a summer solstice in the other. Moreover, more than 80 percent of the selected lines headed off in entirely random directions.

So Hawkins, the great champion of an astronomical explanation for Stonehenge, concluded that at Nazca, "the star-sun-moon calendar theory had been killed by the computer."

ᕫᕙᕠ

In the early 1980s the Canadian archaeologist Persis Clarkson collected the fragments of pottery found along the lines, then compared them to pottery known to come from various eras of Peruvian prehistory. Her striking conclusion was that some of the fragments (particularly those near the drawings of animals) dated back to between 200 B.C. and A.D. 200, while others matched a style prevalent about a thousand years later.

The implications for those seeking an explanation for the lines were dramatic. If the drawings and lines had been created over such a lengthy period, and if they represented the work of people from very different eras, then they might also have served a variety of purposes. In other words, more than one explanation might apply to the lines. Or, to return to Aveni's metaphor, the blackboard may have been covered with the unerased work of not one, but many different geometry classes.

The explanations that followed in the late 1980s frequently had to do with water—not surprising, given its scarcity in the desert. Anthropologist Johan Reinhard argued that some of the lines may have connected particular points in the irrigation system with places of worship, perhaps as part of some fertility ritual. The many bird designs took on a new significance, especially since modern Nazca farmers interpret sightings of herons, pelicans, or condors as signs of rain; perhaps the bird and other animal drawings had been intended to invoke rain.

Two other anthropologists, Aveni and Helaine Silverman, noted that the lines correlated with various geographic benchmarks. Most of the lines were laid out in the same direction that water flowed after the rare desert rainstorm, and many had the same orientation as nearby gullies where water once ran. Aveni and Silverman didn't think the lines had been irrigation ditches—they were far too shallow for that—but they agreed with Reinhard that there was some sort of ceremonial link between the lines and water.

Aveni also teamed up with another anthropologist, Tom Zuidema, an expert on the Incas, who'd ruled much of Peru when the Spanish arrived. Zuidema recognized that Cuzco, the Inca capital, was designed as a network of straight lines emanating from the Temple of the Sun, in the center of the city. The radial layout had religious and social significance to the Incas, according to the early Spanish chroniclers. Zuidema and Aveni concluded that the radial layout of many of the desert lines indicated that the Nazcans had similar beliefs.

ᏣᎳᎩ

Another anthropologist, Gary Urton, looked for parallels in the practices of modern residents of mountain villages near Cuzco. Urton described how the villagers of Pacariqtambo, during certain festivals, took part in a ritual sweeping of long, thin strips of the plaza. To Urton, it didn't seem too much of a leap to imagine ancient Nazcans performing a similar ritual on the desert lines.

Maria Reiche, meanwhile, continued to live in Nazca, acting as not just an expert on the lines but also their protector. After von Daniken's works turned Nazca into a tourist destination, Reiche used her own limited funds to hire security guards. Even as an old woman, she would patrol the desert in her wheelchair, shooing away tourists if she feared they'd damage the lines. In Nazca she was a local hero.

In the early 1990s Reiche and her sister, Renate Reiche, became a bit too vigilant, at least according to some researchers. Maria Reiche's guards temporarily stopped both Clarkson and Urton from working on the desert, accusing the former of stealing potsherds and the latter of willfully harming the plains. Perhaps, Maria Reiche's critics suggested, she was trying to preserve her astronomical theory as well as the lines.

If so, Maria Reiche, who died in 1998 at age ninety-five, might have taken some consolation from the latest astronomical analyses, conducted by Aveni and a British astronomer, Clive Ruggles. Like Hawkins, Aveni and Ruggles found that celestial alignments couldn't account for the majority of the Nazca lines. Unlike Hawkins, however, they concluded that there were too many alignments for all of them to be just a coincidence. Aveni also noted that some of the radiating lines at Cuzco lined up positions of the sun, moon, and stars, leading him to conclude that astronomy did have some role at Nazca, albeit a smaller role than Kosok or Reiche envisioned.

Von Daniken's readers, too, would undoubtedly be disappointed by the latest thinking about the lines. The range of overlapping theories—astronomical, agricultural, religious—don't provide the same kind of satisfaction that a single explanation would. Alas, it's highly unlikely that any single explanation could ever account for all the lines and drawings.

Still, the recent findings of Aveni, Silverman, Urton, Zuidema, and others have a great deal more in common than it might at first seem. Each of these scholars began by looking for connections between the Nazcans and other Peruvian cultures, old or new. And each of these connections helped make sense of the Nazca lines.

The lines have been called a "wonder of the ancient world," implying they were something so remarkable that they could not be understood in the context of anything else known about South American antiquity. But for the most recent archaeologists, anthropologists, and historians of Nazca, the reverse holds true: if the lines are to be understood at all, it can only be in the context of that world.

To Investigate Further

Kosok, Paul, and Maria Reiche. "The Mysterious Markings of Nazca," *Natural History* (May 1947).
   The astronomical thesis, with which everyone who came after had to (and still has to) contend.

von Daniken, Erich. *Chariots of the Gods?* (New York: G. P. Putnam's Sons, 1969).
   The Nazca lines make up just one element of von Daniken's case that aliens once visited Earth; his other "proof" includes the Easter Island statues and the pyramids of Egypt.

Hawkins, Gerald. *Beyond Stonehenge* (New York: Harper & Row, 1973).
   In spite of his negative conclusions about Nazca, Hawkins makes a strong case for the astronomical sophistication of ancient humans.

Morrison, Tony. *The Mystery of the Nasca Lines* (Suffolk, England: Nonesuch Expeditions, 1987).
   A fine popular survey, though with a great deal of not particularly interesting biographical information about key researchers. Superb photos.

Hadingham, Evan. *Lines to the Mountain Gods* (New York: Random House, 1987).
   An excellent summary of others' theories, leading up to Hadingham's own speculation that the drawings were directed at the gods on whom the Nazcans depended for water.

Aveni, Anthony, ed. *The Lines of Nazca* (Philadelphia: American Philosophical Society, 1990).
   A collection of essays by the leading researchers, including Clarkson, Urton, Silverman, Ruggles, and Aveni himself, all offering a pan-Andean approach to the lines.

Did Alexander the Great
Kill His Father?

ALEXANDER THE GREAT owed a great deal to his father. As king of Macedon, Philip extended the reign south into Greece, west to the Adriatic Sea, east to the Black Sea, and north to the Danube River. When his son needed a tutor, Philip hired Aristotle—yes, that Aristotle—to teach him about philosophy and literature and politics. When Alexander was eighteen, Philip gave him command over the Macedonian cavalry and his first taste of military victory. Two years later, in 340 BC, as Philip prepared to invade Persia, he appointed Alexander regent. If Alexander's conquests—by age 26 he ruled Persia, by age 30 pretty much all of the known world—surpassed Philip's, they were to a very considerable extent made possible by his father.

How did Alexander repay this debt?

According to some historians, ancient and modern, by conspiring to murder his father.

⁊〰〰〰〷

Philip's assassination was very much a public event. It took place at Aegae in 336 BC at a festival celebrating the marriage of his daughter (and Alexander's sister) Cleopatra to another Alexander, the king of Epirus. As the king's entourage moved toward a theater, Philip lagged behind the procession so that he could enter more dramatically. His body-guards fanned out around him. One of them, Pausanias, stepped forward, stabbed the king, and fled. Three others chased Pausanias and killed him.

Alexander moved quickly to secure the throne. At Philip's funeral, he put to death several potential rivals. He seized command of the army, subdued rebellions to the south and north, and led his troops into Persia. Clearly, therefore, Philip's death advanced Alexander's ambitions. But just because Alexander benefited from the murder doesn't mean he had a part in it. Indeed, according to Aristotle, Pausanias's actions were the result not of a conspiracy but a personal grudge. "Philip . . . was attacked by Pausanias," Aristotle wrote in his *Politics*, "because he permitted him to be insulted by Attalus and his friends."

Aristotle's brief mention is the only extant account of the assassination by a contemporary of Philip and Alexander. Others who were alive then wrote about it, among them Callisthenes, Ptolemy, Nearchus, and Cleitarchus. But none of their works survived, so we're dependent on later writers who presumably read the original accounts. The main sources are Diodorus Siculus, writing in the first century BC, Quintis Curtius Rufus in the first century AD, Plutarch and Arrian in the second century AD, and Justin in the third century AD.

These sources offer much more detail than Aristotle. Here's Diodorus's version:

Attalus, who was one of Philip's courtiers and had great influence with the king, invited Pausanias to dinner, and there he poured large quantities of neat wine into him and handed him to his muleteers for them to abuse his body in a drunken orgy. When Pausanias sobered up after the drinking bout he was deeply hurt by the physical outrage and brought a charge against Attalus before the king. Philip was angered by the enormity of the deed, but he was unwilling to show his disapproval because of his close ties with Attalus and the fact that he needed his services at that time. Attalus, in fact, was the nephew of the Cleopatra who had become the king's new wife, and he had been chosen as commander of the force that was being sent ahead into Asia—he was a man of courage in the military sphere. Accordingly, the king preferred to mollify Pausanias's legitimate anger over what he had suffered, and he bestowed on him substantial gifts and promoted him to positions of honor in the bodyguard.

Pausanias was not so easily mollified, and "he passionately longed to take his revenge not only on the perpetrator of the deed but also on the man who would not exact punishment for him."

Plutarch, while confirming Pausanias's grudge, introduced the possible involvement of Olympias, Alexander's mother, and Alexander himself. As Plutarch described it, their motives were hatched at another wedding a year before the murder. This time it was Philip himself who was married. The bride was the niece of Attalus, another woman named Cleopatra. Olympias was understandably unhappy about this; though polygamy was common in Macedonia, a new wife could hardly be considered good news to an old one. Alexander, for his part, feared that a son of Cleopatra might displace him as heir. Wrote Plutarch: "The troubles . . . began in the women's chambers . . . spreading, so to say, to the whole kingdom."

Making matters worse, Plutarch added, was "the violence of Olympias, a woman of a jealous and implacable temper . . . exasperating Alexander against his father."

Tensions boiled over at the wedding between Philip and Cleopatra. Here's how Plutarch described it:

Attalus in his drink desired the Macedonians would implore the gods to give them a lawful successor to the kingdom by his niece. This so irritated Alexander, that throwing one of the cups at his head, "You villain," said he, "what, am I then a bastard?" Then Philip, taking Attalus's part, rose up and would have run his son through; but by good fortune for them both, either his overhasty rage, or the wine he had drunk, made his foot slip, so that he fell down on the floor. At which Alexander reproachfully insulted over him: "See there," said he, "the man who makes preparations to pass out of Europe into Asia, overturned in passing from one seat to another."

Justin gave a similar account of an outraged Pausanias, a jealous Olympias, and an insecure Alexander who, after the fight at the wedding of Philip and Cleopatra, left the court along with his mother. Though they publicly reconciled soon after, things were never the same between father and son. "It is thought that Olympias and her son," Justin wrote, "incited Pausanias to proceed to so heinous a crime, while he was making his complaints about the abuse going unpunished." Concluded Plutarch: "Most of the responsibility for [the murder] was attributed to Olympias, but aspersions were cast on Alexander, too."

Arrian, whose portrait of Alexander is by far the most favorable of those in the primary sources, wrote nothing about an incident at the wedding of Philip and Cleopatra, let alone about murder conspiracy. But even Arrian noted that "suspicion existed between Philip and Alexander when Philip married . . . and dishonored Alexander's mother, Olympias."

☙

Arrian provided plenty of other examples of Alexander's resentment of his father, feelings that continued well after the latter's death. In 328 BC, Cleitus, one of Alexander's generals, publicly praised Philip in a way that downplayed Alexander's subsequent achievements. Alexander's response was to run a spear through Cleitus. In 324, faced with a mutiny near Babylon, Alexander addressed his troops. He began by reviewing Philip's achievements—this still according to Arrian—but he did so only to show how much greater were his own.

Alexander's relationship with his mother, in contrast, was a very close one. Indeed, some historians suspected an Oedipus complex. (There has also been plenty of psychologizing about Alexander's love life, with some suspecting he was gay and others that his only true love was his horse Bucephalus, whose funeral procession he led and after whom he named a city.) Oedipal or not, Alexander loved his mother. It was she who raised him while Philip spent much time away from the palace on various campaigns.

Of course, plenty of sons resent their fathers without conspiring to kill them. Polygamy was a common practice among Macedonian royalty; patricide was not. In the absence of hard evidence of Alexander's complicity, therefore, historians have looked to his character. Some, following Arrian, have seen in Alexander the courage of Achilles and the wisdom of Aristotle. This Alexander truly deserved to be called great: he spread Greek culture through the known world, and he sought to unite all people, as he once proclaimed, in a "brotherhood of mankind." Other historians have followed Diodorus and Justin in portraying him as ruthless and amoral, a drunk, a man whose megalomania ultimately extended to a belief that he was a god. This was the Alexander who would not hesitate to murder his rivals, his enemies, and even his father.

In 1977 the archaeologist Manolis Andronikos uncovered three tombs at Vergina, a village thought to be on the site of ancient Aegae, where Philip was killed. The quality and quantity of artifacts, many of gold and silver, were extraordinary. Andronikos also found ivory heads with what might have been representations of Philip and Alexander. The bones and teeth of a male skeleton suggested he was in his forties when he died, as was Philip. Andronikos concluded he had found Philip's tomb.

Was the splendor of the tomb a sign that Alexander wanted to honor his father? Or was it designed to hide the son's crime? There was no way to be sure, and indeed there was no way to be sure these were Philip's bones. His burial place, like his son's role in putting him there, remains a mystery.

To Investigate Further

Aristotle. *Politics and Poetics.* New York: Viking, 1957.
  Translated by Benjamin Jowett.

Heckel, Waldemar, and J. C. Yardley. *Alexander the Great.* Malden, MA: Blackwell, 2004.
  Excerpts from relevant sources, including Arrian, Diodorus, and Justin.

Fuller, Edmund, ed. *Plutarch: Lives of the Noble Greeks.* New York: Dell, 1959.
  The Dryden translation.

Worthington, Ian, ed. *Alexander the Great.* New York: Routledge, 2003.
  A selection of readings, including some of the fragmentary primary sources as well as essays by modern historians.

Fox, Robin Lane. *Alexander the Great.* New York: Dial Press, 1974.
  Alexander as Homeric hero.

Hammond, Nicholas. *The Genius of Alexander the Great.* Chapel Hill: University of North Carolina Press, 1997.
  A genius in statecraft as well as war.

Borza, Eugene. *Before Alexander.* Claremont, CA: Regina Books, 1999.
  A brief guide to Macedonian studies through the reign of Philip.

Worthington, Ian. *Alexander the Great.* Harlow, England: Pearson Longman, 2004.
  Worthington tends to agree with the Persisans who called him Alexander the Accursed.

Cartledge, Paul. *Alexander the Great.* Woodstock, NY: Overlook Press, 2004.
  A thematic rather than chronological study of Alexander's life.

Why Didn't Attila
Invade Rome?

NO PEOPLE HAVE GONE DOWN IN HISTORY as more barbaric than the Huns, who swept across Europe in the fifth century. As portrayed in Edward Gibbon's classic eighteenth-century history, the Huns were one of the main reasons for the fall of the Roman Empire. Admittedly, since the Huns were illiterate, historians had to depend on the biased and incomplete testimony of Romans, who portrayed them as inhumanly fierce. The Huns were so used to raiding Europe on their horses, wrote one fifth-century Roman, that they were unsteady on their feet when walking. "Not even the centaurs," wrote another, "grew closer to their horses."

"The people of the Huns exceed every degree of savagery," wrote the Roman soldier and historian Ammianus Marcellinus. "They all have compact, strong limbs, and thick necks, and are monstrously ugly and misshapen. They eat roots of wild plants and the half-raw flesh of any kind of animal whatever, which they put between their thighs and the backs of their horses, and thus warm it a little."

Most barbaric of all was their leader, Attila. "The haughty step and demeanor of the king of the Huns expressed the consciousness of his superiority above the rest of mankind," wrote the sixth-century Goth historian Jordanes, "and he had the custom of fiercely rolling his eyes as if he wished to enjoy the terror he inspired." He "ground almost the whole of Europe into the dust," wrote Marcellinus.

Attila came to power in 434. By then, the Huns ruled much of eastern and central Europe, having conquered the Germanic tribes in the region. Attila ruled jointly with his brother Bleda until 443, when Bleda died mysteriously. Many suspected Attila had him killed, but Priscus, a Roman historian who visited Attila's court in 459, said nothing about this. During the 440s Attila repeatedly threatened the Eastern Roman Empire, demanding and receiving huge payments from Constantinople. In 450, Marcian became emperor of the east and announced an end to the payments.

Meanwhile, off in the west, Honoria, the sister of the emperor Valentinian III, was engaged against her will to a wealthy senator. Enraged and ambitious, Honoria sent a ring to Attila along with a plea that he rescue her. Attila seized this pretext to transfer his aggressions from the Eastern Empire to the Western. He accepted Honoria's marriage proposal and demanded half the Western Roman Empire as a dowry. When the emperor refused, Attila invaded Gaul, overrunning much of Germany and France before being stopped, in the June 451 Battle of the Catalaunian Fields, by a combined Roman and Visigoth army.

Undeterred, a year later Attila led an army of about 100,000 men into Italy. This time there were no Goths to come to the Romans' aid, nor was the imperial army, exhausted by the defense of Gaul, ready for another fight. Attila laid siege to the city of Aquileia. According to Priscus, Attila considered giving up the siege after three months, but then saw a flock of white storks fly above the city. He took this as a good omen, and the city soon fell. Next he marched west to Milan. In the royal palace there, he found a picture of the Roman emperors sitting on thrones with barbarian princes at their feet. He instructed painters to revise the scene to show the now-prostrate Caesars emptying bags of gold before Atilla. Next he turned south toward Rome itself, pausing on the banks of the Mincio River. Pope Leo's secretary, St. Prosper of Aquitaine, conceded the outlook was bleak.

"In all the deliberations of the emperor, the senate, and the Roman people nothing better was found than to send an embassy to the terrible king and ask for peace," Prosper wrote. "With no other option open to them, they decided to send an embassy to Attila and beg for peace."

The Romans sent three men to negotiate: the senators Trigetius and Avienus and the pope himself.

"Relying on the help of God," Prosper continued, "the most blessed Pope Leo undertook these negotiations. . . . Nor did it turn out otherwise than faith had expected. The king received the whole delegation courteously, and he was so flattered by the presence of the highest priest that he ordered his men to stop the hostilities and, promising peace, returned beyond the Danube."

The Renaissance artist Raphael later produced a famous fresco in which Leo is accompanied not by Trigetius and Avienus, but by St. Peter and St. Paul. To some, divine intervention seemed as good an explanation as any for Attila's withdrawal from Italy. Why else would a barbarian known as the "scourge of God" bow to the will of the pope? "It is unreasonable to suppose," wrote the nineteenth-century historian J. B. Bury, "that this heathen king would have cared for the thunders or persuasions of the Church."

"The apparition of the two apostles of St. Peter and St. Paul," Gibbon wrote, "who menaced the barbarian with instant death if he rejected the prayer of their successor, is one of the noblest legends of ecclesiastical tradition."

Yet legend it clearly was.

∿

Jordanes, following the lead of Priscus, suggested that just because Attila wasn't Christian didn't mean he was immune to religious persuasion. After all, he had taken the storks over Aquileia as a sign to continue his siege. "Attila's mind," wrote Jordanes, "had been bent on going to Rome. But his followers, as the historian Priscus relates, took him away, not out of regard for the city to which they were hostile, but because they remembered the case of Alaric." Alaric was a Goth king who briefly occupied Rome in 410, then died shortly after. Atilla or his followers may have feared the same fate.

In Raphael's version, St. Paul and St. Peter accompany Pope Leo to his meeting with Attila.
(Archivo Iconografico, S.A./Corbis)

Gibbon suggested that "the pressing eloquence of Leo, his majestic aspect and sacer-
dotal robes," may have "excited the veneration of Attila for the spiritual father of the
Christians." Bury suggested that the pope may also have bribed Attila's advisers to remind
him of Alaric's fate.

Problems back home may also have swayed Attila. Marcian, aware that the brunt of
Attila's troops were in Italy, was increasingly aggressive, and Atilla may not have wanted
to fight on two fronts. He may even have feared that reinforcements from the Eastern
Empire were en route to Italy. Or he may simply have redirected his wrath eastward. "For
he sent ambassadors to Marcian, Emperor of the East," wrote Jordanes, "threatening to
devastate the provinces . . . because that which had been promised him by . . . a former
emperor was in no wise performed, and saying that he would show himself more cruel to
his foes than ever."

The Roman chronicler Hydatius provided more evidence that it was Marcian, not Leo,
who turned Attila around. Hydatius never even mentioned Leo's delegation. His only explanation for the Hun retreat was that "auxiliaries were sent by the emperor Marcian,

and . . . they [the Huns] were slain. Likewise they were subdued in their own seats, partly by plagues from heaven, partly by Marcian's army." Hydatius said nothing about the time or place of this battle, so it's hard to gauge its connection to the Huns' retreat, but at the very least it's a reminder that Attila was thinking about Constantinople as well as Rome.

Most historians, picking up on Hydatius's reference to "plagues from heaven," believe famine and disease were also factors. Italy suffered a famine during the winter of 450–451, and Attila may have found there was still a shortage of food for his troops. Some also think his troops may have suffered from disease, possibly malaria. The pope may very well have pointed out to Attila the dangers he faced from natural as well as supernatural forces.

Others have suggested Attila was never particularly interested in conquering Rome. He had, after all, followed a very indirect route toward the city, heading first to Gaul and then to the western part of northern Italy before turning south. By the summer of 452, he may have been ready to go home. The siege of Aquileia had taken three months, and the conquest of northern Italy had taken more time. Winter was approaching. And Attila may have already gotten what he came for: gold and the promise of more gold. A sixth-century letter to Pope Symachus hinted that Leo offered to ransom captured Romans, and that the sums were substantial. Attila may even have been promised Honoria, though none of the Roman chroniclers mentioned it.

Besides, Attila retained the option of returning to Italy. According to Jordanes, the Hun made that clear to the pope: "Attila quickly put aside his usual fury, turned back on the way he had advanced from beyond the Danube, and departed with the promise of peace," Jordanes wrote. "But above all he declared and avowed with threats that he would bring worse things upon Italy, unless they sent him Honoria . . . with her due share of the royal wealth." Gibbon thought "the deliverance of Italy was purchased by the immense ransom dowry of the princess Honoria."

Wrote Patrick Howarth in 1997: "Pope Leo, Trigetius, and Avienus clearly achieved what they wanted, but so, it is quite reasonable to suppose, did Attila. He may indeed have had no intention of advancing further than the river Mincio."

⁓

For historians like Howarth, the withdrawal from Italy exemplified not Attila the scourge but Attila the shrewd. "If he hoped to conquer most of the civilized world, it could be said that he was not granted enough time," Howarth wrote. "But if, having consolidated the Hun kingdom . . . he simply devised a method of enriching its economy by a series of long-distance raids, he may be adjudged a considerable benefactor of his nation."

Pagan, Germanic, and Hungarian traditions were also kind to Attila. In such epics as the ninth-century *Song of Hildebrand*, the tenth-century *Walther's Song*, and the twelfth-century *Song of the Nibelungs*, Attila was, to varying extents, a romantic hero. These works, however, were even more biased than those of the Romans. They were also written centuries later.

Modern historians continued to debate Attila's prowess. Some, like E. A. Thompson, portrayed him as a military and diplomatic incompetent. Thompson stressed that Attila's raids were often against defenseless villages, that he drove the Goths to join the Romans, and that his most famous battle—at the Catalaunian Fields—was a defeat.

Others, notably Otto Maenchen-Helfen, defended Attila. "He was, we are told, . . . a bungler who would not have made such awful blunders had he had a professor of history as advisor," Maenchen-Helfen wrote, mocking Thompson. Attila was not, Maenchen-Helfen conceded, another Alexander, but his military successes created a powerful empire.

Whatever Attila achieved, it didn't last long. A year after withdrawing from Italy, he married Ildiko, the daughter of one of his vassals. (He had many wives, so this didn't necessarily mean that he had given up on Honoria.) The night of his wedding, Attila choked to death while drunk (though, inevitably, there were rumors that Ildiko had murdered him). With Attila dead, his kingdom collapsed.

The kingdom's quick demise has prompted some historians to argue that Gibbon overstated the Huns' role in bringing down the Roman Empire. After all, it was Alaric who sacked Rome, not Attila, and the Eastern Roman Empire survived Attila by a thousand years. Bury went so far as to argue that the Huns "helped to retard the whole process of the German dismemberment of the Empire" by battling those, such as the Visigoths, who would otherwise have attacked Constantinople or Rome.

These arguments underestimate Gibbon, who well understood that Attila alone was not responsible for the decline and fall of the Roman Empire. Gibbon listed dozens of causes—military and political, economic and psychological. The arguments also underestimate the damage Attila caused the empire. Dislodged by the Huns, some Goths and Vandals joined the Romans, but others saw the empire's vast territory as potential new homelands. The Visigoths were more aggressive than ever in attacking Roman outposts in Gaul, while the Vandals pushed into Africa and the Ostrogoths into Italy.

"Even if the Germanic invasions were retarded between 430 and 455, they were accelerated both before and after those dates," wrote Thompson. "That Germans would eventually have set up their kingdoms in Gaul, Italy, and Africa is of course undeniable, but without the Huns they would have done so at a more leisurely pace."

Attila reigned over the Huns a mere eight years, and he turned away from Rome. But during his reign, as Gibbon wrote, "the Huns . . . became the terrors of the world," and "that formidable barbarian . . . alternately insulted and invaded the East and the West and urged the rapid downfall of the Roman Empire."

To Investigate Further

Mierow, Charles. *The Gothic History of Jordanes.* New York: Barnes and Noble, 1966.
  Much of what's survived of Priscus can be found in Jordanes.

Gibbon, Edward. *The Decline and Fall of the Roman Empire.* **New York: Modern Library, 1932.**
Gibbon originally published his masterpiece in six volumes. This edition combines them into three, with the Huns making their appearance in the second.

Bury, J. B. *History of the Later Roman Empire.* **New York: Dover, 1958.**
Bury edited Gibbon but also challenged him on many points, including when the empire fell; Bury believed it continued long after Gibbon's date of 476.

Thompson, E. A. *The Huns.* **Malden, MA: Blackwell Publishers, 1996.**
Originally published in 1948, this was revised by Peter Heather, who also wrote an afterword putting Thompson in the context of more recent studies.

Maenchen-Helfen, Otto. *The World of the Huns.* **Berkeley: University of California Press, 1973.**
Not easy reading (partly since Maenchen-Helfen died before finishing it) but nonetheless the most thorough and important book on the Huns.

Grant, Michael. *The Fall of the Roman Empire.* **Radnor, PA: Annenberg School Press, 1976.**
A tribute to Gibbon that focuses on the internal flaws that led to the fall.

Howarth, Patrick. *Attila, King of the Huns.* **Carlisle, PA: John Kallman, 1997.**
The man and the myth.

PART 3

ZONES OF EXCHANGE AND ENCOUNTER, 500–1000

Did St. Brendan Discover America?

S T. BRENDAN WAS RUNNING A MONASTERY in Ireland when a visiting abbot told him of his voyage across the ocean to the "Promised Land of the Saints." Brendan decided to see it for himself.

So, sometime in the middle of the sixth century, Brendan and seventeen other monks set sail in a small boat they framed with wood, then covered with ox hides, much like the curraghs still sometimes seen in Ireland. Their adventures were many and marvelous.

They came, for example, to one island filled with giant white sheep, and another covered by hymn-singing birds. They found a huge pillar of crystal floating in the ocean, surrounded by pieces of marble, and a whole island on fire, from which they were pelted by hot rocks. Brendan told his fellow monks they'd reached the edge of hell.

Another island appeared rocky and black, and the monks went ashore to cook a meal. As soon as the cauldron began to boil, the island started to move, and the monks scrambled back into their boat. Turns out, Brendan figured, the island was actually the ocean's largest fish.

More pleasantly, there was a spacious and woody island, and one with luxurious colors and fruit unlike anything the monks had seen before. And finally, after seven years, there was the Promised Land of the Saints, where a young man told the monks the land would be given to their successors. Brendan then returned to Ireland.

This is Brendan's story, as told in the *Navigatio Sancti Brendani Abbatis,* a Latin manuscript by an anonymous author. Scholars date the *Navigatio* back to sometime after A.D. 800, at least a hundred years after Brendan's death. The story was tremendously popular throughout the late Middle Ages—understandably, given its mix of maritime romance and Christian theology.

Also understandably, most modern scholars viewed the *Navigatio* as a work of literature, not history. Brendan seemed to have more in common with King Arthur, or perhaps with Odysseus, than with an actual historical figure. Many placed the work in a genre of early Irish literature known as *imrama;* these were generally filled with fantastic sea stories.

But there was a key difference. Unlike *imrama,* the *Navigatio* contained navigational directions and detailed descriptions of the places the monks visited. By plotting their course on a map and comparing the descriptions to actual islands, historians sought to reconstruct Brendan's journey. Some concluded that the Promised Land of the Saints was in North America.

If so, Brendan reached America about a thousand years before Columbus.

⟳

Among those who tracked Brendan's voyage were Geoffrey Ashe in the 1960s and Paul Chapman in the 1970s. Ashe was a medieval historian, Chapman a World War II navigator familiar with the North Atlantic from ferrying planes across the ocean.

Some of the islands were fairly easy to identify, and most historians agreed which of these was which. The sheep and the birds were most likely in the Faroes, an archipelago in the North Atlantic between Scotland and Iceland. True, the sheep there aren't giant and the birds don't sing hymns, but there are plenty of both. Faeroes, in fact, is Danish for sheep, and the island of Vagar is known for its kittiwakes and arctic terns.

The crystal pillar could have been an iceberg, a likely sight as the monks headed north. What appeared to be marble could have been patches of ice that had broken off from the berg. The hot rocks? Molten slag from an erupting volcano near Iceland, according to some speculation, or farther south near the Azores, according to others. Both are areas of volcanic activity.

The moving island is surely a tall tale. But whales are common north of the Faroes, and there were undoubtedly more of them around in the seventh century. So, for Brendan enthusiasts, the story could be seen as confirmation that the monks were in that area.

Now it gets trickier. Brendan and company drifted for twenty days, then were swept west for another forty before reaching the large, wooded island. Chapman concluded this must have been the heavily forested Barbados. Heading north from there, the fruit he soon found may have been grapefruit, which was native to the Caribbean and unknown in Europe. Ashe was less certain of all this, saying only the "effect of the whole passage is West Indian."

The Land of the Promised Saints is even more amorphous. There were another forty days at sea—a number whose recurrence makes one suspect its significance is more biblical than nautical. Equally problematic, Brendan was at this point, according to the *Navigatio,* sailing east, presumably away from America.

Ashe concluded the Land of the Promised Saints was a "literary-religious figment," one that fulfilled the promise of the opening chapter but not the demands of historical reality. Chapman agreed that the *Navigatio* did not prove Brendan reached the mainland. He figured Brendan probably stopped at the West Indies, just as Columbus did.

The *Navigatio* alone, then, could not make the case for the Irish in America. Nor could other medieval Irish texts. Brendan had a minor role in a ninth-century *Life of St. Machutus,* another saint; there was also a tenth-century *Life of St. Brendan.* Both texts were useful in confirming Brendan was a real person, renowned for many sea voyages, but neither offered anywhere near the detail of the *Navigatio.*

There were, however, three medieval texts that did place the Irish in North America. Surprisingly, these came not from Ireland but from Iceland.

⟳

For most of American history, historians treated the Icelandic sagas much as the Irish *imrama*. They were ancient stories, not quite as ancient as the Irish ones perhaps, but equally inadmissible as historical evidence. All that changed when a Norwegian archaeologist, Helge Ingstad, uncovered a Norse spindle whorl amid the remains of a village in northern Newfoundland. Here was proof that the Norse had reached—indeed had settled in—America hundreds of years before Columbus.

The Icelandic sagas, of course, told the stories of Eric the Red and Leif Ericsson and other Norsemen, not of Brendan or the Irish. Yet the Irish did appear in three of the sagas, and each time they were in the New World.

In the *Saga of Eric the Red*, the Norse reached America, captured some natives, and taught them their language. The natives then told the Norse of a land whose people wore white clothes and marched with poles that had cloths attached to them. To the Norse who heard this story, according to the saga, this sounded a lot like a procession of Irish monks. A second saga mentioned a land west of the Norse settlement in America, "which some call Ireland the Great." And a third had a lost Norseman wash up on American shores, where natives spoke a language that he thought sounded like that of the Irish.

In one sense, these stories made a lot of sense. The Norse knew well that the Irish monks were accomplished seamen. The Irish had beaten them to the Faroes and Iceland and Greenland, so why not America? Indeed, it was the Norse who pushed the Irish monks out of Iceland, perhaps prompting them to head west. This was sometime in the ninth century, too late for Brendan to be the first Irishman to reach America, but still well before Leif Ericsson, let alone Columbus.

There were a number of problems with this theory, however. First, the sagas were vague about the location of "Ireland the Great." If the ninth-century Irish monks headed west from Iceland, they would have come to Greenland before America, and they might very well have founded a colony there. Second, there's no archaeological evidence that the Irish made it to America; no one has found an Irish equivalent of Ingstad's Norse spindle whorl.

And third, Leif Ericsson and the Norse didn't reach America before the end of the tenth century, more than a hundred years after the Irish monks left Iceland. So either these monks had reached Old Testament–like ages, or they had met some Native American women and abandoned their vows of chastity.

⌘

Most modern historians, therefore, would deny Brendan's claim. Even some of those who believed the Irish reached the West Indies weren't sure it was Brendan.

"Over a period of two or three hundred years, many Irish monks besides Brendan made actual voyages," wrote Ashe. "And as so often in legend-making, the most famous figure came to be credited with deeds not authentically his."

Ashe concluded the *Navigatio* was not so much the record of a specific voyage as an amalgam of knowledge the Irish accumulated, not only from their own travels but from studying traditions and legends from Plato's Atlantis to the Celtic "otherworld."

Samuel Eliot Morison, the premiere chronicler of the European voyages across the ocean, would grant neither Brendan nor any Irishman an American landing, even in the West Indies.

"We are not straining the evidence to conclude that Brendan sailed for several trips . . . on the circuit Hebrides-Shetlands-Faroes-Iceland, possibly as far as the Azores," Morison wrote in 1971. "But, discovery of America—no!"

"The imagination of certain modern . . . writers, no whit less than that of the early storytellers, has brought Brendan to Newfoundland, the West Indies, Mexico, and even the Ohio River!" Morison continued. "They do not even boggle at peppering the Antilles with Irish monasteries which have disappeared, or ascribing to Brendan's curragh the speed and endurance of a clipper ship."

Tim Severin, a British explorer and writer, believed Morison was wrong, at least about the capabilities of the boat. To prove it, Severin stitched together forty-nine ox hides, stretched them over a wooden frame, put together a crew, and in May 1976, set sail from the west coast of Ireland. The ship—christened *Brendan*—reached the Faroes in June and Iceland in July. There *Brendan* rested until May 1977, when Severin and his crew headed west. Less than two months later, they reached Newfoundland.

Granted, Severin equipped the boat with some modern equipment, including a radio. But the medieval equipment, such as extra hides with which the crew patched leaks in the middle of the North Atlantic, came in just as handy and proved a lot more durable than, for example, the plastic food bags that were quickly inundated by seawater.

The trip did not, of course, prove that the Irish monks had reached America; merely that it was technologically possible.

"A leather boat that some had feared would disintegrate in the first gale off the Irish coast had successfully crossed the Atlantic. Brendan had demonstrated that the voyage could be done," Severin wrote. "But in the final analysis the only conclusive proof that it had been done would be if an authentic relic from an early Irish visit is found one day on North American soil."

⟨∾⟩

Assume for the moment that Brendan reached America. Or, as Ashe did, that the Irish monks at least knew about America. The question then arises: What did Columbus know about Brendan and the Irish?

Since the *Navigatio* was so widely known, Columbus may very well have read about it, or at least heard about it. A pre-1492 globe includes "the Isle of St. Brendan," in what could be construed as the West Indies. Chapman believed Columbus followed Brendan's route, and intentionally hid that fact so that he could claim the New World for Spain.

That seems a stretch, especially since most of Columbus's biographers—including his own son Ferdinand and, more recently, Morison—maintained that the admiral was searching for a new route to Asia, not a New World. Indeed, even after Columbus reached America, he continued to describe it as an island, or perhaps a peninsula, off the Asian mainland.

Still, even the most skeptical historians, such as Morison, don't deny that Brendan may have been an inspiration—and therefore in some sense a forerunner—to later explorers, including Columbus.

"No, here is not a discovery of a New World," Morison wrote of the *Navigatio,* but then added that it was "a captivating tale which led men of later centuries to sail into the unknown, hoping to find Brendan's islands, confident that God would watch over them."

To Investigate Further

Selmer, Carl, ed. *Navigatio Sancti Brendani Abbatis.* Dublin: Four Courts, 1989.
A reconstruction based on 18 of the 120 known Latin versions.

Ashe, Geoffrey. *Land to the West.* New York: Viking, 1962.
Ashe focuses on what the Irish monks knew, as opposed to what Brendan did.

Morison, Samuel Eliot. *The European Discovery of America: The Northern Voyages.* New York: Oxford University Press, 1971.
Morison's elegant prose is informed by his extensive knowledge not just of history, but also of the sea.

Chapman, Paul H. *The Man Who Led Columbus to America.* Atlanta, GA: Judson Press, 1973.
The title has two meanings: Brendan came first, and Columbus used the *Navigatio* as a guide.

Severin, Tim. *The Brendan Voyage.* New York: Modern Library, 2000.
Regardless of its historic import, this is a dramatic and well-told sea story in the tradition of Thor Heyerdahl's *Kon-Tiki.* Originally published in 1978.

Who Was King Arthur?

THE LEGEND OF KING ARTHUR—in stark contrast to the actual man—is easy to track back to its origins. Much of the credit goes to an obscure Welsh cleric named Geoffrey of Monmouth, who taught at Oxford during the first half of the twelfth century. In about 1138 Geoffrey produced *The History of the Kings of Britain*.

The story, as Geoffrey tells it, moves toward its climax in the fifth century. Heathen Saxons, led by the brothers Hengist and Horsa, have invaded and destroyed much of the country. A young wizard, Merlin, arrives on the scene with prophecies of a king who will save Britain.

Meanwhile, King Uther falls hopelessly in love with Ygerna. Unfortunately, she's already married to Gorlois, the duke of Cornwall. Merlin steps in to help out. He transforms Uther into an exact likeness of Gorlois, so the king can slip by the duke's guards and sleep with Ygerna. Thus is Arthur conceived.

Fast forward about fifteen years, when the young Arthur ascends to the throne. He routs the Saxons, confining them to a small section of Britain. Later he conquers the Picts, the Scots, the Irish, and, among many others, the Icelanders. When Roman ambassadors demand he pay tribute to the emperor, Arthur crosses the English Channel and defeats their armies in France.

While Arthur is abroad, his nephew, Mordred, crowns himself king and lives in adultery with Arthur's queen, Guinevere. Arthur returns and slays the traitor but is himself seriously wounded. He's last seen as he's carried off to the "isle of Avalon."

So goes the tale, as told by Geoffrey of Monmouth. Arthur's victory is only temporary, since the Anglo-Saxons eventually do conquer Arthur's Britons (thus making Britain into Angle-land, or England). But this only added to the story's appeal to the Britons, who yearned for a return to a golden age when they ruled the land. For them, Arthur was not dead; he was waiting for the right moment to return from Avalon.

That yearned-for golden age became even more golden in the imaginations of later medieval writers, who enhanced Geoffrey's legend. The French author Robert Wace introduced the Round Table, so that Arthur's knights could sit as equals. Another Frenchman, Chretien de Troyes, brought to the fore Lancelot, Arthur's loyal knight (and Guinevere's passionate lover). The German Wolfram von Eschenbach added Parzival. By the end of the Middle Ages, Arthur's fifth-century foot soldiers had become knights on horses; his fortified hills had become grand castles; and his court had become Camelot, a chivalric utopia.

It was an Englishman, Thomas Malory, whose fifteenth-century *Morte d'Arthur* combined all these elements, giving his countrymen a mythic tradition to match any nation's. There was a certain irony to this, since the original story pitted Arthur's Britons against the Anglo-Saxon ancestors of the English, but such is the nature of classic myths. They can transcend almost any sort of border; witness the revival of the legend in the twentieth century in variations ranging from the feminist (most notably, in the novels of Marion Zimmer Bradley) to the musical (starring Richard Burton, in the Broadway version).

The yearning for a return to a golden age, it seems, is eternal. When journalist Theodore H. White, quoting from the musical, referred to the Kennedy years as "one brief, shining moment," the president's administration was quickly labeled "Camelot."

Yet lost amid his legend was Arthur himself. Even in Geoffrey of Monmouth's own lifetime, it was clear that his *History* was anything but. In about 1197, William of Newburgh called Geoffrey's work a "laughable web of fiction" and calculated that there weren't as many kingdoms in the world as Geoffrey had Arthur conquering.

Since then, historians following in William's footsteps have attempted to sift from the legend the "historical" Arthur—if, indeed, he really existed.

Above all, that meant turning to the (very few) sources that preceded Geoffrey of Monmouth and were thus both closer to Arthur's time and less likely to have been corrupted by later mythologizing. These were mostly Welsh writings, since it was the Welsh who were descendants of the ancient Britons.

These Britons came to power after the fall of the Roman Empire, early in the fifth century. They had wielded considerable power under the empire, so it seemed natural (to them) that they take over after the Roman legions left. That was unlike other areas of the former empire, where the invaders who drove out the Romans seized power. Independent Britain was therefore still in many ways Roman; the Britons, or at least their upper class, saw themselves as the heirs to the imperial culture and civilization.

Unfortunately for them, they also inherited the Roman enemies. The Britons immediately found themselves under attack from groups they thought of as barbarians: the Irish from the west, the Picts from the north, and the Anglo-Saxons from across the North Sea. The invaders saw no reason to withdraw just because the Britons had replaced the Romans.

The situation the Welsh bards described was desperate—every bit as much as that faced by the British in Geoffrey of Monmouth's account. But if we can believe a Welsh monk named Gildas, in about the year 500 the Britons won a great victory at a spot called Mount Badon. In *The Ruin of Britain*, written only about fifty years after that, Gildas described the battle and the two generations of relative peace and prosperity that followed.

Was this interregnum of Gildas the brief, shining moment of Camelot? Perhaps. But, as skeptics have been quick to point out, nowhere does Gildas mention the name of Arthur. Frustratingly, Gildas never says who commanded the Britons.

Glastonbury Abbey, where twelfth-century monks claimed to have found the bodies of Arthur and Guinevere. *(Library of Congress)*

That was left to Nennius, another Welsh cleric. In the *History of the Britons*, which Nennius compiled sometime early in the ninth century, there's no doubt about the identity of the hero: it is "the warrior Arthur." According to Nennius, Arthur defeated the Saxons in twelve battles, at one point slaying 960 of the enemy in a single charge.

But can Nennius be trusted? Such obviously impossible deeds as single-handedly killing 960 of the enemy clearly belong to the traditions of epic poetry, not history. His notoriously disorganized material didn't help, either; the cleric himself described his approach as "making one heap" of all he found. Some historians found comfort in that, arguing that someone unable to organize anything probably also couldn't invent anything. Others just found it frustrating.

Welsh writers who followed Nennius also credited Arthur with the victory at Mount Badon. But, like Nennius, they were all writing at least three hundred years after the actual events. It was impossible to tell whether the oral tradition they recounted was the actual history of fifth-century Britain.

Clearly, the Welsh writings alone would not convince the skeptics. What was needed was some harder evidence that Arthur existed, and that seemed to materialize in 1191 (or, according to some, 1192). That was when the monks of Glastonbury Abbey announced that they had discovered the bodies of Arthur and Guinevere.

∽

The discovery was described by a Gerald of Wales, writing just a couple of years later. Gerald told how the bodies were found at Glastonbury, "deep in the earth, enclosed in a hollow oak." He added that a leaden cross was found "under a stone, not above, as is the custom today."

The inscription on the cross read: "Here lies buried the famous King Arthurus with Wennevereia his second wife in the isle of Avallonia."

Was Glastonbury the isle of Avalon?

There's no clear consensus among historians, but most are inclined to disbelieve the bones were Arthur's and Guinevere's. For one thing, the town of Glastonbury, which is in Somerset, is almost entirely surrounded by meadows. These meadows may once have been swamps, but it's still a bit of a stretch to imagine them as the "isle" of Avalon.

Skeptics also noted that the leaden cross with the engraving was written in a style of letters common in the tenth or eleventh century, not the fifth or sixth—when Arthur supposedly died. This seemed to point to a fraud.

Worse, the monks had a definite motive to fake the discovery. Much of the abbey had recently burned down, and Arthur's grave site would (and did) draw plenty of pilgrims to the abbey. The pilgrims brought with them much-needed funds for rebuilding.

The abbey's defenders have countered that if the monks had wanted to forge an inscription, they would have known enough to choose a properly ancient one. They argued that Arthur's body had first been found in the years after 945, when the abbey demolished a mausoleum on the grounds. Arthur, they surmised, must have been reburied at that point, along with a new cross in contemporary tenth-century letters.

Archaeologist C. A. Ralegh Radford bolstered the monks' story a bit in 1962 and 1963 when he found indications that someone had indeed dug where the monks said they did. But that proved nothing about what they found, and the reburial hypothesis depended on buying into a whole chain of events, each part of which was unproven.

So, barring some dramatic new archaeological discovery, Glastonbury seems unlikely to provide any definite answers about Arthur. Neither the bones nor the cross can be subjected to any modern scientific analysis; the former disappeared sometime during the sixteenth century, and the cross somewhat later.

∽

After finishing his search for Arthur's burial place, Radford turned to his birthplace. Geoffrey had said it was at Tintagel Castle, on the Cornish coast, that Uther and Ygerna had conceived Arthur, and it was there that Radford next dug. Underneath the late medieval castle there, he was delighted to find fragments of imported pottery from the fifth or sixth century. This proved nothing about Uther or Ygerna or Arthur, of course, but it suggested that people of considerable wealth lived there at about the right time.

Even more tantalizing were the results of the search for Arthur's headquarters, the legendary Camelot. Cadbury Castle, just a short distance from Glastonbury, had been been associated in popular legends with Camelot since at least the sixteenth century. Between 1966 and 1970, archaeologists under the direction of Leslie Alcock dug for clues.

Under the high ground known locally as "Arthur's Palace," Alcock uncovered the foundations of a large hall, built with timber and showing signs of skilled workmanship. Alcock also found the remains of an unmortared stone wall enclosing part of the hill, and a gate tower.

All this pointed to a major fortress dating back to about 500. An exultant Alcock wrote that "with every justification, we can think of Arthur and his troops feasting and carousing . . . in a hall similar to that at Cadbury, and riding out to battle through a gate tower like that at the southwest entrance."

Of course, that didn't prove Cadbury was Camelot, as Alcock readily admitted. This was more a fortified hill than a real fort, let alone the castle of the medieval romances. Moreover, nothing found at Cadbury linked the fort with Arthur's name. It could have been the headquarters of any sixth-century military leader.

Radford and Alcock couched their findings carefully, stressing that they'd revealed more about Arthur's Britain than about Arthur himself. Yet their discoveries inevitably placed Arthur at center stage, and some of the media reports on them were quick to equate Cadbury and Camelot.

That, in turn, generated a backlash among academics, who reiterated all of the limitations of the Welsh sources as well as the archaeological finds. Skepticism still prevails among the majority of academics, one of whom described the pro-Arthur case as nothing more than saying there's no smoke without fire.

But smoke there was. Sometime in the fifth or sixth century, we can be pretty sure, there was a brief resurgence of the Britons. At someplace called Mount Badon, someone led the Britons to victory. The Welsh bards, writing at a time closer to the actual events than any subsequent historians, called the Britons' leader Arthur.

So can we.

To Investigate Further

White, Richard, ed. *King Arthur in Legend and History.* New York: Routledge, 1997.
  A handy collection of excerpts from the early sources, including Gildas, Nennius, Geoffrey of Monmouth, William of Newburgh, and Wace.

Chambers, E. K. *Arthur of Britain.* New York: Barnes & Noble, 1927.
  This thorough study initiated the modern quest for the historical Arthur; quite reasonably, Chambers remained an agnostic on the subject of Arthur's existence.

Collingwood, Robin G. *Roman Britain and the English Settlements.* Oxford: Clarendon Press, 1937.
    Arthur as a wide-ranging general and cavalry leader.

Jackson, Kenneth Hurlstone. "The Arthur of History," in *Arthurian Literature in the Middle Ages,* ed. Roger Sherman Loomis. Oxford: Clarendon Press, 1959.
    Responding to arguments that Arthur couldn't have been a major figure because all his battles were in the north, Jackson's linguistic analysis of place names attempted to show he could have fought in southern Britain as well.

Ashe, Geoffrey, ed. *The Quest for Arthur's Britain.* New York: Praeger, 1968.
    Includes archaeological reports from Radford at Tintagel and Glastonbury, and Alcock at Cadbury.

Alcock, Leslie. *Arthur's Britain.* Middlesex, England: Penguin, 1971.
    The case for Arthur as a genuine historical figure and a great soldier.

Alcock, Leslie. *By South Cadbury Is That Camelot.* London: Thames & Hudson, 1972.
    The excavations of Cadbury Castle between 1966 and 1970.

Morris, John. *The Age of Arthur.* New York: Charles Scribner's Sons, 1973.
    A history of the British Isles from 350 to 650, notable for its breadth of scholarship and its acceptance of Arthur as a historical figure.

Dumville, David N. "Sub-Roman Britain: History and Legend." *History* 62, no. 205 June 1977.
    For an academic paper, this is a surprisingly savage attack on Alcock's and Morris's tendency to make too much of the limited evidence of Arthur's existence. Wrote Dumville: "We must reject him from our histories and, above all, from the titles of our books."

Ashe, Geoffrey. *The Discovery of King Arthur.* Garden City, NY: Anchor Press, 1985.
    A clever if not entirely convincing attempt to prove that Arthur led an army of Britons into Gaul, where he was known to Continental sources as Riothamus.

Goodrich, Norma Lorre. *King Arthur.* New York: Franklin Watts, 1986.
    Based on a close reading of Geoffrey and other late medieval texts—an extremely dubious approach—Goodrich locates Arthur and his kingdom near what's now the border between England and Scotland.

Why Did Mayan
Civilization Collapse?

ALL WAS MYSTERY, DARK, IMPENETRABLE MYSTERY."
So wrote John Lloyd Stephens, a best-selling travel book writer, after coming upon the ruins of Copan in 1840. Stephens had traveled by mule and canoe, then hacked his way through the rain forest of Honduras in the hope of finding the lost cities of the ancient Mayans. He would discover more than forty other ruins during the next three years, spent in southern Mexico and Central America. Here, hidden in the jungle, were sprawling complexes of palaces and pyramids, along with monumental stone sculptures carved with a hieroglyphic-like script. These were the remains, Stephens clearly saw, of a remarkable civilization.

The archaeologists who followed Stephens agreed, especially after they were able to decipher some of the markings on the monuments. These turned out to be numbers, and they revealed that the Mayans were sophisticated mathematicians. They'd created calendars stretching back millions of years, and they'd meticulously charted complex astronomical movements. From this, the leading archaeologists deduced that the Mayans, or at least their rulers, were a profoundly intellectual people.

They were also a uniquely peaceful people, as portrayed by Sylvanus Morley, writing in 1946, and J. Eric Thompson, in 1954.

These two prominent archaeologists noted that there were no visible fortifications around the Mayan ruins. They must have been sacred places, Morley and Thompson concluded, where priestly kings contemplated the mathematics of the universe, interrupted only by occasional visits of peasants who brought them their food and depended on them for their wisdom.

The numbers carved on the monuments also revealed when the Mayan civilization ended. The last date recorded at Copan was (translated from the Mayan calendar) A.D. 820, and other Mayan cities followed like dominoes: for Naranjo it was 849, Caracol 859, Tikal 879. But the question remained: Why did the civilization end? Unlike the Aztecs of Mexico or the Incas of Peru, who were destroyed by the Spanish conquistadors, the Mayans abandoned their cities by 900—almost 600 years before Columbus sailed. Nor were there any signs that another Native American civilization—such as the warlike predecessors of the Aztecs—had destroyed the Mayan cities. And wars between the cities themselves seemed inconceivable, at least to Morley and Thompson, whose image of the peaceful Mayans dominated archaeological thinking.

So, at least until the past few decades, the demise of Mayan civilization seemed every bit as impenetrable as the jungle that engulfed it.

⟡

Many scholars assumed that the problem must have been environmental. Morley, for example, speculated that the Mayans kept clearing away the forest for farms until finally they ran out of land. Others assumed that the Mayan farmers wore out the soil. Still others argued for a natural catastrophe, perhaps an earthquake or a hurricane or a prolonged drought. Malaria and yellow fever also were blamed, especially since disease definitely played a destructive role after the Spanish conquest.

The problem with all these theories was that there was no real evidence to back up any of them. Maybe they couldn't be disproven, but an environmental catastrophe that could topple a civilization like the Mayans' ought to have left some signs in the archaeological record—and that just didn't seem to be the case.

Thompson's theory was that some less civilized people, perhaps from central Mexico or from the Gulf Coast, moved into the northernmost Mayan cities on the Yucatan Peninsula and overthrew the rulers there. This was more of a cultural invasion than a military one, he believed, but it nevertheless disrupted the established Mayan political and religious order there, and to the south as well. That in turn may have led to a revolt of Mayan peasants, who'd been perfectly content to serve their own priestly elite but who balked at paying tribute to barbarian outsiders.

There was some evidence for Thompson's theory. Central Mexican–style orange pottery, dating to the tenth century, was found in some Mayan cities on the Yucatan Peninsula, and Gulf Coast–style architecture started showing up there soon after. The problem was that the Mayan heartland to the south showed no sign of foreign influence. As for the pottery and architecture, that could have come from perfectly peaceful commerce. And even if the outsiders had forced their way into the North, the dating of the pottery and architecture was not precise enough to tell whether they'd come before or after the Mayan collapse. Foreigners might very well have done no more than fill a vacuum already vacated by the Mayan rulers.

Still, in the absence of any more viable alternatives, the ideas of Thompson and Morley continued to dominate Mayan scholarship. That lasted until the 1960s and 1970s, when linguists were finally able to decipher words as well as numbers from the ancient Mayan script. The translated texts did more than call into question Thompson's and Morley's ideas about the collapse. In fact, they completely transformed the scholarly view of Mayan civilization.

⟡

Had it not been for Thompson, the scripts would probably have been translated years or even decades earlier. Thompson was certain that they contained only esoteric mathematical concepts and calendars, like those that had already been translated. Anyone who suggested that the Mayan monuments might be inscribed with words or letters as well as numbers or pictures was met with such scorn that he or she quickly abandoned any effort to decipher the script.

So influential was Thompson that scholars largely ignored the work of Diego de Landa. Landa was a Franciscan missionary who traveled through the remains of the Mayan cities in the mid-1550s—almost three hundred years before Stephens arrived at some of the same ruins. Landa made some crude attempts to match the Mayan symbols with letters—incorrectly, it turned out—but he was on the right track. Alas, Landa was a more devoted missionary than scholar; after determining that the Mayan books he'd collected contained nothing but "superstition and lies of the devil," he burned them all.

Only four books survived the combined destructive forces of Spanish missionaries and the soggy tropical environment. One of these ended up in the National Library of Berlin. At the end of World War II, when the library went up in flames, this book almost was reduced to ashes, too. Fortunately, a Soviet soldier named Yuri Knosorov rescued it and took it home with him.

There, far away from Thompson's intellectual tyranny, Knosorov went to work. In 1952 he announced that he'd broken the code: the Mayan script was neither all letters (as Landa thought) nor all numbers and pictures (as Thompson thought); rather, Knosorov wrote, it was a mix of syllables and words.

Thompson, true to form, mocked Knosorov's work. "This could be an authentic example of the effects of strict Party cooperation . . . in Russia," he wrote in his typically contemptuous tone. "For the good of the free world, it is hoped that it is so, as far as military research is concerned."

Gradually, however, other scholars began to question Thompson, and to build on Knosorov's insights. By the time Thompson died in 1975, the general principles of Mayan grammar and syntax were understood, and scholars could get down to translating the Mayan works.

There was still a great deal of work to be done, for though only four books had survived, there were thousands of Mayan texts carved or painted onto stone monuments, as well as on Mayan pottery and building walls. And what was written on these various media, once translated, shattered the image of the Mayans presented by Morley and Thompson. On monument after monument, the translators found detailed accounts of military strategies, of bloody battles, of gruesome sacrifices of enemy prisoners. Gone were the peaceful intellectual-priests; the Mayan rulers, it turned out, were bloodthirsty warriors. Most of the writing documented their military victories.

No longer bound by the Morley-Thompson perspective, archaeologists now started turning up other evidence of Mayan militarism. In Tikal, for example, there were long, narrow ditches and ridges that could have been moats and parapets; at Becan there were walls that could very well have been defensive; at Caracol there were burn marks on buildings and an unburied child on the floor of a pyramid. At Bonampak, vivid murals that were once thought to portray some sort of ritual could now be viewed as real battle scenes.

With the new, militaristic image of the Mayans established, archaeologists could now incorporate it into new explanations for the civilization's collapse. Arlen and Diane Chase found weapons at a site in Belize and concluded that uncontrolled warfare between Mayan cities caused the collapse of the civilization there. Arthur Demarest found mounds of decapitated heads during a dig in northern Guatemala and came to a similar conclusion. He estimated that after 820 or so the Mayan population there fell to just 5 percent of its previous level.

"The collapse," Demarest said, "was due to Bosnia-like endemic warfare."

ᘒ

Just as archaeologists seemed to be reaching a consensus about the impact of inter-city wars, new evidence surfaced, reviving one of the old environmental explanations for the collapse. In 1995, paleoclimatologists examining sediments at the bottom of Lake Chichancanub in central Yucatan found that those from the period between 800 and 1000 were especially rich in calcium sulfate. Calcium sulfate tends to settle to the bottom only when there is too little water in the lake—usually during a drought. This particular drought was so severe, argued David Hodell and his colleagues, that it caused crop failures, famine, and disease, all of which contributed to the Mayan collapse. A 2003 study of the Cariaco Basin off the coast of Venezuela also found evidence of severe drought.

Did that put scientists right back where they started?

Not quite.

For one thing, Hodell didn't argue that the drought was the only cause of the collapse; instead, he argued that it was the trigger that set off a whole series of environmental and cultural crises. Similarly, many of those who believed warfare was to blame also presented it as just one of many factors. Indeed, since the 1970s, scientists on all sides of the issue have been increasingly open to explanations that take into account a variety of interrelated factors—including environmental stresses and warfare, whether with an outside enemy or between Mayan cities. Many different factors could have weakened the Mayans, leaving them increasingly vulnerable to some final crisis. The nature of that final crisis may have varied from city to city.

The past few decades have also seen archaeologists broaden their focus from the Mayan heartlands in the South to the civilization's more northerly outposts on the Yucatan Peninsula. Some of these cities, though nowhere near as grand as those to the south, outlasted their neighbors by hundreds of years; a few even survived until the Spanish conquest. Perhaps some of these northern cities were bolstered by refugees fleeing whatever crisis befell the Mayan heartland to the south.

The latest thinking is that the different Mayan cities suffered many ups and downs, perhaps inevitably, given their constant fighting. The collapse of the great southern cities prior to 900, along with the rise of cities to the north, may have been part of this continuing process, albeit an extreme example of it. Some archaeologists, most notably E.

Wyllys Andrews, have even gone so far as to argue that Mayan civilization didn't collapse, but merely moved north.

Most archaeologists wouldn't go that far. The extent of the southern collapse, after such extraordinary architectural and artistic achievements, was unprecedented in Mayan history, perhaps in all history. That the northern cities subsequently rose to prominence may help explain what happened, but it certainly doesn't fully explain what set it off, or why the Mayans never fully recovered. Those questions remain a mystery— by no means as dark or as impenetrable as it seemed to Stephens back in 1840—but a mystery nonetheless.

To Investigate Further

Morley, Sylvanus. *The Ancient Maya.* **Stanford, CA: Stanford University Press, 1956; originally published in 1946.**

A dated but impressively thorough survey of Mayan culture.

Thompson, J. Eric. *The Rise and Fall of Maya Civilization.* **Norman: University of Oklahoma Press, 1966; originally published in 1954.**

Many of Thompson's ideas have been eclipsed by those of later archaeologists, but the book is still very much worth reading. If only Thompson's successors had shared his talent for popular writing.

Culbert, T. Patrick, ed. *The Classic Maya Collapse.* **Albuquerque: University of New Mexico Press, 1973.**

A collection of papers from a 1970 conference that was important both in reflecting and in advancing the emerging consensus according to which a series of interrelated factors caused the collapse.

Schele, Linda, and David Friedel. *A Forest of Kings.* **New York: William Morrow, 1990.**

Based on their translations of the writings at various Mayan centers, Schele and Friedel present the histories of a number of dynasties. The kings emerge as both sophisticated and brutal.

Coe, Michael. *Breaking the Maya Code.* **London: Thames & Hudson, 1992.**

Coe turns the incredibly technical story of the deciphering into a narrative that's understandable and dramatic, even a bit gossipy.

Sabloff, Jeremy, and John Henderson, eds. *Lowland Maya Civilization in the Eighth Century.* **Washington, DC: Dumbarton Oaks Research Library, 1993.**

A collection of papers from a 1989 conference that included many of the leading thinkers and theories.

Stuart, Gene, and George Stuart. *Lost Kingdoms of the Maya.* **Washington, DC: National Geographic Society, 1993.**

A lavishly illustrated view of the Maya by a husband-and-wife team of archaeologists. The Stuarts' son, David, who first visited Mesoamerica at age three, later became a leading scholar of Mayan anthropology.

Hodell, David, Jason Curtis, and Mark Brenner. "Possible Role of Climate in the Collapse of Classic Maya Civilization." *Nature,* June 1995.

The case for drought.

Diamond, Jared. *Collapse.* New York: Viking, 2005.

Diamond blames human mismanagement of the environment for the end of not just Mayans but also, among others, the Easter Islanders and Anasazi. In the case of Mayan civilization, deforestation, soil erosion, and water management problems were exacerbated by drought.

Who Built the Statues on Easter Island?

FOR SHEER REMOTENESS, hardly any place on earth comes close to Easter Island. South America is forty-three hundred miles to the east, Tahiti twenty-three hundred to the west. Yet somehow, though seemingly isolated from more technologically advanced civilizations, the inhabitants of the island carved hundreds of huge monolithic statues in the shape of men, many of them higher than a three-story building. Somehow these same islanders then transported these moai throughout the land, erected many of them on stone platforms, and topped them off with giant blocks of red stone.

The statues were still standing in 1722 when the Dutch explorer Jacob Roggeveen spotted the island on Easter Sunday (thus the name). Wrote Roggeveen: "These stone images at first caused us to be struck with astonishment, because we could not comprehend how it was possible that these people . . . had been able to erect such images, which were fully thirty feet high and thick in proportion."

Just over fifty-two years later, Captain James Cook stopped briefly at Easter Island while searching for a long-suspected (but nonexistent) continent in the southern Pacific. Cook, too, was amazed: "We could hardly conceive how these islanders, wholly unacquainted with any mechanical power, could raise such stupendous figures, and afterwards place the large cylindric stones upon their heads."

Who built the Easter Island moai, and why?

Most scientists assumed it must have been Polynesian immigrants, who reached shore after a long but not impossible trip from some island to the west, perhaps in the Marquesas. Few took seriously Thor Heyerdahl, a Norwegian scientist who, in the late 1940s, formulated a theory that South American Indians had settled on Easter Island and built the moai.

To prove he was right, Heyerdahl decided to build a primitive raft and cross the Pacific himself.

⚬

Heyerdahl first came to his theory after noting similarities between the legends of the Easter Islanders and the ancient Incas of Peru. The islanders hailed a white chief-god Tiki as the founder of their race, while the Incas told of a white chief-god Kon-Tiki, whom their forefathers had driven out of Peru onto the Pacific.

Heyerdahl recalled that the first Europeans who visited the island in the eighteenth century were struck by the mysterious presence there of some white-skinned inhabi-

Easter Island moai, their backs (as always) to the Pacific. *(Wolfgang Kaehler/Corbis)*

tants who stood out from the normally brown-skinned Polynesians. Tiki and Kon-Tiki had to be one and the same, and the white natives of Easter Island must have been his descendants.

Other oral traditions on the island seemed to buttress Heyerdahl's theory. The islanders spoke of a race of "long-ears" who pierced their ears and put heavy weights into the lobes until they were artificially lengthened. The long-ears ruled the island until, the story went, the short-ears got fed up with them and overthrew them. Since the moai had ears hanging down almost to their shoulders, Heyerdahl naturally assumed that they were built by the long-ears. And where did the long-ears come from? The islanders' stories left no doubt: from the east, toward which there was only ocean . . . and South America.

If the long-ears, and Tiki or Kon-Tiki, could cross the Pacific in a balsawood raft, Heyerdahl thought, so could he.

So he headed to the Ecuadoran jungle, where he and his crew felled the biggest trees they could find. Then they peeled off the bark, Indian-style, and lashed nine big logs together with ordinary hemp ropes, using neither nails nor metal in any form. Atop the raft they added an open bamboo cabin, two masts, and a square sail.

The party smashed a coconut against the bow and christened the boat Kon-Tiki. In April 1947, joined by five men and a parrot, Heyerdahl set sail from the coast of Peru.

Heyerdahl's was a sea adventure to rival *Moby Dick*. With just harpoons, his crew fought off a whale shark so huge that when it swam under the raft, its head was visible on one side while the whole of its tail stuck out on the other side. The drinking water became brackish after two months, but rains replenished the supplies. Breakfast often consisted of the bonitos and flying fish that had landed on deck during the night.

The ocean currents and trade winds pushed the raft farther and farther to the west, well beyond Easter Island, in fact. After 101 days at sea, the raft crashed into an uninhabited South Sea island east of Tahiti. All six men had survived the trip, though a large wave had washed away the parrot.

Heyerdahl was exultant: the Kon-Tiki expedition proved it was possible for a simple raft to cross the Pacific. But just because it could have happened didn't mean it did happen. To prove that South Americans settled on Easter Island, Heyerdahl needed more evidence.

∽

In 1955, Heyerdahl again set off for Easter Island, this time in a converted trawler and accompanied by a crew of professional scientists. Ironically, the scientists who first came under Heyerdahl's aegis, along with those who followed, ended up largely discrediting his theory.

For one thing, their radiocarbon dating placed people on the island by the fifth century A.D., with the earliest moai going up some time between 900 and 1000. Yet the Tiahuanaco culture in the highlands of Peru and Bolivia, where Heyerdahl believed the islanders originated, didn't extend its influence to the South American coast until about A.D. 1000. How could these South Americans cross the ocean before they even descended the mountains?

Moreover, the expedition found no trace on Easter Island of pottery or textiles, the two most characteristic products of Peruvian culture. In contrast, archaeologists on the Galapagos, a chain of Pacific islands far closer to South America, found numerous fragments of pots, at least some of which were clearly the same kind made by the pre–Inca South Americans.

Studies in other disciplines further undercut Heyerdahl. Botanists determined that the island's totora reed was distinct from the kind found in Peru. Sweet potatoes on the island, which Heyerdahl made much of as a link to South America, could have come from elsewhere in Polynesia.

Linguistic analyses also pointed to the west. Many of the islanders' words appeared to be similar to their Polynesian equivalents, and the discrepancies could easily be attributed to the long years of isolation. The island's "Rongorongo" script was also determined to have more in common with Polynesian writing than Peruvian.

Measurements of skeletons, too, showed the islanders had more in common with Southeast Asians than South Americans, and most scientists concluded the early European visitors' descriptions of fair-skinned people must have been exaggerated. After all, only some of the early accounts of Easter Islanders mentioned white skin; others, such as the famously observant Captain Cook, wrote that "in colour, features, and language, they bear such affinity to the people of the more western islands, that no one will doubt that they have had the same origin."

As for the old tales of Tiki and Kon-Tiki, these were just stories, according to most scientists. All of them had to be taken, in the words of Paul Bahn, "with a large pinch of marine salt." Bahn criticized Heyerdahl for his selective use of oral traditions, which allowed him to emphasize those that supported his theory while ignoring other stories—for example, that Hotu Matua, the island's first king, came from an island called Hiva. That's a commonplace name in the Marquesas, twenty-one hundred miles northwest of Easter Island.

Even the dramatic Kon-Tiki voyage wasn't spared from the sober inquisitions of science. Pre-Inca Indians used paddles, not sails, some argued, and the desert coast of Peru had none of the light woods needed for rafts or canoes. Moreover, the Kon-Tiki had been towed fifty nautical miles from shore, thus avoiding the currents that would have carried Heyerdahl somewhere up the coast to Panama, rather than anywhere near Polynesia.

The onslaught of scientific analyses that began with Heyerdahl's 1955–1956 expedition led to an even stronger consensus that Polynesians were Easter Island's first settlers. Unlike the South American Indians, the Polynesians had extensive experience on the seas, colonizing other islands such as Hawaii and New Zealand. Some scientists went so far as to contend that any evidence of a mingling of South American and Polynesian cultures (such as some Easter Island–style spearheads found in Chile) could be attributed to Polynesian sailors who may have ventured to the New World and then returned home.

That was little consolation to Heyerdahl, who continued to maintain that the discoverers were sailing west, not east. He continued to fight the historiographic tide, revisiting the island and defending his thesis even as fewer and fewer listened.

That should not diminish his achievements, however. It was Heyerdahl who arranged for the first scientific expedition to Easter Island and who allowed the scientists who accompanied him to conduct their research free of bias. And it was Heyerdahl's much publicized expeditions that inspired other scientists to go there themselves and to continue the search for the moai's sculptors.

⟨⟩

The consensus view that Polynesians first settled Easter Island provides at least a partial explanation for the giant statues. Ancestor worship was common throughout Polynesia, so the moai may have been some sort of monument set up by the island's tribes or families to honor their dead. The red stone blocks that topped the largest of the moai could have evolved from the Marquesas tradition of placing a stone on the image of a dead man as a sign of mourning.

Yet there was another mystery about these moai, which Cook had noticed during his brief visit. Many of the statues had been toppled from their platforms, and some had apparently been deliberately beheaded.

Why would a people who devoted such a colossal effort to their moai deliberately topple them? What happened between Roggeveen's 1722 visit, when they were apparently still standing, and Cook's arrival in 1784?

Heyerdahl blamed Polynesian immigrants, who he said arrived before the Europeans and went to war against the descendants of the original South American settlers. He turned again to the island's traditions, which recounted a revolt of the "short-ears" against the island's long-eared rulers. Perhaps the short-ears overthrew both the long-ears and their statues, he speculated.

Again, though, the lack of archaeological evidence has undercut Heyerdahl's theory. There are no architectural or artifactual traces of a sudden influx of new cultural influences at that point in Easter Island history, or at any other point, for that matter.

Archaeologists did find large quantities of spearheads and daggers dating from the period prior to the European discovery, leading many to conclude that warfare must have played a part in toppling the moai and the culture that worshiped them. The appearance in rock art of the period of "birdmen" seems also to indicate a new cult that may have replaced ancestor worship.

Most scientists believe an ecological crisis led the islanders to fight for ever-scarcer resources. Overpopulation and deforestation were already serious problems by the sixteenth century, when some of the largest moai were erected. Some archaeologists have suggested that the building spree may have been spurred by an increasingly desperate desire for divine intervention. When their ancestors failed to help, the islanders may have lost faith in them and angrily toppled the statues.

Instead of the islanders' ancestors or gods, it was, of course, the Europeans who soon intervened. By the nineteenth century, missionaries and slave traders had virtually eradicated what remained of the original Easter Island culture and religion. Yet Europeans (and Americans) also deserve credit for their efforts, albeit belated, to preserve the original Easter Island culture. In the 1960s, scientists, including some members of Heyerdahl's expedition, restored several toppled moai to their stone platforms. There they still stand, looking over the islanders (and nowadays, plenty of tourists as well).

Right beyond them, as always, is the Pacific Ocean.

To Investigate Further

Dos Passos, John. *Easter Island*. Garden City, NY: Doubleday, 1971.
A useful anthology of excerpts from accounts of the early European visitors to the island, including Roggeveen and Cook. Dos Passos's own visit, which concludes the book, is of much less interest.

Heyerdahl, Thor. *Kon-Tiki*. Chicago: Rand McNally, 1950.
When it comes to adventures on the sea, Melville has nothing on Heyerdahl.

————. *Aku-Aku.* Chicago: Rand McNally, 1958.

A colorful narrative of the 1955–1956 expedition, no less enjoyable because of the author's iconoclastic views, though slightly marred by his patronizing attitude toward the islanders.

Heyerdahl, Thor, and Edwin Ferdon Jr., eds. *Archaeology of Easter Island.* Chicago, Rand McNally, 1961.

Reports from Heyerdahl's team, many of whom disagreed with their leader.

Heyerdahl, Thor. *Easter Island.* New York: Random House, 1989.

Heyerdahl's final defense of his hypothesis did little to convince skeptics, but his account of how the islanders moved the statues is interesting and the volume is beautifully illustrated.

Bahn, Paul, and John Flenley. *Earth Island.* London: Thames & Hudson, 1992.

The most recent and best popular account of the pro-Polynesian, anti-Heyerdahl position. The book's only flaw is that the authors insist on treating Easter Island's ecological crisis as a metaphor for the earth's, an approach that makes for admirable environmentalism but potentially dubious history.

Fischer, Steven Roger, ed. *Easter Island Studies.* Oxford: Oxbow, 1993.

A useful if specialized collection of essays on the island's natural history, settlement, archaeology, traditions, language, script, and arts.

Van Tilburg, Jo Anne. *Easter Island.* Washington, DC: Smithsonian Institution Press, 1994.

A thorough but somewhat academic overview of the island's archaeology, ecology, and culture.

Fischer, Steven Roger. *Rongorongo.* Oxford: Clarendon Press, 1997.

How Fischer (sort of) cracked the code of the island's mysterious hieroglyphic-like script.

Did Leif Ericsson Discover America?

I F ONE IS TO BELIEVE THE ANCIENT ICELANDIC SAGAS, the first European to discover America was not Christopher Columbus, nor was it Leif Ericsson. It was none other than Biarni Heriulfson.

Biarni was a trader who regularly crossed the part of the Atlantic between Norway and his home in Iceland. In the summer of 985 he left Norway to spend the winter with his father. He arrived to find his father had departed for Greenland—a land recently discovered by Eric the Red. Biarni set off after him. But on his way to Greenland he got lost and came upon some new land. This new land was America—at least according to those who believed the sagas to be historical documents and not just literary epics.

The discovery didn't excite Biarni. "To me this land looks good for nothing," he told his crew, and then he headed back to Greenland. There he was reunited with his father, thus securing his place in history as the world's most devoted son and least venturesome explorer.

Others, however, found Biarni's stories intriguing. These new lands sounded appealing, especially compared to Greenland; in spite of Eric the Red's efforts to attract other settlers by giving the land an attractive name, Greenland was anything but green. Among those stirred by Biarni's stories was Eric's son, Leif Ericsson. He bought Biarni's ship, assembled a crew, and set sail for the land that he would call Vinland. He lived there for a year before returning to Greenland.

Other Norse expeditions soon followed, including one led by Leif's brother, Thorvald. Thorvald spent the winter of 1004–1005 at Leif's settlement but, the sagas say, was killed by "Skrellings." (Presumably these were Indians or Eskimos.) The surviving members of his party then returned to Greenland. Yet another brother of Leif, Thorstein, and a sister, Freydis, then tried to colonize Vinland, but again, the Skrellings drove the intruders away. Only Freydis showed any Viking spirit: after failing to rally the fleeing men, she slapped a sword across her bared breasts and screamed so loud that the Skrellings retreated. But the men had had enough: This land may have been more hospitable than Greenland; its inhabitants, on the other hand, were not. For another five hundred years, the Indians had America to themselves.

Or so the story went. To most historians, however, it was just that—a story. Granted, there were some scholars who argued it was true, but these were mostly Scandinavians whose conclusions were tainted by chauvinism. For the sagas to be accepted as history, there had to be proof.

♒

The search for that proof began in earnest in 1837 when the Royal Danish Society of Antiquaries published the original saga texts. The book's editor, Carl Rafn, also included in the book the results of his correspondence with Americans about various ruined towers and inscribed stones found along the east coast of North America and reputed to be of Norse origin.

Alas, Rafn's enthusiasm overwhelmed his judgment. He included almost anything anyone claimed might be Norse, even though he himself had never even been to America, let alone examined the evidence. On closer examination most of these finds turned out to be crude hoaxes. In towns from Newfoundland to Florida, the claim that "Leif Ericsson was here" became as common and as improbable as the claim that "George Washington slept here."

Among the evidence discovered was the Newport Tower. In one sense the tower couldn't really be discovered: it stood about 25 feet high on top of a hill in Newport, Rhode Island, so you didn't need an archaeologist to find it. The tower certainly looked medieval; with thick floors and round arches, it would have seemed at home in eleventh-century France or Belgium—or Norway. The case for the tower's Norse origins was strengthened when its measurements turned out to be readily divisible by old Norse measures. But something just didn't make sense: if the tower dated back to medieval times, how could Rhode Island's first English settlers have failed to notice it when they arrived? Not one of their writings makes any mention of it. In fact the earliest mention of the tower is in the 1677 will of Benedict Arnold (not the traitor—this Benedict Arnold was the governor of Rhode Island). Arnold referred to it as "my stone built wind mill," and later investigations confirmed it was built, probably by Arnold, around 1675.

The next major find was the Kensington Stone, uncovered in the roots of a 500-year-old tree on Olof Ohman's farm in Minnesota. In an alphabet that was used in medieval Scandinavia, the stone told of "8 Swedes and 22 Norwegians on an exploration journey from Vinland westward." It was dated 1362.

But the word *opdagelsefard* (exploration journey) didn't occur in any Scandinavian language until hundreds of years after 1362. The stone had to be a forgery. As one Icelandic linguist put it: "If a telephone book for the year 1957 were to be found under the roots of a 500-year-old tree, one would admire the skill with which it had been placed there; but one should not find it necessary to accept the antiquity of the volume in question."

♒

By this point most of Leif's boosters were despairing of ever proving their case. One archaeologist—granted, a Norwegian archaeologist—refused to give up. During the 1950s Helge Ingstad traveled thousands of miles up and down the North American coast in search of Vinland. If the sailing times recorded in the sagas were accurate, he reasoned, then the land Leif called Vinland ought to be northern Newfoundland. The sagas' descriptions of these lands also fit.

In 1960, close to the small village of L'Anse aux Meadows near Epaves Bay in northern Newfoundland, Ingstad noted some indistinct overgrown elevations in the ground. They appeared to be sites of houses—very old ones. Their shapes were similar to ancient Norse buildings uncovered in Iceland and Greenland. Could these houses have been built by Leif Ericsson and his crew? Ingstad began excavating.

In 1964 he found exactly what he'd hoped for. In the southernmost room of the largest house site, one of Ingstad's colleagues found a small ring of stone which was clearly a Norse spindle-whorl. It was exactly the kind of spindle-whorl that Norse women had used in Sweden, Norway, Iceland, and Greenland, and it was unlike anything the Indians and Eskimos of Newfoundland would have used. This was as dramatic a find as a Viking sword would have been; in fact it was even better since it proved that the sagas were right—not just about Norsemen reaching America, but about a settlement with Norsewomen (who would have been the ones to use the spindle-whorl) and sheep (whose wool the women would have spun).

There was no question that Ingstad had found a pre-Columbian Norse settlement. But a big problem remained. This was the name Vinland, sometimes translated as Wineland. Leif had named the country after the wild grapes found there. Yet botanists assert that the northern limit for wild grapes along the east coast is somewhere in Massachussetts. Which means: *there are no wild grapes in Newfoundland.*

And one cannot simply ignore the name, since *The Greenlanders' Saga* describes in detail how it was given. Leif, the saga tells us, was very worried when one of his company, a German named Tyrkir, disappeared. When Tyrkir finally returned, the following exchange took place:

> "Why are you so late . . ." Leif asked him, "and parted this way from your companions?"
>
> By way of a start Tyrkir held forth a long while in German, rolling his eyes all ways, and pulling faces. They had no notion what he was talking about. Then after a while he spoke in Norse. "I went no great way further than you, yet I have a real novelty to report. I have found vines and grapes."
>
> "Is that the truth . . . ?" Leif asked.
>
> "Of course it's the truth," he replied. "I was born where wine and grapes are no rarity."

Given how sure Tyrkir was that Vinland was a land of wild grapes, how could it be in Newfoundland?

Historians have ventured a number of guesses.

Farley Mowat, a botanist and climatologist as well as a historian, suggested that even though grapes don't grow in Newfoundland today, they may have grown there between

1000 and 1200. We do know that the vineyards of western Europe at that time extended farther north than they do today.

Ingstad himself offered a number of explanations: that Vinland might be translated as Meadowland rather than Vineland or Wineland or Grapeland; that Tyrkir, for all his apparent certainty, may have mistaken wild berries for grapes; that the saga-writers, in an effort to make Vinland more appealing, may have exaggerated its fertility. (After all, Eric the Red had no qualms about giving Greenland its very misleading name.)

Most historians were convinced for one reason or another. And even if L'Anse aux Meadows isn't Vinland and is simply a different Norse settlement, it's still incontrovertible evidence that the Norse did discover and settle North America five hundred years before Columbus.

To Investigate Further

Jones, Gwyn. *The Norse Atlantic Saga.* New York: Oxford University Press, 1986.
The most widely respected translation of the sagas, along with a history of the Norse voyages. The translation from *The Greenlanders' Saga* is Jones's.

Haugen, Einar. *Voyages to Vinland.* New York: Knopf, 1942.
The history is dated, and the translations have been superseded in scholarly circles by Jones's, but Haugen's account and translations are still the most dramatic.

Holand, Hjalmar. *Explorations in America Before Columbus.* New York: Twayne Publishers, 1956.
The case for the authenticity of the Newport Tower and the Kensington Stone; generally discredited but still fun.

Wahlgren, Erik. *The Kensington Stone.* Madison: University of Wisconsin Press, 1958.
The case against the authenticity of the stone; definitive but dry.

Mowat, Farley. *Westviking.* Boston: Atlantic Monthly Press, 1965.
A fascinating combination of climatology, anthropology, zoology, seamanship, and various other disciplines. Mowat claims he's located Vinland in Newfoundland, though not at L'anse aux Meadows. He also argues—contrary to generally accepted opinion—that Columbus knew of and was influenced by the Norse discoveries.

Skelton, Raleigh, et al. *The Vinland Map and the Tartar Relation.* New Haven: Yale University Press, 1965.
The book features a map from 1440 that included Vinland. If authentic, the map would be the only pre-Columbian document, besides the sagas, to include Vinland. But whether it's "the most exciting cartographic discovery of the century" or a twentieth-century fraud remains a source of heated scholarly debate.

Ingstad, Helge. *Land Under the Polar Star.* New York: St. Martin's Press, 1966.
Ingstad's account of his expedition to Greenland, during which he came to the conclusion that he should search for Vinland in Newfoundland.

————. *Westward to Vinland.* New York: St. Martin's Press, 1969.

Ingstad's account of his discoveries at L'Anse aux Meadows. Scholarly but exciting.

Morison, Samuel. *The European Discovery of America.* New York: Oxford University Press, 1971.

The section on the Norse voyages is a concise yet comprehensive history and historiography. While you're at it, read the rest of the book—there's no better historian of the sea than Morison.

Pohl, Frederick. *The Viking Settlements of North America.* New York: Clarkson Potter, 1972.

Uses the sailing directions and topographical descriptions in the saga to locate Vinland in New England, contrary to most current thinking.

PART 4

HEMISPHERIC
INTERACTIONS,
1000–1500

Why Did the Anasazi Abandon Their Cities?

T HE FIRST WHITE MEN TO EXPLORE CHACO CANYON, in northwestern New Mexico, arrived in 1849, led by Army Lieutenant James Simpson. What Simpson found there convinced him that the Aztec empire of Mexico must once have extended this far north. Only such an advanced civilization, he concluded, could have constructed the massive and beautiful buildings whose ruins he now surveyed. The largest of them—Pueblo Bonito—stood five stories tall and had several hundred rooms. It was larger than any apartment building in North America (and it remained so until 1882, when it was surpassed by one in New York City).

Simpson was wrong: in the twentieth century, archaeologists dated the Chaco Canyon buildings to the end of the tenth century, well before the rise of the Aztecs. From numerous other sites in the area, archaeologists were able to chronicle the rise of the civilization that culminated in these buildings. This was, they determined, a homegrown civilization, one that had been built by a people called the Anasazi by the Indians Simpson encountered.

But who could blame Simpson for looking outside of Chaco Canyon for its architects? The ruins at Chaco Canyon bore little resemblance to the buildings of the Hopi or Zuni or any other Indians then living in the area. At least Simpson, in attributing the Chaco Canyon buildings to the Aztecs, was willing to give the credit to Native Americans, albeit the wrong ones; others would later argue that the buildings must have been a Roman outpost.

In the eleventh century all roads did not lead to Rome; many led—quite literally—to Chaco Canyon. Straight, broad avenues connected Pueblo Bonito to nine "Great Houses" and to some 75 other settlements in and around Chaco Canyon. Archaeologists have mapped more than four hundred miles of roads, many of them 30 feet wide, radiating out from the canyon center. The Anasazi must have used these roads to carry the timber that made up the vast roofs and support systems of their buildings. Judging from the tremendous quantities of turquoise found in the area, the roads were also used to transport the gems from distant mines to Chaco Canyon. After being made into small tiles, the turquoise was then sent as far away as California and Mexico.

The Anasazi were remarkably wealthy: along with exotic gems, archaeologists have found huge quantities of discarded pots—at one Chaco building, a single trash heap contained 150,000 broken pots. This must also have been a remarkably egalitarian society, for there were no palaces or special buildings mixed in among the huge apartment buildings. Supporting all this was a sophisticated irrigation system that used dams and dikes, contoured terraces, and reservoirs to make the most of the sandy soil and limited rainfall.

About one hundred years after they built the Great Houses of Chaco Canyon, the Anasazi moved north into southwest Colorado, creating an architecture that was, if possible, even more stunning. Here they built their homes right inside the caves that sculpt the steep cliffs of the area's canyons. Protected by the caves, many of these cliff dwellings (including the huge Cliff Palace at Mesa Verde) are still largely intact.

But the civilization that built these houses was not nearly so durable. By 1200 Chaco Canyon's houses were empty; by 1300 Mesa Verde's cliff dwellings were, too. Why did the Anasazi abandon their great cities, in many cases only a hundred or so years after they built them? And where did they go? This is a mystery that has intrigued historians—not to mention archaeologists, anthropologists, demographers, biologists, and visitors to the American Southwest—ever since James Simpson and his men first stumbled upon Chaco Canyon.

ᏫᏫᏫ

To the historian and archaeologist Harold Gladwin, writing in 1957, the solution was obvious: the Anasazi were under attack. This would explain why people who had been widely scattered came together in the huge apartment buildings of Chaco Canyon. The large pueblos offered more protection than smaller, scattered villages—hence the building spree in Chaco Canyon at the end of the tenth century. It would also explain why they had abandoned the Chaco Canyon buildings so soon after they'd built them. When the Chaco Canyon towns failed to hold off their attackers, the Anasazi retreated to the cliff dwellings of Mesa Verde, built during the eleventh and twelfth centuries. The cliff dwellings were, to put it mildly, inconvenient—but at least that made them inaccessible to enemies as well.

So, protected by deep canyons and sheer escarpments and warned of the dangers by refugees from Chaco Canyon, the Anasazi held out for another hundred years. But eventually their attackers wore them down, and by the end of the thirteenth century the cliff dwellings of Mesa Verde had gone the way of the pueblos of Chaco Canyon.

Who were the people who drove away the Anasazi? Gladwin believed they were the people who later became known as the Navajo and Apache. Sweeping down from western Canada, they were the last people to reach the Southwest before the Spanish invasion. Navajo tradition seems to confirm this theory: the word "Anasazi" comes from the Navajo word for "ancient enemies." Other historians have proposed it was the Southern Paiute or Ute, not the Navajo or Apache. (Ute legends, too, tell how they conquered people as they moved south.) Whoever their enemies were, the Anasazi outnumbered them, but the raiders' hit-and-run attacks against their settlements and fields eventually took their toll.

There was one major problem with these "military" solutions to the mystery: there is no archaeological evidence that the Apache or Navajo or Ute or Paiute entered the area until long after the pueblos and cliff dwellings had been abandoned. Granted, the Apache and Navajo were traditional enemies of the Pueblo people of the Southwest, but some historians argued that this tradition originated in the seventeenth century after the Indians acquired horses from Europeans (giving them a tremendous tactical advantage). Finally, if the Anasazi went down in battle, why didn't archaeologists find any mass graves or other signs of war? Anyone looking at the ruins of Pueblo Bonito or Cliff Palace today can see they were deserted—not burned or sacked.

◦∽

And so we turn to an alternative solution to the mystery: the great drought.

This theory depends on advances in the science of dendrochronology, which uses the growth rings of trees to supply precise information about past climates. Each year a tree produces a growth ring; the wider the ring, the more rain there was that year. It was A. E. Douglass, on a National Geographic expedition to the Southwest in 1929, who developed new techniques of tree-ring dating, then charted the tree rings in living trees and overlapped and matched them with those found in wooden beams from increasingly older archaeological sites. Douglass found there was a severe drought in the area between 1276 and 1299—exactly the time the Anasazi cities were finally and fully abandoned.

But Gladwin's followers struck back: there had been previous droughts in the area, they pointed out, and the cities hadn't been abandoned. And there were nearby areas with more rainfall—but there was no evidence that the Anasazi had moved there.

So the environmental explanations became more complex, taking into account not just rainfall amounts but the times of the year the rain fell, water table levels, land-clearing practices, the changing mix of subsistence strategies.

Other explanations emerged as well.

Could there have been a massive epidemic? Unlikely: there was no sign of large burial areas.

Could there have been a disruption of the turquoise trade? Perhaps Lieutenant Simpson wasn't so wrong after all; if the Anasazi were dependent, not on the Aztecs, but on some earlier Mexican civilization, then might not the Anasazi demise be tied to problems down south? Also unlikely. Most archaeologists are skeptical of this explanation for the same reason they originally rejected Simpson's theory: the only pre-Aztec Mexican civilization that might have extended so far north was that of Teotihuacán, and that had declined long before the rise of the Anasazi. Although there was trade between the Anasazi and Mexico, there is no evidence that the Anasazi civilization depended on it.

Could the Anasazi have turned on each other? Anthropologist Christy Turner's study of skeletons found evidence of cannibalism, such as sucked-out bone marrow. But others had alternative explanations, and there were still no signs of massive burials or sacked cities. And why wouldn't the victors have stayed on?

Could there have been some sort of religious upheaval? Some archaeologists have argued that the Anasazi may have been drawn south by the emerging Kachina religion. But others question whether the archaeological record of Kachina icons and artifacts puts the religion in the area early enough to have attracted the Anasazi. Besides, why would the religion have required the Anasazi to leave their cities?

And so the debate goes on.

⟡

There are some signs, though, that it may someday be resolved. Most of the archaeologists, anthropologists, and historians working on the mystery today agree that there will never be a single solution, whether military, environmental, or social. Rather, they believe a variety of factors came into play. Perhaps, for example, drought or crop failures set off internal fighting, or undermined people's religious faith. Perhaps a combination of many factors chipped away at a complex system until it could barely maintain itself, and then some final force—a massive drought, an outside attack—was just the last straw.

Almost all scholars agree on one point: the Anasazi did not simply vanish into the sands. Whatever the reason for abandoning their cities, the Anasazi went somewhere. Some probably settled along the Rio Grande, some at the foot of Black Mesa. Some may even have stayed on in Mesa Verde or Chaco Canyon, but in a less structured society that built nothing new to reveal its presence to archaeologists. After all, before Chaco Canyon and Mesa Verde were built, the Anasazi had survived for hundreds of years in smaller, more nomadic groups. That type of life may have seemed as natural and appealing to them as their more complex, urban society seems to us.

Part of the problem, historian Kendrick Frazier points out, is the use of the term "Anasazi." It sounds like a particular tribe of Indians, just like the Navajo or Hopi, and since there are no Anasazi today we think of its people as having disappeared. But they didn't disappear. The Anasazi merged with the tribes who became the modern Pueblo Indians and—though the passage of eight hundred years may make it difficult for us to recognize them—the descendants of the Anasazi are living today in Arizona and New Mexico. To think otherwise is to repeat the mistake James Simpson made almost one hundred and fifty years ago.

To Investigate Further

Douglass, A. E. "The Secret of the Southwest Solved by the Talkative Tree Rings." *National Geographic,* December 1929.

How Douglass advanced the science of dendrochronology and discovered the great drought.

Gladwin, Harold. *A History of the Ancient Southwest.* Portland, ME: Bond Wheelwright Co., 1957.

One of the first comprehensive histories, and still the most dramatic, to make the case that the Anasazi were attacked by outside tribes.

Colton, Harold. *Black Sand.* Albuquerque: University of New Mexico Press, 1962.
The case for an epidemic.

Pike, Donald, and David Muench. *Anasazi.* New York: Crown, 1974.
Striking photos of Anasazi ruins.

Euler, R. C., T. N. V. Karlstrom, J. S. Dean, and R. C. Hevley. "The Colorado Plateaus: Cultural Dynamics and Paleoenvironment." *Science,* September 1979.
A multidisciplinary approach arguing that though the causal relationships were not as direct as previously supposed, environmental factors led to the abandonments. Technical but compelling.

Cordell, Linda S. *Prehistory of the Southwest.* San Diego: Academic Press, 1984.
An anthropology textbook with a useful synthesis of research.

Frazier, Kendrick. *People of Chaco.* New York: Norton, 1986.
A history of Chaco archaeology that succeeds in capturing the mystique as well as the mystery of the Anasazi.

Ambler, J. Richard, and Mark Sutton. "The Anasazi Abandonment of the San Juan Drainage and the Numic Expansion." *North American Archaeologist* 10, no. 1 (1989).
A revival of the case that outside attackers (in this case the southern Ute and Paiute) drove away the Anasazi.

Rafferty, Kevin. "The Anasazi Abandonment and the Numic Expansion." *North American Archaeologist* 10, no. 4 (1989).
Makes the case that the disruption of ties with the Toltec empire in Mexico precipitated the Anasazi collapse.

Gumerman, George, ed. *Themes in Southwest Prehistory.* Santa Fe: School of American Research Press, 1994.
A multidisciplinary collection including a provocative essay on the need to focus on "push" as well as "pull" factors; that is, what drew the Anasazi to new locations as well as what drove them away from old ones.

Turner, Christy, and Jacqueline Turner. *Man Corn.* Salt Lake City: University of Utah Press, 1999.
So much for the image of a peace-loving people.

Why Did Cahokia Fall?

I N 1811, THOMAS BRACKENRIDGE VISITED St. Louis to look at some ancient
mounds and ruins just east of the city.

"When I reached the foot of the principal mound," Brackenridge wrote to his
friend Thomas Jefferson, "I was struck with a degree of astonishment, not unlike that
which is experienced in contemplating the Egyptian pyramids. What a stupendous pile
of earth!"

Earthen mounds of various shapes and sizes were scattered across the eastern half of
the country, but these were exceptional. More than a hundred mounds could be found
within just a few miles of St. Louis, along with other remains from what appeared to have
once been a great city. The mound about which Brackenridge wrote to Jefferson covered
fourteen acres and rose nearly one hundred feet, making it by far the largest man-made
structure in the United States. It looked, as Brackenridge noted, like a pyramid, though
with a flat top. This could have supported "a real palace," speculated George Rogers
Clark, who had visited the site a few years before Brackenridge (and whose brother,
William Clark, was better known for his expedition with Meriwether Lewis). Brackenridge speculated the mounds "were sites of great temples, or monuments to the great
men."

Who built these mounds? And what happened to them?

No one even knew what to call the mounds. The largest was known as Monks
Mound, for a monastery erected on top. But the monks arrived just before Brackenridge,
and even if they hadn't taken a vow of silence, they couldn't have told him anything
about the mound's origins.

As for the city, it was known as Cahokia, for a local tribe, but not one with a particularly long history or significant population in the area. By the time French explorers
sailed down the Mississippi in the late 1600s, only a few Indians lived nearby. Whoever
built Cahokia, it was clear, was gone long before these Indians, let alone any white men,
reached the area.

☙❧

A popular nineteenth-century theory was that the mounds were built by a prehistoric
race that the Indians had somehow eradicated. "The magnitude of the works will ever remain a marvel," wrote Charles Joseph Latrobe in 1835. "They [the builders] were more
civilized, more powerful, more enlightened than the Indian races of our day." Among the
nominees were people from the lost continent of Atlantis and the lost tribes of Israel. A
preacher named Joseph Smith even managed to create a new religion—Mormonism—

based on the belief that a race of white Christians had built the mounds before being driven off, in A.D. 400, by the "red sons of Israel."

There was no archaeological evidence for any of this, of course, but such theories were a good way to justify America's westward expansion. After all, if the Indians had displaced some other civilization, they were no more entitled to the land than white settlers. Indeed, since the moundbuilders were presumed to be white, pushing the Indians onto reservations could be seen as restoring the land to its rightful owners.

Another early but less biased theory was that the moundbuilders came from, or migrated to, Mexico. The pyramids of Mexico looked a lot like these pyramidal mounds, and some scientists still postulate a connection. But the Toltecs and Mayans and Aztecs all built their pyramids of stone, and since there was plenty of limestone near Cahokia, no one could explain why, if these cultures were related, the moundbuilders in Cahokia had chosen instead to use dirt.

Some scientists concluded the mounds hadn't been built by people at all; they were, instead, natural phenomena, perhaps the remains of glaciers or floods. This theory was especially popular in the late nineteenth and early twentieth centuries, when developers found the mounds very inconvenient, except as landfill. Around Cahokia, for example, almost half of the mounds were destroyed, including "Big Mound," which stood until the 1860s in what is now downtown St. Louis.

What all these ideas conveniently ignored was the most logical explanation for the mounds: Native Americans built them. Jefferson himself came up with this answer, after excavating some mounds near Monticello. He found three carefully laid out layers of skeletons, and concluded that the mounds, like the pyramids, were burial sites.

Over the next fifty years, more digs confirmed Jefferson was right. Even the destruction of the St. Louis Big Mound turned out to be helpful in this sense, since just before it was razed, archaeologists uncovered twenty to thirty bodies there. But the question remained: Where did the builders go?

That question became all the more intriguing as excavations turned up all sorts of evidence that the moundbuilders had built a lot more than mounds. The seashells covering the skeletons in Big Mound, for example, came from the Gulf Coast, indicating that Cahokia had traded with, perhaps ruled over, a vast realm. At other mounds, archaeologists found pieces of finely crafted ceramics, statues, and ornaments.

A 1961 dig by a team of archaeologists hinted that the Cahokians were not just rich and powerful, but scientifically sophisticated. Working just ahead of the bulldozers, which this time were there to make way for a new interstate highway, Warren Wittry noticed several bathtub-size oval pits in a circle near Monks Mound. Some contained remnants of cedar, leading Wittry to conclude wooden posts had once been set in the pits. He calculated that when the sun rose due east, it was, viewed from the circle, directly over Monks Mound. Wittry concluded the posts served as a sun calendar, much like Britain's Stonehenge. He named Cahokia's version Woodhenge.

This photo was taken in 1907, more than 500 years after the moundbuilders abandoned Cahokia. *(Library of Congress)*

Other archaeologists found other woodhenges around Cahokia, and came up with other explanations for them. Some suggested their function was architectural, others religious. In any case, the woodhenges were further evidence that Cahokia was once a major Native American center.

Melvin Fowler's 1973 dig into a comparatively small mound near Monks Mound added an unsettling element to our understanding of Cahokian power. Of the three hundred or so skeletons he found, four were headless and more than fifty were those of young women. It was unlikely so many young women would have died naturally at the same time, and the headless skeletons were even more telling. Fowler concluded the Cahokians believed in human sacrifice. Its chiefs, it seemed, held the power of life and death over their subjects.

The most powerful statement of Cahokian power remained, of course, the mounds themselves. Back in 1814, Brackenridge had commented to Jefferson that "to heap up such a mass must have required years and the labors of thousands," and the archaeologists who followed were no less impressed.

Carbon dating allowed archaeologists to set Cahokia in its historical context. Moundbuilding began as early as 500 B.C., as prehistoric Indians established themselves across the eastern part of North America. Indian villages around Cahokia dated back to about

A.D. 700, and Monks Mound was probably begun about 950. Work on Monks Mound continued for about two hundred years.

Cahokia's "golden age" came between 1050 and 1200. This was the period when the area was, as J. W. Porter wrote in 1969, a "prehistoric megalopolis." In 1975, Michael Gregg counted how many houses had been identified in sample sections of Cahokia, and extrapolated that the city's population at its peak must have been more than 25,000—more than London or Rome at the time. Others came up with estimates of up to 40,000.

By the late twentieth century, Cahokia's place in history was firmly established. No longer could serious scientists suggest that its mounds were natural phenomena, or that its builders were not Native Americans. The Cahokian empire was perhaps less famous than the Incan or Aztec, but historians and archaeologists considered it the North American equivalent. Yet this understanding of Cahokia's tremendous power made its fall all the more mystifying. Unlike the Incas or Aztecs, the Cahokians did not fall to Spanish conquistadors. The first Europeans to explore the Mississippi River were the French, and they sailed right by Cahokia, probably assuming that, since there were so few Indians around, the mounds must have been natural hills.

Archaeologists estimated that by 1200, the population of Cahokia was already starting to decline; by the mid-1300s the area was virtually abandoned.

What, they continued to wonder, had happened?

∽

There were plenty of theories.

Some scientists blamed a change in the climate. Temperatures in the Midwest became distinctly colder around 1250, and this may have shortened the growing season. Changing rain patterns could have exacerbated the problem. "The evil twins Flood and Drought alternated their devastating work," wrote William Iseminger, sounding more like a prophet of doom than the archaeologist hired by the state of Illinois to supervise the site.

Others argued the growth of Cahokia was itself responsible for a spate of environmental problems. The Cahokians cut down trees for farms and lumber, causing erosion and rapid runoffs that flooded the crops. Clearing the forests would also have driven away much of the wildlife, increasing their dependence on corn and causing protein deficiencies. Cahokians, William Woods said, committed "an unintended suicide."

Another theory was what war did in Cahokia. Archaeologists have not uncovered any evidence of widespread warfare in Cahokia, but they have turned up some skeletons found with arrowheads embedded in them. Fowler's sacrificial victims could also be interpreted as evidence of warfare. And the discovery of the remains of a massive wooden palisade, apparently built between 1200 and 1250, was the clearest indication that the Cahokians were worried about an attack.

The enemy could have come from within Cahokia, according to some archaeologists. The huge wealth and power of Cahokia's chiefs may have fundamentally changed the city's social structure. Thomas Emerson counted bowls and jars found in the area's largest buildings, and noted that, starting around 1100, there were fewer of the former and more of the latter. Emerson interpreted this to mean there were fewer communal feasts, perhaps a sign that Cahokia's leaders were increasingly aloof. Beheadings wouldn't have endeared them to their public either. Porter surmised a "peasant revolt."

These various theories, their proponents readily admitted, were not mutually exclusive. Warfare could have been accompanied by civil unrest. Environmental problems could have increased political tensions within Cahokia, or with other tribes. And war would surely have exacerbated environmental problems; the palisade, for example, required a lot of trees. But some combination of these elements was undoubtedly to blame.

⟨⟩

If Cahokia could fall so quickly, declining from its peak population to complete abandonment in not much more than a hundred years, maybe it wasn't so powerful after all.

During the last years of the twentieth century and the first ones of the twenty-first, Cahokia's place in history has again come into question. Though a majority of historians still see it as the most powerful civilization of prehistoric North America, many are increasingly skeptical.

"Much is made about very little," wrote George Milner in 1998. "Nothing found at or around Cahokia is out of line with . . . developments elsewhere, except for the number of mounds and the size of some of them, particularly Monks Mound."

Milner and others have argued that Cahokia was not nearly as large as conventional wisdom would have it. Gregg's population estimates, though arrived at honestly, could have been inflated by a dense population in the sample areas, or by counting the remains of houses from a range of periods. In 1997, Timothy Pauketat estimated a peak population of 15,000; a year later, Milner suggested it was in the low thousands.

As for the sophisticated knowledge required to build the woodhenges or mounds, Milner was equally dismissive. "Despite claims to the contrary," he wrote, "the people directing the moundbuilding did not have to be especially knowledgeable to make great piles of dirt."

Are Milner and Pauketat a throwback to the nineteenth- and early twentieth-century scientists who couldn't believe Native Americans built anything of import? Hardly.

Neither they nor any archaeologist today would advocate razing the mounds, nor would they denigrate the value of Native American history and culture. What they are saying is that Cahokia was just one of many moundbuilding societies that rose and fell prior to the Europeans' arrival. Cahokia was the largest, maybe the most powerful, but in many ways more like these others than what Milner referred to, somewhat derisively, as "the mighty Cahokia scenario."

Many who would defend that scenario would agree that an exclusive focus on Cahokia's fall has tended to diminish our appreciation of the various ways Native Americans adapted to their changing environment. That goes not only for the other moundbuilders, but also for Cahokia's descendants. For whatever happened to the city, its people did not vanish. Archaeologists believe some moved north, where they cultivated new strains of corn that grew better there. Some moved south, such as to Alabama's Moundville site. Others probably noticed the growing population of buffaloes to the west, and followed them there.

Cahokia's descendants were undoubtedly among the Indians whites encountered as they settled the West. Like these whites, many Cahokians were pioneers who left the city behind to find a new way of life.

To Investigate Further

Emerson, Thomas, and R. Barry Lewis, eds. *Cahokia and the Hinterlands.* Urbana: University of Illinois Press, 1991.

Seventeen essays by (and for) specialists on Cahokia and its relationship to neighboring cultures.

Kennedy, Roger. *Hidden Cities.* New York: The Free Press, 1994.

How America's founding fathers interpreted the mounds and tried to fit them into their views of the Indians. The portrait of Jefferson is fascinating and complex; not only did he correspond with Brackenridge, but he also excavated a burial mound on his estate and recognized its Indian origins.

Emerson, Thomas. *Cahokia and the Archaeology of Power.* Tuscaloosa: University of Alabama Press, 1997.

Emerson uses Cahokia's "architecture and artifacts of power"—material remains from the mounds to figurines—to trace the increasing power of its chiefs.

Milner, George. *The Cahokia Chiefdom.* Washington, DC: Smithsonian Institution Press, 1998.

Milner's provocative thesis: "The presence of mounds and fancy artifacts, even lots of them, does not require a society as populous, organizationally complex, or powerful as conventional wisdom would have us believe." His writing, though technical, is more readable than that of most archaeologists.

Young, Biloine Whiting, and Melvin Fowler. *Cahokia.* Urbana: University of Illinois Press, 2000.

An entertaining history of Cahokia's archaeology, full of politics and personalities as well as science.

Chappell, Sally A. Kitt, with William Iseminger and John Kelly. *Cahokia.* Chicago: University of Chicago Press, 2002.

Despite its New Age flavor, this is a comprehensive, readable, and beautifully illustrated overview.

Pauketat, Timothy. *Ancient Cahokia and the Mississippians.* Cambridge, England: Cambridge University Press, 2004.

Pauketat locates Cahokia amid other cultural centers while also arguing for its uniqueness.

What Was Joan of Arc's Sign?

The Hundred Years War might never have lasted that long had a seventeen-year-old peasant girl not introduced herself to the heir to the French crown.

In 1429, when Joan of Arc met the future King Charles VII, the on-again, off-again wars between France and England had been going on a mere ninety years, and the end seemed near. The English had routed the French army at Agincourt, then formed an alliance with the duke of Burgundy that gave them effective control of half of France. Paris was in Anglo-Burgundian hands, the Parlement was in exile in Poitiers, and Orleans, the last French stronghold north of the Loire River, was surrounded by British troops.

To make matters worse, Charles was an extremely reluctant champion of his own cause. After his father's death in 1422, Charles had taken the title of king of France, but he'd never been formally crowned, and he continued to be known as the "dauphin," or crown prince. His own mother, Queen Isabeau, had effectively disowned him when she'd joined the Burgundian side. Never decisive, Charles was now paralyzed by doubts about his own legitimacy; he seemed uncertain both about whether he was truly his father's son and about whether he could rule France.

Into this desperate situation stepped France's savior, Joan of Arc. The young maid in armor appeared at the king's castle in Chinon and quickly won his trust and rallied his troops. In May she forced the English to retreat at the Battle of Orleans, and two months later she escorted Charles to Reims for his triumphant coronation.

For Joan, the victory was short lived. She was captured by the Burgundians, sold to the English, tried and condemned as a heretic, and in May 1431, burned at the stake. But she had saved France: though the Hundred Years War would drag on until 1453 (lasting 116 years, to be precise), the British would never again threaten to overrun the entire nation.

How did Joan do it? And, first and foremost, what had convinced the wary Charles to entrust his fate to her—a mere seventeen-year-old, a peasant with no military experience, and a girl to boot? Contemporaries told tales of a "sign" that Joan had shown the dauphin, something that immediately gained his trust. Ever since, historians have been determined to figure out what that sign was.

⚬⚭⚬

The sign was a subject of immediate interest at Joan's 1431 trial for heresy. The official record of the court, of which three copies have survived, indicates that her prosecutors and judges questioned her repeatedly about it.

At first Joan refused to answer, saying the sign was a matter between her king and herself. But this trial was run under the auspices of the Inquisition, and her inquisitors knew how to wear her down. By the trial's seventh session, on March 10, Joan gave in and answered their questions: an angel had given the sign to the king, she told the court. Pressed further, Joan continued to duck questions about what, exactly, the angel had brought. Two days later, she added that the angel had told the king that he should put Joan to work for his army.

At the trial's tenth session, on March 13, Joan was again questioned about the sign. "Do you want me to risk perjuring myself?" she asked, almost as if to warn the court that what would follow would be a lie. Then she launched into a much more detailed description of how a number of angels—some with wings, some with crowns—brought the king a crown of fine gold. One of the angels handed the king the crown and said, "Here is your sign." The crown was now in the king's treasury, Joan added.

Most historians have been understandably reluctant to believe Joan's testimony. The techniques of the Inquisition were hardly conducive to eliciting honest answers; though Joan was never tortured, she was overmatched by more than seventy churchmen and lawyers. Joan's question about perjuring herself indicated she had decided to stop resisting them and to give them what they wanted—namely, evidence that she was in touch with supernatural forces. Once Joan admitted that, it was up to her inquisitors to determine whether these were angels or devils—and there was no doubt they'd choose the latter. Her fate was sealed.

Twenty-five years after Joan's death, a second court overturned its verdict, and these records also survive. Like the original verdict, this one was pretty much predetermined. Charles, who wanted to eliminate any taint of heresy from his reputation, ordered an investigation into the first trial in 1448. The hearings stretched on until 1456, when the second court pronounced the first one "contaminated with fraud, calumny, wickedness, contradictions, and manifest errors of fact and law." Joan was, the court said, "washed clean."

It was at this second trial, which became known as the "trial of rehabilitation," that a now-famous version of Joan's first meeting with the dauphin emerged. Two witnesses recalled that when Joan entered the castle of Chinon, Charles hid himself among his courtiers. Yet Joan, though she'd never before laid eyes on the dauphin, immediately recognized him. Joan then spoke privately with the dauphin, after which he appeared "radiant," according to the witnesses.

The story of the hidden king, later embellished to include Joan's refusal to address a courtier posing as the king, appealed to historians, since it could be explained without recourse to any supernatural power on Joan's part. Many historians noted that even if Joan had never before seen the king, she could have picked him out based on someone else's description. The story was also appealingly theatrical, and it proved irresistible to, among others, Shakespeare, Schiller, Twain, and Shaw.

A victorious Joan of Arc, from an 1833 painting. *(Library of Congress)*

The hidden-king story may very well be true, but it still left unanswered questions. Would Charles have trusted Joan just because she picked him out of a crowd? Wouldn't Charles have realized that someone could have described him to Joan? And what did Joan say to him or show him that made him so "radiant"? To those questions, none of the witnesses at the trial of rehabilitation had an answer.

∞

One theory, which first appeared in print in 1516, was that Joan told the dauphin about a prayer he'd recently made. According to a chronicle written by Pierre Sala, who claimed to have heard the story from an intimate friend of Charles VII, Charles had asked God to grant him his kingdom if he was the true heir, or to let him escape death or prison if he wasn't. When Joan told Charles that she knew about his prayer—a prayer he'd confided to no one—he took it as a "sign" to trust her.

Like the hidden-king story, the prayer story could easily be true. It, too, could be explained without resorting to the supernatural. Joan would not have had to be extraordinarily intuitive to figure out that Charles was insecure about his parentage. The court was full of gossip that he was illegitimate, especially since his mother had disowned him as part of her alliance with the Burgundians and the English. Charles himself must have heard the widespread rumor that his real father was Charles VI's brother, the duke of Orleans. So Joan could easily have guessed that he'd turned to prayers, and Charles would certainly have been relieved that someone had arrived to answer them.

The problem with the secret-prayer story is the same as with the hidden-king story. Even if true, is it enough to explain Charles's decision to put his fate in the hands of an unknown teenager? Charles may have been weak and indecisive, but he was neither stupid nor naive. He would have been as capable as later historians of seeing how Joan might have known what he looked like, or what his prayers were. The appeal of the hidden-king and secret-prayer stories—that a rational, modern historian can make sense of them—is also their weakness, for if Joan's sign could easily be explained away, why did it so sway Charles?

What was required, clearly, was a more dramatic sign, one that could impress the dauphin yet one that didn't involve angels or devils or other supernatural phenomena. In 1805, Pierre Caze came up with a theory that fit the bill: it was Joan, not Charles, Caze wrote, who was the illegitimate offspring of Queen Isabeau and the duke of Orleans. By this account, the infant Joan was smuggled out of Paris to save her from her father's enemies. She was handed over to Jacques d'Arc, who raised her (and who in this version of Joan's story was a country gentleman, not a peasant). The sign she gave Charles at Chinon, then, was some proof that she was his half sister, perhaps a ring or a document or some inside knowledge of their family.

Caze's theory solved all sorts of problems. It explained why the dauphin trusted her. It also explained how Joan had gotten in to see the dauphin in the first place, and how she learned military tactics and strategy. This was no ordinary peasant girl; this was a princess born to command, with royal blood and royal contacts. The theory caught on, especially among monarchists who were never entirely comfortable with the idea of a peasant saving the kingdom. It also appealed to those who liked conspiracies, and it reemerged in various forms during the 1960s and 1970s.

The problem—and neither Caze nor any of his followers could ever overcome this—is that the theory was based on no evidence whatsoever. In fact, it presumed that a good deal of the evidence from both of Joan's trials was somehow falsified. The testimony about Joan's birth came not just from her parents but also from numerous other relatives and neighbors who said they either witnessed her birth or knew her from the day she was born. For Joan to be the king's sister, all of these witnesses—indeed, much of her hometown—must have committed perjury, as part of a grand conspiracy to conceal her royal birth. Caze's theory, though ingenious, simply isn't credible.

🙣

Other proposed conspiracies were less grand, less royal. In 1756, Voltaire suggested that the dauphin's ministers sought out a peasant girl and trained her, in the hope that her dramatic appearance at Chinon would inspire the cowardly Charles and his dejected soldiers to strike back at the English. In 1908, Anatole France's biography of Joan implicated church leaders in the same type of conspiracy. To those who shared their skeptical attitude toward either church or state, such conspiracy theories were very appealing; alas, neither Voltaire nor France had any evidence to back them up.

Another way to explain Joan's influence was to argue that it was never as great as it seemed, and for this position there was some evidence. Charles may have been deeply moved by Joan's sign, but he didn't instantly turn over his troops to her. Instead, in typically bureaucratic style, he appointed a commission to examine her more rigorously. The commissioners met for three weeks at Poitiers. Their report has been lost, but apparently they believed Joan's story, since she then proceeded to Orleans.

Many historians have also disparaged Joan's military contributions, even at the Battle of Orleans. Anatole France, for example, pictured her as little more than a mascot for the French army: brave and inspiring, yes, but with no real role in the battle's planning or execution. And none of the testimony at either of Joan's trials indicated that she was ever in command of the troops at Orleans. There was no point in arguing about how Joan did what she did, some historians argued, since she didn't do all that much anyway.

Such belittling positions had always to compete, of course, with the legend of the savior of France, the young woman whose death at the stake seemed sometimes to rival Christ's on the cross. Through the centuries, Joan became the symbol of France, embraced by all, regardless of their political or religious beliefs. She has stood with revolutionary republicans and Catholic monarchists alike, among others. Even Jean-Marie Le Pen's ultraconservative nationalists made her one of their own.

Not surprisingly, these groups have all been quicker to extol her powers than to offer any credible explanation of them. Yet most historians, though less biased, haven't done much better. Most believe, unlike Anatole France, that Joan was a significant factor in the war, and that she held great sway over the king, at least for a while. But almost all reject any form of a conspiracy theory, whether it be the result of Joan's royal blood or plots of Charles's ministers. That has left historians without any generally agreed-upon explanation for Joan's achievements, starting with her sign to the king.

So, in one sense, after more than five hundred years of historiography, historians are asking the same questions as Joan's inquisitors: Were there angels at work here? Or devils?

To a historian, of course, the answers must be no. But to return to these questions is perfectly appropriate, for to the people of the fifteenth century—and these included Joan and Charles and the French soldiers, as well as the lawyers and churchmen who condemned her—angels and devils were very real. So were the "voices" that Joan believed she heard and that she attributed to St. Catherine and St. Margaret. It was because the French soldiers believed she had saints and angels on her side that they followed her into battle. And it was because Joan's judges believed she had devils on her side that they condemned her to death.

Charles, though a highly educated and sophisticated courtier, was also a man of his times. He may very well have believed that Joan's voices or angels had come to save his kingdom. And that belief, more than anything she said or did at Chinon, was the true "sign" of her power.

To Investigate Further

Jewkes, Wilfred, and Jerome Landfield. *Joan of Arc.* New York: Harcourt, Brace & World, 1964.
   Includes the relevant sections of the original trial and the trial of rehabilitation.

Michelet, Jules. *Joan of Arc,* trans. Albert Guerard. Ann Arbor: University of Michigan Press, 1957.
   The French original, published in 1841, transformed Joan into a republican heroine by stressing that her devotion was to the kingdom, not the king.

France, Anatole. *The Life of Joan of Arc,* trans. Winifred Stephens. New York: John Lane, 1908.
   Joan as the dupe (albeit heroic) of priests who heard about her hallucinations and decided to make use of them.

Sackville-West, Vita. *Saint Joan of Arc.* Garden City, NY: Doubleday, Doran, 1938.
   Both a biography and a meditation on the nature of religious belief.

Pernoud, Regine. *Joan of Arc,* trans. Edward Hyams. New York: Stein & Day, 1966.
   Joan, as seen through her own words and those of the other witnesses at her trial.

David-Darnac, Maurice. *The True Story of the Maid of Orleans,* trans. Peter de Polnay. London: W. H. Allen, 1969.
   In this latest version of the bastardy theory, Joan proves her royal birth by showing Charles a gold ring engraved with the arms of the House of Orleans. She also manages to escape the stake.

Lucie-Smith, Edward. *Joan of Arc*. London: Allen Lane, 1976.
    A psychological approach to Joan that's sometimes insightful, often not.

Gies, Frances. *Joan of Arc*. New York: Harper & Row, 1981.
    A straightforward biography, clear and unbiased, though offering no new interpretations.

Warner, Marina. *Joan of Arc*. New York: Alfred A. Knopf, 1981.
    How Joan fitted into traditions of thought about women, in her own time and after.

Barstow, Anne. *Joan of Arc*. Lewiston, NY: Edwin Mellen Press, 1986.
    Compares Joan to other late-medieval mystics and heretics.

Pernoud, Regine, and Marie-Veronique Clin. *Joan of Arc,* trans. and rev. Jeremy du Quesnay Adams. New York: St. Martin's Press, 1998.
    Pernoud is the leading French scholar on Joan, but it's unclear whether she meant this to be a narrative history or an encyclopedia.

Who Invented Printing?

Y OU WOULDN'T THINK THERE COULD BE much question about an event that was almost immediately recognized as one of the major turning points of world history. Who could question the primacy of Johann Gutenberg? His title as inventor of printing has been so universally accepted that Marshall McLuhan didn't hesitate to refer to the culture he spawned as the "Gutenberg galaxy."

Yet questions abound. For a figure of such historic import, Gutenberg has always been somewhat shadowy. And even in his own times, Gutenberg was by no means the only name put forward as the inventor of printing.

⁜

The earliest reference to the invention of printing comes in a letter dated 1472, just four years after Gutenberg died. It's from a Sorbonne professor named Guillaume Fichet. Writing to a friend, Fichet mentioned that not far from the city of Mainz, "there was a certain Johann who bore the surname Gutenberg, who first of all men thought out the art of printing, by which books are made, not written with a reed . . . nor by pen . . . but by metal letters."

Other early references place the invention in Strassburg, sometimes crediting Gutenberg but at other times another printer, named Johann Mentelin. Claims were also made on behalf of printers in Venice and Milan. Many of these claims seem motivated by little more than local pride.

Something more than that seems to be operating in Avignon, in France, judging from two court documents there. According to two contracts dated 1446, a Prague silversmith named Procopius Waldvogel agreed to teach the secret of "artificial writing" to some local citizens. One of the contracts refers, tantalizingly, to "two alphabets of steel and forty-eight forms of tin, and other forms as well." Could these letters be types for printing, a la Gutenberg's? Waldvogel was undoubtedly working toward a comparable invention, but most scholars have concluded that he had a way to go. The likeliest scenario is that Waldvogel's letters were used for some sort of variation of the traditional woodcut technique—closer perhaps to a manual typewriter than to true typography.

More persistent was the claim on behalf of Laurens Coster of Haarlem, first put forth by a Dutch scholar in 1588. Coster came up with the idea for printing in 1440, according to Hadrian Junius, while Coster was cutting some letters for his grandchildren from the bark of a beech tree. Later Coster exchanged the beechwood characters for lead and then tin. His printing business soon flourished.

Alas, Junius wrote, the growth of Coster's business led him to take on assistants, one of whom—"a certain Johann"—turned out to be unscrupulous. After learning the secrets of the trade, Johann waited until Christmas Eve, when everyone else was at church. Then he stole all the type and equipment and headed off to Mainz, where he set up his own operation.

The Coster story spread beyond the Netherlands, with support coming over the years from French, English, and American scholars. Partly this was because of a substantial body of early though undated Dutch printed works, some from metal type and some from wood blocks. In Haarlem's market square a statue of Coster, "inventor of the art of printing," still stands.

In the past few decades, however, the story has been largely discredited. More precise analyses of the type, inscriptions, and paper have shown that most of the evidence of early Dutch printing dated from after 1465—and ten years after the earliest books known to have been printed at Gutenberg's hometown of Mainz.

The storybook quality of the Coster tale is also suspicious. It's a bit hard to buy that Coster so easily jumped from the idea of cutting letters for his grandchildren to printing books and establishing a flourishing business—all within the six months prior to the Christmas Eve theft.

One reason the Coster legend lasted so long was that it named the villain, "Johann," thus directly answering the claims on behalf of Gutenberg. Waldvogel, too, had some alleged links to Gutenberg: Walter Riffe, who was at one point an acquaintance of Gutenberg, visited Avignon while Waldvogel lived there.

These connections are at best tenuous and serve mostly to indicate that even in the fifteenth century most people associated the invention of printing with Gutenberg. Yet until the eighteenth century, very little was known about Gutenberg's own activities. That changed between 1727 and 1770 as a series of documents pertaining to lawsuits involving Gutenberg surfaced in a variety of archives.

From these emerged a much clearer picture of Gutenberg, as well as a new and by far the most serious threat to Gutenberg's claim to be the inventor of printing.

⚬⚭⚬

The first crucial documents to surface record a lawsuit brought against Gutenberg in 1439, when he lived in Strassburg. Gutenberg, whose inventing ambitions extended beyond printing, had apparently invented some new method of manufacturing mirrors. He'd entered into a partnership with one Andreas Dritzehn to produce and sell them to pilgrims on the way to Aachen, but the deal fell apart. Apparently the partners got wrong the date of the pilgrimage, which was due to take place not in 1439 but a year later. They decided they didn't want to wait a year for the mirror sales, so Dritzehn suggested that Gutenberg should instead teach him another—and unspecified—art. Gutenberg and Dritzehn drew up a new contract to cover Gutenberg's "art and adventure."

The Gutenberg Bible contains no printer's name, no place of printing, no date. *(Library of Congress)*

Was this the art and adventure of printing? The documents are very vague; clearly both parties in the lawsuit intentionally avoided giving away the secret. The documents offer only glimpses, but these include the mention of the purchase of lead and other metals, and of a press and certain "forms."

Whatever Gutenberg was up to, others were convinced it could pay off big. According to testimony from the trial, a woman had visited Andreas Dritzehn one night, and she expressed some reservations about how much he'd invested. Dritzehn conceded he'd mortgaged his inheritance, but he confidently told the woman: "We shan't fail. Before a year is out we shall have recovered our capital and then we shall be in bliss."

Dritzehn's brothers also thought the invention was worth a lot of money, and that's what led to the lawsuit. The contract contained a clause that in the event of the death of one of the parties, his heirs would not take his place. Still, when Dritzehn died in 1438, his brothers wanted in on the deal. Gutenberg refused, and the court found in his favor. As a result, Dritzehn's brothers never learned the secret art his brother was learning from Gutenberg, nor can we know for sure what it was.

The next crucial document is more explicitly about printing. It dates from October 1455, by which time Gutenberg had returned from Strassburg to his hometown of Mainz. Again, Gutenberg faced a lawsuit. (He faced many, perhaps inevitably for an inventor in a prepatent era.) The record of this one has become known as the Helmasperger Instrument, after the notary who signed it, Ulrich Helmasperger.

The plaintiff was Johann Fust, another partner of Gutenberg's and in the minds of some historians, the true inventor of printing.

This much is clear from the Helmasperger Instrument: Fust loaned Gutenberg a large sum of money for what was described as "the work of the books." Later Fust sued for the principal and interest, most of which the court awarded him. The Helmasperger Instrument doesn't say exactly how much, nor whether Gutenberg could pay. Nonetheless, many historians concluded that the decision bankrupted Gutenberg and enriched Fust, who may have taken over the former's printing shop.

Whether in Gutenberg's shop or in one he set up for himself, Fust then went on to become a successful printer. Fust's name, along with that of a new partner, Peter Schaffer, appears on the Mainz Psalter of 1457, of which ten copies still exist. The Psalter is the first printed book whose place, date, and printer is unquestioned, and Fust's supporters cite it as evidence that their man, not Gutenberg, completed the press and first put it to use.

But did Fust actually contribute to the invention of the press, or did he merely capitalize on Gutenberg's invention? Was the Psalter the first book printed, or merely the first book printed with a place, date, and printer?

And what about the Gutenberg Bible? It's the Bible and not the Psalter that many still view as not just the first printed book but also as one of the most beautiful. Who printed that? And when?

ᴑᴕᴕᴑ

About the Bible the Helmasperger Instrument offers no definitive answers. Nor do the extant copies of the book itself, which contain no printer's name, no place of printing, no date. But other clues point to Gutenberg as the printer—and with an earlier date than that of the Psalter.

A note in a copy now at the Bibliotheque Nationale in Paris informs us that the binder and the tinter finished work in August 1456. Working backward, that makes it likely the sheets were printed in 1454 or 1455—before Fust could have taken over Gutenberg's press.

Further evidence surfaced in 1947, in the form of a March 1455 letter from Aeneas Silvius Piccolomini (who later became Pope Pius II) to a Spanish cardinal. Piccolomini described seeing sheets from the Bible printed by this "astonishing man" in fall 1454. The letter didn't say whether the astonishing man was Gutenberg or Fust, but by confirming the earlier print date it made stronger the case that the printer of the Gutenberg Bible was, in fact, Gutenberg.

For most historians, the note and the letter secured Gutenberg's claim to fame.

That's not to deny Fust an important place in the history of printing, however. For centuries Fust has been portrayed as the villain of the story, the evil capitalist who took advantage of Gutenberg, the classic head-in-the-clouds inventor. Fust, according to this view, waited until Gutenberg had invested all of their funds in the production of the soon-to-be-famous Bible. Then, knowing there was no way Gutenberg could pay him back, he called his loan and seized the assets of the business. Fust's name didn't help his reputation, either: it was sometimes spelled Faust, which encouraged some early historians to incorporate elements of the Faust legend into the story.

Modern historians have been kinder to Fust. For one thing, many have noted that Fust grew up in a family of goldsmiths. Even if the invention was Gutenberg's, therefore, Fust ought not to be dismissed as a mere money-hungry exploiter with no interest in a craft.

Nor is it likely that the Mainz judges would have upheld his claim if it hadn't had some merit. It's very possible that, just as Fust claimed, Gutenberg took some of the money that was supposed to go toward their joint Bible project and used it instead to print other works, such as calendars and grammars. Fust had no share in the profits from the other publications, so it's understandable that he'd be angered by the diversion of his funds.

So Fust was no devil and Gutenberg no saint. Perhaps Fust even made some minor technical improvements to the press. Similarly, Gutenberg may have learned some techniques from Waldvogel and Coster, or from others in France or Italy or Germany. He also may have gotten some ideas from the Far East, where some form of metal letters had been in use for centuries and where paper—not to mention silk, gunpowder, and porcelain—was invented. Increasingly, historians have seen all these places, all these artisans and inventors, as part of a gradual process that led to the invention of the printing press.

In 2000, Princeton librarian Paul Needham went so far as to argue that Gutenberg didn't even invent movable type, at least as it's normally understood. By magnifying typefaces, Needham found tiny differences in letters, indicating they may not have come from the same mold.

Still, it was the genius of Johann Gutenberg that synthesized most of the trends and trials of the times. Drawing no doubt on others' work, he brought together paper of the right quality, ink of the right consistency, a press adapted for both, and some form of recyclable and readily available types.

Exactly when it all came together is still a mystery. Some have interpreted the Dritzehn lawsuit to mean Gutenberg pulled it off in Strassburg, perhaps in about 1440. The consensus among historians, however, is that it was in Mainz during the 1450s, not long before the printing of the Bible that's rightly remembered by his name.

Whenever it was, Gutenberg created a method of producing more to read in a day than scribes could write in a year. After that, the world was never the same.

To Investigate Further

Schorbach, Karl, ed. *The Gutenberg Documents.* New York: Oxford University Press, 1941.
    The key documents in translation, including the records from the Helmasperger Instrument and the suit brought by Dritzehn's brothers.

Butler, Pierce. *The Origin of Printing in Europe.* Chicago: University of Chicago Press, 1940.
The case against Gutenberg.

Scholderer, Victor. *Johann Gutenberg.* London: British Museum, 1963.
Not much more than a pamphlet, but the closest thing to an English-language biography.

Goff, Frederick. *The Permanence of Johann Gutenberg.* Austin: University of Texas Press, 1970.
A brief summary of some of the controversies surrounding Gutenberg.

Eisenstein, Elizabeth. *The Printing Revolution in Early Modern Europe.* Cambridge: Cambridge University Press, 1983.
Not much about Gutenberg, but plenty about how he changed the world.

Kapr, Albert. *Johann Gutenberg.* Aldershot, England: Scolar Press, 1996.
Completed in East Germany in 1986 but not translated until ten years later, this is the most recent biography; generally admirable, though it suffers somewhat from having been written prior to the fall of the Berlin Wall, which deprived the author of access to some articles in English and French journals.

Ing, Janet. *Johann Gutenberg and His Bible.* New York: Typophiles, 1988.
A clear and concise historiography.

Man, John. *Gutenberg.* New York: Wiley, 2002.
How Gutenberg set out to make money and preserve Catholicism, and ended losing money and ushering in the Reformation.

Did Richard III
Kill the Princes in the Tower?

Every tale condemns me for a villain," Shakespeare has Richard III complain shortly before his death.

And what a villain he makes! Here was a man who didn't hesitate to murder the saintly Henry VI and his youthful heir Edward . . . or to drown his own brother George (in a vat of Malmsey wine) . . . or to marry the widow of one of his victims, then poison her when another and better-connected potential bride appeared on the scene. Most heinous of all, and what guaranteed Richard's infamy, was the kidnapping and murder of "the princes in the Tower." They were just children, and they were Richard's own nephews, but they stood between their uncle and the throne.

Yet, if Shakespeare's Richard had good reason to worry about his reputation, the real king could take comfort in knowing that he would have more than his share of defenders. Five hundred years after his death, the murder of the princes in the Tower continued to inspire mystery writers, most notably Josephine Tey, author of the best-selling *The Daughter of Time*. The Richard III Society has more than three thousand members dedicated to clearing his name.

To his defenders, Richard was the victim of a propaganda campaign organized by Henry VII, the first of the line of Tudor kings who succeeded their hero. These "Ricardians" paint a strikingly different portrait of Richard: a brave soldier, a concerned king, a loyal brother. And they have their own ideas about who killed the princes in the Tower.

⌒▥▥꙳

More than Shakespeare, the man responsible for the traditional view of Richard as evil incarnate was Thomas More. It was he who set forth the basic plot that Shakespeare and other Tudor writers followed. More wrote *The History of King Richard III* between 1514 and 1518 and revised it in the late 1520s.

Richard of Gloucester, as he was known before he became king, grew up in the shadow of his older brother, King Edward IV. Even More conceded Richard was loyal to Edward, who in turn repaid him with various titles and estates, primarily in northern England.

In April 1483 Edward died at age forty, after a life overly full of food, drink, and women. He left two sons, twelve-year-old Edward and ten-year-old Richard. The dying king's wish was for his son to become King Edward V, with his brother serving as "protector" until the boy was old enough to rule on his own.

This arrangement didn't satisfy Edward IV's queen, Elizabeth Woodville. While Richard was up north, she managed to convince the royal council in London to reject his protectorship. Then she sent an urgent message to her brother, Anthony, telling him to bring the young Edward to London so he could be crowned immediately.

On learning of the plot, Richard moved south quickly, intercepting Anthony Woodville and Edward. After an evening of feasting, Richard had Woodville arrested and sent north, where he was soon beheaded. Richard then accompanied his young nephew to London, where he installed him in the Tower of London—then a royal residence, not a prison.

Still, plans were proceeding for the coronation of the young king, and Richard persuaded the queen to let her younger son join Edward to attend the ceremony. Richard promised to return the boy immediately after the coronation. More persuasive, undoubtedly, were Richard's troops, who surrounded the queen's sanctuary at Westminster Abbey.

Meanwhile, Richard needed some pretext for claiming the crown for himself. That conveniently appeared in June, courtesy of Robert Stillington, bishop of Bath and Wells. Stillington disclosed to the royal council that Edward IV's marriage to Elizabeth Woodville was invalid because he had once been contracted to marry another lady, Eleanor Butler. Therefore the princes in the Tower were bastards . . . and bastards couldn't inherit the throne.

With Edward IV's other brother, George, already drowned in the aforementioned wine, the next in line was none other than Richard of Gloucester.

Richard now felt the crown was within his grasp. In late July or early August he sent a letter to Sir Robert Brackenbury, constable of the Tower, ordering him to kill the princes. Brackenbury refused.

So Richard turned over the job to James Tyrell, an ambitious supporter who enlisted two henchmen. According to More's account, Tyrell waited outside while the others sneaked up to the sleeping princes, "suddenly lapped them up among the clothes," and forced the "featherbed and pillows hard unto their mouths." Then the three men buried the bodies "at the stayre foot, metely depe in the grounde under a great heape of stones."

If Richard was the villain of More's history, the hero was Henry VII, who in 1435 slew Richard on Bosworth Field, bringing to an end the bloody War of the Roses and founding the happy line of Tudor monarchs.

Or so More wrote. But was it true?

⟨∞⟩

It was difficult, even for Richard's supporters, to question the integrity of Sir Thomas More. This was, after all, the man executed in 1535 because his conscience wouldn't let him go along with Henry VIII's plan to divorce Catherine of Aragon and marry Anne Boleyn. More was a writer, a philosopher, and (after his 1935 canonization) quite literally a saint.

Yet question they did. As early as 1768, Sir Horace Walpole described More as "an historian who is capable of employing truth only as a cement in a fabric of fiction." Undeniably, he got certain facts wrong, among them his description of Richard's deformities. The hunchback and withered arm appeared in no other contemporary reference.

Ricardians also questioned More's sources. More was only five when Richard took the throne and only seven when he died, so he obviously wasn't writing about anything he witnessed personally. One source may have been Cardinal John Morton, in whose household More lived as a boy. A more biased source could hardly be imagined: Morton was imprisoned and exiled by Richard III.

Besides, Ricardians noted, More neither finished nor published the *History*. Perhaps, they surmised, he'd dropped the project as he'd learned the truth about Richard and Henry.

Above all, Ricardians argued that More's account didn't make sense. If the royal council had already ruled the princes were bastards and so couldn't inherit the throne, why would Richard have to kill them? If Henry found the princes missing when he took over the Tower in 1485, why didn't he rant and rave about that, or at least search for the bodies?

To Ricardians, all this pointed to Henry as the culprit. His motive was at least as strong as Richard's, they argued. As a fairly distant cousin of both Richard and the princes, his claim to the throne was much weaker than Richard's, and pretty much hopeless if either of the princes were still alive.

To all these questions, traditionalists had answers. Sure, Richard's council had declared the princes illegitimate, but Richard knew that Henry VII could just as easily persuade his council to reverse the decision. As long as they were alive, the princes could always be a rallying point for Richard's enemies and a threat to his crown.

As for Henry, there were several reasons why he might not have done anything about the princes after taking over. Perhaps he didn't know for sure what happened to them. Perhaps he assumed everyone blamed Richard. Perhaps he feared that if he admitted he didn't know where the princes were, it would lead to uprisings on their behalf.

Indeed, that fear was borne out. Twice during Henry's reign, anti- Tudor forces coalesced around leaders claiming to be the princes. The "Edward" who led a 1487 uprising turned out to be Lambert Simnel, the son of an Oxford joiner and organmaker. In 1491 a man claiming to be the younger prince was revealed to be Perkin Warbeck. He may have gained some useful knowledge from his father, who had once earned a living by supplying carpets to the royal court.

So the arguments for and against both Richard and Henry went round and round for centuries, with the prestige of More and Shakespeare generally giving weight to the traditionalists but Richard getting a strong defense, even as early as 1619, from a revisionist history by Sir George Buck. Only one thing seemed sure: the same facts could lead to different conclusions.

Then, in the 1930s, the facts changed.

⟨∞⟩

In 1933, Westminster Abbey finally gave in to pressure from the Ricardians to open the tomb in which the remains of the princes were supposedly interred. Back in 1674, following the instructions of Charles II to clear a site near the White Tower, workmen discovered a chest containing two small skeletons. The location immediately conjured up More's description of the burial site, and Charles concluded that the bones were those of the princes. Velvet found amid the bones lent credence to the conclusion, since it was worn only by persons of the highest rank.

Charles ordered the bodies reinterred at Westminster Abbey, where they remained for another 259 years.

The 1933 study by Lawrence Tanner, Westminster's archivist, and William Wright, president of Great Britain's Anatomical Society, was too early for carbon dating, let alone DNA technology. But Tanner and Wright were able to use dental evidence to estimate that the elder child was twelve or thirteen and the younger nine to eleven. Edward had been twelve and Richard ten when they disappeared.

This was not absolute proof that Richard was a murderer, but it did corroborate at least one aspect of the traditionalists' story.

A year later, more evidence surfaced, this time in the Municipal Library of Lille. This was a report written in 1483 by Dominic Mancini, an Italian monk. Unlike More, Mancini was in London during the critical months when Richard took the throne. The monk stated his intention up front: "to put in writing by what machinations Richard III attained the high degree of kingship."

Mancini described how the princes were moved to the inner apartments of the Tower and were gradually seen less and less, then not at all. As to the way the young king died, Mancini reported only that "already there was a suspicion that he had been done away with."

Ricardians made much of the fact that Mancini didn't come right out and accuse Richard of the murder. They also pointed out that what he reported may have been no more than gossip. Still, at the very least, the report was evidence that the stories about Richard's ruthlessness were not just inventions of later Tudor propagandists. Even in his own time, there were clearly plenty of people who suspected that Richard had killed the princes.

For the majority of historians, the twentieth-century revelations were enough to convict Richard. The evidence is entirely circumstantial, and few historians would deny the Ricardians their reasonable doubt. But history is not a court of law; historians must consider probabilities, not possibilities. Others had a motive to kill the princes, but none so compelling as Richard's. Others had opportunity, too, but so did Richard, and it's hard to imagine someone else doing away with the princes without Richard knowing about it.

Yet if most historians have concluded that Richard was probably guilty of the murder, Ricardians can take some solace in a consensus that he was by no means the monster portrayed by More and Shakespeare. In killing the princes, Richard was following a well-established precedent. Edward II was murdered on the orders of his wife, who took over in the name of her son Edward III. Richard II was starved to death by Henry IV. And Henry VI was killed on the orders of Edward IV.

Richard recalled all of these deaths. Medieval England was no time to be a deposed king, and that's most likely how Richard saw his nephews. Shakespeare's "bottled spider" was very much a man of his times.

To Investigate Further

Mancini, Dominic. *The Usurpation of Richard III.* Oxford: Clarendon Press, 1969.
Mancini may have filled his report with bias and gossip; nevertheless, he was there. Translated and with an introduction by C. A. J. Armstrong, who discovered the document.

Kendall, Paul, ed. *Richard III.* New York: W. W. Norton, 1965.
Brings together the two most prominent early antagonists in the debate, with the full texts of More's *History of King Richard III*, first published in 1543, and Horace Walpole's *Historic Doubts on the Life and Reign of King Richard the Third*, first published in 1769.

Tanner, Lawrence, and William Wright. "Recent Investigation Regarding the Fate of the Princes in the Tower." *Archaeologia* 84 (1935).
If only they conducted a DNA test . . .

Tey, Josephine. *The Daughter of Time.* New York: Macmillan, 1951.
A twentieth-century Scotland Yard inspector concludes that Richard was framed in a novel that's a fine detective story but less convincing as history.

Kendall, Paul. *Richard the Third.* New York: W. W. Norton, 1955.
A readable and sympathetic biography that points the finger at the duke of Buckingham.

Peters, Elizabeth. *The Murders of Richard III.* New York: Warner Books, 1986.
A moderately entertaining English countryhouse mystery, originally published in 1974, in which a bunch of Ricardians dress up as their heroes, then find themselves living through—or rather, dying through—reenactments of his crimes.

Ross, Charles. *Richard III.* Berkeley: University of California Press, 1981.
A comprehensive portrait of Richard's life and his very bloody times.

Weir, Alison. *The Princes in the Tower.* New York: Ballantine Books, 1992.
One of the most persuasive cases against Richard.

Fields, Bertram. *Royal Blood.* New York: Regan Books, 1998.
Fields, a Hollywood lawyer, would definitely have gotten his client off on the grounds that there's reasonable doubt about his guilt, but he's less convincing when he tries to prove Richard's innocence.

Why Did Constantinople Fall?

I N ITALY, THE LAST ROMAN EMPEROR was deposed in the year 476. To the east, the Roman Empire was known as the Byzantine Empire, and it lasted nearly another thousand years. Its capital was Constantinople, named for the first Christian emperor, and for the Christians of Byzantium the city was as central as Rome, its patriarch their pope. Constantinople also held a key economic position along the trade route between the Black Sea and the Mediterranean, and between Asia and Europe.

For most of those thousand years, Constantinople appeared impregnable. Despite more than twenty sieges, the only armies to conquer Constantinople were those of the Fourth Crusade, and they succeeded only by trickery. In 1204 the crusaders, proclaiming friendship with their Christian brethren, anchored their ships in the Golden Horn, the city's harbor. They then scaled the low walls on that side and looted the city. So in 1453, when Sultan Mehmet II and his Turkish armies besieged the city, its defenders blocked entry to the Golden Horn with an iron chain supported by floating pontoons. That meant Mehmet would have to break through the city's western walls. To do this, his armies would have to first cross a moat that was sixty feet wide. Then they'd have to scale a thirty-foot-high, seven-foot-thick stone wall while the city's defenders bombarded them with stones, spears, and boiling oil. Anyone who managed to get through would find himself trapped between the outer wall and an even more imposing forty-foot-high, sixteen-foot-thick inner wall. Interspersed among each wall were ninety-six towers. No one had ever broken through. Even Attila, on seeing the city's defenses, had ordered his Huns to withdraw.

Mehmet was determined to take Constantinople. His advisers, including the Grand Vizier, Halil Pasha, considered the twenty-two-year-old sultan impetuous, his plan reckless. Mehmet ignored them. He built a castle across the Bosphorus from Constantinople, and in early spring set up a blockade. He ordered his men to dig mines underneath the walls, but the Byzantines undermined each one. On April 20, a few Genoese ships pushed through the blockade, and—with the chain lifted in the dead of night—slipped into the Golden Horn. Mehmet then had his engineers build a road on the other side of the harbor, and had his oxen pull seventy ships over land into the Horn.

Still, after seven weeks, no Turk had breached the city's walls. Pasha appeared to have been right. Inside the city, the Byzantines were exhausted but still determined. Then came a series of omens that could not be ignored.

A Venetian doctor, Nicolo Barbaro, witnessed the events from inside the walls. "At the first hour of the night, there appeared a wonderful sign in the sky, which was to tell Constantine the worthy Emperor of Constantinople that his proud empire was about to come to an end," Barbaro wrote. "At the first hour after sunset the moon rose, being at this time at the full, so that it should have risen in the form of a complete circle; but it rose as if it were no more than a three-day moon, with only a little of it showing, although the air was clear and unclouded, pure as crystal."

According to Barbaro, the lunar eclipse occurred on May 22; others placed it on May 24. Either way, it was disturbing. "The Emperor of Constantinople was greatly afraid of it, and so were all his nobles," Barbaro continued, "because the Greeks had a prophecy which said that Constantinople would never fall until the full moon should give a sign."

There were other equally distressing signs. As a statue of the Virgin—the city's holiest icon—was carried through the streets, it fell to the ground. Then there was a sudden thunderstorm, and the procession had to be abandoned. The next morning the city was shrouded in a thick fog, unheard of at that time of year. Then a red glow crept up from the base to the cross atop the dome of St. Sophia. The city's inhabitants interpreted this as a sign that the city would perish in a pillar of fire. A Cardinal Isidore, writing to the pope a month later, noted, "Just as the city was founded by Constantine, son of Helena, so it is now tragically lost by another Constantine [the new emperor was the eleventh of that name], son of Helena." And the monk Gennadios Scholarios observed that May, the month when the city would fall, was the same month in which it had been founded in 330.

The Turks, too, noticed some of these signs. Mehmet was especially disturbed by the red light on the dome of St. Sophia, which he feared was a sign of divine intervention on the side of the city. On May 26, the Turks held a council of war, and again Pasha urged him to withdraw before European reinforcements arrived. But Mehmet had come around to the Byzantines' own interpretations of the signs: it was time for the city to fall.

On May 29, wave after wave of Turks and their vassals assaulted the walls. After four hours, they finally broke through. Just before dawn, the Turks were inside Constantinople.

"[The] prophecies had come to pass," wrote Barbaro, "seeing that the Turks had passed into Greece, there was an Emperor called Constantine son of Helen, and the moon had given a sign in the sky, so that God had determined to come to this decision against the Christians and particularly against the Empire of Constantinople."

⁓

Contemporary chroniclers had good reason to imbue the omens with significance. Gennadios, for example, wrote his account after Mehmet had installed him as the new patriarch of Constantinople. Others, like Kristoboulos of Imbros and Laonikos Chalkokondyles, were also eager to demonstrate their loyalty to the sultan by demonstrating the divine inevitability of his conquest. The sultan rewarded Kristoboulos by appointing him governor of Imbros.

Still, contemporary as well as modern historians recognized that the Turks had more than omens on their side. Mehmet brought with him about 80,000 men, armed with javelins, swords, arrows, battering rams, and a devotion to Islam. Though the sultan didn't know it, Constantine had only about 5,000–7,000 men. Mehmet had about 250 ships, Constantine 26. Mehmet also had the services of a Hungarian cannon-maker named Urban, who built the largest cannons ever constructed. One was twenty-eight feet long with a barrel eight inches thick. According to the Greek chronicler Doukas, it took sixty oxen and two hundred men to move the cannons into position on the European side of the Bosphorus. They could only fire a few times a day, but when they did they sent quarter-ton stone cannonballs across the water and into Constantinople. Ceaselessly, the defenders repaired the walls, but by May the bombardment had taken its toll.

Moreover, the Turks had been on the rise and the Byzantines in decline for centuries. In 1326 the Turks conquered much of Anatolia, and in 1356 they crossed into Europe. In 1402 the Tartars stopped them at Ankara, but the Tartars soon withdrew to the east, while the Turks pushed forward. The Byzantines, meanwhile, had never truly recovered from the 1204 sacking, and their empire had gradually been reduced to little more than Constantinople and its suburbs.

"The Emperor was still, at least in Eastern eyes, the Roman emperor," wrote historian Steven Runciman. "But in reality he was only one prince among others equally or more powerful."

"The last century of the Byzantine Empire was a prelude to the history of the Ottoman Empire," wrote historian Donald Nicol. Well before he captured the city, despite the worries of his advisers, Mehmet was already far more powerful than Constantine.

By 1453, the Byzantines' only real hope was that their Christian allies would rally round. But in the west, the Europeans were busy with their Hundred Years' War and War of the Roses. Further east, the kings of Serbia and Hungary had signed treaties with Mehmet. The pope was supportive but had little to offer. The Venetians and Genoans sent a few ships, but their real interest was in trade, and the Turks seemed as willing a partner as the Byzantines. A few Venetian ships even slipped out of the Golden Horn in February, evading both the blockade and the need to fight the Turks.

⟣⟣⟣

Scientists and historians remain unsure what caused the unusually dark eclipse, the unseasonal weather, and the red lights on St. Sophia. Some thought the lights were a reflection of distant Turkish bonfires. Others speculated that even more distant volcanic activity spewed particles into the atmosphere and caused all three phenomena. Whatever their cause, there's no question that to medieval minds, they mattered. Nor were these omens just the retrospective propaganda of the victorious Turks. There were also plenty of Christian chroniclers, such as Barbaro and Isidore, who, amid their shock and despair over the fall of Constantinople, found some solace in the explanation that it was God's will.

"There was a streak of fatalism in the Byzantine mentality," wrote Nicol. "They had sensed, with growing conviction, that their world would not after all endure until the Second Coming . . . and that the only permanence, the only security, and the only certain happiness were to be found in the true Kingdom above and beyond this vale of tears. When the end came in 1453 they were ready for it. It is surprising that it had not come sooner."

It's even possible that the omens contributed to the city's fall. Coming at a point when the Turks were frustrated and the Byzantines exhausted, they may have bolstered the morale of the former and undercut that of the latter. The superior Turkish artillery and manpower were undoubtedly crucial, but psychological factors may also have played a role in the conquest.

"Mohammed could very well have pointed to each event claiming that they were all portents of victory," wrote historian Robert Martin. "The timing of the final attack on Constantinople certainly lends credibility to this idea."

To Investigate Further

Barbaro, Nicolo. *Diary of the Siege of Constantinople,* trans. J. R. Jones. New York: Exposition Press, 1969.

Jones, J. R. *The Siege of Constantinople.* Amsterdam: Adolf M. Hakkert, 1972.
　　Jones's translations of seven contemporary accounts.

Runciman, Steven. *The Fall of Constantinople.* London: Cambridge University Press, 1965.
　　The most detailed modern history of the events that ended one empire and began another.

Nicol, Donald. *The Immortal Emperor.* Cambridge, England: Cambridge University Press, 1992.
　　The fate of the last emperor remains a mystery. Some accounts report his head was presented to Mehmet as a trophy, while others say he escaped. The most likely scenario is that he was killed in the final battle and buried anonymously along with his fellow Byzantines.

Wheatcroft, Andrew. *The Ottomans.* New York: Viking, 1993.
　　A balanced history of the empire that for almost five hundred years ruled much of the Near East.

Nicol, Donald. *The Last Centuries of Byzantium.* Cambridge, England: Cambridge University Press, 1996.
　　An authoritative synthesis.

Norwich, John Julius. *Byzantium.* New York: Knopf, 1996.
　　The third volume of Norwich's masterful and elegant trilogy covers the decline and fall.

Goodwin, Jason. *Lords of the Horizons.* New York: Henry Holt, 1999.
　　An impressionistic history that attributes the successes of the Ottoman Empire to its tolerance of other cultures as well as its military skills.

Did Columbus
Intend to Discover America?

CONTRARY TO POPULAR MYTHOLOGY, Christopher Columbus had no trouble at all convincing the king and queen of Spain—or anyone else—that the world was round. This was common knowledge among educated Europeans long before 1492. The resistance to Columbus's plan had to do with a different and much more radical idea—that he could discover a new route to Asia by sailing west from Europe.

The standard wisdom was that, if Asia was to be reached by sea, it would be by rounding Africa and heading east across the Indian Ocean. Since Asia was, in fact, east of Europe, this was a perfectly logical plan, and it paid off in 1499 when the Portuguese explorer Vasco da Gama arrived in India. Columbus's "Enterprise of the Indies," in contrast, made no sense. For even if the Indies (as Asia was then called) lay somewhere across the Atlantic, it was far too long a trip for a fifteenth-century mariner. The geographer most sympathetic to Columbus, Paolo del Pozzo Toscanelli, estimated that the Indies were more than 3,500 miles west of the Canary Islands, and most scholars were convinced they were a lot farther.

Columbus, as everyone knows, was not to be dissuaded. He calculated that only 2,760 miles of open water separated Europe and Asia, and he persuaded Ferdinand and Isabella of Spain that it would be worth their while to finance his voyage. So, in September 1492, the *Nina*, the *Pinta*, and the *Santa Maria* set sail from the Canaries. A mere five weeks later—at just about the spot he'd predicted he'd find land—Columbus stepped ashore.

The irony of Columbus's triumphant landing, of course, was that he was nowhere near Asia. The standard wisdom was in this case entirely correct: Asia was a good 6,000 miles farther west than the Bahamian island on which Columbus now stood. Had there not been two continents and numerous other islands between Europe and the Indies, Columbus and his crew would almost certainly have vanished into the seas.

For more than four hundred years this was the story of Columbus told on both sides of the Atlantic, the story of the determinedly heroic, albeit grossly mistaken, discoverer of America. But, starting at about the turn of the twentieth century, the story has come under increasingly skeptical scrutiny.

How, many historians have asked, could Columbus have been so wrong? And how, in the face of the overwhelming evidence that the lands he found were not China or Japan, could he continue to maintain that they were the Indies and that their people were "Indians"? Some historians have concluded that Columbus never intended to go to Asia at all and that his "Enterprise of the Indies" was just a ruse to throw other explorers off the track. They maintain that from the start, Columbus's goal was to discover a New World.

⌒∿

That Columbus was heading for the Indies is certainly what the explorer told the world, and contemporary chroniclers believed him. The most prominent of these was Bartolome de las Casas; he not only wrote the most comprehensive history of Columbus's voyages but also included in it parts of Columbus's own journals. (The originals have been lost.) The prologue to Columbus's journal, as recorded by Las Casas, seems as straightforward a description of Columbus's intentions as anyone could want. "Your Majesties," the explorer wrote to Ferdinand and Isabella, "decided to send me, Christopher Columbus, to those lands of India to meet their rulers and to see the towns and lands and their distribution, and all other things . . . and you ordered me not to go eastward by land, as is customary, but to take my course westward, where, so far as we know, no man has traveled before today."

In Columbus's October 21 journal entry, after he landed on what he described as an outlying island, he reported that he was still determined to reach the Asian mainland to deliver to the "Great Khan"—the Chinese emperor—letters of introduction from Ferdinand and Isabella. And on his way back to Spain, Columbus wrote to Ferdinand and Isabella that the fort he'd established would be convenient "for all kinds of trade with the nearest mainland as well as with . . . the Great Khan."

None of this would seem to leave any room for doubt about where Columbus was headed, or where he thought he ended up.

The second most important contemporary chronicler was Ferdinand Columbus, the explorer's son, and he was equally adamant about his father's intended destination. Ferdinand not only wrote the first biography of Columbus but also preserved his father's books—including marginal notes that were invaluable to future historians. These indicate that Columbus learned about Asia by reading the works of medieval writers such as Marco Polo and John Mandeville. He also apparently consulted Aristotle and Seneca, both of whom discussed the possibility of sailing west to the Indies. Two medieval books in the Columbus library—Pierre d' Ailly's *Imago Mundi* and Pope Pius II's *Historia Rerum*—venture various guesses about how narrow the ocean might be, and the relevant passages are duly underlined, presumably by Columbus himself.

Ferdinand's biography also included copies of the correspondence between his father and Toscanelli, the Italian geographer whose estimates of the distance between Europe and Asia provided Columbus with additional support for his theory. Toscanelli's letter, Ferdinand wrote, "filled the Admiral with even greater zeal for discovery." More dramatically, Las Casas wrote, it "set Columbus' mind ablaze."

But, though neither Las Casas nor Ferdinand Columbus had any doubts about Columbus's intended destination, both included a story that cast a very different light on Columbus's "Enterprise." The story first appeared in print in 1539, in Gonzalo Fernandez de Oviedo's history of the discovery of America. As Oviedo told it, a ship en route from

How could the most famous navigator of all time, here getting his first sight of the New World, have no idea what he was looking at? *(Library of Congress)*

Portugal to England ran into bad weather and was blown far to the west, ultimately reaching some islands inhabited by naked people. On the return trip, all but the pilot died. He washed ashore on the island of Madeiras, where Columbus lived on and off during the early 1480s. The pilot, too, soon died, but just before his death he drew a map of where he'd been and gave it to Columbus.

If the story of the "unknown pilot" is true, then Columbus did not set off into the great unknown bolstered only by an untested theory. If he had a map, he had a pretty good idea where he was going—and a pretty good reason to suspect it wasn't the Indies. But Oviedo, the first to tell the story, concluded that it probably wasn't true, and Ferdinand Columbus didn't believe it either. Las Casas was somewhat more credulous, noting that the story was widely circulated, but it certainly didn't shake his belief that Columbus was seeking the Indies. Later historians followed their lead, dismissing the story if they mentioned it at all.

It was not until the turn of the twentieth century that the unknown pilot found his champion.

ᗡᗡᗡ

Henry Vignaud's startling thesis, boldly stated in a number of volumes published early in the twentieth century, was that Columbus never intended to go to the Indies. The unknown pilot had told Columbus about America, and he wanted those lands for himself. So, knowing full well that the Indies were beyond his reach, he concocted his "Enterprise" merely to make sure no one else would beat him to America. And once the

Columbus myth had been established, Vignaud maintained, historians dared not challenge it, for fear that "the great undertaking which, as Columbus averred, he had organized for the purpose of carrying out a scientific idea . . . would have been reduced to the proportions of a vulgar voyage of discovery."

In other words, Columbus was a liar. And, according to Vignaud and his followers, the unknown pilot wasn't the only thing he lied about.

The journal, for one thing, was a fake, or at least sufficiently rewritten and falsified (by either Columbus or Las Casas) to conceal Columbus's true motive. The Toscanelli correspondence was also forged (either by Columbus or his son); after all, the only evidence of their letters to each other was in Ferdinand's biography, an authorized bio if ever there was one.

Skeptics such as Vignaud also brought to the fore some documents of their own, hitherto ignored or at least brushed aside. The most important of these was the contract between Columbus and the Spanish king and queen known as the "Capitulations." The Capitulations went into great detail about what would be Columbus's share of the profits from his trip, but they never mentioned the Indies. Most suspicious of all, the Capitulations empowered Columbus to "discover and acquire" any islands he came upon, a phrase the emperor of China would certainly not have appreciated. Indeed, it is difficult to imagine the emperor handing over any island to three lightly armed Spanish ships. Much more likely, Vignaud believed, was that Columbus (and Ferdinand and Isabella) had in mind the discovery and acquisition of some new, and to Europeans unknown, territory.

Traditionalists rose to Columbus's defense. Led by Samuel Eliot Morison, whose reputation as a sailor added tremendously to his credibility as a historian, the traditionalists responded that even though the Capitulations didn't mention the Indies explicitly, the references to Columbus's share of pearls, precious stones, and spices—all products of Asia—clearly indicated that was his destination.

As for the story of the unknown pilot, Morison scoffed at the landlubbers who'd swallowed it hook, line, and sinker. Here the historian's sailing expertise proved handy; he argued that the story was meteorologically impossible, since the prevailing winds wouldn't blow a vessel across the Atlantic from east to west.

Sure, Morison conceded, Columbus may have heard tales of islands to the west, and of exotic flotsam washing ashore on islands under Portuguese control. The explorer may very well have been influenced by some of the sea stories he heard. But there was no secret map or unknown pilot; Oviedo's story demonstrated nothing more, Morison wrote, than the "unfortunate tendency to pluck at the laurels of the great."

⸙

Morison's reputation and scholarship ensured that Columbus would not be toppled from his pedestal. But Vignaud and his followers did succeed in creating a great deal of doubt about the traditional story, especially as it pertained to Columbus's later voyages.

Columbus's voyage of discovery was just the first of four trips he made to the New World; he returned in 1493, and then again in 1498 and 1502. Somewhere along the way,

Vignaud's followers asserted, he must have noticed that the islands he found had little in common with anything described by Marco Polo and John Mandeville. Where were the great empires of China and Japan? Where were the streets of marble and the roofs of gold? Here were only primitive villages.

It was on his third voyage, perhaps, that Columbus came closest to recognizing the truth. In July 1498 he reached what is now known as Venezuela's Paria Peninsula, and he began to suspect that this was more than just an island off the coast of China. He looked at the broad delta of the Orinoco River and deduced, correctly, that such an enormous volume of freshwater could only come from a mainland of considerable size. In his journal, as recorded by Las Casas, Columbus wrote, "I believe this is a very great continent, until today unknown."

But after this brief moment of clarity, Columbus leaped to a conclusion far more preposterous than his original "Enterprise of the Indies." The new continent must be, he decided, the "Terrestrial Paradise," the legendary Garden of Eden. His subsequent letter to Ferdinand and Isabella was a strange mix of theology and geography: "I am completely persuaded in my own mind that the Terrestrial Paradise is in the place I have said," he explained, because it is "just above the Equator, where the best authorities had always argued Paradise would be found."

Then came an even stranger concept: the earth was not round, Columbus explained, but it "has the shape of a pear, which is all very round, except at the stem where it is very prominent . . . and this part with the stem is the highest and nearest to the sky." It was at this point nearest the sky that Columbus had found Eden.

Had Columbus lost his mind? Perhaps; he was under a great deal of pressure, and he was ill at the time. But it's more likely, in the opinion of most historians, that his "Terrestrial Paradise" grew out of his long-held conviction that his voyages were divinely inspired. Moreover, Columbus's belief that he'd found Paradise in no way contradicted his claim to be en route to Asia. As he wrote to the Spanish monarchs, Paradise was just where the authorities said it would be; indeed, several medieval Christian writers quoted in *Imago Mundi*, one of the well-read books in Columbus's library, located the Garden of Eden at the farthest point of the Far East.

In any case, Columbus later abandoned the idea of a Terrestrial Paradise. In 1502, during his fourth and final voyage to the New World, he proclaimed that he was searching for a strait by which he could pass through this new continent to reach Asia.

Most historians, still following Las Casas and Ferdinand Columbus and Morison, stressed that Columbus never realized the extent of this new continent; never, in fact, thought of it as a true continent. Rather, in Columbus's mind, it was an extension of the Malay Peninsula. It was, to be sure, larger than he'd anticipated, but Asia lay right beyond it, if only he could find a way through or around.

Most probably Columbus died believing that he'd reached the Indies. If so, Columbus was extraordinarily stubborn and single-minded; otherwise there's no way he could have ignored the evidence of his later voyages—or even, for that matter, his initial voyage.

Then again, it took an extraordinarily stubborn and single-minded man to convince Ferdinand and Isabella to finance his voyage, and to sail into the unknown.

To Investigate Further

Cummins, John. *The Voyage of Christopher Columbus.* New York: St. Martin's Press, 1992.
    The most recent translation of Columbus's journal is especially interesting because it incorporates the sections recorded by Ferdinand Columbus as well as those preserved by Las Casas.

Columbus, Ferdinand. *The Life of the Admiral Christopher Columbus by his Son Ferdinand,* trans. Benjamin Keen. New Brunswick, NJ: Rutgers University Press, 1959.
    Ferdinand, known as a somewhat bookish man, had a tendency to overemphasize the scholarly basis of his father's Enterprise of the Indies, sometimes at the expense of his father's more businesslike qualities. But he's still a remarkable biographer as well as son. The book was first published in 1571, thirty-one years after Ferdinand's death.

Vignaud, Henry. *The Columbian Tradition on the Discovery of America.* Oxford: Clarenden Press, 1920.
    Columbus was a fraud, and historians were his dupes.

Morison, Samuel Eliot. *Admiral of the Ocean Sea.* Boston: Little, Brown, 1942.
    Still the definitive biography.

———. *The Great Explorers.* New York: Oxford University Press, 1978.
    The section on Columbus includes a summary of the traditional view on Columbus's intended destination.

Sale, Kirkpatrick. *The Conquest of Paradise.* New York: Alfred A. Knopf, 1990.
    Sale offers one of the latest (and best) presentations of the Vignaud position as part of a more general attack on Columbus.

Wilford, John Noble. *The Mysterious History of Columbus.* New York: Alfred A. Knopf, 1991.
    An absorbing historiography.

Flint, Valerie I. J. *The Imaginative Landscape of Christopher Columbus.* Princeton, NJ: Princeton University Press, 1992.
    A fascinating, though somewhat academic, interpretation of the medieval sources of Columbus's view of the world; here is, Flint writes, "not the New World Columbus found, but the Old World which he carried with him in his head."

Phillips, William D. Jr., and Carla Rahn Phillips. *The Worlds of Christopher Columbus.* Cambridge, UK: Cambridge University Press, 1992.
    A balanced history of the explorer's life and times, especially strong on his time in Spain.

Davidson, Miles H. *Columbus Then and Now.* Norman: University of Oklahoma Press, 1997.
    A provocative but poorly organized critique of Columbus biographies.

PART 5

THE FIRST
GLOBAL AGE,
1450–1770

Where Did Columbus Land?

L EIF ERICSSON BEAT HIM HERE and perhaps others did as well. But it was Christopher Columbus's discovery of America that mattered most; once Columbus set foot on American soil, the New World and the Old were forever linked. Columbus's landfall was arguably the most momentous occasion in Western history. Yet more than five hundred years later, historians are still arguing about where it took place.

⌒₥₥⌒

To most historians the solution to the mystery was to be found in the *Diario,* a summary of Columbus's own shipboard log of the journey. Unfortunately the original version of the *Diario* has been lost; when Columbus returned to Spain, he presented it to Queen Isabella, and it hasn't been seen since. Fortunately two copies of the log were made. One ended up in the hands of a Dominican friar named Bartolome de Las Casas who included it in his *Historia de las Indias;* that same copy (or the other one) was also at some point in the hands of Columbus's son Fernand, who used it as a source for his biography of his father.

With the *Diario* in hand, historians have attempted three ways of solving what's become known as the "landfall problem." First, they've tried to track Columbus's westbound journey, starting from the Canary Islands off the coast of Africa and following the log's directions to see where he ended up. Second, they've tried going backward, taking as their starting point the north coast of Cuba (which is the first place Columbus visited whose identity is certain) and reconstructing his track between there and his first landing. And third, they've tried to match the log's descriptions of the islands Columbus visited with the current topography of the various possible landing places.

Using all three methods, historians have come up with about a dozen serious candidates for the honor of being the site of the first landfall. Foremost among them is the island of San Salvador, a small island in the northern Bahamas. San Salvador was first cited as the landfall by the Spanish historian Juan Bautista Muñoz in 1793. And San Salvador was also the name Columbus gave to the island of his landfall—but that's irrelevant to the case for this particular island because it was known as Watlings Island until 1926. At that time the island's British colonial government, trying to preempt other claimants, gave it the name San Salvador.

What mattered much more than the local government's endorsement was that of Samuel Eliot Morison in 1942. That was the year Morison published what is still considered the standard biography of Columbus. In it he stated in no uncertain terms that only San Salvador/Watlings fit Columbus's course and description as set down in the log.

Morison's prestige as both historian and navigator—he was a rear admiral in the navy and he scoffed at "dryadusts" who studied Columbus's voyages from their armchairs—all but ended the discussion for 40 years.

Gradually, however, other claimants chipped away at Morison's and San Salvador's position. In 1986 *National Geographic,* after spending one million dollars on a new study, lent its considerable prestige to the case for Samana Cay, a Bahamian island about 65 miles southeast of San Salvador. Samana Cay, too, had had many previous advocates, among them Gustavus Fox, who had been Lincoln's assistant secretary of the navy. (Morison and Fox were just two of the many admirals to be found on Columbus's track.) The *Geographic* study argued that Morison had failed to take into account the effects of currents and leeway (a ship's slow skid downwind), and it enlisted the aid of a computer to resail the routes electronically.

In 1991 other researchers, arguing that neither Morison nor the *Geographic* study had taken into account the effects of magnetic variation (don't ask!), located the first landfall further southeast, on the island of Grand Turk. Grand Turk, too, had had many early advocates, the first being Martin Fernández de Navarette in 1825.

As the landfall's quincentennial approached, the debate intensified, with proponents of one island or another seizing upon different passages in the *Diario* to demonstrate why no other island besides their choice fit the bill. San Salvador, which remained the orthodox position, came under the most attack, but strong cases were made for and against all the leading candidates. The only thing everyone agreed on was that Columbus's landfall took place somewhere in the Bahamas.

⟨∞⟩

Why couldn't all these sophisticated historians and mariners come to some sort of consensus? What was so difficult about comparing Columbus's words with the locations and characteristics of Bahamian islands?

For one thing, it's not so clear what Columbus's words were. Only 20 percent of the *Diario* is in his words; the rest consists of summaries and paraphrases by Las Casas. We can't even be sure that what Las Casas used hadn't been altered before it got to him.

Furthermore, even when you take the words that we're fairly sure are Columbus's own, you run into problems. To take just one example, the *Diario* says the landfall island has *una laguna en medio muy grande*—a very large lagoon in the center. Advocates of Watlings have been especially vehement in pointing out that only Watlings, of all the leading candidates, has a large body of water in the middle of the island. Advocates of Grand Turk and Samana Cay have argued that their islands may have dried up in the past five hundred years, that groundwater is seasonal in the Bahamas, and that we can't know for sure how much water there was on any given island then. But undeniably these are efforts to make the best of a description that favors Watlings.

What neither supporters nor detractors of Watlings take into account is that we have no idea what Columbus meant by a "large lagoon." Large compared to what? Landfall advocates compare the size of their various islands' waters but Columbus couldn't compare them; this was the first New World island he'd seen. What's more, the rest of the phrase—*en medio,* or in the middle—has been taken to mean in the middle of the island as it would be viewed from above; that is, a lake in the middle of the island. But what if you take "in the middle" to mean halfway up the shoreline? Then "laguna" might not mean lake, but "lagoon," as we use the word today. Suddenly Watlings, which has a lake but no lagoon, has lost its most compelling piece of evidence.

The point here is not to make a case against Watlings, or for any other island. Rather, it is to show, as the historian David Henige did most thoroughly in his 1991 book, that all these cases are based on a primary source that may be unreliable and is certainly vague. One revisionist historian has even speculated that Columbus was intentionally vague. Kirkpatrick Sale, a writer who admittedly doesn't like Columbus (he blames him for just about every instance of exploitation of land and people that has taken place in America since 1492), suggests that Columbus's descriptions were vague because he wanted to keep the location secret. If gold and glory were to be found on the landfall island or any other, Columbus wanted it for himself. As evidence, Sale points to a September 1493 letter from Ferdinand and Isabella to Columbus, in which the sovereigns demand more details about "the degrees within which the islands and land you discovered fall and the degrees of the path you traveled." There's no record of Columbus ever answering that letter.

One needn't attribute Columbus's vagueness to greed to admit the *Diario* isn't as useful a source as we'd like it to be. Perhaps it was that Columbus was (understandably) preoccupied. Perhaps he just didn't care about this island; had he returned to it during any of his three subsequent voyages to the New World, this mystery might be easily solved. Alas, the first time Columbus stepped on the landfall island was also the last time he did so.

᠀

So, we can't help asking: if this island didn't matter to Columbus, why should it matter to us?

One answer is that it shouldn't. Neither our understanding of American or European history, nor our understanding of Columbus's character, have changed the slightest bit as the result of conclusions on behalf of one island or the other. Except for a minor blip in a few islands' tourist trade, not much is at stake.

Many historians have, therefore, put the landfall question behind them, moving on to other questions. Perhaps the most hotly contested issue in recent Columbus scholarship has been not where the landfall island is, but where Columbus thought it was. And yet, even as other questions about Columbus have taken precedence, the landfall mystery has continued to intrigue historians, mariners, and others. With its tantalizing mixture of just enough evidence to get us close but not quite enough to get us there, it has again and again proven an irresistible challenge. Columbus's San Salvador, the native's Guanahani: this was, after all, the place where two worlds first collided.

To Investigate Further

Fuson, Robert. *The Log of Christopher Columbus.* Rockport, ME: International Marine Publishing Co., 1987.

Like most translations of the log, this one has an agenda: it was prepared in conjunction with the *National Geographic* case for Samana Cay. Still, it's a lively version.

Morison, Samuel Eliot. *Admiral of the Ocean Sea.* New York: Little, Brown, 1942.

Still the definitive biography, with the case for Watlings/San Salvador.

De Vorsey, Louis, Jr., and John Parker, eds. *In The Wake of Columbus.* Detroit: Wayne State University Press, 1985.

A wide-ranging collection of scholarly essays, with a concise historiography by Parker.

Judge, Joseph, and James StanWeld. "The Island Landfall." *National Geographic,* November 1986.

The case for Samana Cay.

Marvel, Josiah, and Robert Power. "In Quest of Where America Began." *American History Illustrated,* Jan/Feb 1991.

The case for Grand Turk.

Sale, Kirkpatrick. *The Conquest of Paradise.* New York: Knopf, 1990.

Even if you don't buy Sale's argument that Columbus embodies everything wrong with America, from enslaving blacks and Indians to destroying the environment, you'll still find him lively and provocative.

Henige, David. *In Search of Columbus.* Tucson: University of Arizona Press, 1991.

A critique of the flaws of the *Diario* as a primary source, and of the way it's been misinterpreted and manipulated.

Wilford, John Noble. *The Mysterious History of Columbus.* New York: Knopf, 1991.

A readable review of the ways historians from Columbus's time on have mythologized, debunked, and otherwise interpreted the man and his journeys.

How Did Cortés Conquer the Aztecs?

Hernán Cortés and his band of four hundred or so Spanish adventurers first sighted Tenochtitlán, the capital of the Aztec empire, in November 1519. With its busy canals, bustling markets, and beautiful buildings, Tenochtitlán might have reminded some of the Spaniards of Venice. For most of them, though, this was a far larger city than any they'd seen; Tenochtitlán's population of about 250,000 was larger than that of any city in Europe. The city was built on an island in the middle of a large lake near present-day Mexico City. Broad causeways stretched many miles across the lake, connecting the island to the mainland and to an Aztec empire that ruled over nearly four hundred cities and more than 125,000 square miles.

Unlike other Native American groups encountered by Europeans, the Aztecs were a highly organized, highly militarized people. Montezuma II, the Aztec emperor, commanded an army of more than 200,000 warriors, many seasoned in the far-reaching campaigns that had gained the Aztecs their empire. Yet two years after the Spaniards first set foot in Mexico, Tenochtitlán was in ruins and the remains of the empire were presided over by Cortés.

How was it possible for a few hundred Spaniards—acting on their own, with no support or supplies from the crown, and operating in territory that no European had even seen before—to conquer the Aztec empire?

⌀⟋⟋⟍⟍⟍

Most of our knowledge of the conquest comes to us from the conquistadores themselves. Cortés described the events in a series of letters to the Spanish king, Charles I. So did a number of others, most notably the foot soldier Bernal Díaz del Castillo, who participated in the conquest and wrote his recollections twenty years later, and Francisco López de Gómara, who wasn't a witness to the events but who later became private secretary and chaplain to Cortés.

Cortés set off for Mexico in March 1519 under the auspices of the Spanish governor of Cuba, Diego Velázquez. Velázquez ordered him to explore the Mexican coast and trade with any Indians he found there. Cortés, however, had bigger things in mind. Upon reaching Mexico's east coast, he announced (through an interpreter he'd picked up along the way) that he'd been sent by Charles I of Spain, the greatest king on earth, to speak to their leader. This was Montezuma, he learned. Cortés added that he'd also like some gold because, "I and my companions suffer from a disease of the heart which can be cured only with gold." Montezuma's messengers carried this message to Tenochtitlán and then returned with lavish gifts—including gold. But the emperor regretted he would not be able to meet with Cortés, they said.

If Montezuma thought gold would get rid of Cortés, he was tragically mistaken. The gold only whetted Cortés's appetite. He and his motley crew set off for Tenochtitlán, discovering to their delight that many of the cities en route deeply resented the tribute they were forced to pay the Aztecs. Far from resisting the Spanish advance, these people were happy to join forces with Cortés. Most significant of these allies were the Tlaxcalans, fierce enemies of the Aztecs whom the latter had never subdued.

And so it was that on November 8, 1519, Cortés, now accompanied by about five thousand Indian allies, reached the causeway leading to Tenochtitlán. Again, Montezuma chose a policy of appeasement; he welcomed Cortés and his army into his city, put them up in a luxurious palace, and served them sumptuous feasts. Still, after a few days, Cortés became uneasy. Though Montezuma continued to play the generous host, Cortés could sense the growing hostility of other Aztecs. Whatever its emperor's policies, this was, after all, a nation of warriors.

Cortés then came up with one of the most audacious plans in the history of war: he would take the emperor hostage in his own city. In the midst of one of the emperor's social calls, Cortés and his men did just that. For the next six months, with Montezuma as their prisoner, the Spaniards had the run of the city. But trouble was brewing on two fronts. The more hawkish Aztecs, uniting under the emperor's brother Cuitláhuac, seemed increasingly willing to attack the Spaniards, even if it meant risking Montezuma's life. Then, to make matters worse, a Spanish fleet sent by the Cuban governor Velázquez arrived on the Mexican coast. Velázquez was not at all happy that Cortés had turned his little trading mission into a major expedition; if there were riches to be had in Mexico, the governor felt, they were for him to discover, not Cortés.

So Cortés headed back to the coast, taking about 120 soldiers with him. He left just a hundred or so at Tenochtitlán under the command of Pedro de Alvarado. Once he reached the coast, Cortés put to work the same powers of persuasion that had won over so many Indians. And again he succeeded: after some minor skirmishes with Velázquez's soldiers, Cortés convinced most of them to join him. He headed back to Tenochtitlán with his new recruits.

Alas, in leaving Alvarado in charge in Tenochtitlán, Cortés had erred as greatly as Velázquez had when he chose Cortés. Alvarado had none of Cortés's subtlety, and in the midst of an Aztec religious festival he'd attacked and massacred the celebrants. The Aztecs, led by Cuitláhuac, counterattacked, and full-scale fighting had broken out. When Cortés reached Tenochtitlán, he discovered that his carefully cultivated Indian allies had fled, leaving the Spaniards trapped in the palace. Again, Cortés tried to use Montezuma to quell the Aztecs: he sent the emperor up to the palace roof to speak on behalf of the Spaniards. But by now the Aztecs would have none of this, and Montezuma was killed by stones thrown by his own people.

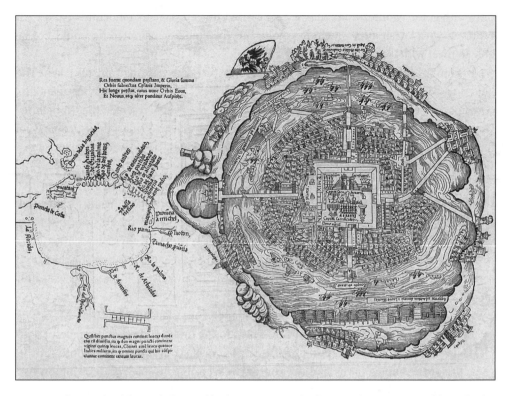

A map of Tenochtitlán and the Gulf of Mexico, made for Cortés in 1524. Although the European-style houses are certainly not authentic, the map does show Aztec temples, causeways across Lake Texococo, and other features of the city prior to its conquest. *(Bettmann/Corbis)*

Cortés then decided his best chance was to sneak out at night. On June 30, 1520, the Spaniards stuffed their pockets with Aztec treasure and headed for the causeways. But the Aztecs discovered them and attacked, killing more than half of the Spaniards. Many drowned in the waters around Tenochtitlán, weighed down by the gold in their pockets. "Those who died," de Gómara wrote, "died rich."

Cortés regrouped at Tlaxcala, his most loyal ally. He set to work building boats, which would cut off all access to Tenochtitlán. In late April 1521, the Spaniards set siege to the city, then began a bloody, house-by-house advance. Three months later, they again ruled Tenochtitlán—or what remained of the once great capital.

∞

This was the Spanish version of the conquest. The Spanish won because they were braver, more tenacious, more resourceful and, when necessary, ruthless in the service of their king and God; the Aztecs, and Montezuma in particular, were indecisive and cowardly. Still, a mystery remained. Why would Montezuma, whose past included many

battlefield victories, suddenly lose all heart when faced by the Spaniards? Cortés's letters
to the king of Spain contain his answer. When Montezuma first welcomed the Spaniards
into Tenochtitlán, the emperor spoke to Cortés, and Cortés's letter quotes him as follows:

> For a long time we have known from the writings of our ancestors that neither I,
> nor any of those who dwell in this land, are natives of it, but foreigners who come
> from very distant parts; and likewise we know that a chieftain, of whom they were
> all vassals, brought our people to this region. And he returned to his native
> land . . . and we have always held that those who descended from him would
> come and conquer this land and take us as their vassals. So, because of the place
> from which you claim to come, namely, from where the sun rises, and the things
> you tell us of the great lord or king who sent you here, we believe and are certain
> that he is our natural lord. . . . So be assured that we shall obey you and hold you
> as our lord in place of that great sovereign of whom you speak.

Montezuma, Cortés explained, had first mistaken Cortés for the Aztec god, Quetzalcoatl, who, according to Aztec legend, would someday return to rule his people. Later, as
in the above speech, Montezuma realized Cortés was not a god but still thought he was
the god's emissary. Either way, Montezuma's superstitious nature prevailed over his military judgment, and Cortés took full advantage of it.

It was not just the conquistadores themselves who explained the conquest thus.
Most historians followed suit, admiring Cortés for his courage and strategy, and ridi-
culing Montezuma's superstition-induced paralysis. Even those historians who have
denounced Cortés as a greedy imperialist, the destroyer of Indian culture, could only
pity Montezuma.

And yet, to many historians today, the above portraits of Cortés and Montezuma
don't ring true. Cortés's letters to King Charles I ought not to be considered an accurate
historical narrative, they argue. Rather, Cortés had a very specific purpose in mind: to
convince Charles that Cortés, and not Velázquez, ought to be granted the right to explore
(and conquer) Mexico. To make his case, Cortés was capable of grossly distorting history:
for example, according to some historians, the speech about Quetzalcoatl that Cortés put
into Montezuma's mouth is entirely apocryphal. Quetzalcoatl was indeed an Aztec god,
but he was worshipped in Cholula, not Tenochtitlán. Cortés may have heard the legend
on his way to Tenochtitlán and used it in his letter to show Charles how well he—as opposed to Velázquez—had mastered and manipulated the Aztecs on the king's behalf.

Alternative explanations for Montezuma's behavior have come from recent studies
of the Indian accounts of the conquest. To be sure, these accounts are also problematic;
they're fragmentary and, since the Aztec language was not a written one, they've come
down to us in versions recorded by Spaniards soon after the conquest. Still, the Aztecs'
own accounts, along with other studies of Aztec culture, do present another side of the
story. The Montezuma who emerges from these studies is reluctant to fight, but not

because he's superstitious or cowardly. This Montezuma shies away from battle with the Spaniards for many reasons: he's not sure whether to trust the Spaniards' talk of peaceful intentions, but he's very aware that they've arrived toward the end of the harvest season, and that many of his warriors are busy in the fields. At the very least, he may have been biding his time, hoping his emissaries could break up the alliances between the Spaniards and other Indian groups.

Historians have spent a great deal of energy debating what was going on in Montezuma's head. We can't know for sure why he let the Spaniards enter Tenochtitlán. In one sense, however, this debate is irrelevant to explaining the conquest: whatever Montezuma's motives, whatever the efficacy of his appeasement strategy, a better understanding of these issues could only help explain the first phase of the conquest—up until the death of Montezuma. After Montezuma's death, the Aztecs were ruled by the openly anti-Spanish Cuitláhuac. There was no longer any question that this was war, and that the Aztec empire was at stake. Yet even at this point, with the massive Aztec forces mobilized by a brave and competent chieftain, it took the Spaniards only a bit more than a year to regroup and return to besiege and overrun Tenochtitlán. To explain this second phase of the conquest, historians have had to shift their focus away from the debate about the relative merits of Cortés and Montezuma to other factors.

One obvious factor was the superiority of Spanish weapons. Against the Aztec arrows, the Spanish had cannons; while the Aztecs were on foot, the Spanish had horses. And the Spaniards' armor rendered Aztec arrows virtually useless.

Another factor was disease. A member of the crew sent by Velázquez had smallpox, and the disease swept across Mexico, whose people had never been exposed to the disease and who had no resistance to it. By 1558, the population of Mexico had been reduced from a preconquest figure of about ten million to a mere two or three million, and disease was undeniably a major factor in this. But smallpox struck down as many of Cortés's Indian allies as it did Aztecs, and it did not spread fast enough to account for the conquest on its own.

Yet another factor was the Aztec tradition of trying to capture, rather than kill, their enemies. This was hardly a compassionate tradition—many of those captured were later sacrificed to the gods and eaten by their captors, a practice that struck terror into the hearts of the most courageous Spaniards. But it did mean that in their efforts to capture rather than kill their enemies, the Aztecs often let them get away. Given the limited number of Spaniards, this undeniably aided Cortés's campaign.

All these factors played a role in the conquest. So, too, did Cortés's courage and strategy. Without a doubt, however, one of Cortés's greatest contributions to the Spaniards' success was his ability to enlist the support of Indian allies. More than anything else, this evened out the numbers on the opposing sides. Cortés admitted this; so did the Indian accounts of the conquest. Reliable numbers are hard to come by, but the Tlaxcalans alone added thousands of warriors to the Spanish ranks.

The empire that the Spaniards conquered was indeed a huge and powerful one. The Aztecs received tribute from far-flung cities and, in the absence of a major competing power, there was little these cities could do about it. But they deeply resented the Aztecs, and when the Spaniards arrived on the scene they offered a rallying point around which these disaffected cities could unite. For all of Cortés's efforts to portray himself as the only figure the king could trust to handle the Indians, it was not Cortés alone who brought down the Aztec empire; it was the Tlaxcalans and their allies, as much as the Spaniards, who were the conquistadores.

To Investigate Further

Pagden, Anthony, translator and editor. *Hernan Cortés: Letters from Mexico.* New Haven: Yale University Press, 1986.
  This translation of Cortés's letters includes a fascinating introduction in which J. H. Elliott convincingly demonstrates how Cortés's accounts of the conquest were slanted by his efforts to gain the king's support.

del Castillo, Bernal Díaz. *The Discovery and Conquest of Mexico.* Translated by A. P. Maudslay. New York: Farrar, Straus and Cudahy, 1956.
  A Spanish soldier's account of the conquest, written in 1555.

de Gómara, Francisco López. *Cortés.* Translated by Lesley Byrd Simpson. Berkeley: University of California Press, 1964.
  Cortés's secretary and chaplain's account of the conquest, written with Cortés's cooperation.

de Fuentes, Patricia, editor and translator. *The Conquistadors.* Norman: University of Oklahoma Press, 1993.
  A handy volume of excerpts from all the major first-person Spanish accounts of the conquest (except Díaz's).

de Sahagún, Bernardino. *Conquest of New Spain.* Translated by Howard Cline. Salt Lake City: University of Utah Press, 1989.
  Sahagún, a Franciscan friar, wrote this history in 1585 based on his interviews with Indians who'd survived the conquest. Though the Aztecs' recollections may have been colored both by Sahagún's mediation and by their own feelings toward the conquest, this is nonetheless the most valuable source of knowledge on the Aztec world.

Leon-Portilla, Miguel, editor. *The Broken Spears.* Boston: Beacon Press, 1962.
  An English translation (from the Spanish, which was itself a translation from the Aztec language, Nahuatl) of surviving Aztec descriptions of the conquest.

Prescott, William Hickling. *The Conquest of Mexico.* New York: Harper & Brothers, 1843; reissued by Modern Library (New York) 1936.
  Though dated by Prescott's nineteenth-century prejudices in favor of Cortés and against Indians, this remains a classic work of narrative history.

Todorov, Tzvetan. *The Conquest of America.* **New York: HarperCollins, 1984.**

Todorov, a French critic, attributes the conquest to the superiority of the Spaniards, not as fighters or strategists, but as communicators.

Hassig, Ross. *Aztec Warfare.* **Norman: University of Oklahoma Press, 1988.**

An ethnohistorian's view of the rise and fall of the Aztec empire, this makes clear the extent to which the empire's downfall was brought about by cleavages that preceded Cortés's arrival.

Clendinnen, Inga. "Fierce and Unnatural Cruelty." *Representations,* **Winter 1991.**

A highly provocative essay emphasizing how both the Spaniards and the Aztecs misunderstood each other and misrepresented the conquest.

Thomas, Hugh. *Conquest.* **New York: Simon & Schuster, 1993.**

Thomas's comprehensive narrative is as close as the twentieth century came to Prescott's history, and the wide range of scholarship incorporated in Thomas's work certainly supplants Prescott's.

Townsend, Camilla. "Burying the White Gods, *American Historical Review,* **June 2003.**

Debunks the idea that Montezuma thought Cortés was a god, and argues that the Aztecs did all they could, given their technological disadvantage.

Did Martin Guerre Return?

THE STORY OF MARTIN GUERRE generally begins with his marriage, in 1538, to Bertrande de Rols. This was meant to consummate a union between the Guerres and the Rols, two prosperous peasant families in the village of Artigat, in southwestern France. The marriage got off to a rocky start.

The problem, though both families blamed sorcery, was most likely the ages of the bride and the groom: Bertrande was only nine or ten; Martin, fourteen. It took eight years to consummate the marriage, a delay that was undoubtedly humiliating to Martin. So was a huge family fight—in 1548—during which Martin's father accused him of stealing some grain. Soon after, the young man abandoned his wife and disappeared without a trace.

Eight years later, after the death of both his parents, Martin Guerre returned to Artigat. He explained that he'd crossed the Pyrenees, joined the Spanish army, and fought in the Netherlands. The experience, it seemed, had changed him: he was a more confident figure, easily adapting to his role as the family's new patriarch, and he was a kinder and more loving husband. His family and his wife were delighted to have him back.

Then, late in 1558, Martin asked his uncle, Pierre Guerre, for his share of the profits from the family farm during his absence. This did not sit well with Pierre. He angrily pointed out that for the eight years Martin was gone, he'd not just run the farm but also taken care of his nephew's wife and son. Pierre's distrust of the prodigal son increased the next year, when two soldiers passing through the village said they'd served with Martin Guerre and that he'd lost a leg during the war. Yet the Martin in Artigat clearly had both legs.

Pierre was now convinced that his adversary was not only greedy but also an impostor. The dispute led to a series of trials, culminating in an appeal before the Parlement of Toulouse in 1560. One of the judges there, Jean de Coras, wrote a book about the case that remains the primary source for most of what historians know about it.

The Toulouse proceedings were extraordinary. Most of the inhabitants of Artigat and many from surrounding villages were called as witnesses. Among those who testified against the defendant were Pierre, Pierre's sons, Bertrande's mother (who had since married Pierre), and the village shoemaker (who declared that the "new" Martin's feet were inexplicably smaller than the "old" Martin's). Also highly damaging was the testimony of a number of inhabitants from the nearby town of Le Pin; they recognized the defendant as a former fellow townsman, a scoundrel named Arnaud du Tilh, alias Pansette.

There was also plenty of testimony on behalf of the defendant. Martin's four sisters stated that the man on trial was without a doubt their brother. The defendant himself answered all questions with confidence, recalling in detail events from his childhood and adolescence. Above all, Bertrande—though she had joined Pierre in signing the complaint that led to the trial—now refused to swear that the accused was not her husband.

The judges, Coras included, were perplexed. But they noted that the financial dispute between Pierre and the defendant created a strong motive for a false accusation by the uncle. They were also swayed by the defendant's perfect recall and by the fact that Bertrande, the one who knew him best, had backed away from her accusation. The judges, Coras wrote, were "more disposed to the advantage of the prisoner and against the said Pierre Guerre."

Then came a denouement that would have left John Grisham shaking his head. As the judges were about to announce their decision, in walked a man with a wooden leg. He said his name was Martin Guerre.

The defendant objected strenuously. He claimed Pierre must have bribed someone to play the part, and he barraged the newcomer with questions, some of which the witness seemed less sure about than the defendant. But the defendant's case was collapsing around him. Martin's sisters deserted him, hugging the newcomer. Then Bertrande was brought into the courtroom, and after one look, she began to tremble and weep. She ran to embrace the newcomer and begged him to forgive her for having been fooled by the impostor.

Coras and his fellow judges were no longer in doubt. Arnaud du Tilh, alias Pansette, was found guilty of "imposture and false supposition of name and person" as well as adultery and was sentenced to be hanged. The sentence was carried out in Artigat on September 16, 1560.

Just before he died, Arnaud du Tilh confessed. He said the idea for the crime had first come to him when some acquaintances of Martin's had mistaken him for Guerre, and that he then learned as much as he could about him. Once Bertrande accepted him, he was able to learn even more from her, though she was entirely unaware of what he was doing.

Even so, questions remained. How could Arnaud have fooled an entire village, including Martin's wife and family? Was Bertrande as completely duped as she claimed? And what prompted Martin's timely return just when Pierre's case seemed lost?

⟨∞⟩

Coras's explanation to the first two questions was that Arnaud was a remarkably talented trickster, and his account of the trial reveals a grudging admiration for the story's villain. "It was truly a tragedy for this fine peasant," the judge wrote, "all the more because the outcome was wretched, indeed fatal for him." Bertrande's gullibility was also easily explained, given "the weakness of her sex, easily deceived by the cunning and craftiness of men." Moreover, Coras believed, she would have put aside any doubts because of her loyalty to the man she believed was her husband and, perhaps, because of her gratitude that he was back.

As for the timely appearance of the one-legged man, Coras admitted it seemed like a miracle. He concluded it was the work of God.

Coras's version of the events satisfied his sixteenth-century readers, of whom there were many. His book *A Memorable Decision* was reprinted five times in the six years after it was published, and several more editions in French and Latin appeared later in the century. An account by a young lawyer named Guillaume Le Sueur was also published in 1561 and presented a broadly similar account of the case.

Still, at least one contemporary commentator expressed some doubts about whether Coras had discovered the full story. This was the renowned essayist Michel de Montaigne. Montaigne suggested that Coras would have been better off following the example of the ancient Athenians who, when they found a case particularly difficult, told the parties to come back in a hundred years. In other words, Montaigne felt, the death sentence was very harsh, given the unanswered questions.

But it was Coras's account, not Montaigne's, that remained the standard for more than four hundred years. Then, in the 1980s, a French moviemaker and an American historian turned the traditional version on its head.

ꝏ

Natalie Zemon Davis, the author of the 1983 book *The Return of Martin Guerre*, was also a consultant to the screenwriters Jean-Claude Carriere and Daniel Vigne on the 1982 movie. In both the movie and the book, Bertrande is dramatically transformed. No longer Arnaud's dupe, she is now his full-fledged partner. She is now sort of a prefeminist heroine, a woman characterized by, in Davis's words, "a stubborn independence and a shrewd realism about how she could maneuver within the constraints placed upon one of her sex."

Bertrande, in Davis's version, knew that Arnaud was a fraud almost from the start. But she saw in him the chance to escape from her shaky and uncomfortable role as an abandoned woman, neither wife nor widow. That Arnaud turned out to be a much kinder man and a better lover than Martin made him "a dream come true, a man she could live with in peace and friendship . . . and in passion." So Bertrande filled in Arnaud on all the details of Martin's life he needed to know, and she made sure everyone else in the village knew that there was no doubt this was her husband.

Once Pierre turned on Arnaud, however, Bertrande's position was again in jeopardy, so she resorted to a delicate strategy. She pretended to side with Pierre by joining him in signing the complaint against Arnaud. That way, if Pierre won, she'd avoid his wrath. At the same time, she attempted—subtly, so Pierre couldn't tell—to undermine his case in court by refusing to swear that the defendant was not her husband. Pierre, like Coras, might attribute her hedging to a woman's weakness, but it was actually a calculated and brilliant performance.

In fact, had it not been for the untimely appearance of the real Martin, Bertrande's strategy might have succeeded, and she and Arnaud could have lived happily ever after. As it was, she recognized that the return of the real Martin Guerre doomed Arnaud, so she quickly abandoned her lover and embraced her husband.

What was most remarkable about Davis's inversion of the traditional account is that it did not depend on the discovery of some new account of the trial that contradicted Coras's. Though she drew upon various other court records, Davis's history was based largely on a careful rereading of Coras's book.

Davis found in Coras's work a profound ambivalence about the case that previous commentators had overlooked and that Coras himself had perhaps tried to suppress. For example, in explaining his reasons for finding Bertrande innocent of any collusion with Arnaud, Coras stressed the need to keep together husband and wife. "In doubtful situations the law commands that the presumption in favor of marriage triumph over any other," he wrote. This sounds more like a pardon than a resounding statement of Bertrande's innocence.

Davis also pointed out that the real Martin Guerre—the man with the wooden leg—was extremely skeptical about his wife's innocence. In response to Bertrande's plea that he forgive her for having fallen for Arnaud's trick, Guerre remained (this still according to Coras) "austere and fierce." Without even looking at his wife, he responded: "Don't excuse yourself by my sisters nor by my uncle: for there is neither father, mother, uncle, sister, or brother who must better know their son, nephew, or brother than wife must know her husband. And for the disaster that has befallen our house, no one has the wrong but you."

Underlying Coras's ambivalence about Arnaud and Bertrande, Davis believed, were religious doubts. Protestantism was spreading throughout southwestern France, and though the peasants of Artigat remained Catholics, Bertrande would have been attracted to the new religion's teaching that a wife deserted by a husband is free to remarry after a year. This was, of course, not her position at the trial, where she maintained Arnaud was her Martin. But privately, she and Arnaud may have drawn upon Protestant ideas to justify their actions.

Coras, too, though nominally a Catholic, was certainly sympathetic to Protestantism, and Davis believed that played a role in his initial impulse to find Bertrande innocent, even though he seemed to have considerable doubts. Coras's Protestant tendencies later became more overt—so much so that, in October 1572, in front of the same Parlement building in Toulouse where Arnaud du Tilh was condemned, Coras himself was put to death on a charge of heresy.

⟨⟩

Davis's version of the story was not universally accepted. Some historians believed she was reading into Coras's text more than was there and that her book was more of a historical romance than a history. Others criticized both the traditional version and Davis's for too readily accepting that the man with the wooden leg was the real Martin Guerre. They, like Arnaud before the court, argued that Pierre could have found a one-legged man, and paid him to show up at just the right moment.

Overall, though, most scholars have accepted Davis's reinterpretation. One of the leading historians of the period, Emmanuel Le Roy Ladurie, said that *The Return of Martin Guerre* was a great book and an even better movie. Even one of her fiercest critics, Robert Finlay, praised Davis's work as "imaginatively conceived, eloquently argued, and intrinsically appealing."

One of the most appealing aspects of Davis's work is that she herself concedes that her interpretation is open to doubt; indeed, her book is to some considerable extent a meditation on the difficulties historians face in trying to figure out what's true and what's not. Those doubts are compounded by a case like Martin Guerre's, where Arnaud and Bertrande and even Coras may have had very good reasons for concealing the truth.

The final words of Davis's book could just as easily apply to most of the other historians discussed in this book. "I think I have uncovered the true face of the past," she wrote, "or has Pansette done it again?"

To Investigate Further

Coras, Jean de. "A Memorable decision of the High Court of Toulouse, containing the prodigious story of our time of a supposed husband, enriched by one hundred and eleven fine and learned annotations . . ." An English translation by Jeannette K. Ringold appears in *Triquarterly* 55 (Fall 1982).

The original was published in 1561.

Montaigne, Michel de. "Of Cripples," in *The Complete Essays of Montaigne*, trans. from the French by Donald M. Frame. Stanford, CA: Stanford University Press, 1965.

Montaigne's comments on the Guerre case appear, fittingly, in an essay on our limited ability to discern the truth. The essay was originally published in 1588.

Zemon Davis, Natalie. *The Return of Martin Guerre.* Cambridge, MA: Harvard University Press, 1983.

Who would have thought that a scholarly study of sixteenth-century peasant life could also be a tragic love story?

Finlay, Robert. "The Refashioning of Martin Guerre." *American Historical Review* 93, no. 3.

In Finlay's view, Davis has perpetrated a fraud almost as ingenious as Arnaud's. "The virtues of *The Return of Martin Guerre* are clear," he writes. "Unfortunately, none of the central points of the book—the knowing Bertrande, the devious court strategy, the tragic romance, the Protestant justification, the self-fashioning peasants, the conflicted judge, the 'multivalent' text—depend on the documentary record."

Davis, Natalie Zemon. "On the Lame." *American Historical Review* 93, no. 3.

Davis's response to Finlay.

Guneratne, Anthony. "Cinehistory and the Puzzling Case of Martin Guerre." *Film & History* 20, no. 4.

Guneratne suggests that Pierre may have worked with Arnaud in an effort to consolidate his landholdings. Later, after their falling out, Pierre may have found another impostor to stage the last-minute courtroom drama.

Did Mary, Queen of Scots, Murder Her Husband?

I T OUGHT TO HAVE BEEN EASY for Mary Stewart to find a suitable husband. She was young (twenty-two). She was beautiful (a countenance," wrote Sir Walter Scott, "the like of which we know not to have existed"). And, unlike her cousin, England's Queen Elizabeth, she was conventionally feminine in her outlook, at least to the extent that she longed for a man on whom she could depend. Perhaps most attractive of all, to any potential suitor, was her dowry: since Mary was queen of Scotland, her husband would be a king.

Yet the man she married in July 1565—Henry Stuart, the earl of Darnley—was about as poor a husband as could be imagined. Superficially, to be sure, he had some fine traits. Like Mary, he was young, good-looking, and a cousin of Elizabeth. The last put Henry close behind Mary in line for the English throne, and Mary therefore had some reason to hope that the marriage would strengthen her own claim to be Elizabeth's successor.

Alas, as Mary quickly learned, Henry's good qualities were all on the surface. He turned out to be spoiled, lazy, and no help at all when it came to governing the country. By the end of 1565 Mary was ignoring her husband and leaning heavily on the advice of other advisers, particularly a onetime musician from Italy named David Rizzio.

Henry, for his part, deeply resented Rizzio's influence, as did many others in the Scottish nobility. That Rizzio was foreign and, like Mary, a Catholic, especially outraged many of the Protestant lords. In March 1566 a group of them broke into the queen's quarters, dragged out the screaming Rizzio, and stabbed him to death. Henry himself did not participate in the murder, but he was definitely part of the conspiracy; to leave no doubt about that, the murderers carefully left Henry's dagger in Rizzio's body.

Still, Mary continued to play the part of the dutiful wife. Even though Henry was suffering from syphilis, she persuaded him to return from his family's home near Glasgow. In February 1567 Henry moved to Kirk o' Field, a house on the outskirts of Edinburgh, where Mary dutifully nursed him back to health.

But the royal reconciliation was short lived. On February 9 Mary left the house to attend a servant's wedding in the city, and a few hours later, Kirk o' Field blew up. Henry's body was found in the garden; he had apparently escaped the explosion, only to be smothered outside.

The man behind the assassination, most observers were convinced, was Henry's longtime enemy James Hepburn, the earl of Bothwell. It was no surprise, then, when Bothwell was indicted for murder in April. The more contentious question was Mary's role in the murder. Contemporary Catholic writers such as Bishop John Leslie instantly rose to her defense, portraying her as more innocent than the Virgin Mary. Protestant writers, most notably George Buchanan and John Knox, were equally vehement that she was guilty.

Mary herself denied that she had anything to do with her husband's death, and many seemed willing to accept her word. But her credibility soon plummeted. On May 15, just three months after the king's murder, the queen remarried. Her new husband was none other than the earl of Bothwell, the prime suspect in Henry's murder.

⸺⸻⸺

The marriage to Bothwell, even more than the murder of Henry, spelled the end of Mary's reign. Bothwell was a powerful lord, but he didn't have the network of alliances with other nobles that was critical for a sixteenth-century Scottish king. As for Mary, her support among the Protestant lords, always tenuous, evaporated entirely after the marriage. In what many considered a desperate attempt to restore her reputation, Mary claimed that she married Bothwell because he abducted and raped her. Few believed the story.

In June 1567, with the support of much of the Scottish public, a band of disaffected nobles defeated the forces of Mary and Bothwell, and imprisoned the queen at Lochleven Castle. A month later, unable to withstand their threats, Mary agreed to abdicate. She turned over the throne to her infant son, James, whose government was led by Mary's half brother, James Stewart, the earl of Moray. A year later, Mary escaped from Lochleven and attempted to regain the throne, but Moray's forces again defeated hers, this time in a decisive battle near Glasgow on May 13, 1568. Three days later Mary fled to England, hoping to convince Elizabeth to help restore her to the throne.

For Elizabeth, Mary's presence created a quandary. On the one hand, the sight of any queen toppled from her throne could only make the queen of England uneasy. On the other hand, to restore Mary to power would require the defeat of the pro-Protestant, pro-English party in Scotland, something Elizabeth was also loath to see. Elizabeth decided to appoint a commission to investigate the whole affair.

The commission was the first chance both sides had to present their cases. (Bothwell's murder trial in April 1567 had shed little light on the crime; with the court surrounded by about two hundred of his armed supporters, his acquittal was assured and meaningless.) The English commissioners met throughout 1568 and 1569, first at York, then at Westminster, and finally at Hampton Court.

Moray himself arrived at Westminster in December 1568 to argue the case against Mary. His evidence electrified the proceedings. Moray brought with him what had up to then been only a rumor—a series of letters and sonnets, allegedly written by Mary to Bothwell, in which she expressed her passionate love for Bothwell and her equally passionate hatred for Henry.

To quote from the letters, Mary wrote to Bothwell that she wanted only to be "between your arms, my dear life." (And this while Henry was still alive.) She would do whatever he asked; he needed only to "send me word what I shall do." As for Henry, the sentiments expressed in the letter were clear: "Cursed be this pocky fellow that troubleth me thus much."

The letters were extremely incriminating, since they made Mary out to be both murderer and adulterer. But Mary denied the letters were hers, and her defenders were quick to label them forgeries. And, indeed, there was much about the letters that was suspicious. For one thing, Mary's supporters demanded to know, why were the letters kept secret until the commission met?

According to Moray, his government had been in possession of the letters since June 1567, when they captured Bothwell's servant, George Dalgleish. Dalgleish had led them to the silver "casket" that contained the documents. Yet, as Mary's defenders pointed out, Moray waited more than a year before making public this vital evidence. This would have given him plenty of time to forge the documents, then present them to the commissioners at the most opportune moment. Moreover, by the time Moray reached Westminster, Dalgleish—the only one who could contradict his story—had been conveniently executed for helping Bothwell murder Henry.

The content of the letters was also questionable. None was dated and none was signed, so there was no way to know for sure that the letters were written by Mary, as opposed to some other lover of Bothwell. The love sonnets were in a style wholly unlike Mary's known poetry, and the poetess, whoever she was, seemed impressed by Bothwell's wealth—an unlikely sentiment for the queen, who was far richer than Bothwell. All this convinced many of Mary's defenders that the Casket Letters were a mix of outright forgeries and actual documents that were doctored to appear to be Mary's.

Elizabeth's commissioners never ruled on the authenticity of the documents, nor did Elizabeth herself. Instead, they decided that there was no proof that either Moray or Mary had acted dishonorably. This was legally illogical, but it made political sense, at least for the short term. Moray could return to Scotland, where he could continue to rule as England's Protestant ally. Mary would remain in England, and in fact would remain in prison, but at least Elizabeth had not passed any judgment against her that would have offended Catholics at home or abroad.

In the long run, however, Elizabeth still had a problem. As long as Mary was alive, she could continue to be a focal point for Catholic plots to regain the British as well as the Scottish throne. Mary willingly participated in at least three such conspiracies, the last of which involved a plan to assassinate the British queen. This was the final straw for Elizabeth; faced with overwhelming evidence of Mary's role in the assassination plot, she reluctantly ordered her execution. Mary was beheaded on February 8, 1587.

As for Bothwell, his end was even grimmer. He sought refuge in Denmark, where the king was as unhappy to see him as Elizabeth was to see Mary. The king threw him into the fortress of Dragsholm, where the prisoner was chained to a pillar half his height. The cruel conditions drove Bothwell insane, and so he remained until his death in April 1578.

⬥

As long as Elizabeth lived, Mary continued to be portrayed in starkly contrasting extremes. To Protestant writers, she was a papist plotter; to Catholics, an innocent martyr. Once Elizabeth died, and was succeeded by Mary's son James, these perspectives gave way to something of a compromise. What emerged was the image, still familiar today, of a romantic heroine brought down by bad luck and bad loves.

The new image served James well. As a Protestant king ruling two Protestant countries (England and Scotland), he could hardly allow a martyred Mary to continue to inspire Catholic hopes and dreams. At the same time, he would have found the venomous Protestant portraits of Buchanan and Knox equally objectionable; after all, this was his mother they were talking about.

Thus was born a convenient and neat compromise. But, though it may have satisfied the political needs of the moment, it ducked the question of whether the Casket Letters were genuine or forged. True to form, James tried to eliminate the question by eliminating the evidence. Sometime early in his reign, and while they were in the possession of his government, the letters disappeared—and they haven't been seen since.

That didn't stop subsequent historians from speculating about them. In the absence of any new evidence, most tended to repeat the same arguments that Moray and Mary raised before Elizabeth's commissioners. Most twentieth-century historians, citing the inconsistencies in the letters' styles and contents, have leaned toward thinking them some combination of outright forgeries and doctored documents. But with the originals gone, the mystery of the letters can't be definitively resolved.

Historians also continue to debate the more fundamental question of Mary's role in Henry's death, about which there is plenty of evidence besides the Casket Letters. Much of that evidence ties Mary to the murder. Her coaxing Henry to return to Edinburgh, in spite of his role in Rizzio's murder and his syphilis; her departure from the house just hours before the explosion; her marriage to Bothwell just months after the murder—all are suspicious. Even if she wasn't aware of the particular plot to blow up Kirk o' Field, she must have known that something was going on. And her eager involvement in later plots to get rid of Elizabeth indicates that Mary had no qualms about political assassinations.

That's not to say that Mary, even if she knew something was going on, was the monster portrayed by Buchanan and Knox. Sixteenth-century royal politics were a dirty business, and Mary's behavior was no dirtier than those of many of her counterparts, Elizabeth included. The difference was that Elizabeth played the game well and won. Mary, for all her beauty and charm, never could keep up with her cousin.

To Investigate Further

Buchanan, George. *The Tyrannous Reign of Mary Stewart*, trans. and ed. W. A. Gatherer. Edinburgh: University Press, 1958.
Includes Buchanan's 1571 *A Detection of Mary Queen of Scots* and the relevant sections of his 1582 *History of Scotland*. A pretty good idea of Buchanan's attitude toward Mary can be gauged

from his tale (completely invented) of how Mary's servant was ordered to haul a half-naked Bothwell up by a rope out of his wife's bed and directly into that of the queen.

Phillips, James Emerson. *Images of a Queen.* **Berkeley: University of California Press, 1965.**
How her contemporaries turned Mary into a symbol of everything good and everything evil.

Armstrong Davis, M. H. *The Casket Letters.* **Washington, DC: University Press of Washington, D.C., 1965.**
Armstrong Davis argues that the letters were forged to frame Mary. So certain is Armstrong Davis of Mary's innocence that he also argues, much less persuasively, that the Kirk o' Field explosion that killed the king was actually Henry's botched attempt to kill Mary.

Fraser, Antonia. *Mary Queen of Scots.* **New York: Delacorte Press, 1969.**
At once scholarly and romantic.

Donaldson, Gordon. *The First Trial of Mary, Queen of Scots.* **New York: Stein & Day, 1969.**
A thorough study of the York, Westminster, and Hampton Court hearings, with a somewhat less sympathetic view of Mary than Fraser's.

Cowan, Ian, ed. *The Enigma of Mary Stuart.* **London: Victor Gollancz, 1971.**
A useful collection of too-short excerpts from various works on Mary, from the sixteenth century to the twentieth.

Plaidy, Jean. *Mary Queen of Scots.* **New York: G. P. Putnam's Sons, 1975.**
Not surprisingly, since Plaidy is also a best-selling writer of romance fiction (under the pseudonym Victoria Holt), this biography presents the Mary of romance, a woman who unwisely let her heart prevail over her head.

Wormald, Jenny. *Mary Queen of Scots.* **London: George Philip, 1988.**
A portrait of Mary as abject failure, so devoid of political judgment and will that she drove her opponents to take action against her.

Weir, Alison. *Mary, Queen of Scots and the Murder of Lord Darnley.* **New York: Ballantine, 2003.**
The case for the defense.

Guy, John. *Queen of Scots.* **Boston: Houghton Mifflin, 2004.**
A superb and sympathetic biography that exonerates Mary and blames many of her woes on Elizabeth's adviser William Cecil.

What Happened
to the Lost Colony?

NINETY MEN. SEVENTEEN WOMEN. NINE CHILDREN.

These were the colonists who landed on Roanoke Island off the coast of what is now North Carolina in July 1587—20 years before John Smith reached Virginia and 35 years before the Pilgrims reached Massachusetts. Among them was Eleanor Dare, the daughter of the colony's governor, John White. She was about to give birth, and that child—appropriately named Virginia Dare—would be the first European child born in the New World, assuming no anonymous Norse child had preceded her.

White stayed in America for the birth of his granddaughter, then set sail for England to arrange additional supplies for the colony. When he returned three years later, the colonists had vanished; the only clues to their whereabouts were the letters CROATAN, carved on a post, and CRO on a nearby tree.

Had the colonists quickly carved these messages while under attack from Indians? White thought not: he'd instructed them to carve a cross if they were in trouble. Did the colonists mean they'd gone to join the friendly Indians on nearby Croatan Island? That, too, perplexed White: he'd discussed with the colonists the possibility of heading north toward the Chesapeake Bay, but Croatan Island was south of Roanoke Island.

Bad weather prevented White from looking further and forced him to return to England, but by no means did that end the search. To the Jamestown settlers later on, the fate of the Roanoke colonists was no mere history exercise; they believed, quite reasonably, that it might be the key to understanding how they themselves could survive in the New World, and John Smith led a number of expeditions in search of his predecessors. More recently, historians and archaeologists have continued the search. And though no white person ever again saw the "lost colonists," those on their trail have turned up some tantalizing clues and proposed some engaging scenarios.

ᏩᎢᏣᎤᎤ

The fate of the Lost Colony is very much bound up with the fate of Sir Walter Raleigh. This was the same Walter Raleigh who, legend has it, spread his best cloak over a puddle before the queen. Perhaps, perhaps not. In any case, whatever he did to charm the queen was worth hundreds of cloaks—for Raleigh became such a favorite that in 1584 Elizabeth granted him an exclusive patent to colonize America.

Within a month he arranged a reconnaissance voyage to North America. It returned later in the year with enthusiastic reports of abundant Carolina resources and friendly

Carolina Indians. Raleigh did not delay: in April 1585 he sent off one hundred colonists in seven ships. They arrived at Roanoke Island later in the year, built a fort, and appointed Ralph Lane as governor.

This, then, was the first Roanoke colony, and the first British colony in America. It was founded two years before the Lost Colony, and its fate, in contrast, is well known.

It was a remarkably ill-conceived colony. Lane was a soldier, as were most of the colonists. What they had in mind for Roanoke was a base for attacking Spanish ships en route from South America. Their plan was to get rich on Spanish treasure; building houses and toiling in the American soil was not for them. They quickly came to depend on friendly Indians for food, and they almost as quickly alienated the Indians. (Lane's idea of diplomacy was to kidnap the favorite son of the powerful chief Menatonon and hold him hostage until the chief gave Lane information about other tribes' defenses.) By the spring of 1586 the colonists were out of supplies and allies and in desperate straits.

Fortunately help appeared on the horizon in the form of a fleet of ships commanded by Sir Francis Drake. But Drake was as much a privateer as the Roanoke colonists. He had come in order to use the colony as a base for his attacks on the Spanish; he could offer the colonists guns but no butter. And when a storm sunk four of his ships he could barely offer them passage home. In fact, to make room for the Roanoke colonists, Drake had to leave behind some African slaves and Indians he had liberated from the Spanish. These slaves and Indians were never heard from again; they were as "lost" as the more celebrated "lost colonists" of John White.

A few weeks after Drake, Lane, and the rest of the colony set sail for England, a relief party sent by Raleigh arrived. (On the way they'd been delayed by an irresistible urge to attack some Spanish ships.) When they found the colony deserted, they turned around, leaving behind a holding party of 15 men. None of them were ever heard from again, either.

✺

Now we get to the "real" lost colony, a colony which ironically was much better prepared to survive in the New World than Lane and company. However greedy a privateer Raleigh was, he was a man who could understand what had gone wrong and act to correct it. For his next colony, instead of the authoritarian Ralph Lane, he chose as governor the artist John White. (White was a superb artist; his drawings of Indian life are still among the best sources for anthropologists and historians.) Instead of soldiers, Raleigh chose colonists whose interest was in building a colony, and he granted them land as incentive to work and stay. Women and children came along, with more planning to follow. And instead of the sandy soil of Roanoke, this new group was to settle in the Chesapeake Bay, not far from where Jamestown would eventually take root. In short, the colony Raleigh sent to America in 1587 was, much more even than Jamestown, the prototype for later successful colonies.

What went wrong?

To begin with, the ships somehow ended up at Roanoke again, instead of on the Chesapeake. Then the ships' pilot, a Portuguese named Simon Fernandes, announced it

If John White made an ineffectual governor of Roanoke, he was nonetheless a superb artist; witness his drawings of Indian life, such as this one engraved in 1590 by Theodor de Bry. *(Library of Congress)*

was too late in the year to take the colonists any further. According to White's letters (one of the primary sources for exploring the mystery of the Lost Colony), greed was the motive of Fernandes; like so many associated with the Roanoke ventures, he was a privateer. He dumped the colonists at Roanoke so he could run off and attack some Spanish ships. More generous interpreters have argued that Fernandes might have been trying to do the colonists a favor. The pilot had had some previous experience in Chesapeake Bay while in Spanish service, and he may have told the colonists (quite accurately) how warlike the Indians in the area were, and how they had wiped out a Jesuit mission there in 1570.

Whatever reasons Fernandes had for staying at Roanoke, White acquiesced. Perhaps he felt Fernandes had the upper hand and there was nothing he could do about it. Perhaps, though he wouldn't admit it, he was happy to be back on familiar ground—despite the inadequacy of the site and the bad relations Lane had generated with the Indians. Perhaps—and this is the most likely explanation—White was an admirable artist but an ineffectual leader.

In any case, Fernandes stuck around for a month, departing in August 1587 and taking White with him. Here's another mystery: why would the colony's governor leave the colony, not to mention his newborn granddaughter? According to White, the colonists insisted that only he could be counted on to make sure that they were not forgotten by their backers. More likely, they were fed up with his vacillating leadership and decided he'd be more use to them back in England.

Again White let them down; it was not until three years later that he returned and by then, as we've seen, it was too late. For this, however, it's not really fair to blame White. He worked tirelessly on behalf of the colonists but his timing couldn't have been worse. For one thing, Raleigh's interest was waning: he had put a lot of money into the venture and didn't feel he could keep doing so, especially since the earl of Essex had replaced him as the queen's favorite. More ominously, the Spanish had grown tired of British privateering and had decided to cut it off at its base. With the Spanish Armada on its way, Elizabeth was taking no chances. In April 1588 she ordered all ships capable of war service—including those White was putting together to go back to Roanoke—to stay put. Even after the Armada was defeated, Elizabeth feared a new attack and was reluctant to let ships go. And so it was not until 1590 that White finally returned to find—or rather, not find—his colony.

∾

What happened to the colonists?

White himself was sanguine. He knew they had planned to move eventually anyway. He found no cross anywhere, and he clearly remembered instructing them "that if they should happen to be distressed in any of those places, they should carve over the letters or name, a Crosse." White couldn't explain why they would have changed plans and gone south instead of north, nor did he explain how they were supposed to carve a cross at Roanoke if they ran into problems elsewhere. Still, everything seemed pretty much in order at the fort and there definitely was no cross there. White was relieved.

Meanwhile, back in England, Raleigh's position was deteriorating. He'd secretly married, and when Elizabeth found out she did not take it well, imprisoning both groom and bride in the Tower of London. When he was released, he found himself exiled from the court. In 1595 Raleigh finally made it to America—but now it was the South American coast that attracted him. Roanoke seemed far away and unimportant. Some historians have argued that Raleigh intentionally abandoned the search to protect his patent, which required him to have a settlement. As long as he could claim the colonists were alive somewhere in the area his patent was safe; further searches might risk proving they were dead. In 1602 Raleigh did send a party to search further but it turned up nothing new.

It was not until after Jamestown was settled in 1607, therefore, that the search continued in earnest. That same year George Percy of Jamestown described seeing an Indian with "a head of haire of a perfect yellow and a reasonable white skinne, which is a Miracle amongst all Savages." And John Smith, in *A true relation of such occurrences and accidents of noate as hath hapned in Virginia,* told of meeting an Indian chief who told him "of certaine men cloathed at a place called Ocanahonan, cloathed like me." William Strachey's 1612 *Historie of Travell Into Virginia Britania* describes how Indians told him of "howses built with stone walls, and one story above another, so taught . . . by the English."

Strachey also told of the slaughter of the lost colonists by Powhatan, the father of Pocahontas. Strachey's story went as follows: The colonists did head north, as White planned, eventually finding their way to the Chesapeake Bay. There they lived in peace for about 20 years with the Chesapeake Indians. Then, just about the time the first Jamestown colonists were arriving, Powhatan went to war with the Chesapeakes, slaughtering both the Indians and the settlers.

This was the story the Jamestown settlers settled on. It explained both the persistent rumors of lost colonists in the area and the failure to actually find them.

Other solutions to the mystery have been proposed in the centuries since then. Some suggested the lost colonists were lost at sea, trying to get back to England. But that's unlikely—they didn't have a large enough boat to cross the Atlantic. Others suggested they were killed by Spaniards. Also unlikely—since Spanish documents show they were still looking for the English colony as late as 1600. Still others claim today's Croatan Indians are the direct descendants of the lost colonists, pointing to some linguistic similarities between the Indians' language and English. But these can more easily be explained by hundreds of years of contacts with European immigrants.

So Strachey's story, which the Jamestown settlers believed, may very well be the truth. One modern historian, David Beers Quinn, has added a new twist. Most of the colonists, he believes, moved north, thus accounting for the rumors and reports that reached Jamestown. At least a few stayed behind for a while longer, however, perhaps to wait for White or to hold the fort, and these were the colonists who ultimately headed south to Croatan, thus accounting for the signs on the tree.

Archaeologists continue to search for clues and they may someday be able to tell us more about what happened to Raleigh's lost colonists, or Drake's lost freedmen. As for Raleigh himself, though he may have given up on his Roanoke colony, he never gave up on America. He found himself even more out of favor with Elizabeth's successor, James I, than he'd been with Elizabeth, and he spent twelve years in the Tower. He was released in 1616, tried to win back his wealth and power with another expedition to South America, failed, and was executed.

And the much maligned John White? A John White, "late of parts beyond the seas," was declared dead in Ireland in 1606. But his was such a common name historians can't be sure this was the former governor. The fate of John White, like that of his daughter and granddaughter, remains something of a mystery.

To Investigate Further

Harriot, Thomas. *A Briefe and True Report of the New Found Land of Virginia.* Frankfort, 1590; reprinted by Dover, NY, 1972.

One of the greatest mathematicians of the Renaissance, Harriot accompanied the 1585 expedition and produced this report, which includes White's drawings.

Hakluyt, Richard. *The Third and Last Volume of the Voyages, Navigations, Traffiques and Discoveries of the English Nation.* London: George Bishop, Ralph Newberie, and Robert Barber, 1600; reissued by Viking (New York), 1965.

What we know about the Lost Colony and about all the British expeditions to America is largely thanks to Hakluyt, who collected the narratives, letters, and reminiscences of Raleigh, White, Lane, and others.

Quinn, David Beers. *England and the Discovery of America, 1481–1620.* New York: Knopf, 1974.

No one has devoted more time and pages to the mystery of the Lost Colony, or to the British explorations and settlements in general. Sometimes Quinn goes way out on a limb, as when he suggests that the British discovered America before Columbus, or (some say) when he explains what happened to the lost colonists. But Quinn always lets you see the evidence on which his theories are based and, given the evidence we have so far, his theory about the Lost Colony is more plausible than anyone else's.

Stick, David. *Roanoke Island.* Chapel Hill: University of North Carolina Press, 1983.

One of a number of very readable histories to appear around the settlement's 400th anniversary.

Kupperman, Karen. *Roanoke: The Abandoned Colony.* Totowa, NJ: Rowman & Alanheld, 1984.

An attempt to present Quinn's ideas in a less academic, more popular style; as such, it's successful, but it's well worth the effort to read Quinn's own work.

Hume, Ivor Noel. *The Virginia Adventure.* New York: Knopf, 1994.

Reports from the area's leading archaeologist; informative and entertaining.

Miller, Lee. *Roanoke.* New York: Arcade, 2001.

Miller blames the colony's failure on conspiracies in England, then presents linguistic and cultural evidence that the colonists ended up scattered among various tribes.

Who Wrote Shakespeare's Plays?

B IOGRAPHIES OF SHAKESPEARE, wrote Mark Twain in 1909, were like the brontosaur that stands in the Museum of Natural History. "We had nine bones, and we built the rest of him out of plaster of paris."

Twain was exaggerating, as was his wont. But he had a point: for all the millions of words written about Shakespeare, not much was known about him. About the only things his biographers could say for sure were that he lived in the town of Stratford-on-Avon; that he was the son of a glovemaker; that he became an actor of bit parts; and that he invested, quite successfully, in a theater company known as the King's Men. There are records of his baptism, his marriage, his lawsuits, his taxes, his death. And that's about it; the rest, as Twain put it, was plaster of paris.

Nothing in the Stratford documentary record gives any indication that Shakespeare was a writer, let alone the world's greatest. There are no manuscripts in his hand, or even letters. There are no signatures, except for six shaky scribbles. There's no mention in his will of books or manuscripts or anything at all literary. There's no record that he attended grammar school in Stratford, or that he traveled abroad, or that he had any close connections to anyone in the queen's court. Yet, somehow, to judge from his plays and poems, Shakespeare acquired an extensive knowledge of Italy, of royalty, of philosophy, literature, history, law, and medicine.

The one obvious link between the man from Stratford and the playwright was the name: Shakespeare. Yet even that raised doubts. In the Stratford documents, the name is spelled a variety of ways—as Shaxper or Shagsber or Shakspere. In the published versions of the works and in the contemporary references to them, it's always Shakespeare or Shake-speare.

To Twain, the explanation was clear: the playwright and the poet was not the same man as the glovemaker's son. Precisely who did write the plays Twain couldn't say for sure. But others could. Through the years, they've proposed scores of candidates, among them Queen Elizabeth, King James, Walter Raleigh, Christopher Marlowe, and (apparently based on the premise that "Sheik" sounds like "Shake") an Arab sheik known as El Spar.

ᏉᎢᎦ

There may have been rumors about Shakespeare in the first two centuries after his death, but it was not until the 1800s that they created a serious stir. This was the heyday of the Romantics, for whom Shakespeare was the very embodiment of poetry, and the more they venerated his works, the harder it was for them to reconcile the plays and the poems with their author's mundane life in Stratford. Even as devout a Shakespearean as

Coleridge was amazed "works of such character should have proceeded from a man whose life was like that."

As the century progressed, the anti-Stratfordians coalesced around a single candidate, Francis Bacon. Bacon had all the credentials that Shakespeare lacked: Bacon was a philosopher, a scientist, a lawyer, and a politician who frequented the courts of both Elizabeth and James. He found his most zealous champion in an American woman named Delia Bacon (no relation), who was convinced that papers proving her namesake's authorship were buried in a hollow space beneath Shakespeare's gravestone in Stratford. In September 1856 she showed up there, shovel in hand. At the last minute her nerve failed her, and she left Shakespeare's bones undisturbed. But she continued to preach the gospel to a growing audience of believers.

Later Baconians dropped the search for buried manuscripts and instead concentrated on the existing ones. It was a strangely narrow scrutiny, however. The Baconians focused almost entirely on the discovery of ciphers, cryptograms, and codes—all purportedly revealing that Bacon was Shakespeare—that were supposedly embedded in the texts. The leading decoder was Ignatius Donnelly, a congressman from Minnesota who took on all sorts of eccentric causes, Bacon's among them.

Much of Donnelly's 1888 book on the subject is too convoluted to follow, involving all sorts of calculations based on adding, subtracting, dividing, and multiplying the page, line, and word numbers of various words in the text, such as "Francis," "William," "shake," and "spear." A few of his findings are pretty straightforward, however; for example, Donnelly noticed that in the *First Folio,* a 1623 collection of Shakespeare's plays, the word "bacon" appeared on page 53 of the histories and also on page 53 of the comedies. For Donnelly, this couldn't be a coincidence; it had to be the author's way of revealing his true identity.

Others followed Donnelly's lead, apparently convinced that whoever wrote Shakespeare's plays and poems was primarily interested in creating elaborate brainteasers for future generations to solve. Walter Begley, for example, studied the last two lines of one Shakespeare poem: "The Romaines plausibly did consent/ To Tarquins everlasting banishment." Begley pointed out that if you combined the first two letters of the last word in the last line (ba) and the first three letters of the last word in the second-to-last line (con) you discovered the poem's true author. Like Donnelly, Begley ignored the role of chance; it apparently didn't occur to him that the letters in Bacon's name are all pretty common and could be found close together in plenty of other texts, Shakespearean and non-Shakespearean.

Inevitably, the cryptographers were especially drawn to a nonsense word used by a clown in Shakespeare's *Love's Labour's Lost.* The word—honorificabilitudinatibus—had enough letters to contain a jumbo assortment of secret messages. One of the best "solutions" came in 1910, when Edwin Durning-Lawrence rearranged the letters to spell "Hi ludi F. Baconis nati tuiti orbi." Translated from the Latin, that read: "These plays F. Bacon's offspring are preserved for the world." What Durning-Lawrence conveniently ignored was that honorificabilitudinatibus was a word that had been around for a while before it appeared in *Love's Labour's Lost,* so Bacon couldn't have designed it to hide his coded message.

By 1920 the Baconians' zest for secret messages had cost them much of their credibility, even among those skeptical of Shakespeare's authorship. Most Shakespeare scholars dismissed the Baconians as cranks and crazies and didn't even deign to comment on their work. But as the Baconian era waned, a new and more credible candidate—Edward de Vere, the seventeenth earl of Oxford—moved to the fore.

ᴖᴕᴕᴖᴖ

The case for de Vere, which was set forth in 1920 by an English schoolmaster with the unfortunate name of J. Thomas Looney, appeared to be a strong one. In addition to being the earl of Oxford, de Vere was a cousin of Queen Elizabeth and the ward and later the son-in-law of the lord treasurer, William Burghley. All this gave him more than a passing familiarity with a courtier's life. Best of all, de Vere was an established poet and playwright; in 1598, a contemporary critic named Francis Meres listed de Vere as "the best for Comedy among us."

Unlike Bacon, de Vere would have had good reasons to keep his authorship secret, since the theater was considered a disreputable venue in the circles in which he traveled. Besides, some of those in Elizabeth's court might not like the way they or their ancestors were being portrayed. So, Looney argued, de Vere used a pseudonym. But the earl couldn't resist dropping some hints about his secret identity, so he chose a name derived from one of his crests, which pictured a lion shaking a spear.

Since the earl was a nobleman, his life was much more thoroughly documented than Shakespeare's, and Looney found plenty there to link de Vere and his alleged works. It was known, for example, that de Vere traveled to Italy in 1575, stopping in Padua, Genoa, Venice, and Florence. This could explain the detailed knowledge of these parts evident in Shakespeare's plays.

The most compelling evidence, Looney believed, could be found in Shakespeare's— or rather, de Vere's—most famous play. Like Hamlet's father, de Vere's died young; like Hamlet's mother, de Vere's quickly remarried. De Vere once stabbed a servant of Burghley, which is how Hamlet killed Polonius. And de Vere, again like Hamlet, was captured by pirates, who then spared his life. By the time Looney had finished his analysis, Shakespeare's tragedy seemed to be de Vere's autobiography.

Looney found reflections of de Vere's life in other Shakespeare characters as well. Like Lear, De Vere was a widower with three daughters, of whom the elder two were married. Like Falstaff, he was known for his sharp wit. And like Prospero in *The Tempest,* de Vere had faced stormy weather—albeit metaphorically—in his life.

As for Shakespeare's sonnets, Looney concluded that Henry Wriothesley, the earl of Southampton, fit the role of Shakespeare's "fair youth." Later Oxfordians took this one step farther, speculating that Wriothesley was de Vere's son and that "fair youth" was a punning reference to "Vere youth."

⌘

By the mid-twentieth century, the Oxfordians had routed the Baconians to dominate the anti-Stratford position. But, to the academic establishment, the new pretender was no less preposterous than the old.

Indeed, the Oxfordians' efforts to find parallels between de Vere's life and Shakespeare's work suffered from the same obsessive tendencies and loss of perspective as the Baconians' codebreaking. The Oxfordians were determined to force fictional characters into historical figures, but they did so very selectively. For example, as many traditional scholars pointed out, the Oxfordians completely ignored the glaring fact that it was Shakespeare, not de Vere, who named his son Hamlet.

Another major problem with the Oxford-as-Shakespeare theory had to do with the dates of Shakespeare's plays. According to most scholars, the King's Men continued to produce new Shakespeare plays until 1614. But de Vere died in 1604. At that point, only twenty-three of Shakespeare's thirty-eight plays had appeared in published editions or been mentioned in printed sources. So there are fifteen plays—including *King Lear*, *Macbeth*, *Antony and Cleopatra*, *The Winter's Tale*, and *The Tempest* (certainly some of the playwright's most accomplished works)—that weren't staged until after de Vere's death.

Some Oxfordians responded to the dating problem by suggesting that de Vere must have started the plays before he died, then someone else finished them. Others went farther, arguing that the dates assigned to the plays were wrong and that almost all of them were written before 1604. The Oxfordians, like all other anti-Stratfordians, had going for them the general dearth of documentation that has plagued all of the traditional biographers. They were correct to assert that some of the plays' dates were based on some speculation and extrapolation, but they were wrong to claim that they were therefore arbitrary.

On the contrary, the traditional dates are based on a variety of contemporary references to Shakespeare and his works. For example, Francis Meres's 1598 work lists twelve of the plays and lauds Shakespeare's works as "most excellent" for comedy and tragedy. This is the same Meres who, you'll recall, the Oxfordians embraced for his praise of de Vere as a writer. But they conveniendy disparage his testimony when it's used to support the traditional dating. Moreover, Meres's work raises another embarrassing question for Oxfordians: If their man wrote Shakespeare's plays, why are de Vere and Shakespeare discussed separately in the same work?

Other contemporary references to Shakespeare also bolster the traditionalists' case. Robert Greene mentions Shakespeare in a 1592 pamphlet, and Ben Jonson does so in a number of works. The Oxfordians have argued that Meres and Greene and Jonson all could have been using de Vere's pen name, just as we might refer to Samuel Clemens as Mark Twain, but this seems unlikely. Jonson's 1623 eulogy of Shakespeare refers to him as the "Sweet Swan of Avon," and it's hard to imagine he was thinking of anyone other than the man from Stratford-on-Avon. For most scholars, Jonson's words clinch the case for Shakespeare as Shakespeare.

Still, the Oxfordians and the Baconians—at least those who have not been carried away by their passions—deserve credit for pointing out the gaps in the record and for raising questions that the Shakespeare establishment would have preferred to ignore. In the past decade, the works of the latest Oxfordians, such as Charlton Ogburn and Joseph Sobran, have gained some grudging respect from traditional scholars. Increasingly, academics have taken it on themselves to respond to the anti-Stratfordians, and those responses have themselves been useful and provocative.

That's not to say that the Oxfordians have won over many Shakespeareans to their side. For the vast majority of scholars, the documentary record, though limited, is clear and sufficient. As Shakespearians often joked, the man who wrote Shakespeare's plays was Shakespeare.

The Oxfordians have accused academics of snubbing them because they were amateurs. But the greater snobbery is to assume that only a university-educated aristocrat could turn out to be a literary genius. Shakespeare should not be denied his achievement just because he was the son of a small-town glovemaker.

To Investigate Further

Bacon, Delia. *The Philosophy of Shakspeare's Plays Unfolded.* London: Groombridge & Sons, 1857.

Nathaniel Hawthorne, who wrote the preface to Bacon's book, was apparently moved by her sincerity but disheartened by her increasingly obsessive need to haunt the graveyards where she was convinced proof of Bacon's authorship would be found. His preface concludes that "it is for the public to say whether my countrywoman has proved her theory." Later Hawthorne came to regret even that tepid support, stating that "this shall be the last of my benevolent follies, and I never will be kind to anybody again."

Donnelly, Ignatius. *The Great Cryptogram: Francis Bacon's Cipher in the So-Called Shakespeare Plays.* Chicago: R. S. Peale, 1888.

According to Donnelly, Bacon wrote not just Shakespeare's plays but also (in his spare time) Spenser's *The Faerie Queene* and Sidney's *Arcadia*.

Twain, Mark. *Is Shakespeare Dead?* New York: Harper & Brothers, 1909.

Twain was actually as concerned with the general question of literary immortality (including his own) as he was with Shakespeare's. But he's always delighted to insult the experts, whom he calls "these Stratfordolaters, these Shakesperiods, these tugs, these bangalores, these troglodytes, these herumfordites, these blatherskites, these buccaneers, these bandoleers. . . ."

Durning-Lawrence, Edwin. *Bacon Is Shakespeare.* New York: John McBride Company, 1910.

Say what you will about Durning-Lawrence, he was a good loser. So confident was he that he'd solved the *honorificabilitudinatibus* problem that he offered a hundred guineas to anyone who came up with another anagram with the same qualities. A Mr. Beevor proposed Abi Invit F. Bacon Histrio Ludit, which translated as "Be off, F. Bacon, The actor has entered and is playing." Durning-Lawrence paid him the money.

Looney, J. Thomas. *"Shakespeare" Identified.* New York: Frederick A. Stokes Company, 1920.
   The Oxfordian Looney should not be confused with George Battey the Baconian.

Hoffman, Calvin. *The Murder of the Man Who Was Shakespear.* New York: Julian Messner, 1955.
   The case for Marlowe, which starts off with the great advantage that he was a much more important writer than de Vere. But, like the Oxfordians, the Marlovians have to get around the basic problem of their hero's death, in this instance a much-publicized murder in 1593. Hoffman's answer is that Marlowe faked his own death to avoid being prosecuted for heresy.

Wadsworth, Frank. *The Poacher from Stratford.* Berkeley: University of California Press, 1958.
   A fair and succinct summary of the rival claims up to that time.

McManaway, James. *The Authorship of Shakespeare.* Amherst, MA: Folger Shakespeare Library, 1962.
   The establishment position, as issued by the establishment.

Schoenbaum, S. *Shakespeare's Lives.* Oxford: Clarendon Press, 1991.
   A scholarly yet highly readable survey of Shakespeare's biographers.

Ogburn, Charlton. *The Mysterious William Shakespeare.* McLean, VA: EPM Publications, 1992.
   Ogburn, the leading Oxfordian, inherited the mantle from his parents, both of whom also wrote books on the subject. Ogburn has been more successful than any of his predecessors in forcing the academic establishment to pay attention, and his book even earned a respectful response in the mainstream journal *Shakespeare Quarterly.*

Matus, Irvin Leigh. *Shakespeare, in Fact.* New York: Continuum, 1994.
   A systematic rebuttal of the anti-Stratfordian arguments.

Michell, John. *Who Wrote Shakespeare?* London: Thames & Hudson, 1996.
   The most recent and most compelling case that Shakespeare's works were a group effort involving Bacon, de Vere, Marlowe, and Shakespeare himself.

Sobran, Joseph. *Alias Shakespeare.* New York: The Free Press, 1997.
   One of the best of the pro-Oxford books.

Greenblatt, Stephen. *Will in the World.* New York: Norton, 2004.
   Greenblatt's deservedly popular biography has been criticized by some scholars for leaping to conclusions based on the limited evidence of Shakespeare's life. Greenblatt makes no apologies, arguing that "to understand how Shakespeare used his imagination to transform his life into art, it is important to use our own imagination."

Did Pocahontas
Save John Smith?

I N December 1607, just a few months after the first permanent British colony in
America was established at Jamestown, Captain John Smith led a trading party up the
Chickahominy River. He was captured by Indians and taken before the great chief,
Powhatan, who ruled over much of Tidewater Virginia. In *The Generall Historie of Vir-
ginia, New-England, and the Summer Isles,* Smith himself told what happened next:

> A long consultation was held, but the conclusion was, two great stones were
> brought before Powhatan: then as many as could layd hands on him, dragged him
> to them, and thereon laid his head, and being ready with their clubs to beate out
> his braines, Pocahontas the Kings dearest daughter, when no intreaty could pre-
> vaile, got his head in her armes, and laid her owne upon his to save him from
> death: whereat the Emperour was contented he should live to make him hatchets
> and her bells.

Is Smith's story true? Did the Indian princess throw herself between Smith and the
tomahawks heading toward his "braines"?

ᠺᠣᠣᠣ

Among the first and most adamant to call Smith a liar was Henry Adams in the mid-
nineteenth century. He pointed out that Smith's earlier histories of Virginia made no
mention of Pocahontas saving him; it was not until the 1624 *Generall Historie* that Smith
published the story. By then, Adams argued, those who could have refuted it—such as
Pocahontas herself—were dead. With no other English-speaking witnesses besides Pocahontas, it came down to Smith's word.

The rest of the *Generall Historie* didn't do much to increase the value of that word.
Smith told some remarkable—some would say incredible—tales. Seemingly least credible
of all was that Pocahontas was just one of four foreign ladies who, unable to resist Smith's
charms, came to his rescue. Before coming to Virginia, Smith had joined the Austrian
armies fighting against the Turks in Hungary. He was captured by the Turks and made a
slave in Constantinople. There his luck improved: his mistress, "the beauteous Lady
Tragabigzanda," took a liking to him, treated him well, and then sent him to her brother in
Tartary, from where he escaped. He ultimately reached a Russian garrison where "the good

189

Lady Callamata . . . largely supplied all his wants." And when Smith escaped some pirates, it was "the good Lady Madam Canoyes" who "bountifully assisted me."

All this from the *Generall Historie*—all this about a very short, bearded, battle-scarred man whose portraits are distinctly underwhelming. No wonder that some of Smith's contemporaries called him a braggart and a liar, and many historians agreed. But then, in 1953, the tide of opinion turned. That year Bradford Smith's biography of Smith appeared, with an appendix on the captain's Hungarian adventures written by Laura Striker Polanyi. Polanyi carefully checked Smith's narrative of the wars against the Turks; to almost everyone's surprise, everything that could be checked turned out to be accurate.

The case for Smith was further strengthened by ethnohistorians. Their work showed that Smith's descriptions of Indian life and culture were realistic. In fact, his works are considered an important primary source for those studying Indian history and culture. Geographers, too, came to admire the accuracy of Smith's maps of Chesapeake Bay and New England.

Smith's defenders took the offense, accusing Henry Adams and his followers of denigrating the man because he was a southerner. After all, Adams was the great-grandson of John Adams and the grandson of John Quincy Adams. Both Adamses were New Englanders to the core and were bitter political enemies of John Randolph, a Virginian—and a descendant of none other than Pocahontas. (Yet another noncoincidence: the first to answer Henry Adams in print was William Hirt Henry, grandson of Virginia's Patrick Henry.)

With Smith's reputation on the upswing, it was time to put aside sectionalist politics and Balkan adventures, and look anew at his relationship to Pocahontas.

◦

The strongest case against the Pocahontas rescue story remained that Smith never published it until his 1624 *Generall Historie.* That he left it out of his 1612 work, *A Map of Virginia,* was fairly easy to explain: that dealt mostly with geography and ethnology and not with Smith's own explorations and adventures.

But why was the story nowhere to be found in Smith's 1608 work, *A True Relation of Such Occurrences and Accidents of Noate as Hath Hapned in Virginia?*

Smith's apologists have offered a number of suggestions. Perhaps, they've argued, it was for the sake of public relations. *A True Relation* was written to encourage investment and settlement in Virginia, and stories of hostile Indians didn't help that cause. Some speculated that the Pocahontas story might have been cut by an over-zealous editor. But, Smith's detractors were quick to point out, *A True Relation* contained plenty of stories about Indians attacking Jamestown settlers—with endings much bloodier and unhappier than that of the Pocahontas story.

So the pro-Smith, pro-truth-of-the-story faction presented a variety of other arguments. In 1608, they said, Smith respected Powhatan; in 1609 he learned of Powhatan's role in killing the Roanoke colonists and his later works therefore portrayed the chief as much more bloodthirsty. Smith's supporters even used his reputation as a braggart to defend him, arguing that he might have left out the Pocahontas story simply because he was embarrassed that he needed an Indian princess—and an eleven-year-old at that—to save him. They also noted that the *Generall Historie* was a longer book with lots of details and stories that weren't in the earlier works. Perhaps Smith left out the Pocahontas story from his earlier works for no particular reason at all; his was a life full of hairbreadth escapes from death and, until Pocahontas later became a celebrity in England, Smith's encounter with her might not have seemed of much importance to him. He had no way of knowing that a few words in the *Generall Historie* were to become the basis of America's version of Romeo and Juliet, or of what Henry Adams called "the most romantic episode in the whole history of his country."

Finally, Smith's supporters pointed out that Smith had included the Pocahontas story in at least one work prior to the *Generall Historie.* This was his letter to Queen Anne, dated June 1616. Pocahontas had by then married the Englishman, John Rolfe, and moved to England. With plans underway for her to meet the royal family, Smith took it upon himself to do the introductions. His letter to the queen tells a story much like that in the *Generall Historie:* " . . . at the minute of my execution, she hazarded the beating out of her owne braines to save mine, and not onely that, but so prevailed with her father, that I was safely conducted to James towne . . ."

The letter was dated 1616, when Pocahontas was still alive and presumably could have denied the story. But it did not appear in print until 1624, as part of the *Generall Historie.* By then, Pocahontas had died. So, again, we have only John Smith's word to go by.

⌀⌀⌀

Perhaps the best way to determine the truth of Smith's story is to ask, simply: does it make sense?

Some of the legend that's surrounded it makes no sense at all and can be summarily dismissed. For one thing, there was never a love affair between John Smith and Pocahontas. In 1607 Pocahontas was eleven years old; John Smith was 27. She may have had a crush on him but there's no evidence it was more than that. It was John Rolfe, not John Smith, whom she married in 1614. If there was any sort of special relationship between Smith and Pocahontas—and, according to the *Generall Historie,* she did come to his aid and the colony's a number of other times—it was not a romantic one. Nor did Smith ever claim otherwise.

As for the claims Smith did make: do they make sense?

No.

Smith said he was spared "to make him hatchets, and her bells." Powhatan had no shortage of hatchets or bells; he knew very well that Smith was a leader of the English and worth a lot more than a few hatchets or bells. Nor is there any reason to believe a powerful warrior and chief would be swayed because of his daughter's plea.

But this does not mean Smith was a liar. More likely, the incident did take place much as Smith described but he misunderstood what was going on. According to Smith's account, Indians prepared to "beate out his braines" by feeding him extravagantly and parading him before the various tribes; right before they were to kill him one Indian woman brought him water to wash his hands and another brought feathers to dry them. All this sounds like a carefully orchestrated ceremony. In all likelihood, the "rescue" of Smith by Pocahontas was also part of the ceremony.

Many historians have suggested that the rescue was part of a traditional ritual of death and rebirth that accompanied adoption into an Indian tribe. The archaeologist and historian Ivor Noel Hume argued that it was not a traditional ritual but a conscious effort on Powhatan's part to try to turn Smith into an ally. To have executed Smith, Hume wrote, would have been to bring down on Powhatan the wrath of the English, and Smith had made clear there were plenty more Englishmen across the water. Better to stage a ceremony that might leave Smith both intimidated and grateful.

Smith, of course, understood none of this. He was indeed intimidated by Powhatan and grateful to Pocahontas. And who can blame him?

To Investigate Further

Barbour, Philip L., ed. *The Complete Works of Captain John Smith*. Williamsburg, VA: Institute of Early American History and Culture, 1986.
  Decide for yourself whether you believe him.

Kupperman, Karen Ordahl. *Captain John Smith*. Williamsburg, VA: Institute of Early American History and Culture, 1988.
  Selected writings for those who don't quite need all of the above.

Smith, Bradford. *Captain John Smith*. Philadelphia: Lippincott, 1953.
  Includes Striker Polanyi's groundbreaking work on the Hungarian episodes and, until Barbour's, the best defense and biography of Smith.

Barbour, Philip L. *The Three Worlds of Captain John Smith*. Boston: Houghton Mifflin, 1964.
  Still the most widely respected biography, this argues that the Pocahontas episode was true (though Barbour later expressed some doubt about it).

———. *Pocahontas and Her World*. Boston: Houghton Mifflin, 1970.
  Adds little to the above.

Vaughan, Alden T. *American Genesis*. New York: Little, Brown, 1975.
  A short—and on the subject of the Pocahontas story, inconclusive—biography of Smith.

Gerson, Noel B. *The Glorious Scoundrel*. New York: Dodd, Mead, 1978.
  Argues that Smith not only made up the story but that he never even met Pocahontas until she came to England.

Lemay, J. A. Leo. *The American Dream of Captain John Smith*. Charlottesville: University Press of Virginia, 1991.

Part of a backlash against the "politically correct" scholarship that has placed Smith at the front of a long line of Europeans who have exploited Native Americans, this polemic portrays Smith as a friend and admirer not just of Pocahontas but of all Indians. However, it doesn't add much substance to Barbour's work and even Smith, braggart that he was, might have been embarrassed by so much praise.

————. *Did Pocahontas Save John Smith?* Athens: University of Georgia Press, 1992.

A history of the controversy, which concludes the answer is yes.

Hume, Ivor Noel. *The Virginia Adventure*. New York: Knopf, 1994.

Reports from the area's leading archaeologist.

Price, David. *Love and Hate in Jamestown*. New York: Knopf, 2003.

A masterful retelling of the nation's start in which both Smith and Pocahontas emerge as key to the colony's survival. On the rescue, Price takes Smith at his word, and rejects the adoption theory on the grounds that his hero was too shrewd a judge of the Powhatans to have misinterpreted the scene.

What Caused
the Salem Witch-Hunt?

IN FEBRUARY 1692 in the town of Salem, Massachusetts, two children in the house of the Reverend Samuel Parris—nine-year-old Betty Parris and her eleven-year-old cousin Abigail Williams—began acting very strangely. They ran around the house, flapping their arms, screaming "Whish, Whish, Whish." They pulled burning logs out of the fireplace and threw them around the room. It was as if, another local minister observed, they "were bitten and pinched by invisible agents; their arms, necks, and backs turned this way and that way, and returned back again, so as it was impossible for them to do of themselves, and beyond the power of any Epileptick Fits, or natural Disease to effect." Local doctors were at a loss to explain what was going on. Finally, Dr. William Griggs suggested the girls were bewitched.

The authorities sprang into action, demanding that the children tell them who was tormenting them. The girls first named Tituba, the Parris family's West Indian slave. Then they added the names of two other local women, Sarah Good and Sarah Osborne. Tituba admitted she'd read palms and told fortunes and perhaps dabbled in some voodoo, but she denied harming the girls; that was the doing of Good and Osborne, she said. Good, in turn, said Osborne was the witch.

So far this was no big deal. There had been other accusations of witchcraft in other New England towns, usually resulting in a lot of gossip and perhaps an occasional arrest or even a conviction. But in Salem this was just the beginning. More and more of Salem's teenage and preteen girls began having fits; more and more of Salem's adults were accused of witchcraft. Even the four-year-old daughter of Sarah Good was accused and sent to prison with her mother, where she remained in heavy irons for nine months. By summer the town's jail was filled with more than a hundred accused witches; by the end of the year, 19 people had been hanged—more than in all the previous New England witch trials. Another victim was pressed to death under heavy stones because he refused to testify before the magistrates.

It was clear things had gone too far. Influential ministers and magistrates, many of whom had been quick to see the devil's work in the girls' behavior, now realized this had gotten out of hand (a realization aided no doubt by the fact that some of them and their wives were being accused). The trials came to a halt, as did the witch-hunt. But the question did not go away: What drove the people of Salem to behavior so extreme that, ever since, Salem has been a metaphor for persecution and intolerance?

⌒

To the rationalists of the eighteenth and nineteenth centuries, the question barely merited analysis. Since there was obviously no such thing as a witch, the girls were simply liars. Those who supported the girls acted out of fear of being themselves accused; those who confessed to being witches and who named other witches did so only to save themselves from the gallows.

In the twentieth century, Freudian interpretations came to the fore. The girls' fits were a classic case of hysteria, the result of repressed adolescent and preadolescent sexuality. It is easy enough to believe the girls were repressed—the Puritans, after all, could be puritanical.

Freudian interpretations reigned until the early 1970s, when social historians began to probe the social and economic background of the witch-hunts. The 1690s, they stressed, were years of extreme instability in Massachusetts. Indian wars had been devastating; so had epidemic illnesses. The king had revoked the charter under which the colony was governed, leaving the entire structure of the government unsettled. And the traditionally agrarian culture of the area was increasingly threatened by the influence of a more cosmopolitan merchant class.

With their world seemingly coming apart, it was not so surprising that New Englanders, steeped as they were in Puritan theology, would blame Satan. Some people took all the fire-and-brimstone talk with a grain of salt, but others undoubtedly believed in witches. In any case, the particular people they accused fit the bill. Tituba was a black slave, an obvious pariah. Sarah Good was a beggar whose pleas had gotten on everyone's nerves. Sarah Osborne was more financially secure than Sarah Good, but she had been involved in some nasty disputes over land with her own sons and was widely suspected of having lived with her husband before they were married—no small transgression in Puritan society. To make matters worse, she hadn't been to church for more than a year. Many of the others accused early on were also conveniently vulnerable scapegoats.

But if all this illuminated the social strains and social divisions that led New Englanders to cry witch, it did little to explain why the witch-hunt materialized in Salem and not elsewhere in New England. To solve that mystery, two social historians, Paul Boyer and Stephen Nissenbaum, took a close look at Salem. What they found was that Salem was actually more like two towns. Near the coast stood Salem Town, a flourishing commercial center dominated by merchants and tradesmen; a little further inland lay Salem Village, a traditional and increasingly impoverished agricultural hamlet. To a remarkable extent, the accusers and their supporters lived in the interior and the accused and their defenders lived near or in town; the former tended to be poorer and more devout; the latter tended to be richer and more secular.

Nowhere else in New England did these two ways of life confront each other so directly and so unavoidably. Had Salem Village been situated somewhat further inland, its

Witchcraft at Salem Village. *(Ridpath, John Clark, Ridpath's History of the World, 1901)*

inhabitants might not have felt so threatened by Salem Town, nor would they have known its residents well enough to accuse them of anything, let alone witchcraft. Had this been the case, the name Salem might today conjure up nothing more than a pleasant coastal village. But with Salem's particular situation, daily contact meant a continual buildup of the Villagers' resentment of their rich and godless neighbors. Worse, some of the Villagers, Boyer and Nissenbaum found, had a particular grudge against their neighbors. In fact, underlying the Salem witch-hunt was a family feud that made the Capulets and the Montagues seem the closest of friends.

ﻌﻌﻌ

On the one side were the Putnams, on the other were the Porters. Both lived in the Village, but the Porters lived on the town side, and the Putnams further inland. Trouble started brewing in 1686, when Thomas Putnam Sr. died, bequeathing the best part of his estate to his second wife, Mary Veren Putnam, and his only son by that wife, Joseph. Like the biblical Joseph, Joseph Putnam was deeply resented by his older half brothers. Thomas Putnam Jr., the eldest, was especially bitter as he watched Joseph become one of the richest men in town with money and land that Thomas felt was rightfully his. His bitterness only deepened in 1690, when Joseph Putnam married Elizabeth Porter, a member of the only town family that rivalled the Putnams' wealth and prestige. To the Putnams, the Porters personified the evils of Salem Town.

No wonder, then, that the Putnams and Porters could be found on opposite sides of almost every issue dividing the town. The Putnams and their wives belonged to the church of Samuel Parris (father and uncle, you'll recall, to the two girls who started the whole witch-hunt). The Porters, on the other hand, led a drive to replace Parris with a new minister. And throughout the witch trials, the Putnam name appeared again and again among the accusers. Eight Putnams were involved in the prosecution of 46 accused witches, and Ann Putnam, the 12-year-old daughter of Thomas Putnam Jr., was by far the most active of all the afflicted girls. Meanwhile, the Porters' friends and family were prominent among the accused.

Three years after the witch trials were over, the feud was still going strong. In 1695 Mary Veren Putnam died, leaving everything that was hers (and that had once belonged to Joseph Putnam Sr.) to Joseph. The Putnams challenged the will, claiming it had actually been written by Israel Porter, Joseph's father-in-law. Furthermore, the Putnams claimed, Mary Veren Putnam had not been of sound mind when she signed the will. And what doctor did they call to testify this was so? None other than William Griggs, the doctor who had first suggested the children in the Parris household had been bewitched.

The Putnam/Porter feud brings to mind not just Bible stories but also fairy tales. Think of Thomas Putnam Jr. and his brothers as Hansel and Gretel, exploited by their father's evil second wife, who abandons them to the forest and its witch. How did Hansel and Gretel survive? The Putnams knew the answer: they killed the witch.

Alas, for the Putnams, it was all in vain. Throughout his life, Thomas Putnam Jr. had to sell off what little land his father did leave him in order to pay his increasing debts. When he died in 1699, there was little left for his three sons, all of whom moved away from the area, or his five daughters, three of whom remained spinsters. Joseph Putnam, in contrast, remained rich, and his sons and daughters prospered in Salem. (The only son who moved away from Salem was Israel Putnam, who became a highly successful soldier, known best for his bravery at Bunker Hill, where he uttered the famous line: "Don't shoot until you see the whites of their eyes.")

∞

Whether the Putnams consciously sought revenge, or whether they actually believed the accused were witches, is unclear. But the Boyer/ Nissenbaum analysis convinced most historians that the social tensions between the two families and communities were at the root of the witch trials. A few historians, however, disagreed.

As Bernard Rosenthal saw it, the trials could only be understood through a study of the surviving trial records. What he found there convinced him that the trials were part of a scam perpetrated by the county sheriff, George Corwin. Rosenthal backed up the charge by demonstrating that Corwin profited from the illegal seizure of the property of the wealthier defendants. More damning still, Corwin's uncle and father-in-law were both among the judges who sent the witches off to jail or to be hanged. Although no evidence exists that they conspired with Corwin, they must certainly have known what was going on, as did the other judges.

Rosenthal's close reading of the records revealed other motives were also at work. For example, the influential minister Cotton Mather backed the court proceedings because he felt that one of the defendants, the dissenting minister George Burroughs, was a dangerous threat to the religious hegemony. Mather, in spite of his fire-and-brimstone image, had mixed feelings about the trials in general, but he was willing to legitimize the other hangings to get rid of Burroughs.

Rosenthal strongly criticized social historians for focusing too much on the background and losing sight of the foreground; namely, the individual motives of people like Corwin and Mather. In this, he was not being entirely fair to Boyer and Nissenbaum; although they certainly paid a lot of attention to socioeconomic factors, they also wrote about the very personal motives of the Putnams and the Porters. So did, more recently, Mary Beth Norton, who illuminated Salem's ties to the Maine frontier, where devastating Indian wars convinced many they were "in the devil's snare."

Nor were the social historians' theses quite so at odds with Rosenthal's evidence as his criticism of it implied. The Salem witch-hunts were caused by both the underlying patterns in the community (which the social historians brilliantly illuminated) and the more immediate motives of the participants (as revealed by Rosenthal). Not all of the participants were driven by the same motive, and some were undoubtedly driven by more than one. Corwin might have been driven by greed, Mather by theology, Putnam by jealousy and resentment, the girls by boredom or frustration. So many different problems converged in 1692 Salem that it didn't take much to cause an explosion. All that was needed was a spark—which appeared in the form of a West Indian slave who dabbled in voodoo.

To Investigate Further

Boyer, Paul, and Stephen Nissenbaum, eds. *Salem-Village Witchcraft.* Boston: Northeastern University Press, 1972.

A documentary record, including transcripts of the preliminary trial proceedings and much of the testimony. (The actual trial records have not survived.)

Upham, Charles. *Salem Witchcraft.* Boston: Wiggin and Lunt, 1867.

This standard "rationalist" approach to the witchcraft was reprinted in 1959 by F. Unger Publishing Co. (New York).

Starkey, Marion. *The Devil in Massachussetts.* New York: Knopf, 1950.

Though it preceded much of the modern scholarship, this remains the most dramatic narrative history of the crisis.

Hansen, Chadwick. *Witchcraft at Salem.* **New York: George Braziller, 1969.**

In a society where most people believed in witchcraft and where many practiced black magic, spells might actually work—if only through the power of suggestion. So, at least according to this iconoclastic work, some of the accused might actually have been guilty of witchcraft.

Boyer, Paul, and Stephen Nissenbaum. *Salem Possessed.* **Cambridge: Harvard University Press, 1974.**

How social tensions between Salem Town and Salem Village led to the witch-hunt.

Caporael, Linnda. "Ergotism: The Satan Loosed in Salem?" *Science,* **April 1976.**

A biologist's proposal that the girls' fits and visions were symptoms of convulsive ergotism, a disease contracted from contaminated grain.

Spanos, Nicholas, and Jack Gottlieb. "Ergotism and the Salem Village Witch Trials." *Science,* **December 1976.**

Disputes Caporael's diagnosis by arguing that the fits and visions seemed to start and stop on cue, thus implying a social rather than physiological cause.

Demos, John. *Entertaining Satan.* **New York: Oxford University Press, 1982.**

Though not exclusively about Salem, this is the most thorough and sophisticated study of New England witchcraft; Demos approaches the subject from the perspectives of biography, psychology, and sociology as well as history.

Karlsen, Carol F. *The Devil in the Shape of a Woman.* **New York: Norton, 1987.**

A feminist investigation, which contends that many of the accused were singled out because they owned or were in line to inherit property that would otherwise go to men.

Gragg, Larry. *The Salem Witch Crisis.* **Westport, CT: Praeger, 1992.**

A straightforward history of the crisis with an excellent chapter on how prison conditions led many to confess.

Rosenthal, Bernard. *Salem Story.* **New York: Cambridge University Press, 1993.**

The case that systematic fraud caused the witch-hunt; also includes fascinating discussions of how the Salem story has been used in American literature and culture.

Norton, Mary Beth. *In the Devil's Snare.* **New York: Knopf, 2002.**

How Indian wars wreaked havoc on Massachusetts as well as Maine.

Was Captain Kidd a Pirate?

IN DECEMBER 1698, in an effort to coax pirates out of the seas, England's King William III offered a pardon to anyone who surrendered. There were two exceptions, pirates whose crimes were so heinous that they were beyond redemption. One was "Long Ben" Avery. The other was Captain William Kidd.

Kidd's reputation for ruthlessness and barbarity continued to spread, even after his death on the gallows in 1701. Many a ballad recalled his deeds and misdeeds; one, for example, has Kidd tell how he disposed of a disgruntled crew member: "I murdered William Moore/ And left him in his gore/Not many leagues from shore." The pirate stories of Washington Irving, Edgar Allan Poe, and Robert Louis Stevenson were all inspired, at least in part, by Kidd.

The Kidd of legend was ill tempered, hugely powerful, and insatiably greedy. He was also rich, and he died without revealing where he'd buried his treasure. In the three centuries since then, treasure hunters have searched the shores and dredged the bottoms of rivers and seas from New York to the Indies, East and West. In 2000, the Discovery Channel financed an expedition to the African coast, where divers found what may be the wreckage of Kidd's flagship. But as for the treasure, they came up empty-handed.

Kidd, for his part, always denied that there was a treasure, and—even more vehemently—that he was a pirate. He maintained that his adventures had been entirely in the service of his country and that his voyage had been sponsored by high-ranking officials, including King William himself.

"My lord," Kidd said after a London jury sentenced him to die for piracy and murder, "it is a very hard sentence. . . . I am the innocentest person of them all."

Surprisingly, quite a few historians reached the same conclusion.

⌖

The record of Kidd's trial, which started on May 8, 1701, and ended the next day, still exists—and offers a close look at the man and his actions.

Both the prosecution and the defense agree on some basic facts. Kidd arrived in London in 1695, looking for someone to sponsor a privateering expedition. Like pirates, privateers robbed ships at sea, but with a big difference: they were licensed by one nation, and they were limited to attacks on the ships of hostile nations. By the late sixteenth century, privateering was a fairly common and inexpensive way to undermine an enemy's trade. Kidd was an experienced privateer, having raided various French ships in the Caribbean.

In London, Kidd gained the support of Lord Bellomont, a member of Parliament and a leading figure in the ruling Whig Party. Bellomont persuaded four other Whig peers to put up the cash for a ship, and the Admiralty granted him a privateering license. The king agreed to put up three thousand pounds, then reneged on the money but still lent his support in return for 10 percent of the profits.

Kidd's commission was somewhat unusual in that it authorized him to capture not just enemy ships but also pirate ships. This may have been added to make the venture involving the king sound a bit less mercenary, though it also indicated that the government was becoming increasingly fed up with pirates who interfered with British trade.

Kidd set sail from London in the thirty-four-gun *Adventure Galley*. In January 1697 he arrived at Madagascar, a well-known pirate base off the eastern coast of Africa. Here were nearly two hundred pirates, including the aptly named Captains Hoar and Shivers, but Kidd made no effort to apprehend any of them.

Almost a year later, having wandered about the coasts of Africa and Asia, Kidd had seized nothing but a few small vessels, and both his crew and his backers were getting itchy. The crew members, who'd signed on for a share of the booty and didn't get paid unless they captured something, were by some accounts near mutiny. Back in London, the government worried that Kidd would soon cross the line from privateer to pirate—if he hadn't already done so. The *Adventure Galley* had made no moves against any of the pirates at Madagascar or elsewhere, and she'd fled from some British Navy ships encountered off the coast of Africa.

With the ship leaking and supplies short, the mood on board was increasingly tense. On October 30, 1697, according to the testimony of crew members at Kidd's trial, the captain got into an argument with a gunner, William Moore. Kidd called Moore a "lousy dog." Moore replied, "If I am a lousy dog, you have made me so. You have brought me to ruin and many more." Kidd then picked up a bucket and slammed it down on Moore's head. The gunner died the next day.

Then, on January 30, 1698, hope appeared on the horizon in the form of the four-hundred-ton *Quedah Merchant*. Here, finally, was a prize worth taking. The merchant ship, flying an Armenian flag, was heading north filled with silk, calico, sugar, opium, guns, and gold. Kidd gave chase and ultimately seized the ship and its cargo.

It's at this point that the prosecution and defense stories, as presented at Kidd's trial, diverge. To prosecutors, this was clearly an act of piracy. The *Quedah Merchant* had an English captain, and it was carrying goods belonging to a leading member of the Indian emperor's court, who had powerful connections with the East India Company—an English venture. What's more, Kidd did not take the ship or his goods home to be judged a legal prize, as the contract with his Whig benefactors required. Instead, he dispersed some of the booty among his crew and kept the rest for himself. Kidd's crew members, taking advantage of the king's offer of immunity, testified to all this. Kidd, for his part, insisted that the *Quedah Merchant* was not an English ship, its captain and connections notwithstanding. Its captain had shown him a "French pass," a document that clearly indicated this was a French ship. The French pass, Kidd maintained, would prove his seizure of the ship was entirely legal.

Kidd cross-examined his ex-crew members, who admitted that they'd heard him speak of the pass, though they hadn't actually seen it. Repeatedly, Kidd asked the court to delay his trial until the jurors could examine the French pass for themselves.

The judges would have none of this, however. The pass was never produced in court, and the trial moved expeditiously forward. The jurors took only an hour to find Kidd guilty of Moore's murder, and another half hour to find him guilty of piracy.

⟨⟩

Many historians were not so sure.

Though Kidd never produced the French pass, there was a great deal of circumstantial evidence indicating that it might have existed. For one thing, Kidd could have hidden out at Madagascar or some other pirate refuge, but he chose to return to America, even though he knew there was a warrant out for his arrest. Why? According to Kidd, it was because he knew the pass would prove his innocence.

Kidd said that before arriving in Boston, he'd sent the pass to Lord Bellomont, his business partner and the newly appointed governor of Massachusetts. Bellomont replied with a reassuring letter, saying that he had no doubts he could get the king to pardon Kidd. Only then did Kidd turn himself in, confident his benefactor would protect him. But Bellomont betrayed him, throwing him in the Boston jail and then shipping him to London in irons.

Bellomont's letter to Kidd, which mentioned the French pass explicitly, convinced many historians that Kidd hadn't made it up. The governor, it seemed, was in a very awkward position. As Kidd's partner, he would have loved to see the *Quedah Merchant* declared a legal prize—for then he'd get his share of the profits. But as governor, he couldn't afford to appear sympathetic to an accused pirate. Ultimately, his political position was more important to him than the profits, so he had Kidd arrested. Kidd's notoriety was a tremendous embarrassment not just to Bellomont but also to his fellow investors—all prominent members of the Whig Party. Their Tory opponents, who saw this as a chance to embroil the Whigs in a scandal, were calling for a vote of censure. For their part, the Whigs were quick to portray Kidd as a privateer turned pirate, to make clear that he'd gone bad after they'd made their deal with him. And, to make Kidd's position even worse, the East India Company wanted to make an example of him, to discourage other pirates and to mollify their friends in India.

To many historians, then, Kidd was no fearsome pirate, but a mere pawn in a political game. Many suspected that Bellomont, or perhaps someone else high up in the government, kept the French pass from Kidd to ensure a guilty verdict. And in 1911, while searching through the Public Record Office in London, a writer named Ralph Paine found the proof: there, for all to see, was the French pass that Kidd had seized from the *Quedah Merchant*. Apparently it had sat in the Public Record Office for the two centuries since Kidd's trial.

The pass convinced Paine that Kidd was an innocent man. True, Kidd had not followed the legal steps for declaring the *Quedah Merchant* a legitimate prize, but that was

After being hanged, Captain Kidd's body was displayed by the Thames, a warning to other pirates. Why was so much attention focused on a man who, in the words of one historian, "never cut a throat or made a victim walk the plank, who was no more than a third-or-fourth-rate pirate?" *(Library of Congress)*

because his crew had mutinied—and absconded with much of the booty. True, too, the *Adventure Galley* had gone on to capture other ships that clearly weren't French, but that was also the work of the mutinous crew and not the captain. And true, Kidd had struck William Moore, but only because he was one of the mutineers. Besides, Paine argued, in an age when captains routinely flogged sailors for trifling misdemeanors, Kidd's blow was downright restrained.

Captain Kidd, in Paine's view, had been "unfairly dealt with by his patrons, misused by his rascally crew, and slandered by credulous posterity."

◉⟋⟋⟍⟍◉

More recently, historians have generally taken a more balanced view of Kidd, portraying him as neither the barbarous pirate of legend nor the entirely innocent victim of unscrupulous politicians. There's no doubt that it was grossly unfair to keep from him the French pass, which would have strengthened his defense against the piracy charge pertaining to the *Quedah Merchant*. But, according to the testimony of various crew members, Kidd had hoisted a French flag on the *Adventure Galley* to trick the *Quedah Merchant*'s captain into showing him the French pass. (It was common for merchant ships to carry papers of various nationalities, in the hope that the right one might turn away a privateer or a pirate.) So, these crew members asserted, Kidd knew perfectly well that the ship wasn't French, even if it did have a French pass.

Moreover, there was the matter of the other, albeit smaller, ships seized after the *Quedah Merchant*. Kidd was charged with—and found guilty of—four other counts of piracy. For each, his defense was the same—his crew had mutinied, and acted without his consent. But there was really no more reason to believe Kidd's version than that of the crew members who testified against him.

Kidd was, the majority of historians now agree, a pirate, though not a particularly successful one. His misfortune, according to his biographer, Robert C. Ritchie, was that he crossed the line from privateer to pirate at just the time when the latter was least likely to be tolerated. Partly this was because of the struggle between the Whigs and the Tories in Parliament. But, Ritchie demonstrated, Kidd's bad timing went beyond that.

During the late 1690s, both parties—Whig and Tory—were increasingly determined to eliminate the threat pirates presented to the trade of the British Empire. That's why King William offered to pardon pirates. That's why the Whig ministers commissioned Kidd to capture pirates as well as enemy ships. And that's why Kidd's piracy, though nowhere near the worst of his era, brought down on him the wrath of the British government.

The concerted effort of the British government to put an end to piracy didn't succeed immediately, but Kidd was by no means the only pirate to suffer. Throughout the empire, the Royal Navy cracked down, as did local forces. In 1718, for example, Virginians and Carolinians converged on the lair of Edward Teach, also known as Blackbeard, who died in a fierce struggle. By 1730, the era when pirates freely roamed the seas was over.

And what of Kidd's buried treasure?

Alas, there was even less to this than to the rest of his legend. Kidd, perhaps because he didn't fully trust Bellomont, left eleven bags of gold and silver with John Gardiner of Gardiner's Island, off the coast of Long Island. But Gardiner didn't want to tangle with Bellomont, and after Kidd's arrest he turned all of it over to the governor, who sent it on to England.

Most of Kidd's treasure probably ended up in the hands of his crew, many of whom deserted long before he reached Boston. Mutinous or not, these men had signed up in the hope of getting rich, and it's hard to imagine they walked away empty-handed. And once they had the money in their hands, they were far more likely to spend it than to bury it.

To Investigate Further

Brooks, Graham, ed. *The Trial of Captain Kidd.* Edinburgh: William Hodge, 1930.
 Transcripts of the trial, with a balanced commentary by Brooks.

Defoe, Daniel. *A General History of the Pyrates.* Columbia, SC: University of South Carolina Press, 1972.
 Originally published in 1724, this classic history was originally attributed to a "Captain Charles Johnson." Only in the twentieth century did most (but not all) scholars conclude that it was written by Defoe, the author of *Robinson Crusoe* and *Moll Flanders.*

Paine, Ralph. *The Book of Buried Treasure.* New York: Macmillan, 1922.
 As the title indicates, Paine was more interested in searching for treasure than a French pass, but it was the latter that he discovered.

Bonner, Willard. *Pirate Laureate.* New Brunswick, NJ: Rutgers University Press, 1947.
 Traces the growth of the Kidd legend, from sailors' ballads to the works of Irving, Cooper, Poe, and Stevenson.

Winston, Alexander. *No Man Knows My Grave.* Boston: Houghton Mifflin, 1969.
 The fine line between privateering and piracy, as exhibited in the lives of Henry Morgan, Woodes Rogers, and William Kidd.

Ritchie, Robert C. *Captain Kidd and the War Against the Pirates.* Cambridge, MA: Harvard University Press, 1986.
 How the British Empire brought an end to the golden age of pirates.

Cordingly, David. *Under the Black Flag.* New York: Random House, 1995.
 An informative and entertaining survey of pirates in fact and faction, based on a 1992 exhibit at the London Maritime Museum.

Zacks, Richard. *The Pirate Hunter.* New York: Hyperion, 2002.
 Kidd as a "reputable New York sea captain."

PART 6

AGE OF REVOLUTIONS, 1750–1914

What Started the Boston Massacre?

D ESPITE A FOOT OF SNOW ON THE GROUND, groups of Bostonians wandered the streets of the town on the evening of March 5, 1770. Some, responding to a fire alarm, carried buckets of water. Others carried clubs to defend themselves—or perhaps to threaten—the despised "lobsterbacks," the redcoated British troops who had been stationed in the town since 1768.

Near the Custom House on King Street, several wigmakers' apprentices taunted Private Hugh White, the lone British sentry. Words soon escalated to snowballs and stones, and White struck back with the butt of his gun. Captain Thomas Preston heard of White's predicament and rushed to the scene with seven other soldiers. By then, hundreds of Bostonians had gathered as well, some still holding their buckets.

There was no fire. But a piece of ice knocked down Private Hugh Montgomery and when he stood up, he fired into the crowd. More shots followed. Three Bostonians were killed on the spot and two others mortally wounded.

Samuel Adams called the deaths a "bloody butcher," and Paul Revere quickly produced an engraving showing soldiers firing point-blank at citizens. Other patriot leaders published a pamphlet, "A Short Narrative of the Horrid Massacre in Boston," and more than ten thousand mourners paraded at the funeral.

Adams made sure the image of the Boston Massacre didn't fade from American memory. He set aside March 5 as a day of mourning. Annual orations recalled the massacre as the direct and inevitable result of British oppression, its victims the first heroes of the revolution to come. Until 1784, when the Fourth of July took its place, Americans celebrated their independence on March 5.

Not surprisingly, the British and Tories had a different view of the day's events. Some London newspapers suggested the Bostonians were after the king's coffers in the Custom House. Others accused patriot leaders of planning the incident, perhaps even with the hope of turning its victims into martyrs. To loyalists, this was not the Boston Massacre but "the riot on the King Street."

This was more than a contest of names. It was, as historian Alfred Young wrote in a slightly different context (he was discussing the loyalist tendency to call the Boston Tea Party "the destruction of the tea") "part of a larger contest for the public memory of the Revolution."

◦◦◦◦

Paul Revere's 1770 engraving is riddled with errors, including the invented "Butcher's Hall" sign and an inaccurate casualty list. *(Library of Congress)*

With patriot leaders like Adams and Revere fomenting rebellion, Massachusetts' royal governor Thomas Hutchinson moved decisively to calm the town. He ordered the British soldiers out of Boston, and he had Preston and the other soldiers arrested and charged with murder.

Preston's case came to court in November. The captain was defended by Samuel Adams's cousin John. Thirty years later, John Adams recalled sitting in his office the day after the massacre.

"Mr. Forrest [a loyalist merchant] came in," Adams wrote in his autobiography. "With tears streaming from his Eyes, he said I am come with a very solemn Message from a very unfortunate Man, Captain Preston in Prison. He wishes for Council, and can get none. I have waited on Mr. [Josiah] Quincy, who says he will engage if you will give him your Assistance.

"I had no hesitation in answering that Council ought to be the very last thing that an accused Person should [lack] in a free Country," Adams answered, somewhat pompously but no doubt sincerely.

Adams was one of Massachusetts's leading attorneys. His cross-examination undermined the credibility of the prosecution's key witnesses, who testified that they heard Preston order the soldiers to fire. Adams argued the captain might have said "fire by no means," even if some in the crowd heard only the first word. He also paraded to the stand a series of convincing defense witnesses; perhaps most effective was Richard Palmes, a revolutionary merchant who had attacked Preston and was standing right next to him when the shooting began, yet conceded he had never heard the captain order the soldiers to fire.

The jury took only three hours to acquit Preston.

Next came the trial of the rest of the soldiers. Here Quincy and Adams, again appearing for the defense, faced a tricky problem. Having established that Preston never gave the order to fire, they had eliminated the soldiers' best defense; namely, that they were just following orders.

Quincy's solution was, essentially, to take the British view of the massacre. He called to the stand a series of witnesses to testify about the hostility to the soldiers throughout Boston, the point being that the mob intentionally provoked the soldiers. This was too much for Adams; whether out of loyalty to the patriot cause or to Boston's reputation, he threatened to quit the case if Quincy continued in that vein.

Adams prevailed, and the remaining defense witnesses focused on the immediate danger to the soldiers, rather than the generally hostile climate. Perhaps most effective was Dr. John Jeffries, a friend of Samuel Adams who had treated Patrick Carr, one of the massacre's victims. Jeffries testified he had asked Carr, as he lay dying, whether he thought the soldiers acted in self-defense. According to Jeffries, Carr answered, "he heard many voices cry out to kill [the soldiers]." Carr added, movingly, "that he did not blame the man, whoever he was, that shot him."

The jury acquitted six of the soldiers of murder and found the other two—Montgomery and Private Mathew Kilroy—guilty of the lesser charge of manslaughter. Kilroy and Montgomery were sentenced to having their thumbs branded, a painful punishment but one that avoided any jail time.

Samuel Adams, writing in the Boston *Gazette,* decried a miscarriage of justice and demanded revenge. For many patriots, though, the trials were more a propaganda victory than a legal defeat. If the massacre proved the evils of British power, the verdicts proved the power of American justice. They should, Samuel Adams's friend Samuel Cooper wrote Benjamin Franklin, "wipe off the imputation of our being so violent and blood thirsty a people, as not to permit law and justice to take place on the side of unpopular men."

For many historians, too, the trials became another symbol of American rectitude. Certainly this was the view enshrined in American textbooks for most of the nation's history. But in the 1960s and 1970s, amidst debate over whether antiwar protesters were peace lovers or rioters, both the massacre and the subsequent trials came under new scrutiny.

☞

In the late 1960s, Hiller Zobel, a lawyer and legal historian, studied the trial records and noted that the jury was packed with British sympathizers, virtually guaranteeing the not-guilty verdicts. So, according to Zobel, the case John Adams later described as "one of the most gallant, generous, manly and disinterested actions of my whole life," was fixed.

Why prosecutors didn't object to a pro-Tory jury remains a mystery. Some historians have pointed to a Tory bias on the part of at least one prosecutor. Others have maintained the prosecutors were patriots, but, like John Adams, eager to show the world how fair they were. Still others have speculated that the prosecutors simply weren't paying close attention, perhaps because they were overconfident that no Boston jury would dare let the soldiers off.

Another theory is that Governor Hutchinson might have pardoned any soldier convicted of murder, and prosecutors feared a pardon would lead to more violence. An acquittal, though hardly likely to satisfy radical patriots, would at least appear to be the result of a fair and legal process.

Whatever the reasons for the prosecution's lapses, the trial was clearly stacked in favor of the defense.

Zobel wasn't satisfied just to debunk the traditional view of the trial. His 1970 book on the massacre argued that the colonists were as much to blame for the violence as the British. He portrayed Samuel Adams as a "demagogic genius" eager to take advantage of the mounting tension between the townspeople and the soldiers.

Other revisionists, such as historian John Shy, went further. Shy resurrected the old loyalist claim that the massacre was a patriot conspiracy, masterminded by Samuel Adams and his fellow revolutionaries. Shy found the timing of the massacre suspicious, coming as it did at the end of a parliamentary session. That meant, he pointed out, that Hutchinson could not count on a strong response from London, so would have no choice but to give in to the patriots' demand that the soldiers leave Boston. And, in fact, that's exactly what happened.

"Circumstances suggest there was as much purpose as spontaneity in the events leading up to the Massacre," Shy concluded.

Shy's evidence, like Zobel's, is largely circumstantial and ultimately unconvincing. What the revisionists failed to take into account was the fact that Boston's "mobs" were perfectly capable of acting on their own. Working-class Bostonians didn't need Sam Adams or Paul Revere to get them worked up about British soldiers in town. Indeed, laborers had more reasons than other colonists to resent the lobsterbacks. Army regulations allowed the soldiers to work part time at civilian jobs, and many took work and pay away from Boston workers.

Tensions between soldiers and workers had been on the rise since 1768, and March 5 was by no means the first time that bands of workers had clashed with soldiers. As recently as March 2, a fight had broken out when some ropemakers asked a passing soldier if he wanted work, and then suggested he clean their outhouse.

Amid all the conflicting reports of the massacre, one fact stands out: none of the revolutionary leaders accused of planning a riot were on the scene until well after the five workers were shot. In fact, as Zobel himself noted, when the first of the prominent revolutionaries arrived on the scene, they immediately began negotiating with Hutchinson to remove the troops from Boston. Their goal was to avoid further bloodshed, not cause more.

Patriot leaders were on the scene for the massive funeral march a few days later, and they did help organize it. But the fact that more than ten thousand Bostonians turned out—the town's population at the time was only about sixteen thousand—seems more an indication of the depth of local anger than of the radicals' organizational skills.

The revisionists deserve credit for showing the not-guilty verdicts to be more than the result of an American sense of fairness or of John Adams's legal genius (though it seems unfair of Zobel not to give Adams some of the credit). More fundamentally, the revisionists put to rest the myth that the massacre was entirely the fault of the British. Workers provoked soldiers as often as the reverse, and when Hugh Montgomery shot into the crowd, he had every reason to believe his life was in danger.

But the revisionists failed to realize that the workers' anti-British fervor had outpaced that of patriot leaders like Sam Adams, not to mention his more conservative cousin John. The patriot leadership wanted the troops out of Boston, but they were not yet ready for all-out revolution. That was still six years in the future.

⌾⌾⌾⌾

In one sense, the traditional and revisionist views of the massacre were not so far apart. Both saw the American Revolution as an essentially conservative movement aimed at protecting the traditional rights of Englishmen, rights threatened by George III and Parliament. Most historians would agree that the Revolution, when it did come, was led by prominent colonists like the Adams cousins, or George Washington and Thomas Jefferson.

In the past thirty or so years, though, historians such as Alfred Young and Eric Foner and Gordon Wood have highlighted some more radical elements of the Revolution, turning it into more of a preview of the one in France than a rerun of the Magna Carta. From this perspective, the five slain workers were not just martyrs (as in the traditional view) or puppets (as the revisionists would have them), but genuine revolutionaries.

Of the five, the most threateningly revolutionary was Crispus Attucks, the first man killed on the scene. During Preston's trial, one witness described Attucks waving "a large cord-wood stick" at the head of a group of "huzzaing, whistling" sailors. Another recalled Attucks grabbing two four-foot logs from a wood pile and handing him one.

Perhaps most threatening of all, Attucks was an escaped slave, the son of an African father and a Native American mother. John Adams was quick to use this against him, calling him a "stout Mulatto fellow . . . to whose mad behaviour, in all probability, the dreadful carnage of that night, is chiefly to be ascribed." Adams went on to describe the mob as "a motley rabble of saucy boys, Negroes and mulattoes, Irish teagues and out-landish jack tarrs."

Most patriot leaders managed to suppress any racist slurs in the interest of revolutionary solidarity, or at least revolutionary propaganda. Attucks was buried alongside the other four victims, in spite of laws prohibiting integrated burials.

In the 1850s, Attucks's radicalism resurfaced. By then, he had become a symbol not of American freedom but of African American emancipation. To abolitionists, he belonged in the company not of either Adams, but of Nat Turner. Black Bostonian leaders lobbied for a monument to commemorate the massacre and Attucks.

Wrote John Rock, an African American doctor: "The John Brown of the Second Revolution is but the Crispus Attucks of the first."

Again, an Adams spoke out against Attucks. This time it was Charles Francis Adams Jr., the president of the Massachusetts Historical Society. Echoing his great-grandfather, Adams called the "so called massacre" a riotous mob, not to be confused with the "peaceful, earnest, patriotic protest and resistance by our wise and resolute popular leaders."

In 1888, after a forty-year campaign by black Bostonians, the monument was erected on Boston Common. Attucks was immortalized as "the first to die, the first to defy."

This was not, by any means, an endorsement of a radical revolution, either for 1770 or 1776 or 1888. By the time the monument went up, Boston had again reimagined Attucks, this time as a symbol of American unity.

At the dedication, Mayor Hugh O'Brien declared "that all men are free and equal, without regard to color, creed, or nationality; and that the memory of the martyrs whose blood was shed in the cause of liberty in 1770 will thus be preserved and honored for all time." The inscription in the upper-right corner of the monument read: "On that Night the Foundation of American Independence was laid."

Those words were originally written by Attucks's first and foremost detractor, John Adams.

To Investigate Further

Wroth, L. Kinvin, and Hiller Zobel, eds. *Legal Papers of John Adams.* **Cambridge, MA: Belknap Press, 1965.**

Volume 3 includes the records of the massacre trials.

Shy, John. *Toward Lexington.* **Princeton, NJ: Princeton University Press, 1965.**

How the British army—and the colonial response to it—led to the American Revolution.

Zobel, Hiller. *The Boston Massacre.* **New York: W.W. Norton, 1970.**

Despite the above criticism, this is the most thorough study of the massacre.

Smith, Page. *A New Age Now Begins.* **New York: McGraw-Hill, 1976.**

The revolution "from the bottom up."

Browne, Stephen. "Remembering Crispus Attucks." *Quarterly Journal of Speech,* May 1999.
A penetrating study of the politics behind the memorial in Boston Common.

Young, Alfred. *The Shoemaker and the Tea Party.* Boston: Beacon Press, 1999.
At once a biography of a revolutionary shoemaker and an elegant essay on historical memory.

Middlekauff, Robert. *The Glorious Cause.* New York: Oxford University Press, 2005.
Originally published in 1982 and still the best one-volume history of the Revolution.

What Caused the Mutiny on the Bounty?

LIEUTENANT WILLIAM BLIGH WAS, if not on a fast track, at least on a clear path to success when he was appointed captain of the HMS *Bounty* in 1787. His mission was to collect breadfruit plants from Tahiti and transport them to the plantations of the West Indies. Bligh was a logical choice for the job: he was an accomplished navigator and mapmaker, and he had served under Captain James Cook, who had explored the South Pacific a decade earlier.

Bligh set sail from England in December. After a month battling storms off Cape Horn, he conceded he couldn't reach the Pacific heading west. Undaunted, he reversed course and headed around the Cape of Good Hope. This added about a thousand miles to his trip, bringing him to Tahiti in October 1788. Bligh encountered further delays preparing the breadfruit plants for transport, but he doggedly pursued his mission. In April 1789, the *Bounty*—loaded with more than a thousand of the plants—left Tahiti.

Twenty-four days later, on April 28, Bligh was rudely awakened. "A little before sunrise," he later wrote, "Fletcher Christian, who was mate of the ship, and officer of the watch, with the ship's corporal, came into my cabin while I was asleep, and seizing me, tied my hands with a cord, assisted by others who were also in the cabin, all armed with muskets and bayonets.

"I was forced on deck in my shirt with my hands tied, and secured by a guard abaft the mizzen-mast," Bligh continued, "during which the mutineers expressed much joy that they would soon see Ottaheite. I now demanded of Christian the cause of such a violent act, but no other answer was given but 'Hold your tongue, Sir, or you are dead this instant.'"

A little more than two hours later, Bligh found himself, along with eighteen of his crew members, in the *Bounty*'s launch, an open rowboat that was a mere twenty-three feet long, not even seven feet wide or three feet deep. Twenty-five others remained on board the *Bounty*, now under Christian's command.

Bligh professed complete surprise at this turn of events. Other than the suggestion that the mutineers had been seduced by the life—and presumably the women—of Tahiti, there was no reason for such treachery, no signs that trouble had been brewing. "The secrecy of this mutiny was beyond all conception," he wrote.

Amazingly, Bligh piloted the launch four thousand miles across the Pacific. Despite little food and no charts, all but one of his men survived. Eventually Bligh made it back to England and was embraced as a hero.

But not by all. Wrote Edward Christian, brother of the mutineers' leader: "There is a degree of pressure, beyond which the best formed and principled mind must either break or recoil. And though public justice and the public safety can allow no vindication of any species of Mutiny, yet reason and humanity will . . . deplore the uncertainty of human prospect, when they reflect that a young man is condemned to perpetual infamy, who, if he had served on board any other ship . . . might still have been an honour to his country and comfort to his friends."

To Edward Christian, the villain was not his brother but Bligh. That's the image of Bligh that's lasted, helped along in the twentieth century by three best-selling novels and two movies in which first Charles Laughton and then Trevor Howard flogged and starved and terrorized their cinematic crews. Bligh's name became a synonym for a sadistic tyrant. Fletcher Christian, meanwhile, was embraced not just by his brother but also by William Wordsworth and Samuel Coleridge (and Clark Gable and Marlon Brando). Christian became the prototypical romantic hero; pushed beyond his breaking point, he sacrifices a promising future in England to lead his shipmates to freedom.

Or so Hollywood would have it.

⌢⋙⌣

The British Navy did not take mutiny lightly. Soon after Bligh's return, Captain Edward Edwards of the *Pandora* was dispatched to bring Christian and his followers to justice. The *Pandora* reached Tahiti in March 1791. Edwards rounded up fourteen *Bounty* crew members and locked them in a box on the *Pandora*'s deck. Another two had died on the island, he learned. The remaining nine, Christian included, had taken the *Bounty* and left Tahiti long ago.

The *Pandora*'s return voyage was not much easier than the *Bounty*'s. The ship ran into the Great Barrier Reef and sank, along with four of the prisoners. The remaining prisoners and crew piled into four small boats and found their way to Timor, the same island Bligh reached in the launch. They eventually made it back to England, where the prisoners faced a court-martial.

For historians, the trial records are somewhat frustrating. For starters, the chief witness for the prosecution wasn't there. In August 1791, Bligh had left England on another—and more successful—breadfruit expedition. When the court-martial began in September 1792, the captain was again in the South Pacific. The captain had left various written documents, such as his log and a narrative based on it, but there would be no opportunity for the defense to cross-examine him. And since Bligh maintained the mutiny came as a complete surprise, his documents offered few clues as to what led up to it. There was the occasional disciplinary action—"I found it necessary to punish Mathew Quintal with two dozen lashes for Insolence and Contempt," he recorded as the *Bounty* headed toward Cape Horn—but nothing uncommon for the British navy of the period.

About his relationship to Christian prior to the mutiny, Bligh had only good things to say. "This was the third voyage he had made with me," he wrote in his narrative. "These

Recent historians have been more sympathetic to Bligh and less to Christian than the 1936 portrayals by Charles Laughton and Clark Gable. *(John Springer Collection/Corbis)*

two [Christian and midshipman and mutineer Peter Heywood] were objects of my particular regard and attention, and I took great pains to instruct them, for they really promised, as professional men, to be a credit to their country."

Indeed, as they forced him into the launch, Bligh asked whether this was a proper return for the kindness he'd shown Christian. "He appeared disturbed at my question," Bligh wrote, "and answered, with much emotion, 'That,—captain Bligh,—that is the thing;—I am in hell—I am in hell."

What drove Christian to hell? Bligh had only this to say: "I can only conjecture that the mutineers had assured themselves of a more happy life among the Otaheiteans, than they could possibly have in England; which, joined to some female connections, have most probably been the principal cause of the whole transaction. . . . They imagined it in their power to fix themselves in the midst of plenty, on the finest island in the world, where they need not labour, and where the allurements of dissipation are beyond any thing that can be conceived.

"The women at Otaheite," Bligh added, "are handsome, mild and cheerful in their manners and conversation."

As the launch pulled away from the *Bounty,* Bligh recalled, the mutineers cried out, "Huzza for Otaheite."

If Bligh had little to say about his alleged cruelty, neither did the defendants. Their situation precluded that: to try to justify a mutiny was a sure way to the gallows. Instead, each defendant stressed that he had nothing to do with the mutiny. Some said they were asleep or below deck and had no idea what was going on until it was too late. Others said they had tried to join Bligh but had been restrained. Still others argued, not unreasonably, that there was no more room on the launch, and to have joined Bligh would have been to condemn themselves and everyone else in his boat to certain death. Many pointed out they'd happily greeted Edwards when the *Pandora* arrived in Tahiti, since they knew they were innocent. Indeed, they asserted, that's why Christian and the real mutineers had dropped them off on the island before sailing into the unknown.

Still, the court-martial provided some hints that life on the *Bounty* was no paradise, and not just compared to Tahiti. John Fryer, the ship's master (who accompanied Bligh on the launch but clearly disliked the captain), testified about the day of the mutiny.

"When I saw Captain Bligh on the ladder," Fryer recalled, "I asked, what they were going to do with him; when [seaman John] Sumner answered, 'Damn his eyes, put him into the boat, and let the bugger see if he can live upon [the crew's allowance of] three-quarters of a pound of yams per day.' I said, For God's sake for what. Sumner and Quintal replied, 'Hold your tongue, Mr. Christian is captain of the ship, and recollect, Mr. Bligh has brought all this upon himself.'"

A judge asked Fryer what he thought Christian meant when he said he was in hell. "From the frequent quarrels that they had, and the abuse which he had received from Mr. Bligh," the master answered.

"Had there been any very recent quarrel?" the judge asked.

"The day before," Fryer said. "Mr. Bligh challenged all the young gentlemen and people with stealing his cocoa nuts."

None of this, however, seemed enough to explain a mutiny, and it certainly wasn't enough to save all the mutineers from the death penalty. After a weeklong trial, the court found four of the defendants genuinely hadn't participated in the mutiny. They were acquitted. Two others were found guilty, but the court found there were enough extenuating circumstances to recommend a royal pardon for those two, and the king granted it. Another got off on a technicality. The remaining three mutineers on trial were found guilty and hanged.

殹

The two mutineers pardoned by the king—James Morrison and Peter Heywood—ended up playing major roles in destroying Bligh's reputation. Morrison's "Journal," which he claimed to have kept during the voyage from Tahiti to England, was probably reconstructed a couple of years after his return. (It's hard to imagine how the original journal could have survived the sinking of the *Pandora* and the open boat trip to Timor.)

Whenever he wrote the "Journal," Morrison wasn't worried about convincing a court he had nothing to do with the mutiny. He was free to tear into Bligh, portraying him as vindictive and corrupt. Soon after the *Bounty* sailed, Morrison wrote, some cheese was discovered missing. When a crew member accused Bligh of having shipped the cheese to his house, the captain ordered the crew's rations cut until the amount was made up. This was a captain who would punish his crew for his own theft.

Heywood, too, once he received his pardon, did much to blacken Bligh's name. Heywood's main contribution was to bring Edward Christian into the fray. In November 1792, Heywood wrote Christian to assure him "that your brother was not that vile wretch, void of all gratitude which the world had the unkindness to think him: but, on the contrary, a most worthy character; ruined only by having the misfortune . . . of being a young man of strict honour." Christian, a law professor at Cambridge, may very well have been worried about his family's reputation before he got Heywood's letter, but this gave him a pretext to rise to his brother's defense. He decided to conduct his own investigation, interviewing both the surviving mutineers and the crew members who'd accompanied Bligh in the launch. In 1794 Christian published a partial transcript of the court-martial along with "an appendix containing a full account of the real causes and circumstances of that unhappy transaction, the most material of which have hitherto been withheld from the public."

According to Christian's appendix, Bligh routinely called his officers "scoundrels, damned rascals, hounds, hell-hounds, beats, and infamous wretches." He threatened "he would kill one half of the people, make the officers jump overboard, and would make them eat grass like cows." He accused Fletcher Christian of stealing his coconuts, then said he'd cut everyone's allowance of yams, this despite the ship having plenty of provisions.

Fletcher Christian, in contrast, was portrayed as a sensitive young man "agonized by unprovoked and incessant abuse and disgrace." He was, everyone agreed, "a gentleman, and a brave man; and every officer and seaman on board the ship would have gone through fire and water to have served him." Unable to tolerate Bligh any longer, Christian planned a near-suicidal escape on a makeshift raft. Other crew members learned of his plan and suggested he instead save them all. Only then, at least in Edward's version of the story, did Fletcher consider mutiny. And even then, Christian made sure that Bligh and the men who accompanied him were given the provisions and equipment they needed. That the launch turned out to be dangerously overcrowded was Bligh's fault, since the captain insisted on taking with him "almost all [his] property in boxes and trunks." And far from celebrating the mutiny with cries of "Huzza for Otaheite," this Christian was thereafter "always sorrowful and dejected." Nor was he drawn to Tahiti by a woman. "It is true that some had what they call their girls," the appendix conceded, "but this was not the case with Christian."

When Bligh returned from his second breadfruit expedition, he found public opinion had shifted dramatically against him. He responded to Christian's appendix by publishing his own "answer to certain assertions." Quite reasonably, Bligh noted that though Christian's appendix named everyone interviewed, it didn't attribute any of its quotes to individuals. That made it impossible to determine the credibility of any given statement. Bligh's pamphlet, in contrast, included affidavits from three crew members and a letter from a fourth, all denying the charges in the appendix.

But it was too late. What Bligh didn't understand was that Christian had history on his side. This was the Age of Revolution, and Christian—even his name—was an ideal standard-bearer. That his family's friends included the Romantic poet William Wordsworth guaranteed that Christian would end up the hero of the story. Moreover, as Christian's supporters were quick to note, Bligh's mission was to transport breadfruit plants to the plantations of the West Indies as a source of food *for slaves.* The purpose of the mission was not solely, as Bligh's backers described it, to improve nutrition. It was to make slavery more economical. This may have had nothing to do with the mutiny, but it was hardly a glorious cause.

"It was Lieutenant Bligh's ill luck," wrote historian Caroline Alexander, "to have his own great adventure coincide exactly with the dawn of this new era, which saw devotion to a code of duty and established authority as less honorable than the celebration of individual passions and liberty."

ᐧᐧᐧ

Bligh's second trip to Tahiti was a success, though breadfruit never really caught on in the West Indies. In 1797, as captain of the *Defiance,* Bligh was again the victim of a mutiny, though this one was part of a general uprising of British seamen and had nothing to do with Bligh personally. In 1805 one of his lieutenants on the *Warrior* charged him with "oppression," and a court-martial urged Bligh to be more careful about his language. This was humiliating, but also not particularly revealing; by then, the lieutenant and the court may well have been reacting to Bligh's reputation as the "Bounty Bastard" rather than to the particulars of the *Warrior* case. In 1806 Bligh became governor of New South Wales, only to preside over another uprising. Again it had little to do with Bligh personally, but again his image suffered.

Christian's romantic image, meanwhile, benefited from the fact that nobody knew what happened to him. That mystery was solved in 1808, when an American ship, the *Topaz,* came upon an uncharted island. As Captain Mayhew Folger headed toward shore, he was amazed to hear three dark-skinned men greet him in English. Soon he met the rest of the island's inhabitants, who turned out to be the Tahitian widows and children of the mutineers. Their leader was Alexander Smith, formerly a seaman on the *Bounty.* Once Folger reassured Smith that he was American, and that he had no interest in hauling him back to England for a court-martial, Smith was happy to tell the mutineers' story. After dropping off the sixteen men at Tahiti, Christian led the remaining eight, along with some Tahitian men and women, to Pitcairn, the island on which Folger had just stumbled.

Folger's story of his visit to Pitcairn generated surprisingly little interest, perhaps because, as one British journal reported, "this interesting relation rested solely on the faith that is due to Americans, with whom, we say it with regret, truth is not always considered as a moral obligation." Soon other ships started calling at Pitcairn, however, and Smith was happy to retell the story of the mutineers, especially once it became clear the British weren't going to prosecute him. With each retelling, Smith changed some of the details, including even his own name (which turned out to be Adams, not Smith). The most extensive record was made by Captain Frederick Beechey of the British ship *Blossom*. In 1825 Beechey spent sixteen days on Pitcairn. To Beechey, Smith offered a few more hints about the cause of the tension between Bligh and Christian, attributing it to the fact that the captain had lent his subordinate money and wouldn't let him forget it. On Bligh, Smith offered a mixed report: he stressed the captain's "remorseless severity" toward Christian and the other officers, but he also admitted that "there was no real discontent among the crew." And Smith confirmed that Christian had planned to escape on a raft before being convinced that "many of the ship's company were not well disposed toward the commander, and would all be very glad to return to Otaheite, and reside among their friends in that island."

What happened to Christian? There too, the details of Smith's account changed over time. But the basic outline remained: for four or five years, the British and Tahitians lived peacefully on Pitcairn, but then the "Otaheite servants" rebelled, killing Christian and all the mutineers other than Smith. In England, Christian was a symbol of liberty. To the Tahitians, he was just another European colonizer.

To Investigate Further

Bligh, William, and Edward Christian. *The Bounty Mutiny.* **New York: Penguin, 2001.**
Includes Bligh's *Narrative of the Mutiny on Board His Majesty's Ship Bounty,* Christian's *Minutes of the Proceedings of the Court-Martial . . . with an Appendix,* Bligh's *Answer to Certain Assertions Contained in the Appendix to a Pamphlet,* Christian's *Short Reply to Capt. William Bligh's Answer,* and various accounts of the Pitcairn islanders.

Nordhoff, Charles, and James Norman Hall. *Bounty Trilogy.* **Boston: Little, Brown, 1985.**
Originally published in the 1930s, these three novels—*Mutiny on the Bounty, Men Against the Sea,* and *Pitcairn's Island*—sold millions and inspired two Hollywood blockbusters.

Hough, Richard. *Captain Bligh & Mr. Christian.* **New York: E. P. Dutton, 1973.**
A dual biography that suggests the mutiny resulted from a broken homosexual relationship between the two. Bligh, jealous that Christian had spent his time on the island with a Tahitian woman, vented his rage; Christian, unwilling to renew his relationship with Bligh, was desperate to escape. Intriguing though unproven.

Kennedy, Gavin. *Bligh.* **London: Duckworth, 1978.**
A thorough and balanced biography.

Toohey, John. *Captain Bligh's Portable Nightmare.* New York: HarperCollins, 2000.

Four thousand miles in a rowboat.

Alexander, Caroline. *The Bounty.* New York: Viking, 2003.

Alexander's well-told retelling shifts some of the blame from Bligh to Christian. "What caused the mutiny on the *Bounty?*" she writes. "The seductions of Tahiti, Bligh's harsh tongue—perhaps. But more compellingly, a night of drinking and a proud man's pride, a low moment on one gray dawn, a momentary and fatal slip in a gentleman's code of discipline—and then the rush of consequences to be lived out for a lifetime."

Was Mozart Poisoned?

SOON AFTER HER HUSBAND'S DEATH, Constanze Mozart told a remarkable story about the *Requiem*, a Mass for the dead that Mozart was working on just before he died in December 1791.

Earlier that year, Constanze recalled, a mysterious messenger had arrived at the Mozarts' apartment in Vienna. He inquired whether Mozart would be willing to write the *Requiem* in return for a generous payment. The composer—whose most recent opera, *Don Giovanni*, had flopped and who was therefore desperately in need of cash—quickly agreed. The messenger paid the first half of the money, then left, staying only long enough to warn Mozart that he shouldn't try to find out who'd placed the order for the piece.

Mozart worked on the *Requiem* night and day. He became obsessed with it, fainting several times but unable to stop composing. Constanze described her husband's state of mind to Friedrich Rochlitz, who published a collection of anecdotes about Mozart in 1798. "He always sat quietly and lost in his thoughts," Rochlitz wrote. "Finally he no longer denied it—he thought for certain that he was writing this piece for his own funeral."

Another of Mozart's early biographers, a confidant of Constanze, was Franz Niemetschek. He told the story this way, also in a 1798 work: "Mozart began to speak of death, and declared that he was writing the *Requiem* for himself. Tears came to the eyes of this sensitive man. 'I feel definitely,' he continued, 'that I will not last much longer; I am sure I have been poisoned.'"

Mozart never finished the *Requiem*, though even in its incomplete form it's considered a masterpiece. Constanze's story undoubtedly added to the aura surrounding the work and its composer; here was Mozart, driven to the heights of creativity, and ultimately driven to his death, by forces neither he nor others could fully understand. What could be a more appropriate ending to Mozart's brief (he was only thirty-five) but brilliant life?

It's a very satisfying story. And there was never any doubt it originated with Constanze; Rochlitz and Niemetschek both said they heard it from her, as did Vincent and Mary Novello, who published a similar account in 1828. But obvious questions remained: Who was the mysterious stranger who commissioned the Requiem? And who, if anyone, poisoned Mozart?

⌘

Rumors that Mozart had been murdered surfaced soon after his death, even before the 1798 accounts by Rochlitz and Niemetschek. On New Year's Eve of 1791, a Berlin newspaper reported that "because his body swelled up after death, people even thought he had been poisoned." One of the earliest suspects was Franz Hofdemel, the husband of one of Mozart's pupils. Hofdemel attacked his wife and committed suicide on the day of Mozart's funeral, leading some to speculate that his wife was pregnant with the composer's child. But there was no real evidence connecting Hofdemel with Mozart's death.

A more credible suspect emerged in the 1820s in the person of a former Austrian court composer, Antonio Salieri. Salieri's name appears in a number of entries in Beethoven's "conversation books," which his guests used to communicate with the deaf composer. Beethoven's son, Karl, and another visitor, Anton Schindler, both wrote in the notebooks that Salieri had confessed to poisoning Mozart; others recorded that the rumor he'd done so had spread throughout Vienna.

What was Salieri's motive?

Envy. Salieri, or so the rumor mill had it, recognized Mozart's genius—and hated him for it. It was unbearable for Salieri to watch Mozart surpass him as the leading composer at the Viennese court, especially since Mozart was often crude and arrogant, while Salieri was always courtly and correct. This was a highly compelling idea, at least as a literary conceit. The first to mine it theatrically was Alexander Pushkin in an 1830 play. Most recently, Peter Shaffer's 1980 Broadway hit *Amadeus*, which was later turned into a movie, again presented Salieri as a mediocre but eminently serious musician unable to bear the spectacle of the brilliant but boorish Mozart. Shaffer stops short of portraying Salieri as a poisoner; instead, the court composer merely hastens Mozart's demise through various plots that leave his victim impoverished and despondent.

The problem with the case against Salieri, either as murderer or intriguer, is the same as that against Hofdemel: there's no evidence. The alleged confession mentioned in Beethoven's conversation books was repeated nowhere else; in fact, according to the diary of one of Beethoven's pupils, the pianist Ignaz Moscheles, Salieri explicitly denied poisoning Mozart. True, Moscheles then went on to say that Salieri "had damaged him morally through intrigues, and thereby poisoned many an hour for him." But other than a few other similar, gossipy references, there's no real evidence that Salieri disliked Mozart, let alone murdered him.

omo

The next poisoner to be proposed was not an individual but an organization: the Freemasons.

The Masons made for a suitably sinister suspect, since they were a secret society with all sorts of mysterious rituals that seemed, to nonmembers, to verge on the occult. Mozart joined a small Viennese Masonic lodge in 1784. He was an active member, composing a number of pieces with Masonic themes, including *The Magic Flute*, his last completed work.

It was not until the mid-nineteenth century that scholars recognized the Masonic allusions in *The Magic Flute*. For example, the number 18, which is of great significance in

Masonic rituals, also plays an important part in Mozart's opera. At the beginning of Act II there are eighteen priests and eighteen chairs, and the first section of the chorus they sing is eighteen bars long. Moreover, the orchestral introduction to this scene contains eighteen groups of notes.

The original printing of the libretto in 1791 provides more explicit evidence that Mozart and his librettist (and fellow Mason) Emanuel Shikaneder meant the opera as, at least partly, a Masonic allegory. The title page of the libretto includes a five-pointed star, a square and a trowel, and an hourglass—all Masonic symbols.

The first to propose that the Masons poisoned Mozart was G. F. Daumer, in 1861. He argued that Mozart had antagonized his fellow Masons by revealing some of their secrets in *The Magic Flute.* So, Daumer argued, the Masons—or rather, an inner circle of Masons—took their revenge. This theory was picked up by many other nineteenth- and twentieth-century writers.

Like the Hofdemel and Salieri theories, however, the Masonic conspiracy theories had no real evidence behind them. True, most (though not all) scholars accepted that there was a Masonic component in *The Magic Flute,* but there was no reason to believe that the Masons weren't perfectly happy to be associated with the opera and its composer. Indeed, after Mozart's death his lodge held a memorial ceremony, and printed copies of the main speech made in his honor. The conspiracy theorists also have never been able to explain why the Masons would murder Mozart but not Shikaneder, who, as librettist, was at least equally responsible for the opera's allegorical elements.

The conspiracy theory is an unfair slur on the Masons who, though undeniably cultish, also included some of the most respected citizens of Vienna. Indeed, the lodges were a meeting place for much of the city's intellectual elite. Similarly, in America, the Masons counted among their members George Washington, Benjamin Franklin, and Thomas Jefferson, and in France many leading republicans joined.

The republicanism of many Masons was hardly reassuring to Austria's Emperor Leopold II, however. Leopold watched the revolutions abroad with a great deal of worry, and responded by cracking down on the Masons at home. He closed many of their lodges and had his police carefully monitor the rest. It was in response to this pressure, some historians have speculated, that Mozart and Shikaneder decided to produce a Masonic opera. Their hope was that The *Magic Flute* would convince the public, and the conservative government, that there was nothing to fear from the Masons.

If so, they hoped in vain; by the mid-1790s Leopold had outlawed the Masons completely, and their membership and influence dwindled. But, to get back to Mozart, he remained a loyal Mason until his death. And there's every reason to believe that his fellow Masons remained equally loyal to him.

⚭

If Mozart was poisoned, the most likely culprits were probably his doctors, albeit unintentionally.

Constanze reported at least one incident of doctors "bleeding" him, and there may have been others, since the treatment was still common in the late eighteenth century. In Mozart's weakened state, especially if he was suffering from a kidney disease, as many medical historians believe, the treatment may very well have contributed to his death.

Other than the bleeding, medical historians don't have much to go on. Mozart's death certificate listed the cause of death as "heated military fever," a diagnosis that means nothing to doctors today. Mozart's visitors, including Constanze, described his symptoms so diversely and so vaguely that he could have been suffering from any number of ailments, among them bacterial endocarditis, Henoch Schonlein syndrome, leukemia, staphylococcal bronchopneumonia, and cerebral hemorrhage.

At a medical symposium held in 1991, on the two-hundredth anniversary of Mozart's death, the top two candidates were clearly kidney failure and rheumatic fever, but there was no clear consensus among the experts—except that none of them believed he was poisoned.

As for Mozart's own belief to the contrary, that could easily have been the result of delirium or depression brought on by just about any of the illnesses that led to his death. No doubt, too, the visit of the mysterious messenger who commissioned the *Requiem* would have focused his mind on death, his own in particular. It's easy to imagine the weakened composer turning the mysterious messenger into a messenger of death. Indeed, Shaffer suggested that Salieri, knowing that Mozart was preoccupied with death, disguised himself as the messenger to drive his rival over the edge.

The truth about the messenger, which was finally revealed 173 years after Mozart's death, was less diabolical but no less strange. In 1964, Otto Deutsch published a document, discovered in the archives of Wiener Neustadt, a town about thirty miles south of Vienna. Titled the "True and Detailed History of the Requiem by W. A. Mozart, from its inception in the year 1791 to the present period of 1839," it was written by Anton Herzog, a musician employed by a Count von Walsegg, a major landowner in the region.

The count, Herzog explained, was a passionate music lover who liked to buy the works of promising composers and pass them off as his own. In February 1791 the count's young wife died, and he decided he wanted to commemorate her death with an especially majestic *Requiem*. So he sent a servant to Mozart, with his usual generous offer and his equally standard admonition not to try to find out who'd commissioned the work.

Herzog and his fellow musicians humored their boss. "That the count wanted to mystify us, as he had done with the [other pieces he'd commissioned], was well known to all of us," he recalled. "In our presence he always said it was his composition, but when he said that he smiled."

So Mozart's final masterpiece, it turned out, was written not for some ghostly harbinger of death, but for an eccentric plagiarist. Constanze, no fool, may have circulated the story of the unknown messenger in the hope that it would add to her dead husband's rapidly growing reputation—not to mention the rapidly growing value of his compositions. If so, she succeeded beyond her dreams, for the *Requiem* came to be seen as one of Mozart's masterpieces. And so it remains, regardless of how it came to be written.

To Investigate Further

Deutsch, Otto E. *Mozart: A Documentary Biography*, trans. from the German by Eric Blom, Peter Branscombe, and Jeremy Noble. Stanford, CA: Stanford University Press, 1965.
    An extensive selection of primary sources.

Nettl, Paul. *Mozart and Masonry.* New York: Da Capo Press, 1970.
    Originally published in 1957, this remains the most comprehensive treatment of the subject.

Hildesheimer, Wolfgang. *Mozart*, trans. from the German by Marion Faber. New York: Farrar, Straus & Giroux, 1982.
    Originally published in Germany in 1977, this is more an extended essay than a traditional biography. The portrait of Mozart as a frivolous boor, albeit a brilliant one, may have partly inspired Shaffer's *Amadeus.*

Shaffer, Peter. *Amadeus.* New York: Harper & Row, 1980.
    A flop with historians, but a hit with theater- and moviegoers.

Robbins Landon, H. C. *1791: Mozart's Last Year.* New York: Schirmer Books, 1988.
    A lively chronicle of the year that portrays Mozart, partly in response to the Hildesheimer/Shaffer image, as a responsible husband and citizen.

Gruber, Gernot. *Mozart and Posterity,* trans. from the German by R. S. Furness. Boston: Northeastern University Press, 1991.
    How Mozart has been interpreted, from the eighteenth century through the twentieth.

Stafford, William. *The Mozart Myths.* Stanford, CA: Stanford University Press, 1991.
    Debunks the myth of foul play, as well as various other myths about Mozart—such as that he was a social reformer or a nationalist.

Dalhousie Review (Summer 1993).
    Most of the issue's contents are devoted to papers given at a 1991 symposium titled "Medicine in the Age of Mozart."

Solomon, Maynard. *Mozart.* New York: HarperCollins, 1995.
    A psychoanalytically influenced biography that focuses, quite persuasively, on Mozart's relationship with his father.

Was Sally Hemings the Mistress of Thomas Jefferson?

"It is well known that the man, *whom it delighteth the people to honor,* keeps, and for many years past has kept, as his concubine, one of his own slaves. Her name is SALLY. The name of her eldest son is TOM. His slaves are said to bear a striking although sable resemblance to the president himself."

So wrote James Callender in the September 2, 1802, issue of the Richmond *Recorder.* The charge that Jefferson had a slave mistress named Sally Hemings was picked up by other Federalist newspapers throughout the country; a Philadelphia magazine even commemorated it in verse, to be sung to the tune of "Yankee Doodle Dandy":

> *Of all the damsels on the green*
> *On mountain or in valley*
> *A lass so luscious ne'er was seen*
> *As Monticellian Sally.*

Stories of his slave mistress haunted Jefferson throughout the 1804 election campaign. Jefferson himself never commented on the charges publicly, though he denied them in a private letter to Robert Smith, his secretary of the navy. Other Republicans vehemently defended the president. They stressed that the stories were politically motivated, and in this they were undeniably correct: not only was the *Recorder* a Federalist paper, but Callender had a personal grudge against Jefferson.

Callender had once been a leading propagandist for Jefferson's own Republican Party. One of his earlier exposés had forced Alexander Hamilton to admit to an affair with a married woman; another of them had landed Callender in jail under the 1798 Alien and Sedition Acts. In 1801, when Jefferson became president, he pardoned Callender. But Callender felt his sufferings merited more than a pardon. He demanded that Jefferson appoint him postmaster at Richmond and that the president personally pay back the fines Callender had paid under the 1798 laws. When Jefferson refused, Callender threatened revenge; in switching to the Federalist side and writing the first of the Sally stories, he made good on that threat.

For Jefferson's defenders, then and since, Callender's blatantly malicious motives discredited his story. But to get to the truth, to determine whether or not Jefferson had a slave mistress, we must look beyond Callender's motives and examine the evidence.

෴

Callender himself had little hard evidence to offer. He never visited Monticello, never talked directly to Sally Hemings or anyone else connected with the story. Nor, apparently, did any other writer of the period. Then, in 1873, an obscure Ohio newspaper, the *Pike County Republican,* published an interview with Madison Hemings, the son of Sally Hemings and—he claimed—Thomas Jefferson. Hemings, in fact, claimed that his mother had told him a great deal about her longtime relationship with Jefferson— namely that the two had first become lovers in Paris in 1787. Jefferson, a widower since 1782, was then minister to France; Sally Hemings was there as a servant to his daughter. Madison Hemings went on:

> During that time my mother became Mr. Jefferson's concubine, and when he was called home she was *enciente* [sic] by him. He desired to bring my mother back to Virginia with him but she demurred. She was just beginning to understand the French language well, and in France she was free, while if she returned to Virginia she would be re-enslaved. So she refused to return with him. To induce her to do so he promised her extraordinary privileges, and made a solemn pledge that her children would be freed at the age of twenty-one years.

This promise Jefferson eventually kept. When Jefferson died, his slaves had to be sold to pay off creditors to whom he owed more than $100,000. But Jefferson made sure in his will that five of his slaves were to be freed; among these five were Madison Hemings and his brother Eston.

Madison Hemings's version of events was confirmed by another ex-slave memoir; that of Israel Jefferson. Israel Jefferson described how for fourteen years he'd cleaned and kept up Jefferson's bedroom and private chamber, and been on intimate terms with both Thomas Jefferson and Sally Hemings. Of Madison Hemings's claim to be the son of the president, Israel Jefferson said: "I can as conscientiously confirm his statement as any other fact which I believe from circumstances but do not positively know."

Israel Jefferson's memoir also confirmed another story that had been passed on for many years; namely, that Sally Hemings's mother, Betty Hemings, had been the mistress of Thomas Jefferson's father-in-law, John Wayles. This meant that Sally Hemings was the half sister of Thomas Jefferson's late wife, Martha Wayles Jefferson.

Strangely, many of Jefferson's defenders were quick to accept Israel Jefferson's testimony about the John Wayles–Betty Hemings liaison. Perhaps this was because the Wayles-Hemings affair provided an alternative explanation for why Thomas Jefferson treated the

Hemings family so much better than other slaves, and why he eventually freed Madison and Eston Hemings. After all, if Jefferson knew they were related to his wife, then his special treatment of them might have had nothing to do with Sally Hemings in particular.

As for the rest of Madison Hemings's and Israel Jefferson's testimony, however, that they adamantly rejected. To discredit it, Jefferson's nineteenth-century biographer Henry Randall produced a letter from Jefferson's grandson, Thomas Jefferson Randolph, in which he revealed that Sally Hemings had indeed been the mistress of a white man—but it was Jefferson's nephew, Peter Carr, and not Jefferson himself who'd slept with her and fathered her children. One of Jefferson's granddaughters, Ellen Randolph Coolidge, came up with a similar story, this time placing the blame on Samuel Carr, Peter's brother, whom she described as "the most notorious good-natured Turk that ever was master of a black seraglio kept at other men's expence." If either Carr brother fathered Sally Hemings's children, that could account for the children's resemblance to Jefferson.

Further mitigating against the Madison Hemings–Israel Jefferson version of events was the fact that both memoirs were published in the *Pike Country Republican*. For a Republican newspaper in 1873, it was good politics to make the antebellum South—with which the Democrats could still be associated—look bad, and the *Republican* was almost as partisan a paper as Callender's *Recorder*. Also suspicious was the language in both the Madison Hemings and Israel Jefferson memoirs; it sounded a lot more like that of a newspaper editor than that of two ex-slaves, and Jefferson's defenders concluded that an editor might have worked on the content as well as the language. Furthermore, they argued, even if Madison Hemings had come up with the story himself, it was clearly in the interest of an impoverished ex-slave to turn out to be the son of Jefferson—and even if Sally Hemings had really told him Jefferson was his father, she might have made up the story for the same reason.

Of course, Jefferson's grandchildren had just as vested an interest in their version of events as his ex-slaves did in theirs. But most historians followed Randall's lead, or at least concluded the conflicting testimonies cancelled each other out. And in the absence of more hard evidence of the affair, most dismissed it as a nasty rumor.

⁙

This genteel consensus was tested with the 1974 publication of Fawn Brodie's "intimate history" of Thomas Jefferson. The first major biographer to accept the Hemings story, Brodie presented a portrait in stark contrast to the traditional image of a monkish Jefferson, a man who, after his wife's death, devoted himself to philosophy and politics. Brodie's Jefferson remained a passionate lover. In France, before the arrival of Sally Hemings, Jefferson met an artist named Maria Cosway, to whom he wrote a remarkable love letter consisting mostly of a debate between "My Head and My Heart." Most biographers have interpreted the letter as a victory for Jefferson's head; Brodie, however, saw the heart as the winner. Brodie was convinced the Cosway-Jefferson relationship was both passionate and sexual.

But it was her portrait of the Hemings-Jefferson relationship that generated the most controversy. In addition to her efforts to rehabilitate the reputations and credibility of Callender and of Madison Hemings, Brodie presented a great deal of psychological evidence. For example, she noted that in his 1788 diary of a tour of Germany, Jefferson used the word "mulatto" eight times to describe the color of the soil; in Brodie's interpretation, it was Sally Hemings's mulatto color and not Germany's soil that was on Jefferson's mind. In a 1789 letter to Cosway, Jefferson described himself as "an animal of a warm climate, a mere Oran-ootan"; Brodie points out that in his *Notes on the State of Virginia,* Jefferson had indiscreetly written that "the Oran-ootan preferred the black woman over those of his own species."

In another letter to Cosway, Jefferson described a painting he'd just seen of Sarah delivering Hagar to Abraham. Jefferson called the painting "delicious" and added: "I would have agreed to have been Abraham though the consequence would have been that I should have been dead five or six thousand years." Brodie was quick to remind readers of the significance of the biblical story: Sarah, who was barren, gave Hagar (whom most artists depicted as dark skinned) to Abraham so that she could bear him a child. To Brodie, Jefferson's lustful description could only be an unconscious admission of his love for Hemings.

Brodie's book was the best-selling nonfiction book of the year, and many general interest newspapers, including the *New York Times* and the *Washington Post,* reviewed it favorably. The historical establishment, however, was unconvinced. Dumas Malone, whose multivolume Jefferson biography won a Pulitzer Prize, said the book ran "far beyond the evidence and carries psychological speculation to the point of absurdity; the resulting mishmash of fact and fiction, surmise and conjecture is not history as I understand the term." Merrill Peterson, author of the most widely respected one-volume biography of Jefferson, called Brodie "obsessive" and concluded there was "no need to charge off in defense of Jefferson's integrity when we have no solid grounds for doubting it."

Indeed, much of Brodie's psychological evidence does seem far-fetched and some of it is just outright wrong; for example, according to the *Oxford English Dictionary,* the use of the word "mulatto" to describe the color of soil was common in eighteenth-century America. Even scholars with no vested interest in any particular image of Jefferson found Brodie's work long on speculation and short on hard evidence.

Still, the vehemence of the attacks on Brodie, and the even more vehement denials that someone of Jefferson's character could have slept with Hemings, were themselves revealing. Malone, for example, wrote that "it is virtually inconceivable that this fastidious gentleman . . . could have carried on through a period of years a vulgar liaison." Clearly, Brodie had done more than repeat some old gossip; she'd touched a nerve.

What Brodie had done was to bring into the foreground of Thomas Jefferson's life the place of slavery and race, something most of his other biographers were loath to do. By focusing on his purported relationship with Hemings, she'd reminded readers that, regardless of whether or not he'd slept with her, he'd owned her. Brodie herself did not believe the relationship was an abusive one; on the contrary, she was convinced

Jefferson and Hemings shared a deep and lasting love. But Jefferson most certainly was not in love with the other two hundred slaves he owned—and his treatment of them and attitudes toward them were not so different from those of other wealthy Virginian slaveowners.

This is not to deny that Jefferson hated slavery, or that his ideals inspired later anti-slavery efforts. But Jefferson's actions definitely did not live up to his ideals. Unlike Washington, whose will freed all his slaves on his death, Jefferson freed only the two Hemings brothers and three others. Jefferson's 1783 draft of a new constitution for Virginia provided for the freedom of all children born of slaves after the year 1800, but that unsuccessful effort was his last on behalf of emancipation. After his return from France, wrote David Brion Davis, "the most remarkable thing about Jefferson's stand on slavery is his immense silence." On one of the few occasions he did speak out, during the Missouri crisis of 1820, he threw his considerable weight behind slavery's expansion. When the chips were down, Jefferson supported the system that supported him.

By 1997, this perspective had spread sufficiently that reviewers were at least respectful when a law professor, Annette Gordon-Reed, systematically exposed the biases that had led historians to dismiss the evidence presented by Madison Hemings and Israel Jefferson, as well as Callender and Brodie. "Jefferson defenders," Gordon-Reed wrote, "having staked their arguments on the notion of the impossibility or improbability of this story, could not afford to set before the readers all the known information." That same year, Joseph Ellis's biography of Jefferson honed in on his flawed and contradictory character. On the Hemings controversy, Ellis concluded it was possible but unlikely. "On the basis of what we know now, we can never know."

Ellis spoke a year too soon. In 1998, writing in *Nature* magazine, a team of scientists announced that the Y-chromosome markers of Jefferson's descendants perfectly matched those of Sally Hemings's last son, Eston. The chances of a random perfect match were less than one in a thousand. The DNA evidence also ruled out any chance that Peter Carr or Samuel Carr was the culprit. The jury remained out on Hemings's other children, but as Ellis wrote in a January 2000 essay in *William and Mary Quarterly,* "the burden of proof has shifted rather dramatically."

Historians continued to debate the nature of the Jefferson-Hemings relationship. Was it consensual, with Hemings gaining some privileged status for herself or her children, or even sharing some form of love, as Brodie thought? Or was it rape, no different from what went on in other plantations of the era? Either way, most scholars agreed, the relationship was both sexual and long-standing.

To Investigate Further

Peterson, Merrill D. *The Jefferson Image in the American Mind.* New York: Oxford University Press, 1960.

The evolution of Jefferson's image in the American imagination.

Jordan, Winthrop. *White Over Black.* Williamsburg, VA: Institute of Early American History and Culture, 1968.

A study of American attitudes toward blacks up to 1812 that includes arguments against the affair.

Malone, Dumas. *Jefferson the President, First Term.* New York: Little, Brown, 1970.

Volume 4 of the Pulitzer Prize–winning set.

Peterson, Merrill D. *Thomas Jefferson and the New Nation.* New York: Oxford University Press, 1970.

The best one-volume biography.

Brodie, Fawn. *Thomas Jefferson, An Intimate History.* New York: Norton, 1974.

Critics conveniently focused on her errors, rather than the rest of her evidence.

Adair, Douglass. *Fame and the Founding Fathers.* Williamsburg, VA: Institute of Early American History and Culture, 1974.

Adair's 1960 essay, "The Jefferson Scandals," is included here and was, until the DNA evidence, one of the most convincing refutations of the affair.

Davis, David Brion. *The Problem of Slavery in the Age of Revolution, 1770–1823.* Ithaca, NY: Cornell University Press, 1975.

A wide-ranging study of the complex and contradictory factors that influenced opinions on slavery, including a very unforgiving analysis of Jefferson's role.

Miller, John Chester. *The Wolf by the Ears.* New York: The Free Press, 1977.

"We have a wolf by the ears, and we can neither hold him nor safely let him go," wrote Jefferson in 1820. "Justice is in one scale, and self-preservation in the other." In Miller's book you can see how Jefferson chose the latter.

Dabney, Virginius. *The Jefferson Scandals: A Rebuttal.* New York: Dodd, Mead, 1981.

A sanctimonious refutation of Brodie.

Ellis, Joseph. *American Sphinx.* New York, Knopf, 1997.

Whatever else you can say about Jefferson, he sure could write. The same can be said of Ellis.

Gordon-Reed, Annette. *Thomas Jefferson and Sally Hemings.* Charlottesville: University Press of Virginia, 1997.

Less damning of Jefferson than of the prominent Jeffersonian scholars who disparaged the sources that undercut their arguments.

Foster, E.A. et al. "Jefferson Fathered Slave's Last Child." *Nature* (November 5, 1998).

The DNA evidence.

Was Aaron Burr a Traitor?

AARON BURR'S ORIGINS would seem to make him an unlikely traitor.

The grandson of Jonathan Edwards, the country's most famous theologian, Burr served gallantly during the Revolution (albeit under the command of Benedict Arnold). His political star rose steadily, and he was elected vice president under Thomas Jefferson in 1800.

The election turned out to be the high point of Burr's career. Though voters clearly intended Jefferson to head the ticket, the ballot did not distinguish between presidential and vice-presidential candidates. As a result, Jefferson and Burr each ended up with 73 electoral votes. Tradition called for one or two of Burr's electors to throw their votes elsewhere, assuring Jefferson the presidency. But Burr, undeniably ambitious, made no effort to see that happen. That threw the election into the House of Representatives.

The House was controlled by Federalists, who were no fans of Burr but who liked Jefferson even less. Suddenly it seemed that Burr, not Jefferson, could become the nation's third president. It was then that Alexander Hamilton stepped in, urging his fellow Federalists to vote for Jefferson. Jefferson, Hamilton said, at least had "solid pretensions to character."

"As to Burr there is nothing in his favour," Hamilton went on. "His public principles have no other spring or aim than his own aggrandizement."

Hamilton was persuasive, and Jefferson, of course, became president. And the Twelfth Amendment to the Constitution was quickly adopted, to make sure that from then on voters would distinguish between presidential and vice-presidential candidates.

Burr's star continued to plummet. Jefferson, understandably unhappy with the man who almost usurped his presidency, made sure that the vice president had no role in his administration. The enmity with Hamilton escalated until Burr challenged him to a duel. In July 1804, the two rowed across the Hudson River to a spot near Weehawken, New Jersey, where the vice president shot and killed Hamilton. Burr was indicted for murder in New Jersey, and for lesser charges pertaining to the duel in New York.

"In New York I am to be disenfranchised, in New Jersey hanged," Burr wrote his son-in-law. "Having substantial objections to both, I shall not, for the present, hazard either, but shall seek another country."

But where?

Dueling was illegal throughout the North. It was more acceptable in the South, but that was Jefferson country. That left the West, where gun fighting was common, and where many saw Hamilton as a symbol of the hated eastern establishment of bankers and land speculators. In April 1805, Burr headed west.

At first, it seemed just the right place for Burr. He began attracting followers for various military expeditions to Texas and Florida. Spanish rule was increasingly unpopular in both places, especially among westerners eager to expand America's (and their own) holdings. Burr bought about 300,000 acres in Louisiana, known as the Bastrop land, and promised a share to many of his followers.

Burr seemed destined to follow the likes of Lewis and Clark, or perhaps Andrew Jackson, another duelist-turned-military-hero against Spain. He met with Jackson, as well as James Wilkinson, commander of the U.S. forces in the West, and impressed both. He may even have received some encouragement from Jefferson, whose own expansionist tendencies were clearly revealed by the Louisiana Purchase.

Yet within a few months of his arrival out west there were already unflattering rumors circulating about Burr's intentions. In August 1805, a front-page article in the widely read *Gazette of the United States* asked: "How long will it be before we shall hear of Col. Burr being at the head of a revolution party on the western waters?"

The clear implication was that Burr was preparing, not to attack Florida or Texas, but to lead a western secession from the United States.

Throughout 1806, Burr gathered men and supplies on Blennerhassett Island, an island in the middle of the Ohio River owned by the improbably named Irish immigrant and Burr-follower Harman Blennerhassett. In October, Wilkinson received a coded letter, dated July and allegedly from Burr.

"I have at length obtained funds, and have actually commenced," the letter read, as Wilkinson decoded it. "The Eastern detachments, from different points and under different pretence, will rendezvous on Ohio on 1 November."

It continued: "Every Thing internal and external favor our view . . . Wilkinson shall be second to Burr only and Wilkinson shall dictate the rank and promotion of his officers. . . . Draw on me for all expenses."

"The gods invite us to glory and fortune," the cipher letter concluded. "It remains to be seen whether we deserve the boons."

What the letter described was clearly more than a military expedition against Spain. It sounded suspiciously like a plot for a revolution in the West, with Burr setting himself up as emperor of a new nation and Wilkinson as his second-in-command.

Wilkinson quickly forwarded the letter to Jefferson, who had by then received reports from numerous others of Burr's alleged plots. Jefferson denounced Burr as the organizer of this "unlawful enterprise." He called his guilt "beyond question," and he ordered his arrest.

And so it was that in August 1807, Aaron Burr—who had come within a single electoral vote of being president of the United States—stood trial for treason.

⌒ﮨﻭ

The presiding judge was John Marshall, chief justice of the Supreme Court, and both Jefferson's cousin and political foe. Jefferson and Marshall had clashed over a number of constitutional issues, since Marshall was a Federalist and eager to protect the judiciary against Jefferson's efforts to expand the power of the executive branch. Not that this necessarily meant Marshall would be prejudiced in Burr's favor, for the chief justice also happened to be a great admirer of Alexander Hamilton.

The prosecution was at something of a disadvantage from the start, because of the dubious credibility of its star witness—Wilkinson. During the grand jury, defense attorneys were quick to point out that the general seemed to know a great deal about Burr's plots; Wilkinson answered, not very persuasively, that he'd pretended to go along with Burr to find out more about his plans. To many, Wilkinson appeared to have turned against Burr to protect himself. After all, the cipher letter named the general as "second to Burr only." Wilkinson further undercut the prosecution's case by admitting he erased portions of the letter that referred to his previous correspondence with Burr.

Still, the government had more than a hundred other witnesses ready to testify about Burr's plans. But they all became irrelevant on August 31, when Marshall ruled that treason required an overt act, and one witnessed by at least two citizens. That meant that Burr's plans, whatever they were, could not be brought into evidence.

Prosecutors now had to limit their case to the goings-on on Blennerhasset Island in December, when Burr's forces assembled and presumably committed some sort of overt act of treason. The problem was, Burr himself wasn't there; in December, he was in Frankfort, Kentucky, a day's journey away. So, Marshall ruled, none of that evidence was relevant either. The next day, the jury took only twenty-five minutes to decide "that Aaron Burr is not proved to be guilty under this indictment by any evidence submitted to us." The phrasing clearly indicates it was a grudging acquittal, but Burr was free to go.

The question, again, was: where should he go?

The press and public thought he was a traitor, even if the jury wasn't sure. The treason trial left him with no base in the West, and in New York there were still charges against him from the duel. In June 1808, Burr sneaked out of Manhattan and set sail for England. He spent two years in Europe before deciding there was no place for him there, either.

Back in America, he continued to maintain his innocence. In Burr's 1836 memoirs, he emphasized his intentions in the West were always, first, "the revolutionizing of Mexico," and second, "a settlement on what was known as the Bastrop lands." Matthew Davis, who co-authored the memoirs, reported that when Burr was asked if he'd ever thought of a "separation of the Union," he responded, "I would as soon have thought of taking possession of the moon, and informing my friends that I intended to divide it among them."

Burr felt somewhat vindicated in 1836, when Sam Houston defeated the Mexicans and Texas declared its independence. "You see? I was right. I was only thirty years too soon," he said. "What was treason in me thirty years ago, is patriotism now."

ᴏᴛᴛᴌᴏ

In 1890, more than eighty years after Burr's treason trial, the historian Henry Adams uncovered new evidence pointing to his guilt. The evidence came not from anything in America, but from British archives.

Adams examined the letters of Anthony Merry, British ambassador to the United States between 1803 and 1806. Merry's letters home were voluminous; one contemporary remarked that if you asked Merry what time it was, he would write his government for instructions. Amidst this correspondence Adams found a short note to the British foreign secretary, dated August 6, 1804.

Wrote Merry: "I have just received an offer from Mr. Burr, the actual Vice President of the United States . . . to lend his assistance to His Majesty's Government in any Manner in which they may think fit to employ him, particularly in endeavouring to effect a Separation of the Western Part of the United States from that which lies between the Atlantick and the Mountains, in it's whole Extent."

Merry warned his government of the "Profligacy of Mr. Burr's Character," but insisted that he could be of much use to the British. "He is now cast off as much by the democratic as by the Federalist Party," Merry wrote, "and where he still preserves Connections with some People of Influence, added to his great Ambition and Spirit of Revenge against the present Administration, [this] may possibly induce him to exert the Talents and Activity which he possesses. . . ."

A March 29, 1805, letter from Merry home seemed even more damning. By then, Burr had already been west, and apparently had reported to Merry on the likely success of a revolution, adding that if England wouldn't help, France might.

"Mr. Burr . . . told me that the Inhabitants of Louisiana notwithstanding that they are almost all of French or Spanish Origins, as well as those in the Western Part of the United States, would, for many obvious reasons, prefer having the Protection and Assistance of Great Britain to the Support of France," Merry wrote. "If his Majesty's Government should not think it proper to listen to this overture, Applications will be made to that of France who will, he had reason to know, be eager to attend to it in the most effectual manner."

Surely, if Burr was attempting to enlist foreign support for a western revolution, this was treason, and that was Adams's conclusion. Yet Burr's defenders had an answer: Burr wanted money from the British, so he told Merry whatever he thought might get him the money. Burr's actual intentions, his defenders maintained, were always a perfectly patriotic (and typically American) expansionism.

"To secure the sum he conceived to be necessary for his purposes," wrote Walter McCaleb in 1903, "he never scrupled at discoursing of treasons, although at the moment every step he was taking looked toward an invasion of the Spanish territories."

More support for Burr was soon forthcoming, this time from Spanish archives.

Here historians found proof that Wilkinson—the man who sent Jefferson the cipher letter and who testified to Burr's treason—was himself a traitor. The Spanish records confirmed a rumor that had circulated even before the trial. Wilkinson, it turned out, was receiving $2,000 a year from the Spanish government, in return for which he regularly supplied the Spaniards with military intelligence. Indeed, just after Wilkinson sent the cipher letter to Jefferson, he sent another copy to the Spanish governor of Florida to let him know of Burr's plans (and to suggest a suitable reward for the information).

Wilkinson's credibility had been suspect during the trial, especially after he admitted to doctoring the letter. With the proof that Wilkinson was on the Spanish payroll, it seemed all the more possible that the general had turned on Burr to deflect suspicion from himself. At the very least, it was clear that the cipher letter to Wilkinson was not grounds for condemning Burr, and some scholars concluded the letter was a forgery.

The most thorough analysis of the letter was by Mary-Jo Kline, who edited Burr's papers in the 1970s and early 1980s. Kline noted that the letter, which still exists in Chicago's Newberry Library, is clearly not in Burr's handwriting. Instead, she found a remarkable resemblance to the writing of Jonathan Dayton, a Federalist senator and Burr associate.

If Dayton was the author, that cleared up one mystery. It explained why the letter referred to Burr as well as Wilkinson in the third person, a usage that seemed strange, even for a letter in code.

But the greater mystery—whether Burr was or was not a traitor—remained unsolved. Sure, it now seemed clear, Burr didn't write the letter. But Dayton, unlike Wilkinson, was Burr's ally and friend. Burr might have asked Dayton to keep Wilkinson informed of the progress of Burr's plans, perhaps to make sure the general was willing to help. Or Dayton might have decided to do so on his own.

Either way, Dayton had no reason to make up stories about Burr's plans, and there's good reason to believe Dayton knew what those plans were.

c²sɔ

From the start, Burr's reputation has been tied to that of his adversaries.

The duel, ironically, gave Hamilton the last word on their feud. As dueling came to be seen as increasingly objectionable, so, too, did Burr. In spite of Burr's adamant denials, most historians believe Hamilton had no intention of shooting Burr, and that Burr shot first.

Similarly, Jefferson once seemed destined to have the last word on Burr's alleged treachery. He was, after all, the president and the author of the Declaration of Independence; of the founding fathers, only Washington's reputation seemed more unassailable.

A majority of historians continue to follow Jefferson in viewing Burr's guilt as "beyond question." But Jefferson's reputation has been tarnished by the now generally accepted evidence that a slave, Sally Hemings, gave birth to his children. More generally, historians have increasingly emphasized the extent to which Jefferson's slaveholding belied his democratic ideals.

Jefferson's fall from grace has meant a corresponding rise in his enemy's reputation, and the latest histories of the period have cast Burr in a decidedly more positive light. For all his character flaws, Burr was a committed abolitionist, and some historians have gone so far as to argue that's why Jefferson wanted him out of the way. When Jefferson called Burr a "threat to the Empire of Liberty," wrote Roger Kennedy in 2000, it was because

Burr's plans for the West threatened "the liberty of . . . those who had slaves to sell into an expanding plantation system."

That's hardly proof of Burr's innocence. The driving force throughout Burr's life was not abolitionism but ambition, and his ambition may very well have encompassed a dream of becoming the Napoleon of the West. Revisionists like Kennedy, in their eagerness to cut Jefferson down to size, are perhaps a bit too eager to build up Burr's stature. But they are absolutely right to look at Burr anew, and through eyes other than Hamilton's or Jefferson's.

To Investigate Further

Kline, Mary-Jo, ed. *Political Correspondence and Public Papers of Aaron Burr.* Princeton, NJ: Princeton University Press, 1983.
> Includes essays on topics such as the cipher letter, as well as the papers themselves.

Reed, V. B., and J. D. Williams, eds. *The Case of Aaron Burr.* Boston: Houghton Mifflin, 1960.
> Documents pertaining to the conspiracy, arrest, and trials.

Davis, Matthew L. *Memoirs of Aaron Burr.* New York: Da Capo Press, 1971.
> Originally published in 1836, this is as close as we'll come to Burr's own version of his life, though it's in the words of his friend.

McCaleb, Walter Flavius. *The Aaron Burr Conspiracy.* New York: Argosy-Antiquarian, 1966.
> Originally published in 1903 and still one of the best cases for the defense.

Abernethy, Thomas Perkins. *The Burr Conspiracy.* New York: Oxford University Press, 1954.
> A persuasive case that Burr, at least initially, was planning to create a new nation in the West.

Lomask, Milton. *Aaron Burr.* New York: Farrar Straus Giroux, 1979, 1982.
> The definitive biography, in two volumes.

Fleming, Thomas. *Duel.* New York: Basic Books, 1999.
> An entertaining retelling of the fateful "interview" at Weehawken.

Ellis, Joseph J. *Founding Brothers.* New York: Knopf, 2000.
> Ellis's opening chapter offers an excellent analysis of the mysteries surrounding the duel, including whether Hamilton shot first, and whether Burr intended to kill him.

Kennedy, Roger. *Burr, Hamilton, and Jefferson.* New York: Oxford University Press, 2000.
> A provocative though sometimes disjointed defense of Burr as abolitionist and proto-feminist.

Melton, Buckner F. *Aaron Burr: Conspiracy to Treason.* New York: John Wiley & Sons, 2002.
> A constitutional scholar's thorough overview of the legal and ethical issues surrounding the trial.

Was Napoleon Murdered?

S T. HELENA, THE SOUTH ATLANTIC ISLAND on which the British imprisoned Napoleon Bonaparte after his defeat at the Battle of Waterloo, featured a reasonably healthy, if damp, climate, and a large country home named Longwood, where the ex-emperor and his entourage could live in comparative comfort. But the island's chief merit, from the British standpoint, was its isolation; prior to being turned into a prison, its main use was as a stopping point for ships en route to India. The British well remembered how easily Napoleon had escaped his previous exile on Elba, an island too near the west coast of Italy, and how close he had come, prior to Waterloo, to reestablishing his empire. St. Helena's forty-seven square miles were enough to house a garrison of 2,250 British troops, without much space left over for those who might gather to gawk at Napoleon, or worse, conspire to free him. The island's cliffs also discouraged any would-be rescuers from landing anywhere other than the port of Jamestown.

Napoleon's first months on the island were fairly pleasant. While Longwood was being readied, he stayed in a house near Jamestown. Passersby witnessed the incongruous sight of the former emperor playing with two giggling English schoolgirls. The girls would blindfold Napoleon, then run around him crying "Boney, Boney!" At Longwood, however, he was rarely playful and often sick. He suffered frequently from stomach aches, chills, coughing, and nausea, despite the comings and goings of six different doctors. By the end of 1820, Napoleon's diet was reduced to fluids, yet he continued to gain weight. He died in May 1821.

The autopsy, carried out by the Italian doctor Francesco Antommarchi and observed by five British surgeons, concluded that the cause of death was cancer, which also killed Napoleon's father but didn't explain why he had gained weight until near the very end. Antommarchi didn't sign the report, blaming instead an enlarged liver caused by hepatitis.

Napoleon himself believed he was poisoned.

"I came to sit at the heart of the British nation, asking only for honest hospitality," he told his latest doctor just weeks before his death. The statement was hardly a full and accurate explanation of how Napoleon came to be under British authority, but Napoleon's immediate point was how the British had treated him. "There is not a single indignity that has not been heaped upon me by my captors. . . . And now perishing on this loathsome rock, I bequeath the name of my death to the ruling house of England."

Around the same time, he revised his will. "My death is not natural," he asserted. "I have been assassinated by the English oligarchy and their hired murderer."

⌒〰〰◡

The hired murderer Napoleon had in mind was Hudson Lowe, governor of St. Helena and thus Napoleon's warden. Lowe offended Napoleon from the start by addressing him as General Bonaparte rather than Emperor Napoleon, and their relationship went downhill from there. In 1818, when the British doctor Barry O'Meara refused to report on his conversations with Napoleon, Lowe fired him. O'Meara took his revenge in his 1822 book, *Napoleon in Exile,* which described the governor as a man of "violent passion" and insinuated he'd ordered the doctor to kill his patient.

Lowe's reaction to Antommarchi's autopsy was also suspicious. He objected to Antommarchi's characterization of Napoleon's liver as enlarged and deleted it from the final report.

Lowe had other enemies as well. In England, a circle of Whigs sympathized with Napoleon, in part because the emperor was also an opponent of the divine rights of kings. They pushed Lowe to help Napoleon escape, and when he refused, they turned against him. The courtiers who accompanied Napoleon to St. Helena also had little good to say about Lowe. Writing home to France, they described the intolerable "cabin" in which they lived, and the "vexatious interference" of the British governor.

Count Charles Tristan de Montholon, Napoleon's closest confidante on the island, recalled Napoleon's words after a visit from Lowe. "Throw away that coffee in my cup," Napoleon told Montholon. "I don't want to drink it, for that fellow has been near it. I think he is capable of anything, even of poisoning me."

By the time of Napoleon's death, Lowe's reputation was in tatters. Even the Duke of Wellington, who defeated Napoleon at Waterloo, described Lowe's appointment as a mistake. "He was a man wanting in education and judgment," said Wellington. "I always thought Lowe was the most unfit person to be charged with the care of Bonaparte's person." When Lowe died in 1844, he was generally despised as at best a petty tyrant.

In reality, there was no evidence that Lowe treated Napoleon cruelly, let alone murdered him. Lowe increased the support for Napoleon's household to 12,000 pounds a year, the same amount he received as governor. Longwood, though hardly a grand palace or the English country estate Napoleon may have envisioned, was more comfortable than Plantation House, where Lowe lived. Napoleon had forty rooms, a stable of horses, his own servants and cook, ample provisions, and a well-stocked wine cellar.

True, there were restrictions on his freedom. He could not walk or ride outside Longwood's grounds except when accompanied by a British officer. But he was, after all, a prisoner, and from the perspective of the British crown, a dangerous one. It was not so long before that he'd escaped from Elba and plunged Europe back into war. Lowe's orders were to make sure he didn't escape again. He obeyed them.

To some extent, the complaints of Napoleon and his courtiers were calculated to create sympathy in France and Europe. Count Emanuel de Las Cases, who accompanied Napoleon to St. Helena to record his thoughts, later explained: "It was necessary to reduce to a system, our demeanor, our words, our sentiments, even our privations, with the intention of exciting a lively interest in Europe and to rouse the political opposition in England to attack their own government regarding their violent conduct towards us."

Lowe may not have been the right person for the job, but he was the victim of a masterful public relations campaign. As Montholon later admitted, "an angel from heaven could not have pleased us as Governor of St. Helena."

⟶

Courts tend to breed intrigue, and Napoleon's was no exception. Indeed, with little else to do on the isle, his courtiers were soon at each other's throats. In 1816 Las Cases stormed off the island after General Gaspard Gourgaud suggested he was taking down Napoleon's stories to sell them and "in order to be talked about" in France. Gourgaud at one point challenged Montholon to a duel, and in 1818, full of resentment over Napoleon's favoritism toward the count, the general left the island. That same year, Napoleon's butler, Cipriani, and a young maid died after the sudden onset of severe chills, burning abdominal pains, and nausea. Those in Napoleon's shrinking circle were increasingly on edge.

The emerging favorite, and—according to the terms of Napoleon's will—the man who would inherit two million francs, was Montholon. This led some historians to suspect that the count, not the governor, poisoned Napoleon. With Cipriani, who'd run the Longwood kitchen, out of the picture, Montholon had easy access to Napoleon's food and drink. The motive may have been to hasten his inheritance, or Montholon may have been disturbed by rumors that his wife was having an affair with Napoleon. Montholon may also have been working for Louis XVIII, who was none too secure in his return to the French throne. As much as the British worried about Napoleon returning to power, Louis worried more.

The count's past was sufficiently shady to lend credence to the theory. He claimed, for example, that he had been honored for his heroism and wounded in various battles at which he wasn't even present. He was charged with stealing the pay of some of the soldiers who served under him. Montholon's explanation was that over the course of four months, he hadn't gotten a chance to pay them.

There was, of course, a great deal of irony in the idea that the French emperor, having evaded the artillery of the Prussians, Russians, and British, was done in by a Frenchman, the man Napoleon called "the most faithful of the faithful." But even if Montholon was not the murderer, more and more historians have concluded someone was. In the 1950s, the diaries of Louis Marchand, Napoleon's valet, and Gratien Bertrand, his grand marshal, were published for the first time. Both included descriptions of Napoleon's symptoms and declining health that were consistent with the gradual introduction of arsenic into his system.

In the 1960s, tests on Napoleon's hair confirmed the presence of arsenic. A decade later, a more sophisticated test indicated not only the presence of arsenic but also the likelihood that it had been ingested over a long period of time. Whoever wanted Napoleon dead, historian Ben Weider concluded, was apparently also eager to make his death look natural.

"The purpose was to . . . weaken and break down the health and immune system of the intended victim," Weider wrote. "Finally, death was caused by the introduction of various medications, which when combined in the stomach, produced a deadly corrosive poison."

᧞

Not everyone agreed poison killed Napoleon. Some historians expressed doubt about whether the hair samples were actually Napoleon's. Others speculated the poison could have been ingested accidentally—there might have been arsenic in the water, or in the ex-emperor's hair cream, or in the wallpaper. Arsenic could also have been added after his death to preserve the hair. Still others questioned whether there was enough arsenic to kill Napoleon. Other factors may also have played a role, such as cancer or hepatitis or even depression.

"There was no need to kill him since he was dying already," wrote travel writer and novelist Julia Blackburn after visiting St. Helena in the late 1980s, "and as one of the English doctors said, the only cure for his sickness, whatever that sickness might prove to be, was freedom from the island."

Even today, the causes of Napoleon's death are still tied, at least in part, to opinions about his life. Those who agreed with Las Casas that his was an "immortal cause," whether French glory or European unity or revolution and freedom, were more likely to portray Napoleon as a martyr, done in by reactionary forces in England or France. Those was saw Napoleon as a tyrant responsible for spilling blood across the continent were less likely to pity his imprisonment or question the official autopsy.

Napoleon himself was fully aware that what happened on St. Helena would be a key part of his legacy. "All eyes are focused on us and this island," he told Las Casas. "We remain the martyrs of an immortal cause."

To Investigate Further

O'Meara, Barry. *Napoleon in Exile.* London: W. Simpkin and R. Marshall, 1822.
    The surgeon's account of life on St. Helena.

Montholon, Charles Tristan de. *History of the Captivity of Napoleon at St. Helena.* New York: E. Ferrett and Co., 1846.
    "I breakfasted and dined with him, and during the night constantly tasted the drink prepared for him," Montholon wrote, explaining why it would have been "impossible to administer poison to him." Unless, of course, Montholon was the poisoner.

Weider, Ben, and Sten Forshufvud. *Assassination at St. Helena Revisited.* New York: Wiley, 1995.

The most persuasive case for poisoning comes from a Swedish dentist (Forshufvud) with a broad knowledge of toxicology, and a Canadian bodybuilding guru (Weider) who couldn't accept that Napoleon could succumb to anything less than treachery.

Blackburn, Julia. *The Emperor's Last Stand.* New York: Pantheon Books, 1991.

A beguiling mix of history and travel writing that vividly evokes life on St. Helena, then and now.

Schom, Alan. *Napoleon Bonaparte.* New York: HarperCollins, 1997.

A comprehensive and lively biography.

Giles, Frank. *Napoleon Bonaparte: England's Prisoner.* New York: Carroll & Graff, 2001.

How British party politics destroyed Lowe's reputation.

Johnson, Paul. *Napoleon.* New York: Lipper/Viking, 2002.

Johnson's brief biography certainly doesn't buy into the immortal cause. His Napoleon "was not an ideologue but an opportunist who seized on the accident of the French Revolution to propel himself into supreme power" and who "unleashed on Europe the most destructive wars the continent had ever experienced."

What Were
Joseph Smith's Golden Plates?

AMERICA, ACCORDING TO THE BOOK OF MORMON, was first settled by Israelites who crossed the Indian Ocean and then the Pacific sometime around 2250 B.C. Then they split into two warring tribes, one led by a prophet named Nephi and the other by his jealous older brother, Laman. For more than two millennia their descendants fought for control of the continent. About A.D. 400, in an epic battle at a hill in upstate New York, the Lamanites defeated the Nephites.

The Lamanites, whose evil ways God had cursed by turning their skin dark, spread throughout America, where they became known to white settlers as Indians. The Nephites were wiped off the face of the earth. But before that final defeat, the Nephite general, Mormon, wrote the history of the two peoples on a set of golden plates, and his son Moroni hid them at the site of the battle. There they remained buried for another fourteen hundred years.

In 1823 (this now according to Joseph Smith's autobiography) Moroni reappeared, this time as an angel. He told the seventeen-year-old Smith where he could find the plates, along with two "seer stones"—the Urim and Thummim—which would enable Smith to read the ancient hieroglyphics. Smith dug up the plates and the stones, and in 1830 published the Book of Mormon.

Thus was born the Church of the Latter-Day Saints, one of the world's fastest-growing religions and the only one whose holy text is set in America. America would also be the site of a new Zion, Smith promised his followers, and in search of it he led them from New York to Missouri and Ohio, then back to Missouri and on to Illinois. There, in 1844, he was gunned down by a mob incensed by his having destroyed the offices of an anti-Mormon newspaper, as well as by a general dislike of Smith's religion and politics. This martyrdom attracted more followers, who (now led by Brigham Young) established another new Zion, this time in Salt Lake City.

To back up his account of how he found the Book of Mormon, Smith allowed eleven witnesses to look at the golden plates. They couldn't keep them since, as Smith later explained, Moroni returned and took the plates with him. But the witnesses all agreed they'd seen the plates, and three swore they'd seen Moroni as well. One of these witnesses, Martin Harris, brought a copy of some of the hieroglyphic-like symbols to Charles Anthon, a professor of classics at Columbia University. This paper, too, has disappeared, amidst conflicting reports of Anthon's verdict. (Harris said Anthon identified the writing as some sort of ancient Egyptian; Anthon later denied this.)

According to Joseph Smith, an angel named Moroni led him to the gold plates that he translated into the Book of Mormon. *(Library of Congress)*

For Mormons, all this was proof that the Book of Mormon was literal truth. For non-Mormons, of course, both the text and Smith's story of how it came to be were met with skepticism from the start. Let Mormon literalists beware: they need read no further, since historians and archaeologists have uncovered no evidence whatsoever that would lead anyone to believe ancient Israelites immigrated to America, or fought a great battle in upstate New York. The Book of Mormon was not written by a general named Mormon, but rather by a farmer named Smith.

Does that mean there's no mystery here? On the contrary: for historians, the intriguing question is not who wrote the Book of Mormon, but how Smith did so. For as Mormon believers have pointed out from the start, Joseph Smith was an uneducated farmboy. His wife, Emma Hale Smith, said he could barely write a letter, let alone a complex literary work. Even his mother, Lucy Mack Smith, described Joseph as the least bookish of her children.

How, then, did Smith do it?

∞

The first and simplest explanation was: he didn't.

As early as 1834, Eber D. Howe argued that Smith had plagiarized the Book of Mormon. The true author, Howe argued in *Mormonism Unvailed* [sic], was an Ohio minister and novelist named Solomon Spaulding. Howe quoted neighbors of Spaulding, who said parts of the Book of Mormon were the same as a story Spaulding had read to them years before. This theory fell apart when Spaulding's papers were discovered and his unpublished manuscript was compared to the Book of Mormon. They had little in common.

Howe's book also provided evidence for another, longer-lasting theory. Much of *Mormonism Unvailed* consisted of testimony from Smith's neighbors, many of whom described how he and his father had tramped around upstate New York using all sorts of divining rods and seer stones to search for gold. This type of folk magic was fairly common in rural parts of the state, and there was nothing inherently disreputable about it. But the portrait of the prophet-to-be as a treasure hunter raised suspicions that, having failed to find gold, Smith chose instead to invent the golden plates.

Nineteenth-century commentators also noted that Smith absorbed many other aspects of rural culture besides magic and treasure hunting. This was a time of much religious revivalism. Just a year after the Book of Mormon was published, for example, another upstate New York farmer named William Miller began preaching to followers who later became known as Seventh-Day Adventists. Smith was thus to some extent just another preacher, albeit an extraordinarily successful one.

His story about Indian origins, too, was a product of his time. Indian mounds dotted much of the eastern half of the country, and were a source of much fascination and speculation. Distinguished preachers like Cotton Mather and Jonathan Edwards had already argued that the mounds were evidence that Indians were descendants of the lost tribes of

Israel, and the same theory was espoused in an 1823 book, *View of the Hebrews,* by Ethan Smith (no relation). Joseph Smith could have read the book, or least have heard the theory. Indeed, with eight mounds within twelve miles of the Smith farm, it would have been surprising if he hadn't heard of it.

Lucy Mack Smith's 1853 family memoir provided more evidence that her son's theory about Indian origins predated his alleged discovery of the golden plates. "During our evening conversations Joseph would occasionally give us some of the most amusing recitals that could be imagined," his mother wrote. "He would describe the ancient inhabitants of this continent, their dress, mode of traveling, and the animals upon which they rode; their cities; their buildings, with every particular; their mode of warfare; and also their religious worship. This he would do with as much ease, seemingly, as if he had spent his whole life with them."

By the end of the nineteenth century, most historians had concluded that the source of the Book of Mormon was the popular culture of the time. Smith may not have been bookish, but his mother's description made clear he had plenty of imagination and intelligence. There was no need to steal Spaulding's manuscript; he was perfectly capable of creating the Book of Mormon himself.

⚭

The twentieth century brought the rise of psychology, and many historians were as eager as therapists to put it to use. Increasingly, they looked inside Smith as well as outside.

Woodbridge Riley's 1902 study was the first to do so. Riley concluded that "the psychiatric definition of the epileptic fits the prophet to a dot." Since then, others have diagnosed Smith as bipolar and manic-depressive. More convincingly, many historians have noted the similarities between the story of the Book of Mormon and Smith's own life, and explained the former as an expression of the latter. Like Nephi, Smith had five brothers, and he fought with them throughout his life. The Book of Mormon begins: "I, Nephi, having been born of goodly parents . . ." Smith's 1832 autobiography starts with: "I was born . . . of goodly parents."

Were Smith's revelations, then, the product of his unconscious mind rather than a conscious hoax? Neither option would please devout Mormons, but the question has shaped Mormon historiography into the twenty-first century.

No one has come closer to a definitive answer than historian Fawn Brodie, whose masterfully subtle biography of Smith, *No Man Knows My History,* appeared in 1945. Brodie brought together the nineteenth-century emphasis on Smith's environment and a twentieth-century understanding of his mind. To the former, she added new evidence that Smith had been an avid folk magician and treasure hunter before becoming a prophet. This evidence included an 1826 court case in which Smith faced charges that he had used these practices to defraud a neighbor. Brodie also noted that Smith's first autobiographical sketch, published in 1834, was decidedly sketchier about the origins of the Book of Mormon than his later versions. Perhaps, she speculated, Smith had started the

Book of Mormon as a secular history of ancient America, and only later decided to sell it as holy scripture.

Brodie was also the first historian to count Smith's wives. She listed forty-eight, a figure that subsequent historians have argued is too high but is nonetheless a reasonable starting point. More importantly, Brodie placed Smith's polygamy in a psychological context, demonstrating how he used his religious doctrine to satisfy his sexual desires.

But Brodie's Smith was more than just a charlatan. She concluded that, gradually, he came to believe in his visions, such as seeing Moroni (and, at other times, God and Jesus Christ). Even his polygamy was in some sense an indication of how fully enveloped he became in his role as prophet. Brodie's 1971 revision added a section on his psychology, clearly implying that Smith was torn by inner conflicts and was not just some ordinary liar.

"The awesome vision he described in later years was probably the elaboration of some half-remembered dream stimulated by the early revival of excitement and reinforced by the rich folklore of visions circulating in the neighborhood," she wrote. "Dream images came easily to this youth, whose imagination was as untrammeled as the whole West."

Brodie's detractors attacked her on all sorts of grounds. Some accused her of focusing too much on Smith's charisma, instead of other causes of Mormonism's growth. (True, but the latter was never her subject.) Some charged she was motivated by her own religious alienation. (Brodie, who was born a Mormon, undoubtedly had a personal interest in her subject, but there's no indication that it affected her objectivity.) Some even criticized her superb writing style, claiming that her use of literary techniques made the book more like fiction than history. (If only all historians could write like her.) The church's review was in no way mixed: soon after the book was published, Brodie was excommunicated.

More moderate Mormons, including such well-known historians as Leonard Arrington and Davis Bitton, responded to Brodie by conceding much of the evidence was on her side but affirming the true nature of Smith's visions a matter of faith. "Historical research can never either confirm or disprove alleged supernatural experiences," the two wrote in 1979. For them, there was no point in arguing about whether Smith believed his own stories. The point was that they—and millions of other Mormons—did.

〜

If Arrington and Bitton seemed to be signaling that the debate over the origins of the Book of Mormon was at an end, they were wrong.

The early 1980s witnessed the appearance of a spate of new documents, most of which further undercut the church's view of its own history. Over a five-year period, a rare documents dealer named Mark Hofmann made hundreds of thousands of dollars selling these documents, mostly to church leaders eager to keep them secret. Hofmann was, as another documents dealer said, "the Mormon Indiana Jones who could lead us to impossible treasures of information and wealth."

One document was a land deed linking Sidney Rigdon, a follower of Smith, to Solomon Spaulding. This reopened the question of whether Smith plagiarized Spaulding's manuscript.

Then there were two letters, not really having to do with the church's origins but nonetheless highly embarrassing. One was signed by Smith on June 23, 1844, just four days before he was murdered. It was addressed to two sisters and it demonstrated that, contrary to the church's claims that he was in the process of abandoning polygamy, he was still very much into it. In another letter, Smith named his son as his successor, effectively undermining Brigham Young's claim.

Worst of all, from the perspective of the church establishment, was what came to be known as the "salamander letter." In it, Martin Harris, one of the witnesses who testified he'd seen not only the golden plates but also the angel Moroni, recalled how Smith initially described to him the discovery of the golden plates: "I hear Joseph found a gold bible and I take Joseph aside & he says it is true I found it 4 years ago with my stone but only just got it because of the enchantment the old spirit come to me 3 times in the same dream & says dig up the gold but when I take it up the next morning the spirit transfigured himself from a white salamander in the bottom of the hole & struck me 3 times & held the treasure & would not let me have it because I lay it down to cover over the hole."

The problem wasn't the lack of punctuation, it was the lack of Moroni. Instead of an angel, there was this white salamander, placing Smith and the Book of Mormon squarely in the folk magic tradition and implying Moroni was a later invention. A loyal Mormon businessman named Steven Christensen paid Hofmann $40,000 for the letter, hoping it would never see the light of day.

Then, in October 1985, a bomb exploded, killing Christensen. Another killed Kathy Sheets, the wife of Christensen's business partner. What had been a historical mystery became a murder investigation.

At first, detectives suspected the murderer was a disgruntled investor in Coordinated Financial Services, the Christensen-Sheets business. They also wondered whether it could have anything to do with the Hofmann deal, and they brought in forensic documents experts to study the paper and ink. The experts concluded that Hofmann had forged the documents—not just the salamander letter but everything the dealer had sold to the church.

Under questioning, Hofmann confessed. He had forged the letters, and he had murdered Christensen because Christensen was onto him, or nearly so. He had intended to murder James Sheets to throw police off track, hoping they'd assume both deaths had something to do with Coordinated Financial Services. Kathy Sheets just happened to be the one who picked up the package with the bomb inside.

Hofmann, it turned out, was motivated by more than money. Raised in a devout Mormon family, he had come to hate the church. He had forged the documents to do double damage: first, by making the church pay him to keep them secret; second, by leaking the documents to the press anyway.

Hofmann was sentenced to life in prison.

Was the church leadership also to blame? Obviously, they had not plotted any murders. But they had conspired to keep the documents secret, and the entire forgery and murder case, wrote journalists Richard and Joan Ostling, "could only have happened in connection with the curious mixture of paranoia and obsessiveness with which the Mormons approach church history."

And what about historians? Robert Stott, the chief prosecutor in the case against Hofmann, didn't hesitate to point fingers in their direction as well. "Mark Hofmann recognized those areas in which you would be the least objective," he told a conference of Mormon historians. "He recognized your interest in folk magic, he recognized that you better accept something in that area than something that wasn't. His deceptions, his creations, then, in part, were fashioned with that in mind, to meet what you wanted."

Stott's criticism certainly shouldn't be applied to all historians, Mormon or otherwise. But it is surely a clear warning that history's mysteries should be approached with the care and objectivity that mark any modern murder investigation.

To Investigate Further

Smith, Joseph. *The Book of Mormon.* Salt Lake City, UT: Church of Jesus Christ of Latter-Day Saints, 1981.

"Chloroform in print," Mark Twain called it, and others have noted that the phrase "and it came to pass" occurs more than two thousand times. But for millions of people, it's the bible.

Brodie, Fawn. *No Man Knows My History.* New York: Alfred A. Knopf, 1945; revised 1971.

The title comes from a line in an 1844 sermon, almost a challenge to future biographers. Perhaps no man does fully know his history, but this woman sure came close.

Arrington, Leonard, and Davis Bitton. *The Mormon Experience.* New York: Alfred A. Knopf, 1979.

The authors' positions as official church historians obviously bias them, but this is nonetheless a thorough and readable history.

Bushman, Richard. *Joseph Smith and the Beginnings of Mormonism.* Urbana: University of Illinois Press, 1984.

Bushman won deserved acclaim for his earlier work on Puritans and Yankees in New England. Here his Mormon faith undermines his objectivity, though not his stylish writing.

Bitton, Davis, and Leonard Arrington. *Mormons and Their Historians.* Salt Lake City: University of Utah Press, 1988.

Portraits of Mormon historians, though the pro-church bias can be quickly judged by the fact that Brodie gets only five pages.

Lindsey, Robert. *A Gathering of Saints.* New York: Simon and Schuster, 1988.
Like the best true crime stories, this is not just about a criminal (Hofmann) and detectives, but also about the society in which they lived.

Naifeh, Steven, and Gregory White Smith. *The Mormon Murders.* New York: Weidenfeld & Nicolson, 1988.
Naifeh and Smith offer more detail about the crime and investigation than Lindsey, and are also more critical of church leaders.

Bringhurst, Newell. *Reconsidering No Man Knows My History.* Logan: Utah State University Press, 1996.
A collection of essays critiquing Brodie's biography, often unfairly but nonetheless interestingly.

Anderson, Robert. *Inside the Mind of Joseph Smith.* Salt Lake City, UT: Signature Books, 1999.
This psychobiography treats the Book of Mormon as, essentially, Smith's autobiography.

Bushman, Claudia, and Richard Bushman. *Building the Kingdom.* New York: Oxford University Press, 1999, 2001.
A brief introduction to Mormon history, made even shorter by the Bushmans' tendency to airbrush most blemishes.

Ostling, Richard, and Joan Ostling. *Mormon America.* San Francisco: HarperSanFrancisco, 1999.
A balanced view of Mormonism, past and present.

Walker, Ronald, David Whittaker, and James Allen. *Mormon History.* Urbana: University of Illinois Press, 2001.
A thorough historiography of Mormon history, biography, and social science literature.

Worrall, Simon. *The Poet and the Murderer.* New York: Dutton, 2002.
Mormon documents weren't the only ones Hofmann forged. Among the other handwritings he faked were those of Daniel Boone, Butch Cassidy, Nathan Hale, John Hancock, Francis Scott Key, Abraham Lincoln, Paul Revere, Betsy Ross, Myles Standish, Mark Twain, George Washington, Walt Whitman, and—the poet of the book's title—Emily Dickinson.

How Did Davy Crockett Die?

T O THE MILLIONS OF AMERICANS who remember Fess Parker in ABC's 1954 *Davy Crockett, Indian Fighter* series or John Wayne in the 1960 movie *The Alamo*, the answer to this chapter's question is no mystery: Davy died fighting at the Alamo, along with all its other defenders. In the television version, he is last seen swinging his rifle like a club, with the bodies of the Mexicans he has slain at his feet; in the movie version he is if anything more heroic, blowing up the fort's powder magazine to make sure a score of Mexicans die with him.

So clear was this image in Americans' minds that when historian Dan Kilgore presented evidence in 1978 that Crockett surrendered at the Alamo and was executed after the battle, Kilgore was branded un-American. Yet Kilgore's evidence was not new, nor were Hollywood's versions the first fictionalized accounts of Crockett's life and death. Crockett himself was famous as a teller of tall tales, and historians attempting to uncover the truth about his death had first to peel away many layers of legends, lies, and half-truths.

సించిలి

The mythic "Davy"—as opposed to the real person historians prefer to call "David"—was at least in part a creation of Crockett's own making. Crockett's autobiography, *A Narrative of the Life of David Crockett*, is more admired by literary critics than by historians. Still, it does present many of the facts of his life and reveals something, at least, of whether he was the type of man who'd fight to the end, or who'd prefer to live to fight another day.

Like Daniel Boone, the Crockett in *A Narrative of the Life* is a great hunter, a superman from the backwoods of Tennessee who killed 105 bears in a single season. So famed was he as a hunter that, so the story went, once a treed raccoon recognized him, it would yell, "Don't shoot, I'm a comin' down!"

Above all, however, the real Crockett was a politician. Using his comic drawl and his log-cabin background as proof that he would fight for the interests of the common man and of the westerner in particular, he was elected to the Tennessee House of Representatives in 1821 and 1823, and to the U.S. House in 1827, 1829, 1831, and 1833. At first he was an ardent supporter of that other "man of the people," Andrew Jackson. But Crockett broke with the president over his policies for disposing of western lands and Indians, and then was embraced by the Whig Party. The Whigs saw in Crockett someone who could match Jackson's image as the common man's protector—and who might even be able to challenge Jackson for the presidency. They began ghostwriting his speeches and books, including his *Narrative of the Life*, which was in one sense a campaign biography.

The Whig propaganda made Crockett a national figure—a sort of western Poor Richard, uneducated but rich in common sense and experience. But Crockett's own constituents were less impressed by him. They noted his failure to pass a land bill protecting the rights of poor settlers and squatters; they noted that, in fact, in his entire congressional career he'd failed to get a single bill passed. With the Jacksonians mobilized against him, the 1835 congressional election promised to be a tight one. Crockett promised his followers that he'd serve them to the best of his ability if they elected him. And if they didn't? "You may all go to hell," Crockett answered, "and I will go to Texas."

They didn't—and so he did.

Crockett was not alone: by the early 1830s, although Texas was a province of Mexico, Americans made up 75 percent of its population. Americans flocked there for land that was available at one-tenth the price of land in the United States. For Crockett, who for all his fame was short on cash, the opportunity to buy cheap land was undoubtedly a factor in his decision to immigrate to Texas. And as a politician, Crockett was also undoubtedly attracted by the possibility that Texas voters would appreciate him more than Tennesseans had.

The Mexican government, on the other hand, didn't like the idea of these Texans voting for anyone at all. Quite reasonably, Mexico saw these increasingly assertive immigrants as a threat to its authority, and decided to outlaw new immigration and ban slavery in the province. The more militant Americans responded by declaring Texas an independent nation and appointing Sam Houston as commander in chief. Like Crockett, Houston was an ex-Tennessean and an ex-congressman; unlike Crockett, Houston remained tied to the Jacksonians in the United States.

By the time Crockett arrived in San Antonio in early February 1836, tensions were near the breaking point. Not only were the Mexican general Santa Anna and his 2,400 troops on the march toward the fort but the Texans at the Alamo were themselves split between those who acknowledged Houston's authority and those who did not. Houston, recognizing that the 183 men in the Alamo could not hold the fort against Santa Anna's troops, ordered its commander, Colonel William Travis, to blow up the Alamo and retreat. But Travis, as part of the opposition to Houston, refused, thus setting up the fateful battle.

It is amidst these political maneuverings that Crockett's decision to stay at the Alamo—and the likelihood of his fighting to the death as opposed to surrendering—must be considered. Crockett had come to Texas because it was a land of economic and political opportunity, not so that he could fight and die. Moreover, Crockett was no soldier. (In his autobiography he readily admitted that he'd hired a substitute to finish out an earlier term of enlistment.) But once he got to Texas he found his past political affiliations threw him in with the anti-Houston, anti-Jackson forces, and these were the forces defending the Alamo. He was stuck there.

Of course, this doesn't prove that Crockett surrendered, or that his heroic death scene is mere myth. Many have died heroically on the battlefield with less evidence of previous heroism than Crockett's life provided. What Crockett's past life proved was merely that he was the type of person who easily *could* have surrendered. To determine whether he actually did so, historians needed some actual witnesses.

ᏃᎳᎳᎾ

The obvious problem with witnesses, at least on the American side, was that they were dead.

Once Colonel Travis used his sword to draw his famous line in the sand, and all those willing to stay and fight to the death crossed the line, the fate of the Americans was sealed. After 90 bloody minutes on the morning of March 6, 1836, they were all dead. (Not quite all: The Mexicans did spare the life of a slave, Joe, and a woman, Susannah Dickinson, and the latter's report of seeing Crockett's mutilated body has often been used to prove he died fighting. But she didn't see his body until well after the fighting had ended—and well after he might have been captured and executed.)

On the Mexican side, of course, there were many survivors. That their testimony was for so long ignored can only be attributed to American chauvinism. In 1975, however, Carmen Perry translated into English the narrative of José Enrique de la Peña, an aide to Santa Anna and an eyewitness to Crockett's death. According to de la Peña, Crockett most definitely did not go down fighting. Rather, he was captured along with six others and brought before Santa Anna. Drawing on his famous ability to tell tall tales, he attempted to talk his way out of his situation. He claimed that he'd merely been exploring the country around the Alamo when he'd heard of the Mexican advance. Then, "fearing that his status as a foreigner might not be respected," he'd sought refuge in the Alamo. Santa Anna didn't buy it. He ordered Crockett and the others killed, and his officers (though not the horrified de la Peña) "fell upon these unfortunate, defenseless men just as a tiger leaps upon his prey."

Other Mexican witnesses offered briefer but similar versions of Crockett's death. Among them were Colonel Fernando Urissa, another aide to Santa Anna; General Martín Perfecto de Cos, Santa Anna's brother-in-law; Colonel José Sanchez Navarro, who led one of the assault columns against the Alamo; and Sergeant Francisco Becerra. Santa Anna's personal secretary also reported the capture and execution of some Americans (though he didn't mention Crockett). In spite of efforts to discredit the testimony of these Mexicans, the sheer number of witnesses to his surrender, and the lack of any reliable eyewitness to his death in battle, clearly favors the surrender story.

At the time, many U.S. newspapers reported the surrender, as did many nineteenth- and early twentieth-century histories. In fact, the story of Crockett's execution was often used as evidence of Santa Anna's barbarity, and it generated comparatively little controversy. Only after the Fess Parker/John Wayne versions were filmed did Crockett's death become a part of American mythology. But mythology, not history, is almost surely what it was.

The revisionist view of Crockett's death can be taken too far, however. Just because he wasn't Parker or Wayne didn't mean he died in vain. Even in its surrender and execution version, Crockett's death focused the attention of the United States on Texas, and money and volunteers rolled into the territory. Six weeks after the Alamo, Sam Houston's men, crying "Remember the Alamo!," overwhelmed the Mexicans. A day later Santa Anna surrendered.

Nor should Crockett's surrender be confused with cowardice: faced with insurmountable odds, Crockett made the only reasonable choice. De la Peña's account of the execution concludes by telling how "though tortured before they were killed, these unfortunates died without complaining and without humiliating themselves before their torturers." Or, to put it another way, Davy Crockett died like a hero.

To Investigate Further

Crockett, David. *A Narrative of the Life of David Crockett of the State of Tennessee.* Knoxville: University of Tennessee Press, 1987.
   This facsimile edition of Crockett's 1834 autobiography includes useful notes and an introduction by James Shackford and Stanley Folmsbee.

Shackford, James. *David Crockett: The Man and the Legend.* Chapel Hill: University of North Carolina Press, 1956.
   Shackford was unaware of some of the Mexican sources on the Alamo; as a result, he argued that Crockett—who was certainly no coward—was likely to have been on the front lines and therefore was likely to have died very early on in the battle. Though he was wrong on this, he was right on most everything else, and his book remains the best biography of Crockett.

Lord, Walter. *A Time to Stand.* Lincoln: University of Nebraska Press, 1978.
   Originally published in 1961 and still the most dramatic history of the Alamo.

de la Peña, José Enrique. *With Santa Anna in Texas: A Personal Narrative of the Revolution,* trans. and ed. by Carmen Perry. College Station: Texas A&M University Press, 1975.
   Written soon after the battle, its translation and publication in 1975 set off the debate about Crockett's death.

Kilgore, Dan. *How Did Davy Die?* College Station: Texas A&M University Press, 1978.
   A concise summary of the case that he was captured and then executed.

Lofaro, Michael, and Joe Cummings, eds. *Crockett at Two Hundred: New Perspectives on the Man and the Myth.* Knoxville: University of Tennessee Press, 1989.
   Most of the essays here are somewhat specialized but the ones by Kilgore and Hutton contain interesting descriptions of the backlash that followed the publication of Perry's translation of de la Peña's book.

Long, Jeff. *Duel of Eagles.* New York: Morrow, 1990.
   The most recent history of the Alamo; worth reading but not quite up to the standard set by Lord's 1961 book.

Derr, Mark. *The Frontiersman: The Real Life and the Many Legends of Davy Crockett.* New York: Morrow, 1993.
   The most recent biography of Crockett; worth reading but not quite up to the standard set by Shackford's 1956 book.

Groneman, Bill. *Defense of a Legend.* Plano, TX: Republic of Texas Press, 1994.

Claims the de la Peña diary was a forgery, and that Crockett was killed at the Alamo.

Davis, William C. *Three Roads to the Alamo.* New York: HarperCollins, 1998.

The converging stories of the Alamo's doomed threesome: Crockett, Travis, and James Bowie.

Brands, H.W. *Lone Star Nation.* New York: Doubleday, 2004.

A colorful history of the battle for Texas independence.

Who Was
Emily Dickinson's "Master"?

In Cave if I presumed to hide
The Walls—begun to tell—
Creation seemed a mighty Crack—
To make me visible—

THUS DID EMILY DICKINSON express her most desperate desire: to hide from the world. Even in her own lifetime, long before her posthumously published poems made her famous, her elusiveness made her the subject of local gossip.

"I must tell you about the character of Amherst," Mabel Loomis Todd wrote to her parents in 1881, just a couple of months after moving to the Massachusetts town. "It is a lady whom the people call the Myth. . . . She has not been outside of her own house in fifteen years, except once to see a new church, when she crept out at night, & viewed it by moonlight. . . . She dresses wholly in white, & her mind is said to be perfectly wonderful. She writes finely, but no one ever sees her."

One of Dickinson's first editors, Thomas Wentworth Higginson, was equally mystified. "I have the greatest desire to see you," he wrote her in 1869, "but till then you only enshroud yourself in this fiery mist & I cannot reach you, but only rejoice in the rare sparkles of light." Higginson did finally meet her, but later confessed that "she was much too enigmatical a being for me to solve."

From the start, her mystery revolved around a thwarted love affair, one whose end was so traumatic that it was the source of both Dickinson's withdrawal from the world and her remarkable poetry. Dickinson herself fueled such speculation by dropping hints about the affair in her poems and letters. In 1862 she wrote Higginson: "I had a friend, who taught me Immortality—but venturing too near, himself—he never returned—Soon after, my Tutor died—and for several years, my Lexicon—was my only companion. . . ."

Scholars in search of Dickinson's secrets have been especially drawn to the drafts of three love letters found among her papers after her death. Addressed only to "Master," they were undated and it's unclear whether they were actually sent.

The first, which on the basis of handwriting analysis has been dated 1858, was the most restrained. Dickinson wrote: "I wish that I were great, like Mr. Michael Angelo, and could paint for you. You ask me what my flowers said—then they were disobedient—I gave them messages. They said what the lips in the West say, when the sun goes down, and so says the Dawn."

The letter was apparently written in response to Master's questions about the meaning of some flowers—presumably poems—Dickinson had sent him. In typical fashion, she answered with a riddle, perhaps even a veiled criticism of Master for not having understood the "messages." She continued: "Each Sabbath on the Sea, makes me count the Sabbaths, till we meet on shore—"

In the second Master letter, which handwriting experts have dated to 1861, there is still longing, and more pain. Began Dickinson: "If you saw a bullet hit a Bird—and he told you he wasn't shot—you might weep at his courtesy, but you would certainly doubt his word." Dickinson clearly felt a bullet had struck her—perhaps in the form of a break-up—and that her lover ought to have seen her agony, even though she tried to cover it up.

"I heard of a thing called 'Redemption'—which rested men and women," she went on. "You remember I asked you for it—you gave me something else. . . . I am older—tonight, Master—but the love is the same—so are the moon and the crescent. . . . if I wish with a might I cannot repress—that mine were the Queen's place—the love of the Plantagenet is my only apology—" Her request for redemption has been interpreted to mean Master might have been a clergyman; her desire to take the place of the Plantagenet's queen that her king, whoever he might be, was already married.

Then: "Vesuvius . . . said a syllable—a thousand years ago, and Pompeii heard it, and hid forever—She could'nt look the world in the face afterward—I suppose—Bashful Pompeii!" Dickinson saw herself both as Vesuvius, whose passion once erupted, and as Pompeii, forever buried by the results of that eruption.

And finally this plea: "I want to see you more—Sir—than all I wish for in this world—and the wish . . . will be my only one . . . Could you come to New England—would you come to Amherst—Would you like to come—Master?"

By the time of the third letter, dated to 1862, Dickinson has apparently lost all hope: "I've got a cough as big as a thimble—but I dont care for that—I've got a Tomahawk in my side but that dont hurt me so much . . . Her Master stabs her more—"

No longer aspiring to be Michelangelo, Dickinson has now been reduced to begging: "Master . . . I will never be noisy when you want to be still. I will be your best little girl . . . I shall not want any more—and all that Heaven only will disappoint me—will be because it's not so dear."

The passion and frustration of the Master letters, especially the second and third, were rivaled only by her poems. Indeed, the letters and poems shared much of the same imagery, and many of the latter seemed written with Master in mind. So one could hardly blame readers for wanting to know who he was.

⌒᷍⌣

The prime candidate was Reverend Charles Wadsworth, a respected Philadelphia minister Dickinson met while passing through that city in 1855. Wadsworth's name first surfaced in a 1931 edition of Dickinson's letters edited by Mabel Loomis Todd. This was the same Todd who had once written to her parents about the "myth" of Amherst. In the intervening years, she learned a great deal more about Dickinson's reality, primarily through a longtime affair with Emily's brother Austin. Todd's edition of Dickinson's letters made clear the latter's great admiration for Wadsworth, whom she described as her "dearest earthly friend" and a man "whom to know was Life." Wrote Todd: "Just what shade of tenderer feeling to ascribe to her attachment, who would presume to guess?"

Wadsworth's name moved further front and center in the 1932 book *Emily Dickinson Face to Face*, by Martha Dickinson Bianchi. Bianchi was Dickinson's niece, the daughter of Austin and Susan Dickinson. According to Bianchi, everyone in the family always knew Wadsworth was her aunt's lover—this came from no lesser authorities than Bianchi's father (Emily Dickinson's only brother), her aunt (Dickinson's only sister), and her mother (one of Dickinson's closest friends).

Wrote Bianchi: "The testimony of her closest contemporaries leaves no doubt that during her visit to Philadelphia . . . my aunt met the man who was henceforth to stand to her for the Power and the Glory . . . These contemporaries were agreed that any further development of what was stated to be their mutual recognition of each other was impossible, owing to the fact that he was already married. According to them, the definite renunciation followed a brief interview in her father's house, and left a permanent effect upon my aunt's life and vision."

Wadsworth fit the bill: he was not just a minister but a renowned orator, which would have impressed someone with Dickinson's appreciation for language; he was married, so the place of his "Queen" was already filled; he briefly visited the Amherst area in 1860, around the time of the Master letters; he moved from Philadelphia to California in 1862, the same year the final Master letter manifested such despair.

The main problem with the Wadsworth-as-Master theory was that the reputed lovers could not have met more than once or twice. She may indeed have heard him preach when she visited Philadelphia in 1855, and he may have visited her in 1860 when he stayed in nearby Springfield, but that was it. Nor, if you don't count the Master letters, was there anything in their correspondence that indicated any intimacy, let alone a grand passion.

Many scholars, therefore, looked elsewhere for Master. The next likely candidate was Samuel Bowles, editor of the nearby *Springfield Republican*, a close friend of Austin and Susan Dickinson, and a frequent visitor to their Amherst home. In contrast to her letters to Wadsworth, Emily Dickinson's letters to Bowles had, if nowhere near the passion of the Master letters, at least many more hints of an actual relationship.

Like Wadsworth, Bowles was married, which might explain this poem she sent him in 1862:

> *Title divine—is mine!*
> *The Wife—without the Sign!*
> *Acute Degree—conferred on me—*
> *Empress of Calvary!*
> *Royal—all but the Crown!*
> *Betrothed—without the swoon!*

It's hard to read this as anything but a love poem, in which the love was off limits (The Wife—without the Sign) and perhaps unconsummated (without the swoon).

There were, alas, as many problems with Bowles-as-Master as with Wadsworth. For one thing, Bowles and Dickinson most likely met sometime after 1858, the approximate date of the first Master letter. Then there was the plea in the second Master letter that he come to New England. This made perfect sense in the case of Wadsworth, who lived in Philadelphia and then San Francisco. Bowles, however, spent most of his life in nearby Springfield and frequently stayed in Amherst. Moreover, Dickinson's request for "Redemption" seemed a lot more appropriate for a minister than a newspaper editor.

With both Wadsworth and Bowles problematic, the search for Dickinson's lover continued. Starting in the 1970s, many feminist scholars concluded that one reason it had been so difficult to identify the man was that it wasn't a man at all.

☙

At the same time that Austin Dickinson was courting his future wife, so was his sister.

I have but one thought, Susie . . . and that of you," wrote Emily Dickinson to Susan Gilbert in 1853. "If you were here—and Oh that you were, my Susie, we need not talk at all, our eyes would whisper for us, and your hand fast in mine, we would not ask for language." In 1858, after Austin and Susan were married, Dickinson wrote her a poem:

> *One sister have I in our house*
> *And one, a hedge away.*
> *There's only one recorded,*
> *But both belong to me.*

This could easily be interpreted as nothing more than welcoming a new sister-in-law to the family. But by the last stanza, it sure sounds like more:

> *I spilt the dew—*
> *But took the morn—*
> *I chose this single star*
> *From out the wide night's numbers—*
> *Sue—forevermore!*

Women's letters of the nineteenth century often sound deceptively intimate to modern readers, but Dickinson's letters and poems to her sister-in-law went well beyond the usual Victorian romanticism. The sheer quantity of letters and poems for her made it plain that Susan Gilbert Dickinson was a key figure in the poet's life. Over the course of their thirty-six-year relationship, there were 153 letters and poems. Though few were explicitly sexual (and even then, subject to alternative interpretations), many were clearly love letters and poems. In one letter, for example, Dickinson compared Susan to Dante's Beatrice; in another, to Eden. For many scholars, Todd's picture of the ethereal, white-dressed recluse who never ventured outside her home was now replaced by that of a lesbian in love with her sister-in-law. Some, among them Ellen Louise Hart and Martha Nell Smith, argued that Todd and other members of Dickinson's family had invented the traumatic love affair with Wadsworth in order to cover up the truth.

To be sure, the lesbian lover thesis had its problems as well. There was the fact that the Master letters were clearly addressed to a man: at one point, for example, she referred to his beard. And some of Dickinson's poems were explicitly heterosexual:

> *He was my host—he was my guest*
> *I never to this day*
> *If I invited him could tell*
> *Or he invited me.*
> *So infinite our intercourse*
> *So intimate, indeed,*
> *Analysis as capsule seemed*
> *To keeper of the seed*

One possibility, of course, was that Dickinson was bisexual, and that she turned to a male Master after Susan chose Austin over her. Another, proposed by Freudian biographers such as John Cody, was that there was no Master, that Dickinson conjured him up out of her own imagination, perhaps in an effort to repress her homosexuality. Dickinson herself, in an 1862 letter to Higginson, wrote: "When I state myself, as the Representative of the Verse—it does not mean—me—but a supposed person." She was referring to her poetry, not her letters, but she was certainly encouraging readers not to take her literally.

One did not have to be a Freudian to grant the poet's right—and her manifest ability—to use her imagination. To paraphrase Robert Frost, poets don't have to go to Niagara Falls to write about falling water. Many formalist critics have gone further than that, criticizing all the attention paid to identifying Master, and arguing that it has detracted from the study of Dickinson's language.

Granted, some of the interest in Master is just a scholarly version of the local gossip Todd reported in 1881. But the relationship between an artist's work and life is surely a legitimate question, and besides, Master is a temptation impossible to resist. And, in the view of most scholars, he almost certainly did exist, in spite of Cody's provocative suggestion. In her letters to Master, Dickinson included enough details that, even if they failed to identify a particular man, made it hard to see him as pure fiction. The current consensus is that Dickinson loved both men and women, and that the Master letters grew out of an actual relationship with a man, though it may have been one-sided and unconsummated.

Regardless of who they think Master was, most scholars see the letters, like the poems, as some mix of fact and fiction. Richard Sewall, author of the most comprehensive Dickinson biography, believed Bowles was Master, but Sewall also stressed that the poet "appropriated the experience to her own creative uses." Alfred Habegger, Dickinson's most recent biographer, thought it was Wadsworth, but he also believed that the characters in poems and letters "sometimes . . . voice her private situation . . . frankly and directly [and] sometimes . . . are actors of her favorite fantasies, fictions, and projections." Habegger settled on Wadsworth for the very reasons that Sewall chose Bowles: the minister and the poet could not have met in person more than once or twice. This, Habegger believed, made him the perfect vehicle for her imagination.

Whoever he (or she) was (or wasn't), Master was certainly that.

To Investigate Further

Franklin, Ralph. *The Poems of Emily Dickinson*. Cambridge, MA: Harvard University Press, 1998.
    She may never have intended anyone to read them, but here are three volumes of them.

Johnson, Thomas, ed. *Emily Dickinson: Selected Letters*. Cambridge, MA: Harvard University Press, 1971.
    Includes the full texts of the Master letters.

Bianchi, Martha Dickinson. *Emily Dickinson Face to Face*. Boston: Houghton Mifflin, 1932.
    Dickinson's niece recalled overhearing, as a little girl, her mother talk about her aunt and "the sacrifice of her young romance."

Patterson, Rebecca. *The Riddle of Emily Dickinson*. New York: Cooper Square Publishers, 1973.
    Originally published in 1951. Patterson was one of the first to argue that Dickinson's lover was a woman; she concluded it was Susan Dickinson's friend, Kate Anthon.

Cody, John. *After Great Pain*. Cambridge, MA: Harvard University Press, 1971.
    Dickinson as psychotic.

Walsh, John Evangelist. *The Hidden Life of Emily Dickinson*. New York: Simon and Schuster, 1971.
    Walsh concluded Master was Judge Otis Lord, a man with whom Dickinson probably did have an affair but many years after the Master letters.

Sewall, Richard. *The Life of Emily Dickinson*. New York: Farrar, Straus and Giroux, 1974.
    Sewall masterfully portrays not just Dickinson, but her family, friends, and world.

Pollak, Vivian. *Dickinson, the Anxiety of Gender*. Ithaca, NY: Cornell University Press, 1984.
    A fascinating combination of literary, psychological, and feminist analysis.

Wolff, Cynthia Griffin. *Emily Dickinson*. New York: Knopf, 1986.
    It was not a man, but God, who abandoned Dickinson (and vice-versa).

Farr, Judith. *The Passion of Emily Dickinson*. Cambridge, MA: Harvard University Press, 1992.
    An incisive analysis of how Dickinson drew on her reading as well as life experiences.

Hart, Ellen Louise, and Martha Nell Smith. *Open Me Carefully*. Ashfield, MA: Paris Press, 1998.
    Emily Dickinson's letters to Susan Huntington Dickinson.

Habegger, Alfred. *My Wars Are Laid Away in Books*. New York: Random House, 2001.
    Insightful and elegant.

Who Lost (and Who Found) the Lost Order?

A s ROBERT E. LEE LED the Army of Northern Virginia across the Potomac River in early 1862, they were singing "Maryland, My Maryland." They had good reason to sing. They were crossing into Maryland—and into Union territory. They were confident that sympathetic slaveowners there would rally round. There was panic in Washington, and even as far north as Pennsylvania.

Indeed, the Confederates were as close to victory as they would ever be.

Reluctantly, George McClellan led the Army of the Potomac out of Washington and into pursuit. McClellan worried about leaving the capital unprotected, and he worried even more about taking on an army that had recently and soundly beaten Union troops near Richmond and then at Bull Run.

Lee halted in Frederick, Maryland, considering where to strike next. Before heading farther north, he wanted to establish a supply line through the Shenandoah Valley. That meant knocking out the federal garrison at Harper's Ferry, about twenty miles to the southwest and held by about twelve thousand Union troops.

The problem was to secure Harper's Ferry without losing his northward momentum.

Lee's solution, typically bold, was to divide his army. On September 10, he issued "Special Orders 191." Some of Lee's forces were to go north toward the Pennsylvania border, under James Longstreet. The brunt of the army, led by Stonewall Jackson, would head toward Harper's Ferry. Other divisions would spread out between Frederick and Harper's Ferry to make sure Union spies didn't find out about Jackson's movements.

This was a very risky plan. If the Union did find out, McClellan could strike the northern parts of Lee's army before Jackson returned. Lee's combined forces were outnumbered by McClellan's troops; spread thin from Hagerstown to Harper's Ferry, the Confederates were extremely vulnerable.

One of Lee's officers pointed out the risk.

"Are you acquainted with General McClellan?" Lee responded. "He is an able general but a very cautious one."

Lee was confident Jackson could take Harper's Ferry and reunite with the rest of the army before McClellan made a move.

Lee was not the only one who thought his opponent overly cautious. McClellan's detractors, among them Abraham Lincoln, thought his caution bordered on cowardice, or at least a ruinous immobility. The president once remarked bitterly that the Army of the Potomac should be renamed "McClellan's bodyguard."

"Place him before an enemy," said Senator Ben Wade, "and he will burrow like a wood chuck." Kenneth P. Williams, whose biography of McClellan appeared in 1949, summed up the general as a man "who sat a horse well and wanted to be President."

What Lee did not know was that fate was about to hand McClellan a break beyond any general's wildest dreams. Three days after Lee signed Special Orders 191, a "lost" copy would find its way to Union headquarters. McClellan now had in his hands a detailed description of Lee's plan, complete with routes and timetable.

"Now I know what to do!" McClellan exulted on first reading the orders. He dashed off a note to Lincoln, telling him "I have all the plans of the rebels." That evening he showed the Lost Order to General John Gibbon, saying: "Here is a paper with which if I cannot whip Bobbie Lee, I will be willing to go home.

"Castiglione will be nothing to it," McClellan added, referring to the 1796 battle in which Napoleon routed a divided Austrian army.

Not surprisingly, given the import of the Lost Order, Civil War historians have spent much time and ink on the case. Their investigations have focused on three mysteries: Who lost the Lost Order? Who found it? And how did it change the course of the war?

∽

It was no mystery whose copy of Special Orders 191 was lost. The copy, which McClellan kept among his papers after the war, was addressed to Confederate General D. H. Hill.

Confederate sympathizers were quick to blame Hill for losing not just the order but the war. One early report had Hill dropping the paper in Frederick. Another had him throwing it away, annoyed by its contents. The recollections of other Confederate generals tended to underscore how careful they were with their copies: General John Walker pinned his in an inside pocket, and Longstreet memorized the contents and then ate the paper.

Hill vehemently denied he had lost the order. He defended himself in an 1868 issue of the magazine *The Land We Love* and again in an 1885 letter to the Southern Historical Society. The gist of his case was the "unfairness of attributing to me the loss of a paper, solely upon the ground that it was directed to me."

As Hill explained, he'd never even gotten the orders from Lee. His copy of the orders came from Jackson (to whom he reported), not from Lee. Hill wasn't even aware anything had been lost until he read about it after the war.

Hill suggested a traitor must have stolen the Lost Order.

For that, he had no evidence. But Hill's alibi was perfectly credible, especially since he had kept (and eagerly showed others) the copy of the orders he received from Jackson. Most historians believed Hill; after all, he couldn't lose something he never had.

The blame for the Lost Order gradually shifted to Colonel Robert Chilton, Lee's chief of staff. Chilton had a reputation for sloppy paperwork, hardly a desirable trait in an officer whose responsibilities were largely administrative. He kept no record of who received Lee's orders, nor did he keep the receipts for the signed orders. So he had no way of knowing for sure whether Hill (or anyone else) actually received the orders. As he lamely explained in a letter to Jefferson Davis, in a "case so important," it would have been the courier's "duty to advise its loss."

Chilton also told Davis he didn't remember who was assigned to take the orders to Hill, and—not surprisingly—no one ever came forward to admit he was the courier. So the details of how the order was lost remained a mystery.

But a year after Hill wrote to the Southern Historical Society, further evidence of his innocence surfaced. It came in an 1886 account of how the Lost Order was found.

⚬⚬⚬

The earliest existing reference to the finding of the Lost Order was a note General Alpheus Williams passed on to McClellan with the order itself. Williams credited a Corporal Mitchell.

More details were revealed in 1886, when Colonel Silas Colgrove, responding to a request from the editors of *The Century* magazine, gave his account of the discovery. According to Colgrove, the Twenty-seventh Indiana Volunteers, under his command, stopped near Frederick on September 13. They set up camp not far from where D. H. Hill's division had been the night before.

"Within a very few minutes after halting," Colgrove recalled, "the order was brought to me by First Sergeant John M. Bloss and Private B.W. Mitchell . . . who stated that it was found by Private Mitchell near where they had stacked arms. When I received the order it was wrapped around three cigars [Hill was known as a cigar connoisseur], and Private Mitchell stated that it was in that condition when it was found by him.

"The order was signed by Colonel Chilton," Colgrove continued, "and the signature was at once recognized by Colonel Pittman, who had served with Colonel Chilton at Detroit, Michigan, before the war, and was acquainted with his handwriting. It was at once taken to General McClellan's headquarters by Colonel Pittman."

Pittman handed it to Williams, who brought it to McClellan.

Six years after Colgrove's account, Bloss weighed in with his own version, in which he and not Mitchell first spotted the order. Bloss's version is suspiciously self-promoting, and Colgrove's seems more credible. The only apparent error in Colgrove's story was Mitchell's rank; he was a corporal and not a private. Since both Williams's contemporaneous note and Colgrove's story credit Mitchell, it seems likely he was the first to spot the orders. And even in Bloss's version, Mitchell was clearly on the scene.

Not that it did Mitchell any good. After handing over the orders to his captain, he was sent back to his unit, in the words of historian Stephen Sears, "without even the reward of the cigars."

Besides crediting Mitchell, Colgrove's story also deflated Hill's claim that a traitor was to blame. The orders, it was now clear, had been found entirely by accident. Mitchell might very well have been more interested in the cigars than the attached paper, which he may have glanced at almost as an afterthought. As Sears put it: "Any turncoat courier or staff officer who deliberately tossed D. H. Hill's copy of Special Order 191 into a meadow near Frederick with the expectation that the Yankees might come along and somehow stumble on it, recognize it for what it was, and get it to McClellan's headquarters must rank as the war's most naively optimistic spy."

Colgrove's account was of some use to Hill, however. For if the orders were found still wrapped around the cigars (and, as McClellan recalled, still in an envelope), that meant no one had opened them before Mitchell or Bloss. Hill, had he received them, would surely have removed the cigars, and probably smoked them. As Hill argued time and again, "the paper was never received."

That it instead reached McClellan was a remarkable stroke of luck.

⟿

After getting the orders, McClellan, typically, hesitated.

Not that he doubted their authenticity; Pittman's testimony that the orders were in Chilton's handwriting took care of that. Nor did McClellan misunderstand the orders' significance. His comment to Gibbon that he could now "whip Bobbie Lee" made that clear, as did his note to Lincoln, sent a few minutes later.

In his memoirs, McClellan wrote that "on the 13th an order fell into my hands issued by Gen. Lee, which fully disclosed his plans, and I immediately gave orders for a rapid and vigorous forward movement."

In reality, he was neither rapid nor vigorous. The problem was that the one thing the Lost Order did not tell McClellan was how many men Lee had. Left to his own imagination, McClellan concluded the Confederates numbered about 120,000 to his 90,000 or so troops. In fact, Lee had barely 50,000, now scattered between Hagerstown and Harper's Ferry.

Still, even McClellan could not entirely squander the opportunity. Reluctantly, he attacked at Turner's Gap and Crampton's Gap on September 14—a full eighteen hours after he'd received the Lost Order. Lee ordered D. H. Hill to block the gaps, and for a day they held off the Union troops, in spite of heavy losses.

When the Union finally did break through, McClellan again hesitated. The delay saved the Confederate army. On September 15, Jackson's troops took Harper's Ferry, still following the plan set forth in the Lost Orders. By September 17, they had rejoined Lee's troops at Sharpsburg, just across the Maryland border.

The stage was now set for the Battle of Antietam, or Sharpsburg, as it was known in the South. (The Northerners, mostly from urban areas, tended to be impressed by nature, such as Antietam Creek. More Southerners lived in the country, and were thus more likely to notice a town like Sharpsburg.)

Even reunited, the Confederates were still outnumbered by two to one. But Lee was unwilling to see his invasion come to naught, and he turned his army to fight. McClellan, finally, was also ready.

The battle began at dawn on September 17. Union troops gradually pushed forward, though they lost three crucial hours as the Confederates stopped General Ambrose Burn-

In October 1862, Lincoln went to Antietam to urge McClellan to pursue Lee's army. When McClellan delayed, Lincoln fired him. *(Library of Congress)*

side's troops from crossing a stone bridge over the Antietam. (Burnside apparently didn't notice that his soldiers could easily have waded across the shallow creek.) By the time Burnside's men broke through the Southern lines, the last of the Confederates had returned from Harper's Ferry, and they pushed the Union back to the creek. There the battle ended.

The next morning, though he still had the numerical advantage, McClellan again hesitated. Lee took the opportunity to lead his worn-out troops back to Virginia.

Who won?

On one level, it was clearly a major Union victory, and McClellan quickly declared it as such.

"Maryland is entirely freed from the presence of the enemy, who has been driven across the Potomac," he wired Lincoln. "No fears need now be entertained for the safety of Pennsylvania."

Lee agreed it was a defeat, and he blamed it on the Lost Order, which he said allowed McClellan "to discover my whereabouts . . . and caused him so to act as to force a battle on me before I was ready for it." The Lost Order, Lee said, was "a great calamity."

Yet there is also no doubt that Lee averted a much greater calamity. Had McClellan not hesitated, had he attacked right after he read the Lost Order and before Jackson's troops returned from Harper's Ferry, the Northerners' huge numerical advantage could have overwhelmed the Confederates. And had McClellan pushed on after Antietam, he might very well have prevented Lee's escape to the South.

Judging from casualties, the Union lost more men, though the South lost a higher percentage of its forces. In the bloodiest day of the war, more than 12,000 Northerners were killed or injured, and more than 10,000 Southerners.

Among the casualties of Antietam was Private Barton Mitchell, who never fully recovered from his wounds. He died in 1868, eighteen years before Colgrove published his account of how Mitchell found the Lost Order.

⁓

Jackson's quick return from Harper's Ferry to Sharpsburg has led many historians to conclude that Lee found out McClellan had a copy of the Lost Order, and ordered him back. By some accounts, a pro-Confederate Maryland man was present when the order was brought to McClellan, and then passed on the news to Jeb Stuart, who told Lee. By other accounts, Lee learned about the Lost Order from the *New York Herald*, which, astoundingly, printed the news on September 14, though there's no evidence Lee read the newspaper.

In his classic 1934 biography of Lee, Douglas Southall Freeman concluded Lee didn't learn about the Lost Order until after the war. But Freeman reversed himself in his 1944 book, *Lee's Lieutenants*, after examining two accounts of conversations in which Lee referred to a Confederate spy in Maryland. In 1868, Lee again mentioned the spy, this time in a letter to D. H. Hill that explicitly said Stuart had informed him about the orders falling into McClellan's hands.

Most major Civil War historians followed Freeman's lead. Bruce Catton assumed Lee knew McClellan had the orders; so did Shelby Foote and James McPherson.

But this particular mystery about the Lost Order remains unsolved. Sears, whose book on Antietam is the standard text, disagreed with Freeman and his followers. Sears argued that the reports of Lee's conversations about the spy were secondhand and vague. As for Lee's 1868 letter to Hill, Sears contended that by then the Lost Order had been so often and so vehemently discussed that Lee must have simply become confused about when he learned about it.

Sears's strongest argument is based on Lee's behavior. Lee did not order Jackson back to Maryland, as he certainly ought to have done if he thought McClellan had the Lost Order. Instead, Jackson continued to follow Special Orders 191, and didn't return to Maryland until after he took Harper's Ferry.

Lee understood his opponent, and he undoubtedly was counting on McClellan's timidity when he issued the soon-to-be-lost order. But if he learned that McClellan had found the order, it would have been foolhardy for Lee to continue to assume McClellan wouldn't attack. And Lee was daring, but not foolhardy.

To Investigate Further

Johnson, Robert Underwood, and Clarence Clough Buel. *Battles and Leaders of the Civil War.* New York: Century Company, 1884.
    Volume 2 includes Hill on the events leading up to Antietam, Colgrove on the finding of the Lost Order, Confederate General John Walker's account on the capture of Harper's Ferry, Longstreet on the invasion of Maryland, and the text of Special Orders 191.

Hill, D. H. "The Lost Dispatch." *Southern Historical Society Papers,* Vol. 13, 1885.
    Hill's case that he didn't lose the orders is convincing, but his argument here—that losing the orders actually helped the South—is not.

McClellan, George B. *McClellan's Own Story.* New York: Charles L. Webster & Co., 1887.
    So determined was McClellan to tell his side that when the single copy of the manuscript was destroyed in an 1881 fire, he sat down and rewrote it in its entirety.

Freeman, Douglas Southall. *Lee's Lieutenants.* New York: Scribner's, 1944.
    Volume 2 includes an appendix with the correspondence that persuaded Freeman that Lee knew McClellan had the orders.

Foote, Shelby. *The Civil War: Fort Sumter to Perryville.* New York: Random House, 1958.
    The first volume of Foote's three-volume history, rightly acclaimed for its narrative power and rightly criticized for its pro-South bias.

Catton, Bruce. *Terrible Swift Sword.* New York: Doubleday, 1963.
    Volume 2 of Catton's still classic *Centennial History of the Civil War.*

Sears, Stephen. *Landscape Turned Red.* New Haven: Ticknor & Fields, 1983.
    This account of Antietam is remarkable in showing the perspectives of both the generals and soldiers. Sears's portrait of McClellan, whose biography he also wrote, is especially damning.

McPherson, James. *Battle Cry of Freedom.* New York: Oxford University Press, 1988.
    The best one-volume history of the war.

Sears, Stephen. *Controversies & Commanders.* Boston: Houghton Mifflin, 1999.
    Sears's essay on the Lost Order comes closer to resolving its mysteries than any other work.

McPherson, James. *Crossroads of Freedom.* New York: Oxford University Press, 2002.
    A succinct history of Antietam that portrays the battle as a turning point in the war.

Were the Dahlgren Papers Forged?

A s THIRTEEN-YEAR-OLD WILLIAM LITTLEPAGE rifled through the pockets of a dead Union officer on the side of a road outside Richmond, he was hoping to find a watch. Instead, he found several documents that came to be known as the Dahlgren Papers. The dead man was Colonel Ulric Dahlgren.

Littlepage passed on the papers to his teacher, Edward Halbach. The next morning, March 3, 1864, Halbach read them. One appeared to be an address to Dahlgren's troops.

"You have been selected from brigades and regiments as a picked command to attempt a desperate undertaking—an undertaking which, if successful, will write your names on the hearts of your countrymen in letters that can never be erased," the address began.

It went on to outline Dahlgren's plan: to lead his cavalry into Richmond from the south, stopping first to release Union prisoners held on Belle Island in the middle of the James River, then continuing across "to burn the hateful city." The address also contained these instructions: "Do not allow the rebel leader Davis and his traitorous crew to escape."

A second set of orders, apparently for Captain John Mitchell, Dahlgren's second-in-command, was even more explicit: "The bridges once secured, and the prisoners loose and over the river, the bridges will be burned and the city destroyed. The men must keep together and well in hand, and once in the city it must be destroyed and Jeff. Davis and cabinet killed."

Halbach was, understandably, appalled. Dahlgren's orders seemed to cross the line from war to terrorism; bloody though the Civil War had been to that point, neither side had resorted to indiscriminate destruction or political assassination. Halbach passed the papers up the Confederate chain of command to President Jefferson Davis, the target of the Union plot.

Davis, recognizing the propaganda value of the papers, released them to the press, which quickly dubbed Dahlgren "Ulric the Hun." The *Richmond Daily Dispatch* headline read "The Last Raid of the Infernals." Another Richmond newspaper, *The Whig*, asked of the Yankees: "Are they not barbarians redolent with more hellish purposes than were the Goth, the Hun or the Saracen?"

Northerners, for their part, were equally righteous and equally adamant in calling the papers a forgery. The *New York Times* condemned "the rebel calumny on Col. Dahlgren," arguing that "no officer of the American army would ever dream of putting to death civil officers . . . and no officer in his senses, even if he were barbarous enough to contemplate such a result, would ever put such orders in writing."

The Dahlgren Papers set in motion more than just propaganda. Incensed, Davis and his cabinet responded in kind, approving plans to free Confederate prisoners and let them loose in Union cities. Their hope was to stave off defeat by spreading fear and undercutting support for the war in the North. The plans failed, but the pretense of civility was now gone from the Civil War.

"In both the north and south there was fury," wrote Bruce Catton, "and the war between the sections, which once seemed almost like a tournament, had at last hardened into the pattern of total war."

The end of the Civil War brought no end to the debate over the Dahlgren Papers.

∽

The raid on Richmond that led to Dahlgren's death originated in the mind of Brigadier General Judson Kilpatrick, an extraordinarily ambitious commander of a division of the Army of the Potomac's cavalry. Kilpatrick was known to his troops as "Kill-Cavalry," for he had few qualms about sacrificing Union as well as Confederate soldiers to achieve his objectives.

Kilpatrick knew Lincoln was impatient with his own commanders. Victories at Gettysburg and Vicksburg and Chattanooga had turned the tide in the Union's favor, but the Army of the Potomac had stalled at the Rapidan River in northern Virginia, and General George Meade appeared reluctant to push farther south. Meanwhile, stories of the suffering of Union prisoners on Belle Island and in Richmond's Libby Prison circulated through the North and in the White House.

Ignoring the normal chain of command, Kilpatrick took his bold plan directly to the president and his secretary of war, Edwin Stanton. He proposed a quick strike on Richmond. With Robert E. Lee's Army of Northern Virginia camped opposite Meade on the other side of the Rapidan, the Confederate capital had only a small contingent of home guardsmen to protect it. Kilpatrick would take his cavalry around Lee and hit Richmond before Jeb Stuart's Confederate cavalry could come to its defense. Even if reinforcements did reach the city, Kilpatrick assured Lincoln and Stanton, by then the freed prisoners would have swelled the Union ranks.

Kilpatrick got the go-ahead, and put together a force of about 3,500 cavalrymen. One was Dahlgren, whose father, Rear Admiral John Dahlgren, was a close friend of Lincoln's. At twenty-one, Dahlgren was the youngest colonel in the Union, and he craved glory every bit as much as Kilpatrick. That he had lost part of his leg chasing Lee's forces from Gettysburg did not deter Dahlgren in the least.

The operation got under way on the evening of February 28, with General George Armstrong Custer leading about 1,500 cavalry toward Charlottesville. This was meant as a diversion and it worked; while Lee worried about Custer, Kilpatrick and Dahlgren sneaked across the Rapidan to the east. At Spotsylvania, the two split. Kilpatrick continued south toward Richmond. Dahlgren led 500 men west toward Jude's Ferry, where he hoped to cross the James. The plan was for them to attack simultaneously, Kilpatrick from the north and Dahlgren from the south.

Now things went seriously awry. At Jude's Ferry, Dahlgren discovered that the past few days' rain had made the river too deep and too fast to cross. He decided to press on toward Richmond anyway, hoping to join Kilpatrick from the west instead of the south. Instead, he ran into Southern troops, and had to turn north.

Kilpatrick, meanwhile, had reached the outskirts of Richmond. He might still have managed to overrun the scant Confederate defenses there, but with no sign of Dahlgren, his nerve failed him. Faced with enemy fire, Kilpatrick decided—wrongly—that the Confederates had somehow managed to get reinforcements to Richmond. He fled toward the east, eventually reaching the Union lines at New Kent.

That left Dahlgren stranded, with the Southerners by now fully aware of his presence. Lost in the dark, he led his men into an ambush. He was shot in the head and left to die, not far from the town of Stevensville, on the road where Littlepage found him.

⌘

On March 30, Lee sent a copy of the Dahlgren Papers to Meade, along with a formal protest and a demand to know whether the orders were "authorized by the United States Government." Meade, in turn, asked Kilpatrick to investigate.

Kilpatrick told Meade he had endorsed Dahlgren's address to his men—but without the offensive parts. "The alleged address of Colonel Dahlgren . . . is the same as the one approved by me," he wrote Meade, "save so far as it speaks of exhorting the prisoners to destroy and burn the hateful city and kill the traitor Davis and his cabinet. All this is false."

Kilpatrick also interviewed survivors from Dahlgren's command, all of whom insisted that Dahlgren had given no such orders.

Meade sent Kilpatrick's statement to Lee, along with his own conclusion: "Neither the United States Government, myself, nor General Kilpatrick authorized, sanctioned or approved the burning of Richmond and the killing of Mr. Davis and cabinet, nor any other act not required by military necessity and in accordance with the usages of war."

So ended the official investigation.

Privately, though, Meade had doubts. He'd never trusted Kilpatrick, especially since he'd gone over his head to Lincoln and Stanton. In a letter to his wife in April, soon after he replied to Lee, Meade described the whole affair as "a pretty ugly piece of business." He told her he regretted implying that, if the papers were authentic, Dahlgren must have written them on his own. "Kilpatrick's reputation," Meade said, "and collateral evidence in my possession, rather go against this theory."

Indeed, relying on Kilpatrick was, as historian Stephen Sears put it, "equivalent to ordering the fox to investigate losses in the henhouse." Kilpatrick, after all, was Dahlgren's superior officer, and may have given him the orders. If so, Kilpatrick had every reason to deny they were authentic.

It's unclear what "collateral evidence" Meade meant, though he could have been re-ferring to a conversation with General Marsena Patrick about Captain John McEntee, who served under Dahlgren and survived the raid. After talking to McEntee, Patrick wrote in his diary: "He has the same opinion of Kilpatrick that I have, and says he man-aged just as all cowards do. He further says that he thinks the papers are correct that were found upon Dahlgren, as they correspond with what D. told him."

It's possible Patrick told this to Meade as well as his diary. Still, McEntee was the only man who rode with Dahlgren and suggested the address could have been authentic. Moreover, McEntee's testimony is secondhand, or thirdhand, if Patrick passed it on to Meade.

One person absolutely convinced of Dahlgren's innocence was his father. The admiral was eager to clear his son's name, and in July 1864, he found some very strong evidence. While studying a photographic copy of the orders that the Confederates had made, the admiral noticed that two of the letters in his son's signature had been reversed. Instead of Dahlgren, it was Dalhgren.

It was inconceivable, the admiral argued, that his son would have misspelled his own name.

"I felt from the first . . . that my son never wrote that paper—that it was a forgery; but I refrained from giving utterance to that faith until I had seen a sample of the infamous counterfeit," he wrote. "I say now, that a more fiendish lie never was invented."

The admiral did not say who had forged the papers, but the implication was clear: someone high up in the Confederate hierarchy, perhaps even Davis himself, had framed his son. The motive may have been to create some potent propaganda, or something even more devious, such as an effort to justify the South's own plans to spread dissension and terror in the North by freeing Confederate prisoners there and letting them loose in Union cities.

It was no coincidence, Dahlgren's defenders noted, that soon after the publication of the papers, the Confederates approved their own plans to bomb the White House and kidnap Lincoln. With defeat on the battlefield only a matter of time, the Dahlgren Papers provided the perfect pretext for Southern leaders, increasingly desperate, to take the war to another level.

Dahlgren's disparagers came up with a variety of responses. In 1879, the ex-Confederate general Jubal Early pointed out that the address had been written on two sides of thin paper. The apparent misspelling, Early argued, was actually the result of ink leaking through from the back of the paper. Others hypothesized that whoever copied the papers had touched them up, and in doing so misspelled the name. Still others speculated that some other Union soldier could have written the orders for Dahlgren.

These theories get a bit convoluted, and historians might reasonably have decided the best way to resolve the questions surrounding the papers would be to examine the originals.

There was only one problem with that: no one knew where the Dahlgren Papers were.

The trail of the papers leads from the Confederate archives in Richmond and then Charlotte, to the federal bureau of the adjutant general in Washington, D.C., which took over the collection after the war. In December 1865, the secretary of war requested the papers, and Francis Lieber, who headed the bureau, sent them to Stanton.

Fourteen years later, Lieber asked for them back, so that he could include them in a multivolume collection of war records he was putting together. The War Department responded that they had no record of the papers.

The mysterious disappearance has led to much speculation about why Stanton wanted the papers, and what he did with them. Some suspected a cover-up; perhaps, they argued, Stanton or even Lincoln himself had authorized burning Richmond and killing Davis. After all, the secretary of war and the president did meet with Kilpatrick, bypassing the normal chain of command.

"Perhaps it is an uncharitable thought," wrote historian James Hall in 1983, "but the suspicion lingers that Stanton consigned them to the fireplace in his office."

Stanton was pushing for a more unlimited war on the South, and it's possible he and Kilpatrick discussed the possibility of kidnapping or even killing Davis.

As for Lincoln, there's no evidence linking the president to the alleged orders, and it's not just uncharitable but unfair to imply the president had anything more in mind than freeing the Union prisoners, and perhaps sowing some chaos in Richmond. These were reasons enough for Lincoln to approve the plan, and they may very well have been all that Kilpatrick—and Dahlgren—ever intended.

Whatever its true intent, the raid on Richmond came back to haunt the Union. Confederate plots to bomb the White House and kidnap Lincoln failed, as did most of the Southern efforts to bring the war home to Northern cities. One of those recruited for the kidnapping plot, however, did not give up, even after the war was over.

His name was John Wilkes Booth.

To Investigate Further

Jones, Virgil Carrington. *Eight Hours Before Richmond.* New York: Henry Holt, 1957.
    A lot can happen in eight hours.

Hall, James. "The Dahlgren Papers." *Civil War Times Illustrated,* November 1983.
    An excellent summary of the mysteries surrounding the papers' origins and disappearance.

Furgurson, Ernest. *Ashes of Glory.* New York: Knopf, 1996.
    Furgurson uncovered an anonymous and undated paper quoting Custer as saying Dahlgren told him "that he would not take Pres. Davis & his cabinet, but would put them to death, and that he would set fire to the first house in Richmond and burn the city." As evidence of Dahlgren's guilt, that seems strained, though overall this is a very vivid portrait of Richmond during the war.

Schultz, Duane. *The Dahlgren Affair.* New York: W. W. Norton, 1998.

A compelling account of the raid on Richmond and the Confederate campaign of terror that followed. Schultz makes a very strong case that the papers were, if not forged, at least altered.

Sears, Stephen. *Controversies & Commanders.* Boston: Houghton Mifflin, 1999.

Includes one of the best cases for the papers' authenticity. For Sears's latest arguments, including his explicit answers to Schultz, go to www.historynet.com/acw/ bldahlgrenpapersrevisited/index.html.

Why Did Custer Attack?

T HE COUNTRY'S TOP TWO GENERALS, William Tecumseh Sherman and Philip Sheridan, first heard about the Battle of Little Bighorn in Philadelphia, where they were attending a celebration of the American centennial. Their first reaction was to deny the reports.

Custer dead? His Seventh Cavalry wiped out by the Sioux and Cheyenne? It was inconceivable not just to Sherman and Sheridan but to most of America in 1876. George Armstrong Custer was the man the Northern press had dubbed the "boy general" for his precocious successes at Gettysburg, during the Wilderness campaign, and outside Appomattox, where he stopped Robert E. Lee's flight and forced his surrender. Custer's blond hair and flamboyant dress, especially the long red tie that flew behind him as he led his men to battle, added to his fame.

Out west, buckskin replaced velvet but not victories. In 1868, Custer led the Seventh Cavalry into the Washita Valley in present-day Oklahoma, where they surprised a Cheyenne village and routed Black Kettle's warriors. Smaller battles against the Sioux and Cheyenne throughout the western plains solidified Custer's reputation as the nation's premiere Indian fighter.

On June 25, 1876, as Custer approached Montana's Little Bighorn River, he must have sensed his greatest victory. His scouts told him the Sioux and Cheyenne had set up a large village along the river, larger even than that on the Washita. As he did at the Washita, Custer divided his troops. He ordered Captain Frederick Benteen south to check for other Indian camps, then to rejoin the rest of the troops near the Indian village. Major Marcus Reno, Custer's second-in-command, would attack the village from the east with 130 men. Custer himself would sweep down from the northwest with about another 220 men, catching the Indians between his forces and Reno's and preventing them from escaping.

It did not, of course, work out that way. Reno attacked, but the Indians vastly outnumbered his men: estimates put the total number of warriors in the village somewhere between 1,500 and 2,000. Reno quickly retreated across the river. There Benteen's forces joined Reno's, and together they were able to hold their position, mostly because the Indians turned west to face Custer's charge.

The next day, infantry under the command of Colonel John Gibbon reinforced Reno and Benteen's men. Slowly, they moved up the valley. The Indians were gone, they discovered, probably to their relief. To their horror, they also found that Custer and all who rode with him were dead.

How could this have happened? Why did the country's most famous Indian fighter ignore his scouts' reports about the size of the Indian village? Why did he divide his forces and then attack, when he was clearly outnumbered? Why didn't he wait for Gibbon and others under the command of General Alfred Terry, who were only a day away from the Little Bighorn?

No wonder Sherman and Sheridan didn't believe the news.

杰

Sheridan, once he got over the initial shock, wrote to Sherman: "I deeply deplore the loss of Custer and his men. I feel it was an unnecessary sacrifice, due to misapprehension, and a superabundance of courage—the latter extraordinarily developed in Custer."

President Ulysses Grant put it much more critically. He described the defeat "as a sacrifice of troops brought on by Custer himself, that was wholly unnecessary."

Granted, Grant was no fan of Custer. Custer had testified against Grant's brother during an inquiry into one of the numerous corruption scandals that plagued the administration, and Grant had not forgotten this. Indeed, much of the contemporary criticism of Custer came from Grant's supporters, defending the president's Indian policies. Custer, wrote the Republican *Chicago Tribune*, "preferred to make a reckless dash and take the consequences, in the hope of making a personal victory and adding to the glory of another charge, rather than wait for a sufficiently powerful force to make the fight successful and share the glory with others."

Custer's critics in the military argued that he had not only exhibited poor judgment but disobeyed orders. Terry's written orders were to wait until Gibbon's troops arrived for a joint attack on the Indians. But this criticism was unfair to Custer; Terry's comments were really just suggestions, and he explicitly told Custer that he had "too much confidence in your zeal, energy, and ability to wish to impose upon you precise orders which might hamper your action when nearly in contact with the enemy." Besides, like the Republicans, the military was a little eager to deflect onto Custer any criticism of its Indian policies.

Still, his critics had a point: it was clear, at least in retrospect, that Custer would have been wise to wait for Gibbon.

The Battle of Little Bighorn also prompted critics to take another look at Custer's history, which wasn't quite as exemplary as it first appeared. The boy general's Civil War campaigns, though always daring and mostly successful, were often costly: at Gettysburg his charge halted a Confederate advance, but 481 Union soldiers were killed or wounded; during the Wilderness campaign of 1864, he lost more than a third of his brigade; even near Appomattox, Custer's command suffered 377 casualties.

Then there was the matter of Custer's 1867 court-martial for being absent without leave and for not stopping to bury the bodies of two soldiers killed while he led his troops across Kansas. Custer claimed he was rushing east to get medicine for cholera victims at Fort Wallace, but the disease had not yet hit there. It appeared more likely—to the mili-

Custer's last stand, portrayed here in Frederick Whittaker's 1876 biography, may never have happened. *(Denver Public Library)*

tary court that found him guilty and to most historians—that he left his post and relentlessly drove his troops simply because he wanted to see his wife, Libbie, who was waiting for him in eastern Kansas. A fine romantic gesture, to be sure, but hardly sound military strategy.

To counter her husband's critics, Libbie Custer enlisted the aid of Frederick Whittaker, a dime novelist who quickly churned out the first biography—really more a hagiography—of Custer. Errol Flynn's 1941 portrayal of Custer in *They Died with Their Boots On* had nothing on Whittaker's 1876 swashbuckler.

"Never was there a life more rounded, complete, and symmetrical than that of George A. Custer, the favorite of fortune, the last cavalier," wrote Whittaker. "To Custer alone was it given to join a romantic life of perfect success to a death of perfect heroism."

Whittaker's villains were Reno and Benteen. Had Reno not retreated when the Indians resisted, had Benteen not dawdled to the south, had either carried out Custer's plan, it would have worked. Reno was a coward and a drunk; Benteen was jealous and vindictive. Whittaker was especially harsh in his treatment of Reno, who outranked Benteen and thus made the final decision not to go to Custer's aid.

Even after the biography was published, Whittaker continued to assail Reno. In June 1878, he released a letter to the press blaming him for Custer's defeat, since "he remained idle with this force while his superior officer was fighting against the whole force of the Indians, the battle being within his knowledge, the sound of firing audible from his position, and his forces out of immediate danger from the enemy."

Reno had had enough of this. He appealed to President Rutherford B. Hayes to convene a special court where he could defend his reputation. At the army's 1879 court of inquiry, Reno and Benteen both maintained they were unaware of Custer's plight and that, even if they'd known, they were too busy defending themselves to help him. "We were at their hearths and homes," Benteen said of the Indians, "their medicine was working well, and they were fighting for all the good God gives anyone to fight for."

Those who served under Benteen defended his courage, arguing that he rallied them to defend themselves amidst the carnage. Reno's subordinates were distinctly less enthusiastic; most claimed to have seen little of him during the battle.

"I don't know whether he rose to the emergency or not," testified Lieutenant Luther Hare, when asked whether Reno was a coward. "I have not much to go upon in making an estimate."

The army court found there was nothing in Reno's conduct that merited its "animadversion." This was not the chastisement Reno must have feared after his men's half-hearted testimony, but it was hardly a ringing endorsement. Nor did it do much to solve the mystery of what caused the debacle at Little Bighorn.

ᐅᙁᙁᐊ

What made the mystery so difficult to solve, most nineteenth-century observers agreed, was that no one had survived Custer's last stand. This was, of course, untrue: there were plenty of Indian survivors. But most of their stories were dismissed as cowardly lies.

There was more than just racism at work here. The Indian reports were confusing and contradictory, and often incompetently translated. Few Indians knew much about cavalry tactics and formations, making it difficult for them to analyze Custer's movements. Most spoke only after they were rounded up onto reservations, and many may have said what they thought the white interviewers wanted to hear. The reports of Custer's heroic stand were especially suspect in this regard.

Still, racism undoubtedly made it easier for late nineteenth- and early twentieth-century historians to disregard the Indian reports. So in the 1960s and 1970s historians made a concerted effort to untangle the Indian testimony. Some of their findings seemed as ideologically motivated as those of their predecessors. Instead of focusing on the Indian reports about how heroic the soldiers were, especially at the last stand, the revisionists emphasized the testimony of mass panic and disorder among Custer's troops. By 1970, the image of Custer as Flynn's swashbuckler had been replaced by Richard Milligan's buffoonish megalomaniac in *Little Big Man*. In that movie, Custer's victory over Black Kettle at the Washita is meant to be seen as a parallel of the My Lai massacre in Vietnam.

"From a symbol of courage and sacrifice in the winning of the West, Custer's image was gradually altered into a symbol of the arrogance and brutality displayed in the white exploitation of the West," wrote Paul Hutton. Evan Connell agreed: "His image has fallen face down in the mud and his middle initial, which stands for Armstrong, could mean Anathema."

Yet the new attention to Indian testimony did bear fruit. Indian participants in the battle had spoken convincingly of their outrage over American Indian policy, their decision to make a united stand, and the strong leadership of such chiefs as Sitting Bull and Crazy Horse. And these factors went a long way toward explaining Custer's defeat. Wrote Robert Utley: "The simplest answer, usually overlooked, is that the army lost largely because the Indians won. To ascribe defeat entirely to military failings is to devalue Indian strength and leadership."

Further evidence of the effectiveness of the Indian warriors surfaced in 1983, after a grass fire swept across the battlefield. At first, historians treated this as a natural and historical disaster. But it turned out the fire cleared the way for a more systematic study of the site than had ever been conducted. Using metal detectors and limited excavation, Richard Fox and a team of archaeologists plotted the distribution of cartridges and bullets around the Little Bighorn. The lack of cartridges on what's now known as Custer Hill—supposedly the site of the last stand—led Fox to conclude the famous stand never happened. Overall, the pattern of artifacts revealed how quickly Custer's forces collapsed under the Indian onslaught.

"Except at the beginning of the battle, the soldiers were in disarray, without much semblance of unified purpose," Fox wrote. "Panic and fear, the prime ingredients in collapse during combat, spread throughout the tactical units.

Custerphiles again rose to defend their man and his troops. Some argued that more than a hundred years of souvenir hunting, especially around Custer Hill, had corrupted the battlefield record. Others maintained there must have been a last stand, though perhaps not at Custer Hill. But Fox's meticulous research convinced most historians that, whatever Custer's strengths or failings as a leader, he and his men were quickly overwhelmed by the Sioux and Cheyenne.

⟨≈⟩

Why did he attack in the face of overwhelming odds?

One theory put forward by some historians is that he hoped a major victory would propel him to the White House. Superficially, this makes sense. Scandals had made Grant vulnerable, and Custer offered the Democrats an alternative war hero. Red Star, one of his Indian scouts, quoted Custer as saying that a victory at Little Bighorn would make him the white's "great father." But there's no other evidence Custer had political ambitions, let alone presidential ones. Red Star could have misunderstood or been misquoted.

More likely, Custer's ambitions were military. The Little Bighorn presented him with an opportunity for an even greater victory than the Washita. To Custer, the circumstances must have seemed similar. At neither the Washita nor the Little Bighorn did he know how many Indians he would face, nor did he care. He had faith that the Seventh

Cavalry could whip any number of them. Besides, experience had taught him that when soldiers attacked an Indian village, the Indians tended to panic and flee. This was exactly what happened at the Washita, where Black Kettle's warriors were generally more worried about getting their families to safety than about setting up an organized defense.

Faced with a large gathering of Indians, Custer's main concern was that they not escape. Waiting for Gibbon or Terry meant not only sharing the credit for the victory, but also risking that the Indians would learn of his presence and scatter. When he spotted the village, Custer reportedly waved his hat and shouted to the troops (this according to a messenger dispatched to Benteen just before the battle): "Hurrah, boys, we've got them!"

"If indeed Custer made such a remark after sighting the greatest concentration of militant Indians in the history of North America," Connell noted, "it sounds like a joke from an old vaudeville routine." But it's perfectly possible Custer said this—or at least thought it. He was not afraid of Indians; he had, as Sheridan put it, "a superabundance of courage." His job was to track them down and attack.

And that is exactly what he did.

To Investigate Further

Custer, George Armstrong. *My Life on the Plains.* Lincoln: University of Nebraska Press, 1966.
   Originally published in 1874, the style is a bit convoluted for modern tastes but shows Custer knew how to generate good publicity for himself. Benteen referred to the book as "My Lie on the Plains."

Whittaker, Frederick. *A Complete Life of General George A. Custer.* Lincoln: University of Nebraska Press, 1993.
   Originally published in 1876, a biography of "one of the few really great men that America has produced."

Custer, Elizabeth. *Tenting on the Plains.* Norman: University of Oklahoma Press, 1971.
   Elizabeth Custer recalled her idyllic life with her husband in three books: *Tenting* covers the marriage through the court-martial (though the latter is not mentioned), *Following the Guidon* covers 1867–1869, and *Boots and Saddles* ends when Elizabeth learns about Little Bighorn. The University of Oklahoma Press reprinted *Boots and Saddles* in 1961, and the University of Nebraska Press reprinted *Guidon* in 1994.

Ambrose, Stephen. *Crazy Horse and Custer.* Garden City, NY: Doubleday, 1975.
   A dual biography set in a background of social and military history.

Connell, Evan. *Son of the Morning Star.* New York: Harper & Row, 1985.
   A meandering but always elegant and evocative narrative that brings to life not just Custer but also Reno, Benteen, Sitting Bull, and Crazy Horse.

Utley, Robert. *Cavalier in Buckskin.* Norman: University of Oklahoma Press, 2001.
   A revised edition of Utley's superb 1988 biography.

Gray, John. *Custer's Last Campaign.* Lincoln: University of Nebraska Press, 1991.
A virtually minute-by-minute account of the battle.

Hutton, Paul. *The Custer Reader.* Lincoln: University of Nebraska Press, 1992.
An anthology of classic articles.

Fox, Richard. *Archaeology, History, and Custer's Last Battle.* Norman: University of Oklahoma Press, 1993.
Anyone who thinks archaeology is just for learning about ancient civilizations will find otherwise here. Highly technical but important.

Welch, James. *Killing Custer.* New York: W. W. Norton, 1994.
A Native American novelist's meditation on the meaning of the Little Bighorn.

Barnett, Louise. *Touched by Fire.* New York: Henry Holt, 1996.
The best parts of this biography are about Libbie Custer, and about the making of the myths surrounding her husband.

Wert, Jeffry. *Custer.* New York: Simon & Schuster, 1996.
An evenhanded biography, though Utley's is better.

Michno, Gregory. *Lakota Noon.* Missoula, MT: Mountain Press, 1997.
A narrative of the battle based on Indian testimony.

Sklenar, Larry. *To Hell with Honor.* Norman: University of Oklahoma Press, 2000.
Argues Custer's attack could have succeeded if Reno and Benteen hadn't betrayed him.

Who Was to Blame
for Wounded Knee?

I
N THE YEAR 1890, at a spot near Wounded Knee Creek in southwest South Dakota, Chief Big Foot and a band of about 120 Sioux warriors accompanied by 230 women and children, met up with 470 members of the Seventh Cavalry, commanded by Colonel James Forsyth. This was the same Seventh Cavalry that had met the Sioux at the Battle of Little Bighorn 16 years earlier; then the cavalry had been commanded by General George Armstrong Custer and the Sioux had wiped out an entire batallion.

At Wounded Knee, it was the Sioux who were almost wiped out. The battle left 25 soldiers and somewhere between 200 and 300 Indians dead, many of them women and children. It also left a number of disturbing questions: Who fired the first shot? Did the Sioux warriors conceal their weapons in order to ambush the soldiers, as many of the latter claimed? Or did the Seventh Cavalry take its revenge on a peaceful band of Sioux families? Was the Battle of Wounded Knee a battle at all—or a brutal massacre?

Eighty-five years later, while historians continued to investigate these questions, Wounded Knee was again the site of an armed confrontation between Native Americans and U.S. government forces. In 1975 two FBI agents found themselves in a shoot-out with members of AIM, a militant organization (its initials stand for American Indian Movement) devoted to Native American rights. When the shooting stopped this time, the two agents were dead. AIM member Leonard Peltier was convicted of murder. His supporters said he was framed by the FBI.

Once again Wounded Knee had become a symbol of Native American resistance. And once again there were disturbing questions to be answered.

◦◦◦◦◦

The path that led Big Foot and his followers to Wounded Knee began about one hundred miles north of there, at a small Sioux village on the Cheyenne River. On the morning of December 23, 1890, the Sioux left their village, heading south toward the Pine Ridge Reservation. According to some accounts, Big Foot had been invited to Pine Ridge to settle some disputes between other Sioux factions; according to others, the Indians were going south to collect the payments due to them under the various treaties by which they'd ceded their land and moved into their reservations.

To Major General Nelson Miles, both Big Foot's destination and his motives were suspect. Miles was well aware that this was a period of intense unrest among the Sioux. Swarms of white settlers had killed off the buffalo, on which the Sioux depended for food. (In 1890 there were so many white settlers throughout the West that the U.S. Super-intendent of the Census could no longer draw a line between those sections of the West that had been settled and those that were still wilderness; the frontier, he conceded, no longer existed.) The move to the reservations had completely disrupted Sioux institu-tions; major crop failures, epidemics of measles and whooping cough, and corrupt and incompetent government agents had further exacerbated their condition.

By 1890 the Sioux were near starvation. About three thousand had left the reserva-tions and congregated in the Badlands, a stark region of plateaus and cliffs north of the Pine Ridge Reservation. There the Sioux danced the "Ghost Dance," a ritual meant to bring about a new world in which the white man would disappear and the buffalo, along with generations of past Indians, would return. The Ghost Dance was a strange mix of traditional Indian beliefs and messianic Christianity, but to a people feeling as helpless and hopeless as the Sioux, it was hard to resist.

In most of its forms the Ghost Dance religion, in spite of the apocalyptic images it called forth, did not call for violence against whites. Still, most whites—and Miles in par-ticular—found it extremely threatening. Miles ordered the arrest of the leading Sioux chiefs who practiced the religion. On December 15, Indian policemen employed by the government arrived at the cabin of Sitting Bull—the chief who, along with Crazy Horse, had led the Sioux in the Battle of Little Bighorn. When Sitting Bull resisted, the police shot and killed him.

That left Big Foot as the most prominent Sioux chief who had taken up the Ghost Dance, and Miles ordered him arrested as well. But before the order could be carried out, Big Foot and his band slipped out of their village. The chief said he was heading to the Pine Ridge Reservation but, Miles was quick to note, the chief's destination might just as easily have been the Badlands, where he could join up with the Ghost Dancers most hos-tile to the whites. More disturbing still, some of Sitting Bull's most militant followers had fled after their chief's death and had reportedly joined Big Foot's band.

Miles ordered his forces to find Big Foot and bring him back. On December 28, a unit of the Seventh Cavalry intercepted the Indians. Big Foot surrendered, and the soldiers es-corted the Indians to Wounded Knee. The next morning the Indians awoke to find them-selves surrounded by even more soldiers, with cannons pointing down at them from a nearby hill. Colonel Forsyth ordered the Indians to disarm, and when the Sioux turned over only a few old guns, Forsyth sent his soldiers in to search the Indian tipis. With ten-sions running high on both sides, not much was needed to spark the conflagration.

⟶

Precisely what set off the fighting is unclear. According to some eyewitness reports, an Indian medicine man named Yellow Bird began walking among the warriors, telling them their sacred "ghost shirts" would protect them from the white man's bullets. Re-portedly, as one of the soldiers lifted an Indian blanket to check for weapons, Yellow Bird threw a handful of dust into the air, signaling the warriors to draw their rifles and open fire. Other eyewitnesses told of how two soldiers grabbed Black Coyote, a deaf warrior who'd been carrying around his rifle, apparently without understanding what was going on. A struggle ensued, the rifle went off accidentally, and the soldiers then opened fire on the mostly disarmed Indians.

Which story did historians believe? It depended, at least partly, on where their sympathies lay. For historians predisposed to finding the Sioux deaths justifiable, the Yellow Bird story demonstrated that the Sioux warriors, or at least some of them, had started the fight. Moreover, it seemed as if they'd planned it in advance; witness the simultaneous appearance of the Indians' weapons upon the signal from Yellow Bird. And these were weapons that had been treacherously concealed after Big Foot had, supposedly, unconditionally surrendered.

For historians more sympathetic to the Indians, the Black Coyote story corroborated their suspicions. The soldiers must have honed in on an Indian who clearly didn't know what was going on, in order to provoke a fight. And, as these historians were quick to remind readers, these were soldiers of Custer's Seventh Cavalry; this was their chance to avenge Little Bighorn.

Viewed objectively, both of these interpretations are unfair: neither the Sioux nor the cavalry plotted in advance to start a fight. For the Sioux, a battle made no sense. They were vastly outnumbered and they had women and children in their midst; however desperate they were, they were not suicidal. Big Foot was suffering from pneumonia and was in no condition to plan a battle. True, he had once been one of the more ardent Ghost Dancers but he'd since lost faith in the religion; besides, he was always more of a peacemaker than a warrior. (Remember, at least according to some accounts, Big Foot was on his way to Pine Ridge to help work out a truce between Indian factions there.)

But if Big Foot and his warriors weren't looking for a fight, neither is there any hard evidence that Forsyth or his soldiers wanted trouble. Miles blamed Forsyth for deploying his troops in such fatal proximity to the Indians but this endangered the troops as well as the Indians; it was more an error of judgment on Forsyth's part than any indication that he was out for blood. Miles himself erred in his initial order to arrest Big Foot; had he left Big Foot alone, he and his followers probably would have ended up on the Pine Ridge Reservation, right where Miles wanted them. But, like Forsyth, Miles hoped to avoid a fight.

So, if neither side planned to fight, who is to blame for starting it? Probably no one. In an atmosphere as highly charged as that of December 29, either Yellow Bird throwing dust in the air or Black Coyote's gun going off could have set off the fight, without any advanced planning on either side. Perhaps both events occurred simultaneously; that would surely have sufficed.

This is not to say, of course, that no one is to blame in any sense. Whatever the immediate cause of the battle, there's no denying that it was preceded by decades of broken treaties, which drove Native Americans from their land. According to an 1868 treaty—the first treaty in which the Sioux agreed to any boundaries on their land—the "unceded Indian territories" would extend, forever, from the Missouri River west to the Big

Horn Mountains in Wyoming and from just below the Canadian border south into Nebraska. By 1890, this had been whittled down to reservations comprised of fewer than 16,000 square miles. Moreover, the slaughter of so many women and children can't be attributed to the heat of battle alone; clearly the fighting released deep fears and prejudices and hatreds on the part of the soldiers. In this fundamental sense, then, the soldiers were to blame.

The fighting at Wounded Knee put an end to the Sioux uprising of 1890. Within two weeks, the remaining Ghost Dancers in the Badlands wandered back to the reservations and surrendered. Years later, a Sioux holy man, Black Elk, recalled the scene at Wounded Knee. "I can still see the butchered women and children lying heaped and scattered all along the crooked gulch as plain as I saw them with eyes still young," he said. "And I can see that something else died there in the bloody mud, and was buried in the blizzard. A people's dream died there."

⌀

In February 1973 Wounded Knee was back in the headlines. A few hundred Oglala Sioux Indians, joined by activists from AIM, seized the church at the tiny hamlet of Wounded Knee, right outside of which the bodies of Big Foot and his followers had been buried. For many of the Oglala, the occupation was a protest against the tribal council leader, Dick Wilson, whom they considered a puppet of the federal government. Wilson, they felt, was more interested in giving his cronies jobs and giving away mineral rights than in protecting the interests of the tribe. Wilson had organized vigilante squads that had terrorized his opponents. (He called his followers "Guardians of the Oglala Nation"; his opponents called them "goons.")

The leaders of AIM hoped to do more than oust Wilson. Fully aware that Wounded Knee remained a potent symbol of white injustice, they saw its occupation as a chance to publicize their broader grievances: against escalating white violence against Indians on the reservation, against exploitation of Indian lands, and against the federal government's Indian policies in general. In March, citing the long-ignored 1868 treaty, they declared Wounded Knee part of the Independent Oglala Nation.

As in 1890 the Indians of 1973 were vastly outnumbered and outgunned. Besides the Bureau of Indian police and Wilson's forces, the Justice Department sent in U.S. marshals, SWAT teams, and FBI agents. The occupiers held out for 71 days before agreeing to a peaceful settlement. Leaders of AIM had obviously failed to establish an independent nation, and in the end they were also unable to capitalize on the national attention the occupation had generated. Like other revolutionary movements of the '60s and early '70s, AIM soon fell apart under the weight of its own internal divisions and under relentless pressure from the FBI. The Wounded Knee occupation turned out to be the movement's high tide.

Compared to the 1973 occupation, the 1975 shoot-out, reputedly involving Leonard Peltier and other AIM members, was a sordid affair. It's unclear how the fight started, or what special agents Jack Coler and Ronald Williams were doing on the Pine Ridge Reservation, but it is clear that they were shot from very close range. This was an execution, not a battle that turned out to be fatal.

In response, the FBI launched the biggest manhunt in its history. Four men were eventually indicted; of these, one was released for lack of evidence, two were acquitted by a jury, and the fourth—Peltier—was convicted of murder in the first degree and was sentenced to two consecutive life terms in prison.

AIM claimed Peltier had been set up by the FBI. Supporting this claim was the testimony of a woman named Myrtle Poor Bear. In order to extradite Peltier from Canada, the FBI presented affidavits from Poor Bear in which she claimed to have witnessed Peltier commit the murders. Later she claimed that she'd never seen Peltier in her life and that the FBI had threatened to kill her unless she testified against him. Peltier's defenders also claimed the FBI fixed the ballistics reports to show Peltier's rifle was the murder weapon.

Peltier's case became a cause célèbre in the 1970s and 1980s. Novelist and naturalist Peter Matthiessen wrote a book about him and Robert Redford made a movie about him. He was compared to Sacco and Vanzetti, to Nelson Mandela, and to Crazy Horse, among others. Whether Peltier deserved this lionizing is unclear; though some of the government's evidence was tainted, not all of it was. Furthermore, the cold-blooded killing of the FBI agents was no act of heroism, and the 1975 killings ought not to be conflated—as they sometimes were in the rhetoric of Peltier's defenders—with either the 1890 massacre or the 1973 uprising.

Still, there's no denying that, even if he's guilty of murder, Peltier landed in jail (where he still is) because of a federal agency's abuses of Native American rights. In that sense, his story fits all too well into the history of Wounded Knee.

To Investigate Further

Mooney, James. *Ghost Dance Religion and Wounded Knee.* New York: Dover, 1973.
    Originally published in 1896, this remains a valuable study of the Ghost Dance phenomenon.

Utley, Robert. *The Last Days of the Sioux Nation.* New Haven, CT: Yale University Press, 1963.
    Though too charitable to the soldiers, this remains the best book on the period leading up to and including the 1890 battle.

Brown, Dee. *Bury My Heart at Wounded Knee.* Orlando: Holt, Rinehart & Winston, 1970.
    The history of the West from the Indians' perspective—so much so that it refers to whites by their Indian names (Custer is at first called "Hard Backsides" because he chased the Indians so long without getting out of his saddle; later he's called "Long Hair"). A best-seller, this was not quite so original in its approach as it claimed, but it is nonetheless a powerful indictment of America's treatment of Native Americans.

Marshall, S.L.A. *Crimsoned Prairie: The Wars Between the United States and the Plains Indians During the Winning of the West.* New York: Scribner's, 1972.

Old fashioned both in its highly entertaining narrative style and in its extremely forgiving attitude toward army actions.

Matthiessen, Peter. *In the Spirit of Crazy Horse.* New York: Viking, 1980.

Though overly long, the book argues convincingly that Peltier was framed by the FBI. Publication was delayed for eight years because of libel suits by FBI agent David Price and former South Dakota governor William Jankow, two of the book's villains.

Jensen, Richard, R. Eli Paul, and John Carter. *Eyewitness at Wounded Knee.* Lincoln: University of Nebraska Press, 1991.

Photographs from before and immediately after the 1890 massacre.

Smith, Paul Chaat, and Robert Allen Warrior. *Like a Hurricane.* New York: The New Press, 1996.

The rise and fall of the American Indian Movement during the 1960s and 1970s.

Ostler, Jeffrey. *The Plains Sioux and U.S. Colonialism from Lewis and Clark to Wounded Knee.* New York: Cambridge University Press, 2004.

"U.S. officials did not deliberately plan a massacre," Ostler concluded, "but their reliance on overwhelming military power to intimidate and coerce eventually had that result."

What Destroyed the Maine?

THE U.S. BATTLESHIP *MAINE* arrived in Havana harbor in January 1898, amidst rising tensions between Spain and the United States. Spain was battling Cuban revolutionaries in an effort to hold on to some of its once-great empire; the United States sympathized with the revolutionaries and was beginning to flex its own empire-building muscles. Officially the *Maine*'s mission to Cuba was a peaceful one, but both Spaniards and Americans recognized the ship was there as a show of U.S. naval strength and resolve.

So when the ship blew up at 9:40 P.M. on February 15 and 266 crew members were killed, jingoistic Americans had few doubts who was to blame. "The *Maine* was sunk by an act of dirty treachery on the part of the Spaniards," wrote the assistant secretary of the navy Theodore Roosevelt. The February 17 edition of William Randolph Hearst's *New York Journal* ran the headline: "Destruction of the Warship Maine Was the Work of an Enemy"; a front-page drawing was captioned: "The Spaniards, it is believed, arranged to have the *Maine* anchored over one of the harbor mines."

Others took a more cautious approach. President William McKinley told a friend: "We must learn the truth and endeavor, if possible, to fix the responsibility. The country can afford to withhold its judgment and not strike an avenging blow until the truth is known." (Roosevelt's response: "The president has no more backbone than a chocolate eclair.")

The navy quickly appointed a court of inquiry to determine the cause of the explosion, and in late March the court reached its verdict: the *Maine* was destroyed by a submerged mine. Though the court was unable to determine who placed or detonated the mine, the verdict released more prowar sentiment than McKinley could resist. Even if the Spanish didn't set off the mine, it was clear to the president that most Americans considered them culpably negligent. The *Journal* had a new war cry: "Remember the Maine! To hell with Spain!" By mid-April the United States and Spain were at war.

Was the court's verdict correct? Was Spain to blame? Or did the United States go to war over what was nothing more than an accident—albeit a tragic one?

⟋⟍⟋

The 1898 court of inquiry was comprised of four naval officers, presided over by Captain William T. Sampson. The first to testify before them was Charles Sigsbee, the captain (and obviously, a survivor) of the *Maine*. Sigsbee testified that all required safety procedures had been followed on the ship. He said that prior to the explosion he had personally checked the coal bunkers in the forward part of the ship (where the explosion had taken place) and they had not been hot enough to set off an accidental fire. The implication was clear: if it hadn't been an onboard accident, it had to have been a mine.

What really swayed the court, however, was not Sigsbee's testimony but that of the next witness, Ensign Wilfred Van Nest Powelson. Powelson had studied naval architecture and he had been working on the scene, interviewing navy divers as they came up from the wreck. He described what the divers had seen. The shattered keel of the battleship appeared to have been bent in the form of an inverted V, where the explosion had been centered. Also, a section of bottom plating had been twisted up to within four feet of the surface.

The upward bending of the metal suggested that an explosion had pushed it up from underneath the ship. This was the first solid evidence of a mine. It was enough to convince the Sampson court.

Meanwhile, the Spaniards were conducting their own official investigation. Not surprisingly, they reached a very different conclusion. Had the explosion been caused by a mine, the Spanish report pointed out, witnesses should have heard a dull concussion rather than the sharp report most reported. Had a mine exploded, there should have been a visible geyser but no one reported seeing any upheaval of water. And had there been a mine, there ought to have been lots of dead fish in the harbor, but there were none.

Granted, the Spanish didn't have the same access to the ship's remains as did the Americans, and they also had an interest in seeing themselves cleared. But they raised some disturbing questions, and doubts about the Sampson court's conclusions lingered, even after the Americans rather easily won the 1898 war.

In 1910, therefore, Congress assigned the Army Corps of Engineers the formidable task of bringing the *Maine* to the surface, and in 1911 President Taft appointed a naval board of inspection to analyze the wreck and determine what caused the explosion. This second naval inquiry, with Rear Admiral Charles Vreeland as its most senior member, examined the evidence in far greater detail than could the first court, but their conclusions were much the same. They dismissed the arguments raised by the Spanish inquiry by noting that a few witnesses did hear a dull concussion and that a column of water might have been thrown up by the explosion but hidden by the dense clouds of fire and smoke that followed almost immediately. As for the dead fish, the Vreeland board suggested fish might only have been stunned by the explosion.

On only one issue did the 1911 Vreeland board differ from the original 1898 Sampson court. Though the second report agreed the explosion had been caused by a submerged mine, it placed the explosion underneath frame 27 of the ship rather than frame 18.

You'd think that would have put an end to, at the very least, the official navy investigations. But 62 years after the Vreeland board issued its report, the maverick Admiral Hyman G. Rickover, the navy's leading nuclear submarine expert, was intrigued by a newspaper article about the *Maine*. He took it upon himself to resolve the mystery once and for all, and he enlisted the aid of an engineer from the Naval Ship Research and Development Center and a physicist from the Naval Surface Weapons Center. After revisiting the 1898 and 1911 evidence, Rickover concluded that both courts had been wrong, and that there had been no mine under the *Maine*. The explosion, he believed, had been caused by an internal, accidental fire in bunker A-16.

Rickover put forth a number of arguments: among them that Sigsbee had taken only ordinary measures to guard against an accident (and, in fact, two other ships had been found to be dirty while under his command); that both the 1898 and 1911 boards had been under a great deal of pressure to exonerate the navy and to blame the Spaniards; and that the inner bottom plating was more mangled than the outer bottom plating at the point where the 1911 board thought the mine had been placed. In addition, Rickover cited his modern experts' findings that the upward folding of the bottom plating could have been caused by an internal explosion.

The response to the Rickover report was largely positive. Most historians were impressed by one of the navy's own admirals taking on the navy's official findings; remember, it was in 1976 that Rickover's report was first published and post-Vietnam mistrust of the military was rampant. A few scientists took issue with his technical analysis, arguing that just because Rickover's experts demonstrated the upward folding *could* have been caused by an internal explosion, that didn't prove it *couldn't* have been caused by an external one. Some questioned whether all of this nuclear-age expertise was relevant to an examination of the workings of antique musket powder. And a 1998 *National Geographic* study, using computer modeling techniques unavailable to Rickover, strengthened the case for a mine, while conceding a coal fire was also a possibility.

Still, most considered Rickover's analysis admirable, if not definitive.

⟨∼⟩

Amidst all the technical analysis, what often seemed lost was the question of motive.

If we assume for the moment that it was a mine that blew up the *Maine*, must we therefore assume that it was the Spaniards who placed and detonated it? The Spaniards were desperate to avoid war with the United States; as they fought to hold on to their colony, the last thing in the world they wanted to see was the United States intervening on behalf of the Cuban revolutionaries. In fact, only a few days before the explosion, the Spanish commander in Havana had taken Sigsbee to the bullfights as his guest. And after the explosion the Spaniards appeared as horrified, if not more so, than the Americans.

In the near century since the explosion, a number of other suspects have been put forward. Though the Spanish government may have been eager to avoid war with the United States, there were many in the Spanish military, especially followers of the hard-line General Valeriano Weyler, who resented the presence of the *Maine* in their harbor. In November 1897 Weyler had been replaced by the more moderate General Ramón Blanco y Eranas, who was actively pursuing some form of autonomy for Cuba. To Weyler's followers, therefore, the *Maine*'s destruction was a double cause for celebration: it was a blow against both the Yankee meddlers and the spineless moderates.

Who else had reason to want the United States in the war? The rebels themselves, perhaps. Their military position had not improved during the two months previous to the explosion and could only be helped by the Spaniards having to defend themselves against the Americans. In addition, the more moderate Spanish government presented a political threat to them as well as to the Weylerites. The limited autonomy offered by the moderates was unacceptable to revolutionaries bent on full independence—and the *Maine*'s destruction guaranteed that compromise would never come to pass.

Who else? Could an American eager to get us into the war be responsible? Ferdinand Lundberg, one of William Randolph Hearst's biographers, pointed a finger at the publisher. Hearst had been involved in other intrigues in Cuba, and a few days before the explosion, when his illustrator Frederic Remington asked permission to return home from Cuba, Hearst wired back: "Please remain. You furnish the pictures and I'll furnish the war." And Hearst certainly profited from the war: two days after the explosion, the *Journal*'s circulation rose to over a million.

But Hearst's blustering and profiting amounted to circumstantial evidence, at best. Without question the most likely culprits were extremists, either of the Spanish or the rebel variety. Both had reason to want to see the ship destroyed. And while it seems unlikely historians will ever know for sure whether it was Spaniards or revolutionaries—or fate—that blew up the *Maine*, almost all do agree that the forces unleashed by that explosion not only propelled us into war with Spain but into a prominent role in world affairs from which we have never retreated.

To Investigate Further

Message from the President of the United States Transmitting the Report of the Naval Court of Inquiry Upon the Destruction of the United States Battle Ship Maine in Havana Harbor. Washington, DC: Government Printing Office, 1898.

Includes the testimony taken before the court as well as the court's report and the president's response to it.

Wilson, Herbert W. *The Downfall of Spain.* New York: Little, Brown, 1900.

Wilson was the first historian to tackle the mystery; his book is a thorough examination of what was then known.

Weems, John Edward. *The Fate of the Maine.* New York: Henry Holt and Company, 1958.

Leans toward a mine, but doesn't rule out the possibility of an accident.

Thomas, Hugh. *Cuba: The Pursuit of Freedom.* New York: Harper & Row, 1971.

Leans toward an accidental explosion, but considers the Cuban revolutionaries the most likely candidate to have detonated a mine.

Rickover, H. G. *How the Battleship Maine Was Destroyed.* Washington, DC: Department of the Navy, 1976.

> Rickover's case against a mine, along with the report of his technical experts.

O'Toole, G. J. A. *The Spanish War.* New York: Norton, 1984.

> One of the most recent and readable histories of the war.

Blow, Michael. *A Ship to Remember.* New York: Morrow, 1992.

> A balanced presentation, which concludes that the *Maine*'s destruction remains an unsolvable mystery.

Samuels, Peggy, and Harold Samuels. *Remembering the Maine.* Washington, DC: Smithsonian Institution Press, 1995.

> The case that Weyler's followers set off a mine.

Allen, Thomas. "Remember the Maine?" *National Geographic,* February 1998.

> "The case remains open," the study concluded.

PART 7

CRISIS AND ACHIEVEMENT, 1900–1945

Why Did
Freud Abandon
His Seduction Theory?

I MUST MENTION AN ERROR into which I fell for a while," Freud wrote in his 1925 autobiography, "and which might well have had fatal consequences for the whole of my work."

Freud's "slip" was his "seduction theory," in which he passionately believed during the early 1890s. The theory's name was misleading, for it had to do not with seduction but with child abuse. Freud formulated the seduction theory while treating eighteen patients exhibiting a range of nervous disorders. Each of these patients, Freud learned, had been sexually molested as a child.

Freud was tremendously excited, for he thought he'd identified the roots of a great many patients' symptoms. In a paper presented to the Viennese Society for Psychiatry and Neurology in April 1896, Freud compared his findings to the discovery of the source of the Nile. Privately, he wrote to his friend and fellow doctor Wilhelm Fliess that he expected his seduction theory to bring him both fame and fortune.

Yet in September 1897, Freud dramatically reversed himself. "I want to confide in you immediately the great secret that has been slowly dawning on me in the last few months," he wrote, again in a letter to Fliess. "I no longer believe in my [seduction] theory." One problem with the theory, Freud admitted, was that the revelations of child abuse hadn't led to a successful treatment of any of his patients. They continued to suffer from the same symptoms. But the theory's biggest flaw was that these symptoms were so common. If everyone who suffered from them had been abused as a child, that would mean— Freud now realized—that child abuse was rampant throughout Viennese society. In fact, since Freud himself shared many of his patients' symptoms, he must also have been abused as a child, if the seduction theory were correct.

Faced with these implications, Freud abandoned the seduction theory. But he continued to believe that there was something to the stories his patients had told him. In 1905, in his *Three Essays on Sexuality*, Freud announced a new and even more revolutionary theory. His patients had not actually been abused, Freud now asserted. Rather, what they had repressed and were continuing to repress were their childhood fantasies. The patients had not had sex, but they had desired sex. More specifically, the patients, as children, had wanted (if they were girls) to sleep with their fathers and (if they were boys) their mothers.

Thus was born the "Oedipus complex." With it came the concepts of infantile sexuality and the unconscious mind, the two pillars of Freud's new science of psychoanalysis. And all this came about, according to Freud, because he had to drop his once-beloved seduction theory.

Freud's disciple and biographer Ernest Jones concurred that this was the crucial turning point in Freud's thinking, and other intellectual historians followed suit. By the 1950s and 1960s Freud was enshrined among the greatest thinkers of all time, and his abandonment of the seduction theory was the prime example of his intellectual courage and honesty.

In the 1970s, however, the consensus view of Freud fell apart. Feminists, offended by some of his misogynistic ideas (e.g., that the driving force in women's behavior was penis envy), led the charge. Other scholars followed with criticism ranging from Freud's use of cocaine to the ineffectiveness of psychoanalysis. Most traumatic of all, for Freud's followers, were a series of works that drastically revised Freud's account of his great breakthrough. The Oedipus complex, according to these revisionists, did not rise from the ruins of the seduction theory. That story was a lie. Even worse, his critics asserted, was Freud's reason for lying. He lied so that no one would ever learn his true—and truly scandalous—reason for abandoning the seduction theory.

⟡

To the dismay of orthodox Freudians, one of the most vociferous critics came from within their own ranks. This was Jeffrey Masson, a young American psychoanalyst who, until 1980, was the heir apparent to the director of the Freud Archives at the Library of Congress.

Masson began looking through Freud's letters to his friend Fliess. A selection, edited by Freud's daughter Anna, had been published in 1950, but Masson's inspection of the archives revealed that many of Freud's letters to Fliess had been omitted. On closer examination it was clear that the missing material had to do with Freud's thoughts on the seduction theory. These letters demonstrated, Masson recognized, that Freud hadn't abandoned the theory as quickly or as certainly as he later indicated; on the contrary, he continued for months and perhaps years to hold out some hope that he could prove it correct.

Masson asked Anna Freud why she'd deleted this material, and she said she didn't want to confuse readers by exposing her father's doubts. To Masson these doubts were of historic import. The letters showed not only that Freud continued to believe his patients had told him the truth about being abused, but also that the seduction theory was, indeed, correct. Freud's patients had been abused, Masson believed.

Why, then, had Freud walked away from his own findings? According to Masson, Freud's male colleagues were scandalized by the theory and its implied allegations of widespread abuse. So Freud, desperate for their approval, backed down. "With the greatest reluctance," Masson wrote in his 1984 book, "I gradually came to see Freud's abandonment of the seduction hypothesis as a failure of courage."

Masson found additional evidence for his position in Freud's letters to Fliess about a patient named Emma Eckstein. Eckstein suffered from painful or irregular menstruation. Freud referred her to Fliess, who decided she needed an operation on her nose. In retrospect it's clear that Fliess, who believed that the nose was the body's dominant organ and that it was the source of Eckstein's menstrual problems, was a quack. To make matters worse, Fliess bungled the operation by leaving gauze in the wound. Eckstein suffered a massive hemorrhage, and she continued to bleed long after Fliess was done with her.

Freud's report on Eckstein, in a letter he wrote to Fliess after the operation, described the continuing bleeding as psychosomatic. It was the result, he added, of Eckstein's sexual desire for Freud. This was a patently absurd diagnosis, almost a parody of the Freudian concepts of repressed sexuality and transference. To Masson such a ridiculous diagnosis also demonstrated how far Freud would go to curry favor with a colleague, and how quick he was to attribute a patient's symptoms to fantasies rather than to an actual traumatic event. The analogy to the seduction theory was clear: Freud was unable to confront Fliess with the uncomfortable truths that his nasal theory was wrong and that he'd botched the operation, just as he was unable to confront his Viennese colleagues with the equally uncomfortable truths that child abuse was rampant and the seduction theory was correct.

Masson's book generated a tremendous amount of controversy. The *New York Times* called it "a Watergate of the psyche," and it was embraced by many feminists and others who believed that the abuse of children, especially girls, had been underestimated and ignored for too long. Masson, who was fired from his job at the Freud Archives, became a hero to the antiabuse movement.

The scholarly response, however, was generally unfavorable—and not just from orthodox Freudians. Even many who were disillusioned with Freud or psychoanalysis were generally unconvinced by Masson's arguments. The Eckstein case, they argued, was an analogy, not proof. Just because Freud had been overly deferential, perhaps even cowardly in his relationship with Fliess, that didn't mean that Freud had acted that way in other situations.

In fact, many scholars pointed out, the abandonment of the seduction theory was an act of considerable courage, for the idea that replaced seduction—that children fantasized about having sex with their parents—was hardly one likely to ingratiate Freud with the medical establishment. The Oedipus complex was at least as radical an idea as widespread child abuse. Indeed it was more radical, since many physicians recognized that at least some child abuse took place, while no one had thought of Oedipus as anything other than an ancient Greek myth.

On only one point did Masson prevail. The newly released letters to Fliess persuaded most scholars that Freud continued to hope he could salvage the seduction theory well after he renounced it in his September 1897 letter to Fliess. After Masson, it became difficult to argue that the Oedipus complex was a direct consequence of the abandonment of the seduction theory; instead, it was clear that he only gradually dropped one and embraced the other. But as to his reason for dropping the seduction theory, the traditional account, in which Freud came to suspect that his patients had not actually been abused, withstood the challenge from Masson.

⌒

If loyal Freudians thought that they could relax, having fended off Masson, they were very much mistaken. A new and more sustained attack was still to come, this time from an assortment of scientists, philosophers, and literary critics. Of these, the literary critic Frederick Crews probably sparked the most debate, partly because his work first appeared in the *New York Review of Books*, long considered a Freudian bastion.

In essays published in 1993 and 1994, Crews agreed with Masson that Freud lied about why he abandoned the seduction theory. Yet unlike Masson, who believed Freud backed away from his patients' stories of abuse because of cowardice, Crews accused Freud of essentially making up those stories in the first place. So eager was Freud to prove his seduction theory, according to Crews, that he encouraged his patients to recall having been abused as children. And the patients, who were none too stable to start with and eager to please their doctor, obliged with descriptions of abuse that, in fact, had never taken place.

To prove his case, Crews delved into Freud's papers from the 1890s. He found repeated admissions that, prior to their analysis, Freud's patients had no idea that they'd supposedly been molested as children. "Only the strongest compulsion of the treatment," Freud wrote in 1896, "can induce them to embark on a reproduction of [the molestation scenes]." It was not that Freud intentionally invented the stories, Crews said, but that he grossly underestimated the extent to which his patients were susceptible to his suggestions.

Gradually, Freud realized that the stories of childhood abuse he was hearing weren't true. Perhaps he also realized that was why his therapy wasn't working, or perhaps some of the patients retracted the stories. But by then it was too late: Freud had already presented the seduction theory to his colleagues, and he was too embarrassed to admit that his findings were the result of a fatally flawed form of therapy. Freud was trapped. If he continued to maintain that the abuse stories were true, some of his disillusioned patients might start contradicting him in public. But if he admitted that he'd planted the abuse stories in his patients' minds, he'd be disgraced as a therapist.

And then the wily Freud found the way out of his predicament. He invented a theory that conceded the abuse never took place but that still attributed the stories to the patients, not the therapist. The stories, Freud explained, were the products of the patients' unconscious and repressed desires. And so was conceived, according to Crews, the Oedipus complex.

Crews's version of the origins of psychoanalysis was even more disturbing than Masson's. Masson's coward was replaced by an outright charlatan. Freud, in short, was a fraud. And, Crews stressed, patients and others continued to suffer as a result.

A particular concern of Crews was the rise, during the 1980s and 1990s, of what became known as "recovered memory" therapies. Many psychologists, seizing on the
Freudian concept of repressed sexual memories, encouraged adults to recall childhood
abuse, and this led to the prosecution of many alleged abusers. Critics of the therapies,
Crews among them, believed that much of this abuse had not occurred and that the recovered memories were, like the stories of Freud's patients, the products of a therapist's
suggestion.

To Freud's defenders, this attack seemed ironic as well as unfair. On the one hand,
they'd finally disposed of Masson, who accused Freud of deserting the victims of childhood abuse. Then along came Crews, who blamed Freud's ideas for encouraging patients
to "recall" abuse that didn't take place. How could Freud be responsible both for letting
abusers get away with it and for accusing innocent people of abuse? Some exasperated
Freudians suggested that the two attacks ought to cancel each other out.

Alas, for Freudians the critics were not so easily dismissed. The various attacks on
Freud damaged both the prestige and the business of psychoanalysis. True, the decline in
the number of pyschoanalytic patients had a lot to do with new drug therapies; Prozac
was quicker and cheaper than analysis. But the attacks on the intellectual underpinnings
of psychoanalysis also took their toll. If Freud couldn't be trusted to tell the truth about
the origins of psychoanalysis, how could patients be expected to trust their emotional
well-being to his successors?

Still, though his most ardent critics would deny this, Freud's status as one of the
most important thinkers of all time remains secure. The critics have succeeded in
proving that Freud's version of his major breakthrough was inaccurate; his abandonment of the seduction theory was neither as immediate nor as complete as he claimed.
But most intellectual historians have been reluctant to attribute to Freud motives as
base as those presumed by Masson or Crews. Equally possible, in the view of some
scholars, is that Freud oversimplified—and yes, misrepresented—the truth for the sake
of a dramatic narrative.

Moreover, regardless of the origins of Freud's ideas, regardless even of what good or
bad they've wrought, their continued influence on science, philosophy, art, and literature—and on the way we think about ourselves—is undeniable. Like it or not, after
Freud, no one had to read Sophocles to know something about Oedipus.

To Investigate Further

Freud, Sigmund. *The Standard Edition of the Complete Psychological Works of Sigmund Freud,*
trans. under the general editorship of James Strachey in collaboration with Anna Freud (London: Hogarth Press, 1953–1974).
　Of these twenty-four volumes, the most relevant are volume 7 (*Three Essays on the Theory
of Sexuality,* published in 1905 and including the first public retraction of the seduction the-

ory) and volume 20 (*An Autobiographical Study*, published in 1925 and with a subtly different recollection).

Masson, Jeffrey, ed. *The Complete Letters of Sigmund Freud to Wilhelm Fliess*, trans. from the German by Masson (Cambridge, MA: Belknap Press, 1985).

The unexpurgated version and, regardless of whether you find Masson's interpretation persuasive, a revealing look at Freud's thoughts in the making.

Jones, Ernest. *The Life and Work of Sigmund Freud, 3 Volumes*. (New York: Basic Books, 1953–1957).

Jones, himself an important figure in the history of psychoanalysis, wrote what remains the most comprehensive biography.

Masson, Jeffrey. *The Assault on Truth* (New York: Farrar, Straus & Giroux, 1984).

Some sense of the Freudians' reception to Masson can be gauged from Janet Malcolm's description of him as "a veritable Iago, papered over with charm yet filled with motiveless malignity."

Gay, Peter. *Freud* (New York: W. W. Norton, 1988).

An authoritative biography that, though it fails to directly address most of the recent Freud critics, reaffirms its subject's intellectual importance and integrity.

Robinson, Paul. *Freud and His Critics* (Berkeley: University of California Press, 1993).

A vigorous defense of Freud.

Crews, Frederick. *The Memory Wars* (New York: A New York Review Book, 1995).

Includes not just Crews's lively essays but also many of the equally interesting responses that also appeared in the *New York Review of Books*.

Crews, Frederick, ed. *Unauthorized Freud* (New York: Viking, 1998).

A collection of essays by many of the leading anti-Freudians, including the literary critics Mikkel Borch-Jacobsen and Stanley Fish, the philosophers Frank Cioffi and Adolf Grunbaum, the psychoanalyst Rosemarie Sand, the biologist Frank Sulloway, the psychologist Malcolm Macmillan, and the mathematician Allen Esterson. The range of contributors shows from how many different sides Freud has come under attack.

Could the Titanic
Have Been Saved?

T HE SMALL OCEAN LINER *CARPATHIA*, with Captain Arthur Rostron at the helm, steamed into New York Harbor on the night of April 18, 1912. It was greeted by the mayor's tugboat and a fleet of other boats, all sounding their bells and whistles and sirens. More than forty thousand people waited on the dock, including a swarm of reporters who immediately surrounded the passengers as they walked down the gangway.

These passengers were the survivors of the *Titanic*, the unsinkable ship that a few days before had, unthinkably, sunk.

The *Carpathia* had first heard the *Titanic*'s SOS just after midnight of April 14. Rostron instantly changed course to rescue the giant ship. Though he had to plot his way through the same ice field that had ripped apart the *Titanic*, Rostron pushed the *Carpathia* up to seventeen knots, faster than his ship had ever gone before.

Four hours later, the *Carpathia* reached the site of the *Titanic*'s last radioed position. They were about an hour and a half too late: the *Titanic*, with 1,502 passengers and crew members still on board, had sunk. Rostron spent the next four hours searching for survivors. By 8:00 A.M. he'd picked up the 705 people who'd made it into the *Titanic*'s lifeboats.

It was at that point that Captain Stanley Lord's ship, the *Californian*, arrived on the scene. Rostron, understandably eager to get the survivors to New York, left it to Lord to make a final search and headed off. Lord found no other survivors, and reset his original course. Nine hours after the *Carpathia* docked in New York, the *Californian* quietly slipped into Boston.

Lord wouldn't avoid the limelight for long. In a few days, the world's attention would shift from the *Carpathia* to the *Californian*. A number of Boston newspapers reported, after talking to members of the *Californian*'s crew, that the ship had been much closer to the sinking *Titanic* than the *Carpathia* had been; indeed, at about 11:00 P.M. on the night of April 14, Lord and his crew had actually seen a ship just a few miles to the southeast. Not long after, some of those aboard the *Titanic* had spotted a ship to the northwest.

Then, soon after midnight (and also soon after the *Titanic* had hit the fatal iceberg), officers of the *Californian* had seen what appeared to be a rocket go off over the other ship. Over the next couple of hours, as the *Titanic* fired its distress signals, the *Californian*'s officers and crew members watched seven more rockets burst in the sky.

The *Titanic* on its first (and last) voyage. *(Library of Congress)*

And yet Lord did nothing. The *Californian* would go down in history—in the words of historian Leslie Reade—as "the ship that stood still." Not until sometime after 5:00 A.M. did Lord set a course toward the *Titanic*'s final position.

Ever since, historians have wondered: Could the *Californian* have saved those aboard the *Titanic?* And if so, why did Lord do nothing?

Among those who greeted the *Carpathia* in New York was Senator William Alden Smith of Michigan, who wasted no time in forming a subcommittee to investigate the disaster. On April 19, the day after the *Carpathia* docked, Smith was already interviewing survivors at the Waldorf-Astoria. Once the reports surfaced in Boston that the *Californian* had seen the sinking ship's distress signals, Smith subpoenaed Lord and his crew.

The *Californian*, according to the testimony of its captain and crew, was en route from London to Boston when, on the night of April 14, it found itself in the same ice-laden section of the North Atlantic as the *Titanic*. Unlike the *Titanic*'s Captain Edward Smith, who doomed his ship by speeding ahead in spite of the ice, the *Californian*'s captain was a very cautious man. Lord ordered the ship stopped for the night.

At about 11:00 P.M., the *Californian*'s wireless operator, Cyril Evans, tapped out a rather informal message to the *Titanic,* which he knew was somewhere in the area: "Say, old man, we are surrounded by ice and stopped."

The *Titanic*'s operator, Jack Phillips, was annoyed by the interruption. He'd been busy all day sending messages for the ship's wealthy passengers, and had no time to chat. "Shut up! Shut up! You are jamming me!" he responded.

Evans, who'd been up all day and who was perhaps a bit put off by the unfriendly response, turned off his set and went to bed. Since the *Californian* had only one wireless operator, it was at this point essentially out of radio contact. When the *Titanic* started sending out its SOS, at about 12:15 A.M., there was no one who could have heard it awake on the *Californian.*

But what of the rockets? Why hadn't the *Californian* responded to the *Titanic*'s distress signals?'

Lord testified that he'd seen only one rocket go off, then went to bed himself. When his officers later informed him that they had seen other rockets, he was half asleep, so he didn't realize they could be distress signals. And since his officers didn't press the point, he slept on.

Besides, Lord told the senators, he still wasn't so sure they were distress signals. Ships routinely used various sorts of flares to greet passing ships. Distress signals were usually bigger and noisier, and no one on the *Californian* had heard anything during the night. Lord had no idea why some ship was sending up rockets that night, but he had no reason to believe, at least back then, that the ship was in trouble.

In fact, Lord continued, he was certain that the ship he and his officers saw was not the *Titanic.* They knew the *Titanic* was in the area, of course, since Evans had been in touch with it by radio. But the ship Lord spotted was far too small, and his officers had seen it steam off—in perfectly good shape—at about 2:00 A.M. That's why it hadn't even occurred to anyone on the *Californian* to wake up Evans and check for an SOS. It was only at about 4:00 A.M. that Lord's officers, perhaps feeling somewhat uneasy about the rockets, woke Evans, who then learned from other ships that the *Titanic* had hit an iceberg. Once Lord was informed, he immediately ordered the *Californian* into action.

Lord's explanation didn't satisfy Senator Smith. He asked the U.S. Navy to check if there was another ship in the vicinity of the *Californian* and the *Titanic* that night, and the navy said it didn't know of any. Smith checked the *Californian*'s log from that night and found there was no reference to any rockets—in spite of the testimony of Lord and his officers. Even more suspicious, the April 15 entry in the scrap log, sort of a rough draft of the official log, was missing. To Smith it looked like Lord, anticipating an inquiry into the *Californian*'s actions, had attempted to cover up its inexcusable inaction.

Smith concluded that the mystery ship described by Lord and his officers never existed. "That ice floe held but two ships—the *Titanic* and the *Californian,*" he announced.

The Senate subcommittee report harshly condemned Lord: "The committee is forced to the inevitable conclusion that the *Californian* was nearer the *Titanic* than the nineteen miles reported by her captain, and that her officers and crew saw the distress signals of the *Titanic* and failed to respond to them in accordance with the dictates of humanity, international usage, and the requirements of law."

A British Board of Trade hearing that followed later in the month was equally damning. "When she first saw the rockets, the *Californian* could have pushed through the ice to the open water without any serious risk and so have come to the assistance of the *Titanic,*" concluded Lord Charles Mersey. "Had she done so she might have saved many if not all of the lives that were lost."

⟨∞⟩

Lord did not take any of this sitting down, and he found plenty of supporters. Many other seamen, especially, were convinced that the shipping establishment had decided to make Lord a scapegoat, in the hope that it would distract attention from the gross negligence of the White Star Line, which owned the *Titanic,* and the British Board of Trade, which was responsible for safety on the seas.

There was no denying that both organizations had plenty to answer for.

For starters, there was the fact that Captain Smith had ordered the *Titanic* to maintain its speed of twenty-two knots, the fastest it had ever gone, in spite of having received eight messages from other ships (including the *Californian*) about the ice in the vicinity. It may have seemed somewhat ungracious to criticize Smith—who did, after all, heroically go down with his ship—but to many it seemed that Captain Lord was taking a lot of the blame for Captain Smith's mistake.

Worst, there was the lingering suspicion that Smith's reckless speed had been a result of pressure, if not a direct order, from Bruce Ismay, the White Star Line's managing director and a passenger on the *Titanic*'s first (and last) voyage. It was not only Lord's defenders who wondered whether Ismay, in his eagerness to prove that the *Titanic* was not only the largest and most luxurious liner but also the fastest, had urged Smith to speed ahead. There were even reports that Ismay had pocketed one of the warnings about ice, so that Smith wouldn't slow down.

That Ismay survived the wreck was itself an embarrassment, for this was an age that still took very seriously the idea of "women and children first." Since more than 150 women and children died on the *Titanic* (along with more than 1,300 men), many felt that Ismay, like Smith, should have gone down with the ship, or at least shouldn't have gotten on a lifeboat until he made sure there were no more women or children on the *Titanic.* But at least Ismay had a chance to deny the charges that he'd in any way influenced Smith's decisions, and neither the Senate nor the Board of Trade hearing found him guilty of anything other than being one of the lucky survivors.

If the company got off easy, in the view of Lord's supporters, the Board of Trade was even more fortunate. The Board of Trade determined how many lifeboats a ship needed by a formula based on a ship's weight; the *Titanic*'s owners had exceeded the board's re-quirements by putting on board 14 regular lifeboats and 4 collapsible ones. Those 18 boats could fit a total of 1,178 people. Yet the *Titanic* itself could hold more than 3,500, and there were more than 2,100 aboard on its maiden voyage.

Whatever else or whoever else was to blame, then, it was clear that the board's grossly outdated regulations also were responsible. Moreover, the agency's mandate was to fur-ther the interests of British shipping, and the White Star Line was among its most power-ful constituents. So it was no wonder that Lord's supporters were outraged that this was the agency empowered to pass judgment over the captain of the *Californian*.

But in fairness to both the Board of Trade and to Senator Smith's subcommittee, nei-ther the British nor the American hearings were the whitewash that Lord's supporters claimed they were. Both hearings examined the failings of Smith, the White Star Line, and the regulations, and though these were not highlighted quite so boldly as Captain Lord's, neither were they covered up. Indeed, both the U.S. and British governments quickly passed new legislation requiring ships to carry enough lifeboats to hold all their passengers and crew members. Similarly, the *Titanic* tragedy—in particular, the image of Cyril Evans asleep in his bunk while the *Titanic* sank nearby—also convinced both gov-ernments to require twenty-four-hour radio watches.

These changes were undoubtedly good for shipping safety, but they did nothing for Stanley Lord. Fired by the *Californian*'s owners, he continued to maintain that the ship seen from the *Californian* was not the *Titanic* and that the ship seen from the *Titanic* was not the *Californian*.

⚬⚬⚬

Lord died in 1962, the same year that his most loyal defender, Leslie Harrison, identi-fied what he believed was the mystery ship that had been seen from both the *Titanic* and the *Californian* that night.

Harrison was the general secretary of the Mercantile Marine Service Association, which represented ship captains and championed Lord's cause. The mystery ship, accord-ing to Harrison, was an Icelandic fishing vessel called the *Samson*. As proof, Harrison pre-sented what was allegedly an old journal in which one of the *Samson*'s crew members admitted that the *Samson* had been between the *Titanic* and the *Californian*. The *Samson*, which had been illegally hunting seals, feared that either the *Titanic* or the *Californian* might catch it with the goods, so it sped away from both as quickly as possible.

Harrison's case fell apart, however, when other investigators placed the *Samson* in Ice-land on both April 6 and April 20. For such a small boat to have made a three-thousand-mile journey almost across the Atlantic and back in just fourteen days was impossible.

Lord's defenders thought they'd finally gotten a break in 1985, when a joint American and French effort, led by oceanographer Robert Ballard, located the wreck of the *Titanic*. The ship, it turned out, was farther east than its final SOS coordinates. That put the *Ti-*

tanic about twenty-one miles away from the *Californian*'s logged position that night—apparently too far away for Lord or any of his officers to have seen it. But, Ballard pointed out, if the *Titanic* had drifted east of where its officers thought it was, the *Californian* probably did the same, putting the two back in each other's view.

The discovery of the *Titanic,* along with Harrison's determined lobbying, finally prompted the British Department of Transport to reopen the case. The department's report, released in 1992, offered Lord a partial vindication. It concluded that the *Californian* was probably seventeen to twenty miles from the *Titanic,* too far to have seen the sinking ship and probably too far to have reached it in time, even if Lord had started up immediately after the first rocket was spotted.

It took Lord more than two hours to reach the *Carpathia* on the morning of April 15, and there's every reason to assume it would have taken even longer to maneuver through the ice in the darkness. And two hours after the first rocket had gone off, the *Titanic* had already sunk. So, the report said, Lord could not have saved anyone aboard.

Still, the report also made clear that Lord's inaction was inexcusable. Even if he couldn't have saved the *Titanic,* he certainly ought to have tried. And even if he hadn't seen the *Titanic,* he had seen one rocket, and his officers had seen seven others. An experienced seaman could not have mistaken these for anything other than distress signals, yet neither Lord nor his officers bothered to wake up their wireless operator to check out what was wrong.

Most recent historians of the *Titanic* have agreed with the 1992 report. The rockets seen from the *Californian* most probably came from the *Titanic;* there's no evidence that any other ship was nearby. But even if they didn't come from the *Titanic,* they came from some ship that was in need of help—and Lord's response was to go to bed. There were many reasons why Lord may have stayed in bed. Perhaps he was a coward. Or perhaps he was such a martinet that his officers were afraid to bother him when they sighted additional rockets. Or perhaps he didn't feel he should have to put his ship at risk just because someone else was more foolhardy than he about speeding through the ice.

Whatever Lord's reason, it wasn't good enough.

To Investigate Further

Kuntz, Tom, ed. *The Titanic Disaster Hearings* (New York: Pocket Books, 1998).
    Transcripts of the 1912 Senate hearings.

Lord, Walter. *A Night to Remember* (New York: Holt, Rinehart & Winston, 1955).
    A real page-turner about the disaster by a popular historian who was no relation and in fact one of the harshest critics of Captain Lord.

Harrison, Leslie. *A Titanic Myth* (London: William Kimber, 1986).
    The case for Captain Lord.

Lord, Walter. *The Night Lives On* (New York: William Morrow, 1986).

Lord revisits the sinking, in the light of new evidence and theories that emerged after *A Night to Remember*.

Ballard, Robert. *The Discovery of the Titanic* (New York: Warner Books, 1987).

A firsthand account of the twelve-year search for the sunken liner, with stunning and eerie photos by the divers.

Davie, Michael. *Titanic: The Death and Life of a Legend* (New York: Alfred A. Knopf, 1987).

A journalist's thorough investigation into the many things that went wrong, from the shortage of lifeboats to the lack of binoculars for the lookouts.

Lynch, Don. *Titanic* (New York: Hyperion, 1992).

Illustrated with haunting paintings by Ken Marshall as well as hundreds of photographs that evoke the ship's Edwardian splendor.

Reade, Leslie. *The Ship That Stood Still* (New York: W. W. Norton, 1993).

The case against Captain Lord.

Gardiner, Robin, and Dan van der Vat. *The Riddle of the Titanic* (London: Weidenfeld & Nicolson, 1995).

The central mystery of the *Titanic* saga, according to Gardiner and van der Vat, is why Captain Smith, who knew there was ice ahead, continued at high speed. The book pursues a conspiracy theory that the White Star Line hoped to sink the ship (which was actually not the *Titanic* but her sister and near twin, the *Olympic*) as part of an insurance scam. After tantalizing readers with the evidence supporting the theory, Gardiner and van der Vat ultimately (and reasonably) reject it as highly improbable.

Butler, Daniel. *Unsinkable* (Mechanicsburg, PA: Stackpole Books, 1998).

A straightforward retelling of the *Titanic*'s story that strips away many myths, not just about the *Californian* but also about how and why the ship sank, and how various individuals and classes behaved that night.

What Sank the Lusitania?

ALTHER SCHWIEGER, COMMANDER of the German U-boat that torpedoed the *Lusitania,* recorded the event, almost matter-of-factly, in his ship's log.

"Torpedo hits starboard side close abaft the bridge, followed by a very unusually large explosion with a violent emission of smoke, far above the foremost funnel," he noted on May 7, 1915. "The superstructure above the point of impact and the bridge are torn apart, fire breaks out, a thick cloud of smoke envelopes the upper bridge. The ship stops at once and very quickly takes on a heavy list to starboard, at the same time starting to sink by the bows. She looks as if she will capsize. Great confusion reigns on board."

Less than twenty minutes later, the great liner went down off the Irish coast. Of the 1,962 people on board, 1,260 died, including 128 Americans. The reaction in America was anything but matter of fact. "Savagery carried to its ultimate perfection," proclaimed the Minneapolis *Journal.* "Humanity is aghast," echoed Denver's *Rocky Mountain News.*

Indeed, the sinking has gone down in history as the outrage that forced the United States to enter World War I. The *Lusitania,* it was said, failed to deliver 198 American passengers to Britain, but ended up delivering two million American soldiers to the Western Front.

Germans, not surprisingly, saw things differently. For one thing, the Americans had been warned. On May 1, the day the *Lusitania* set sail from New York, the German embassy placed an ad in several New York newspapers. It stated: "Travellers intending to embark on the Atlantic voyage are reminded that a state of war exists between Germany and her allies and Great Britain and her allies; that the zone of war includes the waters adjacent to the British Isles; that in accordance with formal notice given by the Imperial German Government, vessels flying the flag of Great Britain, or any of her allies, are liable to destruction in those waters and that travellers sailing in the war zone on ships of Great Britain or her allies do so at their own risk."

The ad didn't specifically mention the *Lusitania,* but the point was ominously clear. In case anyone might have missed it, the embassy placed the ad, in some papers, on the same page as the Cunard Line's own ads for the *Lusitania.*

Moreover, the Germans maintained, the *Lusitania* was no innocent passenger liner. The ship's manifest listed 4,200 cases of rifle cartridges and 1,248 cases of shrapnel shells, along with 50 barrels of aluminum powder and 400 cases of tools and components. That was clearly destined for the British war effort. And it didn't include the items on the manifest that may have been falsified to conceal other contraband. There were supposedly, for example, 205 barrels of fresh Connecticut oysters. The oysters' shelf life would virtually have expired before they reached their destination, and besides, England had plenty of oysters of its own. There were also suspiciously large quantities of cheese.

German newspapers and diplomats argued that the *Lusitania* was fully armed, and filled with explosives and Canadian troops bound for the front. A single torpedo could not have sunk the great liner, they stressed. That second and far greater explosion that Schwieger noted could only have been the result of the torpedo striking a load of munitions hidden on board.

This was not just German propaganda. In the years since the ship went down, many historians and scientists have made similar claims. Some have gone so far as to claim that the British Admiralty, headed up in 1915 by none other than Winston Churchill, intentionally allowed the sinking in an effort to draw America into the war. Searching for answers, some investigators have delved into British archives, while others have dived into waters of the North Atlantic.

∞

The first official inquiry took place on May 8, just a day after the sinking. After some of the bodies washed ashore near the small town of Kinsale, the local coroner, John Horgan, convened a hearing before a jury of merchants and fishermen. This made officials in London very nervous: *Lusitania* captain William Turner's testimony about what the Admiralty had (or hadn't) done to keep this ship safe was potentially embarrassing and certainly classified. The Admiralty quickly ordered the inquiry halted, but the message reached Kinsale too late. The Admiralty was, as Horgan put it, "as belated on this occasion as . . . in protecting the *Lusitania*."

The Admiralty need not have worried. For Horgan's jurors, the guilty parties were clearly in Berlin, not London. "This appalling crime," the jury concluded, "was contrary to international law and the conventions of all civilized nations, and we therefore charge the officers of the submarine and the German Emperor and the Government of Germany, under whose orders they acted, of willful and wholesale murder."

The next official inquiry was that of the Board of Trade, the government agency responsible for merchant shipping. The hearing was chaired by Lord Mersey, a senior judge who had taken the same seat three years earlier, after the *Titanic* sank. For the *Lusitania* hearings, which opened June 15, the Admiralty wasn't taking any chances about the direction in which fingers might be pointed. Captain Richard Webb submitted to Mersey a report that placed the blame for the disaster squarely on the shoulders of Captain Turner.

Turner, Webb charged, invited the Germans to sink his ship by completely ignoring the Admiralty's directives. As the *Lusitania* approached the Irish coast, the Admiralty warned Turner and other captains in the area that German submarines had in the past few days sunk a number of smaller boats near the coast. The Admiralty issued three directives: speed up, zigzag, and stay midchannel. Turner chose to slow down, sail a straight line, and head toward land.

"In taking the course he did, the Master of the *Lusitania* acted directly contrary to the written general instructions received from the Admiralty and completely disregarded the telegraphic warnings received from Queenstown during the hours immediately preceding the attack," Webb wrote. "The Master appears to have displayed an almost inconceivable negligence, and one is forced to conclude that he is either utterly incompetent or that he has been got at by the Germans."

Added First Sea Lord Jacky Fisher: "As the Cunard Company would not have employed an incompetent man, the certainty is absolute that Captain Turner is not a fool but a knave. I hope that Captain Turner will be arrested immediately after the enquiry."

Lest there be any doubt that Webb spoke for his superiors, Churchill scribbled his own note on Webb's report. "The Admiralty case against the Captain should be pressed by a skilful counsel," wrote the First Lord of the Admiralty. "We should pursue the captain without check."

The Admiralty's counsel was indeed skillful. He was Attorney General Henry Carson, who was best known for successfully defending the Marquis of Queensbury in a libel suit that led to the ruin of Oscar Wilde. But Turner, too, was ably represented; his lawyer was Butler Aspinall. Aspinall saw to it that Turner answered each of Webb's accusations.

Why did he slow down? Turner explained it was because of the fog and the tide. Had he pushed ahead at full speed, he would eventually have had to stop and wait for the tide to come in. That standing around he considered more dangerous than a steady eighteen knots.

He didn't zigzag, Turner said, because he thought the Admiralty's instructions were to do so after he saw a U-boat, not as a general precaution, and he never saw Schwieger's sub. Besides, zigzagging would have slowed him down even more, and speed, as the Admiralty itself said, was the *Lusitania*'s greatest defensive asset.

As for the instructions to stay midchannel, Turner argued that's what he was doing. Under normal circumstances, the *Lusitania* would have sailed within a mile or two off the Irish coast, but on her final voyage she was about twelve miles from shore. The Admiralty had never defined midchannel in a way that made Turner question his position.

Mersey's report, issued July 17, exonerated the captain. "It is certain that in some respects Captain Turner did not follow the advice given to him," Mersey wrote. "It may be (though I seriously doubt it) that had he done so his ship would have reached Liverpool in safety. But . . . the conclusion at which I have arrived is that blame ought not to be imputed to the captain.

"The advice given to him," Mersey continued, "although meant for his most serious and careful consideration, was not intended to deprive him of the right to exercise his skilled judgment in the difficult questions that might arise from time to time in the navigation of his ship. His omission to follow the advice in all respects cannot fairly be attributed either to negligence or incompetence."

Except for his refusal to scapegoat Turner, Mersey's report came as a relief to Admiralty officials. Mersey said they, too, had done everything in their power, and they deserved "the highest praise." Mersey also dismissed reports of ammunition exploding on board, in spite of one passenger's testimony that the second explosion sounded "similar to the rattling of a machine gun."

"I did not believe this gentleman," Mersey wrote.

In other words, the *Lusitania,* the Cunard Line, and the British Admiralty were all entirely innocent victims. Mersey's conclusion echoed Horgan's: "The whole blame for the cruel destruction of life in this catastrophe," he wrote, "must rest solely with those who plotted and with those who committed the crime."

The third and final official report came three years later, this time from New York. Survivors and family members of the Americans who died had sued Cunard for negligence. The decisive moment came before the case even went to trial, when the plaintiffs withdrew their allegation that the ship had carried either Canadian troops or any ammunition that might have exploded on board. Unlike the British government, which may have had an incentive to conceal troops or ammo, the plaintiffs had every reason to push for a full investigation, since the findings might add to the company's culpability. Their decision not to pursue those accusations seemed to confirm that there was, in fact, no reliable evidence of troops or ammo.

"That story is forever disposed of as far as we are concerned," said Judge Julius Mayer.

Mayer also absolved Cunard and Turner of any blame, repeating many of Mersey's arguments. By the time Mayer ruled, the United States was at war with Germany, so it was no surprise that the judge found that "the cause of the sinking of the *Lusitania* was the illegal act of the Imperial German Government."

Mayer suggested the survivors and relatives look to Germany for reparations, and in 1925, the defeated nation paid them just over $2.5 million.

◦◦◦◦

Critics of the Admiralty called the official hearings a whitewash. The war muted much of the criticism, but the grumbling started as soon as the Mersey hearings ended and continued long after the war was over. Among the most vociferous critics of the official story was Colin Simpson, a *Sunday Times* reporter who reviewed the court of inquiry records (some of which weren't declassified until the 1960s) and in a 1973 book put together the case against the Admiralty.

It was not Turner, according to Simpson, who was either a knave or a fool; it was Webb, along with the Admiralty whose orders he followed. "The probability is he was both," Simpson contended. "Webb's tactical alternatives are those of a man who would appear likely to have done himself serious injury if allowed to play tactics in his bath, let alone the Western approaches."

Why, critics like Simpson asked, had Mersey and Mayer focused on what Turner did with his orders rather than the orders themselves? If submarines were active off the Irish coast, why not send a destroyer to escort the ship to safety? (Two months earlier, two destroyers accompanied the *Lusitania.*) If a destroyer wasn't available, why not reroute the

Lusitania around the north of Ireland, away from the U-boat-infested waters? Schwieger himself wondered about the latter in his war diary. "It remains inexplicable why *Lusitania* wasn't sent through North Channel," he wrote.

To Simpson and others, the Admiralty's actions—or rather, the Admiralty's failure to act—smacked of a conspiracy. Many pointed to Churchill's February 12 letter to Walter Runciman, president of the Board of Trade. This was just after the Germans announced their intention of blockading Britain with submarines, and three months before the sinking of the *Lusitania*. Wrote Churchill: "It is most important to attract neutral shipping to our shores, in the hope especially of embroiling the U.S.A. with Germany."

To conspiracy theorists, this was proof that Churchill had deliberately exposed the *Lusitania* to danger in order to bring the Americans into the war. Kaiser Wilhelm subscribed to this theory. "England was really responsible," he told the U.S. ambassador to Germany, "as the English had made the *Lusitania* go slowly in English waters so that the Germans could torpedo it and so bring on trouble."

Was Churchill capable of such deviousness? Similar suspicions surfaced after World War II, when he was accused of withholding information from President Roosevelt about an attack on Pearl Harbor in order to bring America into that war. But, for most historians, both accusations were unproven and unfair.

The Admiralty could have ordered a destroyer escort, true, but at the time naval experts still had faith in a large liner's ability to outrun a U-boat. As for the North Channel, that appeared safer but there was no guarantee U-boats weren't there as well.

"The overriding evidence," wrote historian Diana Preston, "is that, whatever the merits of sending an escort . . . and diverting [the ship] out of harm's way, none of these actions was ever systematically considered. The reason why the tragedy was allowed to happen was that the Admiralty at senior levels was preoccupied with bigger issues."

Churchill, in particular, was busy negotiating with Italy and worrying about Britain's failing campaign in the Dardanelles. His subordinates were reluctant to take any dramatic action in his absence. Besides, most doubted the Germans would sink a large merchant ship, especially one carrying a lot of Americans.

As for Churchill's letter to Runciman, less conspiracy-minded historians could interpret it more innocently. "He merely sought to 'embroil' America in a diplomatic or commercial impasse with Germany," wrote David Ramsay. "Such a dispute would have intensified pro-Allied sentiment in America and thus have safeguarded the important munitions purchasing program."

"Far from being the subject of conspiracy," Preston concluded, "the *Lusitania*, in her last days and hours, was the victim of complacency and neglect."

In the days and hours after the sinking, however, there's no doubt that top officials in the Admiralty conspired to make the most of their propaganda bonanza. Not only did they try to scapegoat Turner, but they also worked to suppress any suspicions that the ship's cargo caused the second explosion. It was far better, for British propaganda purposes, that the Germans alone be responsible for the tragedy. Officials carefully selected which crew members would testify before Mersey, and they prepared statements for them emphasizing that the second explosion had been caused by a second torpedo. Many passengers who believed only one torpedo hit the *Lusitania* weren't allowed to testify, and some who did testify about a single torpedo were quickly discredited by the Admiralty's leaks to the press.

The Admiralty may also have pressured Turner to change his story. The captain told the coroner's court he thought there was a single torpedo, but by the time he testified before Mersey he thought there were two. Schwieger, for his part, was consistent. His war diary indicated two explosions, one torpedo. But his diary was, of course, just as susceptible to the manipulations of German propagandists as the testimony of the *Lusitania* crew was to Admiralty pressure.

The only way to figure out what caused the second explosion was to inspect the ship itself.

ꝏ

Divers had no problem locating the wreck of the *Lusitania*, three hundred feet down and twelve miles off the Irish coast. The problem was that, until the 1980s, diving technology didn't allow anyone to stay that far under water for long. Divers who did so suffered from nitrogen narcosis, also known as the "Martini effect" for what it did to their brains. This may have accounted for reported sightings, by U.S. Navy diver John Light and his team in the early 1960s, of a gun barrel and a large hole in the cargo area, supposedly caused by the explosion of contraband ammunition. The team's pictures showed nothing of the gun or the hole.

In 1993 Robert Ballard, who had found and explored the wreck of the *Titanic,* moved on to the *Lusitania.* Ballard had the advantage of much more sophisticated diving and lighting equipment than Light. He found no guns and no hole anywhere near the cargo area.

"We were able to inspect the entire exposed area . . . and it was clearly undamaged," he wrote. "If it held munitions, they were not the cause of the secondary explosions that sank the ship."

What did?

One clue was the coal scattered around the wreck on the bottom of the sea. Ballard's guess was that coal dust, a by-product of the ship's boiler room, caused the explosion. The torpedo, he wrote, could have "kicked up large amounts of coal dust that blanketed the bottom of the bunkers, and that the torpedo ignited, tearing open the side of the ship for the length of one of the starboard bunkers."

Others, like Preston, maintained the torpedo ruptured a steam line. But after Ballard's findings, most historians agreed that the ship's cargo was not to blame. In this sense, Ballard's findings vindicated the British propaganda. The Germans had been telling the truth about there being only one torpedo, but the British were right that a torpedo, and not some explosive cargo, sank the *Lusitania.*

It did not take Ballard's findings, of course, to recognize that the sinking was a major propaganda victory for the British. "In spite of all its horror, we must regard the sinking of the *Lusitania* as an event most important and favorable to the Allies," Churchill later wrote. "The poor babies who perished in the ocean struck a blow at German power more deadly than could have been achieved by the sacrifice of a hundred thousand fighting men."

The United States did not enter the war until almost two years (and many sinkings) later, but Churchill was surely right that the *Lusitania* alerted Americans to the barbarism of German warfare. Back in 1915, Americans could blithely board the *Lusitania*, dismissing the German ad as an idle threat and confident that no nation would attack civilians, let alone those from a neutral country. The year the *Lusitania* sank also brought the introduction of poison gas to the front, the first air raid on civilians, and the recognition that there was no longer any such thing as civilized warfare.

To Investigate Further

Simpson, Colin. *The* Lusitania. Boston: Little, Brown, 1973.
    The case against Churchill and the Admiralty; provocative and lucid, though ultimately unconvincing.

Bailey, Thomas, and Paul Ryan. *The* Lusitania *Disaster*. New York: The Free Press, 1975.
    A scholar and a seaman answer Simpson.

Ballard, Robert D., with Spencer Dunmore. *Exploring the* Lusitania. New York: Warner Books, 1995.
    The juxtaposition of photographs from the ship's glory days and the new underwater images is haunting.

Preston, Diana. Lusitania. New York: Walker, 2002.
    A vivid account of both the human stories and the political consequences.

Ramsay, David. Lusitania. New York: W. W. Norton, 2002.
    Ramsay is extremely thorough in dispelling the myths surrounding the ship.

Did Shoeless Joe Throw the World Series?

THE CAREER OF "SHOELESS JOE" JACKSON—whose talent, according to his fellow players, rivaled that of Babe Ruth—came to an abrupt end when he was banned from the game after the 1919 Black Sox scandal. That was the year gamblers bribed the heavily favored Chicago White Sox to throw the World Series.

A year later, Jackson testified before a Cook County grand jury, and the *New York Evening World* published its famous account of the player encountering a group of boys outside the courthouse.

"A man, guarded like a felon by other men, emerged from the door," reported Hugh Fullerton. "He did not swagger. He slunk along between his guardians, and the kids, with wide eyes and tightened throats, watched, and one, bolder than the others, pressed forward and said 'It ain't so, Joe, is it.'"

Jackson, according to Fullerton, gulped back a sob before answering, "Yes, kid, I'm afraid it is."

Jackson always denied this story. More to the point, he denied he ever played anything but his best, pointing to his .375 Series batting average, his five runs scored, and his six runs batted in. Since then, Jackson has become a mythic figure, sometimes a symbol of guilt and sometimes of innocence. He is the basis for the Faustian Joe Hardy in the musical *Damn Yankees* and the more sinned-against-than-sinning Roy Hobbs in the novel and movie, *The Natural*. As an illiterate cotton-mill worker whose natural ability took him from a small South Carolina town to Chicago, Jackson is a symbol of innocence; corrupted by the big city, he is a symbol of our fall from grace. In the movie *Field of Dreams*, he emerges from an Iowa cornfield, the perfect symbol of a lost America. Even his nickname seemed to fit perfectly his image as bumpkin and phenom, a man without the sense or money to wear shoes but with so much talent that he didn't need them.

Amid Jackson's apotheosis, baseball historians have continued to debate the question whether it actually is or ain't so.

⌒⫴⫴⌒

Rumors that the Series was fixed surfaced even before it began. In fact, by the first game, so much money had been bet on the underdog Cincinnati Reds that White Sox fans could get even odds on their team. After the Reds won the Series, White Sox owner Charles Comiskey offered a $20,000 reward for evidence of a fix.

Almost a year later, the reward tempted Billy Maharg, one of the gamblers involved in bribing players, to tell his story, and a Cook County grand jury convened to investigate. The first player to crack was Eddie Cicotte, a pitcher who told the grand jury he'd taken $10,000 to lose two Series games.

On September 28, 1920, Jackson appeared before the grand jury, and his own testimony is among the most damning evidence against him. Jackson told the grand jury that White Sox first baseman Chick Gandil was the first to approach him about the fix. Assistant state attorney Hartley Repogle questioned Jackson:

Q. How much did he promise you?
A. $20,000 if I would take part.
Q. And you said you would?
A. Yes, sir.
Q. When did he promise you the $20,000?
A. It was to be paid after each game.
Q. How much?
A. Split up in some way. I don't know just how much it amounts to, but . . . it would amount to $20,000. Finally [White Sox pitcher Lefty] Williams brought me this $5,000, and threw it down.

Later the same day, Jackson seemingly contradicted himself. He told the grand jury that he'd always played his best.

Q. Did you make any intentional errors yourself . . . ?
A. No, sir, not during the whole Series.
Q. Did you bat to win?
A. Yes.
Q. And run the bases to win?
A. Yes, sir.
Q. And fielded the balls at the outfield to win?
A. I did.

Still, Jackson's earlier admission, along with similar statements from Cicotte and Williams, seemed enough at least to bring the Black Sox to trial. State's attorney Robert Crowe, who took over the case from Repogle, certainly expected to go to court. But when Crowe examined the grand jury's files, he discovered the critical portions of the players' testimony were missing from the record. This was not just mysterious but also damn suspicious. Gone, too, were the waivers of immunity the players had signed before testifying. And Cicotte, Williams, and Jackson now denied they'd ever confessed to anything.

Crowe proceeded nonetheless, and the fraud and conspiracy trial of eight White Sox, including Jackson, opened in June 1921. Instead of the players, Crowe called to the stand

Maharg and another gambler, Bill Burns, who in return for immunity described their roles in the fix. But the prosecution's case was undercut by the judge's instructions to the jury. There was no law on the books that specifically outlawed throwing baseball games. So Judge Hugo Friend explained that, to find the defendants guilty, the jurors had to be convinced the players had intentionally harmed Comiskey's business and defrauded the public. This was a difficult standard of proof for prosecutors to meet, especially since during the 1920 season, Jackson and his teammates had finished a close second, baseball fans continued to stream into Comiskey Park, and Comiskey was making more money than ever. Besides, even if the Black Sox had thrown the Series, prosecutors hadn't presented evidence that the players were motivated by anything other than greed. It took the jury only three hours to find all eight not guilty.

The celebration, however, was short lived. Baseball's new commissioner, Kenesaw Mountain Landis, didn't think much of the jury's verdict or of leniency in general. (As a judge, Landis once sentenced a seventy-five-year-old to fifteen years in jail. When the man said he couldn't serve that long, Landis told him to "do the best you can.")

The same evening the jurors pronounced their verdict, Landis gave his. "Regardless of the outcome of juries," he said, "no player that throws a ball game, no player that entertains proposals or promises to throw a game, no player that sits in a conference with a bunch of crooked players where the ways and means of throwing games are discussed, and does not promptly tell his club about it, will ever again play professional baseball."

Neither Jackson nor any of the seven other Black Sox would ever again play major league baseball.

⸻

Jackson sued Comiskey for the salary he lost after the owner dropped him and the other Black Sox from the roster. The case went to court in January 1924. This time it wasn't enough for Jackson to show he hadn't damaged Comiskey's business; he had to convince a jury he wasn't in on the fix.

The story Jackson now told differed from the one presented to either the 1920 grand jury or the 1921 jury. Jackson claimed he knew nothing about the fix during the Series; the other players, without his permission, used his name to impress the gamblers. Indeed, Jackson went on, he did not know there was a fix until Lefty Williams gave him the $5,000 after the last game of the Series. Gamblers Maharg and Burns appeared in court again, this time to confirm that Jackson wasn't present at any of their meetings with the players. Williams also testified that he hadn't spoken to Jackson about the fix until he handed over the money.

Moreover, Jackson explained, once he learned of the fix he tried to tell Comiskey about it. With the $5,000 in his pocket, Jackson went to Comiskey's office, but the owner wouldn't see him. Jackson backed up this testimony by producing a letter he'd dictated to Comiskey suggesting that the Series was crooked. Comiskey never responded. The villain of this story was clearly Comiskey, who tried to cover up the fix to protect the value of his team. Only after Maharg blew the lid off the scandal did the owner change course and turn on the players.

Comiskey's lawyer, George Hudnall, struck back with the most startling revelation of the trial. He pulled out of his briefcase the grand jury testimony in which Jackson admitted discussing with Gandil the fix and his $20,000 share. Here was the document that had disappeared after the grand jury hearing. Jackson responded by explaining that, yes, he had sort of confessed, but only because Comiskey's lawyer had advised him no jury would believe the truth. Jackson had taken the lawyer's word that he wouldn't be prosecuted if he confessed.

If the grand jury testimony embarrassed Jackson, it was also awkward for Comiskey. How, after all, did his lawyer come to be in possession of the missing document? Questioned by Jackson's lawyers, Comiskey said he didn't know. But reporters then and historians later couldn't help but note how conveniently the grand jury testimony disappeared when Comiskey was still hoping to hold onto his star players, and how conveniently it reappeared when he was trying to avoid paying back wages to one of those players. Most historians assumed that Comiskey, probably with the help of some of the gamblers, either paid off some clerk or simply stole the documents.

The 1924 jury, like the 1921 one, found for Jackson. They awarded him $16,711.04. Again, however, there was little time to celebrate. Once the jury was out of earshot, Judge John Gregory declared that Jackson was a liar. His 1921 and 1924 stories couldn't both be true, so he must have lied one of those times. Either way, Gregory wasn't going to let a perjurer walk away with a victory in his court. He immediately set aside the verdict.

After the trial, Comiskey offered an out-of-court settlement, thus precluding any more awkward questions about how he happened to have the grand jury testimony. Jackson took an undisclosed (and presumably small) amount of money and went home to South Carolina.

⟨⟩

Comiskey's reputation, deservedly, never recovered. Many baseball historians focused on how he not only covered up the fix, but to some extent also caused it. In an era before big money baseball salaries, Comiskey paid players significantly less than other owners paid theirs. Jackson, clearly one of the best players of all time, never made more than $6,000 a year. Cicotte, according to Eliot Asinof's *Eight Men Out*, was driven to throw the Series at least partly because of Comiskey's penuriousness. In 1917, Comiskey promised the pitcher a $10,000 bonus if he won thirty games; when Cicotte reached twenty-nine, the owner ordered him benched. (Other historians dispute Asinof's story on the grounds that Comiskey would never have promised to pay anyone $10,000.) Even before 1919, some people called his team the Black Sox, because Comiskey, unlike other owners, wouldn't pay to clean their uniforms.

Historians also have done much to put the scandal in its historical context. When Landis banned the eight players, his clear implication was that he had solved the problem, that baseball's record until 1919 was pure and that it now would be again. But these were hardly the first players to get mixed up with gamblers. In addition to the eight Black Sox, fourteen others were banned from the game for similar reasons between 1917 and 1927. The record for the most thrown games probably goes to Hal Chase, a first baseman in New York, Chicago, and Cincinnati. Three of Chase's managers accused him of dishonesty before he was finally banned for bribing an umpire. With a tip of the hat to Asinof's classic, statistician-historian Bill James referred to the players who were banned as the "22 men out." That figure doesn't count the many others who were allegedly involved in gambling, but against whom there wasn't enough evidence to take any action.

But back to Jackson. That some blame has fallen on Comiskey and others does not ultimately answer the question of how much belongs to Jackson. To some of his recent defenders, most notably historian Donald Gropman, Jackson is blameless. The story Jackson told at the 1924 civil trial was the truth; the 1921 grand jury testimony was solely the result of an illiterate mill hand being duped by Comiskey's sophisticated lawyer. Two juries found Jackson not guilty, and so did Gropman. And, as Gropman and others have stressed, there's that .375 batting average. Jackson's twelve Series hits weren't matched until 1960.

A majority of recent historians, however, have found Jackson guilty, though to varying extents. He did take the $5,000 from Williams, even if we accept Jackson's word that he didn't know in advance it was coming and that he tried to tell Comiskey about it. Jackson was illiterate but not stupid. When he returned to South Carolina, he opened a successful dry-cleaning business, employed more than twenty people, and bought a home and two cars. He knew what the money was for, and he kept it.

Whether he actually earned the money by playing less than his best remains a mystery. It's possible, as some historians have suggested, that he intended to throw the games but had so much natural talent and so much love for the game that, once he took the field, he couldn't stop himself from hitting. It's also possible, as others have noted, that he was capable of playing even better than he did. His hits were plentiful, but most of them didn't come with the game on the line. He was not charged with any errors, but three triples fell near him.

In the press box, with rumors rampant during the Series, Hugh Fullerton circled on his scorecard those plays he considered suspicious. Some involved Jackson. But, like so much else about Shoeless Joe, what Fullerton wrote has added as much to the myth as to the reality. Even Fullerton's famous story about the boy who said "it ain't so" has often been questioned, including by Jackson.

"No such word . . . was ever said," Jackson later claimed. "The fellow who wrote that just wanted something to say. When I came out of the courthouse that day, nobody said anything to me. The only one who spoke was a guy who yelled at his friend 'I told you the big son of a bitch wore shoes.'"

To Investigate Further

Asinof, Eliot. *Eight Men Out.* New York: Henry Holt and Company, 1963.
This was a classic of baseball history long before John Sayles made it into a fine movie.

Frommer, Harvey. *Shoeless Joe and Ragtime Baseball.* Dallas, TX: Taylor Publishing Company, 1992.
A less thorough defense than Gropman's, though the appendix—which contains the entire text of Jackson's 1921 grand jury testimony—is useful.

Gropman, Donald. *Say It Ain't So, Joe!* New York: Citadel Press, 1995.
Originally published in 1979, this remains the best defense of Jackson.

Fleitz, David. *Shoeless.* Jefferson, NC: McFarland, 2001.
A comprehensive biography that concludes Jackson was guilty.

James, Bill. *The New Bill James Historical Abstract.* New York: The Free Press, 2001.
James is usually thought of as a statistician, but his history goes way beyond the numbers.

Were Sacco and
Vanzetti Guilty?

NO MURDER CASE—with the possible exception of O. J. Simpson's—has so sharply divided the country as that of Sacco and Vanzetti. To their supporters, Sacco and Vanzetti were, in the words of the latter, "a good shoemaker and a poor fish peddler." They were prosecuted and ultimately executed because they were radicals and immigrants in a society that would tolerate neither. That view was shared by Governor Michael Dukakis of Massachusetts, the state in which Sacco and Vanzetti lived and died. In 1977, 50 years after Sacco and Vanzetti had been executed, Dukakis declared that "any stigma and disgrace should be forever removed from the names of Nicola Sacco and Bartolomeo Vanzetti."

Revisionists have argued that Sacco and Vanzetti were indeed guilty and by the late 1960s the consensus among historians seemed to be that Sacco, at least, was probably guilty, though Vanzetti was probably not. That consensus proved short lived, however. In the late 1980s both sides uncovered new evidence, and both sides claimed their new evidence proved they'd been right all along.

⁊⟋⟋⟋⟍

The murders for which Sacco and Vanzetti were executed took place on April 15, 1920, in the town of South Braintree, 12 miles south of Boston. In the course of stealing the Slater and Morrill shoe factory's $15,776 payroll, robbers shot and killed the paymaster, Frederick Parmenter, and his guard, Alessandro Berardelli. The crime followed a similar but unsuccessful holdup that took place in nearby Bridgewater a few months earlier; in the Bridgewater attempt, it was the L. Q. White shoe factory's payroll that the criminals were after. Both crimes took place in daylight, in front of dozens of witnesses who told police the criminals looked Italian.

Italians were on the mind of Chief Michael Stewart of the Bridgewater police for other reasons as well. The country was in the midst of what came to be known as the Red Scare. In response to the Bolshevik success in Russia as well as a series of strikes, riots, and bombings that took place in America during 1919, local police forces across the country were cracking down on radical immigrant groups. On January 2, 1920, more than four thousand foreigners were arrested, of whom more than five hundred were ultimately deported.

Among those just deported was a local anarchist named Furrucio Coaccio. Stewart recalled that Coaccio's deportation had been very easy; too easy, it now seemed. Was it

322

possible, Stewart wondered, that Coaccio had seen his deportation as an opportunity to get out of the country quickly—with the loot from the South Braintree robbery? Stewart's suspicions were further aroused when he discovered that Mike Boda, who was now living in Coaccio's house, was an employee of the L. Q. White Shoe Company. He went to see Boda but Boda was gone.

Boda, however, had left his car behind at the local garage. Stewart asked the garage owner to let him know right away if Boda came to pick it up. Boda came by on May 5, but, before the police could get there, he took off. Left behind for the police were the two men who had accompanied him to pick up the car: Sacco and Vanzetti.

Soon the police had more reasons to suspect Sacco and Vanzetti. Both were armed, Sacco with a .32 caliber Colt automatic pistol and Vanzetti with a .38 caliber Harrington and Richardson revolver. What's more, both lied to the police; they denied knowing Boda and they denied being involved with any radical groups. Each of these claims was easily shown to be false, since the garage owner had told police they arrived with Boda and since Sacco had on him an announcement of an anarchist meeting at which Vanzetti was to speak.

The trial of Sacco and Vanzetti began on May 31, 1921. The prosecution made much of the lies the defendants had told the police, arguing that it revealed their "consciousness of guilt." More damning, perhaps, was the testimony of seven witnesses who identified Sacco as having been in South Braintree before, during, or after the shooting. No one placed Vanzetti at the shooting, but two witnesses said they saw him in the getaway car and two others said they saw him in or around South Braintree earlier in the morning of the crime.

Most damning of all was the physical evidence against the two. Not only was Vanzetti armed when he was arrested but the Harrington and Richardson revolver was the same kind of gun that the slain guard, Alessandro Berardelli, had owned; the prosecution argued that Vanzetti had taken it from him during the robbery. For Sacco, the situation was worse still: two expert prosecution witnesses, William Proctor and Charles Van Amburgh, testified that one of the bullets taken from Berardelli's body, known as Bullet III, had been fired through the Colt .32 automatic found on Sacco on the night of his arrest.

To all of the prosecution's evidence, the defense had an answer.

To the "consciousness of guilt" argument, Sacco and Vanzetti answered that, yes, they had lied to the police—but the guilt they had been conscious of was that they were radicals and foreigners. In fact, on the night they were arrested, they now admitted, they had planned to pick up Boda's car and use it to move some incriminating radical literature to a safer hiding place. No wonder they had lied to the police; in the midst of a massive roundup of radical foreigners, they assumed that's what they were being arrested for. They were concealing their involvement in a radical anarchist group, not their involvement in a murder.

As for the eyewitnesses, the defense had plenty of its own. A total of eleven eyewitnesses had placed either Sacco or Vanzetti at or near the crime scene, but plenty of other eyewitnesses had seen one or more of the robbers and failed to identify either of the defendants. The defense also attempted to impeach the testimony of the prosecution's witnesses, pointing out, for example, that one of those who identified Vanzetti stated he had spoken in clear English while in fact Vanzetti had a heavy Italian accent. Finally, the defense put on the stand witnesses who claimed to have been with Sacco and Vanzetti at the time of the crime—and nowhere near the crime scene (though the prosecution attempted to discredit the alibis by pointing out that these witnesses were friends of the defendants and fellow anarchists).

On the whole, the eyewitness testimony probably cancelled itself out. For every prosecution witness, there was a defense witness to contradict his or her story; for every defense witness, a prosecution witness told otherwise. That made the physical evidence all the more crucial, and though the defense also had its own experts, the testimony of Proctor and Van Amburgh was persuasive. On July 14, seven weeks after the trial began, the jury found Sacco and Vanzetti guilty of murder in the first degree.

⟊

But the defense had just begun to fight. Defense attorneys submitted a series of motions for a new trial. One included an affidavit from Proctor, whose testimony had been instrumental in securing a conviction. In the affidavit, Proctor stated: "Bullet number III, in my judgment, passed through some Colt automatic pistol, but I do not intend by that answer to imply that I had found any evidence that the so-called mortal bullet had passed through this particular Colt automatic."

This was a far cry from his trial testimony, where he had clearly implied that it was Sacco's specific gun that had fired the fatal bullet. Furthermore, Proctor admitted to arranging the careful phrasing of the trial testimony with the DA in order to leave the jury with the wrong impression. This was virtually an admission that he'd conspired with the DA to commit perjury; it cast doubts not only on Proctor's credibility but on the integrity of the DA. Nevertheless, on October 1, 1924, Judge Webster Thayer denied the defense's motion for a new trial.

The next bombshell came in November 1925. Celestino Madeiros, who was being held in the same prison with Sacco while appealing a conviction for murder during a bank robbery, came forward and confessed to participating in the shoe company robberies. Madeiros would not name his confederates, but he did say that neither Sacco nor Vanzetti had anything to do with the crimes. Defense attorney Herbert Ehrmann undertook his own investigation and determined that Madeiros had been working with a Providence gang under the leadership of Joe Morelli. The gang had been charged with other robberies of the same Slater and Morrill shoe company that Sacco and Vanzetti had supposedly robbed. More remarkable still was the striking resemblance between Sacco and Joe Morelli: when Ehrmann showed prosecution and defense witnesses a picture of Morelli, a number of them identified him as Sacco.

Again, however, Thayer was unmoved. In October 1926, after observing that Madeiros, when questioned, seemed unfamiliar with the scene of the crime, Thayer dismissed the defense motion for a new trial. In April 1927, he sentenced Sacco and Vanzetti to die, and on August 23, 1927, the sentence was carried out.

⟨᠆᠆᠆⟩

Still, the case would not die. Writers on each side continued to research and publish, with defenders of Sacco and Vanzetti especially prolific. These tended to emphasize the prejudices of the judge or jury, and of the country as a whole during the Red Scare.

Then in 1962, Francis Russell published one of the most influential of the revisionist studies. Originally convinced that Sacco and Vanzetti were innocent, Russell came to believe that Sacco, at least, was guilty. Russell's change of heart began after he learned that Fred Moore, the primary defense lawyer during the first four years of the case, thought that Sacco was guilty. He was further persuaded when he learned that Carlo Tresca, a leading Italian American anarchist, also thought Sacco was guilty.

Russell still had to resolve the question of Bullet III. In 1961 he set up new tests during which ballistics experts found that Bullet III had indeed come from Sacco's gun. For Russell, this clinched the case.

But the defense had some new evidence of its own. After the Massachusetts State Police released an enormous file on the case in response to a Freedom of Information Act suit, William Young and David Kaiser discovered that Vanzetti's gun was not that of the guard, Berardelli, as the prosecution had claimed. More shocking still, the prosecution knew this and concealed its findings from the defense. As for Bullet III, Sacco's defenders conceded the bullet came from his gun, but noted that, according to the autopsy report and eyewitness reports in the newly released police files, the same assailant had fired all four bullets into Berardelli. How, then, could only one of the four bullets have come from Sacco's gun? To Young and Kaiser, there could only be one explanation: a bullet was shot from Sacco's gun after the murder, and then was substituted for one of the real bullets.

In short, according to this latest evidence, Sacco and Vanzetti were framed. Whether because they were convinced of their guilt, or just because they wanted to get rid of a couple of troublesome Italian radicals, the district attorney and his assistant used evidence they knew to be false in order to convict Sacco and Vanzetti.

For most historians, the Young/Kaiser conclusions were more convincing than Russell's. Russell assumed Moore and Tresca knew enough to determine whether Sacco and Vanzetti were guilty, but there's no way to test that evidence. Even Russell couldn't question these witnesses; he heard what each said through intermediaries. At best, Russell's evidence was hearsay; at worst, mere rumor.

The new evidence tending to exonerate Sacco and Vanzetti, in contrast, came directly from the prosecution and police files. Even before Sacco and Vanzetti were executed, the defense had questioned the state's credibility on such matters as Proctor's testimony and the reluctance to pursue the Madeiros lead. Now it became even more difficult to trust the state. The new evidence may not have proven Sacco and Vanzetti were innocent, but it certainly left us with reasonable doubts.

So, too, did studies of the pair's anarchist backgrounds. The radical organizations in which both Sacco and Vanzetti were involved were committed to violent insurrections. There's even some circumstantial evidence that Sacco and Vanzetti may have been involved in some of the 1919 bombings that led to the Red Scare (and, indirectly, to their arrest). When Sacco and Vanzetti lied to the police after their arrest, they may have been covering up more than their membership in a radical organization; it's very possible they were planning to use Boda's car to transport some explosives, rather than the radical literature they talked about at their trial. Ironically, however, this violent background also attested to the pair's innocence. Anarchists were committed to violence—but for the sake of revolution, not robbery. And there has never been any sign that the Bridgewater and South Braintree robberies were motivated by anything other than greed.

To Investigate Further

Frankfurter, Felix. *The Case of Sacco and Vanzetti.* New York: Little, Brown, 1927.
    The future Supreme Court justice's passionate argument that the trial was unfair and that Sacco and Vanzetti were innocent.

Frankfurter, Marion, and Gardner Jackson, eds. *The Letters of Sacco and Vanzetti.* New York: Viking, 1928.
    After reading Vanzetti's eloquent and moving letters, it's easy to see why so many believed so strongly that he could not be guilty of murder.

Fraenkel, Osmond. *The Sacco-Vanzetti Case.* New York: Knopf, 1931.
    Includes extensive selections from the court records.

Ehrmann, Herbert. *The Untried Case.* New York: Vanguard, 1933.
    How Ehrmann, one of the attorneys for the defense, put together the case against the Morelli gang.

Joughin, Louis, and Edmund Morgan. *The Legacy of Sacco and Vanzetti.* New York: Harcourt Brace, 1948; reissued in 1971 by Princeton University Press (Princeton, NJ).
    A balanced case for the defense, which also traces how the case was represented in the press and in the arts.

Montgomery, Robert. *Sacco-Vanzetti: The Murder and the Myth.* Greenwich, CT: Devin-Adair, 1960.
    The first of the revisionist studies.

Russell, Francis. *Tragedy in Dedham.* New York: McGraw-Hill, 1962.
    Sacco was guilty, Vanzetti innocent.

Felix, David. *Protest: Sacco-Vanzetti and the Intellectuals.* Bloomington: Indiana University Press, 1965.
A somewhat shrill and unfocused revisionist effort.

Ehrmann, Herbert. *The Case That Will Not Die.* New York: Little, Brown, 1969.
The case for the defense, by one of the defense attorneys.

Feuerlicht, Roberta. *Justice Crucified.* New York: McGraw-Hill, 1977.
A passionate case for innocence, though it adds little evidence to previous studies.

Young, William, and David Kaiser. *Postmortem.* Amherst: University of Massachusetts Press, 1985.
New evidence and one of the best cases for innocence.

Russell, Francis. *Sacco and Vanzetti.* New York: Harper & Row, 1986.
In 1982, Russell received a letter from Ideala Gambera, the son of a radical who had known Sacco and Vanzetti. Gambera said his father had told him that everyone in the anarchists' circle knew Sacco was guilty; for Russell, this was yet more proof that both were guilty. But it's still just hearsay, and except for this letter Russell had little to say that wasn't in his 1962 book. That first book remains the better of the two, and the best of all the revisionist studies.

Avrich, Paul. *Sacco and Vanzetti.* Princeton, NJ: Princeton University Press, 1991.
Though it takes no final position on the pair's guilt or innocence, this is important for its investigation of the political movement of which they were a part.

Who Kidnapped
the Lindbergh Baby?

O F THE MOST FAMOUS TRIALS of the twentieth century—those of Sacco and Vanzetti, Alger Hiss, the Rosenbergs, and O. J. Simpson—the Lindbergh kidnapping trial stands out for its lack of political significance. No one could say the accused, Bruno Richard Hauptmann, was being tried because of his politics or his race. Yet the 1932 crime and trial gripped the American press and public at least as firmly as any of these others. In the days and months following the kidnapping, sightseeing planes circled the scene of the crime, hot dog vendors lined up along the road where the body was found, and among the many thousands of letters the Lindbergh family received were 12,000 just from people eager to recount their dreams about the case.

Partly, of course, this was sheer voyeurism. The father of the kidnapped child was Charles Lindbergh, the first man to fly solo across the Atlantic. In a country that celebrated both individualism and technology, the 1927 flight guaranteed Lindbergh heroic status. This was only enhanced by his 1929 marriage to Anne Morrow, the daughter of a prominent banker and ambassador, and then by the birth of their blond-haired, blue-eyed baby, Charles Jr., a year later. But Lindbergh's status alone cannot explain the fascination with the kidnapping of Charles Jr. In the early years of the Depression, the crime tapped into deeper fears about what the future held for America's children. No wonder that Maurice Sendak, author and artist of some of the spookiest children's stories of any time, once said: "All of my books are really about the Lindbergh kidnapping."

For most Americans, the arrest, conviction, and execution of Hauptmann brought some satisfaction. But it was distinctly less satisfying that Hauptmann went to his death proclaiming his innocence. In the years since then, others have taken up his cause, contending that in their eagerness to solve such a highly publicized crime, the police arrested—and the state of New Jersey put to death—an innocent man.

⚭

The kidnapping took place the evening of March 1, 1932, at the Lindbergh's newly finished house near Hopewell, New Jersey. Normally the family stayed there only on weekends, living the rest of the time at the Morrow family estate. This particular week they decided to stay on. About eight o'clock Anne Lindbergh and her nursemaid Betty Gow put the baby to bed; at ten Gow went to check on him and found he was gone.

Instead, the Lindberghs found a note that read:

Have 50,000 $ redy 25000 $ in 20 $ bills 15000 $ in 10 $ bills and 10000 $ in 5 $ bills. After 2–4 days we will inform you were to deliver the Money. We warn you for making anyding public or for notify the Polise the child is in gut care.

At the bottom of the note were two intersecting circles, with the oval intersection colored red. This, the note said, was a "singnature" by which the Lindberghs would be able to recognize that future notes were from the actual kidnappers and not some other extortionist trying to cash in without actually having the child.

Indeed, the Lindberghs were soon besieged by a variety of shady characters. One was the recently jailed gangster Al Capone, who offered his services as an intermediary between the Lindberghs and the kidnappers—in return for Capone's freedom. The offer was declined.

Others were more successful in convincing the Lindberghs they could help. A former Justice Department agent, Gaston Means, claimed to know the kidnappers and convinced Evalyn Walsh McLean, the owner of the Hope diamond, to donate $100,000 to save the baby's life—after which the money and Means promptly disappeared. (Means was eventually tracked down and convicted of embezzlement.) Another con artist, named Mickey Rosner, moved into the Lindbergh house and spent more than a week there, monopolizing their phone lines with calls to his supposed intermediaries, before the Lindberghs gave up on him and had the police throw him out.

Of all those who offered help, perhaps the most unlikely connection to the kidnappers turned out to be the most legitimate. This was Dr. John Condon, a retired schoolteacher from the Bronx. Condon was in the habit of writing eccentric letters to the Bronx *Home News*, and in one of his letters he offered his services to the kidnappers as an intermediary. Remarkably, they responded: on March 9 he received a letter with the telltale intersecting circles. This ultimately led to a rendezvous with the kidnappers at St. Raymond's Cemetery on the night of April 2. While Lindbergh remained in the car, Condon met with a man who identified himself as "John"; in return for $50,000, John gave Condon a note telling him where to find the baby. Alas, a thorough search of the area described in the note turned up nothing. Seven weeks later the baby's body was found, just a couple of miles from the Lindbergh house.

Though the efforts to save the baby had been in vain, the search for the kidnappers went on. The police had noted all the serial numbers on the ransom notes Condon had given to John; moreover, the ransom was paid largely in gold certificates that, because of new currency regulations, were increasingly rare, and the police hoped this would make them easier to track. Sure enough, about two and a half years later, a gas station attendant was handed a ten-dollar gold certificate. Suspecting it might be counterfeit, he wrote down the car's license number on the certificate. And when a bank identified the certificate as ransom money the police tracked down the car's owner, Bruno Richard Hauptmann. A search of Hauptmann's garage uncovered a shoebox with $13,760 more of the Lindbergh ransom money.

The evidence against Hauptmann seemed overwhelming. Handwriting experts identified Hauptmann's handwriting as the same as that on the ransom note. Condon, after some initial hesitation, identified Hauptmann as the "John" to whom he'd given the ransom money in the graveyard. Lindbergh himself identified John's voice as the same voice he'd heard from the car, as he sat waiting for Condon near the graveyard. Above all, there was the ransom money found in Hauptmann's possession.

Hauptmann's background didn't help his case. He was a German immigrant, and the spelling errors in the ransom note ("gut" for "good," "anyding" for "anything") were consistent with what might be expected from a native German speaker. Worse, Hauptmann had fled Germany to avoid sentencing for crimes that included using a ladder to enter a second-floor bedroom window (as had been the case in the kidnapping), and robbing two women who were pushing baby carriages down the street.

It seemed an open-and-shut case. Certainly the jury thought so: though five jurors favored life imprisonment instead of the death penalty, none doubted his guilt. Hauptmann was electrocuted on April 3, 1936.

⌖

And yet, to his death, Hauptmann proclaimed his innocence. Even when New Jersey's governor offered to convert his sentence to life imprisonment in return for a confession, Hauptmann refused.

Revisionists took up his cause. Anthony Scaduto in 1976 and Ludovic Kennedy in 1985 published books contending the evidence against Hauptmann was at best flimsy. Handwriting analysis was a notoriously subjective science, not the basis for a conviction, they argued. And Condon, though an impressive courtroom witness, had been extremely hesitant about picking Hauptmann out of a police lineup. To revisionists, this was best explained as the result of pressure from the authorities: the police might have threatened Condon that if he didn't identify Hauptmann decisively, they'd prosecute him as an accomplice. As for Lindbergh, he admitted he'd only heard "John" say a couple of words at the graveyard; that he identified the voice as Hauptmann's with such certainty could be another sign that the authorities had inappropriately pressured a witness, perhaps by playing on a father's fear that if he didn't come through at the trial his son's murderer would go free.

According to Scaduto and Kennedy, the case against Hauptmann was based on this kind of trumped-up evidence. The police and prosecutors—under tremendous pressure to solve the most widely talked about crime of the age—had railroaded through a conviction. Scaduto also claimed that the police had interrogated Hauptmann mercilessly, even beaten him, in a vain effort to elicit a confession.

But what about the ransom money? Even if we concede that the authorities trampled on Hauptmann's rights as a defendant, how could revisionists explain the money in his possession? Well, Hauptmann himself always maintained that a friend, Isidor Fisch, had asked him to hold on to the shoebox with the money while Fisch returned to Germany to visit his parents. Only accidentally did Hauptmann discover the box was full of money, and only because Fisch owed him money had Hauptmann spent some of it. Fisch, alas, had died shortly before the arrest.

To revisionists like Scaduto and Kennedy, this was as good an explanation as any. To most historians, however, the Fisch story was just that—a fish story, made up by Hauptmann in a desperate attempt to save himself. A 1987 book by Jim Fisher, a former FBI agent who'd gone through the newly opened New Jersey State Police archives, concluded that, although the police might have violated some of Hauptmann's rights, there was no evidence that they'd cooked up any evidence against him. Most historians have agreed with Fisher—and with the jury—that Hauptmann was guilty.

Many, however, have questioned whether he acted alone. Might Fisch have been a co-conspirator? Or was there another conspirator somewhere inside the Lindbergh house? If not, how could Hauptmann have known the layout of the house? More tellingly, how could he have known that the Lindberghs would be staying there on that particular Tuesday, contrary to their usual custom?

All this pointed to inside help, perhaps from one of the Lindbergh servants. Colonel Norman Schwarzkopf of the New Jersey State Police (the father of the Desert Storm commander) suspected an inside job from the start, but Lindbergh refused to let Schwarzkopf question the servants. He steadfastly maintained they were entirely trustworthy.

Lindbergh's motives for standing in Schwarzkopf's way are unclear. Perhaps it was because he'd been taken in by the various con men claiming to know the kidnappers. One can understand how a desperate parent would want to believe in anyone offering hope. Perhaps, too, it was reassuring to Lindbergh to think that his son was in the hands of professional gangsters—if they were in it just for the money, they would be less likely to harm the child. Or perhaps, as Joyce Milton suggested in her 1993 biography, Lindbergh couldn't bear to think that he'd been betrayed by servants he'd trusted.

Whatever his motives, the restrictions Lindbergh placed on Schwarzkopf frustrated not only police but historians. Because questions about inside help were not asked then, they cannot be answered now. And so, though we can be fairly sure Hauptmann was guilty, we must also suspect that others, equally guilty, went free.

To Investigate Further

Whipple, Sidney. *The Trial of Bruno Richard Hauptmann.* New York: Doubleday, 1937.
   Includes a complete transcript of the trial.

Lindbergh, Anne Morrow. *Hour of Gold, Hour of Lead.* New York: Harcourt Brace Jovanovich, 1973.
   A mother's heartbreaking diaries and letters.

Scaduto, Anthony. *Scapegoat.* New York: Putnam's, 1976.

Even if it doesn't convince you Hauptmann was framed, it will convince you his rights were violated.

Kennedy, Ludovic. *The Airman and the Carpenter.* New York: Viking, 1985.

Kennedy's three previous books resulted in the posthumous pardon or release of convicted murderers; this one didn't succeed in overturning Hauptmann's conviction but it is the most persuasive argument for his innocence.

Fisher, Jim. *The Lindbergh Case.* New Brunswick, NJ: Rutgers University Press, 1987.

A thorough case against Hauptmann.

Milton, Joyce. *Loss of Eden.* New York: HarperCollins, 1993.

A dual biography of Charles and Anne Morrow Lindbergh, including the best statement of the case that Hauptmann was the kidnapper—but not the only one.

Behn, Noel. *Lindbergh: The Crime.* New York: Atlantic Monthly Press, 1994.

Contends the baby was killed in a fit of envy by Anne Morrow Lindbergh's sister, after which—to prevent a scandal—the family concocted the kidnapping story. Though an intriguing explanation for Lindbergh's refusal to let the police question the servants, it's ultimately unconvincing.

Gardner, Lloyd. *The Case That Never Dies.* New Brunswick, NJ: Rutgers University Press, 2004.

A fine summary of the case and its historical context, though nothing dramatically new.

Did Any of
the Romanovs Survive?

T
HE THREE-HUNDRED-YEAR-OLD Romanov dynasty came to a bloody end in
July 1918.

Conditions had steadily deteriorated for the family since March 1917, when
Czar Nicholas II reluctantly abdicated, leaving the government in the hands of Alexander
Kerensky's moderate "Whites." Many of the Whites—in contrast to the Bolshevik
"Reds—favored a constitutional monarchy, and their treatment of the former czar and
his family was accordingly polite, albeit wary. The Romanovs were confined to their
palace near St. Petersburg, but other than that, life went on much as before the Revolution; the family continued their lessons, walks, tennis, and teas. Outside the palace, however, the world had changed. By August, the danger of an angry mob breaking into the
palace forced Kerensky to evacuate the family to the Siberian town of Tobolsk.

In November 1917, with the Bolsheviks now in control, the Romanovs' lives took a
sharp turn for the worse. Gone were the royal routines and the sympathetic White
guards; now the family ate black bread and soup, while hostile Bolshevik guards painted
over the windows, helped themselves to the family's possessions, and scrawled obsceni-
ties on the walls. In May 1918 the family was moved to the town of Ekaterinburg, and it
was there, in the early morning hours of July 18, that they apparently died.

One of the guards, Pavel Medvedev, later described the scene to White investigators.
The family was awakened and ordered into the basement of the house. First came
Nicholas, carrying his ailing son, the thirteen-year-old Alexei. Next came the ex-czarina,
Alexandra, followed by their four daughters, twenty-two-year-old Olga, twenty-one-
year-old Tatiana, nineteen-year-old Maria, and seventeen-year-old Anastasia. Also present were the family doctor, cook, maid, and valet. The Bolshevik officer in charge, Yakov
Yurovsky, arranged the eleven prisoners against the wall, as if for a family portrait. Then
he called in the death squad and informed them that the Ural Executive Committee had
decided to execute them. At that point Yurovsky shot the ex-czar, who died instantly.

Each member of the firing squad had been assigned a victim, but the room was so
small that they were unable to get into position, and their first shots failed to kill the former czarina or her daughters. Their agony was further prolonged by the rows of diamonds they'd hidden in their corsets; bullets ricocheted off them and around the room.
Finally, using their bayonets and rifle butts, the guards finished them off.

The burial of the family was equally chaotic, partly because the guards were more interested in getting hold of the diamonds than in getting rid of the bodies. They dumped

them in some nearby mine shafts, then returned the next day to look for a more concealed spot. When their truck got stuck in the mud, they decided to bury the corpses right there.

The official announcement of the ex-czar's death mentioned none of the gory details. On July 20 *Pravda* reported that Nicholas had been executed on the orders of the local Ekaterinburg Soviets. It added, equally tersely, that the rest of the family had been "sent to a safer place."

That last phrase left the world to wonder about the family's fate. There was, after all, only the single eyewitness—and Medvedev's testimony was given to Whites, who had a vested interest in portraying the Bolsheviks as thugs and murderers. Almost instantly, stories spread about one or another family member having escaped, usually with the help of a compassionate guard. Most of the claimants were easily dismissed as impostors, but not all; some even garnered the support of surviving relatives and acquaintances of the imperial family.

Without any bodies to prove they were dead, it seemed impossible to lay the Romanovs to rest.

⚮

Amid the many Romanov claimants, one stood out. Known by various names at different points in her life, to her supporters she was always "Anastasia."

She first drew the attention of the world in February 1920, a couple of weeks after attempting to commit suicide by jumping into Berlin's Landwehre Canal. After her rescue, she told a fantastic tale about a Polish soldier carrying her out of the cellar in Ekaterinburg, unconscious but alive. With his help, she managed to cross Russia in a wagon. She reached Romania, then decided to go to Berlin to seek help from her aunt, Princess Irene of Prussia. But she despaired of convincing Irene of her identity and decided to throw herself in the river instead.

An impressive number of Russian exiles accepted her, noting the remarkable resemblance between the woman pulled from the canal and the supposedly dead Anastasia. Among the believers were Nicholas II's first cousin, Grand Duke Andrei, and Anastasia's own cousin, Princess Xenia. In New York, where she took the name Anna Anderson, the claimant was the toast of the town; she was wined and dined by various wealthy socialites eager to be seen with the alleged grand duchess.

But most of the living Romanovs quickly lined up against Anderson. In October 1928 twelve Romanovs and three of Alexandra's relatives signed a joint declaration stating that "the woman now living in the United States . . . is not Grand Duchess Anastasia." Contrary to popular legend, the dowager empress, Anastasia's grandmother, refused to meet her, or even to hear her name mentioned.

In 1938 Anderson took her case to court, in an effort to get her share of what remained of the Romanov estate. The evidence against her was substantial: not only did most of her relatives reject her, but in 1927 a woman named Doris Wingender had identified her as Franziska Schanzkowska, a Polish factory worker who had lived with her until 1920.

In their Siberian prison in 1918 (left to right): Olga, Alexei, Tatiana, Nicholas, Anastasia, and Maria. *(STF/AFP/Getty Images)*

For someone claiming a life worthy of a fairy tale, Anderson was a difficult heroine. She was often imperious, antagonizing even her strongest supporters. She refused to speak Russian, further fueling suspicions that she was a fraud. Her supporters offered reasonable explanations: Why shouldn't she be imperious? She was brought up in the imperial family. Why should she speak Russian? This was the language she associated with the traumatic murders of her parents and siblings.

Still, it all made for a weak case. After numerous delays, in 1970 the West German Supreme Court rejected her appeal.

∽

For most historians, the Anna Anderson case was a sideshow; the main events were the investigations within the Soviet Union itself. The first of these was undertaken by the Whites, who recaptured Ekaterinburg just eight days after the executions supposedly took place. The White government assigned Nicholas Sokolov, a professional investigator, to find out what happened to the Romanovs.

Sokolov took six years to finish his investigation. By then, of course, the Bolsheviks had recaptured not just Ekaterinburg but also all of Russia, and Sokolov's report had to be published in Paris. The 1924 book proclaimed that the Reds' initial announcement was a lie; it was not just the former czar, Sokolov claimed, but also the entire family who were killed on July 18. For starters, there was the testimony of the guard Pavel Medvedev, who claimed not to have participated in the shootings but to have heard the shots and seen the bodies in the basement. Sokolov also pointed to a large collection of jewelry and other Romanov belongings found at the scene of the shooting and the nearby mine shaft. And there was a captured telegram, dated July 17, in which the Ekaterinburg Reds informed Moscow that the "family suffered the same fate as its head."

Two years after Sokolov's report, the Soviets issued their own, written by Pavel Bykov. Remarkably, Bykov agreed with Sokolov. The only significant difference in their accounts was that Sokolov said the bodies had been burned, while Bykov said they were buried. Bykov's report reversed eight years of Soviet denials; the government now conceded that the entire family had died in Ekaterinburg, though Bykov continued to maintain that the decision had come from the local Ekaterinburg Soviet, not Moscow. Bykov himself had been a member of the Ekaterinburg Soviet.

The Sokolov and Bykov reports convinced most of the world that no member of the imperial household survived. If the Whites and the Reds could agree on a common story, most historians decided, that alone was a very good reason to believe it. But some remained skeptical, noting that neither Sokolov nor Bykov had found any remains of the bodies themselves.

Among the skeptics were two British journalists, Anthony Summers and Tom Mangold, who tracked down the files on which Sokolov had based his report. They found that Sokolov had "meticulously included all evidence that supported his premise that the en-

tire family had been massacred . . . but omitted evidence that hinted or stated categori-
cally that something else had happened." The latter included testimony from local citizens that the former czarina and her daughters had been spotted in and around
Ekaterinburg after July 18.

Summers and Mangold concluded that the original Soviet announcement—that only
the ex-czar had been shot—was in fact true. In his effort to make the Reds appear brutal
and bloodthirsty, Sokolov had dismissed the evidence that some family members survived. But why would Bykov, writing on behalf of Lenin and the Soviet leadership, want
to cover up the fact that the Bolsheviks had not killed the rest of the family?

The answer, according to Summers and Mangold, had to do with secret negotiations
between the Soviets and the Germans that took place early in 1918. The Germans wanted
to save Alexandra, who was a cousin of Kaiser Wilhelm. And Lenin was perfectly willing
to use the family as a bargaining chip to extract concessions from the Germans. He ordered the family removed from Ekaterinburg, but then the German deal fell apart, and
the family was no longer of any use. At that point the Romanovs either escaped or were
killed; Summers and Mangold weren't sure which. Either way, the whole thing was an
embarrassment to Lenin, so it was easier for Bykov just to go along with the Sokolov
story of an Ekaterinburg execution. Better that than to admit that Lenin had used the
family members as pawns, then either killed or lost them.

Most historians rejected the Summers and Mangold thesis. The evidence of the German negotiations was circumstantial at best—and some of it indicated that the talks, if
they took place at all, fell through before July. That would have left Lenin plenty of time
to switch gears and allow the executions to proceed at Ekaterinburg. As for the newly
found Sokolov files, many historians pointed out that the investigator may have left out
of his report the reported sightings of family members simply because he hadn't believed
them. A close look at the testimony indicated that the witnesses thought they'd seen
some family members, but they weren't absolutely certain.

Still, Summers and Mangold had given new hope to the romantics who hoped that an
heir to the Romanov throne had somehow survived. The only way to extinguish that
hope would be to find the victims' bodies, and in the 1970s a well-known Russian film-
maker named Geli Ryabov set out to do just that.

∽

Ryabov's first big break came in 1978, when he tracked down the eldest son of Yakov
Yurovsky, the man who'd been in charge of guarding the Romanovs in Ekaterinburg. To
Ryabov's delight, the younger Yurovsky handed him a copy of his father's report on the
execution. The report confirmed the Bykov version—in which the bodies were buried,
not burned. Better yet, it included a precise description of the burial place: about twelve
miles northwest of Ekaterinburg.

Ryabov's second break was teaming up with a local man, Alexander Avdonin, who
knew his way around Ekaterinburg and was equally interested in finding the bodies. On

May 30, 1979, again to his delight but also to his horror, Ryabov uncovered three skulls and assorted other human bones just where the Yurovsky report said they'd be. Now Ryabov and Avdonin got nervous; this was still pre-glasnost, and they were none too sure how the authorities would react to the discovery of the Romanov bones, if indeed that's what these were. Ryabov and Avdonin decided to return the bones to their burial place, and they swore not to tell anyone what they'd found until times had changed.

It was not until ten years later that Ryabov decided the time was right. On April 10, 1989, the weekly *Moscow News* broke the story that the Romanov bones had been found in a swamp near Ekaterinburg. Two years later, Russian troops arrived at the site, dug up the reburied bones, and also found some additional skulls, ribs, vertebrae, leg bones, and arm bones.

Were these the Romanovs? To know for sure, scientists had to compare DNA extracted from the bones to DNA taken from the blood of a living relative of the Romanovs. British scientists turned to, among others, Queen Elizabeth's husband, Prince Philip, who in the intertwined worlds of European royalty also happened to be Alexandra's grandnephew. The prince agreed, and donated his blood. In July 1993, after ten months of work, Peter Gill and Pavel Ivanov announced that the DNA evidence made them 98.5 percent sure that these were the Romanovs' bones. Later tests indicated an even higher degree of certainty.

DNA tests also revealed, once and for all, the identity of Anna Anderson. Anderson had died in 1984, after marrying a wealthy doctor in Charlottesville, Virginia. But Gill was able to obtain a tissue sample that a Charlottesville hospital had routinely preserved, after Anderson was operated on there. Gill compared DNA from the tissue with DNA from the Ekaterinburg bones and found they were unrelated. He then compared Anderson's DNA with a sample from a German farmer named Karl Maucher, who was a grandnephew of the Polish peasant Franziska Schanzkowska. It was a 100 percent match.

Only one mystery remained. The Ekaterinburg graves held parts of nine skeletons, even though the imperial household had consisted of eleven people—the seven family members, the doctor, and the servants. That left two members of the imperial party unaccounted for. One of the missing bodies was clearly Alexei's, since none of the skeletons was that of a thirteen-year-old boy. Scientists disagreed about the other: a Russian team concluded it was Maria, while a visiting American team insisted it was Anastasia. Either way, it left open the possibility that an heir to the Russian throne survived the massacre at Ekaterinburg.

But even romantics and monarchists had to concede that it was a very faint possibility. Yurovsky's report, like Medvedev's, described a scene so bloody that it's highly unlikely that Alexei—or Maria or Anastasia—could have survived. The Yurovsky report also offered an explanation for the missing bodies: in the confusion, the chief jailer recalled, two of the bodies were buried separately from the rest. If they're uncovered, as remains possible, that could remove any lingering doubts.

Meanwhile, in July 1998, the bones of Nicholas, Alexandra, and three of their children were reburied, this time in St. Petersburg, and in a dignified though hardly imperial ceremony. For many historians, the Romanovs' deaths signaled the coming of state terrorism, and the millions of other deaths that would mark Soviet rule. The meaning of the Romanovs' return to St. Petersburg was much less clear.

To Investigate Further

Steinberg, Mark, and Vladimir Khrustalev. *The Fall of the Romanovs* (New Haven, CT: Yale University Press, 1995).
A useful collection of documents including letters between Nicholas and Alexandra, parts of their diaries, minutes of government meetings, and other official papers.

O'Conor, John F. *The Sokolov Investigation* (New York: Robert Speller & Sons, 1971).
Includes translations of sections of Sokolov's report, along with a harshly critical commentary.

Summers, Anthony, and Tom Mangold. *The File on the Tsar* (New York: Harper & Row, 1976).
An impressive investigation of the investigator, even though the discovery of the Romanov bones ultimately disproved the Summers-Mangold theory.

Kurth, Peter. *Anastasia* (Boston: Little, Brown, 1983).
An entertaining albeit overly credulous investigation of Anna Anderson.

Radzinsky, Edvard. *The Last Tsar,* trans. from the Russian by Marian Schwartz (New York: Doubleday, 1992).
Radzinsky is a prominent Russian playwright, and that's both the book's strength and its weakness. As literature, it's engrossing and evocative; as history, it's frustratingly vague and undocumented.

Ferro, Marc. *Nicholas II,* trans. from the French by Brian Pearce (New York: Oxford University Press, 1993).
A solid though uninspired biography that's undermined by Ferro's belief that some family members survived.

Massie, Robert K. *The Romanovs* (New York: Random House, 1995).
A thrilling historic and scientific detective story that's especially good at describing the DNA evidence and the rivalries among the Russian, British, and American scientists.

Kurth, Peter. *Tsar* (Boston: Little, Brown, 1995).
A magnificently illustrated portrait of the lost world of Nicholas and Alexandra; even a Marxist historian couldn't help but be moved by the snapshots of the family before and during their imprisonment.

Figes, Orlando. *A People's Tragedy* (New York: Viking, 1996).
A comprehensive history of the Russian Revolution, from the end of the nineteenth century to the death of Lenin. Figes is scholarly and fair, yet he captures the passions of the period.

Did Hitler Murder His Niece?

ON THE MORNING OF SEPTEMBER 19, 1931, a twenty-three-year-old woman, Geli Raubal, was found dead in Adolf Hitler's Munich apartment. Raubal, who was the daughter of Hitler's half sister, had been shot with his pistol. The gun was found next to the body.

For Hitler, the timing couldn't have been worse. The previous year's elections had increased the number of Nazis in the Reichstag from 12 to 107, bringing the party to the brink of power. A scandal now—especially one, as this shaped up to be, involving sex and murder charges—could quickly push Hitler and the Nazis back to the fringes of German politics.

Anti-Nazi newspapers jumped all over the story. Stories soon circulated about how the twenty-three-year-old woman had been Hitler's lover as well as niece. The *Munich Post* reported that Raubal had a broken nose, implying that Hitler had killed her in a fit of rage—possibly because he'd found out she was sleeping with someone other than he, possibly because she'd threatened to tell the public about some of her uncle's unusual sexual practices. Others suggested that Raubal had been driven to suicide, either by Hitler's violent jealousy or his sexual demands.

Questioned by detectives, an apparently shaken Hitler reported that he'd last seen her the day before the body was found. They'd argued about her plan to take singing lessons in Vienna. She was angry that he forbade her to go on her own, but then she'd calmed down. So, Hitler continued, he left for a campaign rally in Nuremberg. It was there that he learned of her death. He immediately rushed back to Munich, stopping only for a speeding ticket that he got near the halfway point.

The staff at Hitler's apartment had little to add to Hitler's story. They recalled Raubal rushing out of Hitler's bedroom, visibly upset, but they had no idea what had upset her or what had happened next.

The police found no signs of a broken nose, or any other evidence that Raubal had been assaulted. They ruled the death a suicide. But since there were many Nazi sympathizers high up in the Bavarian Ministry of Justice, many suspected the police had been pressured to cut short their investigation. The household staff, too, could have been pressured by Nazi officials, especially since party officials were already on the scene when the detectives arrived.

So, at least for historians, the investigation remained open. And their search for evidence that he murdered Raubal has led them into the very dark recesses of Adolf Hitler's mind.

☙

Among those who suspected Hitler of murdering Raubal were some ex-members of his inner circle. The most prominent was Otto Strasser, who published an influential Nazi newspaper and whose brother, Gregor, was the party's deputy führer. Gregor, who later challenged Hitler for the party leadership, was killed in 1934; Otto fled to Switzerland.

In his 1940 book *Hitler and I*, Otto Strasser cited three pieces of evidence for murder: first, a conversation he'd had with a priest who told him that he'd buried Raubal as a Catholic, something he would not have been allowed to do if he believed she committed suicide; second, a conversation with his brother, in which Gregor said that he'd heard directly from Hitler that he'd shot Raubal; and finally, a story (the source of which Strasser didn't give) that Fritz Gerlich, a well-known anti-Nazi editor, had been planning to publish a major exposé on the murder in the March 12, 1933, issue of his newspaper. But on March 9, Nazi storm troopers broke into the newspaper's offices, destroyed all the files, and arrested Gerlich. Gerlich, like Gregor Strasser, was killed in 1934. Otto Strasser didn't spell out a motive for the murder of Raubal, but he implied that it was a result of Hitler's anger about Geli seeing other men.

Ernst Hanfstaengl, once Hitler's foreign press secretary, provided more specifics: Raubal was not only seeing other men, he said, she also was pregnant by one. The prospective father was an art teacher and, worst of all from Hitler's perspective, a Jew. Raubal had met the teacher in 1928, and now she wanted to marry him. For a Jew to take away his niece—his lover—was the ultimate dishonor, personally and politically. So, Hanfstaengl reported, Hitler forced Raubal to commit suicide. How he did so wasn't clear from Hanfstaengl's account, though he implied it had something do with threats about her mother. In any case, Hanfstaengl added, Hitler's family all took this story to be true; he himself had learned it from Brigid Hitler, the wife of Hitler's brother, Alois.

In his 1944 book *Der Führer*, the German historian Karl Heiden argued that it was SS chief Heinrich Himmler, not Hitler, who was responsible for Raubal's death. In fact, Heiden argued, Hitler was in love with Raubal, and wanted to marry her. Himmler feared a scandal, either because he suspected Raubal was sleeping with another man, or because she'd threatened to go public about her uncle's sexual practices. Heiden wasn't sure whether Himmler murdered her or pushed her to suicide, but he was confident the Nazis were to blame. His source, he said, was a friend of Raubal's mother.

The problem with all these accounts was that they were based on unsubstantiated rumors, mostly circulated by relatives and former associates of Hitler, who were often less concerned about the truth than with settling grudges and exonerating themselves. These were people whose testimony later historians, quite reasonably, considered suspect. (It should be quickly added, in fairness to Heiden, that unlike either Strasser or Hanfstaengl, he'd always been an enemy of Hitler. But his story, too, came from an unhappy relative.)

Moreover, Hitler's speeding ticket provided him with an alibi. It was not, to be sure, an airtight alibi, given that the police and other witnesses to the ticket may have sympathized with the Nazis or been intimidated by them, but there was no evidence to contradict it either. As for Heiden's accusation that Himmler was responsible, that seemed illogical; if his motive had been to avoid a scandal, he certainly would not have left the body in Hitler's apartment, or left Hitler's gun beside it.

So, though murder couldn't be ruled out, the police's verdict of suicide seemed more likely. But some crucial (and titillating) questions remained: Did Hitler drive his niece to suicide? And what was the nature of their relationship?

⟡

There was no doubt, in Heiden's mind, that Hitler's intentions toward Raubal were more than avuncular.

One story Heiden told, without naming his source, concerned a letter Hitler wrote to Raubal; in it he "expressed feelings which could be expected from a man with masochistic-coprophil inclinations, bordering on . . . unidinism." More bluntly, what Heiden meant was that Hitler became sexually excited by having a woman urinate on him. The letter never reached Raubal, instead falling into the hands of a blackmailer. In 1929, according to Heiden, Nazi Party treasurer Franz Schwarz paid off the blackmailer and recovered the letter.

Hanfstaengl told the story of a different blackmail attempt, this one a year later. He recalled running into Schwarz in 1930, just after the treasurer had bought from a black-mailer a folio of pornographic sketches that Hitler had made of Raubal. Hanfstaengl glanced at the drawings, horrified, and suggested Schwarz tear them up. Schwarz said he couldn't—since Hitler wanted them back.

Heiden wasn't sure that Hitler moved beyond fantasizing about his niece, but Hanf-staengl thought he did. He quoted a conversation—admittedly one he'd only heard thirdhand—in which Raubal told a friend that her uncle was a "monster" and that "you would never believe the things he makes me do." And, as Hanfstaengl pointed out, there was a precedent for incest in the family: Hitler's parents were second cousins, and Hitler's mother, who was twenty-two years younger than his father, called him "Uncle."

Otto Strasser, like Hanfstaengl, had no doubt that the relationship between Hitler and Raubal had been consummated and that it was by no means a normal sexual rela-tionship. In a 1943 interview with agents of the OSS (the wartime predecessor of the CIA), Strasser was explicit about the unidinism. He claimed he'd heard about it directly from Raubal and that she'd found the whole thing "disgusting."

As with the murder allegations, these stories about Hitler's sex life had to be ap-proached with some skepticism. Neither Hanfstaengl nor Strasser was a particularly reli-able source, and their sources were often unnamed or even less reliable. Nor did Strasser bother to explain why Raubal had supposedly chosen him—at that time a close colleague of the man she supposedly wanted to get away from—as a confidant. So it wasn't surpris-ing that Hitler's most respected biographers of the past two generations—Alan Bullock in 1952 and Ian Kershaw in 1998—both expressed serious doubts about whether Hitler and Raubal ever consummated their relationship, let alone engaged in any sort of un-usual sex. The evidence just wasn't sufficient.

Still, unlike the murder accusation, the rumors of an unusual sexual relationship had a certain logic to them. Psychobiographers, especially Freudians, tended to see sexual secrets lurking everywhere, so they were especially inclined to find them in a psychopath such as Hitler. Walter Langer, a psychiatrist who prepared the 1943 OSS report on Hitler, believed Raubal (and Strasser) were telling the truth about the unidinism. Langer also cited interviews with another woman, the film actress Renate Muller, who reported similarly unpleasant sexual encounters with Hitler in 1932. "From a consideration of all the evidence," Langer wrote, "it would seem that Hitler's perversion is as Geli has described it."

One could hardly fault the Freudians for considering it significant that, of the seven women who were at various times reported to have had sex with Hitler, six either committed or attempted suicide. (The six include Raubal, on the assumption that she wasn't murdered, as well as Eva Braun, who died with Hitler in 1945.) Whatever Hitler was doing to the women he slept with, it seemed, was making them deeply unhappy.

But, as the less Freudian of Hitler's biographers pointed out, none of that proved that sexual issues were the root of the problem for Hitler, or the women he slept with. One did not have to believe Hitler was a sexual pervert to explain why these women would have committed suicide; he clearly had plenty of other disagreeable traits, to put it very mildly. Indeed, one might very well assume that any woman who chose to get into a relationship with Hitler already had some serious problems.

Raubal, of course, did not choose Hitler. She moved in with her uncle because she and her mother had no place else to go, and that remained the case for as long as she lived. She was trapped in the household of a man who was intensely attracted to her and who was ruthless in his efforts to keep her from seeing anyone else. His refusal to let her go to Vienna was just one of a series of escalating restrictions he'd placed on his niece ever since she first moved in with him in 1929.

One did not have to assume that he was forcing her to have some sort of perverted sex to imagine him treating her cruelly. One did not even have to assume they had any sex at all to believe he drove her to suicide.

This was the conclusion Bullock and Kershaw reached, and a majority of historians have followed their leads. Hitler, in the majority view, probably did not murder Raubal. And (though the consensus on this point is much weaker) he probably didn't have sex with her, or if he did, it probably wasn't the nature of the sex that was the direct cause of her death. But he was a tyrant—a domestic tyrant in 1931, even before he became a national tyrant two years later.

For Geli Raubal, death must have seemed the only escape.

∞

For many, including the ex-Nazi memoirists, Raubal's death was a crucial turning point for Hitler. Hanfstaengl, for example, wrote that "with her death the way was clear for his final development into a demon." Hitler's official photographer, Heinrich Hoffmann, echoed those sentiments. "At this time," he recalled, "the seed of inhumanity began to sprout in Hitler. His appetite for carnage grew monstrously only after Geli's death." This kind of analysis was clearly self-serving; if Hitler became a monster only after her death, then they could be forgiven for having allied themselves with him in his earlier, presumably more reasonable, period.

But it wasn't only the ex-Nazis who believed Raubal's death transformed Hitler. Many of the Freudian biographers, whose motivation was certainly purer than the ex-Nazis, tended to see Raubal's death as a crucial stepping-stone in his development as a murderer. Even if he didn't kill her, they've argued, the loss of the woman with whom he was obsessed somehow unleashed the monster in him. The Freudian influence has been considerable; even Bullock, though he found the evidence for an affair insufficient, believed that Raubal's death changed Hitler and that there was "probably something sexual" to Hitler's anti-Semitism.

For most historians, however, Raubal's death doesn't suffice to explain Hitler's genocidal ambitions. Nor have the various other sexually based explanations—which include a supposedly missing testicle and an encounter Hitler allegedly had with a syphilitic Jewish prostitute—satisfied most historians, especially historians of the Holocaust. Indeed, to trace the death of millions back to a single cause presents moral as well as practical problems that historians and philosophers continue to struggle with.

One thing is clear: Raubal's death, however deeply it affected Hitler, did not turn him into a killer. He already had blood on his hands; in spite of the conveniently selective memories of the ex-Nazi memoirists, Nazi thugs had already murdered and beaten hundreds if not thousands of people prior to September 1931, undoubtedly with Hitler's knowledge and approval. By no means was Geli Raubal's suicide the first death for which Hitler was responsible.

To Investigate Further

Strasser, Otto. *Hitler and I,* trans. from the German by Gwenda David and Eric Mosbacher (Boston: Houghton Mifflin, 1940).
    Part history, part self-justification—a combination that's undeniably titillating but by no means trustworthy.

Heiden, Konrad. *Der Fuhrer,* trans. from the German by Ralph Manheim (New York: Lexington Press, 1944).
    Full of details that made it an important source for later historians.

Hanfstaengl, Ernst. *Hitler* (London: Eyre & Spottiswoode, 1957).
    Like Strasser's book, an ex-Nazi's apologia/memoir.

Langer, Walter. *The Mind of Adolf Hitler* (New York: Basic Books, 1972).
    The OSS report from 1943—making this, in a way, the official U.S. government position on Adolf Hitler.

Fest, Joachim. *Hitler,* trans. from the German by Richard and Clara Winston (New York: Harcourt Brace Jovanovich, 1973).

The best German biography of Hitler.

Toland, John. *Adolf Hitler* (Garden City, NY: Doubleday, 1976).

An anecdotal and very readable biography. As for Raubal, Toland's theory was that it was her jealousy, not Hitler's, that led to her suicide. He came to this conclusion after interviewing a couple of the surviving household staff members. They told him that just prior to her death, Raubal had been very upset because she'd found a letter from Eva Braun to Hitler.

Bullock, Alan. *Hitler and Stalin* (New York: HarperCollins, 1991).

Bullock's 1952 biography of Hitler remains a classic, even though this more recent dual biography incorporates new research.

Hayman, Ronald. *Hitler and Geli* (London: Bloomsbury, 1997).

Hayman is the latest to argue that Hitler shot Raubal.

Kershaw, Ian. *Hitler* (London: Allen Lane, 1998).

Arguably the best biography of Hitler to date.

Rosenbaum, Ron. *Explaining Hitler* (New York: Random House, 1998).

An entirely fascinating and often brilliant mix of intellectual history and piercing interviews. Rosenbaum reveals the underlying motivations of historians, and in doing so makes an important contribution to our understanding of Hitler. This chapter is heavily indebted to Rosenbaum.

Was Amelia Earhart a Spy?

WE MUST BE ON YOU BUT CANNOT SEE YOU. Gas is running low." This ominous message from Amelia Earhart reached the coast guard cutter *Itasca* in the early morning hours of July 3, 1937. The cutter was cruising off the coast of Howland Island, a tiny speck in the middle of the South Pacific that was to be one of the final stops on Earhart's record-breaking, round-the-world flight. But Earhart never reached Howland Island and soon lost contact with the *Itasca*. President Franklin Roosevelt ordered a massive naval search. It lasted one week, cost $4 million dollars (no mean sum back then), and covered approximately 250,000 miles, to no avail. Earhart, her navigator Fred Noonan, and her Lockheed Electra aircraft had disappeared.

Officials concluded Earhart had run out of gas and gone down somewhere in the ocean. In the years since then, however, the official story has been repeatedly challenged. One of the most persistent and intriguing of the alternative scenarios recasts Earhart and Noonan as spies for the United States. Their round-the-world adventure was merely cover, with their actual mission being to take pictures of Japanese installations in the Pacific. The Japanese forced them down and (in some versions) took them prisoner or (in other versions) executed them.

The Earhart-as-spy story originated in 1943, in *Flight for Freedom*, a movie starring Rosalind Russell as a famous aviator named Tonie Carter and Fred MacMurray as the navigator she falls in love with. They plan to get lost over the Pacific to give the navy a pretext for searching the area and checking out Japanese fortifications. Just before taking off on the last leg of the journey, Carter learns that the Japanese are on to her, and that they plan to take her prisoner. So she takes off alone and ditches the plane in the ocean, sacrificing her life so the search can go on.

The movie was pure fiction. But it captured the imagination of the public and of generations of journalists, historians, and aviation buffs—some of whom set out to prove it was more than fiction.

∞

Among the leading proponents of the Earhart-as-spy story was CBS reporter Fred Goerner. In 1960 Goerner came across a newspaper article about Josephine Blanco Akiyama, who said that while she was a girl on Saipan Island she'd witnessed a plane crash in the harbor, after which a white woman and man were taken into Japanese custody. Soon after, Akiyama recalled, she had heard shots fired.

Goerner spent six years interviewing hundreds of islanders who claimed to have seen Earhart and Noonan. He concluded that the two landed somewhere in the Marshall Islands, were picked up by a Japanese fishing boat, and were then taken to Japanese Pacific military headquarters on Saipan. Some of Goerner's evidence didn't stand up on closer investigation: the remains in an unmarked grave turned out to be of non-Caucasian origin and parts of a twin-engine airplane he recovered turned out to be made in Japan. Equally problematic were that the islanders' stories about the fliers often contradicted each other: some claimed to have seen just a woman, others a man and woman; some saw the plane wrecked, others virtually undamaged; some saw the fliers summarily executed, others in jail; and the crash itself was apparently witnessed on a whole range of islands.

Still, so many islanders claimed to have seen Earhart and Noonan that their stories couldn't be dismissed out of hand. It is certainly possible, though by no means proven, that two white fliers were captured by the Japanese sometime before the war. But were these two Earhart and Noonan? And were they on a spy mission?

To answer these questions, investigators turned from the Pacific to Washington, D.C. Randall Brink spent thirteen years analyzing documents obtained through the Freedom of Information Act. His conclusion was similar to Goerner's: Earhart was a spy. In Brink's account, Earhart's trip started as a publicity stunt but evolved into a spy mission. As a personal friend of the Roosevelts, Earhart did not hesitate to approach the president for help in arranging for refueling stops during her trip. And the president couldn't risk the temptation to use the trip for military intelligence.

To begin with, Brink pointed out, there wasn't even an airstrip on Howland Island until Roosevelt ordered the Coast Guard to build one for Earhart. This was a major construction job—at taxpayers' expense—and it would be hard to justify it as nothing more than a favor for a friend.

Brink interviewed a Lockheed technician who told him he'd cut holes in the plane so that special cameras could be installed to take pictures of Japanese installations. Brink also argued that Earhart's last-minute change in flight direction, from westward to eastward, could only be explained if hers was a spying mission. According to the original itinerary, Earhart would have flown westward over the Pacific and landed in Lae, New Guinea. There she would have been surrounded by civilians, in foreign territory, and any number of things could have gone wrong, including the discovery of the bulky camera. By going from west to east, she would land on the isolated, U.S.-controlled Howland Island immediately after photographing Japanese installations. On Howland the film could easily be handed over to U.S. agents before she flew on to meet the crowds at Hawaii, her next stop. Earhart's explanation that she was changing the flight direction because of a seasonal change in wind patterns made no sense, Brink said; by flying from west to east she was bucking the prevailing wind.

In addition, Brink uncovered evidence in the files of naval intelligence that, prior to her flight, the navy had secretly installed powerful engines in Earhart's plane that would enable it to take a different, longer flight path than had been announced. This path, Brink concluded, would take her over the Japanese-controlled Marshall and Caroline Islands.

Finally, Brink found that Earhart was heard by radio operators for days after she supposedly disappeared and died. Some of these reports may have been unreliable, but as with the testimony of the islanders gathered by Goerner, there were too many to dismiss them out of hand. Brink believed that Roosevelt was well aware of all the evidence that Earhart had survived, and that he ordered it covered up so that her spying activities, too, would be buried.

Brink's detractors argued that his evidence was circumstantial and that he'd overstated his case. For example, Brink cited a document in which FDR's treasury secretary, Henry Morgenthau Jr., stated that if the full story of Earhart's last flight were made public, her reputation would be ruined. Brink read that as evidence that the administration wanted to cover up Earhart's spying. Tom Crouch of the National Air and Space Museum, however, pointed out that it could just as easily be read to mean that Earhart made some errors in judgment that could have undermined her reputation as a great flyer.

Some of Brink's speculation was, indeed, a bit off the wall. He gave serious consideration, for example, to a long-standing but completely unsubstantiated theory that after being captured by the Japanese, Earhart had become "Tokyo Rose," the infamous wartime disc jockey who beguiled American troops in the Pacific. At one point, Earhart's husband had made a special trip to the front lines to listen to a Tokyo Rose broadcast and had said he would stake his life that it was not his wife's voice.

And though Franklin Roosevelt died without ever publicly discussing Earhart's flight, Eleanor Roosevelt repeatedly denied any spy plot, stating: "Franklin and I loved Amelia too much to send her to her death." So, in the end, the spy theorists had lots of evidence, but all of it circumstantial, and lots of speculation, some of it wild.

⟨⟩

While Brink was searching through files in Washington, other researchers continued to scour the Pacific for evidence of Earhart's landing. The best funded of them was Richard Gillespie, executive director of The International Group for Historic Aircraft Recovery (TIGHAR). Between 1989 and 2001, Gillespie led six expeditions on and around the uninhabited island known as Nikumaroro. It was there that, during the initial search for Earhart, a navy pilot had reported "signs of recent habitation." But after repeated circling and zooming failed to elicit any answering wave, the pilot concluded no one was there.

Gillespie thought the pilot might have missed something, and what he found there convinced him he was right. He returned with a number of objects, among them part of a woman's size nine shoe, consistent with the style Earhart wore; a mid-thirties cigarette lighter, which might have belonged to Noonan (who was a smoker); and an aluminum navigator's bookcase with screwholes that suggested it might have been installed on an airplane. Gillespie believed he'd solved the Earhart mystery: Earhart and Noonan had crashed on Nikumaroro.

Those who thought Amelia Earhart was a spy for the United States pointed to her close friendship with Franklin and Eleanor Roosevelt. Here she is on a night flight over Washington with the first lady. (Eleanor Roosevelt always wanted to take flying lessons but never did.) *(Bettman/Corbis)*

This did not prove, of course, that Earhart died on Nikumaroro; she might still have been captured by the Japanese and she might still have been a spy. But, Gillespie claimed, here at last was some hard evidence to replace the circumstantial evidence and wild speculations of the spy theorists.

How hard was Gillespie's evidence?

His detractors were quick to point out that even though Nikumaroro may be uninhabited now, it had been at times colonized by islanders and military personnel. Shoes might have traveled there by some means other than Earhart's feet, and the same could be said for all the flotsam and jetsam Gillespie collected. Besides, the navy pilot who'd flown over the island was a trained professional on the lookout for any signs of Earhart, Noonan, or their plane—and he'd concluded they weren't there.

So it seems, barring some yet to be discovered evidence, Amelia Earhart is destined to remain a missing person. We simply cannot say for sure where she landed, or whether she was a spy.

What if we put aside the relics of Earhart's trip and look instead at Earhart herself? What clues might be found in her past behavior? Was she the type of person likely to be a spy?

Certainly no one could doubt she had sufficient courage to be a spy. This was, after all, the first woman to fly across the Atlantic as a passenger (in 1928), the first woman to fly solo across the Atlantic (in 1932), the woman who broke her own transcontinental speed record (in 1933), the first person to fly solo from Honolulu to the mainland (in 1935). And her relationship with the Roosevelts was sufficiently close that they might very well have felt comfortable discussing top secret matters with her.

But Earhart was an ardent pacifist, likely to have resisted anything to do with the military. Besides, there were plenty of other motivations for the trip besides spying. Money, for one: Earhart's husband, the publisher George Putnam, was a master publicist with visions of lucrative endorsement contracts for his wife. Indeed, the trip generated more attention than he could have dreamed; alas, without Earhart, there was no way for Putnam to cash in.

Nor need we be so cynical to explain why Earhart took off. This was a woman who loved flying, and a flight around the world was the ultimate aerial adventure. In her journal of the flight (which she cabled to Putnam from various stops along the way so that it would be ready for publication right after the trip was over), Earhart recounted her reasons for the trip: "Here was shining adventure, beckoning with new experiences. . . . Then, too, there was my belief that now and then women should do for themselves what men have already done—and occasionally what men have not done . . . perhaps encouraging other women toward greater independence of thought and action." So feminism, too, propelled Earhart.

Her disappearance, like her motivations for the trip, can be explained without resorting to spy stories. Strictly as an aviation challenge, the trip from New Guinea to Howland Island was plenty dangerous. Howland was tiny and remote and barely above sea level; under the best of circumstances it would be difficult to find. Earhart and Noonan planned to reach it after approximately 18 hours in the air—18 hours that came after having already flown much of the way around the world, in a noisy, vibrating plane with barely room to stretch. To say that Earhart and Noonan were unlikely to be at their most alert under these conditions is no insult to either. And there is also a possibility that Noonan was drunk or hung over; though there's absolutely no evidence that this was the case, he was an alcoholic who'd been fired by Pan American, and suspicions linger.

None of this proves that Earhart wasn't a spy. Nor does it preclude the possibility that, even if Earhart had nothing to do with it, the navy saw her disappearance as an opportunity to survey the Japanese military buildup in the region. But it's worth noting that most of Earhart's biographers have concluded she wasn't a spy. And though other investigators might have looked more carefully at the particulars of Earhart's disappearance, it was her biographers who looked most carefully at the woman herself.

To Investigate Further

Earhart, Amelia. *Last Flight.* New York: Harcourt, Brace, 1937.

Earhart's journal, which was originally to be called "World Flight." Though it was much embellished by Putnam and other editors, and though it obviously ended before the end, it's still the closest we come to Earhart's own account of the trip.

Goerner, Fred. *The Search for Amelia Earhart.* New York: Doubleday, 1966.

The story of Goerner's six-year investigation and the reasons he concluded Earhart was a spy.

Rich, Doris. *Amelia Earhart.* Washington, DC: Smithsonian, 1989.

A thorough, workmanlike biography.

Lovell, Mary. *The Sound of Wings: The Life of Amelia Earhart.* New York: St. Martin's, 1989.

In spite of its title, this is actually a dual biography of Earhart and Putnam.

Gillespie, Richard. "The Mystery of Amelia Earhart." *Life,* April 1992.

Gillespie's own account of his early Nikumaroro expeditions.

Wilkinson, Stephan. "Amelia Earhart: Is the Search Over?" *Air & Space,* September 1992.

A more objective analysis of Gillespie's expedition.

Ware, Susan. *Still Missing.* New York: Norton, 1993.

A feminist biography: the title refers not just to the unsolved mystery surrounding Earhart's disappearance but to her still unfulfilled goal of equality for women.

Brink, Randall. *Lost Star.* New York: Norton, 1994.

Though some of Brink's speculation about what might have happened after Earhart was captured is farfetched, this presents the most thorough case that she was a spy.

Who Was to Blame
for Pearl Harbor?

WHEN FDR DECLARED DECEMBER 7, 1941, "a date that will live in infamy," he left no question about who the infamous party was—the perpetrators of the "unprovoked and dastardly attack" on Pearl Harbor, the Japanese empire.

For many, though, Roosevelt's explanation didn't wash. The world was already at war, all diplomatic efforts to resolve tensions with Japan had failed, the entire Pacific Ocean was ready to boil over. How, with all of this going on, could our army and navy be caught sleeping?

To some revisionists, a more sinister explanation than Roosevelt's seemed called for. They argued that the infamy belonged to Roosevelt himself. They claimed that Roosevelt knew in advance of the attack on Pearl Harbor and deliberately withheld information about it from the U.S. commanders in Hawaii. His motive: to get the United States into the war. Eager to fight the Japanese and Germans, frustrated by isolationists in Congress and the American public, this Roosevelt was a warmonger who would stop at nothing, not even betraying his own forces, to get his way.

☙❧

Among the earliest to point fingers at Roosevelt were his commanders at Pearl Harbor: Admiral Husband Kimmel, the Commander in Chief of the U.S. Pacific Fleet, and Lieutenant General Walter Short, Commanding General, Hawaii Department of the Army. Both, admittedly, had a strong incentive to blame Roosevelt—or, for that matter, anyone but themselves. The humiliation of the defeat at Pearl Harbor had been compounded by a presidential committee that found both Kimmel and Short guilty of "dereliction of duty."

Neither officer took this verdict lying down. Most frustrating of all was that the committee had not considered what they—and all future revisionists—considered the key evidence against Roosevelt. Namely, Magic. Magic was the code name used to refer to the brilliant work of Lieutenant Colonel William Friedman, who in August 1940 cracked the most secret of Japanese codes. From 1940 on, as a result of Friedman's breakthrough, U.S. intelligence officers were reading all of Japan's diplomatic messages.

One of these messages, which U.S. intelligence intercepted on September 24, 1941, was a "strictly secret" message from the Japanese Foreign Ministry to its Honolulu consulate.

This came to be known as the "bomb plot" message. It read: "With regard to warships and aircraft carriers, we would like to have you report on those at anchor . . . tied up at wharves, buoys, and in docks."

That the consulate was spying on American ships at Pearl Harbor was no surprise to anyone; the Japanese had been following U.S. fleet movements for quite a while. Now, however, they were suddenly interested in the locations of the ships in the harbor.

Why the sudden change in the Japanese spies' focus? To many who analyzed it later, including Kimmel and Short, the answer was obvious: the Japanese wanted to know the locations of ships at the harbor because they were planning to attack them there.

Yet no one in the navy or army in Pearl Harbor received a copy of the intercepted message.

Kimmel and Short felt somewhat vindicated when the navy and the army conducted their own investigations and concluded that their commanders had not been derelict. But that satisfied few. For one thing, a lot of people suspected the military was covering up the truth to protect its own people and image. Even for those who did trust the military, the question remained: if Kimmel and Short weren't to blame, who was?

This was a question too pressing to be left to historians. In 1945 a joint congressional committee opened its own investigation.

∞

Testifying about the bomb plot message, Short told the committee:

While the War Department G-2 may not have felt bound to let me know about the routine operations of the Japanese in keeping track of our naval ships, they should certainly have let me know that the Japanese were getting reports of the exact location of the ships in Pearl Harbor . . . because such details would be useful only for sabotage, or for air or submarine attack on Hawaii. . . . This message, analyzed critically, is really a bombing plan for Pearl Harbor.

Kimmel agreed that "knowledge of these intercepted Japanese dispatches would have radically changed the estimate of the situation made by me and my staff."

The testimony mesmerized the nation. How could U.S. intelligence have failed to pass on such a critically important message to Kimmel or Short?

In the 39 volumes of testimony and documents gathered by the congressional committee, there was no definite answer. Various officers confirmed that the bomb plot message was definitely intercepted yet never reached Kimmel or Short. It may have reached the Washington desk of Admiral Harold Stark, chief of naval operations. Stark told the committee he didn't remember seeing the message, but he admitted that even if he had seen it he would have considered it "just another example of their [Japan's] great attention to detail." Also, he assumed (incorrectly) that Kimmel was receiving the same messages directly from Naval Communications.

The congressional committee's verdict was split.

The majority report, signed by six Democrats and two Republicans, blamed the military, both in Washington and in Hawaii. It blamed army and navy intelligence in Washington for failing to pass on this and other intercepted Japanese messages to Kimmel and Short; it blamed Kimmel and Short for failing to appreciate the considerable intelligence and other information that was available to them.

The minority report, signed by two Republicans, blamed not only the military but the administration, including Roosevelt, for failing to put the Pearl Harbor commanders on a full alert for defensive actions, given the increasing tension with Japan. Even the Republicans, however, stopped short of accusing Roosevelt of having known about the attack in advance.

Given the political pressures to which Congress was subjected, a split verdict was hardly surprising. But as time passed, most Americans came to accept the opinion of the majority report. World War II, it was generally agreed, was "the good war." So, just as Republicans dropped their prewar isolationism, they put aside their suspicions about the war's origins. As for Kimmel and Short, they continued to proclaim their innocence, but even in the military fewer and fewer cared.

In retrospect, the preponderance of evidence did support the majority opinion of the committee. No one conspired to keep Kimmel and Short in the dark. Instead, a great many people in Washington and Hawaii—including Roosevelt but also including most other top American officials—grossly underestimated the Japanese. Everyone expected that some skirmish would eventually draw the United States into war; what no one foresaw was that the Japanese would strike so suddenly and decisively. Far from being Roosevelt's pawns, the Japanese military leaders were bold tacticians. They realized war was inevitable and they determined—probably correctly—that a preemptive strike was their best chance to win it.

It was the general underestimation of the Japanese—abetted by bad communication, bad coordination, and bad luck—that was to blame for Pearl Harbor.

ᏩᎥᏫᏬ

Yet the case against Roosevelt has popped up again and again, and it's made for some strange bedfellows. Revisionists have included both anticommunists, who felt the United States should have been fighting the Soviet Union instead of Germany and Japan, and leftist historians of the sixties, who saw sinister parallels between how Roosevelt ensnared the country into World War II and how Johnson and Nixon trapped us into Vietnam.

And in one sense, the case against Roosevelt has stood the test of time. Most historians now agree that, in his eagerness to get the United States into the war, Roosevelt was guilty both of provoking the Japanese and of overstepping his constitutional powers. In early 1941, well before Pearl Harbor and in violation of its own neutrality acts, the United States was providing covert aid to China in its war against Japan. In addition, Roosevelt's "lend-lease" plan, by which he was lending arms to the British and allowing them to pay later, was pure fiction: no one in the administration expected Britain to return the arms or to pay for them. One Republican senator, cutting through the pretense, commented: "Lending arms is like lending chewing gum. You don't want it back."

Roosevelt had no choice. Given the still-prevailing isolationism of the Congress and the public, his deceptions and manipulations were the only means he had to act against Japan and Germany. Still, there's no question that when Roosevelt described the attack on Pearl Harbor as "unprovoked," he was not telling the whole truth.

But did he know about the attack in advance? No.

After all—and this is perhaps the strongest defense of Roosevelt that can be made—Roosevelt wanted America in the war so that we could win the war. And it's a hell of a lot easier to win a war if your Pacific fleet is floating on, and not under, the waters of Pearl Harbor.

To Investigate Further

Hearings Before the Joint Committee on the Investigation of the Pearl Harbor Attack, Congress of the United States, Seventy-ninth Congress, Government Printing Office, 1946.
Still the primary primary source.

Beard, Charles A. *President Roosevelt and the Coming of the War, 1941.* New Haven, CT: Yale University Press, 1948.
Accuses Roosevelt of manipulating the American public and the Japanese, but not of actually knowing in advance about the attack.

Morison, Samuel E. *By Land and By Sea.* New York: Knopf, 1953.
Includes a clear refutation of Beard's arguments.

Barnes, Harry E. *Perpetual War for Perpetual Peace.* Caldwell, ID: Caxton Printers, 1953.
Goes the whole way: not only does it claim Roosevelt wanted the attack, but that he knew about it in advance and then covered that up.

Kimmel, Husband E. *Admiral Kimmel's Story.* Washington, DC: Regnery, 1955.
Kimmel's own defense.

Wohlstetter, Roberta. *Pearl Harbor: Warning and Decision.* Stanford, CT: Stanford University Press, 1962.
How and why American intelligence organizations failed to understand the Japanese messages they intercepted.

Prange, Gordon W. *At Dawn We Slept.* New York: McGraw-Hill, 1981.
The most thorough statement of the orthodox position and of the Japanese side of the story. This essay is much indebted to the book.

Toland, John. *Infamy.* New York: Doubleday, 1982.
Asks some provocative questions but ultimately not a convincing revisionist statement.

Prange, Gordon W. *Pearl Harbor: The Verdict of History.* New York: McGraw-Hill, 1986.

Refutes Toland's arguments but is otherwise a largely unnecessary reorganization of the arguments made quite well in *At Dawn We Slept.*

———. *Dec. 7, 1941.* New York: McGraw-Hill, 1988.

The third, and least necessary, of Prange's Pearl Harbor trilogy.

Thompson, Robert S. *A Time for War.* New York: Prentice-Hall Press, 1991.

A compelling account of Roosevelt's efforts to get the United States into the war.

Rusbridge, James, and Eric Nere. *Betrayal at Pearl Harbor.* New York: Summit, 1991.

Argues that Churchill knew of the attack in advance and, in order to lure the United States into the war, withheld the information from Roosevelt.

Clausen, Henry C. *Pearl Harbor: Final Judgment.* New York: Crown, 1992.

Recapitulating his 1945 investigation for the army, Clausen argues against any conspiracy. Instead, he blames uncoordinated intelligence and serious errors on the part of Kimmel, Short, and others.

Costello, John. *Days of Infamy.* New York: Pocket, 1994.

Accuses Roosevelt of gross strategic miscalculations but not of knowing about the attack in advance.

Stinnett, Robert. *Day of Deceit.* New York: The Free Press, 2000.

More (and convincing) evidence that Roosevelt provoked the Japanese, and that he knew in advance (less convincing).

Why Did Hess Fly to Scotland?

THE BATTLE OF BRITAIN is still recalled as the nation's "finest hour," a time of hardship and heroism. On May 10, 1941, Luftwaffe bombs caused massive damage in the heart of London. That same night, a lone German pilot slipped through Britain's coastal defenses and parachuted to the ground, not far from the duke of Hamilton's estate in Lanarkshire, Scotland.

A Scottish farmer found the pilot nursing a wrenched ankle and, armed with a pitchfork, took him into custody. The pilot would say only that he was on a "special mission" and had to see the duke.

The duke arrived at ten the next morning. Speaking in English, the pilot told Hamilton that Hitler wanted to stop the fighting, and that he had flown to England for peace talks with Hamilton and other sympathetic Englishmen. The pilot also identified himself to Hamilton: he was Rudolf Hess, deputy führer of the German Reich.

Predictably, Hess's flight created sensational headlines around the world. Hess was the Nazi Party chief, the virtual coauthor of *Mein Kampf*, a member of Hitler's inner circle. Surprisingly, the official reactions that quickly followed from Berlin and London were pretty much the same: Hess was a madman, though perhaps an idealistic one. He'd acted entirely on his own, without the knowledge or encouragement of Hitler or Churchill or any responsible person in either government.

From the start, there were many who doubted the official line that Hess acted alone. Some believed Hitler sent his old friend and associate to make peace with England, perhaps so he could turn his armies against Russia instead. Others suspected an even darker secret: that Hess, far from arriving out of the blue, had good reason to believe he'd be met by friends, including some high up in the British government.

⁊⚊⚊⚊⚊⚋

If Hitler knew anything about Hess's mission in advance, he didn't show it. Eyewitness accounts from his mountain retreat, where he called top aides to deal with the crisis, described their führer as grief-stricken and the scene as utter confusion. Chief of Staff General Franz Halder wrote in his diary that Hitler "was taken completely by surprise."

Once it was clear Hess was in British hands, Berlin quickly issued a series of press statements regretting Hess's "hallucinations" and assuring the world that they would have no effect on the war.

Hitler ordered the arrest of various Hess associates, including the deputy führer's valet, Karlheinz Pintsch, and his friend and unofficial adviser, Albrecht Haushofer. Haushofer admitted to the Gestapo that he'd discussed with Hess their mutual interest in peace with Britain, and most historians believe he was the one who planted the idea of a peace mission in Hess's head. Haushofer also admitted that he'd talked to Hess about his many British friends—including the duke of Hamilton.

Also arrested were astrologers and fortune-tellers throughout Germany. According to Nazi press reports, Hess's mental disorder may have left him vulnerable to their influence.

It's tough to say how much of this activity was real and how much was a show. Certainly the Nazis were masters of propaganda, and the Hess affair required all their skills. For the Germans to send a peace emissary in the midst of the Battle of Britain, let alone one as high ranking as Hess, would inevitably be construed as a sign of weakness. So it was clearly crucial that Hitler distance himself from Hess.

Some witnesses, including Pintsch, thought Hitler was acting, and that he knew far more about this mission than he let on. Both Haushofer and Hess's wife, Ilse, said they were under the impression that Hess had discussed the general idea of a peace mission with Hitler, though neither claimed Hitler knew any specifics. Others later recalled a May 5 meeting between Hitler and Hess during which voices were raised, perhaps because Hess was telling Hitler about his plan.

Among those who never bought the official story was Stalin. In spite of his 1939 nonaggression pact with Germany, he didn't trust Hitler. When German forces invaded Russia in June, just a month after Hess's flight, he saw it as proof that he'd been right. Hess, he believed, must have been part of some German-British conspiracy to call off the Battle of Britain and instead jointly destroy the Bolsheviks.

Stalin never relinquished his suspicions. As Churchill recalled in his 1950 history of the war, Stalin confronted him about Hess in 1944, during their meeting in Moscow. Churchill repeated the official version: Hess was a "medical case." Annoyed by Stalin's skepticism, Churchill insisted that he'd stated the facts as he knew them and that he expected them to be accepted. Stalin replied, "There are lots of things that happen even here in Russia which our Secret Service do not necessarily tell me about."

The implication was clear: it was not just Germans but also British spies who were involved in the Hess plot.

⊙〰〰〰৩

With the demise of the Soviet Union and the opening of many KGB archives, Western historians could for the first time get a glimpse of the type of intelligence that fueled Stalin's suspicions. In 1991 British historian John Costello published the results of his study of the KGB Hess files. Costello concluded that Stalin had been right all along.

The files included a report from a Soviet agent who described the Hess flight as "not the act of a madman . . . but the realization of a secret conspiracy by the Nazi leadership to strike a peace with Britain before opening the war with the Soviet Union." Another agent began by explicitly saying that "the disseminated story that Hess arrived in England unexpectedly is not correct."

According to the Soviet spies, Hess had long been in correspondence with the duke of Hamilton—though Hamilton didn't know it. Apparently British spies had intercepted Hess's letters to Hamilton. They'd then sent back answers in Hamilton's name, encouraging Hess to come. The whole thing had been a British trick played on the unsuspecting deputy führer.

Costello found similar theories in a U.S. Army Intelligence file from 1941 that was declassified in 1989. The Soviet and American reports were so similar, in fact, that Costello concluded they must both have had the same source. Both, for example, recounted the same line from a doctor who examined the German pilot soon after his capture. When the pilot announced he was Rudolf Hess, the doctor wisecracked that the hospital also had a patient who thought he was Solomon.

For Costello, the new evidence exploded the myth of heroic England bravely holding out against the Nazi onslaught. Instead, the British government was portrayed as deeply ambivalent about the war, with a significant "peace party" actively working to replace Churchill with a prime minister more likely to appease Hitler. Churchill's opponents held out little hope that they could defeat Hitler; with Pearl Harbor still months away and American isolationists strongly opposed to war, the only certainty was that continuing the fight alone would mean the continuing loss of lives and property. To Costello it made no sense that Hess, however fanatical or naive or crazy he may have been, would drop out of the sky without some reason to believe that the duke of Hamilton would be waiting to meet with him.

Others, most notably the British historian Peter Padfield, found convincing the evidence that the British lured Hess to England, but concluded that it was probably a Secret Service operation, not an anti-Churchill plot. Like Stalin, Padfield suspected that the Hess mission was part of a British campaign designed to persuade Hitler to abandon the Battle of Britain and focus his forces on Russia instead. And, Padfield speculated, Hitler, too, had reasons to send his deputy to England. If the peace mission failed, Hitler may have reasoned, Stalin would assume that ensured the Battle of Britain would continue. That would give Hitler the chance to catch the Soviets off guard.

By this theory, Hess was a pawn of both Churchill and Hitler. Churchill hoped to persuade Hitler to go east, while Hitler hoped to persuade Stalin he was going west.

⁕

Provocative as their books were, neither Costello nor Padfield succeeded in changing the consensus view of the Hess mission. For one thing, just because Soviet and American spies agreed on something didn't mean it was right. More likely, according to most historians, both drew on the same sources, and those sources were wrong. The full story may emerge in 2017, when all the British government files on Hess will be unsealed.

From the British Secret Service files already open, though, it's clear that Hess's friend Albrecht Haushofer (though not Hess himself) had been in touch with the duke of

Hamilton. Some of Haushofer's letters indicate a close relationship between Haushofer and Hamilton—so close that Costello saw homosexual undertones.

In September 1940 Haushofer wrote to Hamilton, inviting the duke's "friends in high places" to "find significance in the fact that I am able to ask whether you could find time to have a talk." Haushofer, probably with Hess's knowledge, was clearly feeling out the possibility of peace talks.

Yet Haushofer's letter never reached Hamilton. It was intercepted by British intelligence, which held on to it for five months. Why they did so is unclear. Perhaps it was because Churchill had made clear peace talks were out of the question. Or perhaps the Secret Service responded in Hamilton's name, intending to bait Haushofer and instead snaring Hess.

Whatever the bait, it's clear the deputy führer was eager to bite. Hess knew of Hitler's grudging admiration for Britain and of his unmitigated hatred of the Russian Bolsheviks. Regardless of whether he'd ever explicitly discussed it with Hitler, Hess knew that a successful peace mission would certainly please the führer. Moreover, this was an opportunity for Hess to regain some of the power he felt slipping away. Hess had been Hitler's number-two man in the early days of Nazism, but by 1941 his influence was declining as a result of rivals such as Martin Bormann and of Hitler's concentration on military matters.

The best explanation of Hess's motives may still be the one Churchill wrote in 1950. After describing Hess's jealousy of the generals who'd overshadowed him, he imagined Hess's thoughts: "They have their parts to play. But I, Rudolf, by a deed of superb devotion will surpass them all and bring to my Fuehrer a greater treasure and easement than all of them put together. I will go and make peace with Britain."

Hess's peace plan was doomed to fail. Driven by loyalty and ambition, and perhaps deceived by the British Secret Service, he failed to see that by 1941 the time for peace had passed. It was not just Churchill, but also the British public who were now firmly committed to the war.

Churchill recognized that the Hess mission was completely irrelevant to the course of the war. That was clear from the moment he first learned that Hess had landed in Britain. After the duke of Hamilton met with Hess, the duke hurried to give his report to the prime minister. Churchill, who had planned to see a movie that evening, listened impatiently, then responded: "Well, Hess or no Hess, I am going to see the Marx Brothers."

To Investigate Further

Churchill, Winston. *The Grand Alliance* (Boston: Houghton Mifflin, 1950).
Volume 3 of Churchill's magnificent history of World War II, full of not just the author's recollections but also his directives, telegrams, and other documents that illuminate the British government's pursuit of the war.

Hess, Ilse. *Prisoner of Peace* (London: Britons Publishing Co., 1954).

Hess's letters to his wife and son from England, Nuremberg, and Spandau Prison.

Douglas-Hamilton, James. *Motive for a Mission* (London: Macmillan, 1971).

As the son of the duke of Hamilton, Douglas-Hamilton grew up immersed in the Hess mystery. Surprisingly, though, his book is more about Haushofer than either Hamilton or Hess. Haushofer emerges as a fascinating and tragic figure: with ties to both the Nazis and the resistance, he ended up despising himself and welcoming his death at the hands of the Gestapo.

Thomas, W. Hugh. *Hess: A Tale of Two Murders* (London: Hodder & Stoughton, 1988).

Thomas, a British surgeon who examined Spandau's inmate, discovered to his amazement that he had none of the scars that should have remained from Hess's World War I injuries. Thomas concluded that the man who died in prison in 1987 couldn't have been Hess. His theory was that Himmler shot down the real Hess over the North Sea, then sent his carefully schooled double to England. Thomas's 1979 book The *Murder of Rudolf Hess* makes many of the same arguments. A 1989 Scotland Yard report reasonably concluded otherwise.

Costello, John. *Ten Days to Destiny* (New York: William Morrow, 1991).

Though Costello didn't succeed in overturning the traditional view of the Hess mission, his book makes a convincing case that at least some British leaders were not averse to a deal with Hitler.

Padfield, Peter. *Hess* (London: Weidenfeld & Nicolson, 1991).

Hess as the pawn of both Hider and Churchill.

Kilzer, Louis. *Churchill's Deception* (New York: Simon & Schuster, 1994).

Goes even farther than Costello in arguing that some inside the British government were behind the German invasion of Russia. Though provocative, Kilzer (like Stalin) is too eager to explain everything by conspiracies. Sometimes (though, of course, not always) the official story also turns out to be the real story.

Why Didn't the Allies Bomb Auschwitz?

OR THE FIRST FIFTEEN OR SO YEARS after World War II, the Holocaust was rarely a subject of historical debate. There seemed little to debate. That the Nazis were guilty of mass murder was beyond dispute; so was the fact that the Allies had saved what was left of European Jewry. Starting in the 1960s, a string of books challenged this straightforward interpretation. The Allies were now denounced for allowing the Holocaust to happen. The revisionists' perspective was spelled out in the titles of their books: Arthur Morse's 1968 *While Six Million Died*, Saul Friedman's 1973 *No Haven for the Oppressed*, Herbert Druks's 1977 *The Failure to Rescue*, Martin Gilbert's 1981 *Auschwitz and the Allies*, Monty Penkower's 1983 *The Jews Were Expendable*. Most influential and most damning of all was David Wyman's 1984 *The Abandonment of the Jews*.

For these scholars, American apathy was the story. "America, the land of refuge, offered little succor," Wyman wrote. "American Christians forgot about the Good Samaritan. Even American Jews lacked the unquenchable sense of urgency the crisis demanded. The Nazis were the murderers, but we were the all too passive accomplices."

The consequences of American indifference, Wyman believed, were most devastatingly evident in the decision not to bomb the gas chambers at Auschwitz. The opportunity to do so was there, starting in May 1943, when the American Fifteenth Air Force began bombing German industrial complexes near Auschwitz. Nor could the administration claim they didn't know what was going on at Auschwitz; in April, two escapees had revealed the full extent of the killings there, along with detailed descriptions of the camp's layout. Some Jewish leaders, among others, pleaded that the Allies bomb the camp, or at least the rail lines bringing Jews there.

Among those persuaded was Winston Churchill. In July, he wrote Foreign Minister Anthony Eden, "There is no doubt that this is probably the greatest and most horrible single crime ever committed in the whole history of the world." He ordered Eden to study the feasibility of bombing Auschwitz, telling him to "get anything out of the Air Force you can and invoke me if necessary." But the Royal Air Force determined it was too risky, and that only the Americans might be in a position to do it.

In America, the official response came from Assistant Secretary of War John McCloy. "Such an operation could be executed only by the diversion of considerable air support essential to the success of our forces now engaged in decisive operations elsewhere and would in any case be of such doubtful efficacy that it would not warrant the use of our resources," McCloy wrote in a letter to the World Jewish Congress. "The War Department fully appreciates the humanitarian motives which prompted the suggested operation, but for the reasons stated above, it has not been felt that it can or should be undertaken, at least at this time."

"To the American military," Wyman concluded, "Europe's Jews represented an extraneous problem and an unwanted burden."

By 1993, Wyman's perspective was so common that no one was startled when it was echoed by Bill Clinton. "For those here today representing the nations of the West, we must live forever with this knowledge—even as our fragmentary awareness of crimes grew into indisputable facts, far too little was done," the president said at the dedication of the United States Holocaust Museum in Washington. "Before the war even started, doors to liberty were shut, and even after the United States and the Allies attacked Germany, rail lines to the camps within miles of militarily significant targets were left undisturbed."

Holocaust historiography, it seemed, had come full circle. The Americans, in particular the Roosevelt administration, had been transformed from the Jews' savior to a not-so-innocent bystander, even a Nazi accomplice. Not all historians, of course, agreed with Wyman. And in the years since the publication of *The Abandonment of the Jews*, both its detractors and defenders have scoured military and political archives to figure out why Auschwitz wasn't bombed.

⚮

Wyman's first critics were military historians and aviators. Wyman may have been an expert on refugee policy and perhaps even political history, they argued, but he didn't understand the intricacies of air warfare.

True, conceded James H. Kitchens of the Air Force Historical Research Agency, American planes might have been able to reach Auschwitz in 1944, but they had neither the intelligence nor the accuracy to hit the gas chambers. "On arriving in the target area," Kitchens wrote, "attackers would have faced a dispersed, dauntingly complex objective . . . that would have had to be identified and attacked in concert with little loiter time and no release error."

"We should have no illusions that any bombing attempt would have significantly damaged the target," agreed Williamson Murray, formerly a professor at the U.S. Military Academy. "In fact, there is every prospect that such bombing, given the inaccuracies of 'precision bombing,' would have killed a significant number of the Jewish inmates."

Murray noted the irony of what he called "Monday morning quarterbacking." The raid could easily have failed and killed many Jews. Then, he argued, "we would now be debating the heartless aerial attack by the Allies on Auschwitz that had only added to the terrible burden of suffering."

Richard Levy, a retired nuclear engineer, noted that many American Jewish leaders feared bombing would do more harm than good, and therefore opposed the idea. Levy also argued that, even if Allied bombers knocked out the gas chambers, that wouldn't stop the killing. The Germans could revert to shooting Jews, or they could march them to death (as they did in November 1944, when Allied armies approached Auschwitz and the Nazis destroyed the gas chambers themselves).

For all these arguments, Wyman and his followers, many with military expertise, had answers. The Air Force had taken photos of Auschwitz, albeit accidentally, during missions to bomb nearby oil plants; these photos provided all the intelligence pilots needed. The British had undertaken an equally difficult mission in February 1944, when they bombed a prison in Amiens to set free members of the French resistance being held there. In September, the Americans had airlifted supplies to beleaguered Polish resistance fighters in Warsaw. Some of them fell into German hands, but the operation had at least boosted Polish morale. And, yes, knocking out the gas chambers wouldn't stop all the killing, but it might at least slow it down.

The technical arguments about the capabilities of various planes raged back and forth. The debate sometimes seems, as historian Henry Feingold put it, "a dialogue of the deaf," and one with little hope of reaching a consensus. Some historians were also frustrated by the very idea of this kind of counterfactual analysis, better known as "what if" history. Since the Allies had decided not to bomb Auschwitz, there was no way to know for sure what would have happened if they had.

For many historians, therefore, answers would not come from military analysis but from probing the motives of the men who made the decision not to bomb Auschwitz. They were especially eager to know what Franklin Roosevelt thought about the idea.

⊙ⱳ⊙

Most historians assumed Roosevelt never thought about the idea at all, because no one ever asked him. "It is likely," wrote Levy, "that widely expressed doubts about the efficacy of the proposed operation discouraged many individuals from pressing the issue at lower levels, or raising it with Roosevelt directly."

In this case, the buck seemed to stop not with Roosevelt but with John McCloy. McCloy himself insisted, in a 1983 interview, that he "never talked" with Roosevelt about bombing Auschwitz. Wrote McCloy's biographer, Kai Bird: "Repeated requests of various Jewish leaders and organizations were not lost in a bureaucratic maze; the request, together with the terrifying evidence, found their way to the right man, probably the only official in the War Department who possessed sufficient power and personal competency to persuade the government to make the rescue of European Jewry a military priority."

Bird did not defend his subject's decision. He believed McCloy was governed not by outright anti-Semitism, but by a fear that bombing Auschwitz might awaken nativist and isolationist sentiments. He didn't want to do anything, Bird believed, "that could suggest to the troops or the American public that the war was being fought in behalf of the Jews." So McCloy decided to do nothing.

The focus on McCloy succeeded in protecting Roosevelt, at least until 2002. Then historian Michael Beschloss offered surprising new evidence that the president himself made the final decision. Beschloss uncovered the tape of a private 1986 interview in which McCloy said Roosevelt "made it very clear" to him that he thought bombing

Auschwitz "wouldn't have done any good," and that the president wouldn't "have anything to do with the idea."

According to Beschloss, McCloy said: "The president had the idea that [bombing] would be more provocative and ineffective. And he took a very strong stand."

That Roosevelt himself made the decision would have been supremely disillusioning for many of his Jewish supporters. So universal was Jewish support for the president that one Republican congressman said Jews had three velten (worlds): "die velt" (this world), "yene velt" (the next world), and "Roosevelt." In 1985, in response to Wyman's criticism of Roosevelt, historian Lucy Dawidowicz recalled that the president was "surrounded by Jewish friends and advisers with whom he talked about the terrible plight of the Jews." Dawidowicz, whose 1975 book, *The War Against the Jews*, is a classic work on the Holocaust, was clearly not someone who would have defended a president who turned his back on its victims.

Admittedly, Roosevelt had failed to change America's immigration quotas prior to the war, thus dooming many Jewish (and non-Jewish) refugees from the Nazis. But this was more Congress's doing than the president's. Besides, this was years before Auschwitz, before anyone in America could have known the full extent of Hitler's genocidal plans.

And yet, if McCloy's 1986 interview was to be believed, it was Roosevelt who, in 1944 and with plenty of evidence of what was going on there, decided not to bomb Auschwitz. Wyman had written that what governed all of Roosevelt's decisions pertaining to the Jews was "political expediency." He had the Jewish vote anyway, so why risk an anti-Jewish backlash? "An active rescue policy offered little political advantage," Wyman explained. "A pro-Jewish stance, however, could lose votes."

Perhaps. Roosevelt was, undeniably, a brilliant politician.

But it was surely possible that Roosevelt also genuinely believed, as he said to McCloy, that the bombing "wouldn't have done any good." The ongoing debate between Wyman's followers and detractors makes clear that military experts, in good faith, could disagree about the merits of bombing Auschwitz. If that's true today, it was all the more so in 1944, when Roosevelt and his generals were fully absorbed by the war effort. Though they undeniably had evidence of the Holocaust, they may not have fully comprehended it, at least as historians do today. Their attention was focused on the Normandy invasion, not a Polish concentration camp. Their objective was to defeat the Nazis, not save the Jews. Anything that distracted them from that objective, including bombing Auschwitz, was likely to get short shrift. To the extent that Allied generals thought about the Jews at all, they probably concluded that the best way to save them was to win the war as quickly as possible.

Many historians, including the Pulitzer Prize–winning Arthur Schlesinger Jr., found that logic compelling. "The best use of Allied bombing—and the best way to save the people in the death camps—was to bring the war to its quickest end," wrote Schlesinger. "FDR, more than any other person, deserves the credit for mobilizing the forces that destroyed Nazi barbarism."

In the end, there were some survivors, and they survived because the Nazis were defeated. And there probably wasn't too much more that could have been done, at least in

1944, by which time millions had already died. But, as World War II historian Gerhard Weinberg put it, "the shadow of doubt that enough was not done will always remain."

For Weinberg, bombing Auschwitz was worth trying, even though it was unlikely to succeed. "Such an action by the Western Allies would have made something of an important assertion of policy, would have encouraged desperate victims in their last days and hours, might have inspired a few additional persons to provide aid and comfort to the persecuted, and might even have enabled a tiny number to escape the fate planned for them by the Germans," he wrote.

British historian Martin Gilbert reached a similar conclusion. Auschwitz would have been a very difficult target, he conceded. But then he asked: "Difficult to hit for what end? For success against crematoria and railway lines? Or for morale and perhaps even morality? The latter two were often at stake during World War II as well."

ᏜᏍᏍᎧ

What the United States could or should have done in 1944 is more than an academic question. It has resurfaced every time Americans have considered military intervention to stop genocide, from Bosnia to Rwanda. Yet it's clear that the nation most entwined in the debate is Israel. The string of books condemning America's abandonment of the Jews started in the late sixties and continued through the mid-eighties, a period that encompassed both the Six-Day War and the Yom Kippur War and during which many Jews feared America might abandon Israel.

For many Jews, the message of these books was, as historian Peter Novick put it, that America had "a compelling obligation to expiate past sins through unswerving support of Israel." Wyman's villains were not just Roosevelt and his administration, but also secular Jewish leaders who, unwilling to criticize the president, didn't put enough pressure on him to act. Wyman's heroes were the religiously orthodox and politically conservative Jews who pushed the hardest for bombing Auschwitz. For religiously orthodox and politically conservative Jews, here was proof that you couldn't count on liberals and Democrats like Roosevelt; here, too, was a clear justification for Israel's increasing militarism.

Ironically, Wyman's arguments appealed to many leftist Jews as well. For them, it demonstrated the dangers of trusting those in power, even liberals like Roosevelt. There was, as Novick put it, "something for everybody in the Holocaust."

None of this is to denigrate the scholarship of Wyman or others who wrote about the abandonment of the Jews. It was not Wyman, but many of his readers, who drew the parallels between Auschwitz and Israel. Nor is there anything wrong with drawing lessons from history, especially if doing so prevents genocide. What's dangerous is using history to make a political point, 8without honestly and openly trying to understand that history. This is especially true of the Holocaust, which is too often and too carelessly invoked for contemporary political purposes.

"Whether it is done by the right or the left," wrote historian Deborah Lipstadt, this "is not only ahistorical, but it will ultimately diminish the memory of those whose lives might have been saved by the bombing of Auschwitz."

To Investigate Further

Morse, Arthur. *While Six Million Died.* New York: Random House, 1968.
An angry indictment of American apathy and bureaucratic inertia.

Feingold, Henry. *The Politics of Rescue.* New Brunswick, NJ: Rutgers University Press, 1970.
Feingold's approach is more scholarly and dispassionate than Morse's, but his conclusions are similar.

Dawidowicz, Lucy. *The War Against the Jews.* New York: Holt, Rinehart and Winston, 1975.
A superb synthesis of Holocaust history.

Gilbert, Martin. *Auschwitz and the Allies.* New York: Holt, Rinehart and Winston, 1981.
What Wyman did for the American response to the Holocaust, Gilbert did for the British.

Wyman, David. *The Abandonment of the Jews.* New York: Pantheon, 1984.
Even those who disagreed with Wyman's conclusions admired his scholarship and style.

Wyman, David, ed. *America and the Holocaust.* New York: Garland, 1990.
Volume 12 of this thirteen-volume documentary history covers the decision not to bomb Auschwitz, including the escapees' report.

Bird, Kai. *The Chairman.* New York: Simon & Schuster, 1992.
A biography of McCloy, the man whose name was synonymous with "the establishment."

Dawidowicz, Lucy. *What Is the Use of Jewish History?* New York: Schocken, 1992.
Includes her 1985 essay, "Could America Have Rescued Europe's Jews?" in which she criticizes America's refugee policy but answers the question with a resounding no.

Newton, Verne, ed. *FDR and the Holocaust.* New York: St. Martin's, 1996.
A useful collection of essays, though the Neufeld-Berenbaum collection is more comprehensive.

Rubinstein, William D. *The Myth of Rescue.* London: Routledge, 1997.
Rubinstein's opposition to Wyman leads him to the other extreme. "No Jew," he writes, "who perished during the Nazi Holocaust could have been saved by any action which the Allies could have taken."

Novick, Peter. *The Holocaust in American Life.* Boston: Houghton Mifflin, 1999.
A provocative analysis of the "uses" of the Holocaust.

Neufeld, Michael, and Michael Berenbaum, eds. *The Bombing of Auschwitz.* New York: St. Martin's, 2000.
A balanced collection of essays by leading participants in the debate, including Richard Breitman, Stuart Erdheim, Henry Feingold, Martin Gilbert, James Kitchens, Walter Laqueur, Richard Levy, Williamson Murray, Deborah Lipstadt, and Gerhard Weinberg.

Beschloss, Michael. *The Conquerors.* New York: Simon & Schuster, 2002.
How Roosevelt and Truman planned the postwar world.

Why Did Truman Drop the Bomb?

I N HIS 1955 MEMOIRS, HARRY TRUMAN devoted only a few pages to his decision to drop an atom bomb on the city of Hiroshima.

"I regarded the bomb as a military weapon and never had any doubt that it should be used," wrote Truman. "The top military advisers to the President recommended its use, and when I talked to Churchill he unhesitatingly told me that he favored the use of the atom bomb if it might aid to end the war."

To end the war: this was Truman's clear and succinct rationale for using the bomb. Its devastating strength would convince the Japanese that an unconditional surrender was their only option, thus saving the lives of the American soldiers who would otherwise have to force that surrender on Japan's home ground. General Marshall had told him that an invasion might cost half a million American lives, Truman added.

Truman's secretary of war, Henry Stimson, wrote a somewhat lengthier defense of the decision to drop the bomb. Published in the February 1947 issue of *Harper's* magazine, Stimson's article recounted his activities as the chief adviser on atomic policy to both Franklin Roosevelt and Truman. In April 1945, as scientists prepared the bomb's final testing, Truman appointed Stimson head of a committee to consider the scientific, political, and military aspects of the bomb. In June, the committee recommended using the bomb as soon as possible. The committee reported that scientists could envision no technical demonstration, such as dropping a bomb over a deserted island, that would convince the Japanese of its power.

On July 26, after meeting with Churchill and Stalin at Potsdam, a suburb of Berlin, Truman issued an ultimatum to the Japanese. This came to be known as the Potsdam Proclamation. Though it didn't mention the atom bomb specifically, the proclamation warned Japan that it must surrender or face "prompt and utter destruction." Two days later, the Japanese premier responded that the ultimatum was "unworthy of public notice." That left Truman with no choice but to show he'd meant what he'd said. "For such a purpose," Stimson wrote, "the atomic bomb was an eminently suitable weapon."

From that point on, events unfolded exactly according to plan: on August 6 the first atom bomb fell on Hiroshima; on August 9 the second fell on Nagasaki; on August 14 the Japanese surrendered. Truman's and Stimson's accounts of the decision-making process seemed unimpeachable; not only had they explained clearly why they'd used the bomb, but history had proved their analysis to be correct.

Yet in the sixty-plus years since Hiroshima, revisionist historians have argued that Truman's decision to use the bomb was not nearly so straightforward as his memoirs or Stimson's article indicated. Revisionists have claimed that nowhere near 500,000 Americans would have died in an invasion; that Japan was at the brink of surrender even before the bomb was dropped; that Truman knew all of this and used the bomb anyway. His motive, according to some revisionists, was not to demonstrate American power to its Japanese enemies, but to its Russian allies. By these accounts the bomb was not the final blast of World War II, but the first blast of the Cold War.

⟅⟆

The first to question the official explanation were hardly leftists or pacifists. Among them was Admiral William Leahy, who presided over the U.S. Joint Chiefs of Staff and was chief of staff to the commander in chief of the army and navy, serving Roosevelt in that capacity from 1942 to 1945 and Truman from 1945 to 1949. A few years after the bombs were dropped, Leahy stated: "It is my opinion that the use of this barbarous weapon at Hiroshima and Nagasaki was of no material assistance in our war against Japan. The Japanese were already defeated and ready to surrender."

Dwight Eisenhower, too, went public with his doubts. He recalled telling Stimson, before the bomb was used, "of my belief that Japan was already defeated and that dropping the bomb was completely unnecessary."

And as early as 1945, the U.S. Strategic Bombing Survey, an extensive and official study established by Stimson, published its findings that conventional bombing would have forced a Japanese surrender by the end of the year.

A variety of scholars have challenged Truman's contention that 500,000 Americans would have died in an invasion of Japan. They've pointed to U.S. military planning documents indicating that an initial landing on the island of Kyushu would have resulted in between 20,000 and 26,000 dead; the highest estimate found in these documents (based on a full-scale invasion of all Japan) was 46,000. Moreover, Truman himself used a variety of figures, with the 500,000 being only the latest and highest.

The debates over these numbers, however, only obscured the revisionists' main point: if the Japanese were at the brink of surrender, there need never have been an invasion— or an atom bombing.

In presenting their evidence, the revisionists turned to an unlikely source: a memo written by the leading defender of the decision to drop the bomb, Stimson himself. For though the secretary of war had undeniably recommended that the bomb be dropped, his proposed draft of the ultimatum to be issued to the Japanese differed in one significant point from the final Potsdam Proclamation.

In a July 2 memo to the president, reprinted right in his *Harper's* defense of the bomb, Stimson called for the ultimatum and then added: "I personally think that if in saying this we should add that we do not exclude a constitutional monarchy under her present dynasty, it would substantially add to the chances of acceptance." In other words, if the ultimatum held out the hope that the Japanese could keep their emperor, they might be more willing to surrender.

Stimson urged Truman to clarify the surrender terms to hold out the possibility of some continuing role for the emperor. So did others, including Acting Secretary of State Grew on May 28, Admiral Leahy on June 18, the State Department in a formal recommendation on June 30, Churchill on July 18, and the Joint Chiefs of Staff, also on July 18. Many pointed to intercepted Japanese documents and peace feelers the Japanese had sent out to neutral countries as evidence that Japan's leaders knew they were nearing defeat and sought only to assure that the emperor would be protected. Of the major administration figures consulting with the president on the bomb, only Secretary of State James Byrnes consistently and adamantly opposed any clarification of the surrender terms.

In the actual Potsdam Proclamation, Byrnes got his way: there was no mention of the emperor. Why did Truman go along with Byrnes—against the advice of so many of his other advisers? And why did the ultimatum not mention specifically that a new and phenomenally powerful weapon would be unleashed on Japan's cities? Wouldn't this, too, have made Japan's surrender more likely?

To some revisionists, the answer to these questions was clear: dropping the bomb was a show of force aimed not at Japan but at Russia. As further support for this thesis, revisionists noted the difference between Truman's behavior toward the Russians before and at Potsdam. Prior to the Potsdam meeting between Truman, Churchill, and Stalin, American policy had been aimed at getting Russia to go to war with Japan. On numerous occasions Truman stated that this was the primary reason he wanted to meet Stalin at Potsdam. In this, he succeeded: Stalin agreed that by the middle of August he'd declare war on Japan. In a letter home to his wife, Truman gloated: "I've gotten what I came for—Stalin goes to war . . . I'll say that we'll end the war a year sooner now, and think of the kids who won't be killed!"

But on July 16, once Truman received word that the atom bomb had been successfully tested in the New Mexico desert, American strategy suddenly changed. No longer did the president see any need for Russian help against the Japanese; no longer, in fact, did he see Russia as a wartime ally. In his mind, the communists were now a postwar rival to be kept out of Japan and anywhere else. On July 17, Byrnes rejected Stimson's advice about including assurances about the emperor in the Potsdam Proclamation. The same day, the newly aggressive Truman faced Stalin across the Potsdam conference table and dismissed the latter's demand for bases in Turkey and the Mediterranean.

As Churchill put it, upon being told of the successful test of the bomb: "Now I know what happened to Truman yesterday. When he got to the meeting after having read this report he was a changed man. He told the Russians just where they got on and off and generally bossed the whole meeting."

∞

The revisionist claims did not go unchallenged. Defenders of the orthodox explanation of the decision countered by arguing that Japan's peace feelers and other evidence

BC 260283
CONFERENCE OF BIG THREE POWERS AT POTSDAM,
NEAR BERLIN, GERMANY, 7 JULY THRU 2 AUGUST
1945, TO DEMAND THE SURRENDER OF JAPAN.
Generalissimo Josef Stalin, facing camera,
shakes hands with Secretary of State James
F. Byrnes near the conference table just
before the opening of the third day's
session. 7/19/45

In which I tell Stalin we expect to drop the most powerful explosive ever made on the Japanese. He smiled and said he appreciated my telling him— but he did not know what I was talking about—the Atomic Bomb!

HST

Truman's note reveals he was thinking about the bomb's impact on Russia as well as Japan. *(Corbis)*

that they might consider surrendering were a far cry from an actual surrender, and that the Japanese cabinet was at best divided on the subject. Others pointed out that even if the 500,000 figure was inflated, the cost of an invasion of Japan's home islands would still be considerable. At Okinawa, the equivalent of just three Japanese divisions had held out for one hundred days against a much larger U.S. ground force that was supported by heavy naval and air bombardment. The Okinawa campaign had left 12,520 Americans dead and another 36,631 injured and, along with kamikaze suicide raids, had left American soldiers and policy makers alike with a very vivid image of the ferocity of Japanese resistance. Under these circumstances, any American president would have to be concerned about the casualties an invasion would bring.

As for the decision not to mention the emperor in the Potsdam Proclamation, Truman may have felt bound by American public opinion. Since Pearl Harbor, Americans had sought revenge; to settle for anything less than unconditional surrender would have seemed a failure of nerve or will. Ironically, dropping the bomb may very well have allowed Truman to offer the surrender terms he couldn't beforehand. With America's mastery so completely established, he could let the emperor stay on. Hirohito remained the titular head of the Japanese nation until his death in 1989.

The debate over the bomb came to a head in 1994 when the Smithsonian Institution in Washington, D.C., prepared an exhibit commemorating the fiftieth anniversary of the Hiroshima bombing. The projected exhibition was fairly evenhanded: it stated that the war *might* have ended without the bombings if the Potsdam Proclamation had guaranteed the emperor's position, but this was by no means a strong revisionist position. Still, it was too strong for organizations like the American Legion, whose protests led the Smithsonian to remove any text from the exhibit. Instead, the *Enola Gay*, the plane that dropped the bomb, was displayed without any explanation or context.

That veterans' organizations were so offended by the exhibit is ironic, given that top military leaders such as Marshall, Eisenhower, and Leahy were among the earliest to argue against the bomb's necessity. Indeed, the veterans' organizations didn't seem to realize that their insistence that the bomb had won the war shifted the credit for that victory away from their own heroic efforts. But all this was lost in a debate that had become so politicized that the traditionalists could only see the revisionists as unpatriotic, and the revisionists could only see the traditionalists as callous and immoral.

What extremists on both sides have too often lost sight of is that the traditionalist and revisionist positions aren't irreconcilable. The traditionalists' claim that the bomb was dropped solely to save American lives was untrue—but that doesn't mean that saving lives wasn't a major concern. Conversely, though revisionists have demonstrated Truman's decision was made with an eye on Russia as well as Japan, that certainly doesn't mean he dropped the bomb solely to position America for the Cold War.

Truman did not drop the bomb for any single reason, traditionalist or revisionist. Many factors pushed him toward his decision—a desire to avenge Pearl Harbor and an ignorance of the bomb's full dangers, to name two more. For an inexperienced and as yet unelected president, the sheer momentum of a $2-billion project must also have been difficult to resist. "He was like a little boy on a toboggan," recalled Major General Leslie Groves, who headed up the project to build the bomb.

Might he have changed course? Perhaps. There were certainly opportunities. But the forces pushing that toboggan downward were very powerful indeed.

To Investigate Further

Stimson, Henry. "The Decision to Use the Atomic Bomb." *Harper's,* February 1947.
    Written by Truman's secretary of war, this was one of the earliest and most influential of the official explanations.

Truman, Harry. *Memoirs.* New York: Doubleday, 1955.
    Volume 1 includes Truman's own account of his decision.

Sherwin, Martin. *A World Destroyed.* New York: Knopf, 1975.
    An account of the interaction between scientists and policy makers and of the origins of the arms race prior to the end of World War II.

Wyden, Peter. *Day One.* New York: Simon & Schuster, 1984.
> An excellent general history of the bomb, before and after Hiroshima.

McCullough, David. *Truman.* New York: Simon & Schuster, 1992.
> A masterful biography.

Allen, Thomas B., and Norman Polmar. *Code-Name Downfall.* New York: Simon & Schuster, 1995.
> A history of America's secret plans to invade Japan, and the latest defense of the traditional position.

Alperovitz, Gar. *The Decision to Use the Atomic Bomb.* New York: Knopf, 1995.
> A comprehensive statement of the revisionist position, this supercedes Alperovitz's influential but more limited 1965 book, *Atomic Diplomacy.*

Takaki, Ronald. *Hiroshima.* Boston: Little, Brown, 1995.
> Takaki adds racism to the revisionist case, arguing that America's image of Japanese as subhuman made it easier to drop the bomb.

Nobile, Philip, ed. *Judgment at the Smithsonian.* New York: Marlowe and Company, 1995.
> Includes the script of the aborted fiftieth anniversary exhibit.

Hogan, Michael, ed. *Hiroshima in History and Memory.* New York: Cambridge University Press, 1996.
> Essays by leading scholars, including Barton Bernstein, Herbert, Bix, John Dower, Paul Boyer, and Seitsu Tachibana on how the decision was made, and how it was resonated in American and Japanese minds.

Walter, Samuel J. *Prompt and Utter Destruction.* Chapel Hill: University of North Carolina Press, 2004.
> A balanced and concise synthesis that concludes the bomb hastened the end of the war and saved the lives of American troops, though it didn't hasten as much or save as many as traditionalists claim.

PART 8

PROMISES AND PARADOXES, 1945–

Were the Rosenbergs Guilty?

L IKE SACCO AND VANZETTI a generation before, Julius and Ethel Rosenberg became a symbol to those on the left of how the American government was ruled by those on the right. To the left, the conviction and execution of the Rosenbergs for "stealing the secret of the atomic bomb" revealed a society caught in the thrall of hysterical McCarthyism. So, when the Rosenbergs' sons sued the government under the Freedom of Information Act, and in 1980 obtained the FBI files on the case, those on the left assumed the couple would be finally and fully vindicated. What the files revealed, however, was not nearly so clear-cut.

⚭

When the Soviet Union successfully tested its atom bomb in August 1949, the United States immediately set out to find those responsible for stealing the classified information. The search led to the British atomic scientist Klaus Fuchs, who was arrested and who confessed that he had given information to the Soviets while working on the bomb at Los Alamos in 1945. Fuchs led the FBI to his American courier, Harry Gold, who was also arrested and also confessed. Gold, in turn, led agents to David Greenglass, an army corporal who had worked in the laboratory at Los Alamos.

It was Greenglass who fingered Julius Rosenberg, his own brother-in-law. According to Greenglass, Rosenberg had dropped out of the Communist Party in 1943 in order to take on a role as a Soviet spy. When Greenglass was sent to Los Alamos, Rosenberg arranged for him to pass on atomic information to Harry Gold. In fact, according to Greenglass, Rosenberg headed up a spy ring whose activities extended well beyond the theft of the atomic information.

At the 1951 trial of the Rosenbergs, the star witnesses were Gold and Greenglass. Gold testified that during the first weekend of June 1945, he traveled to New Mexico, where he met with Greenglass and gave him $500 in exchange for information on the atomic bomb. Greenglass testified that he was following instructions from his brother-in-law. The defense counsel, Emanuel Bloch, focused his efforts on discrediting Greenglass: he charged him with accusing the Rosenbergs to win leniency for his own crimes and to settle some old family grudges. Bloch did not cross-examine Gold at all since, as he explained in his summation to the jury, Gold had not claimed any direct contact with the Rosenbergs.

Later defenders of the Rosenbergs, primarily Walter and Miriam Schneir in their 1965 history of the case, were convinced that Bloch's failure to question Gold's story was a serious error. The Schneirs argued that, apart from the confessions of Gold and Greenglass, the government's sole proof that Harry Gold even met David Greenglass, when the latter supposedly passed on information to the former, was a registration card from the Albuquerque Hilton with Gold's name on it. The card had been placed in evidence during the trial. Yet, when the Schneirs examined it years later, they were shocked to find that the dates on the front and back of the card did not match. Furthermore, when the Schneirs showed the card to a handwriting expert, she expressed "some very real doubts" about whether the initials on the card were actually written by the clerk on duty at the Hilton. The Schneirs could come up with only one explanation for the discrepancies in the date and the handwriting: the card had been forged by the FBI to substantiate a Gold-Greenglass meeting that never actually took place.

Those historians who believed in the Rosenbergs' guilt were not convinced. Handwriting analysis was a notoriously imprecise science. Also, they argued, a simple hotel error could account for the different dates on the back and front of the card as easily as a botched forgery. After all, if the FBI was going to forge a registration card, it would probably have managed to forge one without any error.

So, it seemed, the evidence submitted at the trial could not change anyone's mind. Those who believed in the Rosenbergs' guilt continued to maintain that David Greenglass was telling the truth; it was inconceivable to them that Greenglass would send his own sister and brother-in-law to the gas chamber—not to mention ending up with a 15-year prison term himself—unless he and the Rosenbergs were spies. For those who believed in the couple's innocence, the Rosenbergs were scapegoats for America's anger over the loss of its nuclear monopoly. Greenglass had accused them out of fear or vindictiveness or naivete, and the government was persecuting them because they'd been members of the Communist Party.

So matters stood until Robert and Michael Meeropol, the Rosenbergs' two sons (they'd taken on their adoptive parents' name after their parents' execution), sued the government for the release of the FBI files on the case. When they won that case, some 250,000 pages of FBI and other government documents pertaining to their parents' case were suddenly open to the public.

ᙅᙏᙎ

Supporters of the Rosenbergs celebrated. Among those who assumed the new documents would vindicate the Rosenbergs were historians Richard Radosh and Joyce Milton, both of whom believed the couple had been framed. Their study of the new evidence, released in a 1983 book, convinced them otherwise.

One startling revelation in the documents was that the government had not relied exclusively on Greenglass for reports of the Rosenbergs' spying activities. Another informer, Jerome Tartakow, had supplied a great many details about the Rosenbergs, though he never testified in court. Tartakow, who was serving a two-year sentence for interstate auto theft, was Rosenberg's closest companion in jail; like Rosenberg, he was a former communist and the two spent a great deal of time playing chess together. In return for a reduction of his sentence, Tartakow regaled the FBI with stories of Rosenberg's spy rings. Tartakow reported that Rosenberg had admitted to him that "he played the game and lost." He also tipped off the FBI about a photographer who had taken some passport photos of the Rosenbergs soon after Greenglass's arrest, and whose testimony at the trial was particularly damning. Defenders of the Rosenbergs were quick to assail Tartakow's character (and even his FBI contacts were suspicious about some of his reports). Still, it was no longer just Greenglass's word on which the Rosenbergs' guilt depended.

The newly opened FBI files revealed other evidence against the Rosenbergs as well, including interviews with more reliable informants who claimed to have heard, albeit indirectly, of the Rosenbergs' spy ring. And the files traced the very suspicious disappearances of three of Julius Rosenberg's closest friends soon after his arrest. One, Morton Sobell, was caught in Mexico and tried and convicted (though not executed) with the Rosenbergs. Two others, Joel Barr and Al Sarant, later turned up in the Soviet Union.

Taken together, this new evidence, though circumstantial, convinced Radosh and Milton that the Rosenbergs were indeed spies. The Schneirs continued to defend the Rosenbergs; they issued a revised edition of their book in which they argued that additional evidence from FBI files was meaningless since the FBI was perfectly capable of manufacturing or destroying evidence. But most mainstream historians sided with Radosh and Milton and now accepted the guilty verdict. In 1995, the Rosenbergs' remaining defenders received another blow, when the army released Russian cables it had intercepted and decoded in 1943. Among the Russian agents referred to was Julius Rosenberg.

The government did not emerge from the new investigations with clean hands, either. For one thing, though the new evidence against Julius Rosenberg was damning, the evidence against Ethel Rosenberg was much flimsier. David Greenglass, notably, accused only his brother-in-law and never his sister. Worse, the FBI files made clear that the only reason Ethel Rosenberg was arrested was to put pressure on her husband to confess and name names. When this strategy failed, the government upped the ante, hoping that the threat of executing Ethel would break Julius. Perhaps the most shocking document in the files revealed that FBI agents standing by at Julius Rosenberg's execution had ready a number of questions, should he choose to talk at the last moment. Among the questions was: "Was your wife cognizant of your activities?" Even as it executed her, it was clear the government remained uncertain of her guilt.

This is not to say that Ethel Rosenberg was innocent. The Rosenbergs were a very close couple, and Ethel almost certainly was aware of what her husband was up to. But there was no evidence she participated in his spying, and the government's cynical behavior in executing a wife in order to pressure a husband can hardly be considered a triumph of justice.

Furthermore, the FBI files made clear that even if the Rosenbergs were guilty of spying, the death penalty was a gross injustice. The information they were convicted of passing on to the Russians simply wasn't that important. A few months after describing the case as "the crime of the century," J. Edgar Hoover privately acknowledged to FBI agents that Soviet scientists had undoubtedly developed their bomb independent of any information they'd received through espionage. And a year after the Rosenbergs' execution, General Leslie Groves, the military chief of the Manhattan Project, told a closed meeting of the Atomic Energy Commission that "the data that went out in the case of the Rosenbergs was of minor value."

What David Greenglass passed on to Harry Gold—a crude drawing of part of the plutonium-fired implosion device—could hardly have condensed the results of the Manhattan Project in any technologically meaningful way. At most, the sketch confirmed a small part of what the Russians had already learned from Klaus Fuchs's far more sophisticated information (Fuchs, after all, was an atomic physicist) and from their own research. David Greenglass was a spy and so was Julius Rosenberg, but both were small-time amateurs. Rosenberg couldn't even hold a job, let alone run a major spy ring. To accuse him of having "stolen the secret of the atomic bomb" was either a cynical move on the part of the government, playing to the anticommunist hysteria of the period, or a sign that the government was itself caught in the grips of that hysteria.

The irony of the Rosenberg case, then, is this: the accusers and defenders of the Rosenbergs were both right. The Rosenbergs were spies, and they were also scapegoats. The Rosenbergs were not innocent, but they certainly did not deserve to die.

To Investigate Further

Schneir, Walter, and Miriam Schneir. *Invitation to an Inquest.* New York: Doubleday, 1965. Revised edition Pantheon, 1983.

The case for the Rosenbergs' innocence.

Nizer, Louis. *The Implosion Conspiracy.* New York: Doubleday, 1973.

A day-by-day account of the trial, somewhat biased in favor of the prosecution.

Meeropol, Robert, and Michael Meeropol. *We Are Your Sons.* Boston: Houghton Mifflin, 1975.

The Rosenbergs' sons own stories, including very moving letters from and between their parents, and a much less compelling argument for their innocence. In 2004, having digested the new evidence, Robert Meeropol conceded that "it's quite possible that a grave injustice was done to them without them being totally innocent."

Milton, Joyce, and Ronald Radosh, *The Rosenberg File.* Orlando: Holt, Rinehart and Winston, 1983.

The definitive case for the Rosenbergs' guilt.

Philipson, Ilene. *Ethel Rosenberg.* New York: Franklin Watts, 1988.

Although a biography and not an investigation of the case, this portrait of the Rosenbergs as struggling working-class parents makes it difficult to believe they could have managed to do much more than just get by.

Sharlitt, Joseph. *Fatal Error.* New York: Scribner's, 1989.

Concludes that the Rosenbergs were spies but that they were tried and executed unfairly.

Carmichael, Virginia. *Framing History.* Minneapolis: University of Minnesota Press, 1993.

How the Rosenberg case has been portrayed in the arts; interesting more as a work of criticism than history.

Weiner, Tim. "U.S. Tells How It Cracked Code of A-Bomb Spy Ring." **New York Times**, July 12, 1995.

Among the code names the Soviets gave Julius Rosenberg was "Liberal."

What Has
J. D. Salinger Written?

W HEN A WRITER DOESN'T SHOW HIS FACE," the famously reclusive writer Don DeLillo wrote, "he becomes a local symptom of God's famous reluctance to appear."

Not quite. But to fans of J. D. Salinger, the author's absence has sometimes seemed almost as distressing and perplexing as God's. This was the man, after all, who seemed to have all the answers. More than fifty years after its publication, *The Catcher in the Rye* continues to be a best-seller, as each new generation of teenagers discovers that Holden Caulfield speaks for them. Since 1953, when Salinger moved to the remote town of Cornish, New Hampshire, reporters and readers have sought out his fortress, hoping for a few words or at least a glimpse of the author. In the movie *Field of Dreams,* the hero seeks out a reclusive author, figuring he's the only one who can make sense of things. In the book on which the movie is based, *Shoeless Joe,* the connection is explicit: the character of the guru-author is named J. D. Salinger.

In real life, it's unlikely Salinger's visitor would have gotten through the door. Salinger has completely withdrawn from the public. Unlike DeLillo or Thomas Pynchon, who have simply declined to publicize their work, Salinger has stopped publishing it.

It did not happen all of a sudden. At first, Salinger refused to deal with magazines whose editors had in one way or another offended him. He mocked the author profiles magazines ran with stories, saying that any writer who liked them was "likely to have his picture taken wearing an open-collared shirt . . . looking three-quarter-profile and tragic." Gradually, he ruled out publishing in any magazine other than the *New Yorker,* which ran no notes on contributors and was also known for its extremely sensitive editing.

There were still books, at least for a while, though they consisted of previously published stories about the fictional Glass family. Next Salinger demanded the paperbacks be published between two plain covers with no promotional copy, biographical information, or photo of the author. In 1965, there was a final story in the *New Yorker,* "Hapworth 16, 1924." And then there was nothing.

Salinger has continued to write, or so he said in the author's note to his last book, *Raise High the Roof Beam, Carpenters, and Seymour—An Introduction,* published in 1963. "There is only my word for it," he wrote, "but I have several new Glass stories coming along—waxing, dilating—each in its own way, but I suspect the less said about them, in mixed company, the better."

After the first two printings of *The Catcher in the Rye*, Salinger demanded that his picture be removed from the jacket, and it hasn't appeared there since. This was taken by Lotte Jacobi in 1953. *(Getty Images)*

To the few people who have seen him since, he has also said he was still writing. In 1960, a *Newsweek* photographer found Salinger walking in Cornish. Salinger, perhaps grateful that the photographer asked his permission to shoot, explained why he couldn't allow it.

"My method of work is such that any interruption throws me off," Salinger said. "I can't have my picture taken or have an interview until I've completed what I've set out to do."

In another rare and very brief interview, Salinger spoke to a *New York Times* reporter in 1974. He did so only to stress that a collection of his stories then circulating was unauthorized, but the reporter couldn't resist the opportunity to ask why he wasn't publishing.

"Publishing is a terrible invasion of my privacy," Salinger answered. "I like to write. I live to write. But I write just for myself and my own pleasure."

What he was writing, whether about the Glasses or anything else, he would not say. He showed it to no one. This left readers to wonder, as critic John Wenke wrote, whether he was "composing masterpiece after masterpiece but refusing to publish" or "simply growing vegetables" in New Hampshire.

⁓

Critics tended to look for clues in Salinger's published works. Wenke looked at Salinger's 1950 story, "For Esme—With Love and Squalor," and found hints of the author's early frustration with writing. One character, for example, wrote "fairly regularly, from a paradise of triple exclamation points and inaccurate observations." Silence was clearly better than this.

Others noted that Salinger's work increasingly showed the influence of Eastern religions. The epigraph to his 1953 story collection was the Zen koan, "What is the sound of one hand clapping?" Perhaps, some speculated, Salinger had embraced silence as part of a Zen-like renunciation of the material world. Truman Capote said he'd heard "on very good authority" that Salinger had written five or six novels, and that the *New Yorker* had turned them down because "all of them are very strange and all about Zen Buddhism." The magazine denied this.

One of the most creative theories, from John Calvin Batchelor in 1976, was that Salinger was publishing new work under the pseudonym Thomas Pynchon. This solved two mysteries in one, since Pynchon was almost as much of a recluse as Salinger. Pynchon eventually appeared to deny the story, and Batchelor had to concede he was wrong.

New York Times reviewer Michiko Kakutani noted the solipsism of the Glass family in Salinger's later works. She blamed their solipsism on Salinger's own. "This falling off in his work," she wrote, "perhaps, is a palpable consequence of Mr. Salinger's own Glass-like withdrawal: withdrawal feeding self-absorption and self-absorption feeding tetchy disdain."

Among the most sophisticated critics to take on Salinger's silence was the British poet and biographer Ian Hamilton. Hamilton noted that Salinger was living out Holden Caulfield's dream. In *The Catcher in the Rye*, Holden said he would "drive up to Massachusetts and Vermont, and around there" and "build me a little cabin." Hamilton also made a case that Seymour Glass, one of the main characters in a number of Salinger stories, was the author's alter ego. In the 1948 story "A Perfect Day for Bananafish," Glass—unable to survive in an imperfect world—commits suicide.

"Salinger doesn't commit suicide," Hamilton wrote, "but he does the next best thing: He disappears, he stops living in the world, he makes himself semiposthumous."

It was not, however, Hamilton's literary analysis that generated the brunt of the attention surrounding his biography, *J. D. Salinger: A Writing Life.* In the course of his research, Hamilton found stashes of Salinger's unpublished letters, which he used to buttress his conclusions. Salinger was determined not to allow any of the letters, or even excerpts, to be published. In 1986, just before Random House was to release the book, he succeeded in getting a restraining order. Salinger's right not to publish—and Hamilton's right to publish—was now in the hands of the courts.

Hamilton remained confident. Partly this was because he was willing, albeit reluctantly, to pare down the excerpts from the letters to just about two hundred words. This, he assumed, would help his case. But most of Hamilton's confidence came from the realization that, if Salinger wanted to pursue the case, he would have to face the questions of Random House's lawyers. These questions would be at least as probing as any reporter's.

"I was convinced he wouldn't do it," Hamilton said. "But he did."

⟋⟍⟋

In October 1986, Salinger was interviewed—or, more accurately, deposed—by Random House's lawyer, Robert Callagy. Some of Callagy's questions veered off from the letters to his other writings.

Q: When was the last time you wrote any work of fiction for publication?
A: I'm not sure exactly.
Q: At any time during the past twenty years, have you written a work of fiction for publication?
A: That has been published, you mean?
Q: That has been published.
A: No.

That much everyone already knew. Then Callagy asked whether, during the past twenty years, Salinger had written any fiction that had not been published. Salinger said he had.

Q: Could you describe for me what works of fiction you have written which have not been published?
A: It would be very difficult to do . . .
Q: Have you written any full-length works of fiction during the past twenty years which have not been published?

A: Could you frame that a different way? What do you mean by a full-length work? You mean ready for publication?

Q: As opposed to a short story or a fictional piece or a magazine submission.

A: It's very difficult to answer. I don't write that way. I just start writing fiction and see what happens to it.

Q: Maybe an easier way to approach this is, would you tell me what your literary efforts have been in the field of fiction within the last twenty years?

A: Could I tell you or would I tell you? . . . Just a work of fiction. That's all. That's the only description I can really give it. . . . It's almost impossible to define. I work with characters, and as they develop, I just go from there.

This was as close as Salinger would come to describing his unpublished fiction.

As for the unpublished letters, the first round went to Random House, but an appeals court found for Salinger. As a result, Hamilton's *J. D. Salinger: A Writing Life* was never published, though he rewrote it (minus the letters and much of the analysis of them) as *In Search of J. D. Salinger.* The book, which ended up not so much a biography as the story of the biographer's quest, was finally published in 1988.

Salinger's next biographer was Paul Alexander. Alexander's conclusions were much harsher than Hamilton's. Alexander did not discover any significant new sources, but he compiled a great deal of anti-Salinger talk. In essence, he revived Capote's claim that the author hadn't published anything because he hadn't written anything worth publishing.

Alexander described the author's note in *Raise High* as "insincere," saying it "sounds as if Salinger were trying to overcompensate for the fact that he knew he had no new publishable material in development but didn't want his readers to know it." He had withdrawn from the world, Alexander suggested, to hide the fact that he was finished as a writer.

The withdrawal was even, to some extent, a publicity stunt. "By cutting himself off from the public, by cutting himself off the way he had done, he made sure the public would remain fascinated with him," Alexander wrote. "By refusing to publish any new work, by letting the public know he had new work he was not publishing, he ensured a continued fascination in the four books that were in print. . . . Salinger became the Greta Garbo of literature, and then periodically, when it may have seemed he was about to be forgotten, he resurfaced briefly, just to remind the public that he wanted to be left alone."

As Holden would have put it, Salinger was a "phony."

⌒⌒⌒

Even more disturbing than the idea that it was all a publicity stunt was Alexander's suggestion that Salinger really did have something to hide, namely affairs with teenage girls.

These rumors, too, were nothing new. Many readers had noticed that the wisest characters in many of Salinger's stories are young girls, such as Holden's sister Phoebe. And Salinger clearly liked the company of teenagers. When he first moved to Cornish, he hung out with local teens, Hamilton reported. In 1953, when Salinger was in his thirties, he met the nineteen-year-old Claire Douglas. They married two years later and divorced twelve years after that. In 1972, Salinger, then in his fifties, saw a *New York Times Magazine* story by eighteen-year-old Joyce Maynard, whose picture appeared on the cover. He wrote her an admiring letter. Instead of returning for her sophomore year at Yale, Maynard moved to Cornish, where she stayed for ten months.

Unfortunately for Salinger, Maynard continued to write, and in 1998 she published a memoir, *At Home in the World*. Much of it is about her relationship with Salinger.

"For most of that year I lived with him, in extreme isolation, working on a book and believing—despite the thirty-five years separating our ages—that we would be together always," Maynard wrote. "The following spring, J. D. Salinger sent me away. I remained desperately in love with him."

The Salinger portrayed by Maynard certainly continued to write. Indeed, he seemed more in touch with his fictional characters than the real world.

"He has compiled stacks of notes and notebooks concerning the habits and backgrounds of the Glasses—music they like, places they go, episodes in their history," Maynard wrote. "Even the parts of their lives that he may not write about, he needs to know. He fills in the facts as diligently as a parent, keeping up to date with the scrapbooks."

Salinger, as portrayed by Maynard, was hardly a one-dimensional figure whose sole interest was preying on young women. In fact, during their year together they never had intercourse (though they did have oral sex). But Salinger nevertheless came across as exploiting a vulnerable teenager, and as so absorbed in his work and in himself that he has no patience with anything or anyone else.

A similar view emerged from the 1999 memoir, *Dream Catcher*, by Salinger's (and Claire Douglas's) daughter Margaret. At one point, according to Margaret Salinger, her father defended himself by saying that he never neglected her, even if he was sometimes detached.

"He is detached about your pain, but God knows he takes his own pain more seriously than cancer," she concluded. "There is nothing remotely detached about my father's behavior toward his own pain, in his hemorrhages about anything personal being known about him. There is nothing remotely detached about his passionate defense of any felt infringement on his privacy or in the sanctity of his words and works."

Margaret Salinger's view of her father was by no means entirely negative. "When he chooses to make himself available, he can be funny, intensely loving, and the person you most want to be with," she wrote. "My father has . . . spent his life busy writing his heart out."

The problems arose when real people invaded Salinger's Glass world. "To get in the way of his work," Margaret Salinger wrote, "is to commit sacrilege."

Holden Caulfield imagined a big field of rye where thousands of kids would play. Nearby was a cliff, where Holden stood all day long, catching any of the kids who start to go over the edge. But Holden's creator, according to his daughter, was no catcher in the rye.

"Get what you can from his writing, his stories," she said. "But the author himself will not appear out of nowhere to catch those kids if they get too close to that crazy cliff."

To Investigate Further

Bloom, Harold, ed. *J. D. Salinger.* New York: Chelsea House, 1987.
A useful collection of critical essays.

Hamilton, Ian. *In Search of J. D. Salinger.* New York: Random House, 1988.
Hamilton may not have solved the mystery, but he came closer than anyone else—even in this much-expurgated final version of *A Writing Life.* The book is also fascinating as a study of the moral and legal dilemmas facing biographers.

Rosenbaum, Ron. "The Man in the Glass House." *Esquire,* June 1997.
"In its own powerful, invisible way," Rosenbaum writes, "the silence is in itself an eloquent work of art. It is the Great Wall of Silence J. D. Salinger has built around himself." But Rosenbaum, like others, can't resist the urge to breach the wall.

Maynard, Joyce. *At Home in the World.* New York: Picador USA, 1998.
Salinger's defenders bitterly attacked Maynard for making his private life public, and she didn't help matters by telling all at the same time that Monica Lewinsky did. But it was her life as well as his, and there's no denying it makes fascinating, if disturbing, reading. Salinger, of course, saw only the disturbing side. After she decided to write the book, she returned to Cornish to confront him. As Maynard described it, he pointed his finger directly at her heart. "The problem with you, Joyce," he said, "is . . . you love the world." "Yes," she answered, "I do." "I knew you would amount to this," he said. "Nothing."

Alexander, Paul. *Salinger.* Los Angeles: Renaissance Books, 1999.
It's a bit of a cut-and-paste job, and it's marred by Alexander's tendency to hedge his most sweeping conclusions (such as that Salinger secretly liked attention, or teenage girls) by phrasing them as questions. Still, considering all the obstacles a Salinger biographer faces, this is a worthy effort.

Salinger, Margaret. *Dream Catcher.* New York: Washington Square Press, 2000.
This must have seemed to Salinger even more a betrayal than Maynard's. It was, after all, his Holden Caulfield who said, right at the beginning of *The Catcher in the Rye,* that "my parents would have about two hemorrhages apiece if I told anything pretty personal about them . . . especially my father."

Who Killed JFK?

LIKE PEARL HARBOR, the assassination of President John F. Kennedy on November 22, 1963, traumatized the nation. In both cases the public responded by questioning the official version of what happened. But while the controversy over who was to blame for Pearl Harbor has faded with time, the mystery of who killed JFK is by no means resolved in the minds of most Americans. In the more than two thousand books and tens of thousands of articles on the subject, investigators have argued that Kennedy was killed by, to mention just the main culprits: the CIA, the KGB, the FBI, the Mafia, Fidel Castro, anti-Castro Cubans, and the Joint Chiefs of Staff. Not to mention Lee Harvey Oswald.

Confronted by so much confusing and often contradictory evidence, historians have been tempted to throw up their hands and say that this is one mystery that just can't be solved. Most Kennedy scholars, in fact, have shied away from his death. But they're wrong to do so, for not only is the subject too important to ignore, but the massive accumulation of evidence has moved us a great deal closer (though not all the way) to the mystery's solution.

The first official investigation into the assassination was that of the Warren Commission, headed by the chief justice of the Supreme Court, Earl Warren. The commission's report, released just ten months after Kennedy's death, offered a clear and simple answer to the question of who killed the president: Oswald did it, and he did it alone.

The Warren Commission concluded that Oswald had shot Kennedy from the sixth-floor window at the southeast corner of the Texas School Book Depository Building in Dallas. A construction worker across the street from the Depository saw Oswald shoot and described him to police. Forty-five minutes later, Dallas policeman J. D. Tippit stopped Oswald, who pulled out his revolver and killed Tippit. Oswald fled into a movie theater, from which he was dragged out by Dallas police. Two days later, as Oswald was being transferred from the city jail to a county jail, Jack Ruby broke through the crowds and fired a fatal shot into Oswald.

The Warren Report painted a picture of Oswald as a crazy loner, driven partly by a commitment to Marxism and partly by his own personal madness. Sent by his mother to an orphanage when he was just three, he was committed to a youth center for troubled boys when he was fifteen. He joined the marines, was twice court-martialed, went to Russia, tried to defect, and attempted suicide when the Russians decided to send him home. The Russians then relented and sent him to Minsk, where he spent two years building radios. But Oswald envisioned himself as a revolutionary leader, not a factory worker; he became as disillusioned with communism as with capitalism, and he returned to America. Back home his violent nature manifested itself in beatings of his Russian wife and in his attempted murder of right-wing General Edwin Walker. (Evidence of this previous assassination attempt only surfaced after Oswald's arrest for Kennedy's murder.)

Why did Oswald kill Kennedy? Not because of any long-felt animosity or planning. It was merely chance that Oswald happened to work in the School Book Depository Building. When he learned that the president's limousine would pass within rifle range, he seized his opportunity. Convinced he was destined for greatness, yet a failure at everything he'd tried, Oswald grabbed his place in history.

As for Ruby, he was a failed nightclub and strip joint owner who, like much of the country, was grief-stricken at the assassination. Like Oswald, Ruby loved the spotlight and, on an impulse, he too seized the chance to take center stage. This, at least, was the scenario presented by the Warren Report.

⟋⟍⟍⟍⟍

It didn't take long for skeptics to start chipping away at the commission's credibility.

Early critics pointed out that the commission had been under tremendous pressure, both to issue its report quickly and to assure the country that Oswald acted alone. Reports of Soviet and Cuban involvement in the assassination could lead to war, after all. Besides, Lyndon Johnson didn't want any lingering questions about the assassination clouding his reelection prospects. So, though the commission supposedly worked tirelessly to find the truth, it held its hearings in secret and relied heavily on the FBI and Secret Service reports. Most witnesses appeared before staff members, rather than the commission itself; in fact, not once were all seven commission members present during questioning.

With faith in the Warren Report waning, Jim Garrison, the New Orleans district attorney, undertook his own investigation in 1966. Garrison was convinced that while Oswald was in New Orleans—where he lived before moving to Dallas—he'd hooked up with two local figures, David Ferrie and Clay Shaw. According to Garrison, all three worked for the CIA, which was behind the plot to kill Kennedy. But Ferrie died before Garrison could learn more from him, and Shaw was acquitted a mere 45 minutes after a jury retired for deliberations. And rightly so: Garrison's case against Shaw depended heavily on the testimony of a witness who admitted he had no conscious memory of anything to do with a conspiracy; only after prosecutors had drugged and hypnotized him did his story come out.

Though Garrison's conspiracy theory proved unfounded, more responsible investigators continued to undermine the credibility of the Warren Report. In March 1975 ABC aired, for the first time, the Zapruder film (footage of the assassination taken by a spectator at the Dallas motorcade). Besides shocking the nation with its graphic detail, its image of Kennedy's head snapping back and to the left seemed to indicate a bullet fired from in front, rather than from the rear (where the School Book Depository was located).

Also in 1975, a Senate committee was shocked to learn that the CIA, with the assistance of the Mafia, had repeatedly tried to assassinate Castro during the early 1960s. Immediately this raised questions as to whether the Kennedy assassination might have been Castro's revenge, and what other information the CIA might have withheld from the Warren Commission.

In July came another bombshell: Oswald had been in contact with the FBI before the assassination. FBI agent James Hosty admitted he'd received a note from Oswald shortly before the assassination and had been ordered to destroy it right after the assassination. In addition, the FBI had deleted Hosty's name, address, and telephone number when information from Oswald's address book was sent to the commission.

By 1977 the Warren Commission's credibility was in shreds, and Congress took it upon itself to launch a new full-scale investigation. In contrast to the Warren Report, the House Select Committee on Assassinations took its time, almost three years, and it explored the darkest recesses of the CIA, FBI, and other government agencies. In addition, the committee appointed panels of independent experts who used technology unavailable in 1964. These experts resolved many of the questions about autopsy reports, ballistics matches, firearms tests, and photographic evidence that critics of the Warren Report had raised over the previous 15 years.

After all this, the committee seemed convinced that, though the Warren Commission's investigation was seriously flawed, its conclusion was essentially correct: Oswald alone had killed Kennedy. Then, just before the committee was to issue its report, it heard from three acoustics experts who had analyzed the dictabelt of a Dallas policeman's motorcycle. These experts informed the committee that they'd enhanced the recording and were 95 percent certain that they could detect four distinct shots. Because two of these shots came too close to each other for Oswald's rifle to have fired both, there must have been two riflemen. The experts also said that this additional shot came not from the Depository Building behind Kennedy but from a grassy knoll in front of him.

The committee quickly revised its conclusion. In July 1979 it announced that since there were two gunmen, there must have been a conspiracy to kill JFK. But soon after the committee reached its conclusion, Dallas policeman H. B. McClain, whose radio was supposed to be the source of the dictabelt recordings, came forward with information that indicated that the recording hadn't been from his radio. He'd raced along with the president's limousine to the hospital, sirens blaring all the way—yet on the recording there are no sirens to be heard. So, it seemed, the testimony on which the committee had based its conclusion had been based on the careful analysis of a tape that might have been recording a scene nowhere near and having nothing to do with the assassination.

⌒

This latest twist had only a minor impact on public opinion. Overwhelmed by revelations that government agencies and officials had lied—not only to the Warren Commission but about Vietnam and Watergate as well—the vast majority of the American public had become convinced of a conspiracy. A 1983 *Newsweek* poll showed only 11 percent believed Oswald had acted alone. This conviction was hardened with the release of Oliver Stone's 1991 movie, *JFK,* in which Jim Garrison reemerged as actor Kevin Costner.

Yet, as reporters and a few historians continued to investigate the case, their reports were increasingly less sensationalist. Though the CIA and FBI clearly had covered up information relevant to the assassination, their primary interests had been, in the case of the CIA, to conceal its efforts to assassinate Castro, not Kennedy; and in the case of the FBI, to make sure its reputation wasn't tarnished by its failure to recognize the threat Oswald posed. Gerald Posner's 1993 book, *Case Closed,* was enthusiastically embraced, at least by the mainstream press, for its thorough refutation of much of the evidence conspiracy theorists had gathered over the past 30 years.

Posner was extremely effective in marshalling technical expertise, some but by no means all of which had been presented to the House committee. He presented, for example, a convincing explanation of the "magic bullet." This bullet, identified as having been shot from Oswald's rifle, was found on the stretcher of Texas Governor John Connally, who'd been riding in the presidential limousine and who'd been injured by one of the shots aimed at Kennedy. After analyzing the Zapruder film, the Warren Commission had determined that the time between when Kennedy was first hit and when Connally was first hit was not sufficient for a single gunman to have fired two shots. Therefore, the commission concluded, a single bullet had hit both.

Critics of the commission wondered how a single bullet could have gone through both Kennedy and Connally and emerged, in nearly pristine condition, on Connally's stretcher. To conspiracy theorists, the mysterious appearance of a whole bullet from Oswald's gun smacked of a setup. A more likely explanation of how both Kennedy and Connally were hit one right after the other, they argued, was that a second bullet had been fired by a second gunman. But Posner's experts employed new technology to show that Connally's wounds and the intact bullet were the likely result of a bullet slowed by its passage through both Kennedy and Connally.

More than any technical evidence, however, what has undermined many conspiracy theories are flaws in their own logic. Consider the main candidates:

The CIA. The agency was capable of assassination—it had already admitted its attempts to kill Castro. And some high up in the agency could have feared that Kennedy, embarrassed by the CIA's bungling of the invasion of Cuba at the Bay of Pigs, might try to interfere with other CIA operations and curtail the agency's independence. But: This was the same Kennedy who had approved the CIA's plan to invade Cuba at the Bay of Pigs, who brought the world to the brink of nuclear war during the Cuban missile crisis, and who escalated U.S. involvement in Vietnam. Hardly a president likely to close down the Cold War or the CIA.

The KGB. Oswald was a Marxist who'd defected to Russia. But: KGB files indicated the Russians considered Oswald nothing but a nuisance and were delighted to be rid of him. Besides, Khrushchev would have been crazy to risk nuclear war for the sake of replacing Kennedy with the more hard-line Lyndon Johnson.

Castro. Castro was aware that the CIA had tried to kill him, and in September 1963 he'd threatened revenge. But: Castro himself later insisted that it would have been "tremendous insanity" for him to order Kennedy's assassination and risk the full fury of all America. And, though he undoubtedly hated Kennedy, Castro wasn't insane. It is possible, however, that Oswald read of Castro's threat in the New Orleans *Times-Picayune* and took it upon himself to carry it out.

Anti-Castro Cubans. Many Cubans were unhappy Kennedy had backed away from stronger support during the Bay of Pigs fiasco; some extremists among them may have wanted the president dead. But: Oswald was a communist and an admirer of Castro. It's hard to imagine him working with Castro's enemies.

The Mafia. Attorney General Robert Kennedy was cracking down on organized crime and a number of dons were undoubtedly incensed. Plus Jack Ruby had plenty of mob connections, albeit low-level ones. So, this theory went, Oswald had been hired to kill Kennedy and then Ruby had been hired to make sure Oswald didn't talk. Robert Blakey, chief counsel for the House Select Committee on Assassinations, thought the Mafia was behind the murder and the committee went so far as to discuss particular mobsters—in particular, teamster boss Jimmy Hoffa, Tampa godfather Santo Traficante, and New Orleans godfather Carlos Marcello. All had spoken of hitting the president (at least according to witnesses of questionable reliability). But: There was no evidence that they'd done more than talk. Besides, couldn't the Mafia have found more reliable hitmen than Oswald and Ruby?

Of course, none of this proves there was no conspiracy. And, even if none of the above groups conspired with Oswald, there remains the possibility of a conspiracy between Oswald and other disaffected amateurs, some of whom may have had connections with the CIA, the Cubans, or the mob. For many Americans, Kennedy's death was so traumatic that it seemed unfair that he be the victim of Oswald alone; at least a conspiracy would imbue his death with some greater meaning. And, indeed, there are still too many unanswered questions about the assassination to rule out such a possibility.

But against the illogic of each particular conspiracy theory must be held up the logic, albeit twisted, of Oswald's own mind. Desperately ambitious and deeply tortured, Oswald may have seen the assassination as his chance to punish both America and Russia for not recognizing that he was a great man, destined to change the course of history—which, whether alone or with others, he most definitely did.

To Investigate Further

Report of the President's Commission on the Assassination of President John F. Kennedy. Washington, DC: United States Government Printing Office, 1964.

Even those who disparage the findings of the Warren Commission have found its 26 volumes of testimony and evidence an invaluable source.

Weisberg, Harold. *Whitewash.* New York: Dell, 1966.

The first in-depth attack on the Warren Report, this was originally self-published in 1965.

Lane, Mark. *Rush to Judgment.* Orlando: Holt, Rinehart and Winston, 1966.

Another early attack on the Warren Report, this established a tradition of best-sellers on the subject. Lane also authored a 1991 book, *Plausible Denial,* which argued that the CIA killed Kennedy.

Epstein, Edward Jay. *Inquest.* New York: Viking, 1966.

Of the early attacks on the Warren Report, this stands up best. Epstein presents a convincing case that the commission was unable to insulate itself from political and national security considerations. Epstein's 1968 book, *Counterplot,* is also useful as a refutation of Garrison's theories, and his 1978 book, *Legend,* is an intriguing investigation of the CIA's efforts to establish whether Yuri Nosenko, a KGB officer who defected to the United States and who claimed to have supervised Oswald's case in Russia, was telling the truth. All three books were republished in a single volume, with new material, in a 1992 Carroll & Graf (NY) edition.

Ford, Gerald, and John Stiles. *Portrait of the Assassin.* New York: Ballantine, 1966.

Consisting largely of reprints of testimony before the Warren Commission, this was the first book to defend the Warren Report. Then-Representative Ford was a member of the commission.

Summers, Anthony. *Conspiracy.* New York: McGraw-Hill, 1980.

Claims that a conspiracy involved Oswald, anti-Castro exiles, Mafia members, and CIA renegades.

Lifton, David. *Best Evidence.* New York: Macmillan, 1980.

Claims that Kennedy's body was stolen and surgically altered in order to eliminate evidence of a shooter in front of the president.

Blakey, G. Robert, and Richard Billings. *The Plot to Kill the President.* New York: New York Times Press, 1981.

Claims that the conspiracy involved organized crime and anti-Castro exiles. Blakey was counsel to the House Select Committee on Assassinations.

Davis, John. *Mafia Kingfish.* New York: McGraw-Hill, 1988.

Scheim, David. *Contract on America.* Silver Spring, Maryland: Argyle Press, 1983.

Both Scheim and Davis (see above) claim the Mafia did it.

Garrison, Jim. *On the Trail of the Assassins.* New York: Sheridan Square Press, 1988.

The New Orleans district attorney's story, which was the basis of Oliver Stone's movie *JFK.*

Posner, Gerald. *Case Closed.* New York: Random House, 1993.

A thorough and compelling presentation of the case that Oswald acted alone.

Mailer, Norman. *Oswald's Tale.* New York: Random House, 1995.

More a novelist's portrait of Oswald than an analysis of the evidence; nonetheless, the Oswald who emerges from the (often brilliant, if overly long) portrait is clearly a man capable of shooting the president, by himself.

What Happened at the Gulf of Tonkin?

W ITHIN HOURS OF SUCCEEDING the slain John Kennedy, President Lyndon Johnson vowed: "I am not going to lose Vietnam."

That was easier said than done: the situation that Johnson inherited was already bleak and rapidly deteriorating. By early 1964 about 40 percent of South Vietnam was under Vietcong control, South Vietnamese soldiers were deserting at alarming rates, and the North Vietnamese were in the process of turning the Ho Chi Minh trail into a modern logistical system through which thousands of troops, weapons, ammunition, and other equipment were pouring south. The new regime in Saigon—the result of an assassination that preceded Kennedy's by three weeks—appeared to be even more corrupt and inept than its predecessors. Without a significant increase in U.S. support (there were currently just over 16,000 American troops there, none of whom were directly involved in the fighting), a communist victory seemed inevitable.

On the home front, Johnson was doing much better. His opponent in the upcoming election, Barry Goldwater, was talking about how satisfying it would be to lob a nuclear missile "down into the gents' room in the Kremlin." Voters panicked by Goldwater's extremism were flocking to the Democratic camp in droves, especially after the president promised that "we are not about to send American boys nine or ten thousand miles away from home to do what Asian boys ought to be doing for themselves."

But this presented a problem for Johnson. Unless he did something, Vietnam would fall. Yet, as the peace candidate, how could he escalate American involvement in the war?

Then, in the Gulf of Tonkin, off the coast of North Vietnam, came the solution to Johnson's problem. The administration reported that on August 2 and then again on August 4, while the U.S. destroyer *Maddox* was on a routine patrol mission in the Gulf, it was ambushed by North Vietnamese patrol boats. After the first attack, Johnson was restrained, promising only that patrols in the Gulf would continue and that U.S. forces would destroy any attackers. But a second attack called for a tougher response, which Johnson could now give without undermining his moderate image. He ordered planes from the nearby USS *Constellation* and USS *Ticonderoga* to attack the base of the North Vietnamese patrol boats and a supporting oil complex, and on August 5 they carried out this mission by dropping the first U.S. bombs on Vietnam. The mission was a success: eight boats were destroyed and twenty others damaged, and 90 percent of the oil depot was destroyed.

Still, Johnson and his advisers felt they might need more authority to respond quickly and decisively to the situation in Vietnam. On August 6, the president submitted to Congress legislation officially titled "Joint Resolution to Promote the Maintenance of International Peace and Security in Southeast Asia." The legislation, which was soon dubbed the Gulf of Tonkin Resolution, authorized the president "to take all necessary steps, including the use of armed force, to assist any member or protocol state of the Southeast Asia Collective Defense Treaty requesting assistance in defense of its freedom." On August 7, after Secretary of Defense Robert McNamara appeared before the Senate Committee on Foreign Relations and the House Foreign Affairs Committee to describe the unprovoked aggression against U.S. ships in the Gulf of Tonkin, the House approved the resolution by a vote of 416 to 0 and the Senate by a vote of 88 to 2.

Everything seemed to be going Johnson's way. The election was a landslide, with Johnson receiving 61.1 percent of the vote to Goldwater's 38.5 percent. And, in the Gulf of Tonkin Resolution, Congress had signed a blank check—a check that Johnson cashed in January 1965, when he ordered 100,000 ground troops to Vietnam.

But, as the United States became mired in the Vietnam War, questions arose, not only about whether we ought to be there, but also about how we got there. Some critics of the war claimed the U.S. ships had been the aggressors in the Gulf of Tonkin; others claimed that the battle there had never even taken place. Worse, some contended the administration knew these facts and intentionally misled Congress in order to extract from that body the power to go to war.

♋

Historians of the Vietnam War, and of the Gulf of Tonkin incidents in particular, are fortunate that one of those who came to doubt the administration's story was Senator William Fulbright who, as chair of the Foreign Relations Committee, was in a position to investigate the matter.

Initially, Fulbright was one of the administration's most useful supporters, shepherding the Gulf of Tonkin Resolution through the Senate. When Senator Gaylord Nelson proposed amending the resolution to require congressional approval before the dispatch of troops to Vietnam, Fulbright convinced him that Johnson had no intention of sending the troops and that the amendment was therefore unnecessary. But as the war widened so did the breach between Johnson and Fulbright and by 1966 Fulbright was openly critical of the president's foreign policy.

His suspicions about the Tonkin incidents were heightened in May of that year, when Assistant Secretary of State William Bundy, in secret testimony before the committee, said he'd written a draft similar to the Tonkin Resolution in May or June 1964—several months before the incidents in the gulf. Bundy called the drafts "normal contingency planning," but it was clear that the administration had been preparing to escalate the war well before anything happened in the Gulf of Tonkin.

In September 1967 Fulbright authorized the committee staff to begin an inquiry into the Tonkin incidents, and he requested copies of the official logbooks of the *Maddox*. What emerged from the staff's investigations and the 1967–1968 hearings before the For-

eign Relations Committee was a very different story from the one Johnson and McNamara had presented to the committee in 1964.

First, it became clear that the administration's claim that the *Maddox* was engaged
in a routine patrol was at best misleading, if not downright false. Cables to and from
the *Maddox* repeatedly referred to something called "34-A Operations," which, the
Pentagon eventually admitted, included South Vietnamese raids on the islands in the
vicinity of the U.S. ship. During the brief 1964 hearings before the passage of the resolution, McNamara had stated that "our Navy played absolutely no part in, was not associated with, was not aware of, any South Vietnamese actions, if there were any." Yet
the cables indicated that the captain of the *Maddox*, John Herrick, had been aware of
the operations and that his superiors might very well have been using the *Maddox* as a
decoy to draw the North Vietnamese patrol boats away from the area of the 34-A
Operations.

Second, though the *Maddox* had been pursued by North Vietnamese patrol boats on
August 2, it was the *Maddox* that first opened fire. The North Vietnamese held their
course and then did fire torpedoes at the destroyer. The torpedoes missed the destroyer
but the destroyer's guns were on target; one of the North Vietnamese patrol boats sunk
and the others retreated back to port, briefly pursued by aircraft from the *Ticonderoga*.

It was the revelations about the August 4 incident, however, that most shocked the
committee. It was this attack, remember, that had supposedly prompted Johnson to re-
taliate. Yet what the committee found was that the second battle almost certainly did not
take place at all.

True, the *Maddox* and *Turner Joy* (another destroyer that had joined the *Maddox* after
the August 2 attack) had fired four hundred rounds into the black night, dropped depth
charges, and at one point tried to ram their attackers. But not a single sailor on either
vessel had actually seen or heard North Vietnamese ships or gunfire. Nor had the pilots
of the planes summoned from the *Constellation* seen the enemy. And though the *Maddox*'s sonars counted a total of 26 enemy torpedoes, none scored a hit. Even more suspicious, the sonar man on the *Turner Joy* hadn't reported any torpedoes.

Aboard the *Maddox*, Captain Herrick began to have doubts about the incident even
before it ended. So once the shooting stopped, he conducted an experiment, putting the
ship into high-speed turns. After each, the sonar man reported hearing torpedoes. Herrick concluded that most, if not all, of the *Maddox*'s torpedo reports were probably
caused by the echo of outgoing sonar beams hitting the ship's rudders. He wired his superiors that the "entire action leaves many doubts" and suggested a "complete evaluation" before any further measures were taken.

By then Johnson was in no mood to wait. Even as the Pentagon was sending urgent
messages asking the Pacific commanders for evidence substantiating the attack, American bombers were already en route to their first North Vietnamese targets.

⟶

The navy did not invent the battle of August 4; as Herrick suggested soon after, the weather and an "overeager sonar man" might have accounted for the confusion. Nor did Johnson or McNamara invent the battle, as some later critics of the war contended; both may very well have thought the *Maddox* was attacked. But in their eagerness to use the incident to push through the congressional resolution, both ignored a good deal of evidence that the attack never took place, and both undeniably misled the public and the Congress when they described a complex and ambiguous incident as a clear, unprovoked attack. Only days after the resolution had passed, Johnson admitted he knew more than he'd told. In a private comment to George Ball, his undersecretary of state, he said: "Hell, those dumb, stupid sailors were just shooting at flying fish."

Some of the blame for what followed, however, must be shared by Congress. The Gulf of Tonkin Resolution was only the latest in a series of congressional abdications of its constitutional power to declare war. Congress had stood by as Truman sent troops to Korea without any congressional authorization; it had given permission for Eisenhower to deploy U.S. forces "as he deems it necessary" to protect Taiwan against a communist assault. Like Johnson, many Democrats in Congress were positioning themselves for the upcoming elections, and they feared Republicans would portray a vote against the resolution as unpatriotic or weak.

Later, Fulbright and others contended that they'd never intended to authorize a full-scale war in Asia. As the 1967 Senate Foreign Relations Committee report commented, "the prevailing attitude [in 1964] was not so much that Congress was granting or acknowledging the executive's authority to take certain actions but that it was expressing unity and support for the President in a moment of national crisis." Even hawks such as Senator John Stennis became disillusioned by the administration's broad use of the resolution, and in August 1966 Stennis told Secretary of State Dean Rusk that he thought the administration's deceptions might have invalidated the resolution. But Rusk dismissed the argument and Stennis's legal position was never tested. And, however much Fulbright and Stennis and others in Congress might have later regretted it, they could not deny that they'd voted for a resolution giving Johnson very broad powers; so broad, Johnson later quipped, that it was "like grandma's nightshirt—it covered everything."

To Investigate Further

Goulden, Joseph. *Truth Is the First Casualty.* Chicago: Rand McNally, 1969.
  The first of the revisionist accounts.

Galloway, John. *The Gulf of Tonkin Resolution.* Cranbury, NJ: Fairleigh Dickinson University Press, 1970.
  Especially useful for its inclusion of relevant documents such as the resolution itself, Johnson's addresses to the nation and to Congress, and the transcripts of the Committee on Foreign Relations' 1968 hearings.

Windchy, Eugene. *Tonkin Gulf.* **New York: Doubleday, 1971.**
A thorough reconstruction of the incidents.

Karnow, Stanley. *Vietnam.* **New York: Viking, 1983.**
Given its broad scope, this cannot go into detail about the Tonkin gulf or many other aspects of the war; still, it remains the best general, balanced history of the war.

Stockdale, Jim, and Sybil Stockdale. *In Love and War.* **New York: Harper & Row, 1984.**
Before becoming Ross Perot's 1992 running mate, Stockdale was a navy pilot who took off from the *Ticonderoga* to aid the *Maddox;* his book tells what he saw and what he didn't see—"no boats, no boat gunfire, no torpedo wakes—nothing but black sea and American firepower."

McNamara, Robert. *In Retrospect.* **New York: Times Books, 1995.**
In retrospect, McNamara admits the escalation of the Vietnam War was an error, but he continues to deny (unconvincingly) that he or anyone in the administration deliberately misled Congress about the Gulf of Tonkin incidents.

Moïse, Edwin. *Tonkin Gulf and the Escalation of the Vietnam War.* **Chapel Hill: University of North Carolina Press, 1996.**
A thorough history of both the events and nonevents.

Who Killed Malcolm X?

T O MOST MAINSTREAM HISTORIANS, the assassination of Malcolm X in February 1965 was the work of the Nation of Islam, the black nationalist religious group from which Malcolm had defected a year earlier. In the alternative presses, however, many black writers have questioned this explanation, arguing that U.S. intelligence forces played a role in the conspiracy. Compounding the problem has been the lack of extensive scholarship on Malcolm. In contrast to Martin Luther King Jr., whose life and times have been the subject of a number of major works, Malcolm is still best known through his own autobiography. And while *The Autobiography of Malcolm X* well deserves its place in the back pockets of radicals and rappers—and of any serious student of the period—it is by no means a definitive history of Malcolm's life. Nor, of course, could Malcolm cover his own death.

Does this mean Malcolm's death is destined to remain a mystery? Not entirely.

ᐤᙡᐧᐤ

Whatever else its critics may say about the mainstream account of Malcolm's death, no one can question that the leadership of the Nation of Islam hated Malcolm X. To the Nation, Malcolm was not just an enemy but an apostate and traitor. Malcolm had originally converted to the Nation of Islam in 1949, while serving a term in prison for burglary. The Nation redeemed him from a life of crime: no longer was he Malcolm Little (as he'd been born) or "Detroit Red" (as he'd called himself when he became a pimp and con artist); now he was Malcolm X. "The Muslim's 'X,'" he explained in the *Autobiography*, "symbolized the true African family name that he never could know [and] replaced the white slave master name . . . which some blue-eyed devil named Little had imposed upon my paternal forebears."

What the Nation offered Malcolm (and hundreds of thousands of other blacks) was a radical alternative theology. The Nation's leader, Elijah Muhammad, asserted that all whites were devils (created by an evil black scientist) whose world would be destroyed in the coming racial Armageddon. Malcolm's brilliant rhetorical skills propelled him to the forefront of the Nation, first as the minister of Harlem's Mosque Number 7, the largest in the country, and then as the Nation's National Minister. He became the voice of black nationalism, the angry counterpoint to Martin Luther King Jr.'s preachings about Christian love.

So successful was Malcolm in his role as the Nation's mouthpiece that he became much better known to the press and public than Muhammad himself. This provoked the envy of others in the Nation, including its leader.

Doctrinal disagreements, too, were tearing apart Muhammad and Malcolm. Muhammad's apocalyptic vision provoked fears among whites but what he actually called for was not violence against white society but a complete withdrawal from it. Malcolm's impulses, on the other hand, were more activist. When Martin Luther King led the 1963 civil rights "March on Washington," for example, Muhammad, as part of his nonengagement policy, prohibited his followers from attending. Malcolm went along with Muhammad, part of the way: he derided the integrationists, branding the March the "Farce on Washington" and calling it more of a picnic than a protest. But, in blatant disregard of Muhammad's ban, Malcolm couldn't resist attending the March.

Malcolm's faith became even shakier when he learned that Muhammad had fathered a number of illegitimate children. Malcolm called a meeting of New York Muslim leaders, supposedly in order to prepare them in case the adulteries became public. In the eyes of many around Muhammad, however, this was just another example of Malcolm trying to undermine Muhammad's position.

The rift between Malcolm and Muhammad became public after John Kennedy's assassination. Muhammad had ordered all Muslims to refrain from commenting on the assassination. Malcolm, however, couldn't resist: asked for his comments, he first mentioned the many Third World leaders who'd been killed as a result of American intervention and concluded by saying that Kennedy's assassination was "a case of chickens coming home to roost."

Muhammad was outraged. Not that Muhammad was a fan of Kennedy (who was, after all, the president of a nation of white devils), but Malcolm had disobeyed his direct order. Muhammad suspended his chief minister for 90 days, and before the period was up Malcolm had formally broken with the Nation and started his own rival organization, the Muslim Mosque, Inc.

Now Malcolm presented an even greater danger to the Nation. Not only was he preaching heresy, but he was heading a rival group and appealing to the Nation's own members. Nation ministers denounced Malcolm; he retaliated by going public with the stories of Muhammad's adulteries. So the Nation pushed up its rhetoric another notch. In a three-part series in the organization's newspaper, *Muhammad Speaks,* Minister Louis X of Boston—who had been recruited to the Nation by Malcolm and who later became known as Louis Farrakhan—condemned the "unbelievable treachery" of his former mentor. The December 4, 1964, issue of *Muhammad Speaks* contained the most suggestive attack of all: "Only those who wish to be led to hell, or to their doom, will follow Malcolm," Farrakhan wrote. "The die is set, and Malcolm shall not escape. . . . Such a man as Malcolm is worthy of death."

During the final year of his life, between his March 1964 break with the Nation and his February 1965 assassination, Malcolm was continually harassed by death threats. In his autobiography, he wrote: "Wherever I go . . . black men are watching every move I make, awaiting their chance to kill me. . . . I know that they have their orders. Anyone who chooses not to believe what I am saying doesn't know the Muslims in the NOI [Nation of Islam]."

Hostile, armed Muslims chased Malcolm in New York, Los Angeles, and Chicago. Just a week before his assassination, Malcolm's house in Queens was firebombed. Finally, on

February 21, as he began to speak before his followers at the Audubon Ballroom in Harlem, he was shot to death by at least three and possibly (according to some witnesses in the crowd) five assassins.

⌀∭∿

One of those assassins, Talmadge Hayer, was caught at the scene. The police subsequently arrested two other suspects, Norman 3X and Thomas 15X. Both Norman 3X and Thomas 15X were members of the Nation's mosque in Harlem; both had been accused of shooting Benjamin Brown, another Muslim minister who'd strayed from the fold; and both were placed at the Audubon by eyewitnesses. In March 1966 a jury found all three defendants guilty of murder.

Twelve years later, in 1978, Hayer confessed that he had, indeed, killed Malcolm, along with four fellow Muslims from the Nation's Newark Mosque Number 25. He'd stayed silent so long, he said, to protect Elijah Muhammad; since Muhammad had died in 1975, Hayer could now tell the truth. And, he emphasized, Norman 3X and Thomas 15X were completely innocent.

What to make of Hayer's story? The prosecution didn't buy it, nor did Judge Harold Rothwax, who decided that Hayer was merely trying to get his accomplices off the hook.

But many historians have found Hayer's story convincing. Clearly, Hayer was guilty—and now that he'd admitted he'd done it for the sake of the Nation, his motive was equally clear. As for Norman 3X and Thomas 15X, the case against them had never been as strong as that against Hayer. No physical evidence placed them anywhere near the Audubon on the night of Malcolm's murder and, of the hundreds at the Audubon, only a handful had identified them—this in spite of the fact that Norman 3X and Thomas 15X were well-known members of the Nation (and thus just the type of person for whom Malcolm's followers and bodyguards would have been on the lookout). Hayer's confession swayed Malcolm's biographer Peter Goldman. In the original 1973 edition of his book, Goldman argued that Norman 3X and Thomas 15X were guilty but in the 1979 revision he admitted it was likely they were innocent.

All three men convicted of the murder—Hayer, Norman 3X, and Thomas 15X—have now been paroled and, barring some deathbed confessions, it seems likely that history's verdict will overturn that of the jury. Hayer was certainly guilty; Norman 3X and Thomas 15X were probably not. But more pressing historical questions remain: Who ordered the assassination? Was it Elijah Muhammad? Was it Louis Farrakhan? Or, as Hayer maintained, did he and his accomplices act for the sake of the Nation but without direct orders from any higher-ups?

Elijah Muhammad always denied giving any order to kill Malcolm. So, too, has Louis Farrakhan, though he has acknowledged that his rhetoric contributed to the atmosphere that led to the assassination. But Farrakhan and others in the Nation have stressed that investigators wanting a full understanding of Malcolm's death should look beyond the Nation. The Nation of Islam, they argue, was not the only organization that wanted Malcolm dead.

⌀∭∿

The FBI's history of harassing Martin Luther King Jr.—which included secretly recording his extramarital affairs and threatening to send the tapes to his wife unless he committed suicide—was well documented by the 1975 Senate Select Committee on Intelligence Activities. Unfortunately the bureau's campaigns against the Nation and against Malcolm have not been as fully investigated. Many of the files remain classified, and those that have been released include critical deletions.

But from the files that have been released, a great deal has been learned. FBI surveillance of the Nation dates back to 1956, and its actions included some of the same types of dirty tricks used against King. Between 1959 and 1962, the bureau channeled embarrassing information about Elijah Muhammad's finances and sex life to journalists. When this failed to slow the Nation's growth (perhaps because its members were not quite so puritanical or voyeuristic as J. Edgar Hoover and his agents), the bureau sent anonymous letters with additional information on Muhammad's sex life to "selected individuals" in the Nation hierarchy. Who these individuals were has been deleted from the files, but it's reasonable to assume that Malcolm was among them, and that some of the details about Muhammad's sex life that so upset him came from the FBI.

The files also indicate that at least one and possibly two FBI agents had infiltrated the Nation's top leadership, and that their job was to "plant the seed of dissension" within the organization. A February 1964 memo suggested a move that "could possibly widen the rift between Muhammad and Little and possibly result in Little's expulsion from the NOI." Again, the specifics are deleted from the file, so it's impossible to know what the plan was or even whether it was enacted. But we do know that, as the FBI desired, the rift between Muhammad and Malcolm widened.

Until more FBI files are declassified, it's impossible to say exactly what role the bureau played in Malcolm's assassination. Some, like Farrakhan, have speculated that it was an FBI agent planted in the Nation who gave the order to murder Malcolm. At this point, such speculation remains just speculation; there is no proof that anyone in the FBI actually participated in any way in the murder plot. But—and the revelations about the FBI's campaign against King and others may make this seem less shocking and appalling than it ought to be—it's quite clear that, from J. Edgar Hoover down to his agents in the field, the FBI considered its mission to be one of escalating the feud between Malcolm and the Nation. That the FBI might instead have used some of its intelligence and manpower to save Malcolm's life seems never to have occurred to anyone in the bureau.

An odd epilogue to this sordid tale must have brought at least some satisfaction to Farrakhan. Both Betty Shabazz, Malcolm's widow, and Quibilah Shabazz, his daughter, had blamed Farrakhan for Malcolm's death. In 1995 the FBI arrested Quibilah Shabazz, charging that she had tried to hire a hit man to kill Farrakhan and avenge her father's death. The key witness was a long-time government informant of dubious reliability, and prosecutors and defense lawyers ultimately struck a deal that spared them a trial and let Quibilah Shabazz off with a two-year probation.

Before the deal was struck, however, Farrakhan and Betty Shabazz spoke out together against the government's case. Ironically, this latest federal intervention in the life and death of Malcolm X had brought about what the 30 years since the assassination had not—a reconciliation between Malcolm's family and the Nation of Islam.

To Investigate Further

X, Malcolm, as told to Alex Haley. *The Autobiography of Malcolm X*. New York: Grove Press, 1994.
  A classic of African American letters.

Goldman, Peter. *The Death and Life of Malcolm X*. Champaign: University of Illinois Press, 1979.
  Though Goldman is a little too reluctant to accuse the authorities of wrongdoing, this is nonetheless the best biography of Malcolm.

Garrow, David. *The FBI and Martin Luther King, Jr.* New York: Norton, 1981.
  The revelations about the FBI's war against King had come out during Senate hearings, so this book added little in the way of facts. But Garrow's analysis of the FBI's motives are provocative and convincing.

Carson, Clayborne. *Malcolm X: The FBI File*. New York: Carroll & Graf, 1991.
  Though it is missing a lot of files that were later released (as well as many still classified), what is here is at least suggestive of the mass of intelligence and gossip collected by the FBI.

Breitman, George, Herman Porter, and Baxter Smith. *The Assassination of Malcolm X*. New York: Pathfinder, 1991.
  Originally published in 1976, this is a Marxist view of the assassination. The authors argue that, after leaving the Nation, Malcolm was evolving toward socialism (for which there is some evidence) and that this provoked the CIA into some role in the assassination (for which the evidence is very circumstantial).

Perry, Bruce. *Malcolm*. Barrytown, NY: Station Hill Press, 1991.
  A controversial psychobiography that interprets Malcolm's life and politics as a response not to white racism but to an abused childhood. Though his analysis is often simplistic, Perry raises many issues ignored by other scholars.

Evanzz, Karl. *The Judas Factor*. New York: Thunder's Mouth Press, 1992.
  The Judas of the title is John Ali, a top-level Nation figure who Evanzz thinks conspired with the CIA and FBI to murder Malcolm. Evanzz raises some valid questions but doesn't answer them convincingly.

Friedly, Michael. *Malcolm X: The Assassination*. New York: Carroll & Graf, 1992.
  The most thorough statement of the position that the Nation of Islam was responsible for Malcolm's death, and that the FBI (though actively working to discredit the Nation and Malcolm) did not in any way participate in the plot.

Lee, Spike, with Ralph Wiley. *By Any Means Necessary*. New York: Hyperion, 1992.
  Lee's account of the making of his film about Malcolm includes his tantalizingly suggestive but ultimately frustrating interviews with Farrakhan and others involved in the case.

Gardell, Mattias. *In The Name of Elijah Muhammad*. Durham, NC: Duke University Press, 1996.
  The fullest account of the Nation of Islam's ideology and theology, this also includes the best account of how the FBI attempted to incite the Muslims to violence against one another.

Who Won the Tet Offensive?

ET, THE LUNAR NEW YEAR, is a time to celebrate peace, and in 1968 both sides in the Vietnam War agreed to the traditional truce. So there was some surprise when, on the evening of January 31, the North Vietnamese and Vietcong attacked. But the true surprise was the scope and intensity of the attacks. Just two months earlier, General William Westmoreland, the commander of U.S. troops in Vietnam, had stated that the Americans were winning the war, that American troop withdrawals might begin within two years, and that he could see "some light at the end of the tunnel." Come Tet, some seventy thousand communist soldiers stormed into more than one hundred cities and towns throughout South Vietnam, including Saigon, where they blew a hole into the wall of the U.S. Embassy. Fighting was especially intense around Khe Sanh, a U.S. base in the northwest of South Vietnam where the communists had pinned down six thousand Marines.

The shockwaves were felt across America. Critics of U.S. policy in Vietnam compared the siege of Khe Sanh to that of Dienbienphu, where in 1954 the Vietnamese defeated a French garrison and forced France to abandon its former colony. "The parallels are there for all to see," Walter Cronkite told his CBS audience in early February. The light at the end of the tunnel, many commented, must have been a train headed straight at Westmoreland.

By mid-March, Senator Eugene McCarthy had come within three hundred votes of defeating the incumbent president, Lyndon Johnson, in the New Hampshire primary, and Robert Kennedy, a much stronger peace candidate, had entered the race. On March 31, Johnson ordered a halt to bombing, offered to negotiate with the communists, and—less than four years after having come out on top of one of the largest landslides in American history—declared he would not seek re-election. In May, peace talks began in Paris.

Though the talks would drag on for five years, it was clear that the Tet Offensive was the war's turning point. After Tet, America was no longer looking for victory but merely a way out of Vietnam, or as President Richard Nixon put it, a "peace with honor." Except for its importance, however, there was very little else about Tet on which Americans agreed. For Vietnam doves, Tet was the moment when Americans, overwhelmed by the communists' resolve, realized the war could not be won. For hawks, not only could the war be won but the battle was won; in fact, they argued, Tet was a major military victory for South Vietnam and the United States, which was seen as a defeat only because of the distortions of liberals in the government and media.

The question of who won the Tet Offensive, thus, went right to the heart of the question of who lost Vietnam.

⌒⌒⌒⌒

Not surprisingly, among those who insisted that Tet was an American victory were those in charge of the American war effort.

"There is no doubt in my mind that the Tet offensive was a military debacle for the North Vietnamese and the Viet Cong," wrote Johnson in his 1971 memoirs. "But the defeat the Communists suffered did not have the telling effect it should have had largely because of what we did to ourselves."

"Militarily, the offensive was foredoomed to failure," agreed Westmoreland in his 1976 book. "In terms of public opinion, press and television would transform what was undeniably a catastrophic military defeat for the enemy into a presumed debacle for Americans and South Vietnamese."

To Johnson and Westmoreland, Tet was the North's "last gasp," a desperate effort to salvage a losing cause. After the initial surprise, American and South Vietnamese troops quickly routed the communists. The impact of the hole in the embassy wall was purely psychological; the communists never actually captured the compound. Only in Khe Sanh and Hue, both near the northern border, did the battle last more than a few days. In Hue, it took twenty-five days of house-to-house combat to rout the communists. At Khe Sanh, the siege lasted until early April, but the communists began to pull back in March. Unlike the French trapped at Dienbienphu, the Americans at Khe Sanh could count on the Air Force to carry in supplies and reinforcements, and even more crucially, to drop tons of explosives over the surrounding enemy troops. Westmoreland estimated communist losses there at between ten and fifteen thousand, compared to 205 Marines. Overall, military analysts put enemy losses near sixty thousand, a devastating setback, especially for the southern communists—the Vietcong—who from then on played a comparatively small role in the war.

Johnson and Westmoreland blamed the press for turning a military victory into a psychological defeat.

"There was a great deal of emotional and exaggerated reporting of the Tet offensive in our press and our television," wrote Johnson. "The media seemed to be in competition as to who could provide the most lurid and depressing accounts. . . . The American people and even a number of officials in government, subjected to this daily barrage of near panic, began to think that we must have suffered a defeat."

There were plenty of examples of what hawks considered antiwar and defeatist coverage. On February 2, numerous newspapers, including the *New York Times* and *Washington Post*, featured on their front page a searing Associated Press photo of a South Vietnamese policeman with his arm stretched out and his gun at the head of a Vietcong captive about to be executed. On February 6, Art Buchwald parodied Westmoreland's optimism by recounting his exclusive interview with General George Armstrong Custer at the Battle of Little Bighorn. "We have the Sioux on the run," Custer told Buchwald. On February 7, Peter Arnett built a widely read AP story around a quote from an unnamed American major who, describing the shattered city of Ben Tre, explained that "it

Refugees flee across the Perfume River to escape Tet fighting in Hue. The bridge was soon blown up. *(Corbis)*

became necessary to destroy the town to save it." On February 27, Walter Cronkite—the most respected newsman and perhaps the most respected man in the country—said he was certain that "the bloody experience of Vietnam is to end in a stalemate," and called for negotiations.

The most thorough study of Tet media coverage was made by former *New York Times* and *Washington Post* correspondent Peter Braestrup. Braestrup's *Big Story* was published in 1977. In it, he lashed into his colleagues for taking Hanoi's statements at face value while questioning those of the Americans and South Vietnamese, and for promulgating speculation rather than facts. "At best, this was overwrought instant analysis; at worst, it was vengeful exploitation of a crisis," he wrote. "Rarely has contemporary crisis-journalism turned out, in retrospect, to have veered so widely from reality."

Unlike Westmoreland, Braestrup did not accuse the press of bias. Rather, he blamed its distortions on limited resources and the pressure to sensationalize. Reporters focused on the embassy attack, for example, not just because it was a symbol of America's tottering power, but also because it took place in Saigon, where most of the correspondents were stationed. They focused on Hue and Khe Sanh, not just because that was where the enemy continued to hold the initiative, but also because that's where the heaviest fighting was. They focused on the devastation wrought by American and South Vietnamese counterattacks for the same reason reporters are drawn to fires and earthquakes: as many an editor has put it, if it bleeds, it leads.

⟋∽∽◦

Westmoreland and other critics of the press tended to downplay the many good reasons reporters had to distrust official sources. After all, these were the same American officials who had been proclaiming for years that victory was imminent. Westmoreland's credibility further plummeted in February, when he requested an additional 206,000 troops. The general argued that he needed the troops to take advantage of the opportunity presented by the Tet Offensive, but many could not help but wonder: If Tet was such a great victory, why did the military need 206,000 more men?

As the war continued and after it ended, the military's credibility continued to erode. In 1969, investigative reporter Seymour Hersh broke the story of the My Lai massacre, during which U.S. troops killed hundreds of unarmed citizens. The investigation also raised questions about whether the huge body counts during Tet—which American officials pointed to as a sign that they had won the campaign—included civilians as well as soldiers. In 1982, a CBS exposé charged that Westmoreland doctored intelligence reports of enemy numbers to create the illusion of success. Westmoreland sued the network, but dropped the case after various military officials testified the report was accurate.

The Pentagon Papers, published in 1970 in spite of the Nixon administration's effort to suppress them, revealed that many top-level Johnson aides, military and civilian, had been extremely dissatisfied with the way the war was going. They had reached their conclusions, not because of any press reports, but through their own observations and analyses.

In 1987, Robert Komer, who had been one of the general's top deputies, recalled the mood in 1968: "What really surprised us about Tet—and boy it was a surprise, lemme tell you, I was there at Westy's elbow—was that they abandoned the time-tested Mao rural strategy where the guerillas slowly strangle the city, and only at the end do they attack the seat of imperial power directly. At Tet they infiltrated right through our porous lines."

Komer maintained that the Americans and South Vietnamese ultimately won the battle. But he conceded the offensive shook his bosses. "I mean Washington panicked," he said. "LBJ panicked. Bus Wheeler, Chairman, of the Joint Chiefs, panicked."

The public, too, had had enough. Even before Tet, support for the war had been slipping, and not just among doves. Many hawks, frustrated by policies that made the military fight a war "with one arm tied behind its back," had decided it was time to get out of Vietnam. For dove and hawk alike, the Tet Offensive signaled that current strategies were not working.

"It did not matter to the American public that the platoon of sappers did not actually break into and seize the embassy building," wrote Neil Sheehan in 1988. "It did not matter in the United States that the Vietnamese Communists failed to topple the Saigon regime and foment a rebellion by the urban population. . . . What mattered to the American public was that this defeated enemy could attack anywhere and was attacking everywhere more fiercely than ever before. . . . Nothing had been achieved by the outpouring of lives and treasure and the rending of American society. The assurances the public had been given were the lies and vaporings of foolish men."

The press, then, did not deserve the blame (or the credit, depending on your perspective) for the way the public and the administration reacted to Tet. While newspaper and television reports surely had some influence, it was just as likely that many reporters—even Cronkite—were merely reflecting the increasingly prevalent disillusionment with the war.

"Rather than the press," wrote historian Clarence Wyatt in 1995, "it was the military policies of the United States and North Vietnamese governments that determined public support, or the lack thereof, for the war. . . . In the end, the American people simply tired of pouring more of their blood and money into Vietnam."

Unlike the Americans, the North Vietnamese were willing to pour into the war everything they had. They were willing to incur huge losses that, if not quite as great as Westmoreland's inflated body counts, were nonetheless a severe blow, especially to the Vietcong. For the communists, any sacrifice was worthwhile, if it struck a blow against the Americans and the South Vietnamese, as Tet surely did.

In a 1990 interview with historian Stanley Karnow, General Vo Nguyen Giap, who masterminded the Tet Offensive, explained its rationale. "We attacked the brains of the enemy, its headquarters in Saigon, showing that it was not inviolable," Giap told Karnow. "Our foes destroyed large quantities of the enemy's weapons and other equipment and crushed several of its elite units. We dramatized that we were neither exhausted nor on the edge of defeat, as Westmoreland claimed. . . . We wanted to carry the war into the families of America—to demonstrate . . . that if Vietnamese blood was being spilled, so was American blood. We did all this, and more and more Americans renounced the war."

Giap was undeniably eager to justify his decisions and to claim he foresaw all of their repercussions, at home and abroad. Most likely, Giap hoped Tet would be a decisive military victory, which it most definitely was not. But his main point was credible. Devoted as he and his followers were to their cause, he was willing to sacrifice thousands of lives to strike a psychological blow against the Americans and South Vietnamese. That he did, and there is thus no reason to doubt that he therefore considered the offensive a success.

In another interview with Karnow, General Tran Do, the deputy commander of communist forces in the south during the Tet Offensive, offered what seemed a completely candid analysis. "We didn't achieve our main objective, which was to spur uprisings throughout the south," the general told Karnow. "Still, we inflicted heavy casualties on the Americans and their puppets, and that was a big gain for us. As for making an impact in the United States, it had not been our intention—but it turned out to be a fortunate result."

To Investigate Further

Johnson, Lyndon. *The Vantage Point.* New York: Holt, Rinehart and Winston, 1971.
A surprisingly frank look at presidential decision-making, though those years (and eager readers) await Johnson's preeminent biographer, Robert Caro.

Westmoreland, William. *A Soldier Reports.* Garden City, NY: Doubleday & Company, 1976.
He could have won the war—or so he says.

Oberdorfer, Don. *Tet!* New York: Da Capo Press, 1984.
Originally published in 1971 and still one of the best accounts of the battles, political as well as military.

Braestrup, Peter. *Big Story.* New Haven, CT: Yale University Press, 1983.
An abridged edition of Braestrup's two-volume 1977 indictment of the media's Tet coverage.

Sheehan, Neil. *A Bright Shining Lie.* New York: Random House, 1988.
A riveting history of the war (and of America's changing views of it), as seen through the life of military adviser John Paul Vann.

Wyatt, Clarence. *Paper Soldiers.* New York: W. W. Norton & Company, 1993.
In contrast to the claims of Westmoreland and others, Wyatt argues that most of the time the press did not question official military reports.

McMahon, Robert, ed. *Major Problems in the History of the Vietnam War.* Lexington, MA: D.C. Heath and Company, 1995.
Includes documents and essays on Tet, among them Johnson's news conference of February 2, 1968, General Earle Wheeler's military evaluation of February 27, an early communist evaluation of the offensive, and Komer's recollections.

Gettleman, Marvin, et al., eds. *Vietnam and America.* New York: Grove Press, 1995.
Also a documentary history, this includes Westmoreland's report of June 30, 1968, excerpts from the *Pentagon Papers* pertaining to Tet, Johnson's announcement that he would curtail bombing and not run for re-election, and Hersh's report on the My Lai massacre.

Gilbert, Marc Jason, and William Head, eds. *The Tet Offensive.* Westport, CT: Praeger, 1996.
A collection of essays on the political and military issues surrounding Tet.

Karnow, Stanley. *Vietnam.* New York: Penguin Books, 1997.
Originally published in 1983 as a companion to an Emmy Award–winning PBS series, this remains the most comprehensive and balanced history of the war.

What Did Nixon Know
About Watergate?

SOON AFTER THE WATERGATE BREAK-IN of June 17, 1972, it became obvious this had been some sort of political operation. The burglars were caught, after all, in the Democratic National Committee (DNC) headquarters, in the Watergate office complex, and they had on them bugging devices—hardly the tools needed for a simple burglary. And then police traced the money in the burglars' possession to the Committee to Reelect the President, the aptly acronymed CREEP.

Still, no one in the White House revealed any particular concern. The president's press secretary smugly labeled the incident a "third-rate burglary." Other Republicans were equally quick to point out that no one involved in the president's campaign had any motive for being involved in such a crime. At the time of the burglary, Richard Nixon's political position seemed completely secure. Just eleven days before the break-in, Nixon had delightedly watched George McGovern win the California primary, virtually clinching the Democratic presidential nomination. Nixon realized McGovern was perceived as an ultraliberal, far to the left of the majority of voters, and his nomination made the president's reelection seem inevitable.

With Nixon's reelection virtually in the bag, what could he or anyone associated with him possibly want from the Democratic headquarters? As Nixon himself wrote in his 1978 memoirs: "The whole thing made so little sense. Why? I wondered. Why then? Why in such a blundering way?"

Why, indeed?

ᏇᎶᏁᎸᎤ

To Nixon's question, some historians and journalists have answered that, indeed, neither Nixon nor anyone with his interests in mind had anything to do with the break-in. Some were convinced that the break-in was arranged by the Democrats to frame Nixon. Somewhat more plausibly, others seized on the CIA connections of some of the burglars. According to this theory, the agency felt threatened by the president's policy of détente with the Soviet Union. So its agents planned—and then sabotaged—the burglary in order to embarrass Nixon. Still others believed the Joint Chiefs of Staff were behind the crime, for much the same reason.

In the 1991 best-seller *Silent Coup,* journalists Len Colodny and Robert Gettlin claimed it was the president's counsel, John Dean, who masterminded the break-in. Why

410 <mark>⌘</mark> Mysteries in History

did Dean do it? Because his girlfriend (and future wife) was linked to a call-girl ring supposedly being used by the DNC.

All these theories exculpating Nixon grew out of the entirely false assumption that the DNC held nothing of interest to the president. True, when the break-in was planned in June he was way ahead in the polls. But the operation was planned and approved earlier in the year; at that point the front-runner for the Democratic nomination was not George McGovern but Edmund Muskie—and Muskie was ahead of Nixon in the polls.

Besides, even if the election was secure, Nixon still might have wanted to find some dirt on his opponents. According to some reports, he was especially interested in what might be found from bugging the phone of DNC chairman Lawrence O'Brien. Nixon had disliked O'Brien ever since O'Brien's days as an adviser to President Kennedy, and he'd come to hate him when O'Brien became an adviser to Howard Hughes. Nixon, too, had a relationship with Hughes, including a questionable loan from the industrialist to the president's brother that had been a big embarrassment to the president. Nixon found it galling that the O'Brien/Hughes relationship had never cost O'Brien and the Democrats politically. Nixon was so obsessed with getting O'Brien that in early August, some seven weeks after the Watergate break-in (when it was obviously risky for Nixon to continue to go after him), the president ordered his chief of staff H. R. Haldeman to use the IRS to embarrass O'Brien.

The Watergate break-in might also have revealed how much the Democratic campaign managers knew about a Republican deal with ITT, a corporation that had allegedly offered cash in return for a favorable antitrust ruling. Or it might have been linked to Republican efforts to find out how much the Democrats knew about illegal contributions from Thomas Pappas, a prominent businessman and Nixon supporter. Still another possibility was that the burglars were after evidence linking the Democrats to left-wing radicals.

By his own admission, the plans for the break-in were drawn up by G. Gordon Liddy, an ex-FBI agent and right-wing ideologue who was CREEP's general counsel. On January 27 he presented his plans to John Mitchell, who was at that time the attorney general of the United States but who was preparing to resign from that office in order to run Nixon's campaign committee. Also present at the meeting was John Dean. The plans that Liddy presented included more than just wiretapping the DNC; they also called for kidnapping antiwar demonstrators and sabotaging the air-conditioning system at the Democratic convention.

According to all three present at that meeting, Mitchell rejected the plans: they were unrealistic and too expensive, he told Liddy. (That they were also blatantly illegal seemed never to have crossed the attorney general's mind.)

On March 30 Mitchell met with his deputy at CREEP, Jeb Magruder. Again, the subject was what to do about Liddy's plans. Liddy had revised them, cutting the budget from $1 million to $250,000 but still including the break-in. This time, according to Magruder, Mitchell approved the plan. Mitchell always denied he had done so, but the evidence is against him—for he soon began authorizing large payments to Liddy.

But what of Nixon himself? Did he approve the plan—or even know about it in advance?

∽∽∽

What we know of the president's involvement comes primarily from tapes that he himself made of his White House conversations. No one investigating Watergate even knew about these tapes until July 1973, when Haldeman's aide, Alexander Butterfield, mentioned them in passing to the special Senate committee investigating the crime. From that point on, the legislative and legal investigations focused on getting hold of the crucial tapes.

Nixon considered the tapes his personal property and had no intention of turning them over to anyone. When he was ordered to do so by Judge John Sirica, who presided over the tapes litigation, the tapes started mysteriously disappearing. In October, Nixon's lawyer informed Sirica that two of the subpoenaed conversations had never been recorded. Less than two weeks later, the hapless lawyer told the judge that another of the subpoenaed tapes had an 18 1/2-minute gap—this right in the midst of the very first White House discussion between Nixon and Haldeman on Watergate.

Who erased these crucial 18 1/2 minutes?

Rose Mary Woods, the president's personal secretary, testified before the court that she might have caused a gap by reaching for the telephone while transcribing the tape and accidentally hitting the tape recorder's delete button. But when she was asked to demonstrate how this might have happened, she had to stretch herself into an extremely convoluted position. Stretching credibility even further was her testimony that her telephone conversation lasted only four or five minutes and therefore could not account for the remaining erasures. Nor did the testimony of Nixon's chief of staff, Alexander Haig, alleviate suspicion: it was just like a woman, he said, not to realize how long she'd been talking on the phone.

A court-appointed panel of experts concluded that the 18 1/2-minute gap had been caused by hand operation of the controls, not the foot pedal, as Woods claimed. In addition, the panel stated that the gap had been caused by at least five and perhaps as many as nine separate erasures, and that the evidence was "consistent" with traces left by a deliberate erasure. At this point, even the conservative *National Review* threw in the towel, writing: "Believers in the accidental theory could gather for lunch in a phone booth."

The worst, for Nixon, was still to come. He eventually had to release some of the tapes Sirica requested, and on those tapes he can clearly be heard discussing payoffs and offering advice on how to commit perjury. A tape from June 23, 1972, came to be known as the "smoking gun" and it is indeed that: Nixon can be heard giving explicit instructions that the CIA should tell the FBI to lay off the Watergate investigation.

The June 23 tape proved beyond any doubt that Nixon had been guilty of obstructing justice, and once it was released his resignation was inevitable. But, it must be stressed, it was this involvement in the crime's cover-up that brought Nixon down. Nothing on the tapes he released indicated he'd had any direct involvement or knowledge of the crime itself.

ᴏᴍᴀᴏ

Some Nixon apologists continued to maintain that he was innocent. The 1991 book, *Silent Coup*, portrayed Nixon as a victim not just of Dean (whom it accused, you'll recall, of planning the break-in to find out about his girlfriend's call-girl ring) but also of Alexander Haig, the president's chief of staff. In the Colodny/Gettlin scenario, Haig was "Deep Throat," the anonymous source to whom *Washington Post* reporter Bob Woodward regularly turned when he was stumped in his Watergate investigation. When that wasn't enough to bury Nixon, Haig took it upon himself to put the final nails in the president's coffin by erasing those 18 1/2 minutes. The missing minutes, Colodny and Gettlin speculated, included nothing at all incriminating; Haig erased them solely to embarrass the president.

Many historians found *Silent Coup* intriguing, but most didn't buy its conclusions. The 2005 revelation that Deep Throat was not Haig but FBI associate director Mark Felt further undercut the book's arguments.

Nixon himself worked assiduously to rehabilitate his reputation, writing a series of well-received books on foreign affairs and refusing to release additional tapes from his presidency. In 1996, two years after Nixon's death, hundreds of hours of recordings were released. (Only sixty hours were released in the 1970s.) The tapes provided more evidence of his involvement in the cover-up.

The new tapes did not show Nixon knew in advance about the break-in, but they included plenty of new evidence of his involvement in the cover-up. On August 1, 1972, for example, Haldeman reported that the burglars had received their hush money. "It's worth it," the president responded. "They have to be paid. That's all there is to that."

No amount of revisionism could explain away this obstruction of justice, or all the spying, tricks, and harassment of enemies that characterized the Nixon presidency—and of which Watergate was only a part. For years Nixon's operatives spied on Democrats and reporters. They attempted to break into George McGovern's office. They asked the IRS to harass Nixon's enemies. When they couldn't come up with any dirt on his opponents, they didn't hesitate to invent some—as when E. Howard Hunt forged some cables indicating the Kennedy administration had been responsible for the 1963 assassination of South Vietnamese President Diem. Long before the Watergate break-in, some of the same burglars were working for the White House "Plumbers," a group whose quaint name came from its original task of plugging White House leaks but whose assignments included a variety of other spying jobs.

This, then, was the context of Watergate—a context in which Nixon's apparent bewilderment as to why anyone would want to break into the DNC can only be seen as an extraordinary performance. "In a lifetime of bold and brazen acts, this was the boldest and most brazen, as well as the most successful," wrote Nixon's biographer Stephen Ambrose. "That students, scholars, and the general public continue to ask these questions, as if they were legitimate, as if there were some unsolved mystery here, constitutes a triumph for Nixon." For whatever else he knew or didn't know about Watergate, Nixon understood full well why it happened.

To Investigate Further

The White House Tapes.

Nixon's own edited version, which he made public in April 1974, was subsequently published in paperback by the *New York Times* and the *Washington Post.* Unfortunately, these transcripts were soon shown to be very selective—and not just because of the infamous references to "expletive deleted."

Bernstein, Carl, and Bob Woodward. *All the President's Men.* New York: Simon and Schuster, 1974.

How the two *Washington Post* reporters broke the story. Also worth reading is their second book, *The Final Days* (Simon and Schuster, 1976). The first book puts you inside the *Post* newsroom; the second inside the White House.

Higgins, George V. *The Friends of Richard Nixon.* Boston: Atlantic Monthly Press, 1975.

For Higgins, himself a former prosecutor as well as a master of crime fiction, the heroes of the story are the prosecutors; everyone else—including not just Nixon's friends but quite a few of his enemies—is subject to Higgins's biting wit.

Dean, John. *Blind Ambition.* New York: Simon and Schuster, 1976.

Almost all of the participants in the crime and cover-up penned memoirs; some more than one. Dean's two entries, this and *Lost Honor* (Stratford Press, 1982), are invaluable.

Lukas, J. Anthony. *Nightmare: The Underside of the Nixon Years.* New York: Viking, 1976.

One of the first and best works of Watergate investigative journalism.

Nixon, Richard. *RN: The Memoirs of Richard Nixon.* New York: Grosset & Dunlap, 1978.

Though obviously self-serving, this is nonetheless highly revealing—perhaps more so than Nixon intended.

Haldeman, H. R. *The Ends of Power.* New York: Times Books, 1978.

Like Dean, Haldeman produced two invaluable works, this and the remarkably frank, posthumously published, *The Haldeman Diaries* G.P. Putnam's Sons, 1994.

Hougan, Jim. *Secret Agenda: Watergate, Deep Throat and the CIA.* New York: Random House, 1984.

Much of what made such a splash in the Colodny/Gettlin book was first published here, along with evidence that the CIA's role in Watergate was pervasive.

Ambrose, Stephen E. *Nixon* (Vol. 1, *The Education of a Politician,* 1987; Vol. 2, *The Triumph of a Politician,* 1989; Vol. 3, *Ruin and Recovery,* 1991). New York: Simon and Schuster.

A superb biography of Nixon, including (in Volumes 2 and 3) a thorough presentation of the "orthodox" interpretation of Watergate.

Colodny, Len, and Robert Gettlin. *Silent Coup: The Removal of a President.* New York: St. Martin's Press, 1991.

Even its detractors admit it raised some interesting questions.

Kutler, Stanley I. *The Wars of Watergate.* New York: Knopf, 1990.

There are numerous Watergate books by journalists but this was the first comprehensive treatment by a historian; perhaps as a result, Kutler argues that the role of investigative journalists has been much exaggerated and that most of the Watergate revelations were the result of judicial investigations.

Emery, Fred. *Watergate.* New York: Times Books, 1994.
    The latest history by a journalist, which restores the primacy of the journalistic and congressional investigations. Very thorough.

Kutler, Stanley. *Abuse of Power.* New York: The Free Press, 1997.
    The new tapes.

Who Killed Jimmy Hoffa?

JIMMY HOFFA LEFT his suburban Detroit home in the early afternoon of July 30, 1975. He stopped briefly to see an old friend who ran a nearby limousine service, but the friend had already left for lunch. Hoffa then drove to the Machus Red Fox Restaurant, where he expected to meet Anthony Giacalone and Anthony Provenzano. "Tony Jack" and "Tony Pro" were also old friends, or at least old acquaintances from the days when Hoffa ran the International Brotherhood of Teamsters. At about 2:30, Hoffa called his wife to ask if she'd heard from Giacalone, and then told her it looked like he'd been stood up. It was the last she—or anyone—heard from him.

Few doubted he was dead. Giacalone and Provenzano were mixed up with the Mafia, as was Hoffa himself. The jokes quickly circulated: Jacques Cousteau had spotted Hoffa's body, or it was under the end zone of the new Meadowlands football stadium, where the concrete had just been poured. This was, the FBI agreed, a mob-related execution.

Yet Hoffa's body was never found, Giacalone and Provenzano had airtight alibis, and neither they nor anyone else was ever charged with the murder. Hoffa's disappearance remains one of the most intriguing in American history, partly because Hoffa himself was so intriguing. Was he, as Robert Kennedy put it, the leader of a "conspiracy of evil," a union leader who had "sold out the union membership [and] put gangsters and racketeers in important positions of power within the Teamsters"? Or was he, as many Teamsters believed then and now, persecuted because he stood up for the people he represented? "For what he did for the driver, I'd take a chance on him again," one teamster said, after Hoffa was convicted of misusing union pension funds. "If he robbed a little, what the hell."

Hoffa's connections to the mob, it was clear, were the key to solving the mysteries of his life as well as his death.

⁖

Kennedy's first efforts to connect Hoffa to the mob were distinctly unsuccessful. As chief counsel to the Senate Select Committee on Improper Activities in the Labor or Management Field, Kennedy led an investigation that called 1,525 witnesses over two and a half years. In 1957, after attorney John Cheasty testified that Hoffa had attempted to bribe him to turn over confidential committee papers, Kennedy was confident that he had the goods on the labor leader. "If Hoffa isn't convicted," he announced, "I'll jump off the Capitol Dome." Four months later, after a jury found Hoffa not guilty of conspiring to obstruct the committee's inquiry, defense attorney Edward Bennett Williams offered to send Kennedy a parachute.

The committee's final report was almost fifty thousand pages long, and resulted in the 1959 Landrum-Griffin Act and the first government regulation of internal union affairs. The investigation also led to the expulsion of the Teamsters from the AFL-CIO, and prison terms for several Hoffa associates. But Hoffa himself remained both free and in charge of the union.

When John F. Kennedy became president and made his brother attorney general, it was clear Hoffa would become a top priority of the Justice Department. ("Everyone in my family forgives," the Kennedys' father once said, "except Bobby.") The new attorney general quickly set up a special unit whose lawyers described themselves as the "Get Hoffa Squad." In 1962, prosecutors charged Hoffa with negotiating a sweetheart deal with one trucking company in return for its sending business to another, which happened to be owned by Hoffa's wife. Again, a jury found him not guilty. But that case turned out to be the labor leader's undoing when Hoffa aide Edward Partin told prosecutors that his boss had bribed the jurors. In 1964, another jury found Hoffa guilty of jury tampering. That same year, yet another jury convicted Hoffa of conspiracy and fraud having to do with a Teamster pension fund.

Hoffa was sentenced to eight years. In 1967, his appeals exhausted, he entered the federal penitentiary in Lewisburg, Pennsylvania. It was in Lewisburg, according to FBI reports, that Provenzano (who was serving a four-year term for extortion) decided he wanted Hoffa dead. The two had once been allies. Provenzano, a member of the Genovese crime family, ran Teamster Local 560 in Union City, New Jersey, and had supported Hoffa in his rise to the union presidency. At first, he also protected Hoffa from the dangers of prison, and the two regularly sat together at mealtime. The relationship went awry when Provenzano asked Hoffa for help getting credit toward his Teamster pension, which he was being denied because the Landrum-Griffin Act barred persons convicted of extortion from holding union office until five years after their incarceration. Hoffa refused, telling Tony Pro, "It's because of people like you that I got into trouble in the first place."

The feud intensified after the two men were released from prison, Provenzano in 1970 and Hoffa a year later. (The latter's sentence was commuted by Richard Nixon, one of the few men who resented the Kennedys more than Hoffa did.) The two met several times during 1973 and 1974, and Provenzano once threatened to "pull out Hoffa's guts." Provenzano's friend Giacalone was an equally threatening figure; this was a man who ran an exterminating company and was, as Hoffa biographer Arthur Sloane put it, "thought to be capable of the extermination of humans as well as animal and insect life." Even Jimmy Hoffa, not an easy man to intimidate, must have been unnerved by the promised violence of Tony Pro and Tony Jack. So when the two proposed that they all get together for a "peace meeting" at the Machus Red Fox Restaurant, Hoffa must have been relieved.

He must also have been increasingly nervous when Provenzano and Giacalone failed to show up at the restaurant. Tony Pro, it turned out, was in Union City, New Jersey, playing Greek rummy in plain view of plenty of people. (Provenzano's brother later explained the game: "You knock everybody out, and when one man remains, he's the winner.") Tony Jack was at Detroit's Southfield Athletic Club, having a massage and haircut and noticed by so many people that, an FBI memo concluded, "Giacalone definitely appeared to be establishing an alibi."

According to the FBI's theory, Provenzano assigned the hit to Salvatore and Gabriel Briguglio and Thomas Andretta. Two of them picked up Hoffa at the Machus Red Fox, and killed him. FBI agents accumulated a variety of evidence, including the statements of a prison informant and of an eyewitness who thought she'd seen Salvatore Briguglio on July 30, 1975, in a car parked at the Machus Red Fox. But the Briguglio brothers and Andretta maintained they were in Union City, New Jersey, that day—playing Greek rummy with Tony Pro—and the Bureau never could never shake their alibis, at least not enough to take the case to court.

In any case, many in the Bureau believed Provenzano, Giacalone, and their alleged accomplices wouldn't have killed Hoffa without approval from their higher-ups. The generally accepted theory was that mob leaders had grown very comfortable with Hoffa's successor as Teamster president, Frank Fitzsimmons. True, they'd once worked quite well with Hoffa. But Fitzsimmons lacked his predecessor's temper and independent streak. So when Hoffa started making noises about making a comeback (not at all impossible, given his continuing popularity with the rank and file), the mob decided to eliminate the possibility. They turned to Provenzano because they knew he had his own reasons for wanting Hoffa dead.

Hoffa's son shared the FBI's suspicion that his father was killed to keep him from retaking the presidency. "Dad was pushing so hard to get back in office," James P. Hoffa recalled of the spring of 1975. "I was increasingly afraid that the mob would do something about it."

ᐧᐧᐧᐧᐧ

In 1975, as the FBI investigated Hoffa's death, a Senate committee learned that the CIA, with Mafia help, had attempted to assassinate Fidel Castro. In 1977, as the FBI continued to probe Hoffa's death, a House committee investigated the death of John Kennedy. By the time the congressional committees were done, the assassinations and attempted assassinations of Castro, Kennedy, and Hoffa were all entangled, at least in the minds of some conspiracy theorists.

For starters, Hoffa hated the president. Not as much as he hated his brother, of course, but by extension, plenty. Edward Partin, the Hoffa aide who told prosecutors about his boss's jury tampering, also told them—and later the House Assassinations Committee—that his boss had talked about killing "that son of a bitch Bobby Kennedy." That wasn't the only connection between the labor leader and the president's assassination. Jack Ruby, the man who killed Lee Harvey Oswald, was the number-two man in a Teamster affiliate run by a close friend of Hoffa. And Hoffa was also friendly with Tampa godfather Santo Trafficante and New Orleans godfather Carlos Marcello, both of whom were targets of the attorney general and both of whom had spoken, at least according to some witnesses, of murdering the president. Robert Blakey, the chief counsel for the House committee, believed the Mafia was behind the president's assassination, and he named three suspects: Trafficante, Marcello, and Hoffa.

For some conspiracy theorists, it was only a short jump from Hoffa-as-assassin to Hoffa-as-target. The logic went like this: The Mafia wanted Castro dead, because he was bad for their business in Cuba. The CIA wanted Castro dead, for political reasons. So Castro, in revenge for the joint CIA-Mafia attempts on his life, killed Kennedy. Alternatively, the Mafia, in revenge for Bobby's anti–organized crime efforts, killed John. Then the Mafia killed Hoffa, because they feared he might tell what he knew about either their anti-Castro or anti-Kennedy plots.

With the House and Senate both investigating, the late 1970s were the heyday of assassination conspiracy theories. Among the most persuasive was that of Dan Moldea, an investigative journalist whose 1988 book, *The Hoffa Wars*, stopped short of concluding exactly how the labor leader was involved, but suggested that the solution was "to be found in the consistent cast of characters that threaded its way through Hoffa's life—and through fifteen years of American political violence."

The men suspected of ordering Hoffa's murder, Moldea noted, were the same men suspected of plotting to kill Castro and Kennedy: Trafficante, Marcello, Provenzano, and others. "There is therefore considerable reason to believe," Moldea continued, "that Hoffa was removed for reasons more complicated than mere ambition."

Other conspiracy theorists tied Nixon to Hoffa's murder, alleging that the president feared that Hoffa, if he couldn't regain control of the Teamsters, might reveal secret union payoffs to Nixon. Still others blamed government agents for Hoffa's murder. Hoffa assistant Joseph Franco, for example, claimed in his 1987 book that he was present at the Machus Red Fox, and that he witnessed three men pick up his boss. "They were typical Ivy Leaguers," Franco wrote, "with sports jackets and shirts and ties, and you could see that they were either federal marshals or federal agents." Franco didn't say why the marshals or agents wanted Hoffa dead.

The problem with all these conspiracy theories was that there was no hard evidence to substantiate any of them. There was no evidence that Trafficante or Marcello had done anything more than talk about assassinating Kennedy, or that Hoffa had even talked about hitting the president, as opposed to his brother. Most historians eventually concluded that Oswald acted alone. And as far as Hoffa's own disappearance was concerned, the FBI didn't even have enough evidence to indict Provenzano or Giacalone or Andretta or the Briguglios, let alone other mobsters or Cubans or government agents.

In 2000, the FBI got a break in the form of DNA analysis that hadn't been available back in 1975. They matched hair taken from Hoffa's brush with a strand found in a car owned by Joey Giacalone, Tony's son. This was a car that Hoffa's foster son, Chuckie O'Brien, had already admitted he'd borrowed from Giacalone the day Hoffa disappeared. When the DNA evidence proved Hoffa had been in the car, suspicion focused on

O'Brien. O'Brien's presence that day could explain how Hoffa's murderers got him to leave the restaurant quietly. After all, the labor leader was fully aware of the dangers of dealing with Provenzano or Giacalone or anyone they sent to pick him up. But if his trusted foster son showed up, that would have at least partly allayed his fears.

The FBI suspected O'Brien might have been in on the murder, perhaps because he was angry at Hoffa's refusal to help him repay his gambling debts. Or O'Brien may have been duped by the murderers. "It is quite possible that O'Brien simply thought he was taking Hoffa to just another meeting," one government official told Moldea. "But even if that's true, O'Brien certainly became an accessory to the subsequent cover-up."

Back in 1975, O'Brien told the FBI that he never saw his foster father on the day of his disappearance, and that he borrowed Giacalone's car to run some errands. Grilled by prosecutors twenty-five years later, he stuck to his story. Ultimately, prosecutors decided that the DNA evidence wasn't enough to bring charges against him.

"It has the makings of a whodunit novel, only, unfortunately, without the final chapter being written," prosecutor David Gorcya told the *Detroit Free Press* in August 2002. "But we may someday get lucky, and someone will come forward. Someone involved in the case may want to cleanse their conscience."

That someone turned out to be, according to a 2004 book by attorney Charles Brandt, Frank "the Irishman" Sheeran. Sheeran, a mob hit man who once worked for Hoffa, told Brandt he'd "painted" Hoffa's house. Paint, in mob talk, is the blood that splatters when someone's shot. Sheeran, Brandt said, acted on orders from mob boss Russell Bufalino, after Hoffa refused to drop his bid for the Teamster presidency. Police found blood under the floorboards of the house in which Sheeran said he'd done the job. The blood didn't match Hoffa's, but the rest of the story fit the FBI theory.

Sheeran had only Bufalino's word on what happened to Hoffa's body. "Russell told me that after the two guys got done cleaning the house they put Jimmy in a body bag," he told Brandt. "Protected by the fence and the garage they took him out the back door and put him in the trunk of the Buick. Then they took Jimmy to be cremated [and] flew back to Jersey to report to Tony Pro."

If Sheeran was telling the truth, it was not only his conscience that needed cleansing but Hoffa's. Before turning on his former boss, Sheeran told Brandt, he'd paid off Nixon's attorney general John Mitchell, in return for Hoffa's parole, and he'd carried out many hits on Hoffa's orders. This certainly fit the image of Hoffa as a gangster and racketeer, a Faustian criminal who sold out the Teamsters to the Mafia and who fully deserved the prosecutorial attentions Robert Kennedy heaped upon him. "Jimmy Hoffa's most valuable contribution to the American labor movement," Moldea wrote, "came at the moment he stopped breathing on July 30, 1975."

To most rank-and-file members of the union, however, Hoffa was a true hero, a man who dramatically improved the working conditions of millions in what had once been among the poorest paying and most dangerous of jobs. In 1998, Jimmy's son, James P. Hoffa, was overwhelmingly elected Teamster president, in spite of his notable lack of union experience. Clearly, this was a testament to the continuing power, long after the disappearance and presumed death, of James R. Hoffa.

The middle initial, by the way, stood for "Riddle."

To Investigate Further

Kennedy, Robert. *The Enemy Within.* New York: Harper & Row, 1960.
Considering it's about a Senate committee investigation, this is remarkably dramatic and entertaining.

Brill, Steven. *The Teamsters.* New York: Simon and Schuster, 1978.
Superb profiles of Teamster leaders, including Hoffa and Fitzsimmons.

Moldea, Dan. *The Hoffa Wars.* New York: Charter Communications, 1978.
The many connections between Teamsters, politicians, and the mob.

Franco, Joseph, with Richard Hammer. *Hoffa's Man.* New York: Prentice-Hall Press, 1987.
His rise and fall, as witnessed by "his strongest arm."

Sloane, Arthur. *Hoffa.* Cambridge: MA: MIT Press, 1991.
A solid if somewhat dry biography.

Russell, Thaddeus. *Out of the Jungle.* New York: Alfred A. Knopf, 2001.
Russell concedes Hoffa was corrupt, but he blames more leftist union leaders for putting politics ahead of bread-and-butter issues.

Brandt, Charles. *I Heard You Paint Houses.* Hanover, NH: Steerforth Press, 2004.
"Jimmy Hoffa was one of the two greatest men I ever met," Sheeran told Brandt. The other, alas, was Russell Bufalino.

Was Howard Hughes's
Will a Forgery?

WHEN HOWARD HUGHES DIED in April 1976, no one was sure exactly how much his estate was worth. Partly that was because his holdings were far-flung, encompassing movies, airlines, mining claims, hotels, casinos, and thousands of acres in California and Nevada. Mostly it was because these holdings were almost all private, and Hughes had been extraordinarily secretive. There was no doubt, though, that Hughes left behind a fortune; some estimates put the value as high as $6 billion.

Within days of his death, rumors circulated that there was no will, leaving the money up for grabs. This was, on the face of it, absurd. Hughes hated paying taxes, and in the absence of a will much of the estate would go to the government.

"The tax man who Hughes spent his entire life successfully avoiding would be declared the winner," wrote his biographer Richard Hack. "If Howard Hughes were not already dead, that bit of news alone would have killed him."

The rest of the money would go to relatives Hughes hadn't spoken to in decades.

To avoid just these eventualities, Hughes had spent far more time on his will than most people, even most billionaires. He had signed a will in 1925, just before he married Ella Rice, though that was invalidated after their divorce. During the 1940s, Hughes's personal assistant, Nadine Henley, had spent numerous hours typing and retyping drafts he sent her. From the mid-1950s, he publicly spoke of his plans to leave his money to the Howard Hughes Medical Institute, a charity he set up in 1954. And during his final years, he privately promised his personal aides that he had generously provided for them in his will.

For Hughes to have died without a will seemed entirely out of character. This was not a man who left things to chance. When he wanted to date Hollywood stars like Katharine Hepburn and Lana Turner, Hughes became a movie producer. When he bought RKO, Hughes insisted on re-shooting parts of movies he didn't like. In 1967, when he was staying in the Desert Inn in Las Vegas, the owners asked him to leave because some high rollers had reserved the rooms. Hughes's response was to buy the hotel.

Indeed, Hughes's insistence on total control over his environment was famously pathological. Desperately afraid of germs, he wrote lengthy instructions for aides on how to open a can of fruit salad, how to lift a toilet seat, how to enter and leave a room. In 1955, for example, he explained how to enter his bungalow at the Beverly Hills Hilton, a process that required three men:

"Before opening the door to the room, the third man is to stand with a folded news-paper in his right hand and rapidly wave it for at least one minute to eliminate the possi-bility that flies will enter the room," Hughes wrote. "Using eight Kleenex placed in the left hand, the man who is rapidly waving the newspaper will knock on the door. When HRH responds, the man will open the door, using the hand with the Kleenex. The door is never to be opened further than twelve inches nor longer than ten seconds at a time. This will allow a second man enough time to enter the room."

How could a man so obsessed with power and control leave no will? That he would "die intestate and turn his empire and life's work over to the whims of countless others for dismemberment seemed," wrote the investigative reporters James Phelan and Lewis Chester, "inconceivable."

And yet, as days turned into months, there was no sign of a will.

Executives at the Summa Corporation, which included most of Hughes's holdings, undertook a national search for the will. They broke into filing cabinets and safes, where they found plenty of letters and memos referring to a will, but no will. They placed a classified ad in about forty newspapers, asking anyone with information to call. They even hired a psychic named Peter Hurkos, who claimed all he needed to find a document was a piece of its owner's clothing. The corporation supplied Hurkos with a pair of shoes; alas—maybe because Hughes had a habit of walking around not just shoeless but naked—Hurkos found nothing.

Not surprisingly, the search turned up a series of would-be heirs, among them a man who claimed to be Hughes's son and who said he communicated with his father through a radio transmitter implanted in his brain, and a woman who decided she was Hughes's daughter because she walked like him.

A woman named Martha Graves showed up with a copy of a will, dated July 1960, in which Hughes left 20 percent of his money to the Acme Mining Company, of which Graves happened to be the president and major stockholder. Graves couldn't produce the original document, she explained, because she'd packed it and the airline had lost her luggage. For her efforts, a judge awarded her a year in prison.

Somewhat more credible was the story of Terry Moore, an actress with whom Hughes had an affair in the late forties. The affair was real, and had been recorded in the gossip columns of Louella Parsons and Hedda Hopper. But according to Moore, it was more than an affair.

In her deposition for a Texas court, Moore testified she and Hughes had been mar-ried. The wedding took place on Hughes's yacht, somewhere off the coast of Mexico, and was presided over by the ship's captain. There was no license or ring, Moore conceded, but she had seen enough movies to know that a captain could marry you at sea.

Why did she keep the marriage a secret? "I was the eternal virgin," she said, describing her Hollywood image. "Howard had the reputation of being a roué, and it would be very harmful to my reputation to be married to him."

Moore's story came with no will and with one big hole in it: she had subsequently married three other men. Still, it made Hughes's relatives nervous. They stood to lose everything if by chance the court determined Moore was Hughes's widow (not to mention a bigamist). So they reached an out-of-court settlement, reportedly paying her about $350,000.

Of all the claims to the Hughes fortune, though, the one that most captured America's attention was what came to be known as the "Mormon Will." That's because it was found in Mormon headquarters in Salt Lake City, and it gave one-sixteenth of the Hughes fortune to the Mormon Church. It also left a fourth of his assets to the Medical Institute, a fourth to establish a home for orphans, an eighth to various universities, a sixteenth to Hughes's two ex-wives (not counting Moore), a sixteenth for school scholarships, a sixteenth to be divided among Hughes's aides, a sixteenth to Hughes's cousin William Lummis—and a sixteenth to a former milkman named Melvin Dummar.

ᔕᔕᔕ

Reporters found Dummar in April 1976, working at a small gas station in Willard, Utah, and he told them he didn't know anything about the will. But he did recall that, back in January 1968, he had picked up a bum on a highway south of Tonopah and had given him a lift to Las Vegas. The bum had told him he was Howard Hughes, though Dummar certainly hadn't believed him. Dummar gave him a quarter before dropping him off.

It was easy to see why people wanted to believe Dummar's story of a good Samaritan receiving his just—and surprising—reward. Dummar wanted to be a country singer, and one of his songs was "A Dream Can Become a Reality." His dreams had carried him to three appearances on *Let's Make a Deal,* on one of which he won a car, a freezer, and a range. Now he stood to win a lot more.

Dummar's big break came when Noah Dietrich, the former Hughes executive named in the Mormon Will as executor, pronounced the handwriting and signature genuine. "It's the real thing," Dietrich told reporters.

Hughes's relatives, not surprisingly, disagreed, and they prepared to take their case to court. They pointed out that the will was riddled with spelling and grammar mistakes, even though Hughes was fairly good at both. Moreover, the will donated the *Spruce Goose* to the city of Long Beach, California. The *Spruce Goose* was the popular name for a huge flying boat Hughes had built, but it was a name he hated, and in fact he didn't even own the plane in 1968, when he supposedly wrote the will.

As for Dietrich's validation, the relatives had handwriting experts of their own to contradict it. They also noted that the executive and Hughes had split bitterly in 1957, making him an unlikely choice for executor, and that Dietrich stood to make millions in fees if the will was upheld.

Dummar's case began to fall apart in December, when investigators for the Hughes relatives found his fingerprints on a library copy of *Hoax,* a book about a failed attempt to forge a Hughes autobiography. An insert of the photographs used to copy Hughes's handwriting was missing from the book, leading investigators to suspect Dummar cut out the section. Things got worse when the FBI found his fingerprint on the corner of the envelope in which the will had been found at the Mormon headquarters. This seemed to prove Dummar a liar, since for seven months he had denied having seen the will, or even having heard of it, prior to reporters telling him about it.

In January, Dummar abruptly changed his story. He admitted he was the one who delivered the will to the church, but he continued to deny he had anything to do with writing it. His new account had a mysterious stranger in a blue Mercedes drive up to his gas station, then leave the envelope and the will on the counter. Dummar explained that he'd lied at first, because he feared no one would believe this story. Few did.

A month later, with the case seemingly lost, the stranger in the Mercedes miraculously appeared. This was Levane Forsythe, a construction worker from Alaska who, he announced, had been a secret courier for Howard Hughes. Forsythe said Hughes had given him the will in 1972, along with instructions to deliver it to Dummar after his death.

Was Forsythe telling the truth? Was Dummar? Harold Rhoden, the attorney representing Dietrich, argued they were.

"The will itself is bizarre," he conceded. "Bizarre in what it says, bizarre in the way it was written and in the way it was kept for eight years. And bizarre in the way it was delivered to the Mormon Church. But this was the bizarre way of the man who wrote it."

The eight members of the Las Vegas jury who heard their testimony didn't buy it. In June 1977, they voted unanimously that the will "was not written by Howard R. Hughes."

Dummar did not come out of the affair entirely empty-handed. His country singing career got a boost, albeit a brief one, when he was booked for two weeks in Reno. Unlike Martha Graves, Melvin Dummar was not tried for fraud. And many continued to believe his story, especially after it was turned into a popular movie, *Melvin and Howard,* in 1980, in which Hughes was played by Jason Robards and Dummar by Paul Le Mat. The real Dummar made a brief appearance as a counterman in a bus station cafeteria.

Dummar continued to dream. "What hurts me most about this will, worse than having it ruled a forgery," he said, "is that I didn't get to play myself in the movie."

⤖

Dummar's description of Hughes as looking like a bum was not far from the truth, at least in his final years. Devastated by years of drug abuse, the billionaire died with broken needles in his arms and weighing only ninety-two pounds. This led some, including Texas attorney general Rick Harrison, to suspect that his aides, perhaps with the help of his doctors, had murdered Hughes.

No one was charged with murder, though two of Hughes's doctors pleaded "no contest" to illegally supplying Hughes with drugs. And a murder conspiracy seems unlikely, especially since—in the absence of a will leaving them anything—the aides and doctors had more to gain from Hughes alive than dead.

With no will in sight, the way was clear for Lummis and various other Hughes relatives to inherit varying percentages of his fortune. The total distribution turned out to be, disappointingly, less than a billion dollars, partly because of the huge estate taxes and legal fees.

What would Howard Hughes have thought about that?

Most people pictured him turning over in his grave, distraught to see his fortune go to the government and to relatives he cared nothing about. Some suspected a valid will was destroyed, or might still turn up.

But it's also very possible Hughes never wrote one. Obsessed by his germ-phobia, he spent his final years in various hideouts around the globe. He saw increasingly few people and cared about even fewer. Why, he may have thought, should any of them get his money?

Sure, he had said he would leave the money to medical research, but there's no evidence he really cared about this. The Howard Hughes Medical Institute was in reality little more than a tax shelter; for all his talk about the charity, at no point in his life did Hughes donate any substantial sum to it. As for the promises to his aides and doctors, maybe Hughes was just stringing them along to keep them loyal. Maybe he even feared they'd kill him if he actually wrote them into his will.

"His selfish being knew nothing now of love, of tenderness, of companionship," wrote biographer Charles Higham. "Now he could really show that he cared for nothing."

"He promised [his aides he would] compose an entirely new will. Soon. But he never would," speculated journalist Michael Drosnin. "The nonexistent last testament was his last hold on power."

In the end, that power may have been all he cared about.

To Investigate Further

Fay, Stephen, Lewis Chester, and Magnus Linklater. *Hoax.* **New York: Viking, 1972.**
This is the book from which Dummar allegedly cut out photos of Hughes's signature to copy. It's also the fascinating story of how Clifford Irving forged Hughes's autobiography, a scam that might have succeeded had Hughes not emerged from seclusion, briefly, to deny he had anything to do with Irving's book.

Barlett, Donald, and James Steele. *Empire.* **W. W. Norton. 1979.**
"This is the book," wrote the *New York Times*, "Clifford Irving must wish he had written." It remains the best biography of Hughes.

Rhoden, Harold. *High Stakes.* **New York, Crown, 1980.**
Rhoden, the attorney who represented Dietrich, believed in Dummar, even if the jury didn't.

Drosnin, Michael. *Citizen Hughes.* **New York: Holt, Rinehart and Winston, 1985.**
Focuses on Hughes's final years, especially his political influence and his involvement in Watergate.

Higham, Charles. *Howard Hughes.* **New York: Putnam's, 1993.**
A portrait of Hughes as ruthless, albeit drug-ridden, to the end.

Brown, Peter, and Pat Broeske. *Howard Hughes.* New York: Dutton, 1996.
    Everything you wanted to know about his sex life.

Phelan, James, and Lewis Chester. *The Money.* New York: Random House, 1997.
    The battle for the billions.

Hack, Richard. *Hughes.* Beverly Hills, CA: New Millennium Press, 2001.
    A comprehensive biography.

What Did Reagan Know About Iran-Contra?

THROUGHOUT THE EARLY 1980S, Congress was engaged in a heated debate over whether to support the contra rebels in Nicaragua. Supporters of the contras, among them President Ronald Reagan, portrayed them as anticommunist freedom fighters; opponents decried them for being more interested in profiteering than in democracy or human rights. In the summer of 1984, the contras' congressional opponents prevailed. Capitalizing on public fears that support for the contras could enmesh the nation in another Vietnam, they passed the Boland amendment, which banned any further military aid to the contras. Then in October 1986, Nicaraguan soldiers shot down a cargo plane carrying arms to the contras. The captured pilot, Eugene Hasenfus, confessed that he was part of a covert U.S. government-supported operation—an operation in clear violation of the Boland amendment.

Not true, Reagan assured reporters. Although he adamantly supported the contra cause, his administration had had to abide by the will of Congress. Hasenfus was a private citizen working on behalf of other private citizens. "There was no government connection with that at all," Reagan stressed.

A month later, just as the furor over Hasenfus's statement was dying down, a Lebanese newspaper reported that the Reagan administration had shipped arms to Iran in an effort to win the freedom of American hostages being held in Lebanon. Again the White House was plunged into crisis. In this case, the problem was not so much that such arms shipments were illegal (though they were a violation of the Arms Export Control Act), but that they directly contravened the administration's own oft-stated policy of not negotiating with terrorists. In fact the Reagan administration had been actively pressuring other countries to join an arms embargo against Iran. If the arms-for-hostages story were true, the administration looked like hypocrites, or worse, like fools—for once Iran had the weapons in hand, what was to prevent the terrorists from seizing more hostages?

The administration's response again was to deny the story. Yes, the president said in a televised talk on November 13, the United States had been in contact with some groups in Iran, but this had been purely an effort to bolster those moderates in their efforts to seize power from Ayatollah Khomeini. "We did not—repeat—did not trade weapons or anything else for hostages, nor will we," Reagan said.

Then, on November 25, the president opened a press conference by admitting he had not been "fully informed" of the nature of his administration's dealings with Iran. At that point Attorney General Edwin Meese took the podium and announced that some weapons had indeed been sold to Iran. Even more shocking, Meese continued, was that the profits from these arms sales—approximately $12 million—had been used to finance the contra war efforts. So the Iran and contra stories were not only true, they were linked.

The man responsible for the "diversion" of the $12 million, Meese said, was a mid-level staffer at the National Security Council, Lt. Col. Oliver North. North had now been "relieved of his duties" and his superior, National Security Adviser John Poindexter, had resigned. But if Meese thought that would put an end to the scandal, he was mistaken. Over the next seven years a series of investigations delved deeper and deeper into the Iran-contra affairs, attempting to find out who knew what—and when. Above all, what they wanted to know was this: Did Reagan himself know about—or authorize—the covert operations of his National Security Council?

⸰⸰⸰

Eager to make clear there was no cover-up, the president quickly appointed a commission to investigate the affair. The Tower Commission (named after its chairman, ex-Senator John Tower) interviewed key figures, including Reagan. On the subject of aid to the contras, Reagan was clear: he told the commission he had not known about the activities of the National Security Council staff. On Iran, he was more confused. In his first interview, he said he had approved a shipment of arms to Iran; in his second interview, he retracted this position. Then in a letter to the commission, Reagan wrote: "The simple truth is 'I don't remember.'"

The commission accepted the president's word. After all, Reagan's reputation had always been that of a hands-off manager, one who set broad policy but paid little attention to the details. It was easy to imagine his being oblivious to the actions of the NSC staff members. The Tower Commission report was highly unflattering to the president—the forgetful, confused figure who emerges in the report's pages was hardly the image Reagan wanted to project—but it exonerated him of any wrongdoing or knowledge of wrongdoing.

Next up were the House and Senate, each of which appointed a select committee to investigate the Iran-contra affair. The most dramatic testimony before the joint committee was that of North. Having been granted "use immunity" by Congress—which meant nothing he said could be used against him in any future criminal proceedings—North admitted he'd shredded documents, falsified evidence, and participated in other illicit activities intended to aid the contras and cover up the arms-for-hostages deals. In spite of these admissions, North emerged from the hearings a star—and, to many, a hero. His patriotic fervor, his military bearing, his all-American looks made him seem far more likeable than his congressional inquisitors. Also working in North's favor was the fact that the committee had decided to avoid any substantive discussions on the merits of contra aid (and that seventeen of the twenty-six committee members had voted for aid). North could speechify about freedom fighters without fear of being contradicted.

In addition, North emphasized he was no lone ranger; he was a loyal soldier following orders. When the Boland amendment was passed, North's boss, National Security

Adviser Robert McFarlane (who preceded Poindexter in the job), came to him with instructions directly from the president. These instructions, North told the committee, were to keep the contras together, "body and soul." McFarlane, in his testimony, confirmed that Reagan had said this to him, and that he had passed it on to North.

Did this mean Reagan had ordered the diversion of funds from the Iran arms sales to the contras? North didn't know. Neither did McFarlane, who had been replaced by Poindexter before the diversion. And Poindexter testified that he had not told the president about the diversion. "The buck stops here with me," he told the congressional committee.

After Poindexter's testimony, the committee eased up on Reagan. Its report was harsher than that of the Tower Commission—the president was blamed for creating or at least tolerating an environment where those who did know of the diversion could easily believe they were carrying out the president's policies. But on the key question of whether he ordered the diversion or even knew about it, he was off the hook.

In retrospect, many have speculated about why the committee backed away from investigating what else Reagan did or didn't know, what else he did or didn't order. After all, the diversion was merely the point at which the Iran and contra scandals intersected; it was hardly the entirety of either scandal. Why didn't the committee take a deeper look at Reagan's role in the Iran arms sales themselves, or in the overall National Security Council effort on behalf of the contras? Why did the diversion become the focus of the investigation?

In his autobiography, North suggested one reason why the administration chose to focus on the diversion:

This particular detail was so dramatic, so sexy, that it might actually—well, divert public attention from other, even more important aspects of the story, such as what else the President and his top advisers had known about and approved. And if it could be insinuated that this supposedly terrible deed was the exclusive responsibility of one mid-level staff assistant at the National Security Council (and perhaps his immediate superior, the national security adviser), and that staffer had acted on his own (however unlikely that might be), and then, now that you mention it, his activities might even be criminal—if the public and the press focused on that, then maybe you didn't have another Watergate on your hands after all. Especially if you insisted that the President knew nothing about it.

In other words, the administration used the diversion as a diversion.

Still, the congressional committee went along with the focus on the diversion. This can be explained partly by the committee's makeup. Its members were, by and large, moderates; they had no desire to uncover information that might bring them uncomfortably close to a discussion of impeachment. And partly, the committee was following the lead of the public, which just wasn't that interested in the scandal. At one point, The *New Republic* tried to stir things up by holding a contest to come up with a jazzier name for the "Iran-contra affair." Entries included "Contraversions," "Ronnybrook," and the winner, "Iranamok." None caught on.

The underlying problem was that, in contrast to the dark and brooding Nixon, Reagan remained ever cheerful and popular. The committee's members had no desire to undercut that popularity. Moreover, the committee had early on set a ten-month timetable by which they wanted their hearings and report finished, and time was running out. So the hearings ended and the report came out—with many questions unanswered.

ᗣᗢ

Lawrence Walsh, the independent counsel appointed by a three-judge panel to prosecute any illegal activities associated with Iran-contra, was not burdened by the political or time pressures felt by the congressional committee. His investigations continued until 1993 and resulted in criminal charges against fourteen individuals. Among these were McFarlane, who pleaded guilty to four counts of withholding information from Congress; North, who was convicted of altering and destroying documents, accepting an illegal gratuity, and aiding and abetting in the obstruction of Congress; and Poindexter, who was convicted of conspiracy, false statements, destruction and removal of records, and obstruction of Congress.

Though Walsh was not burdened by the political or time pressures on the congressional committee, he was bound by its grants of immunity. North and Poindexter appealed the convictions, arguing that witnesses at their trials had to have been influenced by the highly publicized congressional testimony. The appeals court admitted that was possible and reversed the convictions. North then declared himself "totally exonerated." That was nonsense. The only reason North went free was that the crimes he'd been charged with were crimes he'd admitted to while under immunity.

The North and Poindexter reversals did not dissuade Walsh from pushing on—up into the highest levels of the Reagan administration. After a lengthy investigation, Walsh concluded that then–Vice President George Bush was not nearly as "out of the loop" as he later claimed. Bush was regularly briefed on the Iran and contra operations, though he probably didn't know about the diversion. In the end though, Walsh decided not to prosecute Bush. Unlike the Tower Commission or the congressional committees, whose job had been to uncover the truth, Walsh's mandate was more limited. His responsibility was merely to prosecute criminals, and Walsh did not have enough evidence to prove that the vice president had violated any criminal statute. Still, the investigation kept Bush on the defensive throughout the presidential elections of 1988 (when he defeated Michael Dukakis) and 1992 (when he was defeated by Bill Clinton).

Walsh also investigated the roles of Secretary of State George Shultz and Secretary of Defense Caspar Weinberger. Shultz and Weinberger, Walsh admitted, were peculiar targets. They were the only high-level members of the Reagan administration who had consistently opposed the arms deal with Iran. But Walsh argued they'd known what was going on and conspired to cover up the Iran arms sales in order to protect the president.

In the case of Shultz, Walsh eventually decided there was a reasonable doubt as to whether he'd willfully given any false testimony, and Walsh decided not to prosecute. In the case of Weinberger, Walsh charged him with four counts of false statements and perjury. Then on the eve of the trial in December 1992, President Bush took his revenge on Walsh. In one of his final acts before turning over the Oval Office to Clinton, Bush pardoned Weinberger. In doing so, Bush argued that Walsh was prosecuting officials because he disagreed with their policies, not because of any actual criminal activities. Walsh, in turn, accused Bush of pardoning Weinberger to cover up his own role, and that of Reagan, in the Iran-contra affairs.

Objective observers, including Theodore Draper, the leading Iran-contra historian, have criticized both Walsh and Bush. Walsh was faulted for pursuing a Shultz and Weinberger conspiracy theory that was never entirely clear or convincing and that was, in any case, tangential to the main Iran-contra issues. And Bush's action was suspiciously self-serving: Had the Weinberger case gone to trial, Bush would certainly have been called as a witness and his claims to have been out of the loop would have been strenuously contested.

As for Reagan, he had slipped beyond Walsh's grasp well before the pardons. Reagan's testimony (via videotape) at the Poindexter trial and his subsequent interviews with Walsh revealed a man who seemed genuinely unable to recall even the main events of Iran-contra. Perhaps, in retrospect, Reagan was already suffering from the early stages of Alzheimer's disease (which was later diagnosed). In any case, Walsh concluded, Reagan's conduct, like Bush's, "fell well short of criminality which could be successfully prosecuted."

Nonetheless, of the three official reports on Iran-contra, Walsh's came down the hardest on Reagan. "The President's disregard for civil laws enacted to limit presidential action abroad," Walsh wrote, "created a climate in which some government officials assigned to implement his policies felt emboldened to circumvent such laws." By directing McFarlane to keep the contras alive "body and soul," by disregarding the warnings of Shultz and Weinberger against selling arms to Iran, by openly encouraging individuals and other countries to fund the contras during the ban on U.S. aid, Reagan set the stage on which Oliver North acted. In this sense, there is no question that the man responsible for Iran-contra was Ronald Reagan.

To Investigate Further

Tower, John, Edmund Muskie, and Brent Scowcroft. *The Tower Commission Report.* New York: Times Books, 1987.
   The first official report.

U.S. House of Representatives Select Committee to Investigate Covert Arms Transactions with Iran and U.S. Senate Select Committee on Secret Military Assistance to Iran and the Nicaraguan Opposition. Report of the Congressional Committees Investigating the Iran-Contra Affair. 1987.
   The second official report.

Cockburn, Leslie. *Out of Control.* New York: Atlantic Monthly Press, 1987.

Contends that well before the Boland amendment was passed, the administration was involved in a wide range of activities that circumvented Congressional restrictions on aid to the contras. Also presents evidence that the contras were involved in drug smuggling and that the CIA knew about it.

Cohen, William, and George Mitchell. *Men of Zeal.* New York: Viking, 1988.

Two senators on the Iran-contra committee tell, among other things, how the television cameras affected their inquiries and why they gave North immunity.

Segev, Samuel. *The Iranian Triangle.* New York: The Free Press, 1988.

Focuses on Israel's role in the Iran-contra affair and on the Israeli side of the triangular U.S.-Iran-Israel relationship.

Reagan, Ronald. *An American Life.* New York: Simon and Schuster, 1990.

The president's own version, or at least that of one of his better ghostwriters.

North, Oliver. *Under Fire.* New York: HarperCollins, 1991.

The number-one best-seller from the man so good at following orders that a fellow Marine once said: "Ollie North's commanding officer should never even think out loud."

Draper, Theodore. *A Very Thin Line.* New York: Hill and Wang, 1991.

A thorough reconstruction of the Iran-contra affair and the numerous crossings of the thin line that separates the legitimate from the illegitimate exercise of government power.

Wroe, Ann. *Lives, Lies and the Iran-Contra Affair.* New York: I. B. Tauris & Co., 1991.

A British journalist's provocative perspectives on the underlying moral and political philosophies.

Kornbluh, Peter, and Malcolm Byrne. *The Iran-Contra Scandal: The Declassified History.* New York: The New Press, 1993.

A useful documentary history.

Walsh, Lawrence E. *Iran-Contra: The Final Report.* New York: Times Books, 1994.

The results of the independent counsel's seven years of investigations.

McFarlane, Robert. *Special Trust.* New York: Cadell & Davies, 1994.

Like the books of most of the principals (almost all of whom wrote one), McFarlane's is somewhat self-serving, but his has more pathos—and perhaps more credibility—since he was the only figure involved to show some remorse about his role in the affair. So much remorse, in fact, that in February 1987 he attempted suicide.

Timberg, Robert. *The Nightingale's Song.* New York: Simon & Schuster, 1995.

An elegant multiperson biography, which traces Iran-contra back to its origins in the experiences of McFarlane, Poindexter, and North at the Naval Academy in Annapolis and later in Vietnam.

Was Gorbachev Part of the August Coup?

T HE RUSSIAN EQUIVALENT of America's legendary smoke-filled rooms—the place where politicians make their secret deals—is the steam bath. So it did not seem extraordinary, on August 17, 1991, that some of the most powerful figures in the Soviet Union gathered to take a bath at the luxurious Moscow facilities of the KGB.

Present were Prime Minister Valentin Pavlov, Defense Minister Dmitri Yazov, Central Committee Secretary for Defense Oleg Baklanov, Central Committee Secretary for Personnel Oleg Shenin, and the president's chief of staff, Valery Boldin. Their host, according to the later testimony of all six, was KGB chairman Vladimir Kryuchkov.

Nowhere to be seen amid the steam was their boss, Soviet president Mikhail Gorbachev. Gorbachev was vacationing with his family in the Crimea. He would first hear about the meeting the day after, when Baklanov and Boldin arrived at the vacation dacha known as Foros. They were accompanied by General Valentin Varennikov, the commander of Soviet ground forces, and General Yury Plekhanov of the KGB.

As Gorbachev later told the story, he was working on the final draft of a speech when his security chief told him he had visitors. That was already a matter of concern, since people didn't just drop in on the Soviet president. Gorbachev's first reaction was to call Kryuchkov to find out what was going on. He discovered the line was dead. So were his four other lines.

At that point the delegation from the steam bath entered the room. Baklanov informed Gorbachev that they represented the "State Committee for the State of Emergency." Gorbachev responded that he'd never authorized such a committee. Baklanov said Gorbachev should sign a decree declaring a state of emergency or turn over his powers to the vice president, Gennady Yanayev. Gorbachev refused.

As he later put it, "using the strongest language that the Russians always use in such circumstances, I told them where to go."

For the next three days Gorbachev was cut off from the outside world, unable to make or receive any calls and surrounded by a double ring of guards. He was able to watch on television the next day's press conference in Moscow, during which members of the emergency committee announced that, since the president was ill, Vice President Yanayev had assumed his duties.

By tuning in to the BBC and the Voice of America on a transistor radio, Gorbachev was able to follow some of the momentous events that followed. Russian president Boris Yeltsin denounced the takeover as an illegal coup and called for popular resistance. The committee declared martial law and ordered large numbers of tanks and armored personnel carriers into Moscow.

By midmorning of August 19, the Russian government building known as the White House was surrounded both by Soviet troops and by tens of thousands of Russian citizens. Some formed human chains to prevent the tanks from moving forward. At noon Yeltsin dramatically mounted a tank near the White House and appealed to the troops to give their allegiance to the elected Russian government, not the emergency committee.

As the day wore on, it became clear that the soldiers were not willing to fire on Russian citizens. Two days later the troops withdrew, Gorbachev returned to Moscow, and the leaders of the coup were arrested. Democrats were euphoric: by the end of the year, the Soviet Union had been disbanded, Gorbachev had reluctantly retired, and Yeltsin—the first democratically elected president of Russia—had replaced him as the most powerful figure in the country.

This fairly straightforward account of the August 1991 coup, featuring Gorbachev as the heroic victim and Yeltsin as the democratic hero, has been accepted by most Western leaders, journalists, and historians. Gorbachev himself recounted the story, in numerous interviews and in two books. Yet the Russian people, even as they celebrated the coup's demise, were much more skeptical. They had lots of questions about the roles played by each of the story's heroes, and these questions continued to plague both Gorbachev and Yeltsin.

⚬⚬⚬

Among the first to challenge Gorbachev's view of the coup were, not surprisingly, the members of the emergency committee.

Not all of them were in a position to do so. Two—Minister of Internal Affairs Boris Pugo and Gorbachev's military adviser Marshal Akhromeev—committed suicide before they could be arrested. Two others—Pavlov and Yanayev—were too drunk to say anything coherent at first.

Once they sobered up, Pavlov and Yanayev joined their coconspirators in insisting that they'd gotten the go-ahead for the state of emergency from Gorbachev himself. According to the committee members, they'd gone down to the Crimea to tell Gorbachev everything was set. Then, to their surprise, he'd backed off, pretending to be sick.

As Pavlov told the Russian prosecutors: "Gorbachev decided to play a game that he could not lose. If he stayed there [at Foros] and the state of emergency worked, he would come to Moscow later, having recovered from his illness and taken charge. If it didn't work, he could come and arrest everyone, and once again as president he would take charge."

The committee members' case depended on proving that, contrary to the president's claim, he was not held incommunicado at Foros. They were helped by some confusion about the timing: one source said phone lines were cut at 4:32 P.M. on August 18, another said it was 5:50 P.M. And a close ally of Gorbachev later recalled speaking to the president at 6:00 P.M. that day—after the lines were supposedly cut.

Two Soviet tank drivers surrounded by protesters in Moscow's Menazh Square on August 19, 1991. *(Reuters/Corbis)*

Of course, all of the conspirators had good reason to blame Gorbachev for the coup: if they could convince people they were just following the president's orders, they could hardly be accused of usurping his power. Still, many Russians found their version of the story as credible as Gorbachev's.

For one thing, the conspirators were all close associates of the president. Indeed, Gorbachev had appointed and promoted them, in spite of the fact that they were all clearly hostile toward his policies of perestroika and glasnost. Publicly, Kryuchkov usually toed the line; he spoke of creating a more open organization (and he even promoted a beauty contest whose winner was crowned "Miss KGB"). But in private he made no secret of his belief that Gorbachev's reforms had gone way too far.

Gorbachev had plenty of warning that his ministers couldn't be trusted. In December 1990 Foreign Minister Eduard Shevardnadze, the leading liberal in Gorbachev's government, dramatically resigned because of the growing power of reactionary forces in the government. "Let this be my contribution, if you like, my protest, against the onset of dictatorship," he said.

In June the U.S. ambassador, Jack Matlock, received an even more specific warning from the mayor of Moscow, Gavriil Popov, a leading democrat. Popov signaled to Matlock that the room was bugged by the KGB and that they couldn't talk freely. Then the mayor handed the ambassador a note that read: "A coup is being organized to remove Gorbachev."

On the same sheet, Matlock asked who was behind it. Popov wrote the names of Pavlov, Kryuchkov, Yazov, and Anatoly Lukyanov, Speaker of the Supreme Soviet—all of whom were involved in the coup two months later. Matlock then passed on the warning to Gorbachev. Since Matlock had only Popov's word to go on, he didn't name any of the plotters, which may have lessened the impact of his warning. Still, Gorbachev's response was disturbingly (and in some minds, suspiciously) nonchalant: the president merely thanked the ambassador for his concern and told him not to worry about it.

Even in public, the hard-liners didn't always try to conceal their strong opposition to Gorbachev's reforms. Pavlov was especially outspoken in his criticism of a new treaty that Gorbachev was negotiating with the leaders of the Soviet republics, and that would have severely curtailed the power of the central government. Many of the conspirators later said they acted to forestall the signing of the treaty, which had been scheduled for August 20.

How could a politician as astute as Gorbachev ignore such clear warning signs? To those who sympathized with the hard-liners on the committee, Pavlov's answer made sense: Gorbachev himself must have been behind the coup. Perhaps he chickened out at the last minute, or perhaps he wanted to let the committee members do his dirty work. But whether he actively participated in the planning or just encouraged the plotters, he was not their innocent victim.

The revisionist interpretation of the coup was unkind to Yeltsin as well. In an open letter to the Russian president, Kryuchkov accused him of staging the heroic defense of the White House to bolster his own reputation. Kryuchkov denied that he ever ordered an attack on the White House. Moreover, he wrote, Yeltsin was fully aware of that, since the KGB chief had called him personally to tell him.

Like the attacks on Gorbachev, the criticism of Yeltsin was to a considerable extent self-serving. The committee members may have been embarrassed to portray themselves as dupes, victims of Gorbachev's manipulations and Yeltsin's histrionics. But, legally and politically, that was a lot better image than the orthodox view of them as power-hungry, bloodthirsty, neo-Stalinist reactionaries.

⚬⚬⚬

The criminal trial against the alleged conspirators brought additional frustration for the supporters of Gorbachev and Yeltsin.

At first, prosecutors charged the leaders of the coup with treason against the USSR. By the end of 1991, however, the USSR had broken up into independent countries. Defense lawyers argued that there was no legal basis for charging their clients with treason against a country that no longer existed.

Prosecutors eventually settled on conspiracy charges, but the trial was delayed again and again because of additional legal arguments and the illnesses of various defendants. Finally, in December 1993, the new Russian parliament—now dominated by an anti-Yeltsin coalition of nationalists and ex-communists—granted amnesty to all the defendants.

Of the fifteen defendants, only one refused the amnesty. Unwilling to concede that he had committed any crime for which he could be amnestied, General Varennikov demanded a trial. Varennikov was also undoubtedly aware that the Military Collegium of the Russian Supreme Court, like the newly elected parliament, was stacked with enemies of both Gorbachev and Yeltsin.

The trial took place in August 1994. An angry Gorbachev took the stand, denying he had anything to do with the coup. The court ignored his testimony and acquitted Varennikov.

Gorbachev and his supporters denounced the verdict, comparing it to Stalin's show trials of the 1930s. The charge had a great deal of merit: both the new parliament and the court reflected how drastically Russian politics had changed since the postcoup euphoria. A disastrous economy and political disarray among the democrats had swept into power a collection of ultranationalists and procommunists who had much more in common with the emergency committee members than with either Yeltsin or Gorbachev.

In the twenty-first century, the legacy of the coup was unclear. President Vladimir Putin, who succeeded Yeltsin, had no qualms about inviting Kryuchkov to his inauguration, and Pavlov bragged that Putin was taking up where the leaders of the coup left off. At the same time, many opponents of the coup, including Gorbachev, also supported Putin.

As for Gorbachev, he continued to argue his case, though it seemed that no one in Russia was listening. His only consolation was that he remained a hero abroad. Western leaders, as well as journalists and historians, emphasized that, whatever Gorbachev's flaws, he implemented a complete reversal of Soviet foreign policy, and he introduced an unprecedented degree of freedom to the Soviet Union, including semidemocratic elections and a multiparty system.

Undeniably, he made all sorts of compromises with and promises to the hard-liners in his government, but that didn't make him one of them. Perhaps some of his conservative ministers genuinely did think they could convince Gorbachev to go along with their coup, or at least held out some hope that he would. Certainly Gorbachev grossly miscalculated how far they'd go to stop his reforms. But that's a far cry from proving he wanted anything to do with the coup.

Gorbachev's memoirs, though often self-serving and sanctimonious, present a convincing defense against the charge that he colluded with the conspirators. "The transformation of the country into a viable democratic federation as well as the general plan of perestroika, the sweeping reforms and the new thinking in the sphere of international politics—these had become my life's work," he wrote.

"Why then would I want to lift my hand against it?"

To Investigate Further

Gorbachev, Mikhail. *The August Coup.* New York: HarperCollins, 1991.
Inevitably, since it appeared just months after the coup, much of the book consists of reworked previous statements and speeches, but these still make for a useful document.

Remnick, David. *Lenin's Tomb.* New York: Random House, 1993.
Intimate and revealing vignettes from the last days of the Soviet Empire.

Dunlop, John. *The Rise of Russia and the Pall of the Soviet Empire.* Princeton, NJ: Princeton University Press, 1993.
Dunlop makes a strong case that the plotters had reason to believe Gorbachev could be convinced to side with them. Somewhat academic in its style but still compelling.

Bonnell, Victoria, Ann Cooper, and Gregory Freidin, eds. *Russia at the Barricades.* Armonk, NY: M. E. Sharpe, 1994.
A collection of documents, interviews, and eyewitness accounts of the coup.

Boldin, Valery. *Ten Years That Shook the World.* New York: Basic Books, 1994.
A venomous and vindictive portrait of Gorbachev, written by his chief of staff while he awaited trial for his part in the coup.

Yeltsin, Boris. *The Struggle for Russia.* New York: Times Books, 1994.
Disorganized and sometimes disingenuous, but entertaining and informative. Yeltsin has little good to say about his archrival, though he stops short of accusing Gorbachev of planning or approving the coup. Instead Yeltsin concludes, somewhat ambiguously, that Gorbachev was its "chief catalyst." As for the revisionist attacks on Yeltsin's own role in the coup, he admits he had a telephone conversation with Kryuchkov during which the KGB chief told him the emer-

gency committee would not use military force. But Yeltsin adds that there were good reasons not to believe him.

Matlock, Jack. *Autopsy on an Empire.* **New York: Random House, 1995.**
Matlock, who was the U.S. ambassador to Moscow under Reagan and Bush, provides a first-hand account of the Soviet collapse. Unlike the works of most diplomats, Matlock's is not just a valuable historical document but also a valuable work of history.

Pryce-Jones, David. *The Strange Death of the Soviet Empire.* **New York: Henry Holt, 1995.**
An unusual and often interesting mix of interviews with former leaders, dissidents, and other Soviet observers.

Gorbachev, Mikhail. *Memoirs.* **New York: Doubleday, 1995.**
Like its author, the book goes on too long but remains important.

Brown, Archie. *The Gorbachev Factor.* **Oxford: Oxford University Press, 1996.**
The best overall defense of Gorbachev's record as a genuine reformer—a better defense, in fact, than Gorbachev's own memoirs.

Knight, Amy. *Spies without Cloaks.* **Princeton, NJ: Princeton University Press, 1996.**
The first chapter is the most recent and most thorough case against Gorbachev. The rest of the book argues that the postcoup KGB continued to be a dangerous and independent force in Russia.

Remnick, David. *Resurrection.* **New York: Random House, 1997.**
A surprisingly hopeful view of postcoup Russia, especially since most of the book chronicles the country's descent into chaos, corruption, and crime.

Was O. J. Simpson Guilty?

E VEN BEFORE THE TRIAL BEGAN, most Americans—certainly most white Americans—believed O. J. Simpson murdered his ex-wife, Nicole, as well as an unfortunate bystander, Ron Goldman. After all, 95 million television viewers followed the slow-motion chase of the white Ford Bronco that ended in his arrest. In the Bronco were O. J.'s passport, a fake goatee and mustache, and more than $8,000 cash, all pretty clear indications that he wasn't heading for the nearest police station. The jury had not yet been selected when a book by Nicole's friend Faye Resnick soared to the number-one spot on the best-seller lists, knocking Pope John Paul II down to number two and informing Americans of Simpson's history of beating his wife. And once the trial finally got under way, Americans saw a parade of expert witnesses present the physical evidence: shoeprints, matching a pair O. J. owned, stamped in the blood at the murder scene; Nicole's blood on a sock in his bedroom; Goldman's blood in O. J.'s Bronco; O. J.'s hair on a cap next to the bodies and on Goldman's shirt; the bloody gloves, one found between the bodies and the other, still holding the victims' hair, outside O. J.'s house. One DNA expert testified that the blood found near the victims, which matched O. J.'s, would match only 1 out of 170 million people. The blood on the sock, which matched Nicole's, would match that of only 1 out of 6.8 billion people—more people, author Dominick Dunne noted, than there are on Earth.

So when, after more than nine months of testimony, the jury took under four hours to reach its unanimous verdict, the reason seemed clear: race. The case was lost, *Newsweek* explained, "virtually the day the predominately African-American jury was sworn in." Prosecutor Christopher Darden agreed: "I could see in their eyes the need to settle a score," he said.

Even defense attorney Robert Shapiro jumped on the bandwagon. "Not only did we play the race card," he told Barbara Walters on the day the verdict was announced, "we dealt it from the bottom of the deck."

In October 1995, when the jurors decided Simpson was not guilty, it seemed certain that time would confirm their bias and his guilt. But the verdict of history has turned out to be far from unanimous.

❦

Resnick's book, *Nicole Brown Simpson: Diary of a Life Interrupted,* was published in October 1994, five months after the murders and right in the middle of jury selection. In one sense, it obviously helped the prosecution by providing a clear motive for the murders. Resnick portrayed O. J. as a womanizer and wife beater, whose jealousy only in-

If it doesn't fit. . . *(Corbis Sygma)*

creased after the divorce. "I can't take this, Faye," Resnick quoted Simpson. "I mean it. I'll kill that bitch." Though Judge Lance Ito temporarily suspended jury selection and pleaded with the television networks to cancel interviews with Resnick, this only made people—including would-be jurors—all the more eager to read it.

Ironically, the book may have done more for the defense than for the prosecution. Prosecutor Marcia Clark was furious with Resnick for having joined the parade of potential witnesses who took "cash for trash." Resnick's tales of her own (and Nicole's) drug abuse tainted her credibility and the victim's image. Fearing what defense attorneys would do with this, Clark decided not to put Resnick on the stand.

The prosecution's case suffered another blow when Ito ruled inadmissible some of the evidence of O. J.'s abuse. This included Nicole's call to the Sojourn Counseling Center, a battered women's shelter in Santa Monica, to complain that O. J. was stalking her. Nicole called the center on July 7, just five days before her death.

Still, Ito did allow some evidence of Simpson's abuse, and that's what prosecutors led with when the trial finally got under way in January 1995. The jury heard about a 1989 beating for which Simpson received a suspended sentence and was ordered to pay $500 to the Sojourn Center. They also heard about a 911 call Nicole made in 1993.

Having established Simpson's propensity to violence (at least in their minds), prosecutors moved on to the physical evidence, which culminated in the trial's most dramatic moment. This was on June 15, when, as millions watched, Simpson put on the pair of gloves police found at the murder scene and at his own home—or, rather, tried to put on the gloves. After struggling with the right-hand glove, he turned to his attorney Johnnie Cochran and told him they were too tight. The moment inspired Cochran's famous line to the jury: "If it doesn't fit, you must acquit."

Prosecutors maintained the gloves did fit, and that Simpson's struggle was an act. "I hoped everyone could see that, hoped the jury could see it," Darden said later. But Clark knew the prosecution was in trouble. She recalled: "I looked down at the bloody, weathered leather, and I said to myself, that's it. We just lost the case."

As if that wasn't enough, prosecutors next had to deal with Mark Fuhrman, the detective who had found the second glove at Simpson's home. Questioned by defense attorney F. Lee Bailey, Fuhrman denied having used the word "nigger" during the previous ten years. Then, in July, the defense got their hands on twelve hours of taped interviews between Fuhrman and aspiring screenwriter Laura Hart McKinney. McKinney had interviewed Fuhrman as part of her research for a screenplay about Los Angeles police. On the tapes, Fuhrman said the word forty-one times.

Fuhrman claimed he was merely playing a role for McKinney, and Ito ruled the jury could hear only two of the excerpts in which the detective used the word. That was damaging enough. Hollywood never showed any interest in McKinney's work, but now her tapes reached a wider audience than any movie. More to the point, even in their much-edited form, the jury could hear that Fuhrman was a liar and a racist. Defense attorneys were quick to accuse Fuhrman of taking the glove from the murder scene, wiping some of Simpson's blood on it, and then planting the bloody glove at Simpson's house. How Fuhrman got his hands on Simpson's blood wasn't clear, but the strategy was brilliant: with Fuhrman's credibility shattered, the gloves, once among the prosecution's strongest evidence, were now a cornerstone of the case for the defense.

The defense team went after other prosecution witnesses besides Fuhrman. Criminologist Dennis Fung, for example, hadn't noticed any blood on Simpson's socks during his initial investigation, and an FBI lab found that some of the blood contained a preservative called EDTA, which is more often found in laboratories than in humans. Someone must have put Simpson's blood on the sock in the lab, the defense concluded. Fung had also neglected to secure Simpson's Bronco at the crime scene, casting doubt on any evidence found there.

Some of the tainted evidence, the defense conceded, might have been the result of sloppy police work rather than a conspiracy to frame Simpson. But it was tainted nonetheless. And, if the police were either crooked or incompetent, none of their evidence could be trusted. Forensic scientist Henry Lee, a defense witness, put it this way: "While eating . . . spaghetti, I found one cockroach. . . . No sense for me to go through the whole plate of spaghetti. . . . If you found one, it's there."

⌒◦

Immediately after the verdict was announced, the fingers started pointing.

Fuhrman blamed Clark for not standing by him, as well as other detectives for mishandling both the physical evidence and their questioning of Simpson. Other detectives blamed Fuhrman for his racism, and Clark for failing to introduce any evidence pertaining to the Bronco chase. Clark defended her decision, arguing that bringing up the chase would have given Simpson's attorneys the chance to counter that he was not fleeing justice but planning suicide—and that the police had driven him to it.

Some blamed Clark for focusing too much on domestic violence, saying she should have introduced other possible motives. What if, some suggested, a jealous Simpson killed Nicole because he suspected she was having an affair? Faye Resnick said Nicole was having an affair with O. J.'s friend and fellow football star Marcus Allen, though Allen denied it. Fuhrman, among others, believed Nicole was having an affair with Goldman. But Clark insisted this was a case of escalating domestic violence. Critics suggested this was because she wanted to keep the victims' images pure, or because Clark herself was in the midst of an ugly (though not violent) divorce. In any case, the jury wasn't buying the connection between the earlier incidents and the murders.

"This was a murder trial, not domestic abuse," juror Brenda Moran told reporters after the trial. "If you want to get tried for domestic abuse, go in another courtroom."

For her part, Clark blamed Darden for demanding that Simpson try on the gloves. (Darden must have been "on a testosterone high," she said.) She blamed Ito for excluding some of the evidence of domestic violence and for allowing Simpson—in a brief statement waiving his right to testify—to tell the jury he was innocent, without having to take the stand and face any cross-examination. She blamed the media for turning the trial into a circus.

Above all, of course, prosecutors blamed the defense team, especially Johnnie Cochran, for making race an issue, and the jury for choosing race over justice. "It wasn't a Dream Team that would acquit O. J. Simpson," said Clark. "It was a Dream Jury." Millions of white Americans shared Clark's outrage.

Gradually, though, these passions subsided. Civil libertarians argued that the jury had plenty of nonracial reasons for its verdict. Two members of the dream team, Barry Scheck and Peter Neufeld, were specialists in the evidentiary use of DNA, and defense experts such as Lee were very effective on the stand. Clark herself conceded that the prosecution had made a fiasco of the glove demonstration and that Fuhrman was a racist. For the jurors to have some doubts about a case in which Fuhrman was a key witness was perfectly reasonable. It did not necessarily mean that they freed Simpson because of his race, or even that they thought he was innocent. It may merely have meant that they had doubts—reasonable doubts—about his guilt. And any criminal jury has an obligation under those circumstances to find a defendant not guilty.

Alan Dershowitz, himself a member of the Dream Team, reflected this emerging consensus in his book *Reasonable Doubts.* Jurors, he argued, were not supposed to be historians.

"The discovery of historical and scientific truths is not entrusted to a jury of laypeople selected randomly from the population on the basis of their ignorance of the underlying facts," Dershowitz wrote. "The task of discovering such truths is entrusted largely to trained experts who have studied the subject for years and are intimately familiar with the relevant facts and theories."

Like historians, jurors are supposed to figure out what happened, but it's by no mean their only goal. "If it were," Dershowitz continued, "judges would not instruct jurors to acquit a defendant whom they believe 'probably' did it, as they are supposed to do in criminal cases."

At least one juror, a white woman named Anise Aschenbach, was apparently thinking along these lines. She said after the trial that she thought Simpson was probably guilty, "but the law wouldn't allow a guilty verdict."

The law did, however, allow the families of Nicole Brown Simpson and Ron Goldman to sue Simpson, and in February 1997 a civil jury found him liable for the deaths and awarded the victims' families $33.5 million. To some, like Dershowitz, this confirmed that the system worked. The civil jury heard much of the same evidence as the criminal one, but its verdict was based on a different standard of proof. The civil jury had only to find that a "preponderance of evidence" pointed to Simpson's liability. In this case, reasonable doubt was not enough to save Simpson.

⟋⟋⟋

The civil libertarian view of the Simpson case is comforting. "O. J. didn't get away with anything," wrote Gerry Spence, seemingly one of the few famous defense attorneys who didn't join the Dream Team. "The system worked. It revealed his guilt and, at the same time, preserved its safeguards for us."

Similar analyses went a long way to ease the tensions that flared up after the criminal verdict, when blacks across the country cheered and whites looked on in horror. It was much safer to see the verdict as an expression of reasonable doubt than of African Americans' contempt for the justice system. Besides, O. J. was no Rodney King. It was one thing for blacks to protest the acquittal of the police officers who beat up the helpless King, quite another for them to rally round a football and movie star who, as the legal scholar Jeffrey Abramson put it, was "more at home on white golf courses than in the black community."

And yet, much as we might like to deny it, this case clearly was about race.

There were other issues, to be sure. Marcia Clark was not wrong to recognize the dangers of domestic violence. Yet, as Brenda Moran's statement made clear, this was not what was foremost in jurors' minds.

Money, too, was an issue. Few defendants, black or white, could have afforded the Dream Team. Few could have hired a renowned expert like Henry Lee, or the private investigators who uncovered the Fuhrman tapes. No wonder critic Diana Trilling argued that the "m" word was as crucial to the outcome of the trial as the "n" word.

Above all and undeniably, though, the issue was race. Shapiro was correct to say the defense had played the "race card," though perhaps wrong to lay the blame on Cochran. Simpson was no Rodney King, but the black community's mistrust of the Los Angeles Police Department was based on a pattern of abuse, not a single beating. Simpson, to many blacks, was merely another a victim, though one with the means to fight back.

"Race had been there all along," commented the legal scholar Paul Butler, "or at least as soon as Fuhrman reported to the scene of the crime."

"Race is not a card," agreed the cultural historian Michael Eric Dyson. "It is a condition shaped by culture and fueled by passions buried deep in our history that transcend reason. That's why many white folk are angry at the verdict, while many black folk feel joy."

Or, as Cochran put it: "I just want to say something about this 'race card.' Race plays a part in everything in America."

To Investigate Further

Resnick, Faye, with Jeanne Bell. *Nicole Brown Simpson: The Private Diary of a Life Interrupted.* Beverly Hills, CA: Dove Books, 1994.
  Ito halted jury selection so he could read the book.

Simpson, O. J. *I Want To Tell You.* Boston: Little, Brown, 1995.
  Simpson's responses to letters he received in jail.

Abramson, Jeffrey, ed. *Postmortem.* New York: Basic Books, 1996.
  A wide-ranging and provocative collection of essays by lawyers, political scientists, historians, and others who address what the case revealed about race, domestic violence, law, money, and the media.

Bosco, Joseph. *A Problem of Evidence.* New York: William Morrow, 1996.
  According to Bosco, Simpson was guilty *and* framed.

Bugliosi, Vincent. *Outrage.* New York: W. W. Norton, 1996.
  The man who prosecuted Charles Manson tells how Clark and company bungled the case.

Darden, Christopher, with Jess Walter. *In Contempt.* New York: Regan Books, 1996.
  The trials of the case's sole black prosecutor.

Dershowitz, Alan. *Reasonable Doubts.* New York: Simon & Schuster, 1996.
  Why the verdict was reasonable.

Schiller, Lawrence, and James Willwerth. *American Tragedy.* New York: Random House, 1996.
  This behind-the-scenes look at the squabbles and strategies of the defense team is surprisingly balanced, considering that Schiller co-authored Simpson's own book.

Shapiro, Robert, with Larkin Warren. *The Search for Justice.* New York: Warner Books, 1996.
  Shapiro is eager to portray himself as the Dream Team's quarterback—except when it came to playing the race card, when he was equally eager to hand the ball to Cochran.

Toobin, Jeffrey. *The Run of His Life.* New York: Random House, 1996.
Authoritative.

Clark, Marcia, with Teresa Carpenter. *Without a Doubt.* New York: Viking, 1997.
Somewhat self-serving (and not just because Viking paid $4.2 million for the book), but nonetheless a fascinating look behind the scenes of the prosecution's case.

Dunne, Dominick. *Another City, Not My Own.* New York: Crown, 1997.
A pointlessly fictionalized memoir of the trial. Stick to his 2001 book, *Justice,* if you like Dunne's take on celebrity murders.

Fuhrman, Mark. *Murder in Brentwood.* Washington, DC: Regnery, 1997.
"The world does not know me," Fuhrman writes. But we know what he said.

Lange, Tom, and Philip Vannatter, with Dan Moldea. *Evidence Dismissed.* New York: Pocket Books, 1997.
Lange and Vannatter were the lead detectives on the case.

Spence, Gerry. *O. J.: The Last Word.* New York: St. Martin's Press, 1997.
Well . . . maybe Spence's last words.

Petrocelli, Daniel, with Peter Knobler. *Triumph of Justice.* New York: Crown, 1998.
Petrocelli, the lawyer who represented the Goldman family, tells the story of the civil suit, including his confrontation with Simpson on the witness stand.

Dunne, Dominick. *Justice.* New York: Crown, 2001.
Dunne's *Vanity Fair* essays chronicle life among the rich and famous and murderous. About half the book is devoted to Simpson's trial, about which Dunne offers plenty of entertaining celebrity gossip, though not nearly as many insights as he thinks.

About the Author

Paul D. Aron is senior editor at The Colonial Williamsburg Foundation. Previously he was a reporter for *The Virginia Gazette,* where he won awards for news and feature writing, and prior to that he was executive editor at Simon and Schuster. His previous books include *Did Babe Ruth Call His Shot?* (2005) and *Unsolved Mysteries of American History* (1997).